THE WPA GUIDE
TO NEW YORK CITY

THE WPA GUIDE
TO NEW YORK CITY

THE FEDERAL WRITERS' PROJECT
GUIDE TO 1930S NEW YORK

WITH A NEW INTRODUCTION
BY WILLIAM H. WHYTE

*A Comprehensive Guide
to the Five Boroughs of the Metropolis—
Manhattan, Brooklyn, the Bronx,
Queens, and Richmond—
Prepared by the Federal Writers' Project
of the Works Progress Administration
in New York City*

PANTHEON BOOKS · NEW YORK

Library of Congress Cataloging in Publication Data

New York City guide.
The WPA guide to New York City.

"A comprehensive guide to the five boroughs of
the metropolis—Manhattan, Brooklyn, the Bronx,
Queens, and Richmond."
Reprint. Originally published: New York City
guide. Rev. ed. New York : Random House, c1939.
(American guide series)
Bibliography: p.
Includes index.
1. New York (N.Y.)—Description—Guide-books.
I. Federal Writers' Project.   II. Title.
III. Title: W.P.A. guide to New York City.   IV. Series:
American guide series.
F128.18.N375   1982   917.47'10443   82-47898
ISBN 0-394-52792-5
ISBN 0-394-71215-3 (pbk.)

Display design by Naomi Osnos

WORKS PROGRESS ADMINISTRATION

FRANCIS C. HARRINGTON, Administrator
FLORENCE S. KERR, Assistant Administrator
HENRY G. ALSBERG, Director of Federal Writers' Project
HAROLD STRAUSS, Director of Federal Writers' Project
in New York City

Preface

THIS volume is a detailed description of the communities and points of interest in all the five boroughs of New York City. It attempts, also, to indicate the human character of the city, to point out the evidence of achievements and shortcomings, urban glamor as well as urban sordidness. It is intended to give both the permanent resident and the visitor an intimate, accurate knowledge of the metropolis.

The *New York City Guide* is the companion volume to *New York Panorama* and is sponsored and published under the same auspices. The two are planned to complement one another. *New York Panorama* draws a large-scale interpretation of the city's life and history; the *New York City Guide* describes the component portions of the city.

The *Guide* represents a collective effort of employees of the Federal Writers' Project. They have been assisted by the suggestions and criticism of many distinguished authorities. The risk of error and omission—always considerable in a work of this nature, despite every precaution—is slightly increased by the fact that responsible authorities sometimes disagree. More serious is the problem of keeping pace, in print, with a dynamic metropolis that overnight replaces a century-old institution with a new triumph in modernity.

Thanks must be given to the hundreds of consultants and experts who generously contributed their advice. We are especially indebted to the Weyhe Gallery and the individual artists for permission to reproduce many prints, and to the Federal Art Project for photographs, prints, and art work. We are grateful, also, for the editorial assistance of the national office of the Federal Writers' Project, and of Harry L. Shaw, Jr., former Director of the Federal Writers' Project in New York City.

The opinions expressed in this book are the opinions of the writers and the editors and are not necessarily shared by the consultants, by the sponsors of the volume, or by the Works Progress Administration.

EDITORIAL STAFF OF THE
NEW YORK CITY GUIDE

Editor-in-Chief: LOU GODY

Editors: CHESTER D. HARVEY, JAMES REED

Editorial Assistants: JAMES BEN. ALLEN, JOHN CHEEVER, HENRY FAGIN, A. BENJAMIN KAUFMAN

The production of this volume would not have been possible without the help of many other staff members of the Federal Writers' Project in New York City—the writers, research workers, checkers, cartographers, the clerical and technical assistants. Among them were Frances Adams, Eugene Burdock, Alexis Chern, Florence Coffield, Samuel Cummings, Irving L. Fishman, Robert Friend, William Garber, Bip Hanson, John Harms, Lillian Krutman, Anthony Netboy, Leba Presner, William S. Rollins, Fred Rothermell, Melvin Shelley, Percy Shostac, Herman Spector, Fred Vigman, Clarence Weinstock, Ruth Widén, Charlotte Wilder, Richard Wright, and Gabriel Zakin.

Contents

The Harbor, The Rivers, and Their Islands

Illustrations and Maps

ILLUSTRATIONS

All photographs and prints not otherwise credited were executed by the Federal Art Project in New York City; photographs whose titles are followed by asterisks (*) were taken by the Federal Writers' Project.

xi

MAPS

Plan of the Guide

UNDER General Information is given practical information about the city and its services: transportation lines to and from New York; motor routes; traffic rules; street arrangement; transit lines; hotel and rooming house accommodations; restaurants; amusements; sightseeing; boat trips, etc. A map showing the principal shopping centers in Manhattan is included. A calendar of Annual Events follows. The subway and elevated systems are shown on a pocket map inside the back cover, and an outline map of the City of New York will be found on pages 6-7.

Each of the five boroughs is treated individually. Manhattan has been divided into five Sections, starting at the Battery and working generally north: Lower Manhattan, Middle and Upper East Side, Middle West Side, The Harlems, Upper West Side and Northern Manhattan. Preceding the description of each Section are given the area of the Section and the stations of transit lines that serve it. The Section introduction sketches the historical background and gives the contemporary description. The Sections are divided into Localities, which are described, under commonly used names, in a general south to north order. A map showing the outlines of Sections and Localities appears on pages 54-55. Transit facilities within each Locality may be readily found by reference to the directions preceding the Section introduction. In general, transit lines follow principal streets, and the names of the lines indicate their routes. Where contiguous Localities merge so subtly that precise definition of them is impracticable, arbitrary boundaries have been established. Points of special interest in each Locality are dealt with in order—again south to north—with the conditions under which they may be visited.

A number of Major Points of Interest have been singled out for separate treatment. This list is not exhaustive; rather it is representative of the many widely known institutions and buildings in Manhattan. Cross reference to these points is made in the stories of the Localities in which they are situated.

Brooklyn, the Bronx, Queens, and Richmond (Staten Island) boroughs are taken up in that order. An introductory essay considers each borough as a whole and traces its history; a map indicating all the communities and main highways within the borough is included. The borough is then split into large Sections for point-by-point description. Transportation directions, boundaries, and a detailed map accompany each Sectional description. Neighborhoods and points of interest follow an order generally away from Manhattan. Hours, fees, and other terms of admission are given for points of interest that are open to visitors. Many old houses in the outlying neighborhoods are privately owned and occupied, but if such a home, or a factory, or an institution, is regularly open for inspection, that fact is noted.

The harbor, the rivers, and their islands have been grouped in one Section. The islands at the western end of Long Island Sound, however, are described with the East Bronx.

This book is completely indexed.

Introduction by William H. Whyte

The *New York City Guide* makes splendid reading. Today, forty-three years after it was written, it is still the most detailed, comprehensive, and diverting guide to the history and geography of the city's places and people. It is so detailed that, when it first came out, the *New Yorker* ventured that it might prove too timely, unless constant revisions were made.

Looking back through the pages of this Guide, and flying in the face of that warning, a number of people who care deeply about this city's past, present, and future became convinced that the original Guide was much more a precious document to be preserved than a packet of information to be updated. This introduction will touch on some of the changes the city has undergone, without attempting any actual revision of its text. Far from being dated, the superb quality of writing found in these pages ensures that the narrative accounts of the city's neighborhoods and how they came to be are as fresh as ever. The Guide's sense of history is in fact what gives it such life. These writers were enchanted—and exasperated—not so much by the particular ways New York was changing even before their eyes as by the constants that suffused that ceaseless change, the cycle of decay and renewal, the leapfrogging vagaries of fashion. They were fascinated by the striking extremes, the best of the city and the worst of it. When they wrote, SoHo was not yet even a name, just a group of cast-iron buildings; Bedford-Stuyvesant a quiet neighborhood of Victorian houses.

The Guide came out in 1939, prior to the unprecedented growth and prosperity of the postwar years. New York had always been the nation's cultural capital, of course, but its performing arts were expanding with the high spirits and strengthened economy of victory, as was the vital base of schools, studios, and Off-Broadway theaters that supported and fed them. As more corporations moved their headquarters to New York, Manhattan was becoming a boomtown for service, technical, and white-collar jobs in general. But there were clouds gathering on this sunny horizon. For an increasing number of blacks and Puerto Ricans jobs were getting further and further out of reach. While the city was gaining jobs for its desk jockeys, its manufacturing was leaving town, and with it a broad range of blue-collar and unskilled employment.

In the meantime the congestion of the city's streets seemed unaffected by its population's turnover. If anything, it only grew more intense, as more and bigger buildings sprang up throughout the business districts. The 1969 Plan for New York City recorded a discernible dynamic from all this bustle, however. Concentration, it affirmed, was the genius of the place, the source of its vitality and excitement. New York's center had become the nation's center, and this concentration of activities its major attraction both domestically and internationally. If this meant crowding, so be it.

In the 1970s, however, things started to go really wrong. The city lost even more of its manufacturing. Top management began moving corporate headquarters closer to home, in suburbia. Office vacancy rates crept up. Building construction collapsed. The subway system that had made the city work began itself not to work; the new Second Avenue line ran out of funds, and the huge trench that had been dug south from Harlem had to be ignominiously filled in. The city's deficits went up. Its credit rating went down. On the verge of bankruptcy, the city asked Washington for help and was scorned. (*Daily News*: "Ford to New York: 'Drop Dead.'") Moralists across the country could take heart; for this wicked and profligate city the end was surely at hand.

But not quite yet. New Yorkers are a resilient lot, and they responded to the contumely with something like patriotic fervor. "Save New York" coalitions were formed. People wore Big Apple buttons and T-shirts saying, "I Love New York." Radio and television ads rang out with catchy songs of self-praise.

Whether or not all this hoopla had much to do with it, things did in fact take an upward turn. The city beat its budget back into shape, though at a terrible cost in reduced services. The exodus of corporations slowed to a trickle and new ones moved in. Foreign businesses and banks opened New York branches at an accelerating clip. By the end of the 1970s, New York City had become the dominant world capital.

Feeling restored if not exactly flush, New York once again launched a number of grandiose projects. Along the Hudson a great landfill would be created so that a tunnel could be built in it, and through the tunnel a superhighway. Opposition to Westway has been fierce, however, and this tunnel may literally never see the light of day. But there will come another time, surely, and another great tunnel.

Buildings and Spaces

Let us take a closer look at the postwar building boom. By any logic, it should not have taken place at all. For one thing, as critics like Lewis Mumford argued, the city was already much too crowded. Secondly, advances in telecommunications and travel were making the necessity of a central marketplace obsolete.

But New York got denser and denser. Stockbrokers, bankers, and lawyers discovered that they, too, loved New York, if not for the ambience, then for the convenience. The guts of their work was still face-to-face communication, and so they clustered in the highly functional congestion of Wall Street's financial district and in Midtown. Midtown takes up only one square mile, not much more space than many a regional shopping mall. Vehicular traffic moves so slowly now in those areas that it is the pedestrian who does the bullying, frequently whacking an offending car or cab on the hood to demand that it stop.

In addition to causing overcrowding, the building boom has at times been charged with homogenizing the cityscape with indistinguishable—and undistinguished—glass boxes. Granted the imposing sameness of many Sixth Avenue skyscrapers, and given the sheer volume of construction that took place, the wonder is that so much of what the Guide describes remains. And the newer buildings, if you know how to read them, are much more idiosyncratic than they first appear to be.

To a remarkable degree, New York's buildings have been shaped by its zoning code, and it by them. It was New York, indeed, that initiated the practice of zoning back in 1919, and it has continued to be the most innovative of cities in that respect—ahead of all others, for ill or good, by about a decade. It is the shift from one zoning innovation to another that gives us our key to the city's postwar architecture: If you know the sequence of the shifts, you can look at a building and gauge its history with some accuracy.

In the late 1940s, zoning was quite prescriptive. Builders could pile up about as much bulk as they wanted to, but there were strict rules governing how the building had to be set back as it went up. Architects were customarily instructed to "fill in the zoning envelope." They did so faithfully, producing a series of nearly identical buildings in the "wedding cake," or ziggurat, form. Then, in 1958, a building came along that was to have a profound new influence on architecture and zoning: the Seagram Building, designed by Mies van der Rohe in collaboration with Philip Johnson. It was a pure tower, rising straight up and set at the rear of a broad plaza. The plaza, fronting on Park Avenue between Fifty-second and Fifty-third streets, proved—to the surprise of everyone, including the architects—to be immensely popular with lunchtime crowds searching for a place to sit, picnic, or sunbathe. New York City's planning commission thought it would be good to prod other architects and builders to provide similarly elegant structures and public spaces. Thus was born New York's incentive zoning. For the next ten years every builder who put up an office tower went for the plaza bonus, which allowed them to build higher as compensation for leaving more space open at ground level. In the process, more new open space was created than in all the country's other cities combined. Unhappily, many of the plazas were sterile and empty, neglecting such essentials as a place to sit. In 1975, however, zoning laws were changed so that essentials would be included. Before long, though, plazas were old hat; arcades, through-block corridors, covered pedestrian areas, and rooftop parks were in. Atriums were especially popular, in part because of the success of the atrium within the Citicorp Center at Lexington Avenue between Fifty-third and Fifty-fourth streets. Before long, Midtown was awash with atrium projects. Some turned out well—indoor parks, essentially, with "waterwalls," cafés, and occasional entertainment. Others looked very much like big office building lobbies. Either way, the builders got lots of extra office space to rent.

Excess piled on excess. As more big buildings went up, east Midtown seemed as if it must soon tilt into the East River. One solution would have been for the builders to head elsewhere—to the neglected west Midtown area, for example. But they didn't. Instead, they got the planning commission to modify the rules so that they could put up bigger buildings on smaller sites. This was done on a case-by-case basis, with much haggling back and forth. In the planners' lexicon, this came to be known as "fine tuning" or "sophisticated zoning." When you see an oversized building adorned with lots of greenhousery and skylights, you can bet it was built sometime between 1977 and 1981.

With bonuses for this and bonuses for that, and air rights as a kicker, developers began putting up "sliver" buildings. Ordinarily, very thin, tall buildings are uneconomical, amounting to mostly elevator banks and stairwells. But space was at a premium and the developers prevailed. If you see such a sliver—some thirty stories high but no wider than a brownstone,—you can date its construction as 1981–1982.

Public criticism mounted. At length, in 1982, the commission downzoned east Midtown. Space bonuses were sharply curtailed. To assure "daylighting" as well as sun, new height and setback procedures have been introduced. The next round of buildings will, in all probability, be configured with the location of the sun in mind—modern-day versions of Stonehenge.

Restoration and Rebirth

With building booms of such magnitude, it is remarkable that any old buildings remain. A surprising number do, and this is, in part, the consequence of New York's penchant for excess. The destruction of old buildings was so wanton, it provoked a vigorous counterattack, and this has led to a preservation movement of outstanding effectiveness, dedication, and guile.

For a while, though, it looked as if nothing would be spared. One after the other, fine old buildings were torn down. Some were mentioned by the Guide as particularly notable—the splendidly rococo Murray Hill Hotel, the Savoy-Plaza and its great green roof (demolished to make way for the singularly unattractive General Motors building). Many were buildings of no special significance but they gave the streets scale and character, and people felt diminished by their loss. The economics seemed inexorable. The protests mounted, but the demolitions continued.

At last, there was one demolition too many. In 1963, the great marble structure of Pennsylvania Station was leveled, and the station itself was reduced from the Baths of Caracalla to a subway concourse. This time people were so outraged, the City was moved to action and, in 1965, set up a Landmarks Preservation Commission with real power.

The commission could designate all sorts of places as landmarks; only structures thirty years old or more could be considered, but otherwise the definition of a landmark was whatever the commission thought should be a landmark. Once a structure was so designated, the owner could not change the exterior without the commission's approval. Demolition of a landmark building was forbidden unless the owner could prove there was no economic alternative. To help provide just such an alternative, the city's zoning stipulated that the owner could sell his air rights to an adjacent property owner.

The commission proceeded to designate many landmarks, a number of them gaining new lives as a consequence. The Jefferson Market Courthouse on Sixth Avenue in Greenwich Village was converted into a library; the old Astor Library on Lafayette Street became the New York Public Theater. The commission also designated key open spaces, like Central Park and Bryant Park, as landmarks, while whole areas, most notably the bulk of Greenwich Village, were designated historic districts.

At length, another railroad station provided a further testing of the commission's authority: Penn Central, owner of Grand Central Station, proposed an office tower that would be built atop the main concourse and obliterate the magnificent facade. The Landmarks Preservation Commission said no. Penn Central sued, holding that the law unfairly stripped them of their property rights to make money. The matter wound up in the Supreme Court.

In a ruling that was vital to preservation programs throughout the country, the Court held the City's landmark procedures constitutional. The majority opinion noted, in passing, that Penn Central could make money by selling its air rights, which subsequently happened. Penn Central sold $2.2 million worth of air rights to the Philip Morris Company, which was then able to add 74,655 more square feet of floor space to the building it was putting up directly across Forty-second Street from Grand Central.

Private groups play an important middleman role in landmark designation. The Fraunces Tavern block, one of the last rows of early nineteenth-century brick houses left in New York is a case in point. The Tavern itself, on Pearl Street, was designated a landmark in 1965. The other houses, however, were not. A developer bought five of them and in 1976 was about to demolish them.

Fortunately, a group of practical preservationists had earlier formed an organization to intervene in such situations. This was the New York Landmarks Conservancy, Inc. A few hours before demolition, this group found a spirited donor who put up $250,000 as a down payment and bought the houses. To raise the balance of what was needed, the conservancy persuaded a developer to put up $300,000 in front money and to draw up plans for the restoration of the houses.

In a related deal, the owners of a new building across the street have given $250,000 for tree planting and the provision of a small park at Coenties Slip alongside the houses. Considering the staggeringly high land values here, the do-gooders' seed money has been made to go very far indeed.

One of the best of landmark deals has been the mating of a brownstone palace and a hotel tower. At Madison and Fiftieth Street, as the Guide notes, are the famed Villard Houses, an imposing complex of Italianate residences designed by McKim, Mead, and White. In 1968 they were designated a landmark. Some years later developer Harry Helmsley acquired them. He could have demolished them on the grounds of hardship, there being no reasonable economic use for them at the time. Instead, he chose to add their air rights to a tall hotel to be built behind them. He would keep the houses as the facade of the hotel. Unhappily, however, he said he would have to gut some of the finest rooms, including a magnificent vaulted room with walls covered in gold leaf. Its floor level was an inconvenient half-level out of kilter with the floor level of the hotel.

There was a tremendous howl from preservation groups. At length, after much kicking and screaming, as Helmsley put it, he agreed not only to keep the rooms but to restore them faithfully. He did so, and well. As a consequence, the Helmsley Palace Hotel has some of the most venerable and elegant public rooms in the City, among them the Gold Room, nine steps up.

Neighborhoods

There have been sweeping demographic shifts since the Guide was written. Some neighborhoods have lost much of their population; some, indeed, have virtually disappeared. Others have taken root where people did not live before. But what is just as notable is the remarkable stability of many neighborhoods.

Greenwich Village is such an example. In 1939, the number of artists and writers living there was declining. Today, most have long since left, and it is professionals and business people who can afford to live there. Yet, physically, the Village has changed very little, and its character has not changed much either. There is a feeling of liberation to the area, of tolerance, and enough odd people to make a stroll in its streets something to savor.

This stability has been hard earned, most spectacularly so in the West Village. In the late fifties, city planners took a long and hard look at the area and found it annoyingly unclassifiable: a jumble of buildings, mostly three and four story brick houses. Commercial and residential uses were all mixed up, with many instances of that fine institution, the apartment over the store.

Urban renewal chief Robert Moses did not like the West Village at all. He had it officially declared a slum and moved to level twenty blocks to make way for colonies of high-rise towers. In cities across the country this kind of urban renewal almost always prevailed. In the West Village, however, lived writer Jane Jacobs. She loved the place, and thought it had all the virtues of mixture, scale, and vitality that planners were ignoring, an argument she was to develop with great power in her *The Death and Life of Great American Cities*. She and her allies took on the City in a bitter three-year battle and won. The West Village today is just about what it was before—mixed up, a bit tacky, and full of life.

Another lively area is the cast-iron district south of Houston Street, or SoHo. It has burgeoned because of another fight the City won by losing. The planned Lower Manhattan Expressway would have cut the heart out of the area, but when the city gave up the project, artists looking for inexpensive loft space began moving in, eventually supplanting much of the industry there. Now there are so many galleries, bars, restaurants, and people looking for lofts that the artists have had to move on—this time to "Tribeca," a triangle of industrial blocks below Canal Street.

By all odds the largest, wealthiest, and most stable of neighborhoods has been the Upper East Side. There have been changes, to be sure. With the dismantling of the El, Third Avenue has seen its fine Irish bars supplanted by new apartment houses, almost all visions of relentless banality. First and Second avenues have become "singles" country, lined with bars and trendy restaurants. Yorkville has a few German cafés and good butchers left, but it is now basically a white-collar, residential district.

But the fashionable parts of the East Side are remarkably stable. In 1939, the Guide reported that the geographic center of the addresses listed in the Social Register was around Sixty-eighth Street and Madison Avenue. To get an idea of what shifts there have been, I have taken the As and the Bs in the 1982 register and plotted their location on a map. Here is what it shows:

1. There has been some northward movement, but not much. The geographic center has moved only slightly, to Seventy-second and Park Avenue.
2. The self-segregation within the Upper East Side is still overwhelming. Of the 333 New York City addresses in the sampling, 88 percent are on the Upper East Side.
3. The address with the highest concentration of Social Register people is 200 East 66th Street, Manhattan House. Many appear to be empty nesters who previously may have had larger quarters on Park or Fifth.
4. Social Register people who live in odd places are often children of families with proper East Side addresses.

The Upper West Side is well beyond this pale and a good thing too, its residents will tell you. They take pride in *not* being society country. The Upper West Side, as they will tell you, has been revitalized by intellectuals, artists, writers, and urbanites of all kinds and is more interesting for that reason. The remodeling of brownstones and limestones in this area has been more extensive than on the East Side and often more imaginatively done. Columbus Avenue, a dull and seedy stretch only fifteen years ago, is lined with a lively mixture of specialty shops, exotic food emporia, service establishments, bars, outdoor cafés, and the kind of restaurants where the menu is on a slate and the waiters all seem to be actors. Broadway is more soulful but similar. At Eigthtieth Street is the incomparable Zabar's, the best deli in New York.

But there is a sad side to this stretch of Broadway. In its rooming houses and single-room-occupancy hotels live the City's largest concentration of elderly poor people; and, with New York State's program for getting mental patients out of hospitals, they have been joined by large numbers of disturbed people. To make matters worse, developers have been forcing these unfortunates out of their buildings so they can be converted to high-priced co-ops and condominiums.

Meanwhile the benches in the middle of Broadway remain. They are the one amenity the older people can count on. Some of the benches are broken; others are taken by drunks and nodding junkies. But every day the older people come, each at their special time, to sit in the sun and watch the people go by.

Harlem has been suffering a population problem of another kind. Not, as the conventional view has it, too many people, but too few. In fact Harlem has been undergoing a severe depopulation. Due in good part to migrations to Bedford-Stuyvesant in Brooklyn, many of its neighborhoods have lost up to a third of their people. There may be overcrowded buildings in a given block; but there are, at the same time, so many burned-out hulks and vacant lots, that the network of people, stores, and activity that makes a block work is simply not there.

But Harlem has some impressive basics in its favor. Bad as the ride may be, subway routes serve Harlem better than any other community. It has broad boulevards, a good part of a great park, and a large stock of fine old houses still in reasonable shape. Lately there has been a trickle back of middle-class blacks.

For sheer hard times, however, nothing can match the South Bronx. In 1939, the Guide cited it as one of the most severely crowded neighborhoods in the City, and the one with the lowest proportion of home owners. It was a depressing-looking place too: block after block of bleak tenements and housing projects. In the years just after the war, there was a large influx of Puerto Ricans, and the place became even more crowded.

Then the devastation began. Landlords stopped making repairs, and finally abandoned the buildings altogether. What the arsonists did not burn, the gangs did. By the 1970s the area looked like a bombed-out city. The population plummeted; in the 1970s that of the Mott Haven and Morrisania districts fell from 289,000 to 132,000.

Today there are few jobs to be had in the South Bronx. This is the key problem, and the clearing of the area has at least had the benefit of providing sites for industrial development that could be more attractive than suburban ones. The close-to-market location is excellent, and there is already in place an infrastructure of utilities and railroad facilities. The South Bronx Devel-

opment Corporation is working hard to bring firms in and has initiated
pilot projects for home-owned, low-rise housing.

Queens is another world altogether. A white-collar borough, its rows of
small houses provide the clearest demonstration that New York is basically
a middle-class city. Queens was the last part of New York to be developed,
the bulk of the housing being constructed in the 1930s by speculative
builders. The Guide was not impressed with the result. In 1939, however,
many of the blocks were still raw subdivisions. Since then the saplings have
become large old trees and the well-kept rows of houses have matured into
pleasant neighborhoods of satisfying stability. Psychologically, the City could
be a million miles away.

Staten Island provides similar satisfactions. With the construction of the
Verazzano Bridge in 1964, it lost its feel of rural self-sufficiency. Staten
Island is now essentially suburban in character and while there are some
large open spaces left, what strikes the eye are the new "town house" and
cluster developments that cover its hills.

Brooklyn, with the City's largest stock of brownstones, has the best
examples of neighborhood revitalization: Park Slope, Boerum Hill, Fort
Greene, Clinton Hill. In some, like Brooklyn Heights, the brownstones have
long since been restored and their prices have soared. But the quest continues; as one area gets resettled, people move on to the still seedy ones in
search of the elusive bargain.

Street Life

Let us conclude with a look at the most elemental of New York's attractions—the life of its streets. Visitors of every era have remarked on this but
never has the street life been more vigorous. The pace is set by New York's
pedestrians and it is fast, now averaging about three hundred feet per minute. They are skillful, too, using hand and eye signals, feints and sidesteps
to clear the track ahead. They are natural jaywalkers, streaking across on the
diagonal while tourists wait docilely on the corner for the light. It is the
tourists, moreover, who are vexing, with their ambiguous moves and their
maddeningly slow gait. They put New Yorkers off their game.

Before I say anything further in praise of New York's street life, let
one point be made. There is a very bad side to it. The streets of the business
districts are safe enough during the day; at night, however, they can be
dangerous. Certain public places, furthermore, are now dominated by undesirables, all day as well as all night. Union Square, for example, once the
site of speeches and rallies has become such a haunt for cut gangs, thieves,
and muggers that some dope dealers fear to go near it anymore.

The heartland of undesirable New York is the block of Forty-second Street between Seventh and Eighth avenues. Here is the national cesspool, so bad, New Yorkers can take perverse pride in it, overflowing with pimps, whores, transvestites, male prostitutes, and the like. At night, roving bands of toughs appear. Saturdays, they take over the subway station at Eighth Avenue, the most dangerous place in the city.

New York's best streets also have their undesirables, or what would be thought so in most parts of the country. No city has on its streets such an array of street professionals: beggars, handbill passers, pickpockets, evangelists, street musicians, pushcart men, merchandise vendors, three-card monte players, bag ladies, characters of every stripe. These people are the despair of merchants' associations, which are forever after the police to chase them away. But New Yorkers themselves are very tolerant of them.

And it is the New Yorkers who provide the best part of the show. Watch them on Fifth Avenue. Ever since Andreas Feininger took his famous telephoto shot of Fifth Avenue all squeezed up, documentaries on the urban plight have used Fifth Avenue as their vision of hell. But it is a glorious street to walk along, and while the 22.5-foot-wide sidewalks are often jammed with as many as eight thousand people an hour walking past a given point, the congestion is functional. Much of it is self-congestion, due to New Yorkers stopping instead of walking; stopping to talk, to say hello, to say good-bye, or, often, just to stand there.

New York's streets are more sociable places than at first they appear to be. Stand in one spot long enough and you will be struck by the high incidence of chance meetings between friends. But they are not chance; with 1.2 million people in the one square mile of Midtown, the meetings are an actuarial probability. You will also note the tendency of people to cluster in the middle of the pedestrian traffic stream for their conversations.

The street is a great place for business. Watch a group of executives go through their post lunch good-byes and you will appreciate how functional the street is as neutral turf. No party has an advantage over the other. As they get around to the real agenda of the lunch, you will witness a series of ballet-like moves and reciprocal gestures, often culminating in a final climactic farewell.

New Yorkers do a lot of shmoozing, most intensively on Seventh Avenue in the garment district. At midday the sidewalks there will be teeming with groups of men. Sometimes they will be exchanging gossip; other times they will be standing in amiable silence, watching the kooks and the screwballs go by. Of course, there is shmoozing downtown and uptown too, most usually in front of office buildings with a large back-office work force.

Shmoozers show a preference for well-defined spots. Flagpoles attract them; so do pillars, perhaps from some primeval instinct for guarding one's rear. They also like to form in a line abreast at the curb, facing inward toward the action.

The regularities of New Yorkers' street behavior are all the more remarkable in view of how very many New Yorkers are newcomers. An astounding number of younger people are still coming to it. They come from all over, some from abroad, and for many the nearest thing to a downtown they've experienced before arriving is a suburban shopping mall. Acclimation is harsh, and quick. Soon they are walking fast, and impatiently, weaving and dashing their way past the dawdling tourists. They shmooze. They learn to block busy street corners with their conversations. They even come to appreciate the tawdriness and inconveniences and danger, reflecting as they do on the heroism of simply coping with New York. Above all, they are fascinated. They are at the center of the universe.

New York City
June 1982

THE WPA GUIDE
TO NEW YORK CITY

D. Spiegel

General Information

(All addresses in the General Information section are in Manhattan, unless otherwise indicated. See map on pages 6-7 for location of boroughs, waterways, harbor, main thoroughfares, bridges, tunnels, and parks; also see map on page 17 for general vicinity of New York.)

The city of New York is the largest in the Western Hemisphere and the second largest in the world, with a population in 1938 of 7,505,068 and an area of 322.83 square miles. It is exceeded in area and population only by London. The metropolis is situated on the Atlantic seaboard in the southeastern corner of New York State, at the mouth of the Hudson River. Its extreme length, north and south, is 36 miles; extreme breadth, 16½ miles.

New York City, chartered in 1898, consists of five boroughs, each also a county: Manhattan (New York County), the Bronx (Bronx County), Brooklyn (Kings County), Queens (Queens County), and Richmond, or Staten Island (Richmond County). Manhattan, the original New York City, founded 1626, is an island; population 1,684,543, area 22.20 square miles. Brooklyn (settled 1636), on Long Island, was formerly an independent city; population 2,798,093, area 80.95 square miles. The Bronx (settled 1641) is on the mainland north of Manhattan; population 1,499,-090, area 41.41 square miles. Queens (settled about 1635) is on Long

3

Island; population 1,346,659, area 121.12 square miles. Richmond (settled about 1638) is in the southwest corner of New York Bay; population 176,683, area 57.15 square miles.

The metropolitan area of New York City is the district within a radius of approximately 40 miles of City Hall and includes parts of New Jersey, Westchester County (N.Y.), Connecticut, and Long Island *(see map on page 17)*. The population of the area in 1930 was nearly 11,000,000.

The city is governed by a mayor and a city council, the latter elected by a system of proportional representation. A president, with certain local duties and powers, heads each of the five boroughs. The county affairs of the various boroughs are conducted independently of the municipal government.

FREE INFORMATION FACILITIES

NEW YORK CITY INFORMATION CENTER, Park Ave. and 42d St., opposite Grand Central Terminal; POLICE DEPARTMENT INFORMATION BOOTH, Broadway and 43d St. (Times Square); DAILY NEWS INFORMATION BUREAU, 220 E. 42d St.; ESSO AND SOCONY-VACUUM TRAVEL INFORMATION SERVICES, RCA Building, Rockefeller Center; AMERICAN AUTOMOBILE ASSOCIATION, Hotel Pennsylvania, 7th Ave. and 33d St.; HOTEL ASSOCIATION OF NEW YORK CITY, 221 W. 57th St.; NEW YORK CONVENTION AND VISITORS BUREAU, 233 Broadway; U.S. TRAVEL BUREAU, 45 Broadway; Y.M.C.A. HEADQUARTERS, 420 Lexington Ave.; Y.W.C.A. CENTRAL BRANCH INFORMATION DESK, 610 Lexington Ave.; TRAVELERS AID SOCIETY, Pennsylvania Station and Grand Central Terminal.

STREETS

Manhattan streets are laid out on the gridiron plan, with avenues running north and south, and cross-town streets running east and west, from river to river. *(See pocket map of Manhattan.)* All cross-town streets are numbered, except those south of Houston Street and some in Greenwich Village, where the gridiron system was not applied. The avenues are also numbered, but include a few with names: Lexington, Park, and Madison Avenues, and Broadway. Fifth Avenue, which begins at Washington Square, divides the cross-town streets into east and west sections and is the starting point of house numbers on those streets.

The designation "downtown" refers to a direction south of a given point; "uptown," north. These terms, together with "midtown," apply also to approximate sections of Manhattan: downtown, from the Battery to Fourteenth Street; midtown, from Fourteenth to Fifty-ninth Street; uptown, north of Fifty-ninth Street.

HOUSE NUMBER KEY TO MANHATTAN. To find the numbered cross-town street nearest a given house number on a north-south avenue, cancel the last figure of the given number, divide the remainder by 2, and then add the key number given below. (Example: For 500 Fifth Avenue, drop the last figure, leaving 50. Divide this by 2. To 25 add the key number, 17. The result is 42 [Forty-second Street], the cross street at 500 Fifth Avenue.) Key numbers:

Amsterdam Ave. ....add 60
Ave. A ....add 3
Ave. B ....add 3
Ave. C ....add 3
Ave. D ....add 3
Broadway ....subtract 31
Central Park W. ....divide the house number by 10 and add 60
Columbus Ave. ....add 60
Eighth Ave. ....add 9
Eleventh Ave. ....add 15
Fifth Ave. ....add 17: from Broadway to 57th Street; opposite Central Park: divide the house number by 10 and subtract 18 add 45: from 110th Street to Mt. Morris Park add 24: from Mt. Morris Park to 140th Street
First Ave. ....add 3
Fourth Ave. ....add 8
Lenox Ave. ....add 111
Lexington Ave. ....add 22
Madison Ave. ....add 26
Manhattan Ave. ....add 99
Ninth Ave. ....add 13
Park Ave. ....add 34
Riverside Drive ....divide the house number by 10 and add 72
Second Ave. ....add 3
Seventh Ave. ....add 12: from Greenwich Ave. to Central Park add 20: north of Central Park
Sixth Ave. ....add 4: from 3d Street to Central Park (old numbers) subtract 13: from 3d Street to Central Park (new numbers)
St. Nicholas Ave. ....add 110
Tenth Ave. ....add 13
Third Ave. ....add 9
West End Ave. ....add 59

The street systems in the other boroughs follow no over-all plan. In the Bronx, Jerome Avenue is the dividing line between east and west sections of numbered cross-town streets, which are approximate continuations of those in Manhattan. In Brooklyn, to avoid confusion note the exact designations of numbered streets, of which there are several groups (for exam-

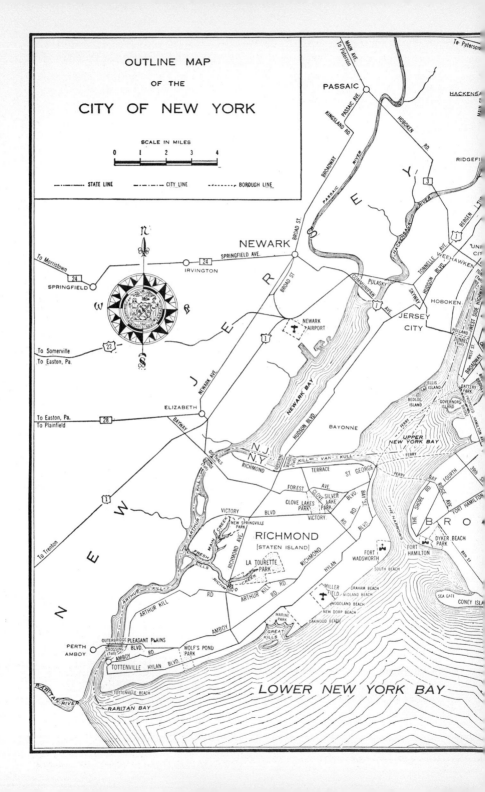

OUTLINE MAP

OF THE

CITY OF NEW YORK

SCALE IN MILES

0   1   2   3   4

········· STATE LINE   ─·─·─ CITY LINE   ─····─ BOROUGH LINE

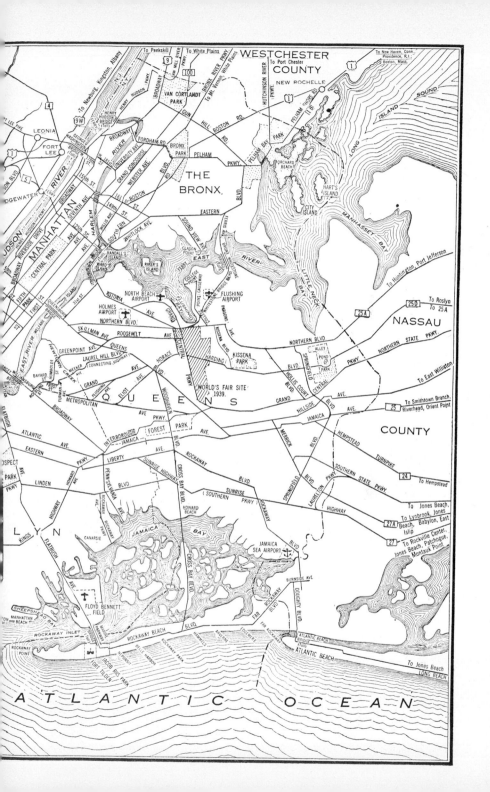

ple, there is a Thirty-seventh Street, an East Thirty-seventh Street, a West Thirty-seventh Street, a Bay Thirty-seventh Street, and a Beach Thirty-seventh Street). In Queens, most of the streets are numbered. House numbers are based on the block system, in which the numbers on a block are preceded by the number of the intersecting street at the start of the block (for example, house numbers on Fifty-eighth Street between Thirty-first and Thirty-second Avenues run 3101, 3103, 3105, etc.).

ACCOMMODATIONS

HOTELS

Prices below (subject to change) are minimum daily rates for a single room with private bath. Asterisk (*) indicates rooms without private bath are available at lower rates.

DOWNTOWN (below 29th Street). *$2.00:* *ARLINGTON, 18 W. 25th St.; *LEDONIA, 42 E. 28th St.; *MARLTON, 3 W. 8th St. *$2.50:* *ALBERT, 65 University Pl.; *BREVOORT, 5th Ave. and 8th St.; *CHELSEA, 222 W. 23d St.; GEORGE WASHINGTON, Lexington Ave. and 23d St.; HOLLEY, 36 Washington Sq.; *MADISON SQUARE, Madison Ave. and 25th St.; PRINCE GEORGE, 14 E. 28th St. *$3.00:* CORNISH ARMS, 311 W. 23d St.; *IRVING, 26 Gramercy Park S.; GRAMERCY PARK, 52 Gramercy Park N.; *PARKSIDE, 18 Gramercy Park S. *$3.50:* BRITTANY, Broadway and 10th St.; *BROADWAY CENTRAL, 673 Broadway; *EARLE, 103 Waverly Pl.; *LAFAYETTE, University Pl. and 9th St.; *SEVILLE, Madison Ave. and 29th St. *$3.75:* FIFTH AVENUE, 5th Ave. and 9th St. *$4.00:* GROSVENOR, 5th Ave. and 10th St.

PENNSYLVANIA STATION ZONE. *$2.00:* *IMPERIAL, Broadway and 32d St.; *YORK, 7th Ave. and 36th St. *$2.25:* *BRESLIN, Broadway and 29th St. *$2.50:* *GRAND, Broadway and 31st St.; *HERALD SQUARE, 116 W. 34th St.; *MARTINIQUE, Broadway and 32d St.; *WOLCOTT, 4 W. 31st St. *$3.00:* *McALPIN, Broadway and 34th St. *$3.50:* GOVERNOR CLINTON, 7th Ave. and 31st St.; NEW YORKER, 8th Ave. and 34th St.; PENNSYLVANIA, 7th Ave. and 33d St.

TIMES SQUARE ZONE. *$2.00:* *CADILLAC, Broadway and 43d St.; CENTURY, 111 W. 46th St.; *FLANDERS, 135 W. 47th St.; FORTY-FOURTH STREET, 120 W. 44th St.; *REX, 106 W. 47th St.; *ST. EDWARD, 70 W. 46th St.; *ST. JAMES, 109 W. 45th St. *$2.50:* ABBEY, 149 W. 51st St.; BELVEDERE, 319 W. 48th St.; *BRISTOL, 129 W. 48th St.; *CHESTERFIELD, 130 W. 49th St.; DIXIE, 241 W. 42d St.; GREAT NORTHERN, 118 W. 57th St.; *KNICKERBOCKER, 120 W. 45th St.; LAURELTON, 147 W. 55th St.; PARAMOUNT, 235 W. 46th St.; PICCADILLY, 227 W. 45th St.; PRESIDENT, 234 W. 48th St.; *REMINGTON, 129 W. 46th St.; *TAFT, 7th Ave. and 50th St.; *TIMES SQUARE, 8th Ave. and 43d St.; VICTORIA, 7th Ave. and 51st St.; WELLINGTON, 7th Ave.

and 55th St.; *WENTWORTH, 59 W. 46th St.; *WOODSTOCK, 127 W. 43d St.; WOODWARD, Broadway and 55th St. $3.00: ASTOR, Broadway and 44th St.; EDISON, 228 W. 47th St.; LINCOLN, 8th Ave. and 44th St.; *MARYLAND, 104 W. 49th St.; SEVILLIA, 117 W. 58th St.; THIRTY-THREE WEST FIFTY-FIRST STREET, 33 W. 51st St.; WEBSTER, 40 W. 45th St. $3.50: *CAPITOL, 8th Ave. and 51st St.; GORHAM, 136 W. 55th St.; PARK CENTRAL, 7th Ave. and 55th St.; PARK CHAMBERS, 68 W. 58th St.; PLYMOUTH, 143 W. 49th St.; SALISBURY, 123 W. 57th St.; SEYMOUR, 50 W. 45th St.; WINDSOR, 6th Ave. and 58th St. $4.00: WYNDHAM, 42 W. 58th St. $4.50: ALGONQUIN, 59 W. 44th St.; SHOREHAM, 33 W. 55th St. $5.00: BUCKINGHAM, 6th Ave. and 57th St.

GRAND CENTRAL TERMINAL ZONE. $2.50: TUDOR, 304 E. 42d St.; *MURRAY HILL, Park Ave. and 41st St. $3.00: BEDFORD, 118 E. 40th St.; BELMONT PLAZA, Lexington Ave. and 49th St.; WINTHROP, Lexington Ave. and 47th St. $3.50: DUANE, 237 Madison Ave.; SAN CARLOS, 150 E. 50th St.; WHITE, Lexington Ave. and 37th St. $4.00: BEVERLY, Lexington Ave. and 50th St.; COMMODORE, Lexington Ave. and 42d St.; LEXINGTON, Lexington Ave. and 48th St.; TUSCANY, 120 E. 39th St. $5.00: NEW WESTON, Madison Ave. and 50th St.; VANDERBILT, Park Ave. and 34th St. $6.00: BARCLAY, Lexington Ave. and 48th St.; *BILTMORE, Madison Ave. and 43d St.; CHATHAM, Vanderbilt Ave. and 48th St.; PARK LANE, Park Ave. and 48th St.; ROOSEVELT, Madison Ave. and 45th St.; WALDORF-ASTORIA, Park Ave. and 50th St. $7.00: RITZ-CARLTON, Madison Ave. and 46th St.

CENTRAL PARK SOUTH. $3.00: BARBIZON-PLAZA, 6th Ave. and 58th St. $3.50: ST. MORITZ, Central Park S. and 6th Ave. $4.00: NAVARRO, 112 Central Park S. $6.00: ESSEX HOUSE, 160 Central Park S. $7.00: PLAZA, Central Park S. and 5th Ave. $8.00: HAMPSHIRE HOUSE, 150 Central Park S.

MIDDLE EAST SIDE. $3.50: ADAMS, 2 E. 86th St.; *BEEKMAN TOWER, 1st Ave. and 49th St.; FOURTEEN EAST SIXTIETH STREET, 14 E. 60th St. $4.00: ALRAE, 37 E. 64th St.; BLACKSTONE, 50 E. 58th St.; GLADSTONE, 114 E. 52d St.; LANGDON, 5th Ave. and 56th St.; SULGRAVE, 60 E. 67th St. $4.50: WEYLIN, 40 E. 54th St. $5.00: BERKSHIRE, 21 E. 52d St.; CROYDON, 12 E. 86th St.; ELYSEE, 60 E. 54th St.; LOWELL, 28 E. 63d St.; WESTBURY, Madison Ave. and 69th St. $6.00: GOTHAM, 5th Ave. and 55th St.; MAYFAIR HOUSE, 610 Park Ave.; RITZ TOWER, Park Ave. and 57th St.; ST. REGIS, 5th Ave. and 55th St. $7.00: AMBASSADOR, Park Ave. and 51st St.; PIERRE, 5th Ave. and 61st St.; SAVOY-PLAZA, 5th Ave. and 59th St.; SHERRY-NETHERLAND, 5th Ave. and 59th St.

UPPER WEST SIDE. $2.00: EMBASSY, Broadway and 70th St.; *ENDICOTT, Columbus Ave. and 81st St.; *MIDTOWN, Broadway and 61st St. $2.50: ALAMAC, Broadway and 71st St.; BRETTON HALL, 2350 Broadway; CLIFTON, 127 W. 79th St.; *EMERSON, 166 W. 75th St.; FRANKLIN TOWERS, 333 W. 86th St.; GREYSTONE, Broadway and 91st St.; KIMBERLEY, Broadway and 74th St.; *MANHATTAN TOWERS, Broad-

way and 76th St.; *MARIE ANTOINETTE, Broadway and 66th St.; *NAR-
RAGANSETT, 2510 Broadway; OLIVER CROMWELL, 12 W. 72d St.; OR-
LEANS, Columbus Ave. and 80th St.; PARK CRESCENT, 150 Riverside
Dr.; *PARK PLAZA, 50 W. 77th St.; ROBERT FULTON, 228 W. 71st St.;
RUXTON, 50 W. 72d St.; *SHERMAN SQUARE, Broadway and 71st St.;
WESTOVER, 253 W. 72d St.; WHITEHALL, Broadway and 100th St.
$3.00: ALEXANDRIA, 250 W. 103d St.; BEACON, Broadway and 75th
St.; *EMPIRE, Broadway and 63d St.; MILBURN, 242 W. 76th St.;
RALEIGH, 121 W. 72d St.; REGENT, Broadway and 104th St.; THERESA,
7th Ave. and 125th St.   *$3.50:* BANCROFT, 40 W. 72d St.; CAMERON, 41
W. 86th St.; CHALFONTE, 200 W. 70th St.; *COLONIAL, Columbus Ave.
and 81st St.; HAMILTON, 143 W. 73d St.   *$4.00:* BROADMOOR, Broadway
and 102d St.; ESPLANADE, West End Ave. and 74th St.; WINDERMERE,
West End Ave. and 92d St.   *$5.00:* MAYFLOWER, Central Park West and
61st St.

THE BRONX. *$3.00:* CONCOURSE PLAZA, Grand Concourse and
161st St.

BROOKLYN. *$2.00:* MONTAGUE, 103 Montague St. *$2.50:* BOS-
SERT, Montague and Hicks Sts.; *ST. GEORGE, Clark and Hicks Sts.;
STANDISH ARMS, 169 Columbia Heights. *$3.00:* *PIERREPONT, 55
Pierrepont St.; TOWERS, 25 Clark St. *$4.00:* *HALF MOON, Boardwalk
and W. 29th St., Coney Island; *MARGARET, 97 Columbia Heights;
TOURAINE, 23 Clinton St.

QUEENS. In addition to the following there are numerous summer ho-
tels in the Rockaways (see summer resort sections of newspapers). *$2.50:*
HOMESTEAD, 82-45 Grenfell Ave., Kew Gardens; *KEW GARDENS INN,
80-02 Kew Gardens Road, Kew Gardens; SANFORD, 140-40 Sanford Ave.,
Flushing; WHITMAN, 160-11 89th Ave., Jamaica. *$4.00:* *FOREST HILLS
INN, 1 Station Square, Forest Hills.

CLUB HOTELS

These offer planned social activities and, in most cases, athletic facilities.
ALLERTON HOUSE, 143 E. 39th St., $10.00 weekly and up; KENMORE
HALL, 145 E. 23d St., $7.50 weekly and up; MIDSTON HOUSE, 22 E. 38th
St., $10.50 weekly and up; PICKWICK ARMS, 230 E. 51st St., $9.00 weekly
and up.

WOMEN'S HOTELS

ALLERTON HOUSE FOR WOMEN (club hotel), 130 E. 57th St., $3.25
daily and up with private bath, $2.25 and up without private bath;
AMERICAN WOMAN'S CLUB (club hotel), 353 W. 57th St., $3.00 daily
and up with private bath; BARBIZON (club hotel), Lexington Ave. and
63d St., $3.00 daily and up with private bath, $2.50 and up without private bath; IRVIN, 308 W. 30th St., $2.00 daily and up without private
bath; MARTHA WASHINGTON, 29 E. 29th St., $3.00 daily and up with
private bath, $2.00 and up without private bath.

Y's

Y.M.C.A.: Executive headquarters and information center, 420 Lexington Ave. Various dormitories throughout New York. Y.W.C.A.: Executive headquarters and information center, 129 E. 52d St. Various dormitories throughout New York. Y.M.H.A.: Dormitory, Lexington Ave. and 92d St. Y.W.H.A.: Dormitory, 31 W. 110th St.

FURNISHED ROOMS AND APARTMENTS

For furnished rooms and apartments consult the classified sections of newspapers, especially the *Herald Tribune, Journal and American, Times,* and *World-Telegram.* The Y.M.C.A., Y.W.C.A., Y.M.H.A., and Y.W.H.A. also have room listings. Types of service include rooms with and without board, or with kitchen privileges. Furnished apartments are available with and without maid service, some with hotel service. These accommodations are found chiefly in the following areas: GREENWICH VILLAGE, Houston to W. 14th St., west of Broadway; CHELSEA, 14th to 34th St., west of 6th Ave.; MURRAY HILL, 30th to 40th St., east of Madison Ave.; TIMES SQUARE, 42d to 57th St., 5th Ave. to 8th Ave.; MIDDLE WEST SIDE, 30th to 40th St., 8th to 10th Ave.; UPPER WEST SIDE, 72d to 110th St., west of Central Park; MORNINGSIDE HEIGHTS, 110th to 125th St., west of Morningside Drive; BROOKLYN HEIGHTS, west of Fulton St., near Brooklyn Bridge.

TRANSPORTATION

There are four types of urban transit in New York City: subways, elevated railways (els), busses, and surface cars. The fare is 5¢ on all lines, except the Fifth Avenue Coach Co. (10¢) and certain routes in outlying parts of the city. Subways link all the boroughs except Staten Island, which is accessible only by the municipal ferry (5¢). One el line serves Manhattan and the Bronx, and five serve Brooklyn and parts of Queens; all points in Queens are also reached by the Long Island Railroad. In Manhattan, surface lines, mostly bus, are the chief means of cross-town travel. Staten Island has a bus system and a railway, the Staten Island Rapid Transit Co. (*see map on page 599*), both with terminals at the St. George Ferry. The Hudson and Manhattan Railroad (Hudson Tubes) is a rapid transit service between New York and Newark, N. J.

SUBWAYS

See pocket map of subway and el lines.
The three subway systems (all municipally owned and operated)— the Interborough Rapid Transit Corp. (IRT), the 8th Ave. (Independent) Subway System, and the Brooklyn-Manhattan Transit Corp. (BMT)— operate in Manhattan and have branches running into the Bronx, Brooklyn and Queens. Both the IRT and 8th Ave. subways run the full length

of Manhattan; the BMT, which is primarily a Brooklyn system, runs only to 60th St. The IRT has two main divisions, the West Side line (Broadway-7th Ave.) and the East Side line (Lexington Ave.-4th Ave.). All subway systems operate 24 hours a day, with express service between 6 a.m. and 1 a.m. Subway travel is facilitated by maps which appear in all stations and cars; by car signs showing name of line and destination; and by numerous directional signs at entrances, in passageways, and on platforms of stations. In the following list of subway lines, the terminals of each are shown in parentheses after the name of the line.

IRT SUBWAY. *West Side:* BROADWAY-7TH AVE. EXPRESS (New Lots Ave.—242d St.-Van Cortlandt Park) serves East New York, Brownsville, Crown Heights, Bedford, Park Slope, Downtown Brooklyn, Brooklyn Heights, in Brooklyn; William St., Varick St., 7th Ave., Broadway, St. Nicholas Ave., in Manhattan; Spuyten Duyvil, Riverdale, Van Cortlandt Park, in the Bronx. BROADWAY-7TH AVE. LOCAL (South Ferry—137th St.) serves West Broadway, Varick St., 7th Ave., Broadway, in Manhattan. 7TH AVE. EXPRESS (Flatbush Ave.—E. 180th St.-Bronx Park) serves Eastern Flatbush, Bedford, Prospect Park, Downtown Brooklyn, Brooklyn Heights, in Brooklyn; William St., Varick St., 7th Ave., Broadway (to 96th St.), Lenox Ave. (to 135th St.), in Manhattan; Mott Haven, Morrisania, Bronx Park S., in the Bronx. 7TH AVE. LOCAL (South Ferry—145th St.-Lenox Ave.) serves West Broadway, Varick St., 7th Ave., Broadway (to 96th St.), Lenox Ave. (to 145th St.), in Manhattan. *East Side:* BRONX PARK EXPRESS (Atlantic Ave.—E. 180th St.) serves Downtown Brooklyn; Broadway (to Fulton St.), Lafayette St., 4th Ave., Lexington Ave., in Manhattan; Mott Haven, Morrisania, Crotona Park, Bronx Park S., in the Bronx. JEROME AVE. EXPRESS (Atlantic Ave.—Jerome Ave.-Woodlawn) serves Downtown Brooklyn, in Brooklyn; Broadway (to Fulton St.), Lafayette St., 4th Ave., Lexington Ave., in Manhattan; Mott Haven, University Heights, Fordham Heights, Jerome Park, Woodlawn, in the Bronx. WHITE PLAINS ROAD EXPRESS (Atlantic Ave.—241st St.-White Plains Road) serves Downtown Brooklyn; Broadway (to Fulton St.), Lafayette St., 4th Ave., Lexington Ave., in Manhattan; Mott Haven, Morrisania, Crotona Park, Bronx Park E., Williamsbridge, Woodlawn, Baychester, in the Bronx. PELHAM BAY PARK LOCAL (City Hall—Pelham Bay Park) serves Lafayette St., 4th Ave., Lexington Ave. (to 125th St.), in Manhattan; St. Mary's Park, Hunt's Point, Unionport, Westchester Heights, Pelham Bay Park, in the Bronx. *Forty-second Street Shuttle* (Times Square—Grand Central Terminal) connects West Side and East Side lines. *Queens Lines:* ASTORIA LINE (Times Square—Astoria) serves 42d St., in Manhattan; Long Island City, Astoria, in Queens. FLUSHING (CORONA) LINE (Times Square—Flushing) serves 42d St., in Manhattan; Long Island City, Sunnyside, Woodside, Jackson Heights, Corona, Flushing, in Queens.

8TH AVE. (INDEPENDENT) SUBWAY. WASHINGTON HEIGHTS EXPRESS (Fulton St.-Rockaway Ave.—207th St.) serves Stuyvesant Heights, Bedford, Downtown Brooklyn, in Brooklyn; Church St., 6th

Ave., 8th Ave., St. Nicholas Ave., Fort Washington Ave., in Manhattan. GRAND CONCOURSE EXPRESS (Hoyt St.—205th St.) serves Downtown Brooklyn; Church St., 6th Ave., 8th Ave., St. Nicholas Ave. (to 145th St.), in Manhattan; University Heights, Fordham Heights, Jerome Park, in the Bronx. GRAND CONCOURSE LOCAL (City Hall—205th St.) serves same route in Manhattan and the Bronx as Grand Concourse Express. QUEENS-MANHATTAN EXPRESS (Church Ave.—Jamaica) serves Prospect Park W., South Brooklyn, Downtown Brooklyn, in Brooklyn; Essex St., Houston St., 8th Ave., 53d St., in Manhattan; Long Island City, Sunny-side, Woodside, Jackson Heights, Elmhurst, Forest Hills, Kew Gardens, Jamaica, in Queens. QUEENS-BROOKLYN CROSS-TOWN LOCAL (Smith St.-9th St.—71st Ave.-Forest Hills) serves South Brooklyn, Downtown Brooklyn, Bedford, North Stuyvesant Heights, Williamsburg, Greenpoint, in Brooklyn; Long Island City, Sunnyside, Woodside, Jackson Heights, Elmhurst, Forest Hills, in Queens.

BMT SUBWAY. SEA BEACH EXPRESS (Coney Island—Times Square) serves Coney Island, East Bensonhurst, South Boro Park, Bay Ridge, Bush Terminal, South Brooklyn, Downtown Brooklyn, in Brooklyn; Broadway, in Manhattan. WEST END EXPRESS (Coney Island—Times Square) serves Coney Island, Bensonhurst, Boro Park, Bush Terminal, South Brooklyn, Downtown Brooklyn, in Brooklyn; Broadway, in Manhattan. BRIGHTON BEACH EXPRESS (Coney Island—Times Square) serves Coney Island, Brighton Beach, Manhattan Beach, Sheepshead Bay, Midwood, Flatbush, Prospect Park, Downtown Brooklyn, in Brooklyn; Broadway, in Manhattan. BRIGHTON BEACH LOCAL (Coney Island—57th St.) serves same route in Brooklyn as Brighton Beach Express; Broadway, Trinity Pl., Broadway, Central Park S., in Manhattan. 4TH AVE. (Brooklyn) LOCAL (95th St.—Queensboro Plaza) serves Fort Hamilton, Bay Ridge, Bush Terminal, South Brooklyn, Downtown Brooklyn, in Brooklyn; Whitehall St., Trinity Pl., Broadway, Central Park S., 60th St., in Manhattan; Long Island City, in Queens. ASTORIA AND FLUSHING LINES (Queensboro Plaza —Astoria and Flushing) serve same routes as IRT Queens Lines. 14TH ST.-CANARSIE LINE (Rockaway Parkway—14th St.-8th Ave.) serves Can-arsie, East New York, Ridgewood, North Williamsburg, Greenpoint, in Brooklyn; 14th St., in Manhattan. BROADWAY (Brooklyn) LINE (Rock-away Parkway—Canal St.) serves Canarsie, East New York, Ridgewood, North Stuyvesant Heights, Williamsburg, in Brooklyn; Delancey St., Cen-tre St., in Manhattan. JAMAICA LINE (Jamaica—Broad St.-Wall St.) serves Jamaica, Richmond Hill, Woodhaven, in Queens; Cypress Hills, Bush-wick, North Stuyvesant Heights, Williamsburg, in Brooklyn; Delancey St., Centre St., Nassau St., in Manhattan. MYRTLE AVE.-CHAMBERS ST. LINE (Metropolitan Ave.-Maspeth—Chambers St.) serves Maspeth, in Queens; Ridgewood, Williamsburg, in Brooklyn; Delancey St., Centre St., in Manhattan. CULVER LINE (Coney Island—Chambers St.) serves Coney Island, West Midwood, West Flatbush, Boro Park, Bush Terminal, South Brooklyn, Downtown Brooklyn, in Brooklyn; Broad St., Nassau St., in Manhattan.

ELEVATED LINES

See pocket map of subway and el lines.
The Manhattan el is operated by the IRT; it extends into the Bronx.
The Brooklyn els are operated by the BMT. The els run 24 hours a day,
except the Second Ave. Line which stops between midnight and 4 a.m.
MANHATTAN. THIRD AVE. LINE (South Ferry—E. 241st St.-White
Plains Road) serves the Bowery, 3d Ave., in Manhattan; Mott Haven,
Morrisania, Crotona Park, East Fordham Heights, Bronx Park W., Wood-
lawn, Baychester, in the Bronx.
BROOKLYN. FULTON STREET LINE (Park Row—Lefferts Ave.)
serves City Hall, in Manhattan; Downtown Brooklyn, Bedford, Stuyvesant
Heights, East New York, in Brooklyn; Ozone Park, Richmond Hill, in
Queens. LEXINGTON AVE. LINE (Park Row—Eastern Parkway) serves
City Hall, in Manhattan; Downtown Brooklyn, Fort Greene Park, Bed-
ford, Stuyvesant Heights, Bushwick, in Brooklyn. CULVER LINE (Sands
St.—Coney Island) serves Downtown Brooklyn, Park Slope, Bush Termi-
nal, Borough Park, West Flatbush, West Midwood, Coney Island, in Brook-
lyn. 5TH AVE.-BAY RIDGE LINE (Sands St.—65th St.) serves Downtown
Brooklyn, South Brooklyn, Bush Terminal, Bay Ridge, in Brooklyn.
MYRTLE AVE. LINE (Sands St.—Metropolitan Ave.) serves Downtown
Brooklyn, Fort Greene Park, Bedford, Stuyvesant Heights, Ridgewood, in
Brooklyn; Ridgewood, Maspeth, in Queens.

SURFACE LINES

All the boroughs are served by surface lines, either busses or trolley
cars, or both, which run on all the principal streets. There are no central
terminals of these lines, except in Queens (168th Street and Jamaica
Avenue), and in Staten Island (St. George Ferry Terminal). In Manhattan, bus lines run on all north-south avenues and on many of the cross-
town streets.

FERRIES

See pocket map of Manhattan.
Fare: passengers 5¢, pleasure vehicles 25¢, unless otherwise indicated.
Between South Ferry and St. George, Staten Island. Between South Ferry
and 39th St., Brooklyn. Between Barclay St. and Hoboken, N. J.; passenger fare 4¢. Between Cortlandt St. and Weehawken, N. J.; passenger fare
6¢. Between Chambers St. and Jersey City, N. J. Between Christopher
St. and Hoboken, N. J.; passenger fare 4¢. Between W. 23d St. and
Hoboken, N. J. Between W. 23d St. and Jersey City, N. J. Between W.
23d St. and Weehawken, N. J. (vehicular traffic only). Between W. 42d

St. and Weehawken, N. J.; passenger fare 4¢. Between W. 125th St. and
Edgewater, N. J. Between Dyckman St. and Englewood Landing, N. J. Between 39th and 69th Sts., Brooklyn, and St. George, Staten Island. Between Howland's Hook, Staten Island, and Elizabeth, N. J. Between Port
Richmond, Staten Island, and Bayonne, N. J. Between Tottenville, Staten
Island, and Perth Amboy, N. J. Between Clason Point, Bronx, and College Point, Queens; vehicle fare 40¢. Between Yonkers, N. Y., and Alpine, N. J.

HUDSON AND MANHATTAN RAILROAD (HUDSON TUBES)

See pocket map of Manhattan.
Stations at Cortlandt and Church Sts., Christopher and Greenwich Sts.,
and on 6th Ave. at 9th, 14th, 19th, 23d, 28th, and 33d St. Serves
Hoboken, Jersey City, and Newark, N. J. Fare 8¢ from Cortlandt St. to
Hoboken and Jersey City, 22¢ to Newark; 10¢ from 33d St. to Hoboken
and Jersey City, 22¢ to Newark.

TAXICABS

The general rate is 20¢ for the first ¼-mile or any fraction thereof,
and 5¢ for each additional ¼-mile. Exceptions to this rate are the meter-
less cabs, which operate at higher tariffs, and those in outlying districts
of Queens and Staten Island where flat zone rates are charged. An
extra fee of 50¢ is charged for trunks. Taxicabs are not permitted to
carry more than five passengers. To recover articles lost in taxicabs, or
to make a complaint, apply at the Police Department Hack Bureau, 156
Greenwich St.

AUTOMOBILES FOR HIRE

Numerous agencies rent automobiles with or without uniformed chauffeurs (see Classified Telephone Directory). Typical rates are: without
chauffeur, from 12¢ per mile; with chauffeur, from $3 per hour.

RAILROADS

Terminals in Manhattan are Grand Central Terminal, 42d St., between
Vanderbilt and Lexington Aves., and Pennsylvania Station, 7th Ave., be-
tween 31st and 33d Sts. Other terminals are in Hoboken, Jersey City, and
Weehawken, N. J., reached by ferry or motor coach from Manhattan. Be-
sides ticket offices at terminals, ticket service for all railroads is available at
City Ticket Offices, 17 John St., 4 W. 33d St., and 3 W. 47th St.

16 GENERAL INFORMATION

ATLANTIC SEACOAST LINE, Pennsylvania Station. BALTIMORE & OHIO, Jersey City; motor coach service to terminal (included in fare); coach stations at 35 W. 33d St., 122 E. 42d St., 15 Columbus Circle, 15 Rockefeller Plaza, and Brooklyn Eagle Building, Washington and Johnson Sts., Brooklyn. CENTRAL OF NEW JERSEY, Jersey City; ferry at Liberty St., Cedar St., and W. 42d St. CHESAPEAKE & OHIO, Pennsylvania Station. CHICAGO, CLEVELAND, CINCINNATI & ST. LOUIS, Grand Central Terminal. DELAWARE & HUDSON, Grand Central Terminal. DELAWARE, LACKAWANNA & WESTERN, Hoboken; ferry at Barclay St., Christopher St., and W. 23d St. ERIE, Jersey City; ferry at Chambers St. and W. 23d St. FLORIDA EAST COAST, Pennsylvania Station. LEHIGH VALLEY, Pennsylvania Station. LONG ISLAND, Pennsylvania Station; Brooklyn terminal at Flatbush and Atlantic Aves.; Queens terminal in Jamaica. MICHIGAN CENTRAL, Grand Central Terminal. NEW JERSEY & NEW YORK, Jersey City; ferry at Chambers St. and W. 23d St. NEW YORK CENTRAL, Grand Central Terminal. NEW YORK & LONG BRANCH, Jersey City; ferry at Liberty St. and W. 23d St.; in summer, ferry at Cedar St. and W. 42d St. NEW YORK, NEW HAVEN & HARTFORD, Grand Central Terminal; Pittsburgh and Washington Divisions, Pennsylvania Station. NEW YORK, ONTARIO & WESTERN, Weehawken; ferry at Cortlandt St. and W. 42d St. NEW YORK, SUSQUEHANNA & WESTERN, Jersey City; ferry at Chambers St. and W. 23d St. PENNSYLVANIA, Pennsylvania Station. RICHMOND, FREDERICKSBURG & POTOMAC, Pennsylvania Station. SEABOARD AIR LINE, Pennsylvania Station. WEST SHORE, Weehawken; ferry at Cortlandt St. and W. 42d St.

BUS LINES

The chief bus terminals in Manhattan are: All American Bus Depot, 246 W. 42d St.; Capitol Greyhound Terminal, 245 W. 50th St.; Consolidated Bus Terminal, 203 W. 41st St.; Dixie Bus Center, 241 W. 42d St.; Gray Line Terminal, 59 W. 36th St.; Hotel Astor Bus Terminal, 220 W. 45th St.; Midtown Bus Terminal, 143 W. 43d St.; Pennsylvania Motor Coach Terminal, 242 W. 34th St.

ADIRONDACK TRANSIT LINES; to Adirondack Mountains; Dixie Terminal. ALL AMERICAN LINES; transcontinental and southern points; All American and Consolidated terminals. ALMA LINES; to Pennsylvania; Dixie terminal. ASBURY PARK-NEW YORK TRANSIT; to Asbury Park; Dixie and Pennsylvania terminals. BEE LINE BUSES; to Jones Beach; Capitol terminal. BERKSHIRE-VICTORIA LINES; to New England; Capitol, Hotel Astor, and Pennsylvania terminals. BLUE WAY LINES; to New England; Dixie and Midtown terminals. BOSTON AND WORCESTER LINES; Boston express; Consolidated terminal. CHAMPLAIN-FRONTIER COACH LINES; to Boston and Montreal; Capitol, Dixie, Gray Line, Hotel Astor, Midtown, and Pennsylvania terminals. DANBURY INTER-URBAN LINE; to Connecticut; Dixie terminal. DeCamp Bus Lines; to New Jersey; Midtown terminal. EAST COAST SYSTEM; to Baltimore and Washington; Dixie

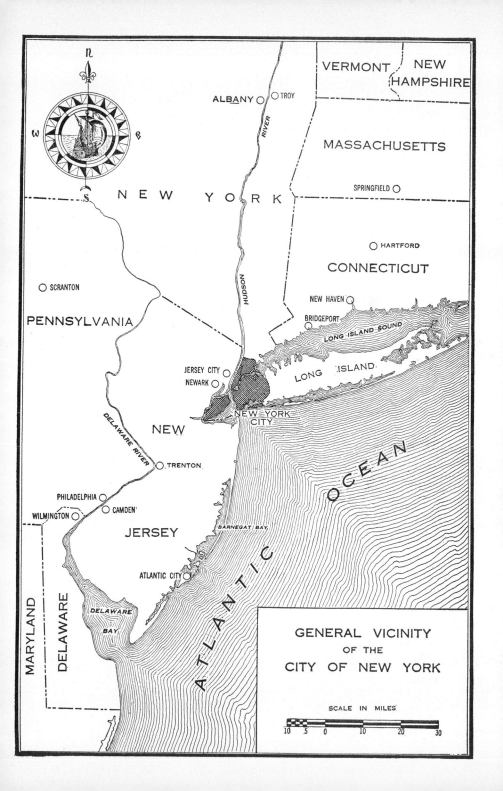

GENERAL VICINITY
OF THE
CITY OF NEW YORK

SCALE IN MILES

terminal. EDWARDS MOTOR TRANSIT; to Pennsylvania; Dixie terminal.
GRAY LINE; to New York and New Jersey points; Gray Line terminal.
GREYHOUND LINES; nation-wide; Capitol, Midtown, and Pennsylvania
terminals. HUDSON TRANSIT; to Sullivan County, N. Y.; Dixie terminal.
LINCOLN TRANSIT CO.; to Atlantic City; Consolidated and Dixie terminals. MARTZ LINES; to upstate New York; Dixie and Hotel Astor terminals. MOHAWK COACH LINES; to upstate New York; Consolidated and
Dixie terminals. NEW ENGLAND LINES; to New England; Capitol, Hotel
Astor, and Pennsylvania terminals. OLD COLONY COACH CO.; to Provi-
dence, R.I.; Dixie terminal. PAN-AMERICAN LINE; Miami express and
southern points; Dixie and Hotel Astor terminals. PUBLIC SERVICE BUSES;
to Atlantic City, N. J., and Philadelphia; Hotel Astor, Midtown, and
Pennsylvania terminals. QUAKER CITY LINES; to Philadelphia; Dixie terminal. ROCKLAND LINE; to Spring Valley and Nyack, N. Y., and other
suburban New York points; Gray Line terminal. SAFE-WAY LINES; to
Chicago and western points; Dixie and Hotel Astor terminals. SULLIVAN
COUNTY HIGHWAY LINES; to Sullivan County, N. Y.; Hotel Astor terminal. YELLOW WAY BUS LINES; to Sullivan and Ulster Counties, N. Y.;
Capitol, Consolidated, and Midtown terminals.

AIRLINES

All major airlines have ticket offices in Manhattan. The Union Airways
Terminal, Park Ave. and 42d St., opposite Grand Central Terminal, is central ticket office and information center for all lines. Airline terminals are
at La Guardia Field, Queens; Newark Airport, Newark, N. J.; and Floyd
Bennett Field, Brooklyn. Passengers are transported (at extra charge) in
limousines between Manhattan ticket offices and airports

AIRLINE OFFICES. AMERICAN AIRLINES, INC., 100 E. 42d St.;
CANADIAN-COLONIAL AIRWAYS, INC., 630 Fifth Ave.; NORTHWEST
AIRLINES, INC., 535 Fifth Ave.; PAN AMERICAN AIRWAYS SYSTEM, 135
E. 42d St. and Pennsylvania Station; TRANSCONTINENTAL AND WESTERN
AIR, INC., 80 E. 42d St.; UNITED AIR LINES, 80 E. 42d St.

STEAMSHIP LINES

The U.S. Passport Agency maintains offices at the Subtreasury Bldg.,
Wall and Broad Sts., and International Bldg., Fifth Ave. and 51st St.
Passport information is also obtainable at travel agencies. See Shipping
News section of newspapers for time of arrival and departure of ships.
For visits to ocean liners see page 36. (*Piers noted below are North
[Hudson] River, Manhattan, unless otherwise indicated.*)

AFRICA. AMERICAN EXPORT LINES, 25 Broadway; AMERICAN SOUTH-AFRICAN LINE, 26 Beaver St.

AROUND-THE-WORLD. AMERICAN PRESIDENT LINE, 604 Fifth Ave.; BARBER LINE, 17 Battery Place; BLUE FUNNEL (BOOTH) LINE, 17 Battery Place; KERR-SILVER LINE, 17 Battery Place.

ASIA. AMERICAN EXPORT LINES, 25 Broadway; AMERICAN PIONEER LINE, 1 Broadway.

ATLANTIC COASTAL. CLYDE-MALLORY LINES, Pier 34, Canal St.; COLONIAL LINE, Pier 11, Cedar St.; EASTERN S.S. LINES, Pier 19, Murray St.; PAN-ATLANTIC LINE, 11 Rockefeller Plaza; SAVANNAH LINE, Pier 46, Charles St.; SOUTHERN PACIFIC CO. (MORGAN LINE), 531 Fifth Ave.; STANDARD FRUIT & S.S. CO., 21 West St.

AUSTRALIA. AMERICAN PIONEER LINE, 1 Broadway.

AUSTRALIA AND NEW ZEALAND. PORT LINE, 25 Broadway.

BERMUDA. AMERICAN-CARIBBEAN LINE, 5 Broadway; FURNESS BERMUDA LINE, 34 Whitehall St.

CANADA AND NEWFOUNDLAND. EASTERN S.S. LINES, Pier 19, Murray St.; FURNESS RED CROSS LINE, 34 Whitehall St.

CENTRAL AMERICA. NEW YORK & CUBA MAIL S.S. CO., Pier 13, Wall St., East River; STANDARD FRUIT & S.S. CO., 21 West St.; UNITED FRUIT CO., Pier 3, Morris St.

EUROPE. AMERICAN EXPORT LINES, 25 Broadway; AMERICAN SCANTIC LINE, 5 Broadway; ANCHOR LINE, 11 Rockefeller Plaza; BELGIAN LINE, 10 Pearl St.; BLACK DIAMOND LINE, 39 Broadway; CUNARD WHITE STAR LINE, 25 Broadway; FRENCH LINE, 610 Fifth Ave.; GDYNIA-AMERICAN LINE, 32 Pearl St.; HAMBURG-AMERICAN LINE-NORTH GERMAN LLOYD, 57 Broadway; HOLLAND AMERICA LINE, 29 Broadway; ITALIAN LINE, 626 Fifth Ave.; NORWEGIAN-AMERICA LINE, 24 State St.; RED STAR (BERNSTEIN) LINE, 17 Battery Place; SWEDISH AMERICAN LINE, 636 Fifth Ave.; UNITED STATES (AMERICAN MERCHANT) LINES, 1 Broadway.

FAR EAST. Same lines as Around-the-World; KOKUSAI LINE, 1 Broadway; MAERSK LINE, 26 Broadway.

INTER-COASTAL. LUCKENBACH S.S. CO., 120 Wall St.; McCORMICK S.S. CO., 17 Battery Place; SHEPARD S.S. CO., Pier 52, Horatio St.

SOUTH AMERICA. AMERICAN REPUBLICS LINE, 5 Broadway; COLOMBIAN S.S. CO., 17 Battery Place; ESSCO-BRODIN LINE, 17 Battery Place; FURNESS PRINCE LINE, 34 Whitehall St.; MOOREMACK S.S. CO., 17 Battery Place; MUNSON LINES, 67 Wall St.; ROYAL NETHERLANDS S.S. CO., 25 Broadway; UNITED FRUIT CO., Pier 3, Morris St.; WILHELMSEN LINE, Pier 6, Middagh St., Brooklyn.

WEST INDIES. AMERICAN CARIBBEAN LINE, 5 Broadway; FURNESS WEST INDIES LINE, 34 Whitehall St.; GRACE LINE, 10 Hanover Square; MUNARGO LINE CO., Pier 3, Morris St.; NEW YORK & CUBA MAIL S.S. CO., Pier 13, Wall St., East River; PORTO RICO LINE, foot of Wall St., East River; STANDARD FRUIT & S.S. CO., 21 West St.; UNITED FRUIT CO., Pier 3, Morris St.

YACHT AND BOAT BASINS

Anchorages, marinas, and landing stages are available for pleasure craft. ANCHORAGES. About 40 anchorages in port of New York. For permits and information apply to Captain of the Port, Barge Office, Battery Park. LANDING STAGES. PIER 9, foot of Wall St., East River; PIER A, Battery Park, Hudson River. For information apply to Department of Docks, New York City. MARINAS. 26TH ST., East River; 79TH ST., 96TH ST., and ENGLEWOOD, N. J., Hudson River; JACKSON'S CREEK BOAT BASIN, Flushing Bay, Queens, Long Island Sound. For information apply to General Superintendent, Department of Parks, New York City; for New Jersey marinas apply to Palisades Interstate Park Commission, 80 Centre St.

TRAFFIC RULES

See map on pages 6-7 for main thoroughfares and highways leading in and out of the city.

A booklet containing all traffic regulations is available at Police Stations. Traffic signs, usually in the form of a white arrow with black lettering, appear on all streets throughout the city. They indicate prohibited turns, one-way streets, no-parking areas, play streets, etc.

SIGNAL LIGHTS. (1) Green means "go." (2) Red means "stop." (3) Red with green arrow means traffic facing such signal may make the movement indicated by arrow. (4) During all red or dark period drivers shall not start. (5) When light turns red drivers shall stop at nearest intersecting street (applies to most main thoroughfares).

TURNS. (1) Complete ("U") turns are forbidden in many downtown and midtown streets (signs indicate these areas). (2) Right and left turns shall be made on a green light only. (3) No turns are permitted on a red light except when permitted by police officer or sign.

SPEED LIMIT. (1) 25 miles per hour except where signs permit greater or lesser speed. (2) 10 miles per hour when turning corner.

ONE-WAY STREETS. Most cross-town streets in Manhattan and some thoroughfares in other boroughs are for one-way traffic only; signs at intersections show direction of traffic. In Manhattan even-numbered streets are usually for eastbound traffic and odd-numbered streets for westbound.

PLAY STREETS. These streets are set aside for children to play in; no traffic is permitted except vehicles having business in such streets. Signs at either end of block indicate such areas.

PASSING STREET CARS. Vehicles are prohibited from passing street cars on the left except when directed by police officer, or when on a one-way street, or when tracks are so located as to prevent driver from passing on right.

EIGHT-FOOT LAW. Vehicles must stop at least eight feet behind rear of street car which has stopped to receive or discharge passengers; if safety isle signs are in place where street car stops, vehicles may pass between signs and curb.

PARKING. (1) No parking is permitted in many streets; these areas are marked by signs. (2) Where parking is permitted signs indicate period allowed. (3) No parking is permitted within fifteen feet of a fire hydrant. (4) No parking is permitted for more than one hour in congested business or residential streets, for more than two hours in a designated parking space, for more than three hours between 12 midnight and 7 a.m.

WHISTLE SIGNALS. One blast means moving traffic shall stop; two blasts mean cross traffic shall move; three or more blasts (emergency) mean all moving traffic shall immediately stop.

HORNS. Horns must not be sounded except to warn a person or animal of danger.

RESTAURANTS

The restaurants listed below are among New York's oldest and best known. The city's thousands of eating places also include self-service cafeterias, lunchrooms, and sandwich shops, drugstore lunch counters and soda fountains, and soft-drink stands that serve light snacks. Almost all hotels have one or more dining rooms; the larger ones offer cocktail, dinner, and supper dancing (see Hotel Restaurants, page 28). For further information consult amusement section of newspapers, or the magazines *New Yorker, Stage,* and *Cue,* or restaurant information bureaus of the *Sun* and *Journal-American.*

Liquor served in all restaurants, unless otherwise noted.

AMERICAN RESTAURANTS

Many foreign restaurants may also be found in the districts named below (see Foreign Restaurants).

FINANCIAL DISTRICT (Battery to Chambers St.). BUSTO'S, 11 Stone St.; Wall Street clientele; lunch, dinner. CAFE SAVARIN, 120 Broadway; old and distinguished; lunch, dinner (in main dining room). CARUSO (see Chain Restaurants). CHILDS (see Chain Restaurants). FARRISH'S CHOP HOUSE, 42 John St.; established 1856; specialties: game and Southdown mutton chops; lunch a la carte, dinner. FRAUNCES TAVERN, Broad and Pearl Sts.; historic structure, erected 1719; scene of Washington's Farewell Address; Colonial interior; open 11 a.m. to 4 p.m.; lunch. HOLTZ POSTKELLER, 233 Broadway; frequented by businessmen; lunch, dinner. HUYLER'S (see Chain Restaurants). LONGCHAMPS (see Chain Restaurants). ROLFE'S CHOP HOUSE, 90 Fulton St.; established 1848; lunch, dinner. SAZARAC, 112 Greenwich St.; Creole cuisine; lunch, dinner. SCHRAFFT'S (see Chain Restaurants). SCHWARTZ'S, 183 Broadway and 54 Broad St.; French and Hungarian specialties; lunch a la carte, dinner. SWEETS, 2 Fulton St., opposite Fulton Fish Market; noted for sea food since 1845; a la carte. WHYTE'S, 145 Fulton St.; frequented by executives; specialty: sea food; lunch a la carte, dinner. YE OLDE CHOP HOUSE, 118 Cedar St.; relic of old New York; established 1800; closes 8 p.m.; a la carte. YE OLDE DUTCH TAVERN, 15 John St.; on site of historic John Street Theater (1767–1798); German specialties; lunch a la carte, dinner.

DOWNTOWN (Chambers to 28th St.) BILLY THE OYSTERMAN, 7 E. 20th St.; well known for sea food; lunch, dinner. CAVANAGH'S, 258 W. 23d St.; established 1876; specialties: steaks, chops, and sea food; a la carte. CHILDS (see Chain Restaurants). ELIZABETH FLYNN'S, 405 W. 23d St.; specialties: lobster and roast prime ribs of beef; sidewalk café; lunch, dinner. GUFFANTI, 274 7th Ave.; established 1892; Italian-American cuisine: lunch, dinner. KARL'S OLD RAVEN, 17 W. 27th St.; well established; closes 9 p.m.; lunch, dinner. LUCHOW'S, 110 E. 14th St.; noted place; established 1882; German-American cuisine; dinner music; lunch, dinner. SCHLEIFER'S, 2 Lafayette St.; patronized by lawyers and judges; lunch a la carte, dinner.

GREENWICH VILLAGE. ALICE MCCOLLISTER, 43 W. 8th St.; lunch, dinner. BARNEY GALLANT, 86 University Pl.; informal entertainment; open to 4 a.m.; dinner. HOTEL BREVOORT, 5th Ave. and 8th St.; old landmark; French cuisine; sidewalk café; lunch, dinner. ROCHAMBEAU, 6th Ave. and 11th St.; lunch, dinner. CHARLES, 452 6th Ave.; well established; French-American cuisine; lunch a la carte, dinner. DICK THE OYSTERMAN, 65 E. 8th St.; well known for sea food; steaks and chops; a la carte. JACK DELANEY'S, 72 Grove St.; specialty: steaks; lunch dinner a la carte. JUMBLE SHOP, 8th and MacDougal Sts.; English specialties; lunch, dinner. HOTEL LAFAYETTE, University Pl. and 9th St.; established 1883; noted French cuisine; luncheon, dinner. LEE CHUMLEY, 86 Bedford St.; resort of the literati; lunch, dinner. LONGCHAMPS (see Chain Restaurants). RENGANESCHI'S OLD PLACE, 139 W. 10th St.; Italian-French-American cuisine; established 1898; lunch and dinner. ROMANY MARIE, 55 Grove St.; quaint, frequented by the literati; specialty: Rumanian dishes; lunch and dinner. SCHRAFFT'S (see Chain Restaurants). STONEWALL INN, 51 Christopher St.; lunch, dinner. WHITE TURKEY TOWN HOUSE, 1 University Pl.; southern cuisine; lunch, dinner.

34TH ST. DISTRICT (28th to 36th St.). CAMPUS, 106 W. 32d St.; sea food specialties; lunch, dinner. CARUSO (see Chain Restaurants). CHILDS (see Chain Restaurants). HUYLER'S (see Chain Restaurants). LONGCHAMPS (see Chain Restaurants). RIGGS, 43 W. 33d St.; well established; lunch, dinner. SCHRAFFT'S (see Chain Restaurants). SHINE'S, 426 7th Ave.; well established; specialties: steaks and chops; a la carte. SOLOWEY, 433 7th Ave.; lunch, dinner.

TIMES SQUARE. ALGONQUIN HOTEL, 59 W. 44th St.; famed as literary and stage rendezvous; lunch, dinner. ANCHOR CAFE, 12th Ave.

and 49th St., opposite Transatlantic Terminal; patronized by crews of ocean liners; open all night when ships are in; a la carte. BLUE RIBBON, 145 W. 44th St.; well established; German specialties; a la carte. BRASS RAIL, 745 7th Ave.; known for sandwiches; lunch, dinner. CARUSO (see Chain Restaurants). CHILDS (see Chain Restaurants). DAVE'S BLUE ROOM, 791 7th Ave.; music publishers and song writers meet here; sidewalk café; lunch, dinner a la carte. "DINTY" MOORE'S, 216 W. 46th St.; old-time Broadway favorite; specialties: corned beef and cabbage, and man-sized steaks and chops; a la carte. GALLAGHER'S, 228 W. 52d St.; known for steaks; a la carte. HUYLER'S (see Chain Restaurants). JACK DEMPSEY'S, 1619 Broadway; the ex-champion plays host; dinner music; lunch, dinner. JACK LYONS CHOP HOUSE, 102 W. 50th St.; specialties: steaks and sea food; lunch, dinner a la carte. LA HIFF'S TAVERN, 156 W. 48th St.; theatrical crowd; specialties: steaks, chops, and sea food; a la carte. LINDY'S, 1626 and 1655 Broadway; rendezvous of music and sporting fraternity; lunch, dinner a la carte. THE LOBSTER, 145 W. 45th St.; lunch, shore dinner. LONGCHAMPS (see Chain Restaurants). MARESI-MAZZETTI, 103 W. 49th St.; American cuisine; specialty: French-Italian pastries; no liquor; lunch, dinner. OYSTER BAY, 8th Ave. and 43d St.; specialties: sea food, steaks and chops; lunch, dinner a la carte. PIROLLE-PILLET, 111 W. 45th St.; French-American cuisine; lunch, dinner. ROSOFF'S, 147 W. 43d St.; plentiful portions; lunch, dinner. SARDI'S, 234 W. 44th St.; popular with stage folk; lunch, dinner. SCHRAFFT'S, (see Chain Restaurants).

MIDTOWN EAST SIDE. BILLY THE OYSTERMAN, 10 W. 47th St.; well known for sea food; lunch, dinner. CAFE CONTINENTAL, 10 E. 52d St.; French-Italian-American cuisine; dinner music; lunch, dinner. CAFE LOUIS XIV, 15 W. 49th St., Rockefeller Center; elegant and quiet; a la carte. CAFE LOYALE, 521 5th Ave.; dancing; lunch, dinner. CARUSO (see Chain Restaurants). CAVIAR, 18 E. 49th St.; known to gourmets; French and Russian specialties; lunch, dinner. CHATHAM WALK, Vanderbilt Ave. and 48th St.; smart outdoor spot; open May to Oct.; lunch, dinner. CHESAPEAKE HOUSE OF NEW YORK, 191 Madison Ave.; southern cuisine; sea food specialties; lunch, dinner. CHILDS (see Chain Restaurants). COLONY, 667 Madison Ave.; de-luxe restaurant frequented by social registerites; a la carte. ELIZABETH FLYNN'S, 143 E. 49th St.; specialties: lobster and roast prime ribs of beef; lunch, dinner. FIRENZE, 6 W. 46th St.; French-Italian cuisine; dancing and entertainment nightly; lunch, dinner. GRAND CENTRAL TERMINAL RESTAURANT, Grand Central Terminal, 42d St. and Park Ave.; noted for its oyster bar; lunch, dinner. HAPSBURG, 313 E. 55th St.; selective continental menu; zither music; lunch, dinner. HUYLER'S (see Chain Restaurants). JANSSEN GRAYBAR HOFBRAU, Lexington Ave. and 44th St.; tavern atmosphere; international menu; specialty: game; lunch, dinner. LONGCHAMPS (see Chain Restaurants). MANNY WOLF'S CHOP HOUSE, 3d Ave. and 49th St.; for hearty eaters; dancing after 10 p.m.; a la carte. HOTEL MARGUERY, Park Ave. and 47th St.; noted French cuisine; lunch, dinner. PRESIDENT TAVERN, Lexington Ave. and 41st St.; specialties: steaks and sea food; lunch a la carte, dinner. REUBEN'S, 6 E. 58th St.; celebrities come here for famed sandwiches; open all night; lunch, dinner. ROSETTA GORDON, 359 Lexington Ave.; no liquor; closes 8:30 p.m.; lunch, dinner. SCHRAFFT'S (see Chain Restaurants). STOUFFER'S, 540 5th Ave. and 100 E. 42d St.; known also in Cleveland, Philadelphia, Detroit, and Pittsburgh; lunch, dinner. THERESE WORTHINGTON GRANT, 284 Park Ave.; southern cuisine; lunch, dinner. TWENTY-ONE, 21 W. 52d St.; renowned gathering place of celebrities; a la carte. WOFFINGTON COFFEE HOUSE, 14 E. 50th St.; quiet tearoom; no liquor; lunch, dinner.

ELSEWHERE IN MANHATTAN. CLAREMONT INN, Riverside Dr. and 124th St.; old landmark; open April to Oct.; outdoor terrace; dancing; lunch, dinner. TAVERN-ON-THE-GREEN, in Central Park, near W. 67th St. entrance; open April to Oct.; outdoor terrace; dancing; lunch, dinner; minimum after 9 p.m.

CHAIN RESTAURANTS. See phone book for addresses. CARUSO; 6 branches in Manhattan; Italian-American cuisine; lunch, dinner. CHILDS; 44 branches in Manhattan; dinner and supper dancing at 1501 Broadway, 12 E. 59th St., and 2689 Broadway; lunch, dinner. HUYLER'S; established 1876; 11 branches in Manhattan, all with soda fountain; liquor served at 9 E. 44th St., 170 Broadway, and 60 Broad St.; lunch, dinner. LONG-CHAMPS; 12 branches in Manhattan; smart atmosphere; specialty: charcoal broiled steaks; sidewalk cafés at 253 Broadway, and 5th Ave. and 12th St.; a la carte. SCHRAFFT'S; 38 branches in metropolitan area; American home food; liquor served at most branches; lunch, dinner.

FOREIGN RESTAURANTS

Native specialties are shown following name of nationality.

ARMENIAN. *Shish kebab* (pieces of lamb grilled on skewers), *pilaff* (steamed rice), *patlijan* (egg plant), honey and rose water pastries. BABA NESHAN'S, 48 E. 29th St.; no liquor; a la carte. BALKAN, 129 E. 27th St.; no liquor; lunch, dinner. OMAR KHAYYAM, 103 Lexington Ave.; no liquor; lunch, dinner. PALACE D'ORIENT, 108 Lexington Ave.; a la carte. *Other Armenian restaurants on Lexington Ave. between 23d and 34th Sts.*

AUSTRIAN. *Wiener schnitzel* (veal cutlet), veal goulash, paprika chicken. HUBER'S, 245 E. 82d St.; Viennese music; lunch, dinner. JOHN STROBL'S, 1256 3d Ave.; specialty: veal goulash; lunch, dinner. *Other Austrian restaurants in vicinity of 3d Ave. and 86th St.*

CHINESE. *Subgum chow mein* (meat and Chinese vegetables with fried noodles), *gai young yuen war* (chicken bird's nest soup), egg rolls. BAMBOO FOREST, 115 Waverly Pl.; well established; North China cuisine;

no liquor; lunch, dinner. CHIN, Broadway and 44th St.; dancing and floor show; lunch, dinner. HANG FAR LOW, 23 Pell St.; a la carte. LUM FONG, 220 Canal St.; lunch, dinner. ORIENTAL, 4 Pell St.; lunch, dinner. PORT ARTHUR, 7 Mott St.; old Chinatown place; no liquor; lunch, dinner. REPUBLIC, 1485 Broadway; no liquor; lunch, dinner. RUBY FOO'S, 161 E. 54th St. and 240 W. 52d St; lunch, dinner. YAT BUN SING, 16 Mott St.; no liquor; lunch, dinner. *Other Chinese restaurants on Pell, Mott, and Doyers Sts.*

EAST INDIAN. Curries, chutneys, *copra* (fried cocoanut), tamarind wine. BENGAL TIGER, 336 W. 58th St.; Hindu instrumental music; no liquor; lunch, dinner. CEYLON INDIA INN, 148 W. 49th St.; no liquor; lunch, dinner. EAST INDIA CURRY SHOP, 117 E. 60th St.; dishes of India and Burma; no liquor; lunch, dinner. RAJAH, 237 W. 48th St.; no liquor; lunch, dinner.

ENGLISH. Beef and kidney pies, mutton chops, puddings. ENGLISH TEA ROOM, 18 W. 48th St.; no liquor; lunch, dinner. KEEN'S ENGLISH CHOP HOUSE, 72 W. 36th St.; old-time theatrical atmosphere; specialty: English mutton chops; lunch, dinner.

FRENCH. Onion soup, frogs' legs, *bouillabaisse* (fish stew), *crêpes suzettes* (light pancakes prepared with burning brandy), pastries. BONAT'S, 330 W. 31st St.; large and popular; lunch and dinner (includes glass of beer or wine, or a cocktail). CAFE CHAMBORD, 803 3d Ave.; Provincial specialties; dinner music; lunch, dinner. CAFE TROUVILLE, 112 E. 52d St.; informal entertainment; lunch, dinner. CRILLON, 277 Park Ave.; attractive surroundings; lunch, dinner. DIVAN PARISIEN, 17 E. 45th St.; many unusual dishes; a la carte. GASTON A LA BONNE SOUPE, 44 W. 55th St.; lunch, dinner. HENRI, 15 E. 52d St.; noted cuisine and wine cellar; lunch, dinner. JANET OF FRANCE, 237 W. 52d St.; intimate atmosphere; lunch, dinner. LE POISSONNIER, 121 E. 52d St.; specialties: sea food and game; entertainment after 10 p.m.; lunch, dinner. PETITPAS, 317 W. 29th St.; established 1895; lunch, dinner. VOISIN, 375 Park Ave.; distinguished and expensive; a la carte.

FRENCH-HUNGARIAN. DUBONNET, 5 E. 45th St.; international cuisine; lunch a la carte, dinner.

FRENCH-ITALIAN. GOLDEN EAGLE, 62 W. 9th St.; old Greenwich Village place; lunch, dinner.

GERMAN. *Sauerbraten, kartoffelkloesse* (sweet-sour pot roast and potato dumplings), potato pancakes, apple cake, German beers. FRANZIS-KANER, 1591 2d Ave.; good selection; a la carte. HANS JAEGER'S, Lexington Ave. and 85th St.; music; lunch, dinner. IVAN FRANK'S HOFBRAU, 1680 Broadway; dancing and Bavarian entertainment; dinner, mimimum week-nights. ORIGINAL MAXL'S, 243 E. 86th St.; singing waiters; opens 3 p.m.; dinner. RUDI AND MAXL'S BRAUHAUS, 239 E. 86th St.; dancing and entertainment nightly; a la carte. ZUM BRAUHAUS, 207 E. 54th St.; established 1890; lunch, dinner. *Other German restaurants in vicinity of 3d Ave. and 86th St.*

GREEK. Balkan cheeses, fried squid, boiled dandelions. APOLLO, 259 W. 42d St.; many native dishes; a la carte.

HUNGARIAN. Goulash, roast goose, apple strudel, Magyar wines. BUDAPEST, 117 W. 48th St.; dancing and floor show nightly; lunch, dinner.

IRISH. Irish bacon, ham, beer. DUBLIN HOUSE, 225 W. 79th St.; a la carte.

ITALIAN. Spaghetti in various styles, *ravioli* (small, meat-filled dumplings), *minestrone* (thick vegetable soup), veal *scallopine* (veal cooked with wine). AMALFI, 115 W. 47th St.; Neapolitan specialties; lunch, dinner. BALILLA, 132 Bleecker St.; northern Italian cuisine; beer and wine; a la carte. BARBETTA, 321 W. 46th St.; well established; a la carte. BAT, 138 MacDougal St.; wine and beer; lunch a la carte, dinner. CASA JOHNNY, 135 W. 15th St.; lunch, dinner. DEL PEZZO, 100 W. 40th St. and 33 W. 47th St.; specialty: sea food; a la carte. ENRICO AND PAGLIERI, 66 W. 11th St.; continental menu; lunch, dinner. GRAND TICINO, 228 Thompson St.; inexpensive Greenwich Village place; a la carte. GROTTA AZZURRA INN, 387 Broome St.; in Little Italy; wine and beer; specialty: lobster and chicken; a la carte. LEONE'S, 239 W. 48th St.; patronized by celebrities; opens 5 p.m.; dinner, minimum. MARTA, 75 Washington Pl.; in Greenwich Village; popular with artists and writers; lunch, dinner. MONETA'S, 32 Mulberry St.; praised by gourmets; northern Italian cuisine; a la carte. PETER'S BACKYARD, 64 W. 10th St.; well-established Greenwich Village spot; lunch, dinner. RED DEVIL, 111 W. 48th St.; specialty: shrimps *alla Fra Diavolo;* a la carte. RESTAURANT DEI LAVORATORI, 92 West Houston St.; inexpensive Bohemian rendezvous; a la carte. VILLANOVA, 106 W. 46th St.; well established; a la carte. ZUCCA'S, 118 W. 49th St.; specialty: chicken cutlet Milanese; lunch, dinner. *Other Italian restaurants on Bleecker and Mulberry Sts., and in vicinity of 1st Ave. and 116th St.*

JAPANESE. *Suki-yaki* (pan-cooked meat and vegetables), *sake* (rice wine). DARUMA, 1145 6th Ave.; well established; wine and beer; lunch, dinner. MIYAKO, 340 W. 58th St.; wine and beer; lunch, dinner. SUEHIRO, 35 E. 29th St.; no liquor; lunch, dinner.

JEWISH. *Gefülte* fish (spiced fish cakes, served cold); sour cream mixed with fruit, vegetables, or pot cheese; chopped liver, usually mixed with fried onions and chicken fat; *kügel* (potato or noodle pudding); noodles and cottage cheese. CAFE ROYAL, 2d Ave. and 12th St.; meeting place of Jewish actors, writers, and intellectuals; sidewalk café; Hungarian-American cuisine; lunch, dinner. MOSKOWITZ AND LUPOWITZ, 40 2d Ave.; Rumanian cuisine; dancing and continental entertainment; lunch, dinner. POLIACOFF'S, 121 W. 45th St.; kosher dishes; lunch, dinner. RATNER'S, 138 Delancey St.; dairy and fish dishes only; beer; a la carte. *Other Jewish restaurants in vicinity of Delancey St. and on 2d Ave. north of Houston St.*

LATIN-AMERICAN. *Sopa de camarones* (shrimp chowder—Peru), *picadillo* (chopped steak with capers—Cuba), *cazuela de ave* (chicken stew—Chile), *asado criollo* (Gaucho beef roast—Argentina). CAFE LATINO, 15 Barrow St.; Pan-American menu; tango and rhumba music; opens 5 p.m.; dinner. *Other Latin-American restaurants in vicinity of 5th Ave. and 110th St.*

MEXICAN. *Tortilla* (corn pancake), *tacos* (rolled *tortilla* with meat), *tamale* (ground corn roll with meat), *mole* (gravy of ground pumpkin seeds, chocolate, chili, and native herbs and spices, served with chicken). EL CHARRO, 4 Charles St.; Mexican and Spanish dishes; opens 5 p.m.; no liquor; dinner. MEXICAN GARDENS, 137 Waverly Pl.; opens 5 p.m.; no liquor; dinner. XOCHITL, 146 W. 46th St.; complete Mexican menu; lunch and dinner. *Other Mexican restaurants in vicinity of 5th Ave. and 110th St.*

POLISH. *Bigos* (cabbage and meat), tripe, sausage. POLISH NATIONAL HOME RESTAURANT, 19 St. Marks Pl.; folk and dance music Sat. and Sun.; lunch, dinner.

RUSSIAN. *Shashlik* (pieces of lamb roasted on spits), *pirojok* (small meat pie), *borscht* (beet soup), *blin* (rolled pancake, usually filled with cottage cheese and covered with sour cream). KAVKAZ, 332 E. 14th St.; no liquor; lunch, dinner a la carte. RUSSIAN TEA ROOM, 150 W. 57th St.; specialties: mushrooms a la Russe, *borscht,* and vodka; lunch, dinner. *Other Russian restaurants in vicinity of 2d Ave. and 12th St.*

SPANISH. *Arroz con pollo* (yellow rice with chicken), *bacalao guisado* (salt codfish), *ameljas frescas* (stewed clams). FORNOS, 236 W. 52d St.; specialty: *pargo al horno a la Habanera* (baked red snapper); a la carte. JAI-ALAI, 82 Bank St.; native Spanish (Basque) and Latin-American dishes; lunch, dinner. *Other Spanish restaurants in vicinity of Cherry and Roosevelt Sts.*

SWISS. CHALET SUISSE, 45 W. 52d St.; specialty: minced veal a la Suisse; lunch, dinner.

SYRIAN. *Yabrak* (stuffed grapevine leaves), *bamiah* (okra and lamb). SON OF THE SHEIK, 77 Washington St.; no liquor; lunch, dinner.

SWEDISH. *Smörgasbord* (buffet appetizer—assorted meat, fish, and cheese delicacies), *biff och lok* (broiled tenderloin),. Swedish pancakes (dessert). CASTLEHOLM, 344 W. 57th St.; dancing; lunch, dinner. GARBO, 148 E. 48th St.; dancing and floor show; opens 5 p.m.; dinner. GRIPSHOLM, 324 E. 57th St.; lunch, dinner. STOCKHOLM, 27 W. 51st St.; dinner music; lunch, dinner. SWEDISH RATHSKELLER, 3d Ave. and 52d St.; lunch, dinner.

TURKISH. *Ajem pilav* (rice with braised meat), *fassouli piaz* (white bean salad), Turkish coffee (black and thick). CONSTANTINOPLE, 9 W. 52d St.; specialty: Turkish wine and liquor; lunch, dinner.

HOTEL RESTAURANTS WITH DINNER AND SUPPER DANCING

Prices shown below are for weeknights; they are usually higher on Saturday and holidays.

AMBASSADOR, Trianon Room, Park Ave. and 51st St.; formal dress required; dinner; minimum. ASTOR, Broadway Cocktail Lounge, Broadway and 45th St.; dinner a la carte; no cover or minimum. BELMONT PLAZA, Glass Hat, Lexington Ave. and 49th St.; dinner; minimum after 10 p.m. Fri; Sat. BILTMORE, Bowman Room, Madison Ave. and 43d St.; dinner a la carte; cover after 10 p.m. BOSSERT, Marine Roof, 98 Montague St., Brooklyn; view of harbor; dinner; no minimum Mon. to Thurs. COMMODORE, Palm Room, Lexington Ave. and 42d St.; dinner; cover after 10 p.m. DELMONICO, Road to Mandalay, Park Ave. and 59th St.; dinner a la carte; minimum. EDISON, Green Room, 228 W. 47th St.; dinner; minimum. ESSEX HOUSE, Casino-on-the-Park, 160 Central Park S.; dinner; minimum after 10 p.m. GOVERNOR CLINTON, The Grill, 7th Ave. and 31st St.; dinner; minimum after 10 p.m. LEXINGTON, Hawaiian Room, Lexington Ave. and 48th St.; dinner; cover after 10 p.m. LINCOLN, Blue Room, 8th Ave. and 44th St.; dinner; cover. McALPIN, Marine Grill, Broadway and 34th St.; dinner; no minimum Mon. to Thurs. NEW YORKER, Terrace Room, 8th Ave. and 34th St.; dinner; cover after 10 p.m. PARK CENTRAL, Cocoanut Grove, 7th Ave. and 55th St.; dinner; cover. PARK LANE, Queen Elizabeth Room, Park Ave. and 48th St.; dinner; minimum after 10 p.m. PENNSYLVANIA, Madhattan Room, 7th Ave. and 33d St.; dinner; cover after 10 p.m. PLAZA, Persian Room, 5th Ave. and 59th St.; formal dress required; dinner; cover after 10 p.m. ROOSEVELT, The Grill, Madison Ave. and 45th St.; dinner; cover after 9:30 p.m. ST. GEORGE, Bermuda Terrace, Clark and Hicks Sts., Brooklyn; dinner; no minimum Mon. to Thurs. ST. MORITZ, Restaurant de la Paix, 50 Central Park S.; dinner; no minimum Mon. to Fri. ST. REGIS, 5th Ave. and 55th St.; Iridium Room: formal dress required; dinner; cover after 10 p.m.; La Maisonette Russe: dinner a la carte; cover after 10 p.m. SAVOY PLAZA, Café Lounge, 5th Ave. and 59th St.; cocktail and supper dancing only; a la carte; minimum. SHELTON, Shelton Corner, Lexington Ave. and 49th St.; dinner a la carte; minimum after 10 p.m. TAFT, The Grill, 7th Ave. and 50th St.; dinner; no minimum. TOWERS, Penguin Room, 25 Clark St., Brooklyn; view of harbor; dinner. WALDORF-ASTORIA, Wedgwood Room, Park Ave. and 49th St.; dinner; cover after 10:30 p.m. WARWICK, Raleigh Room, 6th Ave. and 54th St.; cocktail and supper dancing only; a la carte; minimum after 10:30 p.m.

SHOPPING

For Manhattan shopping areas and description see map on next page.
The chief shopping areas in other boroughs are: Fulton St. from Flatbush

Ave. to Borough Hall, Brooklyn; Jamaica Ave. in the vicinity of 168th St., Queens; 149th St. and 3d Ave., the Bronx.

AMUSEMENTS

For information and current attractions apply to individual theater or night club, or consult amusement section of newspapers or the magazines *New Yorker, Stage,* and *Cue.* Amusement places—legitimate and motion picture theaters, night clubs, and concert halls—are concentrated in the Times Square area, 42d St. to 59th St. between 5th and 8th Aves. (*see map on page 169*).

LEGITIMATE THEATERS

There is no fixed theatrical season, although most new plays open in the fall. The opera season begins in November with the opening of the Metropolitan Opera House. Theater tickets are available at many places other than box offices. Leading hotels have theater ticket agencies. Other agencies are located in the Times Square area, most of the well-established ones charging 75¢ per ticket above the box-office price for their services. Telegraph companies will reserve and deliver tickets at a small charge. Traditional matinee days are Wednesday and Saturday; some matinees are held Thursday.

FOREIGN LANGUAGE THEATERS. Since some of these theaters do not advertise their attractions, it is advisable to phone the individual theater for all information. *Chinese:* NEW CHINA THEATER, 75 East Broadway. *French:* FRENCH THEATER OF NEW YORK, Barbizon-Plaza, 6th Ave. and 58th St. *Italian:* GIGLIO PARKWAY THEATER, 3d Ave. and 172d St., the Bronx; PEOPLES THEATER, 201 Bowery; Sun. only. *Yiddish:* NATIONAL, East Houston St. and 2d Ave.; PUBLIC THEATER, 2d Ave. and 4th St.; SECOND AVENUE THEATER, 35 2d Ave.; YIDDISH ART THEATER, 7th Ave. and 59th St.

MOTION PICTURE THEATERS

Admission prices to most Times Square theaters are lowest before 1 p.m. ("early-bird" matinees) and are raised at 1 p.m. and again at 6 p.m. Many places regularly give midnight performances; almost all do on Saturday. A few remain open until 3:30 a.m. Brooklyn is the only other borough that has a large film theater center; it is in the vicinity of Fulton St. and Flatbush Ave.

MOTION PICTURE HOUSES WITH STAGE SHOWS. PARAMOUNT, 7th Ave. and 43d St.; popular orchestra and specialty artists. RADIO CITY

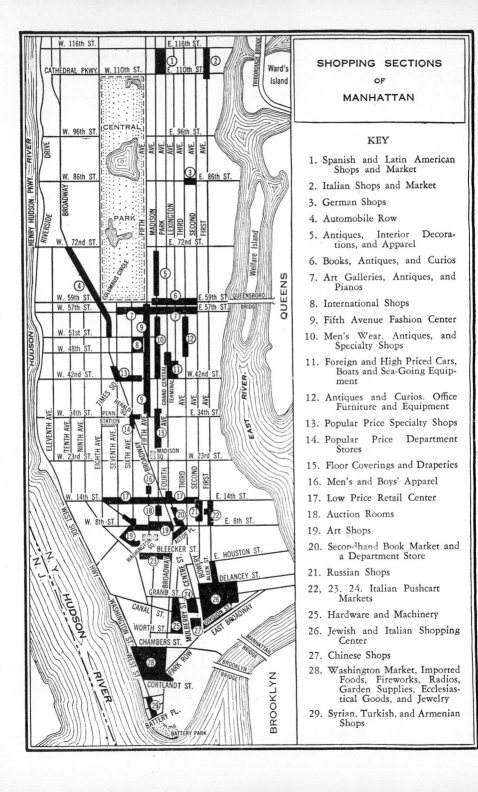

SHOPPING SECTIONS
OF
MANHATTAN

KEY

1. Spanish and Latin American Shops and Market
2. Italian Shops and Market
3. German Shops
4. Automobile Row
5. Antiques, Interior Decorations, and Apparel
6. Books, Antiques, and Curios
7. Art Galleries, Antiques, and Pianos
8. International Shops
9. Fifth Avenue Fashion Center
10. Men's Wear, Antiques, and Specialty Shops
11. Foreign and High Priced Cars, Boats and Sea-Going Equipment
12. Antiques and Curios, Office Furniture and Equipment
13. Popular Price Specialty Shops
14. Popular Price Department Stores
15. Floor Coverings and Draperies
16. Men's and Boys' Apparel
17. Low Price Retail Center
18. Auction Rooms
19. Art Shops
20. Secondhand Book Market and a Department Store
21. Russian Shops
22, 23, 24. Italian Pushcart Markets
25. Hardware and Machinery
26. Jewish and Italian Shopping Center
27. Chinese Shops
28. Washington Market, Imported Foods, Fireworks, Radios, Garden Supplies, Ecclesiastical Goods, and Jewelry
29. Syrian, Turkish, and Armenian Shops

Music Hall, Rockefeller Center, 6th Ave. and 50th St.; elaborate revue, symphony orchestra. Roxy, 7th Ave. and 50th St.; variety revue. State, Broadway and 45th St.; vaudeville. Strand, Broadway and 47th St.; popular orchestra and specialty artists. Capitol, 1639 Broadway.
NEWSREEL THEATERS. One-hour program of newsreels and short subjects. Grand Central, Grand Central Terminal, Lexington Ave. and 42d St.; Embassy, 7th Ave. and 47th St.; Rockefeller Center, 33 W. 50th St.; Seventy-second Street, 2089 Broadway; Trans-Lux, Broadway and 49th St., and Madison Ave. and 60th St.
FOREIGN-LANGUAGE FILM THEATERS. *Chinese:* New Chatham Square, 5 Chatham Square (after 11 p.m.) *French:* Cinema 49, 235 W. 49th St.; Fifth Avenue Playhouse, 66 5th Ave. near 12th St.; Filmarte, 202 W. 58th St. *German:* Eighty-sixth Street Casino, 210 E. 86th St. *Hungarian:* Modern Playhouse, 3d Ave. and 81st St. *International:* Apollo, 223 W. 42d St.; Fifty-fifth Street Playhouse, 154 W. 55th St.; Little Carnegie Playhouse, 146 W. 57th St.; World, 153 W. 49th St. *Russian:* Cameo, 138 W. 42d St. *Spanish:* Teatro Hispano, 5th Ave. and 116th St.; Teatro Latino, 5th Ave. and 110th St. *Swedish:* Forty-eighth Street, 247 W. 48th St. *Yiddish:* Clinton, 80 Clinton St.

Night Clubs

Prices shown below are for weeknights; they are usually higher on Saturday and holidays.

Bal Tabarin, 225 W. 46th St.; Montmartre atmosphere; dinner. Ben Marden's Riviera, Fort Lee, N. J., across George Washington Bridge; on Palisades overlooking the Hudson; summertime favorite; revue; minimum. Bill's Gay Nineties, 57 E. 54th St.; intimate old-time atmosphere and entertainment; a la carte; no minimum. Cafe Latino, 15 Barrow St., Greenwich Village (see Latin-American Restaurants). Casa Manana, 7th Ave. and 50th St.; lavish theater-restaurant; vaudeville show; minimum, including dinner; admission to mezzanine for vaudeville and dancing. Casino Russe, 157 W. 56th St.; Gypsy music; Russian cuisine; dinner. Chez Firehouse, 141 E. 55th St.; intimate doings; dinner. Club Gaucho, Sullivan and W. 3d Sts., Greenwich Village; Argentine atmosphere. Cotton Club, Broadway and 48th St.; Harlem on Times Square; dinner; minimum. Diamond Horseshoe, 235 W. 46th St.; elaborate show; dinner. Dickie Wells, 169 W. 133d St., Harlem; early-morning revelry. Eighteen Club, 20 W. 52d St.; intimate; minimum. El Chico, 80 Grove St., Greenwich Village; Spanish entertainment; dinner. El Morocco, 154 E. 54th St.; a café society resort; formal dress advisable; dinner. Famous Door, 66 W. 52d St.; swing music. Gloria Palast, 210 E. 86th St.; in German quarter; continental entertainment; minimum. Greenwich Village Casino, 5 Sheridan Sq.; well established; dinner; minimum after 10 p.m.

HAVANA-MADRID, Broadway and 51st St.; Cuban-Spanish revue; dinner; minimum after 10 p.m. HICKORY HOUSE, 144 W. 52d St.; swing music; no dancing; menu features steaks and chops; a la carte; no minimum. JIMMY KELLY'S, 181 Sullivan St., Greenwich Village; vaudeville-style show; dinner; minimum after 10 p.m. KIT KAT CLUB, 152 E. 55th St.; Harlem-style show; dinner; minimum after 10 p.m. LEON AND EDDIE'S, 33 W. 52d St.; madcap fun; dinner; minimum. MIDNIGHT SUN, Broadway and 50th St.; show features girls; Swedish food; dinner; minimum after 10 p.m. MON PARIS, 142 E. 53d St.; smart set rendezvous; dinner. NICK'S, 7th Ave. and 10th St.; Greenwich Village; swing music; dinner. NUT CLUB, 7th Ave. and Grove St., Greenwich Village; zany entertainment; dinner; minimum after 10 p.m. ONYX CLUB, 62 W. 52d St.; swing music; minimum. PARADISE, Broadway and 49th St.; extravagant girl-show; dinner; minimum. PEPPER POT INN, 146 W. 4th St., Greenwich Village; well established; dinner; minimum. PLANTATION, Lenox Ave. and 142d St., Harlem; lively music and entertainment; minimum after 10 p.m. QUEEN MARY, 40 E. 58th St.; Swedish food; intimate revue; dinner. RAINBOW GRILL, RCA Building, Rockefeller Center; on 65th floor; informal; dinner; cover after 10 p.m. RAINBOW ROOM, RCA Building, Rockefeller Center; on 65th floor; fashionable following; formal dress required; dinner; cover after 10 p.m. RUSSIAN KRETCHMA, 14th St. and 2d Ave.; well-established, colorful place; dinner; minimum after 10 p.m. SMALL'S PARADISE, 7th Ave. and 135th St.; pioneer Harlem spot; dinner. STORK CLUB, 3 E. 53d St.; a café society resort; dinner; cover after 10 p.m. VERSAILLES, 151 E. 50th St.; features big-name stars; dinner a la carte; cover after 10 p.m. VILLAGE BARN, 52 W. 8th St.; features rustic dances and games; dinner; minimum. WIVEL, 254 W. 54th St.; Swedish food; floor show; dinner.

MUSIC

INDOOR CONCERTS AND RECITALS. BROOKLYN ACADEMY OF MUSIC, Lafayette Ave. and Ashland Pl., Brooklyn; solo, chamber, choral, symphonic music; Oct. to April. BROOKLYN MUSEUM, Eastern Parkway and Washington Ave., Brooklyn; solo, chamber, choral, symphonic music all year; admission free. CARNEGIE HALL, 7th Ave. and 57th St.; solo, chamber, choral, symphonic music; Oct. to May. McMILLIN ACADEMIC THEATRE, Columbia University, Broadway and 116th St.; solo, chamber, choral music; Oct. to April. METROPOLITAN MUSEUM OF ART, 5th Ave.

and 82d St.; symphony concerts, Sat., Jan. and March; admission free. STEINWAY CONCERT HALL, 113 W. 57th St.; solo and chamber music; Oct. to June. TOWN HALL, 123 W. 43d St.; solo, chamber, choral, symphonic music; Sept. to April; occasional evenings in May and June. WASHINGTON IRVING HIGH SCHOOL, Irving Pl. and 16th St.; solo and chamber music; Oct. to April.

OUTDOOR CONCERTS AND RECITALS. CENTRAL PARK, on the Mall; Goldman Band concerts; Sun., Mon., Wed., and Fri., June to Aug.; admission free. LEWISOHN STADIUM, Amsterdam Ave. and 138th St.; New York Philharmonic Orchestra and soloists; June to Aug. PROSPECT PARK, Brooklyn; Goldman Band concerts; Tues., Thurs., and Sat., June to Aug.; admission free.

INDOOR OPERA. METROPOLITAN OPERA HOUSE, Broadway and 39th St.; Nov. to March.

OUTDOOR OPERA. JONES BEACH STADIUM, Jones Beach, Long Island; July to Sept. TRIBOROUGH STADIUM, Randall's Island; July to Sept.

SPORTS

The chief center for indoor sports of all kinds is Madison Square Garden, 8th Ave. and 50th St. There are a number of smaller places, mostly boxing and wrestling arenas, in Manhattan and the other boroughs. Various outdoor sports are held at Baker Field, Columbia University; Lewisohn Stadium, City College; Randall's Island Stadium; and at the baseball parks.

BASEBALL PARKS. Season, April to Oct. EBBETS FIELD (Brooklyn Dodgers), Bedford Ave. and Sullivan Pl., Brooklyn; POLO GROUNDS (N. Y. Giants), 8th Ave. and 155th St.; YANKEE STADIUM (N. Y. Yankees), River Ave. and 161st St., the Bronx.

RACE TRACKS. AQUEDUCT (Queens County Jockey Club), Aqueduct, Queens; meetings June and Sept. BELMONT PARK (Westchester Racing Association), Belmont Park, Long Island; meetings May and Sept. EMPIRE CITY (Empire City Racing Association), Yonkers, N. Y.; meetings July and Oct. JAMAICA (Metropolitan Jockey Club), Jamaica, Queens; meetings April and Oct.

BOAT TRIPS

Steamers operate in summer only.

ATLANTIC HIGHLANDS AND NORTH JERSEY SHORE. SANDY HOOK STEAMERS from W. 42d St. and Cedar St.; four boats daily; fare May and June 91¢ one way $1.25 round trip (slightly higher July and Aug.)

CONEY ISLAND. STEAMERS HOOK MOUNTAIN, DEEPWATER, and FAVORITE from Battery 11 a.m., 1, 2:30, 4, 5:30, and 7 p.m. daily; for fare see newspapers.

HUDSON RIVER. HUDSON RIVER DAY LINE to Yonkers, Indian Point, Bear Mountain, West Point, Newburgh, Poughkeepsie, Kingston Point, Catskills, Hudson, and Albany, from W. 42d St. and W. 125th St.; three to six boats daily; fare weekdays $1.00 round trip to Indian Point and Bear Mountain, and $1.25 to West Point (higher fare to other stops). STEAMER BEAR MOUNTAIN to Bear Mountain from Battery 9:15 a.m. weekdays, 9 a.m. and 10 a.m. Sun; for fare see newspapers. STEAMERS SHOWBOAT and CLERMONT to Bear Mountain from Battery 8:15 p.m. daily; dining, dancing, and floor show; for fare see newspapers.

LONG ISLAND SOUND. STEAMERS WAUKETA and WESTCHESTER to Playland, Rye Beach, from Battery 9:15 a.m., 10:15 a.m., 2:15 p.m., and 8:30 p.m. daily; fare, adults $1.00 round trip, children 50¢. STEAMER MAYFLOWER to Pleasure Beach and Bridgeport, Conn., from Battery 10 a.m. daily; fare Mon. and Fri. $1.00 round trip, Tues., Wed., Thurs., and Sat. $1.25 round trip, Sun. $1.50 round trip. STEAMER BELLE ISLAND to Roton Point, Conn., from Battery 10 a.m. daily; fare Mon. to Fri. $1.00 round trip, Sat., Sun., and holidays $1.25 round trip.

AMUSEMENT PARKS

All parks contain rides, roller coasters, etc.; special features are noted below. Amusements are also available at all beach resorts (*see page 39*).

LUNA PARK, Coney Island, Brooklyn; largest in city; entertainment, dancing, pool bathing; general admission 10¢, individual admission to most amusements. PALISADES AMUSEMENT PARK, Palisades, N. J.; opposite W. 125th St.; entertainment, dancing, pool bathing; general admission 10¢, individual admission to most amusements. PLAYLAND, Rye Beach (Long Island Sound), N. Y.; leading Westchester County park; entertainment, dancing, pool and surf bathing; individual admission to each amusement. ROCKAWAYS' PLAYLAND, Rockaway Beach, Queens; pool and ocean bathing; individual admission to each amusement. STEEPLECHASE PARK, Coney Island, Brooklyn; features many funny amusements; dancing, pool and ocean bathing; admission 50¢ (includes all rides).

SIGHTSEEING

BUS AND LIMOUSINE TOURS. A number of companies providing such tours are located in the Times Square area (see Classified Telephone Directory under "Sightseeing" for addresses). Rates begin at 50¢. The services vary from trips to specific points, such as Chinatown and Coney Island, to all-inclusive tours of the city. Private passenger cars with guide are also available at rates from $5 hourly per person.

STUDY-GROUP TOURS. Among the study-group organizations which conduct combined sightseeing and educational trips are Reconciliation Trips, 503 W. 122d St., and Sloane House (Y.M.C.A.) Tours, 356 W. 34th St.

OBSERVATION TOWERS. BANK OF THE MANHATTAN CO. BLDG., 40 Wall St., 71st floor; open daily 9 a.m. to 5:30 p.m.; admission free. CHANIN BLDG., 122 E. 42d St., 54th floor; open daily 9 a.m. to 11 p.m.; adults 55¢, children 25¢. CHRYSLER BLDG., 405 Lexington Ave., 71st floor; open daily 9 a.m. to 6 p.m.; adults 55¢, children under 15, 25¢, under 8 free. EMPIRE STATE BLDG., 350 5th Ave., 86th and 102d floors; open daily 8 a.m. to 1 a.m.; adults $1.10, children under 16, 25¢. RCA BLDG., 30 Rockefeller Plaza, 70th floor; open daily 10 a.m. to midnight; adults 40¢, children under 16, 20¢. SIXTY WALL TOWER, 70 Pine St., 66th floor; open weekdays 11 a.m. to 5:30 p.m.; Sat. 11 a.m. to 1:30 p.m.; adults 40¢, children under 11, free. WOOLWORTH BLDG., 233 Broadway, 60th floor; open daily 9 a.m. to 6 p.m.; adults 55¢, children 25¢.

AIRPLANE FLIGHTS. Sightseeing planes operate from Floyd Bennett Field, Brooklyn, and Roosevelt Field, Mineola, Long Island. Typical rates: $1.50 for 5-minute trip; $3 for 15-minute trip over the Harbor and Lower Manhattan; $5 for 30-minute trip over Manhattan. Agents for airplane flights include: Airlines Ticket Agency, 41 E. 42d St.; Thomas Cook and Son—Wagon-Lits, Inc., 587 5th Ave.

SIGHTSEEING BOATS. *Around Manhattan:* YACHTS MARILDA, MARILDA II, and MANHATTAN from W. 42d St.; 10 a.m., 2 p.m., and 7:30 p.m. daily, April to Nov.; fare $2. YACHT TOURIST from Battery 10:30 a.m. and 2:30 p.m. daily, May to Oct.; fare $1.50. *Harbor:* GOVERNORS ISLAND; ferry from South Ferry Barge Office at frequent intervals; fare free. STATUE OF LIBERTY (Bedloe Island) boat from Battery every hour; every half-hour in summer; fare 35¢; admission to statue 10¢. STATEN ISLAND FERRY; from South Ferry every 15 minutes; round-trip fare 10¢.

OCEAN LINERS. All the large transatlantic liners may be visited when they are in port. Apply at the pier for pass. See Shipping News section of newspapers for time of arrival. The AQUITANIA and QUEEN MARY (Cunard White Star Line) dock at W. 50th St.; the ILE DE FRANCE (French Line), at W. 48th St.; the CONTE DI SAVOIA and REX (Italian Line), at W. 52d St.; the NIEUW AMSTERDAM (Holland-American Line), at 5th St. Pier, Hoboken, N. J.

RADIO STUDIOS. Apply to sponsor in care of broadcasting company for admission to commercial broadcasts; apply to broadcasting company for admission to sustaining programs. COLUMBIA BROADCASTING SYSTEM (WABC), 485 Madison Ave.; Radio Theater No. 1, 242 W. 45th St.; Radio Theater No. 2, 251 W. 45th St.; Radio Theater No. 3, 1697 Broadway. MUTUAL BROADCASTING SYSTEM (WOR), 1440 Broadway; radio theater: New Amsterdam Theater Roof, 214 W. 42d St. NATIONAL BROADCASTING CO. (WEAF), 30 Rockefeller Plaza; studio tour (not including sponsored broadcasts) 55¢, television tour 55¢, combination 90¢. AMERICAN BROADCASTING CO. (WJZ), 30 Rockefeller Plaza.

MUSEUMS

ART MUSEUMS. AMERICAN ACADEMY OF ARTS AND LETTERS, 633 W. 155th St.; open weekdays 10 a.m. to 5 p.m., Sun. and holidays 2-5 p.m., Nov. to May; admission free. BACHE COLLECTION, 814 5th Ave.: open Tues., Wed., Thurs., and Sat. 11 a.m. to 4 p.m.; closed July, Aug., and Sept.; admission by card on application to the custodian. BROOKLYN CHILDREN'S MUSEUM, Brooklyn Ave. and Park Pl., Brooklyn; open weekdays 10 a.m. to 5 p.m., Sun. 2-5 p.m.; admission free. BROOKLYN MUSEUM, Eastern Parkway and Washington Ave., Brooklyn; open weekdays 10 a.m. to 5 p.m., Sun. 2-6 p.m.; admission free, except Mon. and Fri. (adults 25¢, children 10¢). CHILDREN'S ART CENTER OF UNIVERSITY SETTLEMENT, 184 Eldridge St.; open weekdays 3-5:30 p.m., 7:30-9 p.m., Oct. to June; admission free. THE CLOISTERS, branch of Metropolitan Museum of Art, Fort Tryon Park; open weekdays 10 a.m. to 5 p.m., Sun. 1-6 p.m., closed Christmas morning; admission free, except Mon. and Fri. (25¢). COOPER UNION MUSEUM FOR THE ARTS OF DECORATION, Cooper Square and 7th St.; open weekdays 9 a.m. to 5 p.m.; Oct. to May, 6:30-9:30 p.m., except Sat. and Sun.; closed July and Aug.; admission free. FRICK COLLECTION, 1 E. 70th St.; open weekdays 10 a.m. to 5 p.m., Sun. and holidays 1-5 p.m.; closed Mon., Decoration Day, July 4, month of August, and Christmas; admission free. HISPANIC SOCIETY OF AMERICA, Broadway and 155th St.; open weekdays 10 a.m. to 4:30 p.m., Sun. and holidays 1-5 p.m.; closed Thanksgiving and Christmas; admission free. METROPOLITAN MUSEUM OF ART, 5th Ave. at 82d St.; open weekdays 10 a.m. to 5 p.m., Sun. 1-6 p.m., legal holidays 10 a.m. to 5 p.m.; closed Christmas morning; admission free, except Mon. and Fri. (25¢). MUSEUM OF LIVING ART, 100 Washington Sq.; open Mon. to Fri. 9 a.m. to 8 p.m., Sat. 9 a.m. to 4 p.m.; admission free. MUSEUM OF MODERN ART, 11 W. 53d St.; open weekdays 10 a.m. to 6 p.m., Sun. 12 m. to 6 p.m., closed Decoration Day, July 4, Labor Day, Christmas; admission, adults 25¢, children 10¢, free on Mon. NEW YORK PUBLIC LIBRARY, 5th Ave. and 42d St.; open weekdays 9 a.m. to 10 p.m., Sun. 1-10 p.m.; admission free. PIERPONT MORGAN LIBRARY, 33 E. 36th St.; Main

Building open Tues. and Thurs. 11 a.m. to 4 p.m., Sat. 10 a.m. to 1 p.m., Exhibition Room open weekdays 10 a.m. to 5 p.m.; closed July 1 to Sept. 7; admission free. WHITNEY MUSEUM OF AMERICAN ART, 10 W. 8th St.; open Tues. to Fri. 1-5 p.m., Sat. and Sun. 2-6 p.m., closed Mon. and midsummer months, reopens about Sept. 15; admission free.
HISTORICAL MUSEUMS. CONFERENCE OR BILLOPP HOUSE, foot of Hylan Blvd., Tottenville, Staten Island; open daily, except Mon., 10 a.m. to 6 p.m. May to Oct.; 10 a.m. to 5 p.m. Nov. to April; admission free. DYCKMAN HOME, Broadway and 204th St.; open 10 a.m. to 5 p.m., Sun. and Mon. 1-5 p.m.; admission free. FRAUNCES TAVERN, Broad and Pearl Sts.; open daily, except Sun., 9 a.m. to 4 p.m.; admission free. GRACIE MANSION, Carl Schurz Park, East End Ave. and E. 89th St.; open daily, except Mon., 11 a.m. to 5 p.m.; admission free. HAMILTON GRANGE, 287 Convent Ave.; open Mon. to Fri. 10 a.m. to 5 p.m., Sat. 10 a.m. to 1 p.m., closed Sun. and holidays; admission free. JUMEL MANSION, Jumel Terrace and W. 160th St.; open daily, except Mon., 11 a.m. to 5 p.m.; admission free. KING MANSION, Jamaica Ave. and 153d St., Jamaica, Queens; open Mon., Wed., and Sat. 1-4:30 p.m.; admission free. LEFFERTS HOMESTEAD, Prospect Park, near entrance at Flatbush and Ocean Aves., Brooklyn; open Mon., Wed., and Fri. 1-5 p.m.; admission free. LONG ISLAND HISTORICAL SOCIETY, Pierrepont and Clinton Sts., Brooklyn; open weekdays 9 a.m. to 6 p.m.; closed Fri. and Sat., July 1 to Sept. 3; admission free. MASONIC MUSEUM, 71 W. 23d St.; open weekdays 9 a.m. to 8:30 p.m.; admission free. MUSEUM OF THE AMERICAN INDIAN, HEYE FOUNDATION, Broadway at 155th St.; open weekdays 2-5 p.m., closed July and Aug.; admission free. MUSEUM OF THE AMERICAN NUMISMATIC SOCIETY, Broadway between 155th and 156th Sts.; open daily 2-5 p.m., closed during summer months; admission free. MUSEUM OF THE CITY OF NEW YORK, 5th Ave. at 104th St.; open weekdays 10 a.m. to 5 p.m., Sun. 1-5 p.m., closed Tues.; admission free, except Mon. (25¢). MUSEUM OF JEWISH CEREMONIAL AND HISTORICAL OBJECTS OF THE JEWISH SEMINARY OF AMERICA, Broadway and 122d St.; open daily 10 a.m. to 5 p.m., except Fri. and Sat.; admission free. MUSEUM OF THE STATEN ISLAND HISTORICAL SOCIETY, Court and Center Sts., Richmond, Staten Island; open Mon. to Fri. 10 a.m. to 5 p.m., Sat., Sun., and holidays 2-5 p.m.; admission free. NEW YORK HISTORICAL SOCIETY, Central Park W. between 76th and 77th Sts.; open weekdays 10 a.m. to 5 p.m., Sun. 1-5 p.m., closed during Aug. and on holidays; admission free. OLD MERCHANT'S HOUSE, 29 E. 4th St.; open weekdays 11 a.m. to 5 p.m., Sun. and holidays 1-5 p.m.; admission 50¢. POE COTTAGE, Grand Concourse and Kingsbridge Rd., the Bronx; open weekdays, except Mon., 10 a.m. to 1 p.m. and 2-5 p.m., Sun. 1-5 p.m.; admission free. ROOSEVELT HOUSE, 28 E. 20th St.; open weekdays 10 a.m. to 5 p.m., Sun. and holidays 1-5 p.m., closed Mon., Thanksgiving Day, Christmas, New Year's; admission free, except Wed. and Fri. (25¢). VAN CORTLANDT HOUSE, Van Cortlandt Park, near Broadway and 242d St. entrance, the Bronx; open

Tues., Wed., Fri., and Sat. 10 a.m. to 5 p.m., Thurs. and Sun. 12 m. to 5 p.m.; admission free, except Thurs. (25¢).
SCIENCE MUSEUMS. AMERICAN GEOGRAPHICAL SOCIETY, Broadway at 156th St.; open weekdays 9 a.m. to 4:45 p.m., closed Sat., Sun. and holidays from June to Aug.; admission free. AMERICAN MUSEUM OF NATURAL HISTORY, Central Park W. and 79th St.; open weekdays 10 a.m. to 5 p.m., Sun. 1-5 p.m.; admission free. HAYDEN PLANETARIUM, Central Park W. and 81st St.; performances: Mon. to Fri., 2, 3:30, 8:30 p.m.; Sat., 11 a.m., 1-5 p.m., 8:30 p.m., Sun. and holidays, 2-5 p.m., 8:30 p.m.; admission adults 25¢ (evenings 35¢), children 15¢. NEW YORK MUSEUM OF SCIENCE AND INDUSTRY, RCA Bldg., Rockefeller Center; open daily 10 a.m. to 10 p.m.; admission, adults 25¢, children 10¢. STATEN ISLAND INSTITUTE OF ARTS AND SCIENCES, Stuyvesant Pl. and Wall St., St. George, S. I.; open weekdays 10 a.m. to 5 p.m., Sun. 2-5 p.m.; admission free.
BOTANICAL AND ZOOLOGICAL GARDENS AND AQUARIUM. BROOKLYN BOTANICAL GARDENS, 1000 Washington Ave., Brooklyn; open weekdays 8 a.m. to dusk, Sun. and holidays, 10 a.m. to dusk; library open Mon. to Fri. 9 a.m. to 5 p.m., Sat. 9 a.m. to 12 m., closed Sat., July 15 to Sept. 15; admission free. NEW YORK BOTANICAL GARDENS, Bronx Park; open daily, March 1 to Nov. 1, 10 a.m. to 5 p.m.; Nov. 1 to March 1, 10 a.m. to 4.30 p.m.; admission free. NEW YORK ZOOLOGICAL PARK, Bronx Park; open daily 10 a.m. to dusk; admission free, except Mon. and Thurs. (adults 25¢, children 15¢). PROSPECT PARK ZOO, Flatbush Ave. near Ocean Ave., Brooklyn; open weekdays 11 a.m. to 6 p.m., Sat., Sun., and holidays 10 a.m. to 6 p.m.; closes one hour earlier in winter; admission free. STATEN ISLAND ZOOLOGICAL SOCIETY, Barrett Park Zoo, West New Brighton, S. I.; open weekdays, summer, 10 a.m. to 5 p.m., Sun. and holidays 10 a.m. to 6 p.m.; winter, 10 a.m. to 4 p.m., Sat., Sun., and holidays 10 a.m. to 5 p.m.; admission free.

RECREATION

For facilities other than those listed below see classified telephone directory.
BADMINTON. Rates 50¢ and up. COAST ARTILLERY BRIGADE ARMORY, 120 W. 62d St.; 71ST INFANTRY ARMORY, Park Ave. and 34th St.; 93D INFANTRY BRIGADE ARMORY, 68 Lexington Ave.; 165TH REGIMENT INFANTRY ARMORY, Lexington Ave. and 25th St.
BEACHES. Rates given are for locker or dressing room. ATLANTIC BEACH, Long Island; varying rates. ASBURY PARK, N. J.; rates 50¢ and up. BRIGHTON BEACH, Brooklyn; rates 50¢ and up. CONEY ISLAND, Brooklyn; rates 15¢ and up. JACOB RIIS PARK, Queens; rates 25¢ and up. JONES BEACH, Wantagh, Long Island; rates 35¢ and up. LONG BEACH,

Long Island; varying rates. LONG BRANCH, N. J.; rates 50¢ and up. MAN-HATTAN BEACH, Brooklyn; rates 50¢ and up. MIDLAND BEACH, Staten Island; rates 50¢ and up. ORCHARD BEACH, Pelham Bay Park, the Bronx; rates 25¢ and up. ROCKAWAY BEACH, Queens; rates 25¢ and up. RYE BEACH (Long Island Sound), N. Y.; rates 15¢ and up. SOUTH BEACH, Staten Island; rates 50¢ and up.

BICYCLING. Bicycle paths in Central Park; Ocean Parkway and Prospect Park, Brooklyn; Van Cortlandt and Bronx Parks, the Bronx; Forest and Kissena Parks, Queens; Silver Lake Park, Staten Island. *Bicycle agencies:* Rates 25¢ per hour and up. BICYCLE CLUB, 15 W. 100th St.; BICYCLE CLUB OF AMERICA, 2 W. 61st St.; JACK'S CYCLING SCHOOL, 104 W. 81st St. *For bicycle agencies in other boroughs see classified telephone directory.*

BILLIARDS. Rates 40¢ per hour and up. CAPITOL HEALTH CENTER, 1680 Broadway; DOYLE BILLIARD ROOMS, 1456 Broadway; PARK ROW BOWLING ACADEMY, 31 Park Row; RADIO CITY BOWLING AND BILLIARDS, 1267 6th Ave.; STRAND BILLIARD ACADEMY, 1579 Broadway; JOSEPH THUM, 1241 Broadway.

BOATING. *Motor Boats:* SHEEPSHEAD BAY, Brooklyn; rates 25¢ per ride and up. *Rowboats:* CENTRAL PARK; BRONX, PELHAM BAY, and VAN CORTLANDT PARKS, the Bronx; PROSPECT PARK, Brooklyn; KISSENA PARK, Queens; rates 25¢ per hour.

BOWLING. Rates 20¢ per game and up. CAPITOL HEALTH CENTER, 1680 Broadway; CHELSEA BOWLING CENTER, 244 W. 14th St.; GRAND CENTRAL BOWLING ALLEYS, 40 E. 40th St.; RADIO CITY BOWLING ALLEYS, 1267 6th Ave.; JOSEPH THUM, 1241 Broadway; TUDOR CITY RECREATION CENTER, 239 E. 42d St.

CAMPING AND HIKING. For information apply to State Park Commission, 80 Centre St. The large city parks, such as Bronx Park, Central Park, Forest Park (Queens), La Tourette Park (Staten Island), and Prospect Park (Brooklyn), have long winding paths through attractive wooded areas; hiking trails are found in most state parkways on Long Island and in Westchester County. *Camping:* FIRE ISLAND, ferry from Babylon, L. I.; HARRIMAN PARK, north of Bear Mountain Section; HECKSCHER PARK, Great South Bay, near East Islip, L. I.; POUNDRIDGE RESERVATION, Cross River, Westchester County. *Hiking:* HEMPSTEAD LAKE, Southern State Parkway, L. I.; HUNTER'S ISLAND, along Long Island Sound, the Bronx; OLD CROTON AQUEDUCT, Van Cortlandt Park, the Bronx; PALISADES INTERSTATE PARK, Palisades, N. J.; VALLEY STREAM STATE PARK, L. I.

FISHING. Apply for information to the New York State Conservation Department, Fish and Game Division, 80 Centre St. Consult the daily newspapers for latest information as to boat schedules and kinds of fish running. Deep sea fishing boats leave Sheepshead Bay, Brooklyn, in season at 6, 7, and 8 a.m. daily; rates $2.50. Rowboats and outboard motors are rented at Sheepshead Bay; Broad Channel, Jamaica Bay, Queens; City Island, the Bronx; rates 25¢ an hour and up.

GOLF. *Municipal courses:* Rates, season permit, Mon. to Fri. inclusive, $5.00; single round permit, Mon. to Fri. inclusive, 75¢; Sat., Sun., and holidays, $1.00. All the courses have 18 holes. DYKER BEACH PARK, 86th St. and 7th Ave., Brooklyn; FOREST PARK, Park Lane South and Forest Parkway, Queens; LA TOURETTE PARK, Forest Hill Road and London Road, Staten Island; VAN CORTLANDT PARK, 242d St. and Broadway, the Bronx. *Private courses (open to public):* BAYSIDE GOLF LINKS, Little Bayside Road, Bayside, Queens; rates $1.50 and up. IDLEWILD BEACH GOLF CLUB, Idlewild St., Laurelton, Queens; rates 75¢ and up. MOHANSIC GOLF COURSE, Westchester County Park; rates 75¢ and up. TYSEN MANOR LINKS, New Dorp Lane and Hylan Blvd., New Dorp, Staten Island; rates 50¢ and up.

HORSEBACK RIDING. Bridle paths in Central Park; Prospect Park and Ocean Parkway, Brooklyn; Pelham Bay and Van Cortlandt Parks and Pelham Parkway, the Bronx; Forest and Kissena Parks, Queens. Other paths in state parks and parkways on Long Island and in Westchester County (further information from State Park Commission, 80 Centre St.). *Riding Academies:* Rates $1.00 per hour and up. AYLWARD RIDING ACADEMY, 32 W. 67th St.; CENTRAL PARK RIDING SCHOOL, 924 7th Ave.; CORRIGAN RIDING ACADEMY, 56 W. 66th St.; EQUESTRIAN CLUB, 31 W. 98th St. *For riding academies in other boroughs see classified telephone directory.*

HUNTING. For information regarding State hunting areas and game laws, apply to the New York State Conservation Department, Fish and Game Division, 80 Centre St.

ICE SKATING. *Indoor:* Rates 35¢ and up. GAY BLADES ICE CASINO, 239 W. 52d St.; ICE CLUB, 50th St. and 8th Ave. *Outdoor:* CENTRAL PARK; BRONX, CROTONA, and VAN CORTLANDT PARKS, the Bronx; PROSPECT PARK, Brooklyn; KISSENA and NEW BROOKEVILLE PARKS, Queens; SILVER LAKE PARK, Staten Island; WOODLANDS LAKE, Westchester County. *For other indoor rinks see classified telephone directory.*

ROLLER SKATING. Rates 25¢ and up. PARK AVENUE AUDITORIUM, 101 E. 107th St.; SKATELAND, 53 W. 66th St. *For rinks in other boroughs see classified telephone directory.*

SWIMMING POOLS. *Indoor:* Rates 40¢ and up. PARK CENTRAL HOTEL, 7th Ave. and 55th St.; ST. GEORGE HOTEL, 51 Clark St., Brooklyn; SHELTON HOTEL, 525 Lexington Ave.; WEST SIDE Y.M.C.A., 5 W. 63d St. *Outdoor:* Rates 50¢ and up. CASCADES POOL, 134th St. and Broadway; JEROME CASCADES, Jerome Ave. and 168th St., the Bronx; LUNA PARK, Coney Island, Brooklyn; PALISADES AMUSEMENT PARK, Palisades, N. J.; STARLIGHT PARK, E. 177th St. and Devoe Ave., the Bronx; STEEPLECHASE PARK, Coney Island, Brooklyn. *For other swimming pools see classified telephone directory.*

TABLE TENNIS. Rates 40¢ an hour and up. BROADWAY TABLE TENNIS COURTS, 1721 Broadway; PLAZA TABLE TENNIS CENTER, 2542 Broadway; STRAND BILLIARD ACADEMY, 1579 Broadway.

TENNIS. *Indoor:* JACK BURNS TENNIS COURTS, 244th Coast Artillery Armory, 125 W. 14th St.; rates $1.00 and up. TUDOR CITY TENNIS CLUB, 165th Regiment Armory, 25th St. and Lexington Ave.; rates 50¢ and up. *Outdoor, municipal:* Rates $3.00 a season; apply to Department of Parks. CENTRAL PARK; BRONX, CROTONA, and VAN CORTLANDT PARKS, the Bronx; PROSPECT PARK, Brooklyn; FOREST and KISSENA PARKS, Queens; SILVER LAKE PARK, Staten Island; and numerous other parks. *Outdoor, private:* Rates 50¢ an hour and up. RIPS TENNIS COURTS, 300 W. 96th St.; TUDOR CITY TENNIS CLUB, 41st St. and Prospect Pl. *For nonmunicipal tennis courts in other boroughs see classified telephone directory.*

OUT-OF-TOWN AND FOREIGN NEWSPAPERS

Available for reading at New York Public Library, 5th Ave. and 42d St., and for sale at following newspaper stands: northeast corner 6th Ave. and 32d St.; northwest corner 6th Ave. and 33d St. (out-of-town papers only); southeast corner 6th Ave. and 42d St.; Times Building subway entrance, 7th Ave. and 42d St. (foreign papers only); north end of Times Building (out-of-town papers only); Broadway and 46th St., in the plaza; Union News Stand, lower concourse, International Building, 630 5th Ave.

Annual Events

Events listed here have been selected for their wide general interest. Obviously, the summary presents but a partial review of the city's social, civic, sports, and patriotic events. Specific details and exact dates may be obtained from newspapers or the organizations concerned. *(Note: "nfd" means no fixed date.)*

JANUARY nfd American Water Color Society Exhibition
         nfd Chinese New Year Celebration in Chinatown
         nfd Feast Day (Italian) of St. Francis de Sales in E. 12th St. between 2d and 3d Aves.
         nfd Firemen's Benevolent Association Ball, Madison Square Garden
         nfd Hollywood Ice Revue, Madison Square Garden
         nfd National Motor Boat Show, Grand Central Palace
         nfd National Poultry Show
         nfd Policemen's Benevolent Association Ball, Madison Square Garden

FEBRUARY 5   Feast of St. Agatha Street Festival, Little Italy, between Baxter and Canal Sts.
         nfd Carnation Show, Rockefeller Center
         nfd Milrose A.A. Track Meet, Madison Square Garden
         nfd National A.A.U. Indoor Track Championship Meet, Madison Square Garden
         nfd National Sportsmen's Show, Grand Central Palace
         nfd New York Athletic Club Indoor Track Meet, Madison Square Garden
         nfd Westminster Kennel Club Dog Show, Madison Square Garden

MARCH   17   St. Patrick's Day Parade, 5th Ave.
         nfd Golden Gloves Amateur Boxing Tournament of Champions, Madison Square Garden
         nfd Intercollegiate A.A.A.A. Indoor Track Meet, Madison Square Garden
         nfd International Flower Show, Grand Central Palace

42

	nfd	Knights of Columbus Track Meet, Madison Square Garden
	nfd	Milk Fund Ice Carnival, Madison Square Garden
APRIL	6	Army Day Parade, 5th Ave.
	nfd	Baseball Season opens at Polo Grounds, Yankee Stadium and Ebbets Field
	nfd	Beaux Arts Ball
	nfd	Father Divine's Peace Parade in Harlem
	nfd	Fifth Avenue Easter Parade
	nfd	General Grant Birthday Exercises at Tomb
	nfd	Society of Independent Artists' Exhibition, Grand Central Palace
	nfd	Jamaica Race Meet opens, 22 days
	nfd	Lamb's Club Gambol
	nfd	Pratt Institute (Brooklyn) Art Exhibition
	nfd	Ringling Brothers, Barnum and Bailey Circus, Madison Square Garden
	nfd	Westbury Horticultural Society Show
	nfd	Women's National Exposition of Arts and Industries, Grand Central Palace
MAY	1	May Day Labor Parade
	10	Rumanians celebrate Independence Day
	15	Hungarian Independence Day Parade in honor of Kossuth, from E. 82d St. to Riverside Drive and 98th St.
	nfd	Belmont Park Race Meet opens, 24 days
	nfd	Coney Island and other shore resorts open
	nfd	Intercollegiate A.A.A.A. Outdoor Track and Field Meet, Randall's Island
	nfd	Model Boat Races, Central Park
	nfd	New York Athletic Club Spring Games, Travers Island
	nfd	Outdoor Art Exhibition, Washington Sq.
	nfd	Tulip Show, American Museum of Natural History
JUNE	5	Danes celebrate Constitution Day
	nfd	Aqueduct Race Meet opens, 21 days
	nfd	Lewisohn Stadium Symphonic Concerts, June to Aug., Amsterdam Ave. and 138th St.
	nfd	Madonna delle Grazie Festival in Cherry St.
	nfd	Outdoor Rose Show, Pelham Parkway, the Bronx
	nfd	Summer Operetta Season opens at Jones Beach, L.I.
	nfd	Swedish Festival and Folk Dances in Van Cortlandt and other parks

| | | nfd | Sweet Pea and Rose Show |

JULY 15-17 Celebration in honor of Our Lady of Mt. Carmel in Italian Harlem

      nfd Empire City (Yonkers) Race Meet opens, 24 days

      nfd Polo at Meadowbrook, L.I., and Governors Island

      nfd World Labor Committee's Track and Field Meet at Randall's Island Stadium

AUGUST nfd Fete of San Rocco in all Italian Quarters

SEPTEMBER

    1st Mon. Labor Day Celebrations

      19 Feast of San Gannaro in Little Italy, Mulberry St.

      22 Hungarian Grape and Folk Festival in National Bohemian Park near 69th St., Queens

      nfd Aqueduct Race Meet opens, 15 days

      nfd American Ballads Contest

      nfd Belmont Park Race Meet opens, 15 days

      nfd Camera Art Exhibit, Rockefeller Center

      nfd Coney Island Mardi Gras

      nfd Dahlia Show

      nfd National Electrical and Radio Exposition

      nfd National Graphic Arts Exposition, Grand Central Palace

      nfd New York Athletic Club Fall Games, Travers Island

      nfd Outdoor Art Exhibition, Washington Sq.

OCTOBER nfd American Indian Day Ceremonies

      nfd Auto Races at Roosevelt (L.I.) Raceway

      nfd Drug Trade Exposition

      nfd Empire City (Yonkers) Race Meet opens, 12 days

      nfd Jamaica Race Meet opens, 12 days

      nfd Model Yacht Regatta, Conservatory Lake, Central Park

      nfd National Business Show

      nfd National Funeral Directors' Exhibition, Grand Central Palace

      nfd Philharmonic Symphony Society Concert Season opens, Carnegie Hall

      nfd St. Francis of Assisi Festival in 38th St. between 8th and 9th Aves.

      nfd World's Championship Rodeo, Madison Square Garden

NOVEMBER nfd Chrysanthemum Show, New York Botanical Garden, Bronx Park
          nfd Horticultural Society Exhibition, American Museum of Natural History
          nfd Ice Follies, Madison Square Garden
          nfd Macy's Thanksgiving Day Balloon Parade, Broadway, 110th St. to 34th St.
          nfd Metropolitan Grand Opera Season opens, Nov. to March
          nfd National Academy of Arts and Letters Exhibit
          nfd National Automobile Show, Grand Central Palace
          nfd National Horse Show, Madison Square Garden
          nfd National Hotel Exposition, Grand Central Palace
          nfd Poultry Industries Show, Port Authority Building

DECEMBER nfd Chemical Industries Show, Grand Central Palace
          nfd International Salon of Photography, Rockefeller Center
          nfd International Ski Meet and Winter Sports Carnival, Madison Square Garden
          nfd National Exposition of Power and Mechanical Engineering, Grand Central Palace
          nfd Press Photographers' Exhibition

Manhattan

D. Spiegel

Manhattan

THE liner steams through the Narrows (the Normandie, Queen Mary, Bremen; the dozen greatest ships of the world, sailing from Liverpool, Southampton, Hamburg, Rotterdam, Havre, Genoa, head for that narrow strip of water and steam dexterously through it, turn precisely toward the slender island toward the north). Out of an early morning fog come brooding, ghostly calls. A dark blotch appears, takes form—an anchored tramp: *coffee from Brazil, rubber from Sumatra, bananas from Costa Rica*—and slowly disappears; another liner is suddenly moving alongside, also steaming northward, and then dissolves into the white nothing. Invisible ferries scuttle, tooting, across the harbor.

The Limited, bearing a sight-seeing family (there are 115,000 of them daily—from Waco, Mobile, Los Angeles, Kansas City), the literary genius of Aurora High School, the prettiest actress in the Burlington dramatic club, a farm boy hoping to start for Wall Street, and a mechanic with an idea, pounds across the state of New Jersey. They cross the meadows, see far off the great wall of the city and dive into the darkness beneath Jersey City and the Hudson River. Or perhaps the train comes from Winnipeg, Gary, Erie, and follows the Hudson toward its mouth or crosses the Hell Gate from New England.

In the city, night workers, their footsteps sharp, irregular on the quiet streets, return home. A water wagon rolls by. Bands are still playing in half a dozen night clubs. In the Upper East Side, in the Upper West

Side, in the Gashouse and Hell's Kitchen, in Chelsea and Greenwich Village, the faint and broken ringing of alarm clocks comes to the empty street. *Another day, another dollar. Don't forget to tell the laundryman not to starch my shirts!* Slowly the air between the buildings fills with light.

The crowd increases with the light, a black moving mass, workbound; a million pale faces; a clicking of heels that swells to one sustained roll of thunder. The roar of the city shoots up to encompass it. A rivet overhead pierces the sultry sky; another shakes the earth. *He took me to the Paradise. He's been to college. We came home in a taxi.* The voice is lost in the rumble of an elevated train jammed with work-going clerks gazing at a woman leaning out of the window at 124th Street, 123d, 122d, 121st, 120th . . .

The morning sun picks out an apartment house, a cigar store, streams through the dusty windows of a loft. The racket swells with the light. *These shoes are killing me,* she said, taking the cover off the typewriter. *Main Central is up to forty-six. Did you read about the earthquake?* Looms, shears, jackhammers, trolley cars, voices, add to the din. And in the quieter streets the hawker with the pushcart moves slowly by. *Badabadabada O Gee!* Hawkers of vegetables, plants, fruit. *Badabadabada O Gee!*

In half a million rooming-house rooms the call penetrates ill-fitting windows. The boy who came to be a writer is waked in his mid-town room and dresses for his shift on the elevator. In Chelsea the girl who came to be an actress launders her stockings. The boy who was going to Wall Street sprawls on his bed, wincing as each cry cuts into his dream of the smell of fresh hay and warm milk. A deep blast rises, drowning the sound of hawkers, children, automobiles. *The Conte di Savoia steams up the river; wine from Capri, olive oil from Spain, figs and dates from North Africa.*

Shouting screaming kids fill the streets, playing baseball, football, hopscotch, jump-rope, dodging swift-moving trucks and taxis. Down Fifth Avenue marches a May Day parade sixty thousand strong. Solidarity forever, solidarity forever, the portentous tramp, tramp of regimented feet; slogans called, banners flying. Up lower Broadway an open car moves slowly through the yelling throng and on its pulled-back hood, laughing, waving into the snowstorm that flutters thickly downward from high-up windows, sits a returned aviator, explorer, movie actor, champion chess player, the first man to walk the length of Manhattan backwards.

The late afternoon sunshine glitters on windshields, chauffeurs' caps, on Parisian gowns, Chinese ivories, ebony from Africa, Mexican pottery, and furs from Siberia. *Driving back from Southampton in the fall we used to sit up in front with the chauffeur. Aunt Helen had a staircase in her house that cost fifteen thousand dollars. He died right in the middle of the depression.* Smells of cooking fill the corridors. The lights go on in a loft on a side street, in an office on the thirty-fourth floor of the Empire State Building, along the streets and the bridges. The tugs are riding with port and starboard lights.

The sun leaves the highest of the city's buildings. There are no steamship blasts but loud now are the hoarse pipings of tugs, the yap of ferries with homeward-bound crowds. *I've worked overtime three nights in a row. Two martinis. Did you see the way he looked at me when I put on my hat and walked out?* The light burns out at the foot of 23d Street, 22d Street, 21st, 20th, 19th . . .

The light leaves the flat roofs of the ghetto along the river. Here is the greatest city of the Jews. Here, all unconscious of exoticism, thousands of persons celebrate *bar mitzvah*, sit *shiva* for their dead. Streets littered with papers, bags of garbage shooting out of windows, lines of pushcarts selling food, neckties, pictures, bric-a-brac.

East Side, West Side, all around the town, boys and girls together hanging around shop doors; whispering, giggling in tenement hallways, in courtyards smelling of backhouses. The world's most populous Italian city outside of Italy spends the sultry night on doorsteps, standing, sprawling on sidewalks of broken cement. So with the world's third Irish city. The world's Negro metropolis is the most crowded of all. Home has scarcely room to hang one's hat, which instead is hung in churches, club rooms, rent parties. And in the Upper West Side fifty thousand families will be reading the newspaper by the sitting room table; fifty thousand Upper East Side families will be finishing a quiet game of bridge or sitting at the library table; and among the thousand already asleep on the Lower East Side will be a large number of old timers who have never seen Broadway.

With final blast, quivering over the harbor, a liner moves out of its docks; southern cotton for Liverpool, northwestern wheat for Bordeaux, Kansas City hides for Brazil, Virginia tobacco, Massachusetts shoes, Chicago canned meats, lumber from the Pacific Coast.

The ship moves along the path of a thousand living steamers, past the ghosts of ten thousand sailing vessels and steamships; vessels that brought the Dutch, the English and their goods, Negro slaves, West Indian rum, British textiles, Australian wool, German machinery.

Night draws to a close. Bands are still playing behind the closed doors of half a dozen night clubs. The river wind lifts yesterday's paper the length of a block. A water wagon rolls by. A solitary taxi tracks the wet paving. *Goodnight darling, goodnight, goodnight.*

A blast from the far-off Narrows whispers through the dead streets; spruce from Norway, asbestos from South Africa, German, Austrian, Polish, Italian refugees.

FACTS ABOUT MANHATTAN

It's a tight little island, $12\frac{1}{2}$ miles at its longest, $2\frac{1}{2}$ at its widest, covering 14,211 acres, rising from its surrounding rivers to a height of about 268 feet near Fort Tryon Park, and standing at about latitude 40° N., longitude 73° W. 1,688,769 persons were listed as living here in 1938. 217,976,370 commuters in 1936 traveled into and out of town by way of Manhattan's 20 bridges, 18 tunnels, and 17 ferries, while an average of 115,000 noncommuting visitors are said to pour into town daily through the great railway terminals. For the accommodation of these visitors there are 326 hotels which have a total assessed valuation of $479,793,500.

Transportation within Manhattan is furnished by rapid transit systems of subways and elevated lines (owned by the city but operated both municipally and privately), which in the year ending June 30, 1938, carried 1,038,499,269 passengers; by street surface railways, which in the same year carried 70,936,650 passengers; by busses carrying 312,426,522 and by the 6,893 taxicabs licensed to operate in the borough in 1938.

Two districts, the first lying between the Battery and City Hall, the second bounded by Twenty-third and Fiftieth Streets and lying approximately between Ninth and Park Avenues, contain a high percentage of blocks in which a population of more than 5,000 work during the day. It was estimated in 1936 that 62.6 per cent of Manhattan's land was used for residential purposes and 22.9 per cent for nonresidential. Nearly all the remainder, 14.25 per cent, is given over to parks, of which there are 93 with a combined area of 2,303.897 acres.

In 1937, 24,550 Manhattanites were born, 29,441 couples were married, and 25,228 died. The number of church members was estimated as 853,972. The foreign-born white population was set at 641,618 in 1930. In 1927 there were 465,000 Jewish residents, or 25.71 per cent of the total population. Negroes in 1930 numbered 224,670; Italians, 117,740; Free State Irish, 86,548; Russians, 69,685; Germans, 69,111; Poles,

59,120. These were the principal race and language groups in Manhattan. The borough lost 170,821 of its residents between 1930 and 1938, and this shifting of population represents a trend that is likely to continue as a result of the development of cheap transportation to the suburbs. Though realtors have been shaking their heads, Manhattan land was assessed at $3,962,738,145 in 1938. The largest rental group of tenants, 36.5 per cent, paid from $30 to $59 a month in 1936, while 20.7 per cent paid $19 a month or less and 18.6 per cent, $60 or more. In 1937, 297 new buildings were erected at an estimated total cost of $60,775,350.

297,446,059 shares of stock, worth $1,859,525,825, changed hands at the New York Stock Exchange in the year 1938. Retail trade amounting to $1,462,499,000 was carried on in 41,233 stores in 1935. 18,694 manufacturing establishments in 1935, employing throughout the year an average of 288,036 workers and paying them $359,893,432 in wages, added $1,322,533,066 to the worth of materials which had already cost them $1,110,223,156. Manhattan docks received a large percentage of the 3,547 vessels of a net tonnage of 20,291,204 which entered the port of New York in the year ending June 30, 1938, while a proportionate share of the $650,252,600 in gold and silver and $1,160,726,960 in merchandise imported, and of the exports amounting to $50,780,694 in gold and silver and the $1,238,331,380 in merchandise was handled here.

In 1937 there were 231 homicides in the borough. In 1936, 78 were convicted of homicide; 274, felonious assault; 485, burglary; 422, robbery; 493, grand larceny; 94, forgery; 8, arson, and 76, rape. Fire Department engines and trucks in 1937 went shrieking to 9,042 fires and kept the losses down to $2,647,970. Seventy-three hospitals looked after the islands' sick and incapacitated. The home relief case load as of October 22, 1938, was 68,121. 243,899 students were enrolled in various public institutions of learning, of whom 126,375 attended elementary school; 39,284, junior high school; 55,231, high school; and 23,009, vocational schools.

Of the city's water supply gushing down from 22 reservoirs, Manhattan and the Bronx consumed in 1937 545,400,000 gallons a day. 2,794,445,326 kilowatt hours of electricity and 20,530,875,700 cubic feet of gas were used in Manhattan in 1937, and in 1938, 897,579 telephones were in active operation.

The 40 to 50 legitimate theaters in Manhattan are patronized yearly by about 8,500,000. It is reported that 218 motion-picture houses were doing business as of April, 1937, and 1938 saw something like 300 night clubs

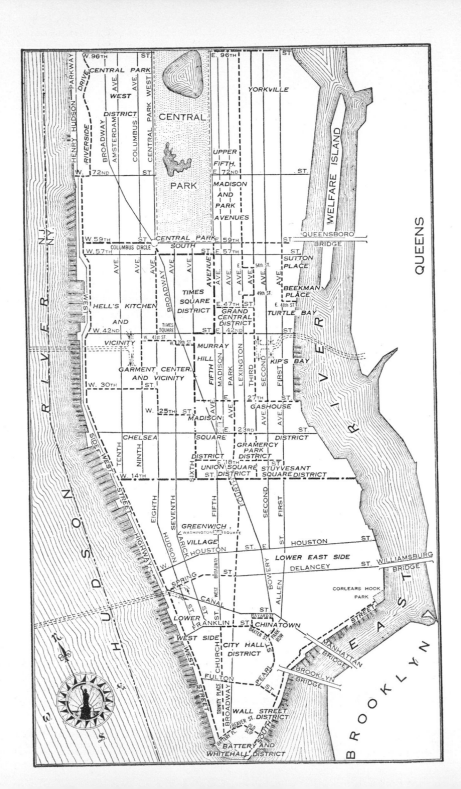

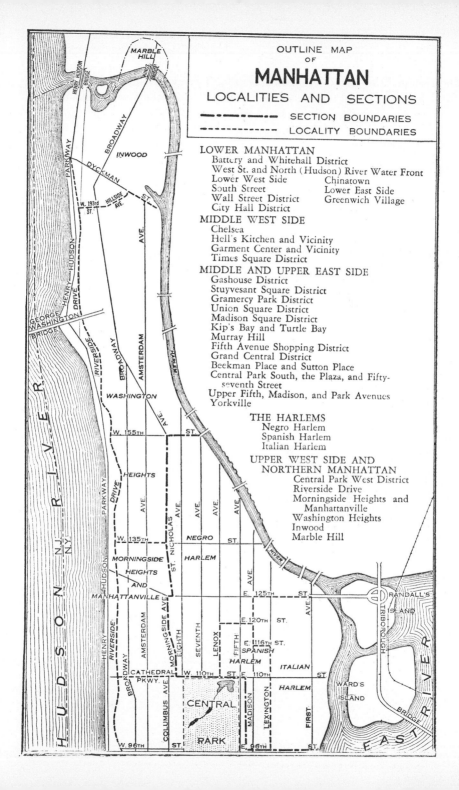

OUTLINE MAP
OF
MANHATTAN
LOCALITIES AND SECTIONS

—--—--—--— SECTION BOUNDARIES
---------------- LOCALITY BOUNDARIES

LOWER MANHATTAN
Battery and Whitehall District
West St. and North (Hudson) River Water Front
Lower West Side Chinatown
South Street Lower East Side
Wall Street District Greenwich Village
City Hall District

MIDDLE WEST SIDE
Chelsea
Hell's Kitchen and Vicinity
Garment Center and Vicinity
Times Square District

MIDDLE AND UPPER EAST SIDE
Gashouse District
Stuyvesant Square District
Gramercy Park District
Union Square District
Madison Square District
Kip's Bay and Turtle Bay
Murray Hill
Fifth Avenue Shopping District
Grand Central District
Beekman Place and Sutton Place
Central Park South, the Plaza, and Fifty-
seventh Street
Upper Fifth, Madison, and Park Avenues
Yorkville

THE HARLEMS
Negro Harlem
Spanish Harlem
Italian Harlem

UPPER WEST SIDE AND
NORTHERN MANHATTAN
Central Park West District
Riverside Drive
Morningside Heights and
Manhattanville
Washington Heights
Inwood
Marble Hill

in more or less continuous operation. Twenty-nine museums and a zoological garden furnish educational recreation for the more serious-minded, and 73 art galleries were listed in December, 1938.

"It is as beautiful a land as one can hope to tread upon," said Henry Hudson.

D. Spiegel

Lower Manhattan

BATTERY AND WHITEHALL DISTRICT—
WEST STREET AND NORTH (HUDSON)
RIVER WATER FRONT—LOWER WEST SIDE
—SOUTH STREET—WALL STREET DISTRICT
—CITY HALL DISTRICT—CHINATOWN—
LOWER EAST SIDE—GREENWICH VILLAGE

Area: Battery on the south to 14th St. on the north; Hudson River to East River.
Map on pages 54-55.
Principal north-south streets: Broadway, West St., Hudson St., Varick St. (and
7th Ave.), 6th Ave., Chrystie St. (and 2d Ave.), Allen St. (and 1st Ave.).
Principal cross streets: Fulton St., Chambers St. (and New Chambers St.), Canal
St., Broome St. (and Delancey St.), Houston St., and 14th St.
Transportation: IRT Broadway-7th Ave. subway (local), South Ferry to 14th St.
stations; IRT Lexington Ave. subway (local), Bowling Green to 14th St. stations;
BMT subway (local), Whitehall St. to Union Square stations; 8th Ave. (Independent) Grand Concourse or Washington Heights subway, Broadway-Nassau St.
to 14th St. stations; 8th Ave. (Independent) Queens-Church Ave. subway, East
Broadway to 14th St. stations; Third Ave. el, South Ferry to 14th St. stations;
busses on all principal north-south and cross streets except West St., Fulton St.,
and Broome St.

THE FLAT lower end of Manhattan, between the Battery and Fourteenth
Street, is the oldest section of the city and the richest in historical associations. Today it has become a commercial, financial, and industrial center

57

where steamship docks crowd one another, and ferries, subways, elevated lines, bridges, and traffic arteries converge and spread fanwise, distributing people and merchandise to every section of the Nation.

In the extreme south is the Battery and Whitehall district, in whose skyscrapers, overlooking the Goddess of Liberty and the ships that pass out to sea, are concentrated the executive offices of transatlantic lines, of exporters and importers, and of consular representatives of foreign nations. West Street, fronting the Hudson River, and edged with busy docks, is the main highway for the city's incoming and outgoing supplies. On the Lower West Side are the produce markets, the dark streets of Manhattan's Syrian colony, and numerous warehouses interspersed with tenements.

Broadway, the nation's foremost thoroughfare, starts at the Battery and bisects lower Manhattan. Below Chambers Street it reflects the varied character of the downtown neighborhood; then it becomes a street of bare lofts and garment factories, whose aspect has changed little in half a century. East of Broadway, above the Battery, the tall buildings of the financial district surround Wall Street; skirting them to the east is South Street, the city's maritime center in the days of sailing ships where now railroad and freight barges are warped into dock by puffing tugs, and the smell from anchored fishing boats drifts inland.

City Hall Park and Foley Square, with their municipal, State, and Federal buildings, lie to the north of Wall Street; and beyond is little, crowded Chinatown. The Bowery, sinister street of lurid fiction and drama, starts below the eastern edge of Chinatown and runs northward beneath the rumbling elevated. Stretching approximately from Broadway to the East River and north to Fourteenth Street is the Lower East Side, crowded slum area of many nationalities, but noted chiefly for its concentrated Jewish population. Greenwich Village, with meandering streets, tenements, and charming old houses, marks the northwest terminus of lower Manhattan.

Prior to the completion of the Erie Canal, the story of Lower Manhattan was largely that of the whole city. In contrast to Boston, Philadelphia, and other Colonial settlements, New Amsterdam, belonging to the Dutch West India Company, was founded in 1626 mainly for commercial reasons. As time passed, the little trading post became the market place and financial capital of the rapidly expanding colony. Almost from the first, commercial establishments began a ceaseless march northward, encroaching upon steadily retreating residential districts. The Wall Street stockade, built in 1653 by the Dutch at the town's northern limit, was removed by the British in 1699; by 1771 the city, with 22,000 population, extended to Grand Street; and after the Revolution the movement northward reached Greenwich Village, accelerated by the yellow fever epidemics at the turn of the century.

Under English rule, following New Amsterdam's surrender in 1664, two great steps toward freedom were taken here. A free press was assured in 1735 as a result of the trial of John Peter Zenger, editor of the *New-York Weekly Journal*, and liberty of worship was firmly established early in the eighteenth century.

The history of New York during the Revolution is less notable than that of Boston and other large towns, since the British occupied Manhattan for almost the entire duration of the war. Early in the conflict, however, liberty poles had been erected on the Common (now City Hall Park), and the lead statue of George III in Bowling Green had been melted into bullets for the Colonists' cause. After the Revolution, New York (the city still consisted of the lower part of the island) boasted of being the first capital of the United States of America. Though suffering temporary setbacks, New York, like several other major American cities, grew rapidly in the next fifty years. In 1792 an embryonic stock exchange was modestly inaugurated under a Wall Street tree. The opening of the Erie Canal in 1825 and the expansion of the West began the process which soon made New York the market place and banker of half a continent, and the primary gateway to Europe. By 1830 the population was 202,589; by 1860 the rising tide of immigration, which was to sweep the city in successive waves for another half-century, had helped to raise the total to 813,669. After the Civil War the Erie Canal lost much of its importance, but by this time New York, with its superb harbor formation, had already attracted a tremendous foreign commerce, and it now became also a railroad center, with many of its freight terminals located across the Hudson.

The more spectacular side of nineteenth-century New York history is associated with lower Manhattan. As early as the 1830's Tammany Hall had discovered the advantages to be derived for itself from the vote of the unassimilated immigrant, and City Hall became the pawn of a group of men whose main object was to deplete the public treasury. The infamous operations of the Tweed Ring in the 1860's and early 1870's, and of other early Tammany politicians, belongs to the past of this older part of the city. Following the Civil War, Wall Street, only a few short blocks south of City Hall, began its more ambitious career as financial controller of the nation.

The history of Lower Manhattan has, however, another side. In the late nineteenth and early twentieth centuries "Newspaper Row" was situated on Park Row. Here James Gordon Bennett, Joseph Pulitzer, and William Randolph Hearst fought their sensational battles. Lincoln Steffens discoursed on political corruption, and Richard Harding Davis and O. Henry spun their tales—O. Henry finding in this exciting, chaotic, sordid section of the city much material for the stories of "Baghdad on the Subway."

With increasing rapidity, the residential areas receded northward. About the 1850's aristocratic St. John's Park began to yield to commerce, and the well-to-do were to be found only in the purlieus of Lower Manhattan, around Greenwich Village. By the time the World War was declared, only a small number of the city's more prosperous residents remained below Fourteenth Street, chiefly in mansions around Washington Square and lower Fifth Avenue.

Beginning in the 1880's Greenwich Village was occupied by the Irish and Negroes, and later by Italians. At approximately the same time, the Germans and Irish of the Lower East Side were supplanted by Italians, Russians, Poles, and to an even greater extent by East European Jews, who, despite poverty, filth, and overcrowding retained their native gaiety and hope. Today, a change is appearing in the Lower East Side; though it is still a slum area, the old "lung" blocks are slowly giving way before widened avenues and new apartment houses.

The settlement there of an increasing number of artists and painters in the 1910's gave Greenwich Village national prominence as an artistic and literary center.

Except for the East Side and Greenwich Village, lower Manhattan is now almost entirely devoted to commerce and finance. In the Wall Street district skyscrapers multiplied rapidly after the turn of the century until building was halted by the stock market crash of 1929. Park Row is no longer Newspaper Row, but an adjunct to the commercial district. Old landmarks were erased by the postwar building boom; and a solid wall of giant structures, almost unbroken from the Battery to Fourteenth Street, hides the busy traffic of the Hudson River.

BATTERY AND WHITEHALL DISTRICT

Area: South of Battery Place, Beaver St., and Old Slip. Map on page 63.

The Battery, threshold of Manhattan, spreads in a decided arc along the North River shore at the southernmost extremity of the island, where

East and North rivers empty their sediment into the Upper Bay. West Street (*see page 68*), rumbling with the trucks that serve almost a hundred North River docks, extends northward from the Battery. Massive blocks of office buildings fill the rest of the northward view until, at the northeast corner of the park, Bowling Green opens out in an irregular plaza; from here Broadway cuts a clean northbound way through the towering stonework of the lower island. Squared ponderously against Bowling Green, south, is the U.S. Custom House. North, nearest the river, is the Whitehall Building. The name "Battery" derives from a British fort built along the river in 1693.

The curve of the highway on the park's east border and Pearl Street, extending east, mark the original shore line. The rest of the area is filled-in land. Beyond the el structure are State Street and the conglomerate skyscraper contours that mount toward Broad and Wall Streets. At the southeast corner of the park opens the great plaza of South Ferry, where all forms of Manhattan's transportation—subway, el, ferry, bus, and taxi—have a compact major terminus, and where the heavy traffic artery, South Street (*see page 80*), opens out opposite, bordering the docks to the east.

The BATTERY is as attractive to water gazers now as when Herman Melville wrote of "Men fixed in ocean reveries. . . . Landsmen: of week days pent up in lathe and plaster—tied to counters, nailed to benches, clinched to desks. Nothing will content them but the extremest limit of the land. They must get just as nigh the water as they possibly can without falling in. And there they stand. Inlanders all, they come from lanes and alleys, streets and avenues—north, east, south, and west. Yet here they all unite."

But the park is more than a Sunday and holiday attraction; it is a welcome breathing space in an area dominated by marine commerce. From the sea wall that bounds its twenty-one acres can be viewed the busy traffic of the North River—liners, tugs with tows of barges and scows, low-riding Diesel cargo boats from the Barge Canal, passenger steamers of the Hudson lines, and ferries plying cross-river and cross-harbor from the row of terminal rail and marine docks on the Jersey shore. Only one railroad has entry for its freight into Manhattan by land; the bulk of the railroad freight must be transshipped by tug and barge.

Southwest appears the Statue of Liberty on Bedloe Island (*see page 411*), and beyond it is Ellis Island and the great immigrant station (*see page 415*). Five miles down the bay rise the abrupt hills of Staten Island. South by southeast lies Governors Island (*see page 413*), military reservation, with Castle Williams, twin fort to Castle Clinton—the old Aquarium—standing grimed and grim on its highest headland. Between Staten Island and Brooklyn is the Narrows, the strait connecting the Upper Bay with the Lower Bay and the sea. Plans for a suspension bridge, between the Battery and Hamilton Avenue, Brooklyn, were approved by the City Council early in 1939. The estimate of the cost was $41,200,000.

Central in popular attraction as well as in prominence among the buildings of Battery Park was the Aquarium (*see page 307*), set close beside the river. At one time it served as an immigration station.

Some immigrants are still landed at the Battery after examination at Ellis Island. A Government (Department of Labor) ferry disembarks them at the BARGE OFFICE, at the southeast extremity of the park. A second ferry, operated by the Army, plies between the Barge Office and Governors Island. From Colonial times to the Civil War a barge served as transport between the office and the island, and it was this circumstance that gave the office its name. The original Barge Office was a charming Colonial structure surmounted by a tall cupola from which a beacon shone at night. The present building is an exceptionally interesting work in the style of the Venetian Renaissance, and it is one of the few buildings in Manhattan with a street arcade. The Barge Office building contains branch offices of the Customs Service, Coast Guard, and Immigration Service. Here, too, ship-news reporters gather to meet incoming liners, for it is from the Barge Office that Customs cutters leave to meet those ships that heave to at Quarantine for sanitary inspection on entering the port. A TABLET at the western end of the building bears the names of radio operators lost at sea.

Southeast of the Barge Office is the bow-roofed, painted building of the SOUTH FERRY TERMINAL, its upper deck invaded by the el structure. From here, powerful steam ferries carry trucks, pleasure cars, and passengers to St. George, Staten Island, in about twenty minutes (*see page 410*).

At the north end of the park is PIER A, second oldest structure on the water front, occupied by the Department of Docks and the Police Department's Harbor Precinct. A clock tower at the edge of the pier is a memorial to soldiers and sailors killed in the World War. The clock sounds the signals for the watches kept on shipboard, and also shows the time by dial. Adjacent is a boat basin where police boats are tied beside pleasure craft. At the end of the sea wall is the two-story city FIREBOAT STATION, its tower overlooking the harbor. This is the headquarters for a fleet of ten fireboats protecting about 771 miles of New York and New Jersey water front. The 130-foot *Fire Fighter,* powerful enough to throw a stream over George Washington Bridge, is berthed beside the building.

Midway along the sea wall is a squat building used as a TICKET OFFICE for excursion boats. Craft bound for the Jersey side of the Lower Bay and steamboats for Coney Island leave from this point. The Battery boatmaster, Peter (Buck) McNeill, who has his office here, keeps a sharp watch for would-be suicides to whom this is a favorite spot.

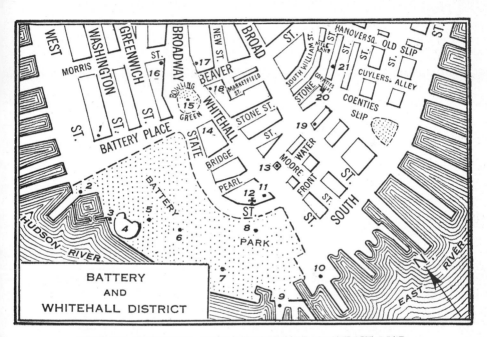

KEY TO BATTERY AND WHITEHALL DISTRICT MAP

1. Whitehall Building
   U.S. Weather Bureau
2. Department of Docks
   Police Harbor Precinct
3. Fireboat Station
4. Aquarium
5. Statue of Giovanni da Verrazano
6. Statue of John Ericsson
7. Flagpole (Evacuation Day)
8. Oyster Pasty Battery Cannon
9. Barge Office
10. South Ferry Terminal
    Staten Island Ferry Slip
11. South Ferry Building
12. Mission of Our Lady of the
    Rosary
13. U.S. Army Building
14. U.S. Custom House
15. Statue of Abraham de Peyster
16. Cunard Building
17. Standard Oil Building
18. New York Produce Exchange
19. Fraunces Tavern
20. Site of First Tavern and City
    Hall in New York
21. Site of the First Printing Press

It was on the original rocky finger of land that the first Dutch colonists built their huts and a simple breastwork—later called Fort Amsterdam. In 1626 Peter Minuit, governor of the new settlement, "bought" the island from the Manhattoes for cloth and fripperies worth about twenty-four (gold standard) dollars. Administered by the Dutch West India Company, New Amsterdam was the scene of frequent disputes between its inhabitants and its governors. Englishmen, Jews, and other colonists, traders, and adventurers from many lands, had, however, settled there among the Dutch by 1664, when a British war fleet appeared to demand the surrender of the town to the Duke of York, who had received from his brother, Charles II, a grant embracing the present state of New York, the islands off the New England coast, and part of the present state of Maine. Despite the efforts of Director Peter Stuyvesant, the burghers refused to defend New Amsterdam, and the English flag was run up without opposition. It remained there until the Revolution, except for one year, during which the armed naval forces of the Dutch Republic retook it and undertook to carry on under Dutch rule; the settlement was returned to England under a treaty made in the Old World.

Names, plaques, and statues in the park recall the early history of the Battery. A bronze STATUE OF GIOVANNI DA VERRAZANO, Florentine navigator who is said to have entered the harbor in 1524, stands in the park. On a granite FLAGSTAFF base, Minuit is shown making his deal with the natives. A CANNON believed to have been part of the armament of the Oyster Pasty Battery (1695–1783) has been preserved. A FLAGPOLE commemorates the one greased on Evacuation Day, November 25, 1783, to prevent the hauling down of the British flag by the American troops. And a bronze FIGURE OF JOHN ERICCSON honors the memory of the designer of the *Monitor,* first turreted battleship, and the screw propeller. The street bordering the park on the north is Battery Place.

From the Battery, streets wind their way in erratic angles. Colonial brick, nineteenth-century sandstone, and modern steel-skeletoned office buildings stand side by side. Clerks, maritime employees, Custom House officials, stenographers, sailors on shore leave, Army and Navy men, South Street lodging house indigents, commuters to Staten Island and Brooklyn, and tourists move along together.

The sea dominates this virile neighborhood. Sou'westers, sea boots, pea jackets, and dungarees are displayed in the shop windows along the side streets. Model ocean liners and colorful posters advertise offices of the great STEAMSHIP AGENCIES along Broadway, while sandwich men mutely call attention to passport photo studios.

State Street, bordering Battery Park on the east, was the town's most fashionable thoroughfare until the beginning of the nineteenth century, when the wealthy residents began moving uptown. Here were the homes of the merchant princes, known as the "Peep-o'-Day Boys," because they arose at dawn to peer across the harbor at Staten Island where signal staffs flashed news of ships sighted beyond the Narrows. One residence, No. 7, between Pearl and Whitehall Streets, survives, almost merged with the contemporary drabness of neighboring buildings under the winding el. Its tall white columns and delicate ironwork balcony still suggest the opulence of another day. The interior, with its fine old hand-carved mantelpieces, may be seen by permission of the Mission of Our Lady of the Rosary, which for many years has maintained the dwelling as a HOME FOR IMMIGRANT GIRLS. The house, it is believed, was built according to plans drawn by John McComb, one of the architects of the present City Hall. On the site of the South Ferry Building near by, at 1 State Street, once stood the homes of Peter Stuyvesant and Robert Fulton, the inventor. Opposite the main entrance of the South Ferry Building, is the U.S. ARMY BUILDING, 39 Whitehall Street. This red-brick structure with a two-story granite foundation, conservatively built in 1886 in the style of a generation earlier, houses many Army departments of the New York district, such as the recruiting, information, and pictorial services, and an engineers' unit.

Facing Bowling Green, between State and Whitehall Streets, is the CUSTOM HOUSE, in which are the offices of the Collector of Customs of the Port of New York, and the headquarters of Custom Collection District No. 10 (which embraces the sub-ports of Albany, Newark, and Perth Amboy). Other offices in the building are those of the Comptroller of Customs, the Surveyor of Customs, the Collector of Internal Revenue for the Second New York District, the Coast Guard, the Tariff Commission, the U.S. Navy Hydrographic Office, the Bureau of Statistics of the Department of Commerce, and Station P of the New York Post Office.

The building, somewhat ponderous in its neoclassic treatment, was designed by Cass Gilbert. It was completed in 1907 at a cost of more than seven million dollars, including the price of the land. Seven stories high, the masonry is Maine granite, heavily embellished with dolphins, tridents, and other nautical symbols. On pedestals advancing from the front of the building are four heroic sculptured groups by Daniel Chester French, representing Asia, America, Africa, and Europe. Across the sixth story are twelve statues dedicated to commercial centers of the world: *Greece* and *Rome,* by F. E. Elwell; *Phoenicia,* by F. W. Ruckstull;

Genoa, by Augustus Lukeman; *Venice* and *Spain,* by F. M. L. Tonetti; *Holland* and *Portugal,* by Augustus Saint-Gaudens; *Denmark,* by Johannes Gellert; *Germany,* by Albert Jaegers; *England* and *France,* by Charles Grafly. A cartouche by Karl Bitter, on the seventh floor, depicts two winged figures bearing the shield of the United States. Ten paintings by Elmer E. Garnsey, representing world ports as they appeared in 1674 when the Dutch flag last floated over Fort Amsterdam, are on the walls of the reception room in the main corridor.

The Custom House occupies the site of Fort Amsterdam, whose four bastions, corresponding to the points of the compass, commanded both the North and East rivers. The fort, including a governor's house built for Peter Stuyvesant, was demolished in 1790. On its site a mansion, known as the Government House, was erected. At the time, ambitious New Yorkers, hoping their city would become the nation's capital, intended the mansion for the President's home. It was used by Governors Clinton and Jay, and later did service as a customhouse until destroyed by fire in 1815.

In Colonial days Battery Place, which bounds Battery Park on the north, was a much wider street and was known by its Dutch name, *Marcktveldt;* later this was anglicized to Marketfield. This thoroughfare was the site of New Amsterdam's first cattle market. The WHITEHALL BUILDING at No. 17, which occupies the entire block between West and Washington Streets, comprises two buildings. The original twenty-story edifice, facing the park, was built in 1900; a thirty-two-story addition was completed in 1910. Many leading shipping companies and a number of consulates have their offices in this building. Above these is the office of the U.S. WEATHER BUREAU, with an instrument shed on the roof.

Standing at the foot of the deep sunless canyon of lower Broadway is BOWLING GREEN, probably the city's oldest public park. Here, according to the legend, astute Peter Minuit made the bargain that gave Manhattan to the white man. In 1638–47 this oval spot was part of the hog and cattle market of *Marcktveldt.* Later, it served as a parade ground for the Dutch militia. The English fenced off the plot and in 1732 leased it to three citizens for use as a private bowling ground. The rent was set at one peppercorn a year. During the Revolution, the royal crowns ornamenting the fence pickets disappeared. A bronze STATUE OF ABRAHAM DE PEYSTER, merchant and one-time mayor of the city (1691–5), by George Bissell, has stood here since 1896.

East of Bowling Green is the dark red-brick and terra-cotta building of the NEW YORK PRODUCE EXCHANGE erected in 1881–2 from plans by George B. Post. The design of the exterior bearing walls is derived from

that of a Roman aqueduct: the arched openings, arranged in long orderly lines, double in number as they rise. Inside, the produce brokers busy
themselves trading and watching the quotation boards from the floor.
The boards display Chicago, Winnipeg, Minneapolis, Duluth, St. Louis,
and Kansas City grain prices, and New York and New Orleans cotton
prices as well as those of foreign markets. The Produce Exchange is
the oldest incorporated exchange in the country, having been chartered
in 1862 by special act of the State Legislature. Its trading floor is the
largest in the world, measuring 220 feet long, 144 feet wide, and 60 feet
to the skylight.

The STANDARD OIL BUILDING, 26 Broadway, incorporates two structures of different age and height. It is surmounted by a massive pyramidal
tower, once one of the most imposing of the New York sky line. A bust
of the first John D. Rockefeller by Jo Davidson is on the left side of the
corridor. Crowds swarming through the building and along the street in
the daytime are in the main unaware of its existence, but at night the
lighting of the marble gives the bust a strange appearance, and people
passing through the now deserted region often stop before the entrance
and gaze curiously inside.

The CUNARD BUILDING, at 25 Broadway, is still one of the city's most
luxurious structures. Its interior, with its vast domed hall, is decorated
with murals by Ezra Winter, depicting the voyages of Leif Ericson,
Sebastian Cabot, Christopher Columbus, and Sir Francis Drake.

Beaver Street, east of Bowling Green, is lined with commercial and
maritime houses, and restaurants. The original Delmonico's, which eventually moved to Madison Square, is part of the neighborhood's tradition.
At the end of Beaver Street is Pearl Street, so named because of the sea
shells found there in the days when the East River almost reached this
street. The inlet, filled in more than a hundred years ago, was known as
Coenties Slip, a corruption of the Dutch nickname *Coentje,* a combination of the given names of Conraet and Antje Ten Eyck, whose home
was near by. At the head of the slip, on what is now the northwest
corner of Pearl Street and Coenties Alley, Governer Kieft, tired of playing host to traders in his own home, built in 1641 the *Stadt-Herberg,* or
City Tavern, a five-story stone structure with an unobstructed view of
the East River. Twelve years later, when the community rose to the dignity
of a municipality, New York's first hostelry was converted into the *Stadt
Huys,* or City Hall. A TABLET high on the wall of 73 Pearl Street marks
the site of the building, demolished in 1790. Near by at No. 81
another TABLET marks the site where William Bradford established in

1693 the first printing press in New York, "At the sign of the Bible." A quaintly carved female figure is set above the street in the building at No. 88 over a TABLET commemorating the great fire of 1835 which destroyed most of the buildings of Coenties Slip. The blaze, which raged for nineteen hours, destroyed 650 buildings with a loss of twenty million dollars. Ten years later a fire in the same neighborhood destroyed 345 buildings and caused property damage amounting to six million dollars.

At the corner of Pearl and Broad Streets is FRAUNCES TAVERN, one of Manhattan's most cherished landmarks and a notable restoration of early Georgian Colonial work. The relatively square proportions, regular window spacing, brickwork, white portico, hipped roof with its light balustrade, and the interior paneling, are all characteristic of the style, but Dutch influence is echoed in the shape of the dormers, which differ from the gabled English type. It was erected in 1719 as a residence by Etienne de Lancey, a wealthy Huguenot. The merchant firm of his grandson Oliver (De Lancey, Robinson, and Company) turned it into a store and warehouse in 1757. The building was bought in 1762 by Samuel Fraunces, a West Indian of French and Negro blood, who opened it as the Queen's Head Tavern. Washington bade farewell to his officers in 1783, in the tavern's Long Room, faithfully restored in 1907 by the Sons of the Revolution (not to be confused with the Sons of the American Revolution). A museum, exhibiting Revolutionary relics, is on the third floor, and on the fourth is a small historical library with paintings by John Ward Dunsmore. *(Open daily except Sunday 9 a.m. to 4 p.m.; admission free.)* Headquarters of the Sons of the Revolution occupy much of the building; a restaurant patronized by Wall Street bankers and shipping and business men is on the ground floor.

WEST STREET AND NORTH (HUDSON) RIVER WATER FRONT

Area: Battery Place to 72d St. along North River. Maps on pages 75, 127, and 149.

Although the western rim of Manhattan is but a small segment of New York's far-flung port, along it is concentrated the largest aggregate of marine enterprises in the world. Glaciers of freight and cargo move across this strip of North (Hudson) River water front. It is the domain of the super-liner, but it is shared also by the freighter, the river boat, the ferry, and the soot-faced tug. Great trunk line railroads from the hinterland, barred from the city by the Hudson, transship their passengers to ferries at the Jersey railheads and their freight cars to scows. In consequence, the railroads use nearly as many North River piers as the steamship lines.

The broad highway, West Street and its continuations, which skirts the North River from Battery Place to Fifty-ninth Street, is, during the day, a surging mass of back-firing, horn-blowing, gear-grinding trucks and taxis. All other water-front sounds are submerged in the cacophony of the daily avalanche of freight and passengers in transit. Ships and shipping are not visible along much of West Street. South of Twenty-third Street, the river is walled by an almost unbroken line of bulkhead sheds and dock structures. North of Twenty-third, an occasional open spot in the bulkhead permits a glimpse of the Hudson and the Jersey shore beyond. Opposite the piers, along the entire length of the highway, nearly every block houses its quota of cheap lunchrooms, tawdry saloons and water-front haberdasheries catering to the thousands of polyglot seamen who haunt the "front." Men "on the beach" (out of employment) usually make their headquarters in barrooms, which are frequented mainly by employees of lines leasing piers in their vicinity.

In Revolutionary days what is now West Street was under water. About 1811 the bank was extended and raised to allow the building of docks. A number of water grants, or permanent leases, were given at nominal rentals to individuals and corporations who later profited greatly when the city reclaimed the property. Not until 1870, however, did this western water front come into considerable use, and it was 1890 before West Street displaced South Street as the main gateway for water-borne traffic. Today it is worth $470,000 an acre, with a pier value of $1,500 per linear foot, and is the most lucrative water-front property in the world.

Passenger lines use many North River terminals. Transatlantic, South American, West Indian, and intercoastal ships dock north of Fourteenth Street, while the terminals of the coastwise and Long Island Sound lines are scattered between this point and the Battery. The most notable exception is the "Great White Fleet" of the United Fruit Company, whose steamers, engaged in the West Indian fruit and passenger trade, are berthed at the famous "banana docks," Piers 2, 3, 7, and 9, near the foot of West Street.

In this section, water-front shipping operates literally in the shadow of Manhattan's downtown sky line. Opposite the United Fruit terminal, two red-brick structures, the thirty-seven-story DOWNTOWN ATHLETIC CLUB at 18 West Street and the thirty-one-story OFFICE BUILDING adjoining it at No. 21, both designed by Starrett and Van Vleck, contribute peaks to the architectural sierra. Their modern appearance is accentuated by the more conventional aspect of the near-by Whitehall Building *(see page 66)*. Not far to the north, somewhat more modest heights are reached by the NEW YORK POST and WEST STREET BUILDINGS. The former, a seventeen-story structure of buff-colored brick at 75 West Street, houses the daily paper which was founded by Alexander Hamilton in 1801. The twenty-three-story West Street Building, at No. 90, was designed by Cass Gilbert and completed in 1905. Its elaborate pinnacles, decorative chimneys and gables disclose the late French Gothic influence.

Just north of the West Street Building, a pedestrian footbridge provides safe passage from the foot of Liberty Street to the ferry terminal of the Central Railroad of New Jersey. Between this point and Forty-second Street, the railroads maintain eleven ferry services to Jersey City, Hoboken, and Weehawken. These are used by more than sixty million passengers, and between ten and eleven million vehicles, annually.

In the block between Liberty and Cortlandt Streets, at 107 West Street, is the WATCH MUSEUM of Fred W. Jensen and Son, managed by three generations of the Jensen family. Its collection contains timepieces of every known variety, the most intricate being a mechanism that splits seconds and records the passing minutes, hours, days of the week and month, and phases of the moon.

In 1807, Robert Fulton's *Clermont* cast off from a pier at Cortlandt Street and steamed up the Hudson to Albany, demonstrating the practicability of steamship transportation.

The NEW YORK TELEPHONE COMPANY SKYSCRAPER at No. 140 is an unusually successful attempt to obtain the maximum spatial benefits under the restrictions of the zoning law. Designed in 1926 by Ralph Walker of the office of McKenzie, Voorhees, and Gmelin, it is the largest telephone building in the world, thirty-two stories high and covering an area of 52,000 square feet. Despite difficulties raised by its irregular-shaped site, the building masses are exceptionally well related, endowing the structure with a silhouette of great strength. The exterior, of buff brick and limestone with a granite base, is enriched by ornamental flowers and elephant heads. This building is the headquarters for the largest of the component companies of the Bell Telephone System, serving New York State and part of Connecticut.

From the World-Telegram Building, between Barclay Street and Park Place, to the great Pennsylvania Railroad pier for perishable freight, between Hubert and Watts Streets, West Street bounds the Washington

Market *(see page 74)*. At 260 West Street stood the Phoenix Foundry where Captain John Ericsson in the late 1830's constructed America's first iron sailing boats and steamships with screw propellers. Opposite Duane Street, the ramps of the newest extension of the WEST SIDE (Elevated) HIGHWAY slope into West Street. A 350-foot parabolic bridge over the wide intersection at Canal Street links this segment with the four-and-one-half-mile elevated roadway that follows the water front to the Henry Hudson Parkway *(see page 284)* at Seventy-second Street. This magnificent express drive, which provides the motorist with an unexcelled view of the Jersey water front, the mid-town sky line, and the liners berthed along the North River, leads by means of Canal Street ramps directly to the Holland Tunnel *(see page 79)*. Eventually the highway will be extended south, curving around the Battery and South Street to the East River Drive.

ST. JOHN'S PARK FREIGHT TERMINAL, a three-story structure covering three city blocks between Charlton and Clarkson Streets, marks the southern terminus of the New York Central's West Side line. The terminal, which was opened in 1934, is the principal delivery station for dairy freight in the city.

In a group of buildings which occupy the block around 463 West Street and a portion of the adjoining block are consolidated the RESEARCH LABORATORIES OF THE BELL TELEPHONE SYSTEM. Here scientists have made many contributions to the telephone and to allied means of communication, such as sound films, picture transmitters, and public address systems. To visit these laboratories special permission must be obtained.

GANSEVOORT MARKET, or "Farmers' Market," as it is generally known, occupies the block between Gansevoort and Little West Twelfth Streets. Farmers from Long Island, Staten Island, New Jersey, and Connecticut bring their produce here at night for sale under supervision of the Department of Public Markets. Activities begin at 4 A.M. Farmers in overalls and mud-caked shoes stand in trucks, shouting their wares. Commission merchants, pushcart vendors, and restaurant buyers trudge warily from one stand to another, digging arms into baskets of fruits or vegetables to ascertain quality. Trucks move continually in and out among the piled crates of tomatoes, beans, cabbages, lettuce, and other greens in the street. Hungry derelicts wander about in the hope of picking up a stray vegetable dropped from some truck, while patient nuns wait to receive leftover, unsalable goods for distribution among the destitute. The market closes at 10 A.M. and is not open Sundays or holidays.

In a wharf at the foot of Gansevoort Street, Herman Melville, the author of *Moby Dick,* once served as customs inspector. Across West Street is the WEST WASHINGTON MARKET, comprising ten quaint red-brick buildings which house a live poultry market patronized mostly by *kosher* butchers. Since poultry requires ample heat in winter, every stall is equipped with a furnace, so that each roof adds more than a dozen chimneys to its picturesque architecture.

From this point to Twenty-second Street, Eleventh Avenue (as the water-front street is here called) skirts the weather-beaten CHELSEA PIERS designed by Warren and Wetmore. These nine great docks, built by the city between 1902 and 1907 for the transatlantic ships of that period, serve such lines as the United States, Grace, Cunard White Star, Panama Pacific, and American Merchant, and are among the busiest on the river. SEAMEN'S HOUSE, an eight-story Y.M.C.A. building at the corner of Twentieth Street and Eleventh Avenue, furnishes up-to-date living and recreational facilities for more than 250 sailors.

Because of the heavy concentration of shipping at the Chelsea Piers, this area has been a strategic sector in the industrial conflicts that break out periodically between maritime labor and shipowners. During the 1936–7 strike, when rank and file seamen tied up the ships in their struggle for a better agreement, Eleventh Avenue was the scene of frequent clashes between pickets and scabs, "goon squads" (thugs) and defense squads, strikers and police. The NATIONAL MARITIME UNION OF AMERICA, established after the termination of the strike, has its headquarters at 126 Eleventh Avenue.

Unlike their sea-going brothers, the port's "dock-wallopers" (longshoremen), thousands of whom live in slum areas adjoining West Street, have been quiet in recent years, although they steadily oppose the hiring system, called the "shape-up," whereby the boss stevedore selects his working force several times daily from crowds of longshoremen massed before the dock gates.

At Twenty-second Street the North River shore line bends sharply westward. The highway is called Thirteenth Avenue from this point to Thirtieth Street, whence it extends northward to Fifty-ninth Street as Twelfth Avenue. Not far beyond the great Twenty-third Street ferry terminal, in the block between Twenty-sixth and Twenty-seventh Streets, the STARRETT LEHIGH BUILDING dominates the water front. The building, erected in 1931, represents an effort to solve the problem of freight distribution in a congested metropolis. It comprises a huge railroad yard, loading platforms for trucks and trailers, and facilities for the storage, repacking, redistribution, manufacturing, and display of goods. Although the first three floors and central portion are steel-frame in construction, the rest of the building follows a cantilevered concrete design. The great horizontal bands of concrete floor, brick parapet, and continuous windows sweep majestically to meet the service portion, which rises, framed in steel, near the center of the block. The building has unusual power and constitutes an important step in the development of contemporary architecture. The architects were Russell G. and Walter M. Cory.

The railroads have burrowed deeply into the water front between Twenty-fifth and Seventy-second Streets, pre-empting most of the piers and nearly all the property opposite. The New York Central's THIRTIETH STREET YARD straddles ten city blocks, and its SIXTIETH STREET YARD, thirteen blocks, constituting two of the largest privately owned areas in the city. The latter is the main receiving, classification, and departure yard for the only all-rail freight line on Manhattan Island. Both yards were being arranged in 1939 to provide for building construction over the tracks (see page 157).

Sandwiched among this welter of railroad sidings are the piers of the Hudson River lines and the terminals of many of the world's greatest liners. The new TRANSATLANTIC DOCKS of the Cunard White Star, French, Hapag Lloyd, Italian, Swedish American, and Furness Bermuda lines extend from Forty-fourth to Fifty-seventh Street, and were especially designed to handle luxurious ships like the *Queen Mary, Normandie, Europa, Rex,* and other greyhounds of the Atlantic. Piers 88, 90, and 92, each of which is 1,100 feet long, make this terminal the largest in the world.

LOWER WEST SIDE

Area: Battery Place on the south to Spring St. on the north; from West St. east to Trinity Place, Church St., and Broadway (Franklin to Spring St.). Maps on pages 75 and 127.

Though this district has a few modern skyscrapers with impressive marble façades, the character of the neighborhood is derived from produce sheds, crates, smells of fruit and fish of Washington Market, and the amazing variety of retail shops selling radios, pets, garden seeds, fireworks, sporting goods, shoes, textiles, and church supplies. There is an endless flow of traffic through the streets, whose buildings, grimy with age, reveal their pre-Civil War glory in carved lintels, arched doorways, and ornate cornices.

Five streets—Washington, Greenwich, Hudson, West Broadway, and

Church—form the main north and south thoroughfares, but the narrow, transverse streets leading to the Hudson River carry the burden of the traffic, much of which heads for New Jersey through the ferries at the end of Chambers, Barclay, Cortlandt, and Liberty Streets, or via the Holland Tunnel. Beneath the streets roar the subways and above them hurtled the Ninth Avenue el, which created an atmosphere like Milton's "darkness made visible," until its demolition.

Tunnels, railroads, ferryboats, subways, and road traffic have made this section one of the most important transit centers. Close to the river and harbor, it is also easily accessible to all parts of the city, making it a natural site for the largest fruit and produce market in the world. Location, too, accounts for the flourishing retail trade: New Jersey commuters returning home after a day's work in the city often find it practicable to buy their necessities here.

The markets inject a rude vitality into the district. While most of the city sleeps, WASHINGTON MARKET, north of Fulton Street and spreading to many side streets between West and Greenwich Streets, reaches the peak of its activity. Perishable products must be distributed quickly; in this concentrated market they pass from jobbers to wholesalers and retailers. Streets free of daytime traffic are taken over by trucks of dealers and farmers. Freight cars discharge their burdens; produce is moved, stored, stacked, boxed, and crated. A weird spatter of lights provides illumination, and in the glow truck drivers, farmers, tally-keepers, and inspectors work at a swift pace. In winter the streets are lined with bonfires around which the men warm themselves.

The name Washington Market is used to designate the entire wholesale produce section and the city-owned RETAIL MARKET, a block-square building between Washington, West, Fulton, and Vesey Streets. The Bear Market, established in 1812, was the predecessor of the original Washington Market. The latter, built in 1833, was also known as Country Market, Fish Market, and Exterior Market. The present Retail Market building was reconstructed in 1914. Its interior is split into stalls that are leased. An entrancing array of food is offered including caviar from Siberia, Gorgonzola cheese from Italy, hams from Flanders, sardines from Norway, English partridge, native quail, squabs, wild ducks, and pheasants; also fresh swordfish, frogs' legs, brook trout, pompanos, red snappers, codfish tongues and cheeks, bluefish cheeks, and venison and bear steaks.

In the vicinity of Cortlandt and Greenwich Streets, two blocks east and south of Washington Market, is the retail radio district. Seed and pet shops, largely patronized by suburban commuters, are south of Barclay

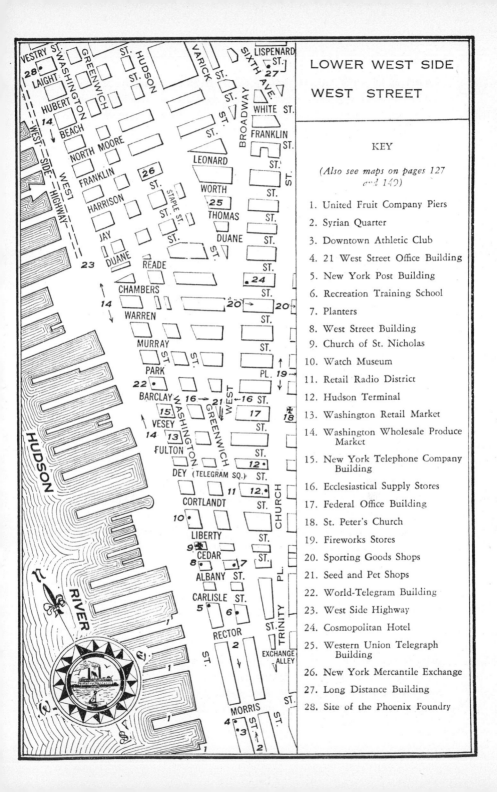

LOWER WEST SIDE

WEST STREET

KEY

(Also see maps on pages 127 and 142)

1. United Fruit Company Piers
2. Syrian Quarter
3. Downtown Athletic Club
4. 21 West Street Office Building
5. New York Post Building
6. Recreation Training School
7. Planters
8. West Street Building
9. Church of St. Nicholas
10. Watch Museum
11. Retail Radio District
12. Hudson Terminal
13. Washington Retail Market
14. Washington Wholesale Produce Market
15. New York Telephone Company Building
16. Ecclesiastical Supply Stores
17. Federal Office Building
18. St. Peter's Church
19. Fireworks Stores
20. Sporting Goods Shops
21. Seed and Pet Shops
22. World-Telegram Building
23. West Side Highway
24. Cosmopolitan Hotel
25. Western Union Telegraph Building
26. New York Mercantile Exchange
27. Long Distance Building
28. Site of the Phoenix Foundry

Street, on West Broadway and Greenwich Street. Barclay Street has a number of ecclesiastical supply stores, originally attracted there because of the presence in the neighborhood of old St. Peter's Church.

Dealers in fireworks who also stage the pyrotechnic spectacles—*Niagara Falls, Flying Eagles, Pyramids of Fire,* and the like—for carnivals and celebrations throughout the country and in South America, have stores near Church Street and Park Place. Their factories are in New Jersey, and the proximity to the ferries has been a factor in the location of the business here since the 1880's. On the south side of Chambers Street between Broadway and West Broadway, are many sporting goods shops. Wholesale grocery houses line Greenwich Street near Beach Street.

The trading center for the 7,500,000 cases of eggs and 3,500,000 tubs of butter which New Yorkers consume each year is the NEW YORK MERCANTILE EXCHANGE at Hudson and Harrison Streets. Prices are based upon daily receipts and open market conditions. The dairy and poultry commission houses are near Reade Street and a little farther north are huge warehouses from which emanate a pungent aroma of coffee, tea, and spices.

Not far away from the Exchange, in the vicinity of Church, Reade, and Duane Streets, is the shoe jobbing center, and east of West Broadway from Thomas to Franklin Streets, the wholesale textile market.

In the market section, comprising a world of its own, is the SYRIAN QUARTER, established in the late 1880's at the foot of Washington Street from Battery Place to Rector Street. A sprinkling of Turks, Armenians, Arabs, and Greeks also live here. Although the fez has given way to the snap-brim, and the narghile has been abandoned for cigarettes, the coffee houses and the tobacco and confectionery shops of the Levantines still remain.

Using the same methods and types of implements as native Syrian bakers, the confectioners make delicious sweets such as *baclawa* (chopped walnuts or pistachios, wrapped in forty layers of baked dough of gauze-like thinness flavored with goat's milk butter and drenched in honey), *knafie* (twisted hank of fried dough with a core of chopped pistachios flavored as *baclawa),* sweet-sour apricot paste sprinkled with pistachios, strings of walnuts dipped in grape syrup, and "Syrian delight" scented with attar of roses. Restaurants feature *shish kebab* (spit-broiled lamb) and rice cooked in salted vine leaves, and furnish narghiles upon request. Other neighborhood stores sell graceful earthen water jars; brass, silver, and pewter trays; tables inlaid with mother of pearl; brass lamp shades fringed with variegated beads, and Syrian silks of rainbow hues.

LOWER MANHATTAN SEEN BENEATH BROOKLYN BRIDGE

THE BATTERY, 1679

THE BATTERY, 1939

LINER NIEUW AMSTERDAM IN THE HUDSON

EAST RIVER DOCKS BELOW BROOKLYN BRIDGE

SOUTH STREET PIER AND WALL STREET TOWERS

OLDEST HOUSE IN MANHATTAN, 11 PECK SLIP

NEW YORK STOCK EXCHANGE, BROAD AND WALL STREETS

WALL STREET CANYON

The tiny CHURCH OF ST. NICHOLAS (Greek Orthodox), at 155 Cedar Street, between Washington and West Streets, was built in 1820. Each January 6, on the Day of Epiphany, the chapel observes the colorful ceremony of the Rescue of the Cross but not as in the old days, when a small wooden crucifix was thrown into the harbor from the Battery landing to be rescued by the most agile Greek youth. The waters proving too cold, the custom was changed in 1937, and now the cross may be drawn ashore by a white ribbon attached to it.

Near the Syrian Quarter stands the RECREATION TRAINING SCHOOL at 107 Washington Street. Organized in 1936 under the direction of the WPA, it gives instruction in more than one hundred courses, and has an enrollment of about twelve hundred.

Greenwich Street, as Greenwich Road, skirted the shore of the Hudson until about the nineteenth century when the river was pushed back by dumping fill. Now it is heavily walled with merchandising warehouses.

A relic of the old days, the PLANTERS, at Albany and Greenwich Streets, was established as a hotel in 1833. It closed when the Civil War broke out, but after being remodeled in 1922 was opened as a restaurant. In its heyday the hotel was patronized by Southern planters, its location being convenient to the Perth Amboy ferry, and thus to the Washington Post Road and the railroads connecting with the South. Near by, at 113 Greenwich Street, is the rear entrance to the New York Curb Exchange Building *(see page 86)*.

The twin twenty-two-story structures connected by a bridge at 30 and 50 Church Street, were among the first skyscrapers. Designed by Clinton and Russell, these red tapestry-brick buildings were erected in 1908 at a cost of $12,000,000. Their name, the HUDSON TERMINAL, derives from the downtown station of the Hudson and Manhattan Railroad (the Hudson Tubes) underneath the buildings. The station is connected by way of tunnels with BMT and IRT subways. A block north, on the east side of Church Street, is the graveyard of St. Paul's Chapel *(see page 98)*, a subsidiary of Trinity Parish.

The imposing FEDERAL OFFICE BUILDING, a $7,697,000 structure of limestone, occupies the block from Church Street to West Broadway, and from Vesey to Barclay Street. Cross and Cross, and Pennington, Lewis, and Mills, associate architects, designed the heavy fifteen-story structure, a pretentious example of the "classic-without-columns" style of some recent public buildings. It houses branches of the New York Post Office, the Foreign and Domestic Commerce Bureau of the Department of Commerce, the Federal Housing Administration, and the Treasury Department.

Hemmed in by modern business structures, ST. PETER'S, on the southeast corner of Barclay and Church Streets, is the oldest Roman Catholic church building in Manhattan. The edifice was erected in 1786, three years after the congregation was organized, and was rebuilt in 1838. Steps lead to the six massive columns supporting a pediment in whose center stands a figure of St. Peter holding the keys of heaven and hell.

Old Columbia College, founded in 1754 as King's College (see page 383), stood until 1857 between Barclay and Murray Streets, and West Broadway and Church Street. West Broadway, then Chapel Place, was a wandering lane which led from Canal Street to the college chapel.

During the early eighteenth century, the vicinity of Greenwich and Warren Streets was the site of Vauxhall Garden. A reproduction of a contemporary London resort, it flourished about forty years, and was the rendezvous of most fashionable Colonials.

The COSMOPOLITAN HOTEL, at Chambers Street and West Broadway, the oldest hotel in the city, was opened in 1850 as the Gerard House, drawing steady patronage from near-by steamship piers and the first Grand Central Terminal, then across the street. Among the patrons were bearded 'Frisco gold miners who staggered into the lobby after a trip around the Horn, dumped their gold-dust, went out to the barber, and came back "unrecognizably clean." The hotel survives, a ramshackle building, with stores crowding its entrance, and an incongruous neon sign flashing from its façade.

Many buildings on the block between Church Street and Broadway, and Thomas and Worth Streets represent the florid architectural style of the post-Civil War period when decorative feats, structurally impossible in stone, were accomplished in cast iron. These white buildings were erected by Griffith Thomas in 1869 for the flourishing textile trade, in which many of the town's wealthiest citizens were engaged.

This block was the first site (1773–1870) of the New York Hospital (see page 246). One of the great riots in the city occurred here in 1788 when a mob stormed the hospital to attack medical students and doctors who, it was claimed, had used for dissection the cadavers of "respectable people, even young women of whom they made an indecent exposure." The militia, summoned by the governor and mayor, removed the students to a near-by jail for safekeeping, and when the crowd gathered in front of the prison, the troops fired, killing five and wounding scores.

The WESTERN UNION TELEGRAPH BUILDING, at 60 Hudson Street,

rises twenty-four stories high in thirteen shades of brick, like a huge red rock projecting out of the city; Voorhees, Gmelin, and Walker were the architects. The LONG DISTANCE BUILDING of the American Telephone and Telegraph Company, 32 Sixth Avenue, near Walker Street, designed by the same firm, is the world's largest communication center and the junction point of many important telephone trunk routes. It has direct circuits to important cities and radio telephone circuits to points in every part of the world. All private wires from New York to other cities, whether telephone, telegraph, or teletypewriter, lead through the building, which is also the main control point for the great radio broadcast series.

The land west of Broadway to the river, between Fulton and Christopher Streets, was once known as the Queen's Farm. In 1705 Queen Anne granted it to Trinity Church. Since 1731 descendants and alleged descendants of Annetje Jans, an early owner of the farm, have sued Trinity, either for the return of the land or for pecuniary compensation. William Rhinelander in 1794 obtained ninety-nine-year leases of a large part of Trinity land; the Common Council in 1797 augmented these holdings by granting him all rights to the water front adjoining his property. With the rapid northward expansion of the city in the nineteenth century, the area became the site of large commercial structures and yielded millions in rent annually to the Rhinelander family.

For many years Trinity land was ignored by builders because of its leasehold status, and not until the Lower East Side of Manhattan had been built up did they turn to this section. In 1803 the streets from Warren to Canal were laid out. Four years later, St. John's Church, a chapel of Trinity parish, was erected on Varick Street near Beach, and St. John's Park, named for the chapel, was set up on the block bounded by Varick, Hudson, Laight, and Beach Streets. The park was open only to residents of the houses facing it. From 1825–50 this district was the home of the city's wealthy aristocrats. When the plebeian population encroached upon it the wealthy moved northward. The park was razed in 1869 to make way for the freight terminal of the Hudson River Railroad which later was merged with the New York Central Railroad; in 1936 the terminal was moved to West Houston and West Streets.

Canal Street, named for and following the course of a stream that ran from Collect Pond (the site of the present Foley Square district) to the Hudson, is the main traffic artery connecting New Jersey and Long Island by way of the Holland Tunnel and the Manhattan Bridge.

The HOLLAND TUNNEL, named for its chief engineer, Clifford M. Holland, begins at Watts Street, between Hudson and Varick Streets, a block north of Canal, and bores underneath the Hudson River to Twelfth Street, Jersey City, New Jersey *(toll: passenger cars 50¢)*. A spacious and impressive plaza leads to a narrow tunnel entrance, whose dingy masonry lacks the exciting quality of the glistening interior. The tunnel is made of cast iron lined with concrete and the side walls are inset with white vitreous tiles, with markers at quarter-mile points. East- and westbound tubes are separate, each two lanes wide, together carrying a traffic of 12,000,000 cars a year. (The exit of the eastbound traffic tube is on Canal Street.) Catwalks in each tube are paced by guards who keep vehicles at the required speed of thirty miles an hour. The tunnel was constructed by the states of New York and New Jersey at a cost of fifty million dollars. Work was begun on October 12, 1920, and the tunnel opened on November 13, 1927. It is operated by the Port of New York Authority.

Old SPRING STREET PRESBYTERIAN CHURCH, founded in 1811, stands at Varick and Spring Streets. In 1834, a mob spurred by prominent politicians, almost destroyed the original frame building because Dr. Henry G. Ludlow, the pastor, was a firm advocate of abolition. Two years later, the present brick structure was erected.

The firearms firm of FRANCIS BANNERMAN AND SONS, still active at 501 Broadway, near Broome Street, was founded in 1865 by a former naval officer in the Civil War. It has a remarkable collection of military arms and war relics. *(Open Monday to Friday 8:30 a.m. to 5 p.m., Saturday 8:30 a.m. to 12 m.; admission free.)* Chronological arrangements of the exhibits lucidly indicate the stages in the development of modern lethal weapons. Prized possessions include such objects as the headquarters flag of Major General "Light Horse" Harry Lee, famous Revolutionary cavalry leader and father of General Robert E. Lee; a double-barreled flintlock shotgun that belonged to Napoleon I, and the guidon of the Seventh U. S. Cavalry used in the battle of Little Big Horn (General Custer's last stand).

SOUTH STREET

Area: South Ferry to Corlears Hook along the East River. Map on page 91.

The bowsprit of many a clipper—Baltimore, California, McKay—and Liverpool packet once jutted over South Street, now visited by ungainly scows, fishing smacks, lighters, and car floats from Long Island and Jersey City. This famous "street o' ships," a two-mile stretch of bumpy stones skirting the East River from the Battery to Corlears Hook, is historically associated with New York's development as a great port; though today but few ocean-going craft breast the piers that once berthed whole fleets of gallant windjammers. The *Lightnings* and *Comets* and *Flying Clouds* of a later day, requiring deeper water, steam up the broad fairway of the North (Hudson) River, leaving South Street to the traffic of the ten-ton truck. Viewed from the piers near the Battery end of South Street, the East River bridges—Brooklyn, Manhattan, and Williamsburg—form a superimposed pattern of steel and stone, like a photograph from a camera that was jarred during exposure. Across the river, on a bluff overlooking the plebeian harbor activities, are the staid residences of Brooklyn Heights, for more than a century the center of wealthy conservative society.

The rumble of speeding trucks, the blasts from near-by steam shovels, and the intermittent whistles from passing river traffic join in crescendos of dissonance. Sailors in pea jackets and dungarees, workmen in overalls, neat office clerks and shabby drifters throng the highway. On mild sunny days the drifters sit along the docks with their "junk bags," share cigarette butts, and stare endlessly into the water. In winter they cluster in little groups about small bonfires; many sleep at night in doorways with newspapers for covering. Others join the homeless men who sleep in the MUNICIPAL LODGING HOUSE, ANNEX No. 2, in the old ferry shed at the foot of Whitehall Street, which can accommodate about 1,200 nightly.

The majority of the piers along South Street are leased or owned by railroad companies. Pier 4, at the foot of Broad Street, marks approximately the site of the first dock—built by the Dutch—on Manhattan Island. What is now South Street was then under water, so the exact location is inland. The NEW YORK STATE BARGE CANAL TERMINAL occupies Pier 6 where arklike, weather-beaten Erie Canal barges are moored. Many of the barge captains are married, and their families live on board the year round. In winter the boats sometimes lie for months along the river banks farther north.

At 61 Whitehall Street is the old EASTERN HOTEL, now used as an office building. In 1822 the owner, Captain John B. Coles, remodeled the original structure, a warehouse, and named it the Eagle Hotel. It was renamed the Eastern in 1856. The frame of the building reputedly contains mahogany beams that were used as ballast in eighteenth-century merchantmen. Among the hotel's guests were Robert Fulton, Jenny Lind, P. T. Barnum, and many of the illustrious entertainers who appeared in Castle Garden, now the Aquarium *(see page 307)*.

The two blocks between Whitehall and Broad are typical of the lower length of South Street. Here, dilapidated brick and brownstone structures crowd the sidewalks, upper floors forlornly vacant, street floors occupied by cut-rate "drink and food" stores, low-priced barber shops, secondhand clothes stores, sail lofts, and chandleries.

Broad Coenties Slip, which was filled in about 1835, encloses JEANETTE PARK, a rendezvous popular with South Street's army of beached seamen and homeless unemployed. The park was named for the ill-fated vessel of the Jeanette Polar Expedition, promoted in 1880 by the elder James Gordon Bennett. The concrete and chromium structure within the park houses the famous OYSTER BAR, established in the neighborhood in 1849. Its founder, Robert Peach, opened up shop by the simple device of setting three planks across two barrels. In 1898, Patrick O'Connor, age twelve, became his assistant, and, five years later, his partner. Peach retired in 1917, but O'Connor carried on. He now operates the park bar.

The SEAMEN'S CHURCH INSTITUTE OF NEW YORK occupies a thirteen-story brick and stone-trimmed structure at 25 South Street (latitude 40° 42' 10" N, longitude 74° 00' 35" W). Surmounting the roof is a small lighthouse tower erected in 1913, by public subscription, as a memorial to the passengers, officers, and crew of the S.S. *Titanic,* luxury liner that sank April 15, 1912, after striking an iceberg on her maiden voyage to America. Standing guard over the main entrance of the building is a gilded figurehead of Sir Galahad, reminiscent of the carvings on the prows of the clipper ships which docked near by during the nineteenth century. Above the figurehead is a ship's bell rescued from the S.S. *Atlantic* which foundered off Fisher's Island on Thanksgiving Day, 1846, with a loss of seventy-eight lives. The bell, connected with a clock, rings ship's time every half-hour. The institute was founded in 1834, and in 1843 established churches on the water front. In 1854 activities were expanded to include provision for sailors' lodging and entertainment. Several missions, floating churches, and boarding houses were operated throughout the port until 1913 when the present building was opened as the institute's center. An annex with accommodations for a thousand guests—making a total lodging capacity of about fifteen hundred at the institute—was completed in 1929. Seamen are charged moderate rates for lodging and meals; privileges include admission to moving pictures and other entertainment, and the use of libraries, club, game, and writing rooms. A merchant marine school, conducted by the institute, is the oldest surviving school of its kind in New York. It was founded in 1916.

In the middle of Old Slip is the FIRST PRECINCT POLICE STATION, a grim, solid structure reminiscent of a fortified Florentine Renaissance palazzo. North, across the street, is the UNITED STATES ASSAY BUILDING, a five-story granite building with a massive chimney. The public is not admitted to this sanctuary where scrap gold and silver are melted into bullion.

The thoroughfare's only skyscraper is at Wall and South Streets, 120 WALL STREET. It is a huge, white, thirty-three-story building, uncompromising in its literal conformance to the setback ordinance. Ely Jacques Kahn was the architect. A bronze PLAQUE identifies the site as that of Murray's Wharf, where George Washington landed April 23, 1789, on his way to Federal Hall for his inauguration as President. Private seaplanes of Wall Street commuters land at the MUNICIPAL DOWNTOWN SKYPORT between Piers 11 and 12.

The squat fortress-like WAREHOUSE on the corner of De Peyster Street is one of the oldest buildings on the street. It was built of rough-hewn granite blocks more than one hundred years ago by the Griswold brothers, East India merchants.

FULTON MARKET, largest wholesale fish mart on the Atlantic Coast, was established in 1821 as a retail market to "supply the common people with the necessities of life at a reasonable price." The market covers an area of six city blocks bounded by Fulton, Water, Dover, and South Streets, and includes two large markets on the South Street docks near Fulton. Before daybreak tons of fish are unloaded from the holds of stubby-sticked trawlers and draggers and from refrigerated trucks from New England and New Jersey. Six days a week, from 2 to 9 A.M., the section is a bedlam as rubber-booted men in the street and in narrow stalls clean, bone, ice, unpack, and repack approximately one hundred varieties of fish. After a section of the market structure collapsed in 1936, the city undertook the modernization of this landmark. Three new market buildings have been planned.

SWEET'S, a restaurant established almost a century ago, is on the southwest corner of Fulton and South Streets. In old days it was especially popular among shipmasters and South Street merchants, and from 1850 to 1860, when "blackbirders" flourished along the East River, many nefarious slave-running deals were transacted in this South Street "Delmonico's."

From a pier near the present Peck's Slip, the first licensed Brooklyn ferry began operations in 1654. Fares were three stivers for whites, and six stivers for Indians. Between Dover and Roosevelt Streets, South Street passes under the Brooklyn Bridge (see page 313). Near by, at 174 South Street is the BIRTHPLACE OF FORMER GOVERNOR ALFRED E. SMITH.

Almost the entire block between Catharine Slip and Market Slip is occupied by the HEARST PUBLICATION PLANT which houses the editorial and press rooms of the New York *Journal and American* and the *Sunday American*. The *American Weekly* is also printed here.

The stretch of shore from Catharine Slip to Corlears Hook was occupied by the shipbuilding industry during the War of 1812 and in the decade preceding it. Many of New York's privateers that harassed British sea-traffic during the war were constructed in the local shipways. And from these yards was recruited Noah Brown's heroic band who fashioned Commodore Perry's fleet for the Battle of Lake Erie.

South Street gradually assumes a quieter tempo at Market Slip as trucks and pedestrians become less frequent. Farther on, at Rutgers Slip, there is a pathetic little park more liberally supplied with benches than with shade. From Clinton Street to Corlears Hook Park the East River is walled from view by a continuous line of railroad pier sheds, and only an occasional blast from an unseen tug reminds one that water-borne traffic is passing.

WALL STREET DISTRICT

Area: Battery Place, Beaver St., and Old Slip on the south to Fulton St. on the north; from Trinity Place and Church St. east to South St. Map on page 91.

Wall Street, financial heart of the nation, is itself but little more than a third of a mile long from its head at Broadway to its foot at the East River, although its name is applied to a small district lying to the north and south. Functionally, Wall Street is a complex mechanism developed to provide the centralized banking and credit facilities and the efficient securities market place that modern industry and commerce demand. Walled in by towering structures, the street, by historical coincidence, is well named.

At this place in 1653, Peter Stuyvesant, governor of New Amsterdam, ordered a protective wall built across what was then the colony's northernmost limit. It was not long before the city had pushed past this barrier, and under British rule the district flourished as a center of government and fashion. Following the Revolution, Wall Street became for a year the seat of the Federal Government, and here were located the establishments of such statesmen and leaders of commerce as Alexander Hamilton and John Jay.

The four buildings of the famous NEW YORK STOCK EXCHANGE cover the area between New, Wall, and Broad Streets and Exchange Place —one block east of Broadway. The original building, designed by George

B. Post, was finished in 1903, and the twenty-two-story addition, in 1923, from the plans of Trowbridge and Livingston. The adjoining BLAIR BUILDING and COMMERCIAL CABLE BUILDING were bought in 1928. The Exchange building proper, with its well-proportioned Corinthian order and sculptured pediment, shows an expressive use of the "temple" form of façade. The Exchange is owned and administered by 1,375 member brokers, each of whom possesses a "seat." In the boom year of 1929, seats sold for as much as $625,000; the top price in 1938 was $85,000. During 1937, the Exchange had on its trading list some 1,200 stock issues, valued at almost sixty billion dollars, as well as 1,400 bond issues valued at more than forty-two billion dollars.

The Exchange was established shortly after the formation of the United States. In 1790, the first Congress authorized the issue of eighty million dollars in bonds. Three large banking institutions were incorporated about this time, and for the public sale of their stock, a market was developed under a buttonwood tree at what is now 68 Wall Street. Here, in 1792, a group of twenty-four brokers drew up a trading agreement. Financing the next war, in 1812, gave the exchange a new importance and the New York Stock and Exchange Board was organized with offices at 40 Wall Street. It was as a result of financing the Civil War, however, that the board began to approach its full power. The organization was combined with the Open Board of Brokers and the Government Bond Department to form the present New York Stock Exchange early in 1863.

There followed a half-century of unprecedented expansion. Money was needed for railroads, telegraph lines, factories, for building cities over night and exploiting the resources of the West. Financial titans arose: Jay Gould, Jim Fisk, Daniel Drew, Jim Hill, E. H. Harriman, and the elder J. P. Morgan. After Gould, Fisk, and Drew, with the help of bribed New York legislators, had succeeded in their struggle with Commodore Vanderbilt for the control of the Erie Railroad, Gould and Fisk conceived the plan of cornering the gold market, counting on the United States Treasury not to sell from its gold reserve. But when the price of gold reached 162 on Black Friday (September 24, 1869), President Grant ordered the Treasury to sell, breaking the corner. The panic of 1869 resulted, followed by a depression which lasted ten years. Banks, brokers, merchants suspended business; nearly one hundred railroads failed, and the Stock Exchange closed its doors.

With the fall of men like Fisk came the rise of Morgan, Harriman, and others, unbridled expansion, larger fortunes, and further battles for personal financial dictatorship. It was in this period that Morgan's and

Harriman's struggle over the great Northern Pacific Railroad was followed by the collapse of the market and the nation-wide panic of 1901. Again, in 1907, Morgan's struggle with the Knickerbocker Trust Company brought about the failure of that and other institutions.

The World War brought further prosperity to the Exchange and necessitated the erection of a twenty-two-story addition to its building. After the war, except for the depression of 1920–22, the market rose to new heights, and with it the expectations of an expanding nation. The panic of October, 1929, and another depression were the inevitable reactions.

One radical result of this depression was the creation of the Securities and Exchange Commission (SEC) in 1934, which for the first time attempted governmental regulation of the influential Stock Exchange.

The function of the Exchange is to provide a liquid market where securities can at all times be disposed of or acquired virtually without delay. Trading in America's greatest securities market is conducted on the floor of the Great Hall, one of the largest rooms in the world. Orders to buy or sell, telegraphed and telephoned from all over the world, are relayed through brokerage houses to their active members on the floor, who transact business orally with traders stationed at numerous horseshoe trading posts. Despite the informal nature of these transactions, they are quickly recorded in meticulous detail on the Exchange's ticker tape and are communicated by telegraph and cable to other markets.

Trading operations may be viewed from the visitor's gallery. Admission was comparatively easy until 1933, when a visitor unkindly deposited a tear gas bomb in the ventilating system. Today admission is available only to guests of an Exchange member firm.

The visitor, standing in front of Trinity Church *(see page 310)*, Wall Street and Broadway, shortly before nine o'clock in the morning, will see the empty "street" fill suddenly with swift-moving clerks, tellers, stenographers, and office boys pouring from subways, ferries, and elevated trains; while bankers and brokers arrive almost as promptly in chauffeured automobiles or by planes landing at a ramp near the foot of Wall Street.

Directly behind Trinity Church, is the NEW YORK CURB EXCHANGE, 78 Trinity Place, second largest securities market in the nation. Here certain other securities not listed by the New York Stock Exchange are traded. The Curb Exchange's two buildings, designed by Starrett and Van Vleck, were opened in 1921 and 1931 respectively. The 550 regular and more than four hundred associate members include many members of the Stock Exchange.

Before 1921, the Curb conducted transactions in the open street, from which comes its name. The brokers, known originally as "Curb brokers" in Wall Street, met at the northern end of Broad Street and communicated by violent gesticulations with their colleagues in the windows above. In 1908 the New York Curb Agency was organized, and reorganized in 1911 as the New York Curb Market, with fixed trading hours. The present name was adopted in 1929. The lowest price accepted in 1929 for a Curb seat was $150,000; the 1938 minimum was $8,000.

At the entrance to Wall Street are two skyscrapers, the IRVING TRUST COMPANY, at No. 1, and the FIRST NATIONAL BANK, at No. 2. The former, completed in 1931, from the plans of Voorhees, Gmelin, and Walker, is fifty stories high, and resembles a solid shaft of stone. Fluted walls and chamfered corners (an expensive device on land worth $520 a square foot) help create this illusion. The site is about 180 by 110 feet and is assessed at $10,250,000 without improvements. The twenty-one-story First National Bank, erected in 1933 from a design by Walker and Gillette, is marked by a flat, unimaginative use of classic precedent. At No. 14, is the entrance to the thirty-nine-story BANKERS TRUST COMPANY, designed by Trowbridge and Livingston, and erected in 1911. The twenty-five-story addition, facing Pine Street, was completed in 1933. Shreve, Lamb, and Harmon designed the addition.

Opposite the Stock Exchange at the corner of Wall and Nassau Streets is the SUBTREASURY BUILDING, a dignified structure designed in Greek-Revival style by Ithiel Town and A. J. Davis. Built in 1842 as a Custom House, it was remodeled in 1862 for use as a Subtreasury. The Federal Reserve Bank used it until 1925. Now the building houses the New York Passport Agency of the Department of State, several departments of the U.S. Public Health Service, and the Bureau of Accounts of the Interstate Commerce Commission. It stands on the site of the Colonial City Hall, built in 1699 and torn down in 1812. Here, in 1735, John Peter Zenger, imprisoned editor of the *New-York Weekly Journal,* was tried on charges of libeling the administration of the royal governor, William Cosby, and was acquitted after the country's first major battle for freedom of the press. The Stamp Act Congress met here in 1765, and the Continental Congress in 1785. In the expectation that New York would be the national capital, Major L'Enfant, who later planned the city of Washington, was commissioned to remodel the building in 1788 as the Federal Hall, and here Washington took oath, April 30, 1789, as President of the United States. The place above the steps where it is claimed he stood on this occasion is marked by J. Q. A. Ward's STATUE OF WASHINGTON erected in 1883. The actual stone on which Washington stood is preserved in a glass case within the building.

Near the Subtreasury, in front of the adjoining old Assay Office, a horse-drawn wagon, loaded with explosives, blew up shortly before noon, September 16, 1920. Thirty of the noonday crowd were killed and one hundred wounded. Scars of the explosion are still visible on near-by buildings. Occurring during a period of anti-radical hysteria, the disaster was said by some to have been a protest dynamiting of this important financial corner. Others held that the wagon had belonged to an explosives company and had been using a prohibited route when its load of dynamite was accidentally discharged. Neither theory ever was proved.

At 23 Wall Street, across from the Stock Exchange, is the diminutive MORGAN BUILDING, home of America's most powerful private banking firm. Erected in 1914, the gray five-story building is impersonal to an almost forbidding degree. It was designed by Trowbridge and Livingston.

East, at 40 Wall, is the BANK OF THE MANHATTAN COMPANY, the city's second oldest bank. By-product of the feud between Aaron Burr and Alexander Hamilton, the Manhattan Company was organized by Burr in 1799, and though chartered as a water company, the bank was opened almost immediately. The water service ceased in 1842. The present building, called the Manhattan Company Building, was designed by H. Craig Severance in association with Yasuo Matsui. Seventy-one stories in height, it was intended to be the world's tallest structure when construction was begun in 1929, but the last-minute addition of a spire to the Chrysler Building *(see page 224)* defeated the plan. Within five years it had dropped to fifth place in height. The observation tower stands 830 feet above the street. *(Open daily 9 a.m. to 5 p.m.; admission free.)* Solid glass automatic doors in the lobby are an unusual feature.

Hamilton's bank, the BANK OF NEW YORK AND TRUST COMPANY, the city's oldest, is just east, at No. 48; it was organized in 1784. The present thirty-two-story structure was erected in 1928, from the plans of Benjamin Wistar Morris III.

The NATIONAL CITY BANK, the second largest bank in the country, has offices at No. 55. The building's lower part, with its four-story colonnade, was built in 1842, and served as customhouse from 1862 until 1907, when it was taken over by the bank, and the second tier of four stories and another colonnade were added under the direction of McKim, Mead, and White, architects. The simple power of the composition of the north façade is most effective. The bank, chartered in 1812, was an outgrowth of the First Bank of the United States, established in Philadelphia in 1791.

A block to the north, at 18 Pine Street, is the CHASE NATIONAL BANK, the nation's largest bank since its merger with the Equitable Trust Company in 1930. At its Cedar Street entrance is a free exhibit of more than forty thousand coins. *(Open weekdays 9 a.m. to 4 p.m., Saturday 9 a.m. to 12 m.)*

The tallest building in lower Manhattan, and third highest in the city, is SIXTY WALL TOWER (the Cities Service Building), at 70 Pine Street. An underground passage and a bridge connect with older quarters at 60 Wall Street. Sixty-seven stories (965 feet) high, it was designed by Clinton and Russell, and erected in 1932. A complicated play of overlapping forms emphasizes long vertical lines that accentuate the height of the building. There is an observation room in the tower. *(Open weekdays 11 a.m. to 5 p.m.; admission 40¢, children under eight, free.)*

The TONTINE BUILDING, northwest corner of Wall and Water Streets, is on the site of the Tontine Coffee House, erected in 1794, a favorite meeting place for merchants and political groups. The Merchants' Coffee House, erected about 1737 on the southeast corner of Wall and Water Streets, was a rendezvous for Revolutionary plotters, and is memorialized by a bronze plaque on the present building.

Hanover Square, where Hanover, Stone, Pearl, and William Streets converge on Old Slip, south of Wall Street, was a public Common as early as 1637. On the southwest side of the square is INDIA HOUSE, built in 1837 by Richard Carman, and headquarters since 1914 of a group of foreign traders. Ship models, prints, and other relics are housed here. Nicholas Bayard built a house on this site in 1673, while across the square (119-21 Pearl Street) in about 1691 lived his friend Captain William Kidd. The Bayard House, together with a greater part of the square, was destroyed in the great fire of 1835.

The lower end of William Street has probably undergone more changes of name than any other street in the city. It has been known as: The Glass Makers' Street, The Smith Street, Smee Street, Smit Street, Suice Street, De Smee Street, Burghers Path, Burger Jorisens Path, King Street, Berger Joris Street, and Borisens Path.

The NEW YORK COTTON EXCHANGE, at 60 Beaver Street, two blocks south of the Stock Exchange, is the most important cotton market in the world; it was organized in 1871. Its present building, designed by Donn Barber, was erected in 1923. Other exchanges in the vicinity include the MARITIME EXCHANGE at No. 80 and the COMMODITY EXCHANGE at 81 Broad Street, three blocks south of the Stock Exchange; and the NEW

KEY TO MAP OF SOUTH STREET, WALL STREET DISTRICT, CITY HALL DISTRICT, AND CHINATOWN

SOUTH STREET

1. Hearst Publication Plant
2. Birthplace of Alfred E. Smith
3. Fulton Market
4. Sweet's
5. The Old Griswold Warehouse
6. 120 Wall Street Building
7. Municipal Downtown Skyport
8. U.S. Assay Building
9. First Precinct Police Station
10. Seamen's Church Institute
11. Jeanette Park
12. State Barge Canal Terminal
13. Site of the First Dock
14. Municipal Lodging House
15. Site of the Eastern Hotel

WALL STREET DISTRICT

16. Maritime Exchange
17. Commodity Exchange
18. India House
19. Cotton Exchange
20. Coffee and Sugar Exchange
21. Site of Merchants' Coffee House
22. Tontine Building
23. Sixty Wall Tower
24. Bank of N.Y. and Trust Company
25. National City Bank Building
26. Manhattan Company Building
27. U.S. Subtreasury Building
28. Morgan Building
29. New York Stock Exchange
30. Irving Trust Company Building
31. Aldrich Court Building
32. New York Curb Exchange
33. New York's Oldest Restaurant
34. Trinity Church
35. First National Bank Building
36. Bankers Trust Company Building
37. Chase National Bank Building
38. Equitable Building
39. New York Clearing House
40. Mutual Life Insurance Company
41. Federal Reserve Bank
42. Chamber of Commerce
43. Singer Building
44. Site of John Street Theater
45. Golden Hill
46. Old John Street Church
47. Washington Irving's Birthplace

CITY HALL DISTRICT

48. St. Paul's Chapel
49. Woolworth Building
50. Statue of Nathan Hale
51. Civic Virtue
52. Statue of Benjamin Franklin
53. Newspaper Row
54. Tribune Building
55. Old Beekman (Tavern)
56. Pulitzer Building
57. Brace Newsboys' House
58. Municipal Building
59. Statue of Horace Greeley
60. City Hall
61. City Court Building
62. Stewart Building (The Sun)
63. Hall of Records
64. Court Square Building
65. St. Andrew's Church
66. U.S. Court House
67. Site of Tea Water Pump
68. Supreme Court Building
69. State Office Building
70. Health Department Building
71. Tombs
72. Criminal Courts Building

CHINATOWN

73. Chinese School
74. Wall Newspaper
75. On Leong Tong
76. Joss House
77. Tom Noonan's Rescue Society
78. Bloody Angle
79. Hip Sing Tong

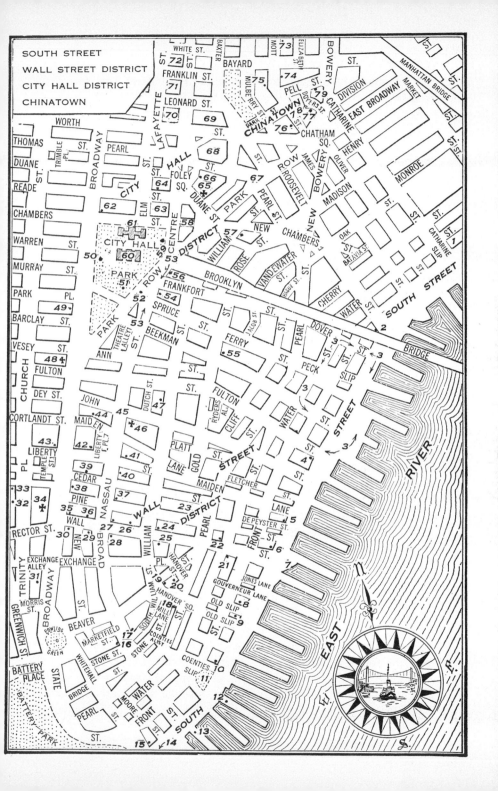

YORK COFFEE AND SUGAR EXCHANGE at 113 Pearl Street. The New York Produce Exchange *(see page 66)* is at 2 Broadway.

At 45 Broadway, between Morris Street and Exchange Alley, is the ALDRICH COURT BUILDING, housing the United States Shipping Commission, the Bureau of Marine Inspection and Navigation and other Federal agencies. A TABLET in the building's façade marks what is said to be the site of the first residence of white men on Manhattan. In November, 1613, the ship *Tyger* burned offshore, and the captain and crew landed here and built four huts.

Running north of the Stock Exchange, Nassau Street, known originally as "the Street that Runs by the Pye Woman," a continuation of Broad Street, is the retail shopping center of the financial district. Here in low old buildings are shops and restaurants catering to the noonday crowd.

At 77 Cedar Street, between Nassau and Broadway is the NEW YORK CLEARING HOUSE, a five-story building with a marble front, erected in 1896. R. W. Gibson was the architect. In this important institution many millions of dollars in checks and drafts drawn on member banks are cleared daily. Although constant mergers have reduced member banks from a maximum of sixty-seven to twenty, the volume of business has expanded enormously since it was organized in 1853.

New York's oldest restaurant, YE OLDE CHOP HOUSE, is located at 118 Cedar Street, and for more than 130 years has catered to men in the Wall Street area. At 120 Broadway, between Cedar and Liberty Streets is the EQUITABLE BUILDING, planned by E. R. Graham. Erected in 1914, before the setback law, it shoots up forty-one stories, unrelieved and formidable. Its total of 1,200,000 square feet of rentable floor space makes it the second largest building in floor area in the city. The MUTUAL LIFE INSURANCE COMPANY of New York is at 34 Nassau Street, between Cedar and Liberty Streets. Chartered in 1842, it is the oldest organization of its kind in America. The insurance section of the financial district is now largely concentrated in the neighborhood of Fulton and William Streets.

The FEDERAL RESERVE BANK OF NEW YORK, 33 Liberty Street, occupies the block bounded by Maiden Lane, Nassau, Liberty, and William Streets. The fourteen-story building, completed in 1924 from plans by York and Sawyer, is constructed of heavy limestone blocks. It strongly suggests the fortified palaces of the Florentine Renaissance. The rusticated stone exterior is almost without ornament except for iron lanterns, and the iron grilles of the great arched windows complete the picture of a building ready for a siege. Five stories are below street level. Subterranean vaults are barred by doors weighing as much as ninety tons. The NEW YORK CHAMBER OF COMMERCE, 65 Liberty Street, occupies a five-story building designed by James B. Baker and completed in 1902. This, the oldest commercial organization of its kind in the world, was founded in 1768 in the Long Room of Fraunces Tavern *(see page 68)* and chartered by George III in 1770 with the aim of encouraging commerce and supporting industry. Its resident membership, limited to two thousand, includes many of the city's prominent bankers and industrialists.

Maiden Lane, one block north of Liberty Street, was so named when, as Maagde Paatje (the Dutch equivalent), it was a footpath used by lovers along a rippling brook. Once the city's noted retail jewelry center, the street is now given over to wholesale trade and manufacturing. A TABLET in the Jewelers' Building, 17 Maiden Lane, marks the location of the John Street Theater, built in 1767, and frequently attended by President Washington.

One block north, John Street, center of insurance and jewelry business, was known before the Revolution as Golden Hill and was the scene of the "Battle" of Golden Hill where, in January, 1770, two men were wounded in a skirmish between citizens and British soldiers. A TABLET at the northwest corner of John and William Streets marks the site of this early encounter. The SINGER BUILDING, 149 Broadway, at the head of John Street, was built in 1908 and remained the city's tallest edifice for eighteen months; forty-one stories (612 feet) high, today (1939) it ranks sixteenth. Ernest Flagg, the architect, gave it the first slender skyscraper tower. At 46 John Street is the OLD JOHN STREET METHODIST EPISCOPAL CHURCH, mother church of American Methodism. The present edifice, Federal in style, and erected in 1841, is the third on the site since 1768.

In 1783, Washington Irving was born at 131 William Street, corner of Fulton—an appropriate birthplace for the man who coined the phrase "the Almighty Dollar." One block east, at the corner of Pearl Street, Holt's Hotel, later known as the United States Hotel, was erected in 1833. It was considered "the pioneer of the 'great' hotels of New York City and of America." The roof contained a promenade and an observatory whence the city's traders could watch for incoming vessels.

CITY HALL DISTRICT

Area: Fulton St. on the south to Franklin St. on the north; from Church St. east to Pearl St. Map on page 91.

One mile north of Battery Landing, the imperfect triangle of CITY HALL PARK is wedged into Broadway's steep eastern wall. Here is the venerable seat of the municipal government, and the scene of important historical events. Broadway clips the park precisely on the west—as does Chambers Street on the north—and hems it in with a palisade of commercial buildings whose architectural distinction, except for the Woolworth Building, lies mainly in their renovated store fronts. The apex of the park's ten-and-one-half-acre triangle points to St. Paul's Chapel, the oldest church in the borough and probably the only building that presents its back to Broadway. The eastern boundary of the park is fixed by two streets: Park Row, which slants northeast from Broadway past old "Newspaper Row," and Centre Street, which runs north from the end of Brooklyn Bridge *(see page 313)* through the new civic center at Foley Square.

Paved walks subdivide the park into small grassy areas set with trees. Rows of benches bordering the walks accommodate strollers and idlers who pause to rest, to read, to have their shoes shined, to feed the pigeons, or to enjoy the transient sunshine. This is a restless park: six days a week crowds of office workers stream to and from the IRT subway kiosks on both sides; elevated trains rattle and screech in a rambling shed at the approach to Brooklyn Bridge; well polished automobiles bearing low license numbers nudge into a parking space "For Official Cars Only"; policemen ceaselessly patrol the grounds; lunch-hour crowds, released from near-by office buildings, fill the paths at noontime.

There are but two buildings in the park proper, although a third, the triangular post-office building that was called "Mullett's monstrosity," occupied the southern segment until 1938. In the north central section of the park is City Hall, and to the rear and fronting Chambers Street is the City Court Building, formerly known as the Old County Court House.

CITY HALL houses the offices of the Mayor, chief executive and magistrate of the city, and his staff; the City Council, the municipal legislative body; the Board of Estimate, the general administrative body; and the Art Commission, the agency that passes on the designs for all public buildings and works of art.

Architecturally, City Hall is an exceptionally well-executed design of the post-Colonial period showing clearly the fact, noteworthy in its day, that professional rather than amateur architects planned it. The design, a beautiful adaptation of French Renaissance and American Colonial influences, was essentially the work of Joseph F. Mangin, a Frenchman, but his partner and co-winner of a competition for the commission, John McComb, a Scotsman, supervised the work in New York and received most of the contemporary credit. He was paid six dollars a day, a very good salary at the time. Construction was under way for nearly a decade; it took three years to settle on the plan alone. To save $15,000 the city fathers, tempering their recklessness in spending a half million dollars for the structure, insisted that brownstone be used for the rear. City Hall was completed in 1811.

Reminiscent of the Hotel de Ville of the eighteenth century, the dignified marble structure, chastely embellished with Louis XVI pilasters between arched windows, is noteworthy for its unusual grace and delicate scale. The two wings are balanced on either side of a central portico that is surmounted by a cupola. Its finial is a figure of *Justice,* said to have been executed by John Dixey. The interior is marked by McComb's fine attention to detail, especially in the rotunda, in the superb double curve of the self-supporting marble stairway with its delicate wrought-iron railings, and in the slender columns of the upper gallery.

Portraits of former governors crowd the walls of the corridors, and mayors' portraits are hung in the mayor's antechamber and reception room on the first floor. Over the mantelpiece in the mayor's office is a portrait of Lafayette, painted by Samuel F. B. Morse on the occasion of the general's visit to America in 1824. The Governors' Suite, on the second floor, was originally intended for the official use of the State's chief executive when in New York, but its three rooms have been converted into a museum. *(Open Monday to Friday 9 a.m. to 4:30 p.m., Saturday 9 a.m. to 12 m.)* A mahogany writing table used by George Washington during the first days of his Presidency is exhibited along with other historic pieces of furniture. In the Governors' Room of the suite are Trumbull's portraits of such noted personages as John Jay, Alexander Hamilton, and George Washington (valued at more than a quarter of a million dollars), and in the other two rooms are hung paintings by John Wesley Jarvis, Henry Inman, John Vanderlyn, Thomas Sully, George Catlin, and others. The portrait of Henry Hudson is the work of Paul van Somer, a seventeenth-century Flemish master; the identity of the subject is doubtful, however, for there is no authenticated portrait of the navigator. This valuable collection is under the care of the Art Commission.

The mahogany-lined City Council chamber, once the aldermanic chamber, on the second floor, contains portraits of Henry Clay and George Washington, a statue of Thomas Jefferson by Pierre Jean David (d'Angers), and a pretentious ceiling mural, *New York City Receiving the Tributes of the Nations,* by Taber Sears, George W. Breck, and Frederic C. Martin. The adjoining committee room is decorated with portraits of General George B. McClellan, by William H. Powell, and of William Bainbridge, by John Wesley Jarvis. The former Common Council chamber, on the second floor, is now the meeting place of the Board of Estimate. Corinthian columns and pilasters give the room an atmosphere of dignity. A bust of John Jay, on the north side, is the work of John Frazee; that of John Marshall, on the south side, is by an unknown artist.

The steps of City Hall are worn smooth by official public receptions and ceremonies. Here the mayor welcomes distinguished visitors, awards promotions to members of the fire, police, and sanitation departments, and makes contributions opening charity campaigns.

The CITY COURT BUILDING is a white marble structure with Corinthian columns and pilasters. Built (1861–72) by the Tweed Ring at the cost of more than $12,000,000, it provided the opportunity for one of the most gigantic steals in the city's history.

City Hall Park is New York's approximation of a courthouse square or village green. This little plot of land is all that survives of one of New York's earliest municipal gathering places. The site was once part of the common lands. Whenever the community peace was threatened or cause for celebration arose, the populace gathered there. An oak planted near City Hall in 1911 does honor to the memory of Jacob Leisler, who fought against the tyranny of English rule and was hanged for treason in 1691 close to this spot. Near the front of the building the Sons of Liberty erected five successive "liberty poles" between 1766 and 1776. In 1776 the Declaration of Independence, brought by courier from the Continental Congress in Philadelphia, was read here, for the first time in New York, in the presence of George Washington.

On February 13, 1837, the "Flour" or "Bread Riot" took place during a financial panic then threatening the country. The price of flour had advanced from six dollars to fifteen dollars a barrel amid widespread speculation. A placard was carried through the streets announcing a meeting at the park, and declaring: "All friends of Humanity, determined to resist Monopolists and Extortionists are invited to attend, rain or shine. Bread, Meat, Rent, Fuel—the voice of the people shall be heard." The six thousand who attended vented their anger by breaking into the flour stores, dispersing only after the militia had been called out. The distressed gathered again in ominous protest during the lean days of the 1850's.

The park was the scene of a peculiar riot in 1857 when opposing bands of policemen cracked one another's heads. The Municipal Police, venal and inefficient, had been abolished by an act of the State Legislature and a new body, the Metropolitan Police, established under State control. The Municipals refused to disband, however, and when a large force of Metropolitans attempted to serve warrants for the arrest of Mayor Fernando Wood, the two groups clashed in a savage battle that stormed through the corridors of City Hall and was finally checked only by a show of bayonets by the Seventh Regiment of the National Guard.

During the Civil War, food for the soldiers went out across the park from the supply base at City Hall. A ceremony held here on March 24, 1900, marked the commencement of construction of the subway transit system.

A STATUE OF NATHAN HALE, the work of Frederick MacMonnies, is on the west side of the park. The FIGURE OF BENJAMIN FRANKLIN, near the east side of the park, was sculptured by E. Plassman and was erected in 1872 as the gift of Albert de Groot to the press and printers of New York. Another journalist, Horace Greeley, is honored by a heroic STATUE in bronze by Henry Bonnard. But the MacMonnies statue, *Civic Virtue,* erected in 1922, is the one generally associated with City Hall Park. Said to be the largest piece carved from a single block of marble since Michelangelo's *David,* the central figure is a gigantic muscular youth, nude except for a dash of foam (or seaweed) encircling his middle: a sword over his right shoulder, he fixes his gaze forward, seemingly unaware that he is trampling on two sirens writhing at his feet. In summertime children splash in the basin of the monument. Protests against the unembarrased nudity of the group and the conception it presents of virtuous man's chivalry have brought a promise of removal to Foley Square, where, presumably, criticism is less stringent.

The region north of City Hall Park is a district of wholesale commerce, where caps, pants, and woolens are manufactured and sold.

For almost a score of years before 1930 the sixty-story WOOLWORTH BUILDING, erected in 1913 west of the park's apex, at Broadway and Park Place, was the world's tallest building; its architect was Cass Gilbert. Intended as a huge "sky s¹gn" to advertise Frank W. Woolworth's chain of five-and-ten-cent stores, it was acclaimed a masterpiece, the first "cathedal of commerce." Its tower rises without a setback from the center of the Broadway front to 792 feet above the curb. The lower and broader section of the building mounts thirty stories to a height of about four hundred feet. This section has been criticized as being too high in comparison with the tower, when seen from the west. All the horizontal elements of the building are subdued in color to strengthen the soaring quality of the vertical lines.

The color is as delicately graded as the modeling. The chief effect is a glistening white, set off by the weathered green of the copper peak and copper roof; but as many as six different colors were used on a single terra-cotta ornamental detail. Pinnacles, carved canopies, and gargoyles soften the silhouette and impart an atmospheric lightness.

Crisp and delicate terra-cotta surface ornament drops over the building like a veil. All the details are Gothic, even to the tourelles that surround the peak, the finial that surmounts it, and the flying buttresses.

Despite its Gothic decorations, the Woolworth Building was a genuine contribution to the development of an American skyscraper style. It represents one of the earliest attempts to express the steel-frame structure—a departure from the "immobility of mass and weight of masonry" that characterized the classic type of building.

Below the Woolworth Building, on Broadway between Vesey and Fulton Streets, is St. Paul's Chapel of Trinity Parish, the oldest church building in Manhattan. Its cornerstone was laid May 14, 1764, in a field sloping to the Hudson River. The architect, James McBean, a Scot, is said to have been a pupil of James Gibbs. Gibbs designed the Renaissance church of St. Martin's-in-the-Fields, in London, which greatly influenced the design of St. Paul's.

The church was constructed of stone quarried from the site which is now the graveyard. Its original, lovely warm color has been greatly dulled by age. The church is surmounted by a tower at the west end, to which a wooden spire, more elaborate than the rest of the church but of excellent design, was added in 1794. At the east end, facing Broadway, is a carriage portico with a pediment and slender but well-proportioned Ionic columns. The light, spacious interior is handsomely decorated, with a barrel vault carried on slender columns, and a gallery on each side. On the north side of the interior a painting of the arms of the United States marks George Washington's pew; opposite, on the south, the arms of New York State mark Governor Clinton's pew. Immediately after Washington's inauguration, April 30, 1789, both houses of Congress accompanied him to St. Paul's, where Bishop Samuel Provoost conducted a service.

On the Broadway side is a monument to Major General Richard Montgomery, killed in the attack on Quebec, December 25, 1775. It was executed by J. J. Caffieri, French sculptor, on order from the Continental Congress. Montgomery's grave is beneath the monument. Among the memorials on the west wall of the interior is a bust of John Wells (1770–1823) by John Frazee, the first known portrait bust by a native American sculptor.

The graveyard, which flanks the church on three sides, is a favorite noonday retreat of office workers in the neighborhood. It contains the weatherbeaten tombs of many historic personalities. The churchyard gates are closed during the two days preceding the Feast of the Conversion of St. Paul, as they have been since the chapel's founding, to remind the public that the property belongs to Trinity Parish, and that it is open only by the courtesy of that body.

Newspaper Row

Across Park Row from City Hall Park, near the approach to the Brooklyn Bridge, stands the brownstone PULITZER BUILDING, once the proud home of the *World;* its gilded dome makes it one of the section's most imposing buildings. George B. Post designed the structure in 1890; it was enlarged in 1908. This was an early example of buildings whose walls carry only their own weight; the floors are supported by columns. Nevertheless, the exterior walls are, in places, more than nine feet thick.

Today the *World* is dead, the dome in which Joseph Pulitzer had his office is deserted, and the structure has become merely another office building—a relic of New York's NEWSPAPER ROW. In the late decades of the nineteenth century Park Row and northern Nassau Street constituted the publishing center for the great metropolitan dailies. Today only the *Sun,* housed in the Stewart Building, flanking City Hall Park on the northeast corner of Chambers Street and Broadway, remains in the vicinity.

A little to the south of the Pulitzer Building, at Spruce and Nassau Streets, is the red-brick, clock-towered TRIBUNE BUILDING, former home of the *Tribune* and one of the earliest elevator buildings. Dana's *Sun* was once next to the *Tribune*—in the same building, incidentally, which for a time housed Tammany. The modest building that housed the *Times* in the days of its humble beginnings occupies the site of the old Brick Presbyterian Church at Park Row and Nassau Street. The nonpartisan CITIZENS UNION, founded in 1897 for the purpose of obtaining honest, efficient municipal government, is now one of the tenants of the building. A little off the Row, on near-by William Street, were quartered Hearst's *Evening Journal* and *American.* The *Evening Post,* edited by William Cullen Bryant, had its home at Broadway and Fulton Street. James Gordon Bennett's

Herald had its workshop on the southeast corner of Ann Street and Broadway, site of the old Barnum Museum.

Long a familiar feature of the Row was the 120-year-old building of the Roman Catholic CHURCH OF ST. ANDREW, famed for its 2:30 A.M. Mass for night workers, most of them printers from the great dailies. In 1938 a new church structure was erected on the original site at Duane Street and Cardinal Place, behind the Municipal Building. The site also includes 15 Cardinal Place, birthplace of Patrick Cardinal Hayes.

On New Chambers, corner of William Street, is the BRACE MEMORIAL NEWSBOYS' HOUSE, founded in 1853 by Charles Loring Brace and now one of five shelters maintained by the Children's Aid Society. It provides food and lodging at low cost for homeless boys. Horatio Alger is said to have found material for his rags-to-riches stories there.

This section was New York's Rialto before it became the domain of the Fourth Estate. Its theaters presented the first American dramas as well as the most famous stars of the English and American stage. Through the Park Theatre's stage entrance—the narrow lane still known as Theatre Alley, parallel to Park Row and connecting Ann and Beekman Streets— passed such celebrated stars as Edwin Booth, Edmund Kean, Edwin Forrest, and Fanny and Charles Kemble. In 1825 the first formal opera presented in America, Rossini's *Elisabetta,* was performed here.

Other playhouses in this section were the Anthony Street Theatre, Anthony Street (now Worth Street) near Broadway, which presented Joseph Jefferson, the elder, and James Wallack; the Old Broadway Theatre at Broadway and Pearl Street, which opened in 1847 with Sheridan's *School for Scandal;* and Palmo's Opera House, 39 Chambers Street, renamed Burton's, which opened in 1844 and presented opera intermittently during two decades.

South of the Brooklyn Bridge and east of Park Row is the "Swamp," center of the city's wholesale leather market since the late 1690's. When the tanning industry was expelled from Broad Street, the mart followed it to Beekman Swamp—the site bounded approximately by Frankfort, William, Beekman, and Cliff Streets. During the nineteenth century, an encroaching population gradually drove the tanneries from the neighborhood, but the leather merchants remained.

Beekman Street, southern boundary of the "Swamp," is the center of downtown New York's job printing industry, which took root in this section when most of New York's newspapers were published on near-by Newspaper Row. (The printing and publishing industry is the second largest in the city.)

On the northeast corner of Beekman and Gold Streets is THE OLD
BEEKMAN, a tavern and coffee house where General Grant is said to have
imbibed his favorite Peoria whisky.

The Civic Center

Despite the northward expansion of the city, the vicinity of the City
Hall has remained the center of governmental activities in New York.
This concentration of official business—municipal, State and Federal—
occurs in an impressive group of buildings erected within the past decade
in and around Foley Square, the neighborhood northeast of City Hall Park.

On the two triangular blocks bounded by Park Row, Centre, and Duane
Streets, and looking down on City Hall, is the forty-story MUNICIPAL
BUILDING, designed by McKim, Mead, and White. It straddles Chambers Street, forming an arcade through which flows west-east vehicular
traffic; this passageway has been called the "Gate of the City," the title
of an oil painting of the scene by William Jean Beauley. The building
has a flattened U-shaped plan, with its open side toward Centre Street. It
gains dignity through the bold treatment of the intermediate stories, despite the poorly related tower and the disturbing character of the Corinthian colonnade at the base. In themselves the elements are well designed,
but their combination lacks unity. It is surmounted by a heroic figure of
Civic Fame, by Adolph Alexander Weinman, who was also the sculptor
of the relief on the lower part of the building.

The building, opened in 1914, cost about twelve million dollars. Despite its size (650,000 square feet of floor area), it has proved inadequate,
and several departments have been housed in buildings on Foley Square
proper. The municipally owned and operated RADIO STATION, WNYC,
on the twenty-fifth floor, broadcasts no commercial programs; performers
are supplied by government agencies and educational institutions. The
MUNICIPAL REFERENCE LIBRARY, on the twenty-second floor, a branch
of the New York Public Library, contains documents, pamphlets, maps,
directories, and reports from all important cities. On the second floor,
across the hall from the marriage license bureau, is the MARRIAGE CHAPEL,
a sunny room decorated with flowered wallpaper and potted palms.

The seven-story granite structure at Chambers and Centre Streets is the
HALL OF RECORDS, repository for all legal records relating to deeds of
Manhattan real estate and to court cases—some of the documents were
drawn as early as 1653. It contains offices of the New York County
Register, Surrogates' Court, and Commissioner of Jurors. Designed by
John R. Thomas and opened in 1911, it is New York's best example of

the eclectic baroque style used in French nineteenth-century municipal buildings. Heroic statues of distinguished New Yorkers on the ornate granite façade and symbolic figures representing such conceptions as Philosophy, Poetry, and Industry are by Philip Martiny and Henry K. Bush-Brown. The interior is sumptuously decorated.

Beyond the Municipal Building and the Hall of Records lies Foley Square proper, a plot of land shaped somewhat like a hatchet head, around which several public buildings have been grouped to form a civic center. Unfortunately, this group lacks a unifying architectural design. Several city departments are housed in the COURT SQUARE BUILDING at 2 Lafayette Street, a commercial office building.

Across, on Centre Street between Duane and Pearl, is the new UNITED STATES COURT HOUSE, last architectural work of Cass Gilbert, and completed in 1936 by his son, Cass Gilbert, Jr. The architects attempted the difficult task of harmonizing their work with the neoclassic structures on either side. The tower, thirty-two stories high, is crowned by a pyramidal roof covered with gold leaf. The offices of the United States Attorney for the Southern District of New York as well as the United States District Court and Circuit Court of Appeals are in the building.

A block east, at Pearl Street and Park Row, was the famous Tea Water Pump, which was the chief source of water supply for the city until 1789. Its water, so housewives declared, was excellent for brewing tea. Carted about in casks, it was sold from door to door.

North of the United States Court House on Centre Street is the eight-story, neoclassic SUPREME COURT BUILDING, designed after the drawings submitted in competition by Guy Lowell, of Boston, in 1912. Skillfully planned for a difficult site, the hexagonal building has a refreshing robustness. Unlike the other columns of Foley Square, its great Corinthian order presents a real portico of convincing form and scale. It is approached by a sweep of granite steps one hundred feet wide. The elaborately decorated central rotunda is three stories high. The building houses one of the country's finest law libraries.

Various New York State departments centered in Albany have offices in the granite-faced, nine-story STATE OFFICE BUILDING which stands on the northeast corner of the square (Worth and Centre Streets). Built (1928–30) under the supervision of W. E. Haugaard, State commissioner of architecture, it is of "chastened classic" design. Its walls are relieved by flat carving and at its four entrances are black granite lighting standards. The offices are grouped around two large courts. The main floor halls are finished in gray marble with green marble pilasters and bronze capitals, and plaster cornices and ceilings decorated with gold leaf.

The building to the west, occupying an entire block and with its main entrance on Worth Street, contains offices, laboratories, and clinics of the CITY HEALTH, HOSPITAL, AND SANITATION DEPARTMENTS. It was designed by Charles B. Meyers to conform with the State Office Building, and was completed in 1935. It is ornamented with metal grilles and lanterns, and a series of panels depicting medical subjects.

Occupying the two blocks between Centre and Lafayette Streets, a few steps north of Foley Square, are the bleak structures of the TOMBS and the CRIMINAL COURTS BUILDING connected by the famous BRIDGE OF SIGHS. The Tombs, a prison for men awaiting trial, derives its funereal name from its predecessor on this site, which resembled an Egyptian tomb. The present huge gray pile, with its rounded ends and high pitched roof, is more suggestive, however, of a gloomy medieval fortress. Notorious criminals have been incarcerated within these somber walls before being led across the enclosed bridge for trial in the Criminal Courts. The long career of both structures neared an end in 1938, when the State Legislature authorized the expenditure of $15,000,000 for the erection of modern buildings. The new site is directly across Centre Street from the old one.

This entire area in the eighteenth century comprised marshland and a pond known as the Collect. It was on this pond that John Fitch, in 1796, conducted experiments with a steamboat. In the depression of 1808, municipal authorities established a work relief project to drain the section. It became a recreational center for holiday-making laborers, sailors, and oystermen. But when the land began to sink into the imperfectly drained swamp, the houses and taverns of the region were abandoned to freed slaves and hapless immigrants.

Such was the origin of the historically infamous Five Points section. The territory derived its name from the intersection of five streets forming a triangular area, with Paradise Square, now the southwest corner of Columbus Park (opposite the State Office Building at Baxter and Worth Streets), in the center. It reached its peak in disorder and debauchery about the middle of the nineteenth century when the first gangs of New York made their appearance in the congested slum with such picturesque names as the "Forty Thieves," "Kerryonians," "Chichesters," "Plug Uglies," "Shirt Tails," and "Dead Rabbits." The most unsavory place was the "Old Brewery," a converted tenement swarming with thieves, prostitutes, and degenerates. In one room called the "Den of Thieves" more than seventy-five men and women made their home. This warren was vividly described by Charles Dickens in his *American Notes*.

CHINATOWN

Area: Baxter St. east to Park Row and New Bowery; south of Bayard St. Map on page 91.

New York's Chinatown is trying to live down a myth; a myth kept alive by the sight-seeing companies that pile tourists into Chinatown busses, transport them to prepared points of interest, and frequently prime them with tales of mystery and crime. The truth is (and the policemen on the beat will verify it) that no safer district is to be found in New York City. Yet guides have been known to warn tourists to "hold hands while walking through the narrow streets."

Tourist trade, which supplies a small part of its income, is but a secondary concern of the Chinese quarter; for though its population is only 4,000 the district serves as "home town" for the 18,000 Chinese of New York City and for the 30,000 in the metropolitan area. Laundrymen, restaurant workers, servants, shopkeepers, and professionals come here, especially on Sunday, to meet their friends, do their shopping, see a Chinese movie, eat a holiday dinner, play fan-tan, or arrange a marriage or burial.

The first Chinese known to have visited New York was Pung-hua Wing Chong, who arrived in 1807, the year the embargo on foreign trade was established. Later he became known as John Jacob Astor's mandarin because Astor got permission from President Jefferson to send out a ship, despite the embargo, on the pretense of taking "this prominent mandarin" home.

Historians differ as to the identity of the first Chinese resident of New York City. Some say it was Quimbo Appo, who came to San Francisco in 1844 and arrived here a few years later; others state it was Ah Ken, a Cantonese merchant who made his home on Mott Street in 1858. Still others contend it was Lou Hoy Sing, a sailor who shook off his wanderlust and settled in New York in 1862. (He married an Irish lass who bore him two stalwart sons, one of whom became a policeman and the other a truck driver.) From 1875 until shortly after the Chinese Exclusion Act of 1882, Chinese migrated in large numbers to the city, displacing well-to-do families in the neighborhood of Mott and Pell Streets. The colony soon overflowed into Bayard and Canal Streets, and at its peak numbered 6,000 residents.

For many decades Chinatown kept intact the religious and cultural customs of old China. The younger generation, however, like that of other immigrant groups, no longer adheres strictly to the traditional mores;

changes in China have been an added factor in the weakening. Though the joss houses, shrines of Buddhist worship, still exist, they are rarely attended by Chinese, certainly not by the youth. The Chinese New Year is still celebrated in traditional paper-dragon-and-firecracker style but the more rigid ethical customs, such as suicide because of failure to pay debts, are being ignored or abandoned. No longer is American citizenship frowned upon; and mixed marriages cause little comment. So far has the process of assimilation progressed that in the 1936 Democratic National Convention Wong Lee was seated as a New York delegate.

The tongs, Chinese equivalent of American fraternal societies, which for so many years ruled the quarter with iron discipline and fought each other with hired gunmen, now share influence with newer groups. The *Chinese Journal* and the *Vanguard,* recently established liberal-progressive newspapers, are steadily gaining in circulation, and the *Chinese Republic News* and the *Nationalist Daily* reflect the new trend.

Since the Japanese invasion of China in 1937, a new spirit of unity has developed in Chinatown which has eliminated social and political friction and discouraged tong wars. Old and young, conservatives and moderns, have joined in raising funds for the homeland and in promoting the boycott against Japanese goods.

One custom, however, the devout Chinese still retains; he arranges that when death comes his remains shall be sent to China for interment. This is accomplished with characteristic patience and thrift. The deceased is first buried in this country, an identification tag sealed in a bottle being placed in the casket. Ten years later the grave is opened and the remains, removed to a zinc-lined box two feet by one, are shipped to China for reburial. Freight charges are thus brought within the means of the dead man's family.

A leisurely stroll at sundown through Chinatown's winding streets is an interesting experience. Throughout the neighborhood Chinese importing houses and groceries, like the New England "general stores," offer a wide variety of goods. Neatly stacked in the windows are Chinese vegetables (grown on Long Island)—tender green Chinese cabbage, blanched bean sprouts, fibrous brown lily roots, crinkly bitter melons, great squashes resembling watermelon covered with a white bloom, water chestnuts, young pods of peas—with smoked squid, shark fin, blubber, roast ducks, and roast pork hanging from hooks.

In these shops, patronized almost exclusively by Chinese, many articles for use and decoration may be purchased: hexagonal and fluted green bowls, native spoons of China, simple brown paper fans, packets of joss

sticks, sturdy black cotton slippers without backs, strangely shaped but unusually durable toothbrushes, kites shaped like butterflies or dragons,
wooden flutes, beautiful green-leaved Chinese lilies, wall pockets for
flowers, long-handled wooden back-scratchers.

Mott Street, entered from Worth Street, which extends west of Chatham
Square, gives the first colorful view of the quarter. The large Chinese signs
of a native temple at No. 5 emphasize the oriental style of the façade of
the adjoining PORT ARTHUR RESTAURANT BUILDING (No. 7). The
CHINATOWN EMPORIUM in the Port Arthur Building attracts souvenir
buyers, and near by at No. 13 the JOSS HOUSE presents for curious
passers-by and the herded throngs from the "rubberneck wagons" an in-
accurate but highly dramatic lecture on Chinese religious customs. At No.
37 the oldest JEWELRY STORE in Chinatown offers gold objects hammered
according to the design requested by the customer. The headquarters of
the powerful ON LEONG TONG are at No. 41, and beyond is the LIQUOR
STORE of Wing Lee Quon at No. 53, where authentic Chinese wines and
cordials, medicated with snakeskin and tiger bone, are available.

At No. 58, Wah Kue sells Chinese books, brushes, and writing material; at No. 64 is the CHINESE SCHOOL where, after regular public-school
hours, children are taught Chinese culture and language according to the
traditional method. Just north of Pell Street on Mott hangs the WALL
NEWSPAPER. Sheets of brilliant red and orange paper flecked with gold
are covered with characters which inform knots of readers that a business is
for sale or has been sold, that a job is available or is wanted, and of the
latest war news from China.

At 32 Pell Street, the MEE TUNG COMPANY announces "Ladies Dresses
Made to Order in Chinese Styles." The ESTABLISHMENT OF MAN GAR
CHUNG at No. 26 offers an assortment of Chinese drugs and ingredients
for an assortment of love potions: dried sea horses, blanched snakes, preserved bears' testicles, neat slices of deer's horn, and ginseng root. The
last-named sells for as much as a hundred dollars an ounce.

The headquarters of the HIP SING TONG are situated appropriately
near the corner of Pell and Doyers Streets, for just beyond is the BLOODY
ANGLE, the bend in Doyers Street where henchmen of this tong fought
the On Leongs in the early 1900's. The Hip Sings, led by Mock Duck, a
gambler, battled the On Leongs, captained by Tom Lee, for control of the
lucrative gambling and opium rackets. At this bend, occupying the quarters of the old Chinese theater, is Tom Noonan's famous RESCUE SO-
CIETY. The ex-convict sponsored the mission for twenty-three years, until
his death in 1935. Near by, at 6 Doyers Street, is a building once occupied

by the Chatham Club, where a young singing waiter, Isadore Baline (Irving Berlin), occasionally performed. Here, too, Chuck Connors, whom the movies years later made king of Chinatown lobbygows, Bowery thespian and philosopher, served as bouncer.

Each night the Chinese take over the ten-cent movie house on Chatham Square just north of Mott Street, and Chinese pictures made either in China or in San Francisco replace the customary Westerns. At 8 Chatham Square the old-fashioned TOBACCO EMPORIUM of Seckler Brothers is crowded with smokers' oddities. The next building houses the establishment of Rocks Grillo, the artist who makes "black eyes" look normal. Two doors north is the studio of Charlie Wagner, "champion tattooing artist in the world."

A visit to Chinatown should include dinner at one of the numerous restaurants, declared by the Board of Health to be among the cleanest in the city. Some of the less prominent places, many of which are on the second story or in unpretentious basements, are as good as the larger ones. The food in most of the quarter's restaurants is authentically Chinese and of a uniformly high quality, and most places specialize in one or more native dishes.

Chop suey came into existence in Chicago in 1896 during the visit of Li Hung Chang, famous "ambassador of good will." Literally translated the name means "hodge-podge." As prepared by the restaurants in Chinatown the dish is far superior to that served in drug stores and cafeterias. A good Chinese meal consists of soup, fish, and of preparations of sea food, pork, or chicken, served with Chinese vegetables and sauces. When a group dines together it is advantageous to order "by the table," fixing a price beforehand with the waiter.

The most delicious soups are won ton soup, made with little dumplings filled with duck; water-cress soup, tart with quantities of fresh water cress; chop suey soup, rich with chicken gizzards, livers, and oddments. Shrimp is usually fried and served with egg or lobster sauce or with steamed Chinese vegetables, or combined with chopped lobster and seasoning as the filling for the fried dough cakes known as egg rolls. Stuffed crab, served in deep-sea crab shells, is a pungent and exotic delicacy, and fish-balls covered with delectable sauce and with native vegetables is a favorite dish. Roast pork prepared by Chinese chefs is famous. Soft noodle chow mein, Canton style, and chicken diced with almonds and fresh peas with a Chinese white sauce, are two other appetizing dishes. A Chinese meal is not complete without one sweet and pungent dish, preferably spareribs prepared with a rich sauce of ginger, pineapple, and spices.

LOWER EAST SIDE

Area: Fulton St. (South St. to Pearl St.) and Franklin St. (Baxter St. to Broadway) on the south to 14th St. on the north; from the East River west to Pearl St. and Broadway; excluding Chinatown. Map on page 111.

The dramatic, intensely human story of the Lower East Side is a familiar chapter in the epic of America; a host of writers—some seeking out the Lower East Side and others originating there—have described its people. Here have dwelt the people whose hands built the city's elevateds, subways, tubes, bridges, and skyscrapers. Its two square miles of tenements and crowded streets magnify all the problems and conflicts of big-city life. The inhuman conditions of its slums and sweatshops brought about the first organized social work in America. Crowded, noisy, squalid in many of its aspects, no other section of the city is more typical of New York.

The district is best known as a slum, as a community of immigrants, and as a ghetto; yet not all of the district is blighted, not all of its people are of foreign stock, and not all are Jewish. From its dark tenements, generations of American workers of many different national origins and an amazing number of public figures have emerged; politicians, artists, gangsters, composers, prize fighters, labor leaders.

One of the first New York tenements designed for multifamily use was erected in the Lower East Side in 1833, on Water Street near Corlears Hook. The most notorious "modern" slum, however, was Five Points—centered at the intersection of Baxter, Worth, and Park Streets—flourishing when Charles Dickens described it in 1842. The southern part of the Lower East Side soon shared the conditions if not the notoriety of Five Points and, thanks to potato rot, political oppression, and pogroms, the northern part took on the same character, as the last great waves of the "old immigration" and the first great waves of the "new immigration" surged in. The overwhelming majority of the tenements still standing are of the kind banned in 1901. Many antedate the Civil War, but most were built in the 1880's and 1890's.

Two million Irish, fleeing famine, migrated to America between 1846 and 1860, and many of them settled, at least temporarily, in the Lower East Side. It was the Lower East Side that produced Alfred E. Smith, four-time Democratic governor of New York State, Democratic candidate for President in 1928, and a founder of the American Liberty League; and three of the best-known sachems of the originally anti-Irish Tammany

Hall: "Boss" Tweed, leading figure of the infamous Tweed Ring, "Honest John" Kelley, and Charlie Murphy. From 1811 to 1867 the Tammany Wigwam was located at Chatham and Frankfort Streets. Large numbers of Irish workers went into the shipping and building trades, and later into the police, fire, and other city departments.

The first of thousands of Germans came to the Lower East Side at the middle of the nineteenth century. Many of them were skilled workers with a background of labor organization, and they played an important role in the trade union movement in New York: they formed the General German Workingmen's Union, which in 1867 affiliated with the International Workmen's Association (The First International); they founded the Free Workers' School (housed in Faulhaber's Hall on Second Avenue), one of the first of its kind in the United States; they established labor and progressive newspapers. German Jews became traders, professionals, clothing manufacturers, furriers, jewelers. By 1880 they were the dominant element in New York's Jewish community of eighty thousand.

In 1881 the great influx of Italians, Russians, Rumanians, Hungarians, Slovaks, Greeks, Poles, and Turks, into the Lower East Side began. Between 1881 and 1910, 1,562,000 Jews came to America. Many of these Jewish emigrants, chiefly from Russia, settled on the Lower East Side, forming the world's largest Jewish community. The Jews, like other peoples in the region, grouped themselves in more or less compact colonies determined by language, customs, country or province of origin. Little Rumania, for instance, centering around Allen Street, was one of the most distinct and interesting quarters during the 1890's.

Most of these new Jewish immigrants worked as peddlers or entered the expanding needle trades. Workshops, established in the tenements, enslaved entire families, and the sweatshop era began, with its disease and degradation. Many of these workers succeeded after a time in improving their position, and a few became large-scale employers themselves. Through appalling sacrifice, some Jewish families realized their fondest aspiration: a son became a doctor, teacher, or lawyer. Those who rose above poverty moved to more desirable localities, but "greenhorns"—new and bewildered immigrants, Jew and Gentile—continued to augment the population of the East Side until the third decade of this century, when quota laws severely restricted further immigration. During that decade the population remained between five and six hundred thousand.

An East Side family was often divided against itself by the conflict of the old and the new. "Many of us were transient, impatient aliens in our parents' home," Samuel Ornitz records in *Haunch, Paunch and Jowl*

(1923), a semi-autobiographical novel of the Lower East Side. There were almost no play areas. Boys formed themselves into gangs, roamed the streets in search of mischief and money; many became gangsters. One of the toughest thugs in the city's history, "Monk" Eastman, rose at the turn of the century, commanding hundreds of gunmen. From his headquarters on Chrystie Street came in a later period, Johnny Torrio, "Legs" Diamond, and Jacob ("Little Augie") Orgen.

During the latter part of the nineteenth century the writings of Jacob Riis and others stimulated the housing reform movement and social-welfare work. The Neighborhood Guild, first of the many settlement houses established in the Lower East Side, was founded in 1886 at 147 Forsythe Street. Two years later East Siders themselves took an important step toward combating their intolerable living conditions by forming the United Hebrew Trades, a trade union body. Today such centers as Christadora House, the Church of All Nations, the Educational Alliance, Grand Street Settlement, Henry Street Settlement, Stuyvesant Neighborhood House, and University Settlement are invaluable community agencies.

Unionism, anarchism, capitalism, socialism, and communism have been thoroughly discussed in the streets and parks of the East Side. Yet Tammany Hall has reigned almost uninterruptedly over the actual political life of the area. Anarchist and Socialist papers and periodicals, some short-lived, others continuing to appear for many years, have been issued in

---

KEY TO LOWER EAST SIDE MAP

1. Lavanburg Homes
2. Bed Linens Market
3. Orchard Street Pushcart Market
4. Henry Street Settlement Playhouse
5. Amalgamated Dwellings
6. Henry Street Settlement (Main House)
7. Educational Alliance
8. Jewish Daily Forward
9. Division Street Shopping Center
10. Knickerbocker Village
11. Oldest House in Manhattan
12. Franklin Square
13. Spanish-Portuguese Cemetery
14. Columbus Park
    Mulberry Bend
15. Olliffe Pharmacy
16. Secondhand Clothing Market
17. Manhattan Bridge Plaza
18. Bowery Outdoor Jewelry Market
19. Mott Street Pushcart Market
20. Police Headquarters
21. "Thieves' Market"
22. Salvation Army Hotel
23. Bowery Mission
24. First Houses
25. Condict Building
26. Old Merchant's House
27. Colonnade Row
28. Statue of Peter Cooper
29. Cooper Union
30. Secondhand Book Market
31. St. Mark's In-The-Bouwerie
32. Jewish Theater District

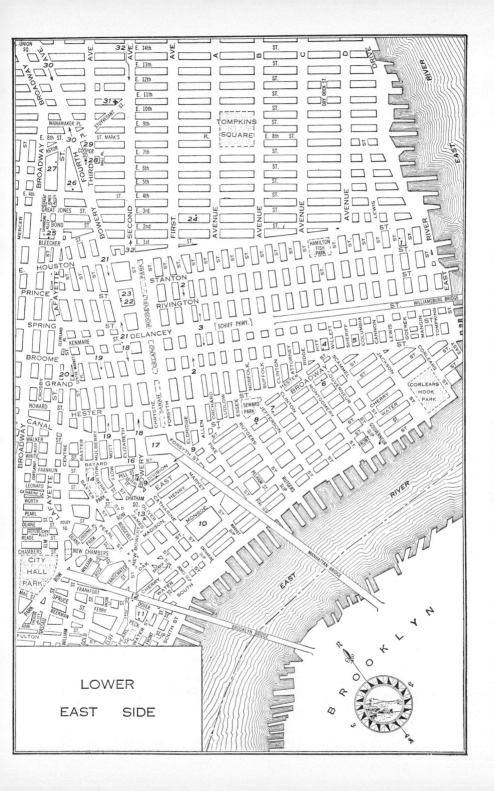

LOWER

EAST SIDE

many languages. Johann Most published *Freiheit,* and later (1906) Emma Goldman founded *Mother Earth.* Under the editorship of Abraham Cahan, the *Jewish Daily Forward,* a labor paper in Jewish, has been most influential, and still has a circulation of about 170,000. The Socialist Party's work was rewarded when Meyer London was elected to Congress in 1914, and again in 1918 when three Socialist assemblymen were elected. Morris Hillquit, leader of the Socialist Party for many years after the war, was from the locality. B. Charney Vladeck, of the *Forward,* was elected majority leader of the City Council in 1937, the year the East Side assembly districts cast 14 per cent of their votes for the American Labor Party as against 8.5 per cent in the rest of Manhattan.

The intellectuals among the immigrants brought with them their old-world avidity for culture, and their influence on the East Side provided thousands with their first contact with art and literature. A lunch hour at a garment factory would find many of the workers absorbed in Tolstoy, Kropotkin, or Heine. Maeterlinck, Hauptmann, Sudermann, Gorky, and other European dramatists had their American premiers in the ghetto. While Broadway was receiving Ibsen coldly, the East Side was enthusiastically applauding Nazimova in *Ghosts.* The ghetto has produced a remarkable Jewish literature of its own, much of it mirroring the harsh life of sweatshop and slum. The Yiddish poet, with his relatively small public, ordinarily sells many more copies of his works than a poet who writes in English. Probably the two most widely read books in English about the East Side by East Siders are Abraham Cahan's novel, the *Rise of David Levinsky* (1917), and Michael Gold's autobiographical *Jews Without Money* (1930). Fannie Hurst, born in St. Louis, lived in the East Side while gathering material for her stories. "Humoresque," dealing with this locale, is perhaps the best known.

Jo Davidson and Jacob Epstein, sculptors, and Max Weber, the painter, are from the East Side, as are scores of younger artists whose works have gained wide recognition. Jazz owes much to the district where George and Ira Gershwin and Irving Berlin started their careers. The wise-cracking brand of humor, and much language which has become part of popular speech, have roots in the Lower East Side. Such expressions as *gabfest, plunderbund, it listens well, bum, dumb* (in the sense of stupid), come from the Germans; the Jews have given words like *kibitzer, kosher, mazuma, phooey;* and the Irish, *shillelagh, smithereens, ballyhoo,* and *shebang.* The district's environment has influenced Jimmy Durante, Al Jolson, Eddie Cantor, Fannie Brice, George Jessel, Lionel Stander, Milton Berle, and the Marx brothers.

Immigration quotas at the beginning of the 1920's brought a great change to the district. No longer maintained by new arrivals, the population dropped from well over a half million in 1920 to less than a quarter million in 1938. Land values have declined and many of the rookeries are no longer profitable. Some have been condemned and demolished, leaving vacant lots used as playgrounds. The building of the Williamsburg and Manhattan bridges (opened in 1903 and 1909) cut swaths through the close-packed dwellings; and recently Chrystie, Allen, and part of East Houston Streets have been widened, removing blocks of tenements. The East River Drive and its park have transformed the water front north of the Williamsburg Bridge. The Amalgamated Dwellings, built in the 1920's, and Knickerbocker Village, built in the 1930's, replaced some of the worst houses.

But throughout most of the section the smothering heat of summer still drives East Siders to the windows and fire escapes of their ill-ventilated dwellings, to the docks along the river or to the crowded smelly streets, where half-naked children cool themselves in streams from fire hydrants. In winter, basement merchants sell coal and kindling in minute portions for the stoves of unheated cold-water flats.

In 1939 a $19,500,000 Federal-financed housing project was considered for the Lower East Side. Other changes are in prospect and even the push-carts may yet be housed in respectable markets. But the tenements that have been home to so many generations will probably be home to many more. Shored up with great beams against their sagging walls or vacant and crumbling, they still seem defiant. Great slums die hard.

East Side Neighborhoods

Several well-defined neighborhoods, with different backgrounds, distinct populations, and varied street plans, make up the Lower East Side. Along the East River above Fulton Street, bounded on the north by Division and Grand Streets, and roughly corresponding to the outlines of the old Fourth Ward, lies the oldest of these neighborhoods. Between Division and Houston Streets, and from the Bowery to the East River is the Jewish quarter with its small shops and markets. The Little Italy district lies west of the Bowery as far as Broadway, bounded on the north by Houston, and on the south by Franklin and Bayard Streets. Its Italian population now occupies only those four streets closest to the Bowery, the rest being given over to prosaic small businesses. Northward, from Houston to Fourteenth Street and between Broadway and Third Avenue, the Astor Place district retains, among second-rate commercial buildings, a few relics of its aristocratic days in the early 1880's. Lastly, between Third Avenue and the river, and between Houston and Fourteenth Streets, lies a district populated by a mixture of many nationalities (which for convenience will be named for its large park, Tompkins Square). The Lower East Side is connected with Brooklyn by the Brooklyn, Manhattan, and Williamsburg bridges. Automobiles bound for Holland Tunnel cross the neighborhood in great numbers by way of Canal and Delancey Streets.

Old Fourth Ward District

Four blocks east of City Hall, an abandoned building at 11 Peck Slip (near Pearl Street) is reputed to be the oldest house in Manhattan. It was built in 1725. Constructed of roughhewn stone and faced with plaster, the structure is still in good condition. At No. 7 is a tumbledown clapboard house, now serving as a junk shop, which was the farmhouse in which David Thomas Valentine, famous editor of *Valentine's Manual,* lived during his youth.

In Revolutionary days the rich and influential built their mansions on fashionable Cherry Hill. The center of this section, Franklin Square, originally called St. George Square, at the junction of Pearl, Frankfort, Dover, and Cherry Streets, was named for Walter Franklin, a wealthy importer in whose home President Washington resided, from his inauguration on April 30, 1789 to February 23, 1790. One of the piers of the Brooklyn Bridge covers the site of the house.

Near by, at 326 Pearl Street, stood the Walton House, home of William Walton, one of the city's richest merchants. The display of wealth at Walton House was cited in the British Parliament as incontestable proof of the Colonists' ability to pay higher taxes. The house was destroyed by fire in 1853, and its site is now occupied by a warehouse.

John Hancock lived at 5 Cherry Street, and Captain Samuel Chester Reid, a hero of the War of 1812, made his home at No. 27, now the site of a parking lot. Here Mrs. Reid is said to have sewed the first American flag in its present-day design, with a star for each state. The house was the first (1823) in America to have gas lighting. The old mansions, gradually abandoned by their owners, became tenements in the early 1800's and the district degenerated into a slum area.

At 36 Cherry Street, in 1850, was erected Gotham Court, hailed as a private venture in model housing. It covered an entire lot, with only two narrow alleys for sunshine and air, the wider of which the neighbors ironically nicknamed Paradise Alley. In cholera epidemics the death rate in this house was highest in the city. It was torn down in 1896, but the name

Paradise Alley lingers on in one of the sentimental songs of the period, the *Sunshine of Paradise Alley,* which, like the *Sidewalks of New York,* and *Maggie Murphy's Home,* was written about life among the Irish immigrants in this district in the 1890's. Near by, at 25 Oliver Street, lived Alfred E. Smith. The population of this former Irish district is chiefly Italian and Russian; a Greek colony occupies the lower end of Madison Street, while a small group of Spaniards lives in the neighborhood of Roosevelt and Cherry Streets. Today Cherry Street itself for the most part is a dismal-looking quarter of lumberyards and many abandoned tenements.

Among rancid tenements, at Cherry and Catharine Streets, stands the immense KNICKERBOCKER VILLAGE, a housing project completed in 1934 by a limited-dividend corporation with assistance from the Federal Government's Reconstruction Finance Corporation. Built on the site of a notorious "lung" block, it rents 1,600 apartments for an average of $12.50 a room a month to better-paid white-collar workers. The average rental elsewhere in the district is nearer five dollars and the former occupants of this site have moved to other slums. With a total of twelve floors, the buildings form an overcrowded group whose essential monotony is barely relieved by the sparse planting which differentiates it from hundreds of equally undistinguished apartments farther uptown. At the fourth floor level a projecting band of bricks hints at the parapet that should have marked the termination of the buildings.

Four blocks north of Cherry Street, at 175 East Broadway, standing head and shoulders above its neighbors, is the building housing the liberal *Jewish Daily Forward,* founded in 1897. It is the largest Yiddish daily newspaper in the world. On the next corner, East Broadway at Jefferson Street, the EDUCATIONAL ALLIANCE, a non-sectarian social settlement maintained by Jewish societies, organizes educational and recreational activities for the neighborhood.

The famous HENRY STREET SETTLEMENT, at 265 Henry, a block south of East Broadway, still maintains its modest main house. Opened in 1893 by one of the great pioneers in social work, Lillian Wald, the settlement has attracted world-wide attention through its work in nursing the sick, aiding in the solution of domestic and social problems, and striving for better housing, recreation, and education facilities in the slums of the Lower East Side. Buildings at 301 Henry Street and 8 Pitt Street have been acquired and the settlement employs 265 nurses working from sixteen branches throughout the city. During the depression of the early 1930's, before public relief was taken over by the Federal Government, the settlement issued thousands of food tickets, gave aid, and directed relief. Lillian Wald retired in 1933 and the work is being carried on under the guidance of Helen Hall.

Three blocks north, at 466 Grand Street, is the Henry Street Settlement's PLAYHOUSE, once famous as the Neighborhood Playhouse. Organized in 1915 for the purpose of staging productions of the settlement's dramatic groups, it branched out into professional production under the leadership of Alice and Irene Lewisohn. The Playhouse saw the American premieres of *The Dybbuk* and of James Joyce's *Exiles*. Yvette Guilbert; Roshanara, the Hindu dancer; Ratan Devi, the Hindu singer and musician; Rabindranath Tagore, the Indian poet; and the Isadora Duncan dancers appeared here. A satiric revue, the *Grand Street Follies,* was such a success that in 1927 it moved uptown. The theater now serves its original function.

Jewish Quarter

Here tiny shops huddle between wide-fronted chain shoe stores and clothing establishments. Housewives carrying shopping bags walk to the dimly lighted food stores; shriveled old women sit on the steps before the tenements; an occasional elder in beard and *yarmalka* (skull cap) climbs the steps to a tiny synagogue maintained by some struggling congregation; a Jewish passerby may be solicited to come into the synagogue to make up a *minyan* (quorum of ten) so that the service may start. In this district may be found some of the marriage brokers who advertise "rich and professional connections" in the Jewish newspapers.

At 504 Grand Street, between Columbia and Sheriff Streets, stands AMAL-GAMATED DWELLINGS, a co-operative apartment house sponsored by the Amalgamated Clothing Workers of America. The architecture diverts the eye with parabolic archways, and a surface patterning of brick designs and stucco inserts. An early development, it has a certain charm and human quality notably lacking in its more famous neighbor, Knickerbocker Village. Designed by Springsteen and Goldhammer, and completed in 1930, it was the first housing development built in Manhattan under the State Housing Law of 1926. Rents average $12.23 a room a month, and it is said that few clothing workers can afford to live there. Four blocks north at Goerck and Stanton Streets are LAVANBURG HOMES, a semi-philanthropic venture, built in 1927 and administered by the Fred L. Lavanburg Foundation to furnish modern housing at reasonable cost to families with small children.

Two blocks south of Stanton is Delancey Street, the district's main traffic and shopping artery. The WILLIAMSBURG BRIDGE, a steel suspension structure, runs through its center as far as Clinton Street. It was opened in 1903, the second to span the East River. Its designer was L. L. Buck. The bridge has a 1,600-foot over-water span and cost $23,278,000, including land. With its two roadways, two sidewalks, and six tracks for surface and elevated cars, it carries more than fifty thousand vehicles a day.

A number of interesting markets lie west of Clinton Street. In the famous ORCHARD STREET PUSHCART MARKET, which stretches for several blocks above and below Delancey Street, fruits, vegetables, bread, hot *knishes* (boiled buckwheat groats or mashed potatoes, wrapped in a skin of dough and baked), *bagel* (doughnut-shaped rolls), and hot *arbes* (boiled chick-peas) are offered for sale; also tools, hardware, work clothes, and many odd types of merchandise. It may not be long before this and other open-air pushcart markets will disappear, for the Department of Markets, more interested in sanitation than in the picturesque, plans to house them all indoors.

A block west, on Allen Street, under the elevated tracks, red, green, and purple quilts hanging on poles advertise a market for bed linens between Stanton and Grand Streets. A few Rumanian restaurants and night clubs contrast with these surroundings. South of Delancey on Allen Street, the little shops feature copper coffee urns, silver vases, and candlesticks, ornate Victorian lamps and mantel clocks, and an occasional porcelain shepherdess. Antique metalware is sold here as well as the shoddiest machine-made articles. The brass and copper market ends at Grand Street. The three blocks south on Division Street, from Eldridge Street to the Bowery, are occupied by an unbroken series of women's apparel shops with gleaming plate-glass windows. In the doorways *schleppers* (pullers-in, a recognized profession on the East Side) stand ready to draw prospective customers into the stores. Some nationally known clothing firms started here.

One block west is Chatham Square, a jagged confluence of streets over which clatter two old elevated lines. South a block on New Bowery, between James and Oliver Streets, is the oldest JEWISH CEMETERY in Manhattan. The plot, once covering all of Chatham Square, was purchased in 1682 by a band of Spanish and Portuguese Jews who had fled to New Amsterdam from the Inquisition. Gershom Mendez Seixas, one of the great rabbis of early America and a patriot during the Revolution, is buried here. The little triangle is owned today by the uptown Spanish-Portuguese congregation of Shearith Israel.

Little Italy and the Bowery

According to a 1932 survey, 98 per cent of the heads of households in this area were of Italian birth or parentage, mainly from Sicily and the south of Italy. During church festivals the streets are festooned with colored electric lights, the sidewalks lined with booths selling souvenirs and delicacies, and there is music, along with dancing, and a parade in the streets.

The old Mulberry Bend—on Mulberry Street between Bayard and Park, two blocks west of the Bowery—one of the worst slums in the city, was torn down in 1892 and replaced by Columbus Park, after drawing the fiery criticism of the reformer, Jacob Riis. However, many five-story tenements remain decked with cluttered fire escapes, washlines, and crowded stoops. The pushcarts on Mott Street from Canal to Broome, a block east of Mulberry Street, are relics of a thriving market that once embraced the four streets west of the Bowery. They sell ripe and green olives, artichokes, goats' cheeses, finochio (sweet fennel), and ready-to-eat *pizza,* an unsweetened pastry filled with tomatoes and cheese, meat, or fish.

At 240 Centre Street, between Grand and Broome Streets, is NEW YORK POLICE HEADQUARTERS, a large stone building designed by architects Hoppin and Koen in the French Baroque manner of the nineteenth century. A profusion of carved ornament gives it a somewhat pretentious aspect. Until this building was completed in 1909, headquarters was at 300 Mulberry Street.

From offices on the second floor, the Police Commissioner and his deputies direct the activities of 19,346 police officers operating from eighty-three precinct houses scattered throughout the five boroughs. Detectives, patrolmen, policewomen; a great fleet of radio cars, three motorcycle divisions, twenty emergency squads, two mounted squads, thirteen traffic and two bridge traffic units, and a flotilla of launches are controlled from this building by means of an intricate system of telephone, telegraph, teletype, and radio communication. Three short-wave radio stations, WPEE, WPEF, and WPEG, provide almost instantaneous contact with all units.

The daily "line-up" of arrested criminals takes place in a large, semi-darkened room on the fourth floor. Offenders parade across a brilliantly lighted stage to be questioned through a public address system, while detectives memorize their appearance and mannerisms. Criminologists from many countries come to witness the procedure. The building also houses the Traffic Division, the Surgical and Medical Bureau, the Traffic

Safety Bureau, the Legal Bureau, the Missing Persons Bureau, the Head-quarters Detective Division, a law library, and a disciplinary trial room. In the Police Academy, directly across Broome Street, police specialists give elementary training to rookies and advanced instruction to veterans of the force. Also housed in this building are the Criminal Identification Bureau (fingerprints and photographs), the Technical Research Laboratory, and the offices of a number of specialized detective squads. The Bureau of Equipment is maintained on the ground floor where members of the Department may buy all kinds of police equipment, from guns, nightsticks, and "nippers," to uniform caps, shirts, and shoes.

THE BOWERY, dividing line between the Jewish Quarter on the east and Little Italy on the west, was once an Indian trail used by aborigines in their expeditions against New Amsterdam. In the days of the Dutch it became known as "the road to the *bouwerij* (farm)," Peter Stuyvesant's country estate. The street was later part of the highroad to Boston and figured in many a Revolutionary incident as the only land entrance to New York City.

From 1860 to 1875 the city's theatrical life centered here. At the Bowery Amphitheatre (37 Bowery), the first blackface minstrel group made its appearance. At the National Theatre (104 Bowery) Frank S. Chanfrau, actor-manager, appeared with his brother in a long series of plays about Mose, the Bowery Paul Bunyan, an epic slugger, eye-gouger, and hobnail-stamper in New York's rowdy history. The legendary Big Mose was eight feet tall, with hands as big as hams. In his belt was thrust a butcher's cleaver, and in summer a keg of beer hung there for his refreshment. He loved to lift a streetcar off its track and carry it on one hand as a waiter carries a tray, the horses dangling from their harnesses; and Big Mose laughing thunderously at the terrified passengers. Another of his favorite jests was to stand in the East River, and blow back approaching vessels with a few puffs from his mighty lungs. The first stage version of *Uncle Tom's Cabin* appeared at the National on August 23, 1852.

Harrigan and Hart with their idealized pictures of East Side life, Weber and Fields, George M. Cohan, and Eddie Cantor are a few of the many actors who first succeeded in Bowery theaters. The Jewish theater in the United States had its beginnings here, and the well-known *Eli, Eli* by Jacob Sandler was first sung in a Yiddish play at the old Windsor Theatre in 1896.

After 1870 came the period of the Bowery's celebrated degeneration. Fake auction rooms, saloons specializing in five-cent whisky and knockout drops, sensational dime museums, filthy and rat-ridden stale-beer dives,

together with Charles M. Hoyt's song, "The Bowery, the Bowery! . . .
I'll never go there any more!" fixed it forever in the Nation's consciousness as a place of unspeakable corruption.

The Bowery today is chiefly given over to pawnshops, restaurant equipment houses, beer saloons, and miscellaneous small retail shops. Here flophouses offer a bug-infested bed in an unventilated pigeonhole for twenty-
five cents a night, restaurants serve ham and eggs for ten cents, and students in barber "colleges" cut hair for fifteen cents. Thousands of the
nation's unemployed drift to this section and may be seen sleeping in
all-night restaurants, in doorways, and on loading platforms, furtively
begging, or waiting with hopeless faces for some bread line or free lodging
house to open. No agency, at present (1939), provides adequate food,
shelter, and clothing for these wanderers. Missions furnish food and lodging for a few, and try by sermon and song to touch the souls of the down-
and-outers and the sympathies of generous tourists.

The Bowery begins at Chatham Square, and at No. 6 stands the
OLLIFFE PHARMACY, established before 1803 and reputed to be the oldest
drugstore in America. At No. 15 is the twenty-five-cent lodging house
where Stephen C. Foster, author of *Swanee River* and *My Old Kentucky
Home,* lived in 1864. To the west of the Bowery is Chinatown *(see page
104).* West for a block on Bayard Street to Elizabeth Street is a secondhand
clothing market occupying the basements. A suit or overcoat hangs out on
the street by way of a sign, and the proprietor stands halfway up the cellar
steps, peering eagerly for customers.

Two blocks north, at Canal Street, is the MANHATTAN BRIDGE, opened
in 1909. The approach was designed by Carrère and Hastings, and the
bridge proper, by Gustav Lindenthal, the engineer. The triumphal arch
and curved colonnade are combined in a vigorous baroque composition,
inspired by the Porte St. Denis, a gateway in Paris, and the Bernini colonnade that forms the Piazza of St. Peter's in Rome. Beginning here, and for
several blocks north, the Bowery is a row of jewelry stores displaying diamonds. On the sidewalks, braving the weather, stand diamond dealers
whose whole stock in trade may consist of one diamond, wrapped in tissue
paper and carried in the vest pocket.

The stretch between Delancey and Houston Streets is jocularly known
as the THIEVES' MARKET. Those who have any small objects to sell or
exchange congregate here. At No. 227, between Rivington and Stanton
Streets, stands the BOWERY MISSION, which has been in existence for more
than fifty years. It is now guided by Dr. Charles St. Johns, who conducts
a radio broadcast from his chapel every Sunday afternoon. Guest singers

perform and men from the audience appeal for jobs and testify to their conversion. At No. 225 is the SALVATION ARMY HOTEL, which runs a buttermilk bar where beef stew, oatmeal, and coffee sell for five cents.

Astor Place District

This was quite an aristocratic neighborhood in the early 1880's. William Cullen Bryant lived here, as well as Isaac M. Singer, improver of the sewing machine. Five blocks north of the Salvation Army Hotel and west of the Bowery, at 29 East Fourth Street is one of the old mansions, a red-brick structure in late Federal style, known sometimes as OLD MER-CHANT'S HOUSE. Built about 1830 by the nephew of the Reverend Samuel Seabury, first Bishop of the Episcopal Church in America, it has a richly detailed interior that shows the dominant influence of the Greek Revival. The house was purchased in 1936 by the Historic Landmark Society and re-opened as a museum. *(Open weekdays 11 a.m. to 5 p.m., Sunday 1 to 5 p.m.; admission 50¢.)* Bronze whale-oil mantel lamps, old gaslight fixtures, and Duncan Phyfe furniture are on view.

On Lafayette Street, south of Astor Place, the Greek Revival style finds expression in COLONNADE ROW, formerly La Grange Terrace. Only four out of the eight original houses remain, but they serve to give some idea of the handsome proportions of a fashionable residence of the 1830's.

The CONDICT BUILDING, 65 Bleecker Street (near Lafayette Street) is New York's sole example (1898) of the work of Louis H. Sullivan, whose buildings in Chicago and the Middle West counted among the leading structures in the development of modern architecture here and abroad. A minor example of his work, it displays some of Sullivan's clarity of expression and inimitable ornament.

The department store of JOHN WANAMAKER *(see page 136)* consists of two buildings between Broadway and Lafayette Street, separated by Wanamaker Place (Ninth Street). Across Lafayette Street and slightly to the south, is COOPER UNION, founded in 1859 by Peter Cooper, philanthropist, reformer, and inventor. His purpose was to establish a center where all public questions might be openly and freely discussed, and where young people might receive the technical education which he had been denied, and which was becoming increasingly important in that era of industrial expansion. Cooper Union Forum has often been the meeting hall of reformers gathering their forces against corrupt city administrations. Henry Ward Beecher, William Cullen Bryant, William Lloyd Garrison, and others thundered there against slavery and in defense of the Union, and Lincoln, in 1860, made the speech that is credited with winning for him the nomination for the Presidency. Cooper Union today offers to students, irrespective of race, creed, or color, courses in engineering and other technical subjects, secretarial training, and art. It has about ten thousand applicants a year, of whom only 3,500 can be accommodated. Augustus Saint-Gaudens, Adolph A. Weinman, and Leo Friedlander are three illustrious graduates of the art school. The main library, open to the public, contains 67,000 books; the art library, 17,000. The MUSEUM FOR THE ARTS OF DECORATION includes textiles, drawings, and designs, and musical instruments. *(Open weekdays 9 a.m. to 5 p.m., from the day following Labor Day to June 30; 6:30 to 9:30 p.m. from October 1 to May 1; admission free.)* The institution was supported entirely by the Cooper family until 1900; since then other philanthropists have helped. The innovations used by Peter Cooper in the construction of the school were important developments in the history of building. To support the flooring, he used rolled, wrought-iron beams arranged in a light grid; and by replacing heavy stone arches with thinner piers, he increased the usable space. In the tiny green triangle south of the building is a STATUE OF PETER COOPER by Augustus Saint-Gaudens.

Just east of Third Avenue, at 15 East Seventh Street, is McSorley's Old Ale House, which was established in 1854. No women are served at McSorley's. Fourth Avenue, from Eighth to Thirteenth Streets, is faced with the longest row of secondhand bookstores in the city. The outside tables, displaying bargain items, attract browsers at all hours.

Tompkins Square

The population here is composed of Italians, Slavs, and East European Jews. Some of the Greek Orthodox churches are under the guidance of priests who wear long beards, according to the custom of the Slavic countries. The grocers, merchants, and mechanics of the district are Russian; and their language is heard in a dozen basement cafés where men sit drinking tea. Politically, the colony is violently divided between pro- and anti-Soviet.

On Avenue A and Third Street, three blocks east of the Bowery, rise the FIRST HOUSES, the first project of the New York City Housing Authority, opened in 1935. Of the old slum tenements which formerly occupied this space, some were torn down and others were completely rebuilt by WPA labor, using the old materials. Unfortunately the attempt to utilize old structures has forced the new ones into a dull scheme. Bathrooms, sound-proofed partitions, gardens, and playgrounds promote the health and comfort of the occupants, who pay five dollars to seven dollars a room a month.

Four blocks north is TOMPKINS SQUARE PARK. Within the park, near the East Tenth Street side, a small MONUMENT depicting a boy and girl looking at a steamboat commemorates the tremendous loss sustained by this district, in the sinking of the excursion steamer, *General Slocum,* on June 15, 1904. Most of those who lost their lives, more than a thousand in number, came from this neighborhood, then predominantly German, and the disaster changed the character of the district. A large number of German families, overwhelmed by painful memories, moved to other parts of town.

Second Avenue, from Houston to Fourteenth Street, is known as the JEWISH RIALTO. The theaters specialize in melodrama and musical comedy, leaning heavily on success themes in which the immigrant makes good. Bertha Kalich, Jacob Adler, Molly Picon, David Kessler, Boris Thomashefsky, Sigmond Mogulesco, Jenny Goldstein, Morris Moscovitch, and Ludwig Satz are famous Jewish players who have performed here. Two of Adler's children, Luther and Stella, now famous on Broadway, had their start on Second Avenue. This Rialto is also famous for its foreign restaurants. Just below Fourteenth Street several Russian eating places offer entertainment and dancing to balalaikas, and a menu including *borscht, pirojski* (pastry), and *shashlik* (chunks of roasted lamb). There are Polish restaurants near St. Mark's Place that serve stuffed pig and *bigos mysliwski* (cabbage and game). And there are many reasonably priced Hungarian-Jewish and Rumanian-Jewish restaurants where a meal includes chicken soup with *mandlen* (a kind of crouton) and stuffed *kishkes* (intestines).

In the incongruous setting of the theater and restaurant district is ST. MARK'S IN-THE-BOUWERIE, Second Avenue and Stuyvesant (East Tenth) Street. Erected in 1660, as a Dutch chapel, on the farm of Governor Peter Stuyvesant, it was rebuilt in 1799. The steeple and portico were added in 1826 and in 1858. Pagan-looking frescoes fill the pediment above the porch. They recall the pastorate of Dr. William Norman Guthrie. In an effort to make the church attractive to progressive parishioners, Dr. Guthrie worked out a ritual based on the theory of the essential unity of all religions, which included Greek folk dancing, American Indian chants, and many other things which the conservative element in the diocese heatedly declared to have no place in an Episcopalian church. A Body and Soul Clinic was attached to the church with the aim of combining physical and spiritual treatment.

In the graveyard lie buried Governor Stuyvesant and Commodore Matthew C. Perry. A statue of the Dutch governor, presented by Queen Wilhelmina of Holland in 1915, stands near his grave. In 1878 the graveyard was the scene of a sensational body snatching when the remains of A. T. Stewart, well-known merchant and owner of a store which is now part of Wanamaker's, were stolen and held for $20,000 ransom. They were not returned till two years later.

On Second Avenue at Twelfth Street is the CAFÉ ROYAL, forum and meeting place of the Jewish intelligentsia. Behind the box hedges that make it a sidewalk café in summer, or in the big inside room on Friday nights, vehement arguments are carried on for and against a new play, book, or art movement. Managers on the road telephone the café by long distance to fill some sudden need, and unemployed actors eat there in the hope of attracting the eye of some impresario.

GREENWICH VILLAGE

Area: Spring St. on the south to 14th St. on the north; from West St. east to Broadway. Map on page 127.

A nation, coming into its own artistically after an era of ruthless industrial expansion, of materialism and strait-laced conventionality, seized upon Greenwich Village as a symbol of revolt in the ferment of postwar years. The "Village" was the center of the American Renaissance or of artiness, of political progress or of long-haired radical men and short-haired radical women, of sex freedom or of sex license—dependent upon the point of view.

Greenwich Village, actually, is a cross section of American urban life. Here are old families in their gracious mansions; bankers and clerks in tall apartment buildings; and a foreign-born population of some twenty-five thousand, largely Irish and Italian, in tenements. If in 1939 there were more serious artists and writers, more "bohemians" in renovated old houses, more colorful tea rooms and wild night clubs than in other American centers, the number each year was lessening.

In the years just preceding and following the World War the political, artistic, and literary rebels who flocked to the Village gave it a character unique in this country. The literary history of Greenwich Village, however, begins much earlier. Here Tom Paine spent the last years of his life. Poe lived, drank, and worked at several Village addresses. Walt Whitman lived in the vicinity, Henry James was born near Washington Square (he named

LOWER MANHATTAN

BROOKLYN BRIDGE

HANOVER SQUARE

DERELICTS (*East River Water Front*)

CHERRIES — 5C

CHATHAM SQUARE EL

SALVATION (*A Bowery Mission*)

RAIN (*The Bowery*)

ST. PAUL'S CHAPEL

one of his books for the square), and Mark Twain adopted the neighborhood for his city home. In 1896 John Masefield, English poet laureate, made his living here by scrubbing the floors of a saloon.

But the story of Greenwich Village is the rounded story of an old and lively American community, at once typical and individual. Here exploring parties were entertained by the natives of the hamlet of Sapokanican; and, in return, with the earliest settlement of lower Manhattan, the Dutch drove the Indians from this neighborhood. In 1633, while most of the island north of Wall Street was still a wilderness, Governor Van Twiller was cultivating here a large tobacco plantation—*Bossen Bouwerie* (Farm in the Woods)—and built his home at the foot of the present Charlton Street. During the fall of 1679, the Labadist missionaries, Danckaerts and Sluyter, visited what had grown to be a small village, where they drank "some good beer." In 1740, Sir Peter Warren, vice admiral of the British Navy and at that time commander of the fleet in New York, chose the locality for his home.

The Village grew throughout the Colonial period as a community of the wealthy. Here was the great Brevoort estate, sold in 1762 to one John Smith, a large slaveholder; the Bleecker farm; and the mansions of the Bayards, the Jauncys, and the De Lanceys. A popular drive for New York's fashionable reached the Village by way of Greenwich Street, which then ran along the river; when wet weather rendered this route impassable, the drive was made along the Bowery to an extension of what is now Greenwich Avenue, with a monument erected to General James Wolfe, hero of the French and Indian War, as its goal.

A spurt was given to the growth of the community following the Revolution, particularly in the neighborhood of the State prison, erected at the foot of Tenth Street; that institution, like the Bedlam Madhouse of Elizabethan days, was considered a residential attraction.

An epidemic of smallpox in 1739 in the Battery region gave impetus to the first hasty migration of the well-to-do to the healthier climate of the Village; scourges of yellow fever in 1797, 1799, 1803, and 1805 resulted in similar stampedes northward in crowded stages, and goods-piled carriages and pushcarts. Some drifted south again when conditions became normal, but others remained in their new homes. The greatest of all the yellow fever plagues, in 1822, brought such a rush of refugees that the Brooklyn ferry changed its course from New York to a point opposite the Village. Makeshift dwellings and business houses were thrown up almost overnight; lanes and cowpaths winding haphazardly through the neighborhood became busy streets. One of these lanes, during the 1822 epidemic, quartered temporarily the counting houses of Wall Street, and still bears the name Bank Street.

From 1825 to 1850, the population of Greenwich Village quadrupled, its inhabitants being largely of middle-class and well-to-do American stock. But for the next half-century, its growth, although steady, was slower than that of New York as a whole. While the city moved steadily northward, along Broadway, Fifth Avenue, and other great arteries, the Village, with its narrow erratic streets, remained a quiet backwater. As late as 1875, since only 32 per cent of its population was foreign-born—unusual for Manhattan—the section was known as the "American Ward."

An area so central, however, could not escape the ever encroaching poorer classes. Already numbers of Irish immigrants had moved into the neighborhood, and later a Negro invasion, starting at the southeastern edge of the Village and moving north to Washington Square itself,

KEY TO GREENWICH VILLAGE MAP

1. Salmagundi Club
2. First Presbyterian Church
3. Church of the Ascension
4. Grace Church School
5. Grace Episcopal Church
6. Hotel Lafayette
7. Home of Mark Twain
8. Hotel Brevoort
9. One Fifth Avenue
10. Clay Club
11. Whitney Museum of Art
12. A.C.A. Gallery
13. MacDougal Alley
14. The Row
15. Rhinelander Mansion
16. Washington Mews
17. Wanamaker House
18. Washington Arch
19. Bust of Alexander Lyman Holley
20. Judson Memorial Baptist Church
21. World War Memorial Flagpole
22. Statue of Giuseppe Garibaldi
23. New York University Museum of Living Art
24. Broadway Central Hotel
25. Bannerman Museum
26. Holland Tunnel
27. Spring Street Presbyterian Church
28. St. John's Park Freight Terminal
29. Hudson Park Playground
30. Little Red School House
31. Narrowest House in New York
32. Cherry Lane Theater
33. St. Luke's Chapel
34. Grove Court
35. Greenwich House
36. Site of Tom Paine House
37. Statue of General Sheridan
38. Northern Dispensary
39. House of Detention for Women
40. Jefferson Market Court
41. Patchin Place
42. Rhinelander Gardens
43. Milligan Place
44. Spanish-Portuguese Cemetery
45. New School for Social Research
46. St. Vincent's Hospital
47. Downtown Gallery
48. Bell Telephone Laboratory
49. Gansevoort Market
50. West Washington Market

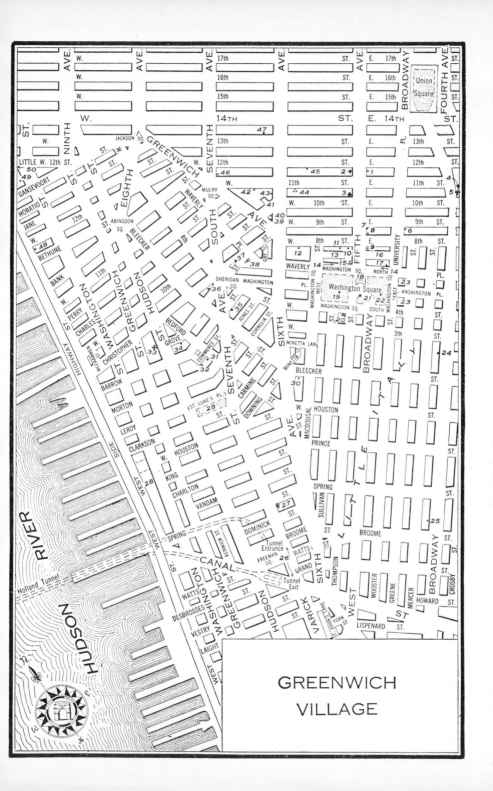

GREENWICH

VILLAGE

heralded the first major change in the district. Property values decreased. Save for the families in the aristocratic stronghold of Washington Square and north of it, and a few tenacious ones scattered throughout the southwest, the older and wealthier inhabitants joined the continual migration uptown.

Then, in the 1890's, came another invasion of Irish lower in the economic scale than the compatriots who preceded them. The Italians—displacing the Negroes who left their last stronghold in Gay Street in the early 1920's—moved up from the south in even greater numbers than the Irish, meeting them in the neighborhood of Sheridan Square.

By 1910, the transformation of Greenwich Village had been completed. The American Ward had become Ward 9, a foreign ward, leading its life of pushcart, café, fiesta, and bar, its land values as cheap as in nearly any settled section of the city, its people faithful followers of the Roman Catholic Church and of Tammany.

A second change of a different nature began in Greenwich Village shortly before 1910. It had a slow, quiet beginning, scarcely perceptible to the neighborhood itself; yet it was to make that dingy backwater celebrated wherever the English language is spoken. At that period materialism had assumed an unprecedented importance in American life. Ambition not directed toward the goal of a large bank account was almost alien to thought and education, and, like most things alien, was regarded with distrust and scorn. Above all was this attitude adopted toward the struggling artist seeking satisfaction from completion of a poem or picture.

A natural result was the withdrawal of the rebel artist into protective groups. Many of these groups gravitated to the larger cities—Kansas City to St. Louis, St. Louis to Chicago—and finally, from all over the country to the metropolis.

In Greenwich Village the earliest rebels found comparative quiet, winding streets, houses with a flavor of the Old World—and cheap rents. The local people existed largely to be traded with; otherwise they were passed unnoticed as the Villager moved from group meeting to group meeting.

These meetings—after a day of hard work or of grandiose planning—at first took place in their homes, in a back room in Washington Square South, in an attic on West Fourth Street. The room was often sparsely furnished, partly for lack of funds to buy furniture, partly as a revolt from overfurnished, late-Victorian backgrounds. Often candles replaced electricity. A few pictures of their own or of their friends' painting and a batik hung on the walls. They talked of their work, of the arts, or of sex and Freud; and were secretly thrilled at doing so in mixed company.

They discussed Socialism, the I.W.W., woman's suffrage, and the philistinism of the folks back home. The conversation ranged from brilliant to silly, but always, instinctively or consciously, it was unconventional. And throughout, they drank endless glasses of tea—for these were the days before Prohibition and bath-tub gin.

As their numbers grew, they found outside meeting places of their own, places more esoteric than the Italian restaurants they first frequented, such as Bertolloti's on West Third Street, Renganeschi's on West Tenth Street, Gallup's on Greenwich Avenue. The first of these new meeting places was Polly Holliday's, on the north side of Fourth Street, between MacDougal Street and Sixth Avenue. Here commercialism, even on the part of the proprietress, scarcely existed. Meals were written on the cuff, never to be erased; but all "true" Villagers were welcome so long as they kept the conversation flowing well into the night. The Mad Hatter was another such eating place; with Polly's it entertained many who were later to become noted in art, science, and politics. There was the Samovar, Sam Swartz's TNT, the Purple Pup, the Pirate's Den, and Romany Marie's, the last-named still in existence. For drinks, at the corner of Fourth Street and Sixth Avenue, there was the Golden Swan, popularly known as the "Hell Hole," frequented by Villagers and toughs alike, and on Greenwich Avenue, Luke O'Connor's bar, where John Masefield worked. Finally, as a degree of affluence came to many of the Villagers, the cafés of the Brevoort and Lafayette—hotels continental in flavor and esteemed by cosmopolitans—were invaded, for drinks, cards, chess, and for discussion. Always the line between groups was sharply drawn; there were as yet no big business neighbors, no white-collar workers, no respectable well-to-do drawn here by the love or the glamor of the arts. There were only the Villager and Ward Niner, and the former walked from home to Polly's and from Polly's to the Brevoort through a little world of his own.

In the theater, from modest beginnings, the Villagers all but revolutionized the American stage. A group, loosely organized at first, gave performances in a converted stable at 133 MacDougal Street. Its members, sometimes actors, sometimes playwrights, called themselves the Provincetown Players, after their so-titled wharf theater in Cape Cod's Provincetown, and included such people as George Cram Cook and his wife, Susan Glaspell, Eugene O'Neill, Edna St. Vincent Millay, her sister, Norma, and Robert Edmond Jones. And if this group gave the country modern playwrights, the group that preceded it for a short while at the same address—the Washington Square Players—with Helen Westley,

Philip Moeller, Lawrence Langner and others—gave America an organization, which, moving uptown as the Theater Guild, taught the incredulous Broadway producers that living art could bring box-office receipts. A later venture, Eva Le Gallienne's Civic Repertory, in the old Theatre Français, 105 West Fourteenth Street, carried on the tradition of a "different" theater until 1933, when it gave way to the Theater Union, which produced plays with a pronounced social theme.

Literature, in group form, found expression in a number of papers and magazines of varying worth. They ranged from purely literary to primarily political, and lasted from one issue to several years. Two of them, the *Seven Arts* and the *Masses,* were forced to discontinue publication because of their opposition to the World War. The former, edited by Louis Untermeyer and James Oppenheim, with a number of now noted contributors, was revolutionary in content. The *Masses* was radical politically; following its suppression in 1918, Max Eastman, Art Young, John Reed, and Floyd Dell, were placed on trial, charged with a conspiracy to obstruct recruiting and prevent enlistment. The trial was an event of nation-wide interest, the tension of which on the climactic day was disturbed only by the snoring of the defendant Young. The *Masses* reappeared in 1919 as the *Liberator,* and later, after another lapse, as the present *New Masses.*

First, however, among organized groups expressing the revolt of the Villagers was the "A" Club, at One Fifth Avenue, with the writer, Mary Heaton Vorse, Rose O'Neill, creator of the Kewpies, and Frances Perkins, later Secretary of Labor under Franklin D. Roosevelt, among its leaders —a group devoted to the advancement of woman's suffrage and social reforms. The Liberal Club, with a similar membership, followed, moving from East Seventeenth Street to 133 MacDougal Street, at which address it gave houseroom and financial aid to the Washington Square Players and, later, to the Provincetown Players.

The liberals were beginning to exert an influence not only on New York but on American thinking, when the entrance of the United States into the World War altered radically the intellectual aspects of the Village. Repression of liberal and radical activities during and for several years following the war was, of course, the major cause of the change. Some Villagers had been ardent supporters of the war; the nebulous liberalism and radicalism of many others were dissipated. Meanwhile, however, fame had come to some of these early rebels, success to many others, maturity to all. Many of the successful moved, with their families, to Connecticut, Westchester County, and farther afield; the unsuccessful trekked back home to take up their old life where they had left off a decade earlier. A nucleus remained to greet the postwar rebels attracted to a now celebrated Bohemia.

By 1939 there were more Greenwich Villagers than in the days preceding the war, but these young people were leading a life not greatly dissimilar to that of many of their contemporaries throughout the country. The Village tearooms and night clubs, for the most part no longer the haunts of the Bohemian, were patronized largely by out-of-town tourists and sensation seekers from outlying boroughs. Large apartment buildings and rents were rising as the well-to-do and white-collar workers, attracted by the central location, by vastly improved transportation facilities, and, perhaps, by the glamor associated with the address, moved in.

And as the foreigner had for two decades retreated before the advance of the Villager, so already the Villager had begun to retreat to outlying districts before the wealthier newcomer. The passionate individualism of the Village was giving way to community singing and similar neighborhood activities. Bobby Edwards' erratic, "villagy" *Quill* was replaced by the highly successful commercial *Villager,* which exalted the conventional, small-town aspects of the district. If such institutions as the semiannual open-air art show in Washington Square—where three-quarters of the exhibitors have been non-Villagers—still exist, they are inspired by the legend rather than by the actuality of the community.

Much of the old aspect, and many of the old people, such as Theodore Dreiser and Vilhjalmur Stefansson, returned, however. Papa Strunsky still rails at the tenant in arrears in his West Third Street building—and at times lets the promising writer or painter stay on, the bill unpaid. Literary teas (with tea scarcely in evidence) are still popular. The easy unconventionality, the charming old houses, comfortable as an old shoe, still invite the Villager, emerging from the subway after a visit to more formal neighborhoods, to drag off his or her hat and swing along home.

Washington Square

The district roughly known as Greenwich Village has two focal points: Washington Square and Sheridan Square, each the center of a neighborhood fairly distinct in architecture, in the character of its activities and in the type of its people. Sheridan Square can best be described as the "Times Square" of Greenwich Village. WASHINGTON SQUARE, on the other hand, is striking for its dignity, still undestroyed by the commercial and tenement advances that swept around it, while many of the streets to the north, between Fifth and Sixth Avenues, have scarcely changed through the decades. Although some of the private homes have been converted into rooming houses, large numbers of charming dwellings are still occupied by their owners.

The site of the square served as the city's potter's field in 1789, and the use of its trees—some still standing—as the public gallows during that period was an attraction drawing large crowds of holiday makers on execution days. In 1823, however, the potter's field was closed. Four years later a park was laid out and the first of the impressive mansions which give the square its present character was erected.

The square today is well shaded by trees: pin oaks, oriental planes, yellow locusts, ash, and American elm. Benches line its paths, and here meet Italian workers, mothers and their broods from the south, apartment dwellers from the north, university students from the east, and young Villagers from the west.

Dominating the park is the white marble WASHINGTON ARCH, eighty-six feet high, with a span thirty feet wide, designed by Stanford White. Rising at the foot of Fifth Avenue, it forms an imposing gateway to New York's most imposing thoroughfare. It was completed in 1895 at a cost of $128,000, and commemorates the first inauguration of George Washington. Two statues of the first President, one in the uniform of commander-in-chief, by Hermon A. MacNeil, the other in civilian garb, by A. Sterling Calder, face the north on bases projecting from the east and west piers, respectively.

On the east side of the square is a bronze STATUE OF GARIBALDI by Giovanni Turini, erected in 1888 and presented by the Italians of New York. Directly south of the arch is a WORLD WAR MEMORIAL FLAGPOLE, forty-five feet high, and near by is a bronze BUST OF ALEXANDER LYMAN HOLLEY, Bessemer steel pioneer. It is the work of J. Q. A. Ward and was erected in 1890.

Annual events in Washington Square include the folk festival and the open-air art and pottery exhibits. The first, an outdoor pageant of folk dancing and singing, is held on Labor Day. Art exhibits, inaugurated in 1931, are held in May and September, with pictures lining the building walls on the blocks near the western half of the square—Thompson, Sullivan, and MacDougal Streets, and Washington and Waverly Places. Painters living within the confines of the city may exhibit their wares free, and receipts from sales range from less than a dollar to several hundred dollars. In May, the Ravens tack their verses on a fence along Thompson Street—the Fifth Avenue extension south—and sell them for quarters and half dollars.

Washington Square North, part of the old Warren estate, retains almost intact its line of fine early nineteenth-century Greek Revival homes of red brick with white limestone trim. Each mansion was built on a generous plot with a ninety-foot garden in the rear. One of the earliest of these was the RHINELANDER MANSION, designed by Richard Upjohn, architect of Trinity Church, and built at the west corner of Fifth Avenue in 1839.

Across Fifth Avenue is the WANAMAKER HOUSE, built in 1833–7 as two separate houses by James Boorman, a merchant, and purchased by Rodman Wanamaker, a merchant's son, in 1920. The twelve houses extending between Fifth Avenue and University Place are known as THE ROW, one of New York's most elegant residential areas, and occupy land owned by Sailors Snug Harbor, an organization to aid indigent seamen. Once part of the Minto farm of twenty-one acres, which included most of the land between Washington Square North and Tenth Street, from Fifth Avenue to the Bowery, the area was acquired by Captain T. Randall, a privateer, in 1790. His son, appropriately and sentimentally, gave it to men of the sea, and stipulated in his will that none of the land was ever to be sold. The sailors benefiting from the income live in a home on Staten Island *(see page 618)*. These houses, among the most lavish of the 1830's, with brick, ivy-covered walls, fine doorways, and quaint and carefully tended front yards, did not acquire their extraordinary harmony by accident. Though built by lessees, and with varying interior schemes, their exteriors were controlled by a master plan dictating the cornice and window heights. Some of the city's leading families and some of the country's best-known writers and artists have occupied the houses. Among the latter were Henry James, Edith Wharton, William Dean Howells, and Francis Hopkinson Smith. In No. 3, a studio building, lives Frederick W. Stokes, the artist, who went to the North Pole with Peary; some of his paintings of the Arctic regions are in the Smithsonian Institution in Washington, but many are in his studio, which, like others in the building, is still heated in winter by pot-bellied stoves.

Waverly Place, running east and west of Washington Square North, honors through its name Sir Walter Scott. At No. 108 Richard Harding Davis lived during his early newspaper days.

The beauty of the square is marred on its east side by the tall drab buildings of NEW YORK UNIVERSITY. The Main Building, erected in 1894, replaced the original building of the university, which was founded in 1830. Albert Gallatin, Jefferson's Secretary of the Treasury, was one of the leaders in the move to establish this nonsectarian institution for the dissemination of practical as well as classical education among the middle and poorer classes. The use of stone cut by Sing Sing convicts for the buildings precipitated one of New York's first labor demonstrations—the Stone Cutters' Riot. Masons, parading in protest, were dispersed by the Seventh Regiment. At the school Morse conducted successful experiments with telegraphy, Draper made the first daguerreotype of the human face, and Colt perfected the revolver. The first two men were faculty members. Morse, a portrait and landscape painter, was professor of art; George Inness was one of his pupils. Colt was one of the lodgers in the Gothic tower of the university. Others who had rooms there were Brander Matthews, Winslow Homer, and Walt Whitman. New York University has another campus in the Bronx *(see page 521)*.

On the ground floor, right, of 100 Washington Square East is the MUSEUM OF LIVING ART. *(Open Monday to Friday 9 a.m. to 8 p.m., Saturday 9 a.m. to 4 p.m.)* Founded in 1927, the gallery contains works of Man Ray, Lachaise, Cézanne, Brancusi, Matisse, Picasso, and Juan Gris, owned by Albert E. Gallatin, a descendant of the New York University's first council chairman. Three of the paintings are critically acclaimed as being among the most important of this century: *The Three Musicians,* by Picasso, *The City,* by Leger, and *Composition in White and Red,* by Mondrian. The exhibits also include the work of American artists such as Marin, Demuth, Sheeler, Hartley, and Knaths. Near the university, at 22 Washington Place, was the Triangle Waist Company, where in 1911 occurred a disastrous fire which took a toll of 150 lives. As a result of the investigation that followed, State laws were enacted to improve working conditions in the factories.

Washington Square South, with its remodeled and newer studio buildings, is far less elegant than the north side. Beginning shortly before the war, many Villagers who later became noted lived on this street. Adelina Patti, Theodore Dreiser, Frank Norris, Stephen Crane, Willa Cather, Gelett Burgess, John Dos Passos, James Oppenheim, Pierre Matisse, Guy Pene duBois, and Alan Seeger were tenants at No. 61, Madame Branchard's Rooming House. At the west corner of Thompson Street stands the $450,000 JUDSON MEMORIAL BAPTIST CHURCH, of amber-colored brick, with slender Lombardian campanile surmounted by a lighted cross. The church was designed by Stanford White; its twelve stained-glass windows were executed by John La Farge.

Tall, modern apartments pre-empt Washington Square West, a threat to the old open atmosphere that attracted them. In the court of the Holley Chambers spouts a fountain fed by the subterranean Minetta Brook. Its winding, erratic course beneath Greenwich Village has been a repeated cause of distress to apartment builders and subway constructors.

MacDougal Street, bordering the west side of Washington Square, swarms with tearooms, night clubs, and Villager memories. The Liberal Club and the Provincetown Players occupied No. 133—a half block south of the park.

Around Washington Square South and extending west to Sheridan Square are numerous Village night clubs, patronized mostly by outsiders. Many of them, such as the Black Cat, established in 1888, between the square and Third Street, were early meeting places of Village intellectuals.

One-half block north of Washington Square, the blind MACDOUGAL ALLEY, a lane of century-old mews converted into studios, runs east from MacDougal Street. Privately owned, the Alley is lit by New York's only remaining gas street lamps.

Fifth Avenue and University Place

On Fifth Avenue, north to Twelfth Street, rise tall, modern apartment buildings and hotels, along with a few old renovated mansions. In the summer a number of sidewalk cafés give this quarter-mile the flavor of a South European boulevard. At Christmas time it is ablaze with lighted trees and decorations.

ONE FIFTH AVENUE, built in 1927, is the twenty-seven-story apartment hotel by Helmle, Corbett, and Harrison in association with Sugarman and Berger. The structure is interesting for its cut corners and setback, a change from the rectangular massing of the period. An amusing attempt was made to simulate vertical piers by the use of "shadow brick." Below the skyscraper, running east, is WASHINGTON MEWS, a row of converted stables, now the homes of the well-to-do, resembling a secluded lane in the Chelsea district of London with cobblestones, door shrubbery, and green shutters. Half a block north is the HOTEL BREVOORT, at Eighth Street. Built in 1854, it is noted for its distinguished intellectual and cosmopolitan clientele. New York's first marble house, at No. 8, was built in 1856 by John Taylor Johnston, first president of the Metropolitan Museum of Art. On the southeast corner of Ninth Street stands the house where Mark Twain lived during the early years of the twentieth century. This three-story brick house betrays the largely ecclesiastic practice of its architect, James Renwick.

The CHURCH OF THE ASCENSION (Protestant Episcopal) is on the northwest corner of Tenth Street. Built in 1841 in English Gothic style after the design by Richard Upjohn, it was redecorated about 1888 from the plans of Stanford White, the chancel being the work of well-known artists of the late nineteenth century. John La Farge's mural, *The Ascension* (behind the altar), is considered his finest work. Here, on June 26, 1844, President John Tyler was married to Julia Gardiner. Between West Eleventh and Twelfth Streets is the FIRST PRESBYTERIAN CHURCH, an example of English Gothic architecture, built in 1845 from plans of Joseph C. Wells.

The SALMAGUNDI CLUB, at 47 Fifth Avenue, was founded in 1871 as a sketch class. Its members are artists and sympathetic "amateurs of art." The name recalls the interest in the "Salmagundi Papers" published by Washington Irving. The club occupies the last surviving high-stooped brownstone (built in 1854) of the block. The gallery, just beyond the spacious entrance, hall, exhibits work by Salmagundi members, and the library has a valuable collection of costume books. The club's auction exhibition—the Mug Sale— is held annually in January; a summer show is usually held from May to October.

Paralleling Fifth Avenue to the east, University Place runs from Washington Square to Fourteenth Street. The HOTEL LAFAYETTE, founded in 1883, at the southeast corner of Ninth Street, is known for its French cuisine, while its café, like that of the Brevoort, is a meeting place of intellectuals, American and foreign. The district to the north is given over largely to auction rooms for the sale of antique and modern furnishings.

Broadway

Broadway, a block east of University Place, is at its drabbest in this sector. At Tenth Street and Broadway rises the lacelike GRACE EPISCOPAL CHURCH consecrated in 1846. It was designed by James Renwick, architect of St. Patrick's Cathedral. Typically English are the square east end, the elaboration of the ribbing of the vaulting, and the arrangement of tracery in the windows. The carved ornament of the exterior is crisp and incisive. The adjoining GRACE CHURCH SCHOOL, organized in 1894, was New York's first institution for training choir boys. In 1934 a day school was also inaugurated which now offers a complete secondary school curriculum.

The swerve of Broadway at this point attests to the stubbornness of Hendrick Brevoort, whose tavern stood on the present church site and who refused to allow the street to be cut through (1847) because it would mean the destruction of a favorite tree. One block south is JOHN WANAMAKER, one of the oldest and foremost department stores in New York. It passed into the hands of its present owners in 1896. The original (north) store, erected by A. T. Stewart in 1862, is believed to be the first building in the city with a cast-iron front. A skylighted "open well" in the center of the old store recalls the days before electricity made good illumination possible. Upon the completion of the new building in 1905, the two were joined by a bridge similar in design to the Bridge of Sighs in Venice. Attractions offered by the store include Christmas concerts by famous choirs, exhibits by the American Artists Congress in May, and marionette shows.

At No. 673 stands the BROADWAY CENTRAL, built in the 1870's to be "America's most palatial hotel." The National Baseball League was organized here in 1876. In this hotel Edward S. Stokes shot and killed James Fisk, president of the Erie Railroad, in January, 1872, in a quarrel over Josie Mansfield, actress.

Little Italy

South of Washington Square and stretching to Spring Street lies a section of LITTLE ITALY. Numerous Italian cafés and restaurants, some small and wholly native, several—particularly on West Houston Street —having city-wide fame, cater to the needs of the residents and visitors. Here are held minor fiestas, with streets strung with lights, with singing and dancing, and the sale of candies and ices. On Bleecker Street between Sixth and Seventh Avenues is a pushcart market displaying fruits and vegetables, many, such as finochio and zucchini, exotic to Americans. Fortunio, a proprietor of a restaurant on this street, is said to have imported the first broccoli in the country. The LITTLE RED SCHOOL HOUSE, an experimental school for children, is at 196 Bleecker Street.

Eighth Street and the Art Galleries

Eighth Street, between Fifth and Sixth Avenues, with its bookshops, antique shops, food shops, tearooms, bars, and art galleries, has been called the "Main Street" of Greenwich Village. At No. 4 is the CLAY CLUB, working headquarters and gallery for a group of sculptors. The building, originally the stable belonging to the marble house on Fifth Avenue *(see page 135)*, was remodeled by the owner, John Taylor Johnston, as an exhibition gallery for his private collection. Impressed by his success, a group of wealthy collectors organized the Metropolitan Museum of Art *(see page 368)* in 1870. At Nos. 8-12 is the WHITNEY MUSEUM OF AMERICAN ART, founded in 1931 "to help create rather than conserve a tradition." *(Open Tuesday to Friday 1 to 5 p.m., Saturday and Sunday 2 to 6 p.m.; closed during August.)* It exhibits the works of Whistler,

Ryder, Homer, Eakins, and La Farge, as well as the works of living American artists of greater and lesser fame, including the painters Sloan, Gropper, Davis, and Kuniyoshi, and the sculptors Davidson, Lachaise, Noguchi, Robus, and Zorach. Murals by Thomas Benton decorate the library. The museum was founded and endowed by the sculptor, Gertrude Vanderbilt Whitney (Mrs. Harry Payne Whitney). The building, remodeled from three residences, has a pink stucco façade. The A.C.A. GALLERY (American Contemporary Art), at No. 52, exhibits the work of contemporaries who have concerned themselves with present-day life. Among artists represented are Gropper, Evergood, Tromka, Joe Jones, and Harriton.

Sixth Avenue

Sixth Avenue, the dividing line between that part of Greenwich Village dominated by Washington Square and that dominated by Sheridan Square, is an uninspiring thoroughfare. The old Sixth Avenue elevated structure, which darkened the street, was removed in 1938-9; and with the completion of the Sixth Avenue branch of the municipal Independent Subway, the character of the street may change. Running east, between Sixth Avenue and MacDougal Street, is Minetta Lane, with Minetta Street leading south from it. Considered in the latter part of the nineteenth century one of New York's most notorious slums, it has been improved through the renovation of some of its houses, which form an interesting group.

In the triangle formed by West Tenth Street, Sixth Avenue, and Greenwich Avenue are the HOUSE OF DETENTION FOR WOMEN and JEFFERSON MARKET COURT, which handles cases of women's delinquency. The jail, which in 1932 replaced the picturesque Jefferson Market, resembles a bleak apartment building. Modern in all its equipment, probably its most striking feature is the turntable altar in the chapel, one sector fitted for Protestant service, the second for Catholic, and the third for Jewish. The court itself was designed by Frederick C. Withers and Calvert Vaux, in 1876. The fantastic Victorian Gothic building with its array of weird turrets, traceried windows, and its patterns of brick and carved stone is an exceptionally interesting work of its period.

The oversized, odd-shaped block just north of the court, bounded by West Tenth Street, Sixth Avenue, West Eleventh Street, and Greenwich Avenue, is the result of the meeting at a slight angle of two gridiron systems of streets. To utilize the interior of the property the owners developed the land in an unusual way. From West Tenth Street and from Sixth Avenue blind alleys—PATCHIN PLACE and MILLIGAN PLACE—run into the block at right angles to the street, and give access to the houses which front on them. Patchin Place resembles a bystreet in Old London. In its modest little brick houses, only recently modernized, have lived Theodore Dreiser, John Masefield, Dudley Digges, John Reed, John Howard Lawson, and e. e. cummings. Milligan Place, whose houses were built in the 1850's, was named for Samuel Milligan, who acquired the property, part of the Warren farm, in 1799. His granddaughter married Aaron Patchin, to whom was deeded what became Patchin Place in 1848. George Cram Cook and Susan Glaspell lived here, and Eugene O'Neill came frequently when the three worked on his play, *The Emperor Jones.* Here, as throughout the Village, grows the ailanthus—the "back-yard" tree, indigenous to India. It is a city tree, one that flourishes with little soil, water, and light. In the days of the pestilence it was believed that the tree absorbed "bad" air.

On Eleventh Street, a few doors east of Sixth Avenue, is the tiny second SPANISH-PORTUGUESE JEWISH CEMETERY OF NEW YORK, opened in 1805 and closed in 1829. West of the avenue, from 112 to 124 West Eleventh Street, is RHINELANDER GARDENS, part of the Rhinelander estate, which utilizes the deep lots on the north portion of the block by setting the buildings far back from the street line and thus getting a pleasant front garden. Built in the 1850's, this distinctive line of houses with cast-iron balconies reminiscent of New Orleans is the only remaining example of its type in the city.

The NEW SCHOOL FOR SOCIAL RESEARCH, founded in 1919 by James Harvey Robinson and Charles A. Beard, is at 66 West Twelfth Street, just east of Sixth Avenue. Thorstein Veblen was a faculty member. It is devoted chiefly to adult education in political and social sciences and psychology, but advanced courses in the arts are also given. Here, in 1934, was organized the "University in Exile," its teachers being drawn from the brilliant political and racial exiles from Nazi Germany. The building, designed by Joseph Urban and erected in 1931, illustrates in striking fashion some of the characteristics of modern architecture. The central portion of the exterior is cantilevered out to form a shelter for the entrance doors below and is accented by continuous horizontal windows. An interesting feature is the progressive narrowing of the space between windows as the building rises and the inward inclination of the front wall; seen in perspective these tend to give the building additional height. On the first floor of the interior is a small auditorium of skillful design. Murals by Thomas Benton and Camilo Egas, Ecuadorean artist, and the only frescoes in New York City by the Mexican, Orozco, decorate other parts of the interior. Benton's work, the artist's first important mural decorations, are in the reception room on the third floor. The three on the west wall depict the old agricultural South, lumbering, and the growth of the West; the three on the east, phases of the coal and iron industries; the one facing the entrance, power; and those on either side of the entrance, phases of city life. Egas' work is in the Caroline Tilden Bacon Memorial Room on the mezzanine floor and in the foyer. Those in the foyer depict the harvest festivals of the Indians of Ecuador; the two panels on the mezzanine floor, harvests in South America and Minnesota (Mrs. Bacon's native state). The Orozco Room is on the fifth floor. The fresco on the south wall is entitled *The Table of Universal Brotherhood* and embodies the theme of the group. Those on the west wall are concerned with attempts to achieve this brotherhood, one in the Soviet Union, the other in Mexico. A portrait of Lenin, leader of the Russian Revolution, is in the first, and in the second, one of Felipe Carillo Puerto, Yucatan hero. On the north wall is a representation of the Universal Family, the worker and his wife. Gandhi is portrayed in the painting on the east wall, which depicts the plight of India and its enslaved masses.

The DOWNTOWN GALLERY, 113 West Thirteenth Street, always has examples of the work of six outstanding painters on view: Marin, O'Keeffe, Sheeler, Karfiol, Laurent, and Kuniyoshi. *(Open weekdays 10 a.m. to 6 p.m.; closed July and August.)* An excellent collection of folk art is exhibited on the upper floors.

Sheridan Square

SHERIDAN SQUARE, at the intersection of Seventh Avenue and West Fourth Street, is reached from Washington Square by Waverly Place. This is the focal point for tourist night life in Greenwich Village; revelers from the Bronx, Brooklyn, and Queens arrive, as evening approaches, on the IRT subway, by bus, taxi, and private car to visit night clubs and bars that abound in the square itself, line West Fourth Street to Washington Square, and dot the neighborhood north and west. This, too, is a center for Villagers who frequent more modest establishments—unpretentious saloons, lunch wagons, and cafeterias. A cafeteria, curiously enough, is one of the few obviously Bohemian spots in the Village, and evenings the more conventional occupy tables in one section of the room and watch the "show" of the eccentrics on the other side.

The square, named for General Philip H. Sheridan, though a blaze of light by night, is, by day, an uninteresting hodgepodge of buildings of varying sizes and ages, suggesting little of the charm that lies beyond its limits. At the northeastern end is a small park, containing a bronze STATUE OF GENERAL SHERIDAN, sculptured by Joseph P. Pollia and erected in 1936. Beyond the park is the NORTHERN DISPENSARY, a simple triangular brick building, erected about 1830, and curious for the fact that two of its sides are on one street (Waverly Place) and the third side on two streets (Christopher and Grove Streets). A block south of the square at 27 Barrow Street is GREENWICH HOUSE, a seven-story structure of Georgian Colonial design, a settlement house. Its social and educational activities and its powerful influence for civic improvement have given it a national reputation. Among its experiments in education and sociology is the Nursery School, founded in 1921 to provide a place for working mothers to leave their children.

Wide Seventh Avenue, running north, offers little of interest. On the northeast corner of Eleventh Street is ST. VINCENT'S HOSPITAL, established 1849, New York's first charity hospital depending on voluntary contributions. Across the avenue a PLAQUE on the Sheridan Theater designates the site where Georges Clemenceau, who later became the wartime premier of France, lived in 1870 practicing and teaching medicine. At the juncture of West Twelfth Street and Eighth Avenue is ABINGDON SQUARE, named for a daughter of Vice-Admiral Warren, Charlotte, who married the Earl of Abingdon. This large, irregular square is surrounded by tall, modern apartment buildings and older warehouses and business establishments.

At Sheridan Square Fourth Street turns northwest, and to the bewilderment of visitors, crosses all the westbound streets, from Tenth to Thirteenth. In the late 1890's the region thus traversed was the domain of a notorious but colorful gang of thugs known as the Hudson Dusters. A high percentage of them were cocaine addicts and thus especially vicious and ferocious. Their exploits were favorite grist for the journalists' mill and the Dusters became one of the best-known gangs of the time.

It is perhaps in the district southwest of Sheridan Square that one finds best the atmosphere of Greenwich Village. Along winding streets, interspersed with ugly tenements and occasional apartment buildings, are the age-worn dwellings of the burghers of the early nineteenth century who fled from the pestilence-ridden city—houses with steep roofs, often of slate, with old chimney pots; old brass knobs on handsome doors; high-ceilinged rooms, small-paned windows; carved mantels over huge fireplaces; "ship carpenter's" woodwork, and gates and area-fences with Georgian ironwork. Informal gardens in the rear are much in use, as are the Italian garden restaurants that thrive throughout the Village.

On narrow Grove Street, just west of the square, at No. 59, a bronze

PLAQUE memorializes the site where Tom Paine, greatest literary force of the Revolution, died in 1809. It was then the home of Mme. Nicolas de Bonneville, whose husband had befriended Paine after his release from prison in France. When the De Bonnevilles came into disfavor with the Napoleonic government Paine invited them to America. He provided for them as best he could but, toward the end, impoverished himself, he lived in a rooming house on Herring Street (now Bleecker Street) until Madame de Bonneville brought him under her care. His last days were made miserable with the importunings of religious fanatics who wanted the old deist to recant his "atheistic" teaching. His last request, that he be buried in a Quaker churchyard, was refused.

GROVE COURT, entered from the bend in Grove Street, is used for access to the houses around it. Of charming scale and simplicity are the frame and brick houses of the 1830's. At the corner where Grove Street intersects Bedford, there is a bizarre group—a farmhouse remodeled with high twin gables, a stable converted into a small house, and a prosaic old three-story frame building.

Facing the foot of Grove Street, on Hudson Street, on land that was part of Trinity Church farm, ST. LUKE'S CHAPEL was opened in 1822. It is a simple low building of yellow brick with an effective square tower. Under the approach to the baptismal font, reminiscent of old England, is a wooden figure of Saint Christopher, brought from South America in the sixteenth or seventeenth century. The vicarage to the north is the oldest existing in the city. The Leake Dole of Bread, distributed every Saturday after ten o'clock service, was provided for in the will of John Leake, who, in 1792, bequeathed one thousand pounds for "sixpenny loaves of wheaten bread" to be distributed to "such poor as shall appear most deserving."

Barrow Street, below Grove, was originally named Reason Street, in honor of Paine's famous *Age of Reason*. The street's name was corrupted to "Raisin Street," and some time later it became Barrow.

Commerce Street, a block south, is a short, backwater street, hardly deserving of its name. Near the bend of Commerce Street is the CHERRY LANE THEATER, a converted barn, which, in the postwar period, served the experimental New Playwrights group. A group of two-story-and-dormer houses, near Bedford and Commerce Streets, dates from the early nineteenth century. Said to be the narrowest house in New York, 75½ Bedford Street is nine and one-half feet wide, thirty feet long, and three stories high. Its stepped gable recalls the old Dutch architectural detail. Among the tenants of the building have been John Barrymore and Edna St. Vincent Millay.

The HUDSON PARK PLAYGROUND, south of St. Luke's Place, was converted from a graveyard in the 1890's. Here, it is claimed, was buried the oft-found lost Dauphin of France, above whose body was placed a stone bearing the simple description—Leroy (The King).

On Varick Street (continuation of Seventh Avenue) at the corner of Charlton Street, stood Mortier House, one of Washington's headquarters during the Revolution. While Washington was living here Thomas Hickey, one of his bodyguards, was hanged for his participation in a Tory plot that involved firing the city, inciting the troops to mutiny, and feeding the general a dish of poisoned peas. Aaron Burr later lived in the house and in 1831 it was opened as the Richmond Hill Theatre. It was razed in 1849 to make room for business, which today dominates this neighborhood with tall loft and office buildings. Only south of Charlton Street does an occasional dingy red-brick house now serving as a tenement remain as a vestige of the old village.

D.SPIEGEL

Middle West Side

Chelsea—Hell's Kitchen and Vicinity —Garment Center and Vicinity— Times Square District

Area: 14th St. on the south to 59th St. on the north; from the Hudson River east to 6th Ave. (14th to 42d St.) and 5th Ave. (42d to 59th St.); excluding area east of Broadway, between 57th and 59th Sts. Maps on pages 54-55 and 149.
Principal north-south streets: Broadway, 7th, 8th, 9th, 10th, and 11th Aves.
Principal cross streets: 14th, 23d, 34th, 42d, and 57th Sts.
Transportation: IRT Broadway-7th Ave. subway (local), 14th to 59th St. stations; 8th Ave. (Independent) Grand Concourse or Washington Heights subway (local), 14th to 59th St. stations; BMT subway, 34th to 57th St. stations; bus lines on all principal north-south and cross streets except on 11th Ave. and 42d St.; 42d St. crosstown and Broadway surface cars.

THE HUDSON RIVER water front *(see page 68)* of the Middle West Side, an important sector of the New York port, includes the docks of the transatlantic luxury liners. In the adjoining localities, Chelsea on the south and the Hell's Kitchen district on the north, live the largest group of underprivileged families in the city. The Times Square area, east of upper Hell's Kitchen, contains the showrooms of café society and the auditoriums of night clubs as well as the famed congeries of legitimate theater houses and motion-picture palaces. Below the Rialto lies the Garment Center, the home of the cloak-and-suit, women's dress, and fur trades. The Thirty-

fourth Street zone houses some of the great department stores of the city
—Macy's, Gimbels, Saks—and the eastern terminus of the Pennsylvania
Railroad. Clustered around the station are skyscraper hotels which are frequently used by the garment industry for fashion shows and business transactions.

The most characteristic feature of the Middle West Side section is the
residential belt extending from the Twenties through the Fifties between
Eighth and Tenth Avenues. Row after row of three-, four-, and five-story
grimy brick tenement houses proclaim one of New York's worst slum areas.
Significantly, the city health center district that includes the Middle West
Side area has the highest general mortality rate in the city and ranks first in
pneumonia and cancer, second in tuberculosis, and third in infant mortality.

A large number of brownstones, originally built as private residences,
have been converted into lodginghouses, particularly in Chelsea and in the
eastern part of upper Hell's Kitchen. Many others have been extensively
altered and remodeled into apartment homes for families of moderate
means, and here and there, notably in the Times Square district, in Hell's
Kitchen above Forty-second Street east of Tenth Avenue, and in Chelsea
near Seventh Avenue between Fourteenth and Twenty-first Streets, modern
apartment houses have been erected. These, however, serve to accentuate
rather than relieve the surrounding drabness.

Ethnically the section is a typical metropolitan melange. Since the late
1840's, the Irish have been the predominant group in Chelsea and Hell's
Kitchen. Not so numerous perhaps, but constituting a sizable minority in
each of these localities, are the Italians. The northern part of the Hell's
Kitchen district also contains small French, German, and Negro groups,
while Chelsea also houses Spanish, Puerto Rican, Greek, and Balkan colonies. On the whole, however, the long process of assimilation, accelerated
by immigration restrictions, is rapidly transforming the Middle West Side
into a native American community. According to the 1930 census, native-
born residents of the district outnumbered the foreign born by nearly two
to one.

Eighth Avenue, in the throes of a minor boom that was stimulated by
the construction of the Independent Subway system, may be termed the
Middle West Side's "Main Street." Broadway, which enters the district at
Herald Square, Thirty-fourth Street and Sixth Avenue, cuts northwesterly
across the Garment Center and Times Square, and meets Eighth Avenue at
Columbus Circle.

In the days of the Dutch, what is now the Middle West Side comprised the southern section of Bloomingdale (the area between 14th and 125th Streets)—fertile, rolling fields, for the most part free of crags or clumps of underbrush. For nearly two hundred years successive generations of Dutch farmers tilled the land and provided garden truck for the thriving town at the lower end of the island.

In 1667, soon after English occupation, Governor Nicholls issued a patent to several citizens, among whom was Jans Vigne, probably the first white child born on Manhattan, granting them "a certain tract or parcel of land on the Island Manhattans lying and being to ye North of ye Great Creeke or Kill alongst ye River commonly known and called by ye name of Hudson's or ye North River." The Great Kill was a small stream that emptied into the Hudson at the foot of what is now Forty-second Street; the territory north of this stream was subsequently called the Great Kill region. By the end of the eighteenth century most of the upper Great Kill region had been acquired by the Hopper family and was known as Hopperville. The original Hopper farm in the lower Great Kill district was called the Hermitage; the name is perpetuated by a hotel at Forty-second Street and Seventh Avenue which occupies part of the site of the farm. The land between Forty-first and Thirty-second Streets in the second half of the eighteenth century belonged to the famous Glass House Farm—it contained a glass bottle factory—while most of the territory to the south, now Chelsea, was the property of Captain Thomas Clarke, veteran of the French and Indian wars. Within twenty-five years following the adoption of the City Plan in 1811, all these estates were subdivided into lots.

Manhattan's early railroads and the natural Hudson River water-front facilities played major roles in the development of the Middle West Side. In 1851, when Broadway between Twenty-third and Forty-second Streets was but a winding road through pleasant countryside, the Hudson River Railroad was opened to traffic, with a station at Thirtieth Street and Eleventh Avenue. A year later, the Eighth Avenue Railroad announced the opening of a line between Fifty-first and Chambers Streets.

When friends cautioned Commodore Cornelius Vanderbilt against building the Hudson River Railroad through sparsely settled country, he curtly rebuked them, declaring, "Put the road there and people'll go there to live." Vanderbilt's assertion proved correct. In the 1850's, lumberyards, brickyards, lime kilns, stables, warehouses, and distilleries moved into the old farm land north of Chelsea, crowding the malodorous slaughterhouses in the upper Thirties; and with the industrial plants came the workers, swarming into wooden shacks and shanties and, during the 1860's, into the jerry-built tenements of Chelsea and what is now Hell's Kitchen. As early as 1864 public indignation at these housing conditions resulted in a vigorous but ineffectual reform movement.

Throughout the 1860's and 1870's the industrial influx into the westerly half of the Middle West Side section continued, pushing northward. Gashouses, swill-milk cow stables, glue manufactories, freight yards, stockyards, piano factories, new slaughterhouses, and dozens of other establishments employing unskilled labor took advantage of the cheap swampy land near the foot of Forty-second Street and the drier and even cheaper land beyond. By 1850 a cotton factory had been established as far north as Fifty-first Street. In 1871 the Ninth Avenue el, the first rapid transit system in the city, began operating north to Thirtieth Street, destroying the charm and property values of Chelsea's most sedate avenue, but making possible additional profits for successful speculators engaged in building tenements. Five years later the system was extended northward.

Shackled by low-wage industry to desperate poverty and barbarous living conditions, the early Hell's Kitchen residents resorted at times to violence and crime. Occasionally, the spirit of protest assumed mass proportions, as in the Draft Riots of 1863 when thousands of workers marched down Eleventh Avenue and destroyed property of the Hudson River Railroad. More generally this spirit found expression in such organizations as the Gophers, the Parlor Mob, and the other predatory West Side gangs.

During the heyday of Mayor Fernando Wood and the Tweed Ring, organized vice had completely taken over the area between Twenty-fourth and Forty-second Streets and from Fifth to Seventh Avenue. The district, known later as the Tenderloin, became the scene of such wickedness that one crusading minister, the Reverend T. DeWitt Talmage, denounced the city that tolerated it as "the modern Gomorrah." So ineffectual were law enforcement agencies that in 1866 Bishop Simpson of the Methodist Episcopal Church complained that prostitutes were as numerous in the city as Methodists. The Tenderloin, however, continued to prosper. As late as 1885 one-half of all the buildings in this district were reputed to cater to vice.

Retail trade, rather than industry, started the development of the eastern half of the Middle West Side. During and following the Civil War, the northward march of the fashionable residential and trading district had reached Fourteenth Street and Union Square, and by 1875 these neighborhoods were well-established trading centers for prosperous contiguous East and West Side communities. When the aristocracy moved into the Madison

Square section, the merchants followed. During this period Sixth Avenue, Chelsea's eastern border, replaced Broadway as the principal street for stores, mainly owing to its newly built elevated. Before the turn of the century, Twenty-third Street, which had already become famous as the city's theatrical center (Jim Fisk's Grand Opera House, Proctor's, etc.), was the retail shopping center as well.

In the 1900's the Rialto began shifting to the Herald Square vicinity. Chelsea's great department stores soon followed, finding quarters hard by the newly constructed (1910) Pennsylvania Station. The converging rapid transit systems here rendered the stores accessible to an unlimited market, and the shopping center rapidly expanded to its present proportions. The theaters did not remain long in Herald Square and moved with the Tenderloin to the "Roaring Forties" of the Times Square area. The original Tenderloin, abandoned by vice as well as commerce, stagnated forlornly for many years until the World War period, when the needle trades took possession of the Thirties.

KEY TO MIDDLE WEST SIDE MAP

TIMES SQUARE DISTRICT

1. Merchant's Gate
   Maine Memorial
2. Statue of Christopher Columbus
3. General Motors Building
4. Broadway Tabernacle
5. Park Central Hotel
6. Mecca Temple
7. Grand Street Boys' Club House
8. Rockefeller Apartments
9. Manhattan Storage Warehouse
10. Fifty-second Street Night Clubs
11. American Federation of Musicians, Local 802
12. St. Malachy's Church
13. Madison Square Garden
14. Union M. E. Church
15. Statue of Father Duffy
16. American Federation of Actors
17. Church of St. Mary the Virgin
18. Variety Building
19. Actors' Equity Association

20. Harvard Club
21. General Society of Mechanics and Tradesmen
22. New York Yacht Club
23. Twelfth Night Club
24. New York Bar Association
25. Hotel Algonquin
26. City Club
27. Criterion Theater Building
28. Astor Hotel
29. Ascension Memorial Chapel
30. New York Times Annex
31. Paramount Building
32. Police Information Booth
33. Lambs' Club
34. Town Hall
35. Times Building
36. Bush Terminal Sales Building
37. Herald Tribune Offices
38. Metropolitan Opera House
39. Site of the New York Casino

Continued on Page 150

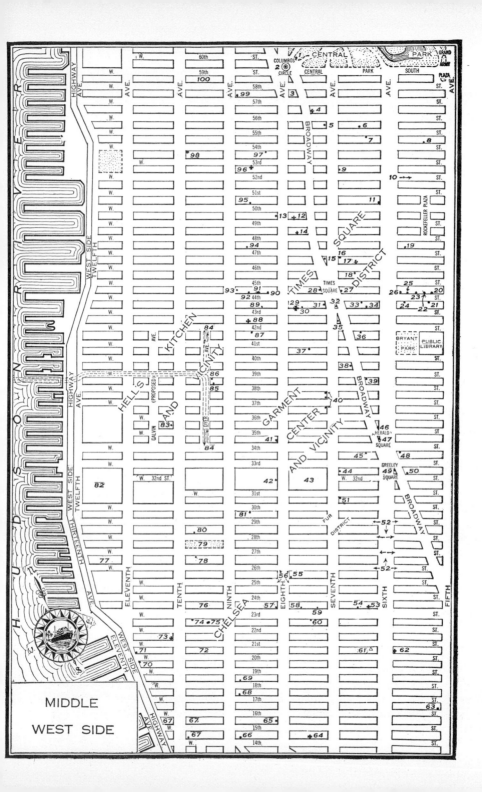

MIDDLE

WEST SIDE

Continued from Page 148

GARMENT CENTER AND VICINITY

40. Garment Center Capitol
41. Hotel New Yorker
42. New York General Post Office
43. Pennsylvania Station
44. Hotel Pennsylvania
45. Herald Square Hotel
46. Old Herald Building

47. Statue of William E. Dodge
48. McAlpin Hotel
49. Statue of Horace Greeley
50. Hotel Martinique
51. Hotel Governor Clinton
52. Wholesale Flower Market

CHELSEA

53. Church of St. Vincent De Paul
54. Old Proctor's 23d Street Theater
55. Spartacus Greek Workers Educational Club
56. Greek Quarter
57. Old Grand Opera House
58. Central High School of Needle Trades
59. Y.M.C.A., 23d Street Branch
60. Hotel Chelsea
61. Spanish-Portuguese Cemetery
62. Church of the Holy Communion
63. International Ladies Garment Workers Union
64. Spanish Church of Our Lady of Guadalupe
65. Port Authority Building
66. Spanish-American Workers Alliance

67. National Biscuit Company's Plant
68. Catholic Youth Organization
69. Straubenmuller High School
70. Seamen's House (Y.M.C.A.)
71. National Maritime Union
72. General Theological Seminary
73. Church of the Guardian Angel
74. Chrystie Street House
75. Site of Birthplace of Clement C. Moore
76. London Terrace
    École Maternelle Française
77. Starrett-Lehigh Building
78. Hudson Guild
79. Chelsea Park
80. Model Tenement House
81. French Hospital

HELL'S KITCHEN AND VICINITY

82. New York Central Railroad, Thirtieth Street Yard
83. WPA Federal Theatre Project Workshop (Bethany Church)
84. Lincoln Tunnel
85. West Side Children's Center
86. Schermerhorn Playground
87. McGraw-Hill Building
88. Church of the Holy Cross
89. Troupers' Club Association
90. Vitaphone Building

91. Paramount Pictures Building
92. Twentieth Century Fox Films
93. Film Center
94. 18th Precinct Police Station
95. Polyclinic Hospital
96. Church of St. Benedict the Moor
97. 7th District Magistrates' Court
98. Fox Movietone News
99. American Women's Association
100. Roosevelt Hospital

CHELSEA

Area: 14th St. (6th to 11th Ave.) on the south to 25th St. (6th to 8th Ave.) and 30th St. (8th to 13th Ave.) on the north. Map on page 149.

Chelsea is known as a conservative Irish Catholic community despite the presence of Spanish, French, Scottish, and other national groups. Although typical Manhattan tenements, small business establishments, and apartment houses make up most of the district, here and there an old theater or café reminds Chelsea of its past as an amusement center in the 1880's, and a relatively large number of local ancients helps give the neighborhood a "preserved" quality.

In 1750 Captain Thomas Clarke established his home on what is now the block from Ninth to Tenth Avenue between Twenty-second and Twenty-third Streets and named it for a soldiers' hospital (near London) called Chelsea. The house, which was rebuilt by his widow, Mistress Molly Clarke, was the birthplace of his grandson, Clement C. Moore (1799–1863), compiler of the first Hebrew and Greek lexicons published in the United States, and author of the perennially favorite poem, *A Visit from St. Nicholas.* Moore broke up his patrimony, selling it in building lots, and on the site of the old estate the village of Chelsea grew. In 1831 streets were cut through.

The English-village character of the neighborhood began to change in the middle of the nineteenth century. The Hudson River Railroad laid its tracks along Tenth and Eleventh Avenues in 1847. Industrial plants moved in. People of many nationalities settled here, including a large number of Irish, many of whom came here as a result of the potato famines of 1845–8 in Ireland. The votes of these immigrants increased Tammany's strength and Chelsea gave the "Wigwam" a number of leaders including Richard B. ("Slippery Dick") Connolly, of the Tweed Ring. The neighborhood is still a Tammany stronghold.

Among the immigrants were Spaniards, who gathered in the vicinity of Fourteenth Street. Since 1920 the SPANISH COLONY has declined, but *bodegas* (grocery stores), *carnicerias* (butcher shops), Spanish benefit societies, the SPANISH-AMERICAN WORKERS ALLIANCE at 349 West Fourteenth Street, and the SPANISH CHURCH OF OUR LADY OF GUADALUPE at 229 West Fourteenth Street still preserve the Iberian flavor.

The NATIONAL BISCUIT COMPANY'S PLANT on Fourteenth Street near Tenth Avenue is the largest factory in the neighborhood. It has about forty-six acres of floor space and employs several thousand workers.

The Port of New York Authority, which owns and operates the three bridges between Staten Island and New Jersey (Bayonne, Goethals, Outerbridge Crossing), the George Washington Bridge, the Holland and Lincoln tunnels, erected in 1933 the PORT AUTHORITY COMMERCE BUILDING, a fifteen-story, block-square structure between Eighth and Ninth Avenues, Fifteenth and Sixteenth Streets. It was designed by Aymar Embury II. The ground floor and basement make up Union Inland Freight Station Number 1, the first of a projected series of strategically placed truck terminals for the collection and distribution of freight. Eight trunk railroads jointly operate the station. The upper fourteen floors are used for general commercial and manufacturing purposes; Commerce Hall, on the second floor, is used for large exhibitions. Four great elevators carry loaded trucks weighing as much as forty thousand pounds to any upper floor.

The MANHATTAN CENTER OF THE CATHOLIC YOUTH ORGANIZATION, 353 West Seventeenth Street, also serves as a neighborhood settlement house for lower Chelsea. In 1890 Father John C. Drumgoole opened a boys' club on near-by West Fifteenth Street, which eventually led to the establishment in 1936 of the C.Y.O., an influential youth group.

The STRAUBENMULLER TEXTILE HIGH SCHOOL at 351 West Eighteenth Street trains its students in modern industrial arts. The school's museum has extensive collections of wool, silk, rayon, cotton, and lace fabrics. A Federal Art Project mural in the library—thirteen panels by Paul Lawler—illustrates the history of the textile industry. Groups interested in visiting the museum may obtain permission from the school office.

The GENERAL THEOLOGICAL SEMINARY occupies the entire block between Twentieth and Twenty-first Streets, Ninth and Tenth Avenues. When Clement C. Moore left his old apple orchard to the General Convention of the Protestant Episcopal Church in 1817, he did so on the condition that the church build a seminary on the site. Of the original group only the west building, erected in 1835, still stands. Most of the other existent structures were erected in the 1880's and were designed by Charles C. Haight. Of red brick with brownstone trim, they form a simple and charming Collegiate Gothic group. The seminary has in its possession one of the priceless Gutenburg Bibles.

The CHURCH OF THE GUARDIAN ANGEL (Roman Catholic), 191 Tenth Avenue, is an interesting architectural adaptation based on the Romanesque style of churches in Lombardy. It was designed by John V. Van Pelt and built in 1930. This church is called the Seamen's Institute, and its pastor, the Reverend John J. O'Donnell, is the Port Chaplain of the Archdiocese.

The little brownstone CHURCH OF THE HOLY COMMUNION (Protestant

Episcopal), Sixth Avenue and Twentieth Street, was built in 1846 through the efforts of William Augustus Muhlenberg, who was its first pastor. The building shows a harmonious proportioning of its tower and wings, windows and doors. The pleasing stone interior contains finely carved church furniture and a sturdy timber ceiling, and is lighted by well-designed stained-glass windows. The first "boy choir" in America and the first Sisterhood in the Anglican Communion were established here.

On Twenty-first Street near Sixth Avenue is the third CEMETERY OF THE SPANISH AND PORTUGUESE SYNAGOGUE, Congregation Shearith-Israel (the oldest Jewish congregation in New York).

Edwin Forrest, famous actor of the pre-Civil War period, who did much to stimulate interest in the development of native American drama, resided at 436 West Twenty-second Street.

Along Twenty-third Street, the main cross-town street of Chelsea, and in the 1880's the Times Square of the city, are found hotels, movie houses, dignified apartment buildings, restaurants, and residence houses for young men, such as the CHRYSTIE STREET HOUSE at No. 456 and the Y.M.C.A. at No. 215. The HOTEL CHELSEA, at No. 222, has been a landmark since 1882. Its boldly placed wrought-iron balconies are conspicuous among less venerable façades.

Near Sixth Avenue Edwin Booth's theater was opened in 1869. Booth played Shakespearean roles to an admiring public there until 1873. PROCTOR'S TWENTY-THIRD STREET THEATRE, now a motion-picture house, was also popular, first as a legitimate playhouse, and later for its vaudeville. Beautiful Lily Langtry, "the Jersey Lily" who was a friend of Edward VII, lived near by. Three restaurants, famous in the 1880's and 1890's, are still operating in the neighborhood: CAVANAGH'S at 258 West Twenty-third Street, GUFFANTI'S at 274 Seventh Avenue, and PETITPAS at 317 West Twenty-ninth Street.

The RKO theatre at Twenty-third Street and Eighth Avenue, built in 1868 at a cost of a million dollars, was known as Pike's Opera House. James Fisk and Jay Gould bought it in 1869 and changed the name to the Grand Opera House. Fisk extended the repertoire to include plays, light opera, and vehicles for his sweetheart, Josie Mansfield. Her neighboring mansion was connected to the theater by an underground tunnel. When the abortive attempt of Fisk and Gould to corner the gold market resulted in the panic of Black Friday in 1869, Fisk barricaded himself behind the doors of the opera house. Later when Fisk's partner, Edward S. Stokes, shot him in a quarrel over Mansfield's favors, "Jubilee Jim's" body lay in state in the opera house lobby.

Several early cinema companies had studios in this part of Chelsea, and by the time of the World War the locality was considered a center of the industry. Some of Mary Pickford's first pictures, including *Good Little Devil* (1913) and *Tess of the Storm Country* (1914), were made on the two top floors of an old armory building at 221 West Twenty-sixth Street. In the World War period, the Reliance and Majestic studios of Adam and Charles Kessel and Charles Baumann occupied a building owned by Stanford White at 520 West Twenty-first Street, and such well-known players as Wallace Reid, Florence Hackett, and Henry Walthall worked there. Alice Joyce began her career with the Kalem Company at 235 West Twenty-third Street.

The sixteenth-story LONDON TERRACE building, one of the largest apartment houses in the world, occupies the full block between Ninth and Tenth Avenues, Twenty-third and Twenty-fourth Streets. Designed by Farrar and Watmough, and built in 1930, the project contains 1,670 apartments, a swimming pool, solarium, gymnasium, and a central garden. Its doormen are costumed as London "bobbies." This block was the site of the original London Terrace and Chelsea cottages, both groups of fashionable homes in the middle-nineteenth century.

In London Terrace is the ÉCOLE MATERNELLE FRANÇAISE, partly supported by the French government, and directed for forty years by Mme. Anna Frégosi, whose original pedagogical methods have won the attention of many educators. Other evidences of the once large French population of Chelsea are the CHURCH OF ST. VINCENT DE PAUL (Roman Catholic) at 127 West Twenty-third Street, the oldest French church in the city (founded in 1841), and the FRENCH HOSPITAL at 330 West Thirtieth Street.

On Twenty-fourth Street between Seventh and Eighth Avenues is the new CENTRAL HIGH SCHOOL OF NEEDLE TRADES, being completed in 1939 at an estimated cost of nearly three million dollars. It represents the renewed interest of educators in skilled occupations and may indicate a trend away from the professions.

The GREEK QUARTER centers about Twenty-fifth Street and Eighth Avenue. On the northeast corner is the SPARTACUS GREEK WORKERS EDUCATIONAL CLUB. The walls of its building bear bullet scars sustained in a riot in 1871 when a procession of Orangemen escorted by the Sixth, the Ninth, and the Eighty-fourth Regiments were sniped at as they marched down Eighth Avenue. A battle involving police, infantry, rioting Hibernians, and parading Orangemen resulted in fifty-four deaths.

The best-known social agency in Chelsea is the HUDSON GUILD, at 436

West Twenty-seventh Street since 1905. It was founded in 1895 by its present head, Dr. John L. Elliott, Senior Leader of the Society for Ethical Culture and a descendant of Elijah P. Lovejoy, the abolitionist. Its model tenement house, built in 1916 at 441 West Twenty-eighth Street, helped to focus attention upon the need for adequate low-rent housing.

The MORGAN ANNEX, New York Post Office, with its huge parcel-post station, fills the block from Ninth to Tenth Avenue, between Twenty-ninth and Thirtieth Streets. A railroad spur enters the western end of the building at the third-floor level.

HELL'S KITCHEN AND VICINITY

Area: 30th St. (9th to 12th Ave.) and 41st St. (8th to 9th Ave.) on the south to 59th St. (8th to 12th Ave.) on the north; from 12th Ave. east to 9th Ave. (30th to 41st St.) and 8th Ave. (41st to 59th St.). Map on page 149.

Freight yards, factories, garages, warehouses, stock pens, and tenements today cover the area of Hell's Kitchen, a district that bears one of the most lurid reputations in America. The neighborhood's proximity to Manhattan's railroad and water terminals still fixes its industrial working-class character. Indeed the only characteristic of the traditional Hell's Kitchen that has completely disappeared is the organized hoodlumism, which, according to one authority, made the locality "one of the most dangerous areas on the American continent." To the north is a drab region of tenements, churches, factories, and garages deriving a little color from near-by Times Square. Scattered throughout the district are modern apartment houses and renovated brownstone dwellings.

Hell's Kitchen acquired its reputation as one of the toughest areas in the city shortly after the Civil War. According to Herbert Asbury, who recorded many exploits of Hell's Kitchen hoodlums in his book, *The Gangs of New York,* the section deserved its notoriety. Its name, originally applied to a dive near Corlears Hook on the East Side, came from the Hell's Kitchen Gang, organized in about 1868 by Dutch Heinrichs. Although this gang specialized in raids on the Thirtieth Street yard of the Hudson River Railroad (now part of the New York Central), its repertoire included extortion, breaking-and-entering, professional mayhem, and highway robbery. It merged with the Tenth Avenue Gang, which had held up and robbed a Hudson River Railroad express train, and for decades terrorized the neighborhood. From its ranks rose the desperadoes who organized the Hudson Dusters and the Gophers.

After the decline of the Hell's Kitchen Gang, the Gophers achieved hegemony in the Hell's Kitchen underworld. They made their headquarters in saloons such as one on "Battle Row" (Thirty-ninth Street between Tenth and Eleventh Avenues) operated by "Mallet" Murphy, who won his pseudonym by bludgeoning disputatious customers with a mallet. Leaders of the Gophers included "Happy Jack" Mulraney, "Goo Goo" Knox, "Stumpy" Malarkey, and "One Lung" Curran. Besides the Gophers, whose membership numbered nearly five hundred men, several smaller affiliated gangs such as the Gorillas, the Rhodes Gang, and the Parlor Mob waged consistent warfare against what was left of law and order in the neighborhood.

Gangster rule of Hell's Kitchen continued until 1910, when a special police force organized by the New York Central Railroad launched a counter-offensive. Clubbing, shooting, and arresting indiscriminately, they soon had most of the Gopher leadership in hospitals or behind the bars and a majority of the lesser lights in flight. Remnants of the mobs functioned throughout the Prohibition era, but the backbone of Hell's Kitchen gangsterdom had been effectively broken.

Two developments, the Lincoln Tunnel and the New York Central Railroad West Side Improvement, have altered the appearance of the Kitchen. In the construction of a seventy-five-foot wide approach to the tunnel—Dyer Avenue—buildings midway between Ninth and Tenth Avenues from Thirty-fourth to Forty-second Street were demolished; and in the execution of the grade crossing elimination project of the railroad, structures midway between Tenth and Eleventh Avenues from the Thirtieth Street freight yard to the Sixtieth Street yard were razed.

The LINCOLN TUNNEL, owned and operated by the Port of New York Authority, connects Thirty-ninth Street and Weehawken, New Jersey *(passenger automobile toll 50¢)*. On the Manhattan side its approaches permit easy access to and from six transverse streets and the ramps of the West Side Highway *(see page 71)* that leads by way of the Henry Hudson Parkway to US 9 and the Westchester County Parkway system. A projected cross-town roadway underneath Manhattan will eventually link the Lincoln Tunnel with the Queens Midtown Tunnel *(see page 209)* now under construction (1939). On the Weehawken side, an express highway joins the Lincoln Tunnel with US 1 and 9W and important New Jersey arteries.

The south double-lane tube of the Lincoln Tunnel, 8,218 feet long, was opened to traffic in December, 1937, and now carries east- and westbound vehicles. When the north tube is completed, it will take over the westbound traffic. An approach lane to this tube will run between Thirty-seventh and Forty-second Streets over the depressed New York Central right of way previously mentioned. The cost of the project, including ventilation, buildings, equipment, approaches, and real estate, is estimated at $75,000,000.

For nearly ninety years the tone of the community has been determined by the New York Central Railroad's THIRTIETH STREET YARD, which includes all the property between Eleventh and Twelfth Avenues from Thirtieth to Thirty-seventh Street and the two additional blocks bounded by Tenth and Eleventh Avenues, Thirtieth and Thirty-second Streets. Prior to the completion of the company's West Side Improvement Plan, the Thirtieth Street yard was linked to the Sixtieth Street yard by means of surface trackage on Eleventh Avenue; a "cowboy" would ride in advance of the train to warn pedestrian and vehicular traffic. The endless movement of freight trains through the neighborhood added hazards, congestion, noise, and dust to surroundings that were already grim, and Eleventh Avenue became known as "Death Avenue." Now the tracks between the two railroad yards have been dropped below street level, and south of Thirtieth Street the line has been elevated. Most of the New York Central's costly new right-of-way will be covered over eventually as the "air rights" are utilized for the construction of modern industrial plants. Several warehouses already have risen over the tracks.

SCHERMERHORN PLAYGROUND, on Thirty-eighth Street between Ninth and Tenth Avenues, is the only recreation center in the lower part of Hell's Kitchen. Although pathetically inadequate in equipment and open space, it provides children with a safe play area. Intelligent adult direction is provided by the WEST SIDE CHILDREN'S CENTER, an affiliate of the Children's Aid Society, which occupies the four-story brick building at 419 West Thirty-eighth Street.

The vari-hued façade of the BETHANY CHURCH, 455 Tenth Avenue, contributes a splash of color to the area. This building, formerly occupied by the Salvation Army, serves as the workshop of the WPA Federal Theatre Project.

Thirty-ninth Street, west of Ninth Avenue, was popularly known as "Abattoir Place" when the slaughterhouse industry was concentrated here.

For nearly fifty years a large pushcart market known as PADDY'S MARKET was maintained under the Ninth Avenue elevated between Thirty-ninth Street and Forty-second Streets. It supplied a variety of foodstuffs to the poor of the Middle West Side and became one of the best-known landmarks in the Kitchen. Then the Lincoln Tunnel was built, and it became necessary to clear and widen streets for the increased traffic. In

1937 the Department of Public Markets, co-operating with the Port of New York Authority, ordered the pushcart merchants to move. They refused, and took their case to court, but in 1938 they were finally evicted. The disgruntled hucksters split into two groups; one group moved to West Thirty-ninth Street, the other to West Forty-first Street. Business slumped in the new locations, however, and early in 1939 the merchants petitioned the Commissioner of Public Markets for an enclosed market building.

The thirty-three-story McGraw-Hill Building, 330 West Forty-second Street, built in 1930 from Raymond Hood's design, is the Middle West Side's most imposing edifice. It is notable for an experimental use of exterior materials, for the simplicity of its main outlines, and especially for its alternation of horizontal bands of blue-green terra-cotta tile with bands of windows. The horizontal accent contrasts strongly with the vertical emphasis of Hood's Daily News Building *(see page 210)* at the other end of Forty-second Street.

The adjoining amusement district has influenced the character of many of the blocks north of Forty-second Street. The Church of the Holy Cross, opposite the McGraw-Hill Building, arranges special services and masses for the theatrical people and entertainers in its congregation, as well as for workers in mid-town factories, offices, and shops. The church is popularly known as "Father Duffy's Church," in memory of the Reverend Francis P. Duffy who was Roman Catholic chaplain of the "Fighting Sixty-ninth" during the World War, and pastor here until his death in June, 1932. Father Duffy's rehabilitation work among the survivors of the old gangs and their successors was a considerable factor in reforming the Kitchen's folkways.

The Troupers' Club Association at 327 West Forty-third Street is run by stagehands "to foster and cultivate social relations and aid one another in sickness and distress, free of politics and religion." Unemployed members who live at the club pay nothing, but share in the housework and cook their own meals.

Seventy-two motion-picture distributors occupy the Film Center on Forty-fourth Street and Ninth Avenue. Twentieth Century Fox Film Corporation has its sales and distribution offices at 345 West Forty-fourth Street, and on the same street, at No. 331, is the Paramount Pictures Building, and, at No. 315, Warner Brothers' ten-story Vitaphone Building. Farther uptown at 420 West Fifty-fourth Street are the headquarters of Fox Movietone News where newsreels are edited for release. Shots taken in the afternoon can be made ready for a Broadway showing on the same evening.

The ugly, yellow-brick EIGHTEENTH PRECINCT POLICE STATION, 345 West Forty-seventh Street, was put into service January 1, 1862, in good time to play a part in the Draft Riots of 1863. The district was not densely settled then, and most of its crimes were unspectacular; the single blotter entry for the first day recorded the return of a lost child to her parents. By the early 1900's, however, the gambling dives and the gangsters of the West Side had made the station house one of the busiest in New York. Later, following occasional raids on theaters and night clubs, such names as Texas Guinan and Mae West would appear among hundreds of underworld aliases on the blotter. Before the advent of the police radio car, reporters maintained headquarters in a basement across the street from the station. Among the newspapermen who worked this coveted "fly-beat" were David Graham Phillips, Charlie Somerville, Richard Harding Davis, and Louis Weitzenkorn.

In 1939 the WPA was building a new station house for the precinct beside the Men's Night Court on West Fifty-fourth Street, and the old Forty-seventh Street building was destined to be abandoned at a time when its force of more than 500 men are issuing 30,000 summonses and making 15,000 arrests a year.

Whenever a heavyweight boxer in Madison Square Garden (see page 330) takes too many right-hand punches, or a circus trapeze performer misses his safety net, or a rodeo rider falls under the hoofs of a steer, the victim is carried across the street to POLYCLINIC HOSPITAL, 345 West Fiftieth Street. The 346-bed hospital serves the ordinary people of the neighborhood, for the most part, but because of its location it receives an unusually large number of well-publicized patients. During the Prohibition era the bullet wounds of such notorious figures as Arnold Rothstein and Jack "Legs" Diamond were treated here.

One of the city's oldest Negro communities is concentrated on West Fifty-third Street near Ninth Avenue. It was first settled by Negroes who worked on the Croton Aqueduct (1840–42). The CHURCH OF ST. BENEDICT THE MOOR, a small white-brick building, stands at 342 West Fifty-third Street, in the shadow of the Ninth Avenue el. The original church building, the first for Negro Catholics north of the Mason-Dixon Line, was erected on Bleecker Street in 1883.

Although every block in this neighborhood contains a broad mixture of nationalities, in the West Forties and Fifties there is a French population large enough to form a true FRENCH QUARTER. Bastille Day and other French national holidays are celebrated here and many restaurants serve Gallic dishes. French cultural, professional, social, sporting, educational, and culinary organizations have their headquarters in the building at 349 West Forty-fourth Street.

The Seventh District Magistrates Court, better known as the MEN'S NIGHT COURT, occupies the gray stone building at 314 West Fifty-fourth Street. Petty offenders in Manhattan and the Bronx are brought before a magistrate who presides here from eight o'clock in the evening to one in the morning. Before rubbernecking was officially discouraged, Park Avenue in evening dress used to drop in to gape at the tragic parade of drunks, panhandlers, pickpockets, wife beaters, and brawlers.

The clubhouse of the AMERICAN WOMEN'S ASSOCIATION, 353 West Fifty-seventh Street, was completed in 1929 from designs by Benjamin Wistar Morris at a cost of eight million dollars. This imposing twenty-seven-story structure is open to transients and non-members. Miss Anne Morgan heads the board of governors of the association, one of the most influential women's organizations in the country.

ROOSEVELT HOSPITAL, which occupies a group of red-brick buildings along Ninth Avenue from Fifty-eighth to Fifty-ninth Street was founded in 1871. Nationally known for its surgical work, the hospital has 387 beds, and treats in its clinics some fifty thousand patients a year. A monument stands on the grounds, erected to the memory of James Henry Roosevelt (1800–1883), "the generous founder of the hospital."

A Negro community, west of Columbus Circle, has been popularly known since the turn of the century as SAN JUAN HILL, a folk tribute to the exploits of Negro soldiers in the Spanish-American War.

GARMENT CENTER AND VICINITY

Area: 25th St. (6th to 8th Ave.) and 30th St. (8th to 9th Ave.) on the south to 39th St. (6th to 7th Ave.) and 41st St. (7th to 9th Ave.) on the north. Map on page 149.

New York's garment center, housing the city's foremost industry, and America's fourth largest, crowds the middle of Manhattan between Sixth and Ninth Avenues, from Thirtieth to Forty-second Street. Here are produced three out of four of the ready-made coats and dresses, and four out of five of the fur garments worn by American women. Immediately north of Twenty-fifth Street, between Sixth and Eighth Avenues, are the quarters of the fur industry. The wholesale flower market borders Sixth Avenue from Twenty-sixth to Twenty-eighth Street. In the mid-section of the district are the Pennsylvania Station, hotels, and the city's most concentrated shopping market, the hub of which, at Broadway and Thirty-fourth Street (Greeley and Herald Squares), is dominated by three famous department stores: Macy's, Gimbels, and Saks-34th Street.

The location of major industries—fur and garment—in the heart of Manhattan near the passenger terminals and the hotels is dictated to a considerable extent by their need for being easily accessible to both resident and out-of-town buyers. Moreover, the peculiar character of the garment industry, with its constant, intimate contact between selling and manufacturing departments, apparently makes it difficult to move the workrooms to less congested districts.

The garment industry, which concentrated on the Lower East Side late in the nineteenth century, followed the city's every move northward and westward until it reached its present location in the World War period.

Garment Center

Sixth, Seventh, and Eighth Avenues, main routes for heavy-duty traffic, are packed with trucks and busses. The curbs of side streets are lined with trucks unloading bolts of materials and loading finished garments while other trucks wait for an opening. Through narrow traffic holes along the curbs, "push boys" guide handtrucks with garments swaying from racks made of metal pipes. Into these crowded streets at noon, thousands of workers, East and South European by origin, Italians and Jews mostly, descend for food, fresh air, and sun. (Few women workers appear in the noonday crowd, for most of them bring food from home and eat in the workrooms.) They pour from the buildings, congregate in groups, jam into lunchrooms and cafeterias, and gather around pitchmen. A few minutes before one they take a final puff at the cigarette, look fondly once more at the warming sun, throw away the butt, and crowd the doors to the buildings.

The garment trade, as represented in this area, may be divided into two main parts: the cloak-and-suit business and the women's dress business. Cloak-and-suit firms are centered above Thirty-fourth Street and Seventh Avenue, while the dress houses, for the most part, are farther to the north, although the geographical division is general, not sharp. While other branches of the trade are represented in the district, they are concentrated, in the main, in other parts of the city.

Almost every building in the district is filled with shops, most of which employ no more than thirty workers. Three tall buildings at Nos. 498, 500, and 512 Seventh Avenue, from Thirty-sixth to Thirty-eighth Street, form the GARMENT CENTER CAPITOL. Constructed as a co-operative venture by leading manufacturers, the structures cover a ground area of 38,000 square feet and contain the most modern manufacturing facilities. Nos. 498 and 500, built in 1921, were designed by Walter M. Mason; No. 512, tallest of the three and built in 1929, was designed by Sugarman and Berger.

The average shop has two main sections: showroom and workroom. The former is generally long and ornately decorated, with one side partitioned into booths. In these, buyers for stores sit and appraise the latest fashions displayed by mannequins.

Refinements of the showroom are totally lacking in the workroom. Walls and ceilings are whitewashed; floors are bare. Placed close to the many windows are long cutting tables where a motor-driven blade can cut through as many as four hundred thicknesses of some materials in a single operation; and rows of electric sewing machines can needle fabrics at the rate of three thousand stitches a minute. The workers are Negro and white, native and foreign-born; women outnumber men three to one.

The great number of independent shops in the garment center is illustrative of the industry's peculiar make-up. The process of centralization and monopoly that shaped other large industries has not operated to any great extent in the garment trade, largely because the style factor makes it an extremely speculative business. Instead of the assembly-belt system that obtains, for example, in the automobile industry, garment production is relatively dependent on the skill of the operator, who in most cases sews the entire garment. The so-called manufacturer, or jobber, may do only a portion of the actual manufacturing. Contractors assume the responsibility for the sewing and finishing of whatever "cut work" the various manufacturers send to them. This subdivision of the industry has increased competition all along the line, among manufacturers, contractors, and workers. The result has been a chaotic system of production, reflected each year in the amazing rate of bankruptcy that has been as high as 20 per cent among "inside" manufacturers, and 33⅓ per cent among contractors.

A strong stabilizing force, admittedly, is the INTERNATIONAL LADIES GARMENT WORKERS UNION, whose union halls stud the district and whose main New York office is at 3 West Sixteenth Street. It has established wage levels tending to halt ruinous price competition at the expense of the workers. The union, founded in 1900, has a firm hold upon the affection and loyalty of its members. To it is attributed the eradication of the sweatshop conditions forced upon the immigrant workers during the rapid rise of the needle trades, which had their origins in the invention of the sewing machine in 1846 and of the cutting machine twenty years later. The union's general strikes in 1909 and 1910 against sweatshop conditions was a mile-stone in the American labor movement. It has consistently fought for higher wages and better working conditions and has developed a remarkable educational program—economic, cultural, and political in nature. The social life of many garment workers also centers around the union. The ILGWU maintains a million-dollar summer camp for its members; in the fall of 1937, the union produced a musical comedy success, *Pins and Needles,* with a cast of garment workers, in its own Labor Stage Theater on Thirty-ninth Street. Less spectacularly the union serves the workers daily through its business agents. Even more than manufacturers' groups, it functions as the "chamber of commerce" for the industry, maintaining research and statistical divisions. Highly respected by employer groups, it often initiates policies generally accepted as beneficial to the industry as a whole.

Fur District

Although the street scene of the fur district—Twenty-fifth to Thirtieth Street, between Sixth and Eighth Avenues—is less turbulent than that of the garment center, the neighborhoods are similar in many respects: trucks backed to the curb, loading and unloading; scurrying delivery boys carrying pelts dangling from hangers; salesmen, buyers, and union agents bent on business. Pelts are piled high behind dealers' windows, frequently reinforced with iron grillwork. Sometimes a tiger skin is displayed among mink and ermine.

The dealer acquires the furs directly from trappers or at the auctions held here quarterly, and he sells them in turn to the manufacturer for fabrication into wraps, scarves, trimmings, and accessories. Unlike the highly mechanized garment industry, fur manufacture consists, in large part, of work done by hand. Fur and fur products valued at $195,000,000 were handled in New York City in 1936, retail prices ranging from about a dollar for an undyed rabbit "choker" to several thousand for a sable wrap. Of the ninety varieties of pelts used, muskrat is most common, with rabbit and fox next in commercial importance.

There are approximately two thousand shops in the district, employing 15,000 workers. The trade is a seasonal one: during June and July shops operate at top speed to meet the demand of the winter sales and in November there is a short spurt to supply the needs of the Christmas trade. All in all the fur worker averages twenty weeks of employment a year. Eighty per cent of the workers are members of the powerful International Fur Workers Union (CIO).

Flower Market

Millions of flowers—some of rare species—are sold annually in the wholesale flower market in the vicinity of Sixth Avenue between Twenty-sixth and Twenty-eighth Streets. Seventy per cent of these flowers are grown within one hundred miles of the city, although about thirty thousand tulips are imported annually from Holland, and from one-quarter to one-half million Easter lilies from Bermuda.

The market had its origin before 1870, when Long Island growers gathered each morning at the foot of East Thirty-fourth Street to sell their blossoms to both retail and wholesale trade. In 1873 a commission business was started at Third Avenue and Twenty-eighth Street. Before long, wholesale commission merchants had set up stores in the present location, chosen for its proximity to the retail flower market and to the center of business, then at about Fourteenth Street.

In the 1880's and 1890's the area between Twenty-fourth and Fortieth Streets, from Fifth to Seventh Avenue, was notorious as the wickedest and gayest spot in the city. Reformers of the day referred to it as "Satan's Circus." On the southeast corner of Sixth Avenue and Thirtieth Street flourished the Haymarket, a post-Civil War variety theater remodeled into a combined dance hall and café. Sisters' Row, near here, was run by seven sisters of reputedly great physical charm. On certain nights only gentlemen in evening dress were admitted, and all the proceeds taken in on Christmas Eve were donated to charity. This district was known as the "Tenderloin" after Captain (later Inspector) Alexander C. Williams, newly transferred there, was quoted as saying, "I've had nothing but chuck steak for a long time, and now I'm going to get a little of the tenderloin."

Pennsylvania Station and Vicinity

The large-scale production of the garment industry has its counterpart in the retail selling of department stores in the shopping sector around the intersection of Broadway, Sixth Avenue, and Thirty-fourth Street. The amount of retail business transacted yearly in this neighborhood far exceeds that of any comparable area in the city.

MACY'S, founded in 1858 by a Nantucket whaling captain, describes itself as the largest department store in the world. Its ten acres of selling space have a daily capacity of 137,000 customers, who may buy anything from diamonds to raspberries. Macy's, GIMBELS, and SAKS are giants in the midst of scores of small specialty shops devoted to women's or men's wear. Thirty-fourth Street is almost entirely a woman's precinct, while Broadway has the men's shops.

The intersection of Broadway and Sixth Avenue at Thirty-fourth Street creates two triangles: GREELEY SQUARE on the south and HERALD SQUARE on the north. The former contains a STATUE OF HORACE GREELEY by Alexander Doyle; the latter, named for James Gordon Bennett's New York *Herald,* contains a STATUE OF WILLIAM E. DODGE, noted New York merchant, by J. Q. A. Ward. In 1894 the publishing plant and offices of the *Herald* were moved into a handsome building—a McKim, Mead, and White reproduction of an Italian palace—on the irregular block directly north of Herald Square. The northern part of the structure has since been replaced by an office building; the original southern portion is occupied by a men's clothing store. Plans for the renovation of the two squares, announced in 1939 when the Sixth Avenue el was removed, include shifting the statues and surrounding them with trees. The great Bennett clock, whose two figures (nicknamed Stuff and Guff) had long struck the hours from the front of the Herald Building until they were exiled to New York University, was to be returned to a place of honor. Until about 1910 Herald Square was the city's Rialto, and diners-out frequented hotels such as the MARTINIQUE, Broadway and Thirty-second Street, and the HERALD SQUARE, 116 West Thirty-fourth Street, and ordered lobster in the neighborhood's sea-food restaurants. The McALPIN HOTEL, Thirty-fourth Street and Broadway, carries on the tradition in the modern manner.

At Herald and Greeley Squares a maze of transit lines—subways, interstate busses—helps to feed this congested district. Latest addition to the underground tangle is the Sixth Avenue subway, under construction in 1939, which lies fifty-two feet below the street, sandwiched between the BMT subway and the Pennsylvania Railroad tunnels. New Jersey crowds enter and leave the square by the Hudson Tubes.

The south side of Thirty-second Street, between Sixth and Seventh Avenues, has become a center for dealers in cameras and photographic equipment.

PENNSYLVANIA STATION, Seventh Avenue between Thirty-first and Thirty-third Streets, is one of the city's two great passenger transport centers. It is the terminus of the Pennsylvania and Lehigh Valley railroads, which reach Manhattan by way of tunnels under the Hudson River, and of the Long Island Railroad, which enters through tubes under the East River. Both sets of river tunnels, a cross-town link sixty feet underground, and the station itself were completed in 1910. A connection with the New York, New Haven and Hartford, over the New York Connecting Railroad (Hell Gate) Bridge, enables trains to run from Maine to Miami—the only continuous direct rail route from New England to the South.

The design of the station, by McKim, Mead, and White, was inspired by Roman Classical architecture. For the two-block façade on Seventh Avenue the architects chose the most monumental of compositions—a great central element flanked by colonnaded wings and end pavilions. The central portion is the main pedestrian entrance; the end pavilions are used by passenger vehicles.

The interior is a sequence of tremendous spaces. From a long, barrel-vaulted arcade, lined with shops, a marble stairway and escalators lead to the floor of the main hall. In this vast hall, which is a copy of the Tepidarium of a Roman bath, are ticket booths and the information desk. Six murals by Jules Guerin depict scenes of the area served by the Pennsylvania Railroad. Along the west side are twin waiting rooms. Beyond them a great glass-roofed concourse gives access to the track platforms. The Long Island Railroad waiting room and ticket offices are on a lower level.

The station yard, part of which is beneath the concourse floor, covers three hundred thousand square feet and accommodates a network of twenty-seven tracks. Six hundred and fifty steel foundation columns support the building.

Directly across Eighth Avenue from Pennsylvania Station, the NEW YORK GENERAL POST OFFICE, the largest in the country, rests on steel and concrete stilts above the railroad yard. It was designed by McKim, Mead, and White. The simplicity of the main outline is beautifully enriched by the well-proportioned Corinthian colonnade above a two-block sweep of granite steps. Across the frieze a quotation from Herodotus is inscribed: "Neither snow nor rain nor heat nor gloom of night stays these couriers from the swift completion of their appointed rounds."

The main lobby ceiling, subtly arched to avoid the illusion of sagging, is decorated with the coats-of-arms of nations that belong to the postal union.

Forty-five per cent of the city's mail is handled here. In the basement, belts, chutes, and other mechanical devices transfer mail to and from trains directly beneath. An intricate system of underground pneumatic tubes, the first units of which were installed in 1896, carries mail between the New York General Post Office and branches in Manhattan and the Brooklyn General Post Office.

Around the Pennsylvania Station are grouped several large satellite hotels, to two of which, the Pennsylvania and the New Yorker, it is connected by underground passages. The huge HOTEL PENNSYLVANIA, facing Seventh Avenue between Thirty-second and Thirty-third Streets, is the scene of frequent fashion shows, for it is the New York headquarters of buyers for many out-of-town department stores. The architects were George B. Post and Sons. The HOTEL GOVERNOR CLINTON, two blocks south, was designed by Murgatroyd and Ogden. On Eighth Avenue between Thirty-fourth and Thirty-fifth Streets is the forty-three-story NEW YORKER, the second tallest hotel in the city. Completed in 1930 from plans by Sugarman and Berger, the structure is a fine example of setback design, conforming to the zoning law without loss of artistic effect.

TIMES SQUARE DISTRICT

Area: 42d St. (5th to 6th Ave.), 39th St. (6th to 7th Ave.), and 41st St. (7th to 8th Ave.) on the south to 57th St. and Columbus Circle on the north; from 8th Ave. east to 5th Ave. Maps on pages 149 and 169.

A belt of white electric bulbs girds the Times Building at Forty-second Street and Broadway, spelling out spot news in moving letters that can be read several blocks away. And to the north a wall of light and color, urging the onlooker to chew gum, drink beer, see the world's most beautiful girls, or attend the premiere of a Hollywood film, lights the clouds above Manhattan with a glow like that of a dry timber fire.

This is the Great White Way, theatrical center of America and wonder of the out-of-towner. Here midnight streets are more brilliant than noon, their crowds on ordinary evenings exceeding those of large town carnivals. Scarcely a day passes that does not inaugurate some notable event, and in these theaters, cafés, and hotels, personages mentioned daily in the newspapers are everywhere at hand. It is the district of glorified dancing girls and millionaire playboys and, on a different plane, of dime-a-dance hostesses and pleasure-seeking clerks. Here, too, in a permanent moralizing tableau, appear the extremes of success and failure characteristic of Broadway's spectacular professions: gangsters and racketeers, panhandlers and derelicts, youthful stage stars and aging burlesque comedians, world heavyweight champions and once-acclaimed beggars. An outer shell of bars and restaurants, electric signs, movie palaces, taxi dance halls, cabarets, chop suey places, and side shows of every description covers the central streets.

By day, Times Square is a jumble of skyscrapers, antiquated and remodeled commercial structures, and shabby taxpayers topped by the huge

KEY TO TIMES SQUARE THEATER DISTRICT MAP
(The following are theaters, except Nos. 20, 33, and 89.)

1. Labor Stage
2. Maxine Elliott
3. Empire
4. Metropolitan Opera House
5. National
6. Mercury
7. Cameo
8. New Amsterdam
9. Sam H. Harris
10. Liberty
11. Eltinge
12. Wallach
13. Selwyn
14. Apollo
15. Times Square
16. Lyric
17. Republic
18. Rialto
19. Henry Miller
20. Town Hall
21. Hippodrome
22. Belasco
23. Hudson
24. Loew's Criterion
25. Paramount
26. Forty-fourth Street
27. Nora Bayes
28. Little
29. St. James
30. Majestic
31. Broadhurst
32. Shubert
33. Shubert Alley
34. Booth
35. Plymouth
36. CBS Radio Theater No. 1
37. John Golden
38. Martin Beck
39. CBS Radio Theater No. 2
40. Imperial
41. Music Box
42. Morosco
43. Bijou
44. Astor
45. Loew's State
46. Lyceum
47. Gaiety
48. Fulton
49. Forty-sixth Street
50. Mansfield
51. Central
52. Globe
53. Embassy
54. Palace
55. Cort
56. Vanderbilt
57. Loew's Mayfair
58. Strand
59. Ethel Barrymore
60. Biltmore
61. Longacre
62. Forty-eighth Street
63. Ritz
64. Rivoli
65. Windsor
66. Playhouse
67. Belmont
68. Center
69. World
70. Translux
71. Forrest
72. Cinema 49
73. CBS Radio Theater No. 4
74. Capitol
75. Winter Garden
76. Roxy
77. Music Hall
78. Continental
79. Hollywood
80. Alvin
81. Guild
82. Cine Roma
83. Loew's Ziegfeld
84. Adelphi
85. CBS Radio Theater No. 3
86. New Yorker
87. Fifty-fifth Street Playhouse
88. Little Carnegie Playhouse
89. Carnegie Hall
90. Filmarte
91. Yiddish Art

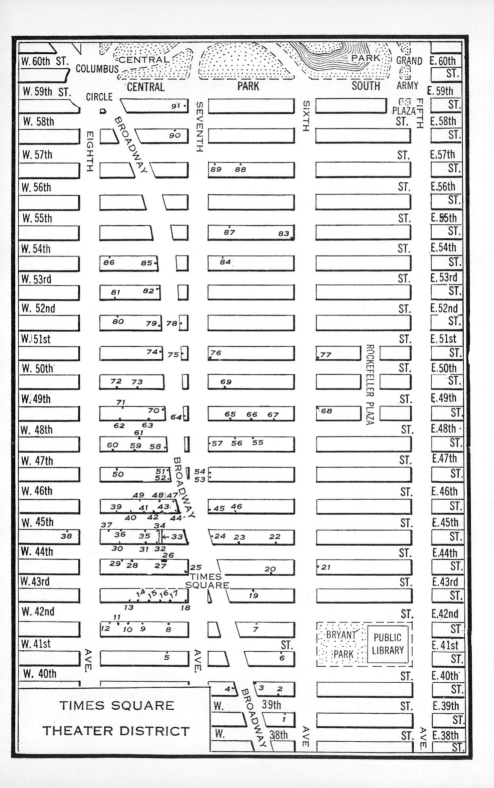

skeletons of electric signs. Without the beneficent flood of light descending from above, the area exhibits greater variety and at the same time a certain drabness. Adjoining elaborate hotel and theater entrances and wide-windowed clothing shops are scores of typical midway enterprises: fruit juice stands garlanded with artificial palm leaves, theater ticket offices, cheap lunch counters, cut-rate haberdasheries, burlesque houses, and novelty concessions. Streams of shoppers, movie-goers, and tourists move across the sidewalks, and members of the theatrical professions congregate on favorite street corners.

The name Times Square District designates the rectangle extending from Thirty-ninth Street to Fifty-seventh Street and from Fifth to Eighth Avenue. Below Forty-second Street the Metropolitan Opera House and a handful of theaters hold out against the intrusion of the mid-town business section. Times Square proper is the core of the neighborhood; it includes the roughly triangular area bounded by Forty-second Street, Broadway, Seventh Avenue, and Forty-seventh Street. The side streets east and west of Broadway between Forty-second and Fiftieth Streets are lined with hotels, theaters, restaurants, and boarding houses. In the upper Forties between Sixth and Seventh Avenues are many well-known eating places. Sixth Avenue, conditioned until 1939 by the el structure, was the dark border of the district. Eighth Avenue on the west takes its character from the sporting world attracted by Madison Square Garden. From Fiftieth to Fifty-seventh Streets between Fifth and Seventh Avenues are expensive night clubs, a number of substantial residential hotels, and a scattering of garages and parking lots. Northward from Fiftieth to Sixty-first Street west of Broadway, the area rapidly changes character. The theaters, restaurants, and crowds thin out, the hotels become smaller and shoddier, and the rooming houses multiply. The intersection of Fifty-seventh and Broadway is the focal point of a great cluster of automobile sales rooms. To the north is windy Columbus Circle.

Since early in the nineteenth century when New York could count but five playhouses, the theatrical district has kept close to Broadway, following it uptown with the changing city. By 1902, the theater had begun to concentrate itself about Times Square. The district was then occupied chiefly by old brownstones, carriage and harness shops, and livery stables. The northern end of this quiet quarter was called Longacre Square after the street in London.

The phrase, the Great White Way, is supposed to have been coined in 1901 by O. J. Gude, an advertising man, who is said also to have been the first to see the tremendous possibilities of electric display. A modest sign at

Broadway and Twenty-third Street advertising an ocean resort was New York's first experience with this phenomenon. The present show of light has never been dimmed in the evening, except for a brief period during World War I and the dimout of World War II.

Rapid transit reached Times Square in 1904 with the opening of the first IRT line to 145th Street, and since then the growth of the city's transportation has played a vital part in the development of the district. Every twenty-four hours, two hundred thousand passengers emerge from the IRT and BMT subways to the cement passageways of the underground stations extending from Fortieth to Forty-third Street. A shuttle connects the East Side IRT lines at Grand Central with Times Square, and the Eighth Avenue (Independent) subway has a station from Fortieth to Forty-fourth Street on Eighth Avenue. Forty-second Street surface cars carry riders from the New Jersey ferries; north- and southbound Manhattan busses cross the square; interstate busses arrive at many terminals in the Forties; Pennsylvania Station and Grand Central Terminal are near by—all the city's boroughs, every state, and many foreign countries contribute to the crowds that overflow the sidewalks and gape enchantedly at the tall buildings, the shop windows, and the gyrating sky signs.

Once a year sees the Times Square district as jammed as a rush-hour subway train. On New Year's eve crowds fill the bars, restaurants, and theaters of the square and block the streets and sidewalks. Prices in restaurants soar to premiums. A tremendous wave of joviality and good will, in which even the police participate, carries the crowds along. At midnight a lighted globe on the roof of the Times Building falls, and a shout goes up from the square. Boat whistles, tin horns, rattles, and klaxons swell the racket until it can be heard all over the island.

Election night is a milder and less jubilant occasion. On other nights the lights and noise of the Rialto begin to dim at four o'clock (at three on Saturday), the official closing hour for bars. By six, in the gray light of morning, Broadway is momentarily empty of life. Soon the flow of workers begins; and at high noon the sun beats down upon the heads of the first matinee-goers.

Times Square

At the southeast corner of Broadway and Thirty-ninth Street a modern office building marks the SITE OF THE NEW YORK CASINO, the theater that introduced the "Florodora" girls to New York on November 10, 1900. Occupying the entire block across the street behind a rather dingy front of dark buff brick is the Metropolitan Opera House *(see page 322)*. On Broadway at Fortieth Street the old-fashioned lobby of the EMPIRE THEATRE, decorated with portraits of the many stars who played there under Charles Frohman, is a reminder of the years when this stretch of Broadway was the northern outpost of the amusement center. More recent is the building housing the PUBLISHING OFFICES OF THE NEW YORK HERALD TRIBUNE on Forty-first Street near Eighth Avenue. This paper was formed in 1924 by the combination under Ogden Reid of the New York *Herald* and the New York *Tribune*. The latter was founded by Horace Greeley in 1841 several years after he had rejected the offer of James Gordon Bennett to join the *Herald* staff. At Forty-second Street and Broadway is the KNICKERBOCKER BUILDING, formerly the Knickerbocker Hotel, where Enrico Caruso lived and entertained.

The austere, white TIMES BUILDING, erected in 1903 at Forty-second Street and Broadway, now seems an intruder in the area that was named for it. The architects, Eidlitz and MacKenzie, surfaced the tall wedge with glazed terra cotta, designed in an eclectic combination of Gothic and Renaissance details. A weather observatory surmounts the tower. The publishing offices of the paper have moved to Forty-third Street and the building is leased for offices.

At the north end of the building is a newsstand where home-town newspapers may be purchased; and foreign papers are sold at a stand in the subway entrance on the Forty-second Street and Seventh Avenue corner. The Police Department maintains an INFORMATION BOOTH north of the Times Building. Within Times Square proper a traffic fence runs north and south from the booth to Forty-sixth Street, discouraging jaywalkers.

The west side of the square has undergone many changes in recent years. The RIALTO at Forty-second Street, a small movie house and the only one with a separate entrance in the subway, occupies the site of Hammerstein's Victoria Theatre, the leading vaudeville house in the 1900's.

The PARAMOUNT BUILDING, which houses the palatial Paramount Theatre, extends from Forty-third to Forty-fourth Street on the west side of Broadway. Its thirty-five stories rise upon the site of the Putnam Building, in which was Shanley's, a famous restaurant in the early years of the century. The NEW CRITERION THEATER BUILDING between Forty-fourth and Forty-fifth on the east side of the street commands attention because of its showy façade and the sign on its roof, the largest animated sign in the world.

The ASTOR HOTEL, whose French Renaissance façade has been a New York landmark since 1904, occupies the block from Forty-fourth to

SOUTH STREET

MUNICIPAL BUILDING FROM CHATHAM SQUARE EL STATION

CITY HALL

HOLLAND TUNNEL

MANHATTAN BRIDGE ENTRANCE

WEST WASHINGTON POULTRY MARKET

RADIO ROW, CORTLANDT STREET

PATCHIN PLACE, GREENWICH VILLAGE

ST. MARK'S IN-THE-BOUWERIE

BACKYARDS, LOWER EAST SIDE

POLICE HEADQUARTERS

Forty-fifth Street on the west side of the square. Headquarters and convention center of many organizations, from national political parties to beauticians' associations, it has been the scene of many picturesque and significant events.

LOEW'S STATE, north of Forty-fifth Street, is now the only theater in the square regularly presenting vaudeville. The PALACE, at Broadway and Forty-seventh Street, was until recently the nation's leading vaudeville house and headliners like Pat Rooney, Eddie Leonard, Elsie Janis, and Sophie Tucker played two-a-day here. The theater now shows motion pictures. BILLBOARD, a publication devoted to the amusement world, has offices in the building, and the street corner is still a camping ground for minor members of the theatrical profession. Owners and managers of carnival shows also meet there. In the building at 1560 Broadway are the OFFICES OF THE AMERICAN FEDERATION OF ACTORS, a union of variety entertainers.

At the base of a small triangle of pavement at Forty-seventh Street is the bronze STATUE OF THE REVEREND FATHER FRANCIS DUFFY, dressed in his uniform as chaplain of the 69th Regiment (now 165th Infantry). The figure, the work of Charles Keck, stands in front of a granite Celtic cross. Father Duffy, who died in June, 1932, was a familiar character on Broadway. His church was the Holy Cross on Forty-second Street between Eighth and Ninth Avenues.

Broadway North of Forty-seventh Street

North on Broadway a row of low drab buildings becomes at night, when the signs on the roofs light up, an extension of the Rialto. Seventh Avenue with the elaborate supper clubs and dine-and-dance palaces also stretches the white way northward; at Forty-seventh Street is the half-block marquee of LOEW'S MAYFAIR where until 1929 the Columbia "Wheel" (circuit) presented the great comedians of burlesque.

LINDY'S RESTAURANT, a contemporary landmark of black and red, set off by yellow, is at 1626 Broadway. Like the PARADISE, a night club diagonally across the street at Forty-ninth Street, it has acquired a national reputation through the Broadway columnists—Lindy's for the gossip and celebrities, the Paradise for the genuine blue-eyed blondes in the chorus line. JACK DEMPSEY'S BROADWAY BAR, near Forty-ninth Street, is the Churchill's of 1939, a favorite with the sporting crowd. The old Churchill's was near the spot in 1900, as was also Rector's after it had moved out of the square proper.

Built at a cost of more than a million dollars, the STRAND THEATRE, near Forty-eighth Street on the west side of Broadway, claimed the record for opulence when it opened in 1914 with a motion-picture version of Rex Beach's *The Spoilers*. The COTTON CLUB, the former Harlem night club made famous by Duke Ellington and Cab Calloway, is opposite the Strand between Broadway and Seventh Avenue. At about four o'clock every afternoon the swing musicians gather on the west side of Broadway near Forty-eighth Street to gossip and to exchange ideas for new variations in hot music.

The RIVOLI, north of Forty-ninth Street on the east side of Broadway, revolutionized theater architecture when it opened in 1917 with a cooling system and balconies without posts. "Roxy" (S. L. Rothafel), who initiated the lavish presentation of a motion picture, was managing director, a position he held at one time or another at the old Rialto, the Strand, the Capitol, the Roxy, and the Radio City Music Hall.

The WINTER GARDEN, its long marquee still advertising the wares of legitimate show business, is near Forty-ninth Street. The leg-shows once presented here were as famous as any in burlesque. Al Jolson was in the show that opened this theater in 1911, and in 1913 New Yorkers had a foretaste of New Orleans music when the original Creole Band played here.

One block east, at Fiftieth Street and Seventh Avenue, is the CASA MAÑANA, a lavish night club, directed by Billy Rose, creator of stage and outdoor spectacles. Prior to 1935, Earl Carroll's *Vanities* was located here, advertising that "Through These Portals [the stage door] Pass the Most Beautiful Girls in the World." The BRASS RAIL, 745 Seventh Avenue, was opened during Prohibition years as a counter sandwich shop. The restaurant has grown until it occupies four floors with a seating capacity of more than one thousand. The ROXY, Seventh Avenue and Fiftieth Street, is the most elaborate of the first-run motion-picture houses in the Broadway district. The huge oval lobby, highly ornate in its decorations, can accommodate three thousand patrons, about half as many as the auditorium itself. The Roxy opened in 1926, representing an investment of fifteen million dollars.

The dome sign of the CAPITOL on Broadway at Fifty-first Street identifies the first-run house of Metro-Goldwyn-Mayer. On the opposite side of the street is the CONTINENTAL, formerly the Warner, where on October 6, 1927, the sound film was introduced by the *Jazz Singer,* with Al Jolson. At Fifty-first Street on the east side of Broadway is ROSELAND, largest of the dance halls and since the 1920's the downtown headquarters for hot music and such urban dance steps as the cake and collegiate, the Lindy and the Shag.

The BROADWAY TABERNACLE at Fifty-sixth Street was built in 1903. The Gothic structure of brick and terra cotta is dominated by the heavy tower at the rear of the building. A progressive factor in the church life of today, the congregation was an Abolitionist center when it was located downtown a century ago. Nor is this church's preference for a theatrical atmosphere a recent development: "It is but a few years," wrote Asa Greene in 1837 *(A Glance At New York)*, describing its early Chatham Street chapel, "since it was captured from the Arch Enemy; and it still bears evidence of its profane origin: for the boxes, tier above tier, remain precisely as in the days of its theatrical glory; the pit and the stage only being changed into something more of a churchlike appearance."

Side Streets, Forty-second to Fifty-sixth

The depression emphasized the midway side of the Times Square district. Theaters closed one after the other, and contract bridge games, chess tournaments, and side shows occupied the vacant stores and restaurants. Long before, however, the decisive factor of popular support had shifted from dramas and musical plays to motion pictures. Hollywood had taken over the most desirable locations, relegating the legitimate theater business to the side streets. Only two legitimate houses remain on Broadway.

On Forty-second Street west of Broadway, once the show place of the district, famous theaters have been converted into movie "grind" houses devoted to continuous double feature programs or burlesque shows. Among cut-rate haberdasheries, cafeterias, and bus stations are tokens of a not-so-distant past—the photographs of the Ziegfeld *Follies* in the lobby of the New Amsterdam, the exterior of the Republic, and the names above the brightly lighted marquees: Eltinge, Wallack's, Sam H. Harris, Liberty, Times Square, the Selwyn, the Lyric. . . .

Forty-second Street east of Broadway has only one theater, the CAMEO, now used as the American first-run house for Russian films. The hotels and bars of this block have been replaced by office buildings, retail stores, and restaurants. Impressive architecturally is the BUSH TERMINAL SALES BUILDING, designed by Helmle and Corbett in 1917. Thirty-two stories high and only fifty feet wide, the building gives an impression of greater height because of the sheer lines of its unbroken piers. The chamfering at the corners and the treatment at the top are notable as antedating the set-back laws.

On Forty-third Street east of Sixth Avenue at No. 51 was the stage door of the HIPPODROME, the architectural pachyderm of the amusement world. It was built in 1905 by Frederick Thompson and Elmer S. Dundy, who also built Coney Island's Luna Park. For many years theatrical extravaganzas were produced there under the management of Charles B. Dillingham, among whose famous presentations were the diving girls who mystified thousands when they walked down a flight of stairs into a huge tank and slowly disappeared beneath the surface of the water. Tenanted by opera companies, prize fighters, elephants, and chorus girls, the theater has also served as a *jai alai* court where Cuban, Spanish, and Mexican champions gave exhibitions of "the fastest game in the world."

Restaurants and hotels crowd Forty-third Street between Sixth Avenue and Times Square. TOWN HALL, designed in the Georgian Colonial style, was opened in 1921 as a civic concert auditorium. Its weekly radio forums have achieved national importance. A large panel on the front of the building bears the inscription: "You Shall Know the Truth and the Truth Shall Make You Free."

In the quiet block of Forty-third Street west of Times Square the stage doors of the Lyric and other formerly legitimate theaters have a ghostly air. On the north side of the street is the NEW YORK TIMES ANNEX, a white terra-cotta office building where all the publishing activities of the newspaper are carried on. Under the management of Adolph S. Ochs, the dignified and encyclopedic *Times* grew from a daily circulation of 19,000 to 490,000 and took its position as the foremost American newspaper. Distinguished for its foreign news coverage and its superior reliability, the *Times* today is as sedate and exhaustive as it was in the earlier years when Ochs described it as "the sort of paper which no one needs to be ashamed to be seen reading." Guides are provided on application to groups who wish to tour the building.

ASCENSION MEMORIAL CHAPEL, a plain, steeple-less building of dark-red brick, lies in the shadow of modern office buildings on the north side of Forty-third Street near Eighth Avenue. In 1911 the late Reverend Dr. John Floyd Steen told the press: "I now have as regular churchgoers many chorus girls." The interior of the chapel, Colonial in design, may be seen only by special permission.

At Forty-fourth Street the true "west of Broadway" theater area begins It was to these side-street theaters that the legitimate shows retired when they were driven from Times Square itself by the movies. Here, surrounded by medium-price hotels, they seem to have found a more or less permanent sanctuary. The heart of the area is the famous SHUBERT ALLEY which splits the block between Eighth Avenue and Broadway from Forty-fourth to Forty-fifth Street. Here are the executive offices of J. J. and Lee Shubert, who together with their brother, the late Sam Shubert, broke the hold of the theatrical trust headed by Klaw and Erlanger which controlled legitimate theaters throughout the country in the decade 1900–1910. Actors and chorus boys and girls still throng the alley when shows are being cast. Across Forty-fourth Street at No. 234 is SARDI'S RESTAURANT, a favorite of stage stars, writers, and their agents. In the near-by building are the offices of the GROUP THEATRE, founded in 1931. J. Edward Bromberg, Frances Farmer, Clifford Odets, and Franchot Tone have been associated with this theater which represents both a vigorous social outlook and the acting traditions of Stanislavsky.

On Forty-fourth Street east of Times Square a marquee with hanging lanterns extends across the front of the BELASCO THEATRE where David Warfield appeared in 1907 in *A Grand Army Man*. Belasco of the clerical collar and white hair lived in a magnificently furnished apartment above the theater.

At 128 West Forty-fourth Street is the LAMBS CLUB, a select actors' club known widely for its private and public shows, the *Gambols*.

The HOTEL ALGONQUIN, associated with the theatrical and literary life of the city, is east of Sixth Avenue on Forty-fourth Street. Under the management of Frank Case this French Renaissance structure has served as headquarters for the Round Table, the Thanatopsis and Literary Inside Straight Clubs, and the Forty-fourth Street Chowder and Marching Club. A tiny annex to the Hotel Iroquois, farther east in the same block, is maintained by the TWELFTH NIGHT CLUB, which admits visitors only by special permission. The parlor walls are crowded with signed photographs of such distinguished persons as Booth, Modjeska, John Drew, Daniel Frohman, and Lily Langtry.

The block between Fifth and Sixth Avenues is crowded with landmarks. The CITY CLUB is at No. 57; at No. 42 the BAR ASSOCIATION OF THE CITY OF NEW YORK, with a law library of more than two hundred thousand volumes, occupies a heavy classical building. The façade of the NEW YORK YACHT CLUB at No. 37 is highly characteristic of the work of the Parisian Beaux Arts Academy at the turn of the century. The façade, frankly treated as a piece of sculpture, is carved to symbolize yachting. Three curious bay windows represent the sterns of eighteenth-century sailing ships, complete with waves and dolphins.

The HARVARD CLUB at No. 27 is in Colonial red brick, designed after the early American buildings of the college itself. But what is probably the oldest organization in the block is the GENERAL SOCIETY OF MECHANICS AND TRADESMEN OF THE CITY OF NEW YORK in an undistinguished building at No. 20. The society was founded in 1785.

Forty-fifth Street west of Broadway has been called the "street of hits," because of the many long-run shows in its theaters. The MARTIN BECK THEATRE is the newest and most impressive of the numerous legitimate theaters on this street. Beck's business is the theater; his hobby, painting. Van Dyck's *Samson et Delilah* hangs in the lobby. The old-fashioned LYCEUM THEATRE east of Broadway was put up for Daniel Frohman. He maintains an apartment in the building, reached by an elevator which barely admits his tall spare body.

The polished brass, white paint, and evergreen shrubs of "DINTY" MOORE'S, as famous for its Broadway celebrities as for its corned beef and cabbage, front on Forty-sixth Street west of Times Square. Farther up the street is the CHURCH OF ST. MARY THE VIRGIN where the rites of the Anglican Communion are observed. At No. 154 are the offices of VARIETY, trade paper of show business, known to the public chiefly for its peculiar jargon. Typical of this writing is the headline, "Stix Nix Hick Pix," once used to designate a crisis in the film industry.

The ACTORS EQUITY ASSOCIATION, affiliated with the American Federation of Labor, and the first union organization in the American legitimate theater, maintains headquarters at 45 West Forty-seventh Street, east of Sixth Avenue. In 1919 when Frank Bacon led his company out, during Equity's struggle for the Equity shop, the newspapers headlined it: "Lightnin' Has Struck!" It was at the BILTMORE THEATRE on Forty-seventh Street that the first living newspaper, *Triple-A Plowed Under,* had its premiere under the auspices of the WPA Federal Theatre Project.

On Forty-eighth Street west of Times Square are three theaters. The UNION METHODIST EPISCOPAL CHURCH, midway in the block, dates from 1894. Civic, social, and union meetings are frequently held here and the church has an attic theater. The name Actors' Church was given to it in 1920–21 when the Professional Children's School had quarters in the building. During the depression unemployed actors and actresses were fed in the basement restaurant.

In the block west of Broadway on Forty-ninth Street is ST. MALACHY'S CHURCH (Roman Catholic), whose chapel was one of the first in the country for actors. At Forty-ninth Street and Eighth Avenue is the new Madison Square Garden *(see page 330),* which extends up to Fiftieth Street and midway to Ninth Avenue. Gymnasiums, managers' offices, and the bars and restaurants of the sporting crowd—Jack Dempsey's, Mickey Walker's, Jack Sharkey's—cluster around the Garden.

On the northwest corner of Sixth Avenue and Fiftieth Street, a plain office building houses LOCAL 802, AMERICAN FEDERATION OF MUSICIANS, whose 25,000 members represent every phase of the city's musical life.

Fifty-second Street gained some prominence in the 1920's when the THEATRE GUILD set up house near Eighth Avenue. The Theatre Guild, formerly the Washington Square Players, moved uptown under the present name in 1919 when Otto Kahn leased them the old Garrick on Thirty-fifth Street for a nominal rental. The present theater, Florentine in character, was built in 1925 from plans by C. Howard Crane, Kenneth Franzheim, and Charles H. Bettis in consultation with Norman Bel Geddes and Lee Simonson, stage designers. An invigorating force, the Guild has produced plays by known and unknown dramatists, and some of the finest acting talent in the contemporary theater has appeared in them.

The long block of Fifty-second Street lying in the shadow of Rockefeller Center *(see page 333)* between Fifth and Sixth Avenues has won recent renown for its night clubs. This block is the swingman's Rialto and the source of much of the gossip of columnists and radio commentators. At No. 72 is the LITTLE CLUB at the address of the original Onyx Club, already famous for its jam sessions during the Prohibition era. "I'd rather drink muddy water, Lord, sleep in a hollow log," Jack Teagarden sang here, "than be up here in New York treated like a dirty dog." The FAMOUS DOOR, with its glass brick vestibule, is at No. 66. At No. 62 is the black and white of the ONYX. Out-of-towners favor LEON AND EDDIE'S where Eddie packs them in with his shady ballads. The TWENTY-ONE CLUB, behind the grilled fence of the old Hockstader estate, and TONY'S, a once famous speakeasy, are culinary high spots where celebrities go to see and be seen. The HICKORY HOUSE, noted for swing music and steaks, is west of Sixth Avenue.

The MANHATTAN STORAGE WAREHOUSE extends from Fifty-second to Fifty-third Street, fronting on Seventh Avenue. The plain brick building, designed by McKim, Mead, and White, is undecorated save for the fortress-like machicolations at the top. The new ROCKEFELLER APARTMENTS, built in 1936 from designs by Harrison and Fouilhoux, run through the block from Fifty-fourth to Fifty-fifth Street between Fifth and Sixth Avenues. For decoration the architects have relied upon the interesting shapes of circular dining-bays and upon the play of light on many surfaces of glass. Despite the juxtaposition of windows differing in height, the buildings are distinguished for their simplicity and clarity of design.

At the corner of Sixth Avenue and Fifty-fourth Street is the ZIEGFELD THEATRE, the bulging limestone of its façade intended to suggest a proscenium arch. The theater was designed by Joseph Urban. Built for the *Follies,* it is now a regular theater.

The GRAND STREET BOYS ASSOCIATION, on Fifty-fifth Street west of Sixth Avenue, sponsors many civic and philanthropic activities, and claims many famous New Yorkers in its membership. MECCA TEMPLE, the largest

Masonic Shrine in the city, is at 135 West Fifty-fifth Street. The mosque-like façade is framed with shallow-arched recesses in blue, green, and orange mosaic. The hall itself, which seats 3,500, is crowned by a tiled dome surmounted by the Scimitar and Crescent.

Columbus Circle

Broadway enters Columbus Circle at Fifty-eighth Street, crossing it diagonally. The GENERAL MOTORS BUILDING towers above the Circle taking up the entire block on the west side of Broadway between Fifty-seventh and Fifty-eighth Streets. It was designed by Shreve and Lamb and completed in 1928; it includes the original three-story Colonnade Building. The structure, with its simple piers, has a directness of expression evident in few commercial buildings.

The imitation Corinthian pillars above the dime store on Eighth Avenue, opposite the General Motors Building, recall Reisenweber's Restaurant, which brought the cover charge and the Original Dixieland Jazz Band to Broadway in 1916.

At the center of the Circle is a seventy-seven foot granite column supporting a marble STATUE OF COLUMBUS, completed by Gaetano Russo in 1894. Three bronze ships' prows, representing the ships in Columbus' fleet, ornament the shaft, and before the pedestal is the figure of a winged youth, studying a terrestrial globe. Until the United States entered the World War, Times Square was the scene of many outdoor forums. When the square became too crowded these activities shifted northward; now in the open space below the monument impromptu discussions are held and groups listen to oratory on every conceivable subject from Thomas Paine and the *Age of Reason* to the advantages of a vegetable diet. At night advertising signs on the near-by buildings light the scene.

Columbus Circle gives an impression of monuments and space, the expanse of Central Park *(see page 350)* spreading north and east beyond the Merchant's Gate, with towering apartment hotels on Central Park West, and Broadway—the old Bloomingdale Road—stretching north. Boomed for a time as an outpost of Times Square, the Circle gradually took on a somewhat abandoned appearance. The western arc of the Circle is dominated by a huge old-fashioned theater, originally the Majestic, now called the Park and showing motion pictures. Beside this theater stood Pabst's Grand Circle, a prewar restaurant famed for its free lunch, orchestra, and oyster bar.

The MERCHANT'S GATE to Central Park is an imposing pylon of marble, set between two roadways flanked by smaller pylons. The center pylon serves as a background for the heroic bronze and marble of the

MAINE MEMORIAL, unveiled in 1912 in honor of those who lost their lives on the battleship *Maine*. In the basin, where neighborhood children duck for pennies in summer, figures grouped on the prow of a wooden battleship symbolize Courage awaiting the Flight of Peace, the Feeble supported by Fortitude, and the Atlantic and the Pacific coasts. The whole is topped by a robed figure of Columbia Triumphant, riding in a shell drawn by three sea horses. Members of the City Art Commission were forced to come to the defense of Attilio Piccirilli's sculptural group when a high wind ripped the burlap off before the official unveiling and artists living near by questioned its artistic merit.

Middle and Upper East Side

GASHOUSE DISTRICT—STUYVESANT SQUARE
DISTRICT—GRAMERCY PARK DISTRICT—
UNION SQUARE DISTRICT—MADISON
SQUARE DISTRICT—KIP'S BAY AND TURTLE
BAY—MURRAY HILL—FIFTH AVENUE
SHOPPING DISTRICT—GRAND CENTRAL DIS-
TRICT—BEEKMAN PLACE AND SUTTON
PLACE—CENTRAL PARK SOUTH, THE
PLAZA, AND FIFTY-SEVENTH STREET—UPPER
FIFTH, MADISON, AND PARK AVENUES—
YORKVILLE

Area: 14th St. on the south to 96th St. on the north; from 6th Ave. (14th to 42d
St.) and 5th Ave. (42d to 96th St.) east to East River. Maps on pages 54-55, 193,
and 237.
Principal north-south streets: 5th, Madison, 4th, Park, Lexington, 3d, 2d, and
1st Aves.
Principal cross streets: 14th, 23d, 34th, 42d, 57th, 59th, 72d, 86th, and 96th Sts.
Transportation: IRT Lexington Avenue subway (local), 14th to 96th St. stations;
3d Ave. el, 14th to 96th St. stations; BMT Broadway subway (local), Union
Square to 34th St. stations; bus lines on all principal north-south and cross
streets.

IN THE Middle and Upper East Side, virtually every facet of cosmopolitan life is represented in famous hotels, churches, clubs, department stores,
shops, skyscrapers, apartment houses, and amusement centers.

Perhaps the contrast between wealth and poverty is more heightened in the Middle and Upper East Side than in other parts of the city. The Gashouse District on the East River front above Fourteenth Street, for example, has been a slum area since the 1840's, while Stuyvesant Square, adjoining on the west, has maintained a middle-class calm which is accentuated by the presence of several hospitals. Slightly farther to the west, the children of exclusive Gramercy Park play behind a high fence that is locked against the public. South and west of this lies the popular low-price shopping center of Fourteenth Street, from Union Square to Sixth Avenue. Union Square itself is used as a rallying point by New York's labor and radical organizations.

As in all Manhattan, the narrow cross streets of this district are cut by broad avenues. Broadway, coming in from the south, shoots north and west from Union Square, crossing Fifth Avenue at Twenty-third Street, where the Flatiron Building looks down upon the tangled traffic of Madison Square. Broadway leaves the district at Thirty-fourth Street, having contributed few reminders of its lurid past in the 1880's.

Above Twenty-third Street the land begins to rise and reaches a summit between Thirty-second and Forty-second Streets, where Murray Hill, once a center of large private residences, now rears its sky line of expensive apartment buildings.

The Fifth Avenue shopping district also begins in Murray Hill. It is paralleled on the east by Madison Avenue, lined with shops specializing in men's wear and interior decoration, and by wealthy Park Avenue, a continuation of Fourth Avenue. Impressive skyscraper hotels, Rockefeller Center, and a number of fashionable churches, such as St. Patrick's and St. Thomas, stand in this mid-town area. On and near Fifty-seventh Street are gathered many of the art galleries that make Manhattan the art center of the country. North of its intersection with Central Park South (Fifty-ninth Street) at Grand Army Plaza, Fifth Avenue still retains a few of the millionaires' villas and castles that faced the park before the apartment house boom. In fact, there are more single-family residences in the neighborhood of upper Fifth, Madison, and Park Avenues than remain in any other part of Manhattan.

The eastern flank of this entire mid-town section is of less prepossessing character. Along the East River, north of the Gashouse District, the Kip's Bay-Turtle Bay neighborhood presents a welter of depressing tenements and small stores that follows the shore to Forty-eighth Street, breaks west around the low bluff of small, opulent Beekman Place and Sutton Place, and then turns north again to Fifty-ninth Street. Forty-second

Street, with its clean-lined News Building, injects almost the only distinctive element in this strip; at the end of the street the tall apartment buildings of Tudor City surround large gardens.

The region east of Third Avenue between Sixtieth and Ninety-sixth Streets is known as Yorkville, a crowded section of tenements and brownstone houses, invested with a diluted Old World flavor by people from Middle Europe. Also in Yorkville, beside the East River between Sixty-third and Seventy-first Streets, are the Rockefeller Institute for Medical Research and the New York Hospital and Cornell University Medical College.

In the seventeenth century, the estate of Peter Stuyvesant extended into the southern part of this section, the region now known as Stuyvesant Square. Gramercy Park was a swamp. Along the East River shore the area that is now the East Thirties was the property of Jacob Kip, while the East Fifties was the Spring Valley Farm.

In pre-Revolutionary days the Eastern (later called Boston) Post Road ran north from the Bowery past what is now Union Square, crossed the Madison Square region diagonally to Fourth Avenue and Twenty-eighth Street, and there branched into two roads. The east one, bound for Boston, followed irregular Indian trails, crossing the intersection of present-day Park Avenue at Eighty-second Street and continuing north to a junction with Kingsbridge Road near Ninety-first Street. The western branch, called Middle Road, in 1811 became Fifth Avenue. A road known only as Cross Road connected the two thoroughfares in the neighborhood of what is now Forty-second Street. There were two "kissing bridges" across Saw Mill Creek (or Saw Kill) at Fifty-second and Seventy-seventh Streets, on which gentlemen were privileged to salute chastely the ladies in their company.

The Quaker Robert Murray held title to almost all of Murray Hill. In 1776, the fleeing Continentals streamed up this way after the British landed on Manhattan, and it was at the Murray mansion (Thirty-seventh Street and Park Avenue) that Mary Lindley Murray detained General Howe for tea while Putnam's army made good its escape. British frigates were stationed in near-by Kip's Bay for the duration of the war. After the evacuation of the British in 1783, the Common Council voted to have the Murray Hill region surveyed and divided into lots for sale by the acre, and as the nineteenth century began, this section took its place alongside Bloomingdale and Harlem as an area for summer homes and country estates. Jones' Wood, part of an estate that extended from Sixty-sixth to

Seventy-fifth Street, was owned prior to 1803 by Samuel Provoost, the first Protestant Episcopal bishop of New York.

In 1834 the village of Yorkville, which then occupied the territory on the Boston Post Road in the middle Eighties, was brought within commuting distance of the city by the partial completion of the Harlem Railroad. Its engines chugged (or, when the boilers had blown up and demolished the engines, its horses galloped) from Prince Street, along the Bowery and what is now Park Avenue, to Yorkville and later to Harlem, through miles of rocky wasteland overrun by pigs and goats. There, after 1850, unemployed Irish immigrants squatted in great numbers, picking up a hand-to-mouth existence in wretched hovels by milking the goats and salvaging coal out of the ashes dumped by the railway engines.

When Commodore Vanderbilt erected the Grand Central Depot at Forty-second Street in 1871, it was considerably north of the center of the city. But Manhattan was growing rapidly if irregularly. Businesses requiring water transportation (brick, stone, and lumberyards; factories, and machine shops) were first established on the river front. Soon the adjacent streets inland were filled with tenements for workmen and their families. Then, the leading avenues on each side of town, such as Third and Eighth Avenues, became great marts, selling the necessities of life to the workmen. Lastly, in the center of town, shifting occasionally, but in general taking the same northward trend, came the four-story brownstones of the well-to-do.

The development of the mid-town came to a standstill during the Civil War. On Saturday, July 11, 1863, the opening of the first conscription office on the corner of Forty-sixth Street and Third Avenue precipitated the famous Draft Riots among the impoverished residents of the neighborhood, who resented the ease with which more fortunate conscripts could buy exemption.

Postwar prosperity set the stone masons to working again. The buildings they created, though substantial enough, showed a singular lack of imagination. Mrs. Trollope in her *Domestic Manners of the Americans,* published in 1832, said, "The great defect in the houses [of New York] is their uniformity—when you have seen one, you have seen all." This was equally true of subsequent decades. Builders were contractors, and journeymen were underpaid handymen. The brownstone fronts, which appeared by the hundred in the last half of the century, may still be seen on nearly all the side streets of mid-town Manhattan, but the cast-iron fronts which were greatly in vogue for the business buildings clustering around Union Square and its environs in the 1860's, '70's, and '80's have now vanished almost entirely.

Fifth Avenue during these decades saw building on a scale of elaborate grandeur never before known in the city. In the early 1880's the brownstone tradition was broken by a desire for French chateaux. The frenzied search for art works, for the epidermis and entrails of medieval castles and cathedrals, made it difficult to tell a fashionable mansion from a museum. By the 1900's commerce had crept up lower Fifth Avenue largely in stores disguised as baronial dwellings, country villas, and medieval castles.

The Squatter Town where some five thousand people were said to have lived in the 1880's, extended up Park Avenue (so named in 1888) and upper Fifth Avenue as far as Mt. Morris Park (120th St.). The squatters yielded gradually to the steam shovel, a new tool which made it profitable to level the rocky terrain for building sites. The opening of the Third Avenue elevated in 1878 also effected a change. With the electrification and roofing over of the New York Central tracks, which ran along Park Avenue, in the first decade of the present century, the boulevard was ready to become the new home of the Fifth Avenue residents driven out by the intrusion of commerce. Land had become so valuable, however, and transportation between the city and the suburbs so swift—owing in part to the development of the automobile—that large town houses went out of favor. Many of the new Park Avenue buildings were luxurious apartment houses, whose managerial staffs assumed some of the responsibilities of housekeeping.

The eastern fringe of this entire section will undergo drastic changes in the near future, when the Queens Midtown Tunnel, and the East River Drive are completed. By 1941 the water front will be beautified by the projected East River Drive, part of a continuous express highway around the edge of Manhattan, which will pick up traffic from the West Side Highway at the Battery and route it to South Street and through Corlears Hook Park and then along the river. By widening existing streets, cutting new ones, and building highways where necessary, the Drive will be extended up the irregular water front to the Triborough Bridge, and beyond to the Harlem River Driveway, in order to connect by means of tunnels with the George Washington Bridge and the Henry Hudson Parkway. As on the West Side, this program includes an extensive parkway development, with appropriate landscaping and recreational facilities. With this development may come demolition of slum tenements and construction of riverside apartments similar to Tudor City and Beekman Place.

GASHOUSE DISTRICT

Area: 14th St. on the south to 27th St. on the north; from 1st Ave. (14th to 18th St.), 3d Ave. (18th to 23d St.), and 4th Ave. (23d to 27th St.) east to East River. Map on page 193.

The "gashouse district" today is largely a reminiscent term. Though four large tanks still rise near the East River, their domination of the neighborhood is passing, and the notorious gashouse gangs have gone. The area now is a drab extension of the Lower East Side, a district of ". . . powerful ugliness and devastation . . . with its wasteland rusts and rubbish, its slum-like streets of rickety tenement and shabby brick, its vast raw thrust of tank, glazed glass and factory building . . . lifted by a powerful rude exultancy of light and sky and sweep and water such as is found only in America." So Thomas Wolfe remembered this neighborhood, particularly that part near the East River.

The first of these great gashouses was raised in 1842 at the foot of East Twenty-first Street; and before long a cluster of giant structures, the skyscrapers of their day, overshadowed the landscape. "Their tracery of iron, against an occasional clear lemon-green sky at sunrise," writes Lewis Mumford, "was one of the most pleasant aesthetic elements in the new order."

Another element in the new order, however, was its disregard for human comfort and health. Gas, leaking from the tanks, made the neighborhood a pesthole. Only the poorest families—at first predominantly Irish, later joined by Germans and Jews—could be drawn into the district, and flimsy tenements were built to accommodate them. The young men reared in this slum environment formed gangs that terrorized the Gashouse district for half a century. In their lighter moments they organized courageous volunteer fire companies and dallied with "the girls with the swinging handbags" who inspired the song, the *Belle of Avenoo A.*

One of the original plants—now called the O'CONNELL PLANT in honor of an employee of seventy-two years service—is still standing, though bigger units have been built in other parts of the city. Slovaks and other East Europeans have largely replaced the earlier settlers. Although old-law tenements are still in the majority and the public baths at Avenue A and Twenty-third Street are still the only bathing facilities available to many, an increasing number of modern apartment houses are being erected and many of the more substantial older buildings are being renovated.

This district, like the adjoining Stuyvesant Square *(see page 189),* contains many important hospitals. WILLARD PARKER HOSPITAL for contagious diseases, at the foot of East Sixteenth Street, has made several contributions to medical science, including the now universally accepted suction treatment for diphtheria. COLUMBUS HOSPITAL, 227 East Nineteenth Street, is patronized largely by Italians. At 303 East Twentieth Street is NEW YORK POST-GRADUATE MEDICAL SCHOOL AND HOSPITAL, affording study to physicians in the latest medical practices; its NEW YORK SKIN AND CANCER UNIT, 301 East Nineteenth Street, ranks among the foremost in the country. The hospital and shelter of the AMERICAN SOCIETY FOR THE PREVENTION OF CRUELTY TO ANIMALS has quarters at Avenue A and Twenty-fourth Street.

Twenty-fourth Street, between Second and Lexington Avenues, is known as "OLD STABLE ROW." Here, before the advent of the automobile, a horse mart flourished. The street was littered with straw, oats, and manure. On auction days, the strength of draft horses was demonstrated by hitching the animals to wagons with locked wheels and then whipping them up the block and back. Only two stables remain, along with H. KAUFFMAN AND SONS SADDLERY COMPANY, at No. 139, where the tiny coach of General Tom Thumb, P. T. Barnum's famous dwarf, is exhibited.

At 432 East Twenty-fifth Street is the MUNICIPAL LODGING HOUSE, established in 1908 to accommodate homeless men. It has a capacity of 2,500. The covered pier at the foot of East Twenty-fifth Street serves as an annex. Here are the dining room, where three free meals are served daily; two recreation rooms; and facilities for washing and drying clothes.

The 165TH REGIMENT INFANTRY ARMORY, headquarters of the former "Fighting 69th," fronts on Lexington Avenue between Twenty-fifth and Twenty-sixth Streets. This regiment draws its recruits from the neighborhood. It carried through the World War a distinguished tradition begun in the Civil and Mexican wars. A statue to its noted World War chaplain, Father Duffy, stands in Times Square *(see page 173)*.

Since 1915 Butler Davenport has operated a small THEATER at 138 East Twenty-seventh Street. Productions of Molière, Racine, Maugham, and Galsworthy have been given. General admission is free, and only the few reserved seats are paid for.

Many of Manhattan's ten thousand Armenians—one of the largest groups in the country—live in the upper Twenties, between First and Lexington Avenues. At 221 East Twenty-seventh Street is ST. ILLUMINATOR'S ARMENIAN APOSTOLIC CHURCH, American see for Armenian Gregorian Catholics. This section of Lexington Avenue has a number of

Near Eastern restaurants, serving dishes such as *shish kebab* (skewered lamb), *pilaff* (steamed rice), stuffed grape leaves, and Armenian wines and spirits.

STUYVESANT SQUARE DISTRICT

Area: 14th St. on the south to 18th St. on the north; from 1st Ave. west to 3d Ave. Map on page 193.

Staid old Stuyvesant Square, although its neighborhood has changed drastically, is still the quiet park it was in its opulent days of the 1860's. It was originally part of the farm owned by "Pegleg" Peter Stuyvesant and the Dutch were most numerous in the section until 1700. The Germans and Irish came during the last half of the nineteenth century, to be followed later by Italians, Jews, and Slavs. In the early 1900's it was the bailiwick of Charles F. Murphy, Tammany chieftain and overlord of the adjoining gashouse district.

The pleasant four-acre park, bisected by Second Avenue, is landscaped with elms, catalpas, ginkgos, sycamores, hawthornes, and ailanthuses. Walks follow the pattern of two elongated ellipses. In the center of each half is a small flower-bordered pool.

Bordering the park are several hospitals: the WILLIAM BOOTH MEMORIAL HOSPITAL of the Salvation Army, 314 East Fifteenth Street; BETH ISRAEL, Stuyvesant Park East; MANHATTAN GENERAL, 307 Second Avenue; ST. ANDREW'S CONVALESCENT HOSPITAL, 237 East Seventeenth Street; and NEW YORK INFIRMARY FOR WOMEN AND CHILDREN, 321 East Fifteenth Street. The infirmary, staffed entirely by women, was founded in the early 1850's by Dr. Elizabeth Blackwell, pioneer woman physician. At Second Avenue and Fifteenth Street is the CONVENT OF THE LITTLE SISTERS OF THE ASSUMPTION, a nursing order. From 1902 until 1928 the Lying-In Hospital, now a part of New York Hospital *(see page 247),* occupied a building on Second Avenue between Seventeenth and Eighteenth Streets. Doctors occupy many of the brownstones facing the park. In early days unscrupulous midwives and medical quacks had their quarters in this vicinity, conducting a lucrative business among gullible immigrants.

Wedged between weathered brownstones is the GERMAN MASONIC TEMPLE, 220 East Fifteenth Street, a building of blue-gray cast stone designed in neoclassical style.

Rutherford Place, the west side of the square, long associated with the

Society of Friends, retains its peaceful character. In the FRIENDS MEETING HOUSE, between Fifteenth and Sixteenth Streets, monthly meetings are held, and at Easter, large sectional and national gatherings; in the adjacent FRIENDS' SEMINARY, a private school, with courses from kindergarten through college preparatory, is conducted. To obtain quiet for their annual meetings, the Friends used to spread tanbark, six inches deep, in the streets to muffle the noise of horses' hoofs. A granite hitching post that once stood in front of William Penn's home in Philadelphia is at the southeast corner of the house.

The charmingly simple buildings, constructed in 1860, are reminiscent of the post-Colonial style. The two-story meeting house, at the south end, is of red brick, trimmed with gray sandstone lintels. The details—the wide cornice of simple Greek profile, the broken pediment with louvred segmental openings in the tympanum, the high window frames, the wooden porch of slender Doric columns—are painted white. The seminary, a two-story building with a three-story extension, is of similar design.

At the northwest corner of Sixteenth Street is the ivy-covered ST. GEORGE'S CHURCH (Protestant Episcopal). It was erected in 1847. A fire gutted the structure in 1865, but it was rebuilt two years later according to the original plans of Blesch and Eidlitz. The pleasant brownstone building is highly eclectic in style, with its northern French Romanesque, two-towered façade, its heavy, unnecessary buttresses that belie the English timber roof within, its basilica-like plan with French Gothic *chevet* in place of the circular apse, and its Renaissance balconies. Dr. Tyng, the rector at the time the church was rebuilt, insisted that the effect of the interior should be evangelical, and this tradition has always been maintained: in place of the usual altar and reredos there is a simple table; on the west wall of the vaulted chancel the Lord's Prayer is printed in large plain lettering. Adjoining the church on the north is the Centennial chapel, designed in a modified Byzantine Romanesque style by M. L. and H. G. Emery. To the west is the dignified and well-composed parish house, by Eidlitz. St. George's was originally a Chapel of Ease of Trinity Church, but in 1811 its connection with the latter was severed. When J. P. Morgan the elder was senior warden the church was sometimes known as "Morgan's Church."

One door north of St. George's Chapel is ST. DUNSTAN'S HOUSE, a rest house and city headquarters of Old Catholics, a monastic sect. Its two-story porch in Italian Renaissance style has a frieze of garlands and Della Robbia cupids. Among the sect's treasures are a fourteenth-century

statue of St. Francis, an Italian Bible of 1477, and part of the original
English Coverdale Bible. Chapel and reception walls contain tiles from
Glastonbury Abbey in England.

The UNITED HOMING PIGEON CONCOURSE, one of the largest racing
pigeon organizations in the city, meets at Teutonia Restaurant, Third Avenue near Sixteenth Street, a block west of the square. A block north is
the GERMAN-AMERICAN RATHSKELLER, known in riper days as Scheffel
Hall and later as Allaire's. Many noted writers quaffed its foaming pilsener,
among them James Huneker, H. C. Bunner, Bayard Taylor, and Brander
Matthews. O. Henry called the place *Rheinschlossen* and wrote some of
his best stories in the old taproom. Taylor and Oliver Herford lived near
by on Eighteenth Street, while Bunner and Matthews had quarters with
other writers at 330 East Seventeenth Street, an early apartment house.

GRAMERCY PARK DISTRICT

Area: 18th St. on the south to 23d St. on the north; from 3d Ave. west to 4th Ave.
Map on page 193.

The "golden keys" to Gramercy Park, symbol of the exclusiveness
guaranteed by a real-estate operator about a century ago, are still required
to open the gate to New York's most important privately owned park.
A forbidding eight-foot iron fence encloses this oblong tract two blocks
square that is "forever" locked to the public.

The park's creator, Samuel B. Ruggles, was among the first of New
York's early real-estate operators to offer for sale a development with
building restrictions. He caught the fancy of the rich by guaranteeing to
a selected group—those who bought his property—the exclusive use of a
private park as a permanent privilege. Keys—no longer golden—to the
iron gates are distributed to owners and tenants under the close scrutiny
of the trustees of Gramercy Park. Residents in near-by streets who have
been approved by the trustees are given keys for annual fees. All others
must be satisfied with a glimpse through the gate.

The Dutch named the locality *Krom Moerasje,* meaning "little crooked
swamp," which also designated the brook that used to twist from Madison
Square to the East River near Eighteenth Street. Later, in 1692, the section
was called Crommashie Hill. By the usual process of corruption the name
became Gramercy.

Gramercy Park was a marsh in 1831 when Ruggles drained it, laid out
the green and the streets on the model of an English square and offered

KEY TO MIDDLE EAST SIDE MAP

UNION SQUARE DISTRICT

1. Lincoln Building
2. Amalgamated Bank Building
3. Bank of Manhattan Company
4. Union Building
5. Hartford Building
6. Statue of Abraham Lincoln
7. Liberty Pole
8. Statue of Lafayette
9. Statue of George Washington
10. Luchow's
11. Site of old Academy of Music
    Consolidated Edison Building
12. Irving Place Theater
13. Tammany Hall

STUYVESANT SQUARE DISTRICT

14. United Homing Pigeon Concourse
15. Scheffel Hall
16. St. Andrew's Hospital
17. Manhattan General Hospital
18. St. Dunstan's House
19. St. George's Church
20. Friends Seminary
21. Friends Meeting House
22. German Masonic Temple
23. Convent of the Little Sisters of the Assumption
24. William Booth Hospital
25. New York Infirmary for Women and Children
26. Beth Israel Hospital

GASHOUSE DISTRICT

27. Willard Parker Hospital
28. Columbus Hospital
29. New York Skin and Cancer Unit
30. New York Post-Graduate Medical School and Hospital
31. American Society for the Prevention of Cruelty to Animals (Hospital and Shelter)
32. Municipal Lodging House
33. St. Illuminator's Armenian Apostolic Church
34. Davenport Theater
35. "Fighting Sixty-ninth" Armory (165th Regiment Infantry)
36. Old Stable Row

GRAMERCY PARK DISTRICT

37. City College (School of Civic Administration and Business)
38. Children's Court
39. Home of Peter Cooper
40. Statue of Edwin Booth
41. Friends' Meeting House
42. 112 East 19th Street Building
43. The Players
44. National Arts Club
45. Netherland Club
46. Calvary Episcopal Church
47. Russell Sage Foundation
    New York School of Social Work
48. Madison Square Station, New York Post Office
49. United Charities Building

MADISON SQUARE DISTRICT

50. Theodore Roosevelt House
51. 900 Broadway Office Building
52. Flatiron Building
53. Site of old Fifth Avenue Hotel, Franconi's Hippodrome, and Madison Cottage

Continued on Page 194

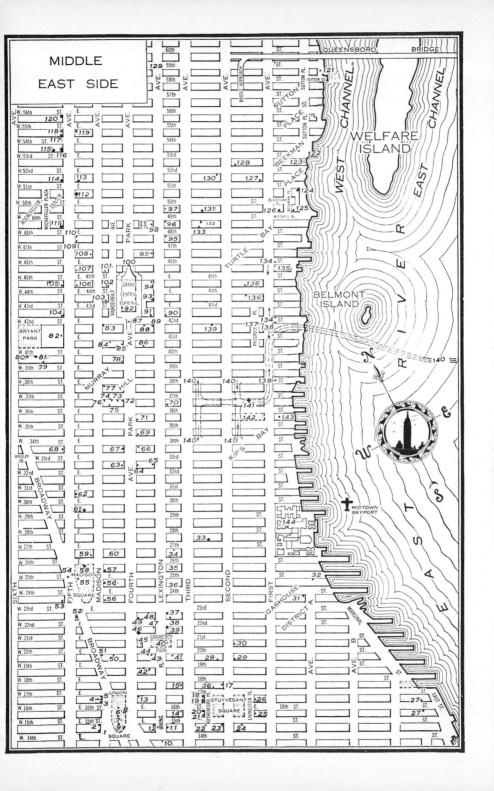

Continued from Page 192

54. Memorial to General William Jenkins Worth
55. Eternal Light
56. Metropolitan Life Insurance Building
57. Building of the Supreme Court Appellate Division
58. Statue of Admiral Farragut
59. American Society for the Prevention of Cruelty to Animals (Offices)
60. New York Life Building Site of old Madison Square Garden

MURRAY HILL AND GRAND CENTRAL DISTRICT

61. Little Church Around the Corner (Church of the Transfiguration)
62. Textile Building
63. Two Park Avenue Building
64. One Park Avenue Building
65. Furniture Exchange Building
66. Seventy-first Infantry Armory
67. Vanderbilt Hotel
68. Empire State Building
69. Residence of Mrs. Robert Bacon
70. Amherst Club
71. Advertising Club
72. Union League Club
73. Dartmouth College Club
74. Williams Club
75. Morgan Library
76. J. P. Morgan Home
77. Midston House
78. Princeton Club
79. Engineering Societies Building
80. National Republican Club
81. Engineers' Club
82. New York Public Library (Central Building)
83. Lincoln Building
84. Chemists' Club
85. Murray Hill Hotel
86. Architectural League
87. New York City Information Center (Pershing Square)
88. Bowery Savings Bank Building
89. Chanin Building
90. Chrysler Building
91. Hotel Commodore
92. Grand Central Terminal
93. Graybar Building
94. Grand Central Station, New York Post Office
95. Lexington Hotel
96. Shelton Hotel
97. Belmont Plaza Hotel
98. Barclay Hotel
99. Grand Central Palace
100. New York Central Building
101. Hotel Roosevelt
102. Yale Club
103. Hotel Biltmore

FIFTH AVENUE SHOPPING DISTRICT

104. 500 Fifth Avenue Building
105. Fifth Avenue Bank Building
106. Ruppert Building
107. Fred F. French Building
108. Hotel Ritz-Carlton
109. Finley J. Shepard Home
110. Robert W. Goelet Home
111. Collegiate Church of St. Nicholas
112. St. Patrick's Cathedral
113. Grand Central Galleries
114. Cornelius Vanderbilt III Home
115. Museum of Modern Art
116. St. Thomas Church
117. University Club
118. Hotel Gotham
119. Hotel St. Regis
120. Steuben Glass Co. Building

sixty-six lots for sale. The privacy of Gramercy Park was violated only once, when troops encamped within this sacrosanct area during the Draft Riots in 1863. In 1890 the State Legislature passed a bill embodying plans for bisecting the square by the extension of a cable car line down Lexington Avenue, but it was vetoed by Governor David B. Hill. Again in 1912 the park was threatened by a proposal to extend Irving Place northward into Lexington Avenue; the Gramercy Park Association, however, defeated the plan, as it has defeated many such threats to the neighborhood's quiet.

While skyscrapers in adjacent streets and tall apartment houses, erected recently on the north and east sides of the park, cast shadows over the sunlit patch of greenery, a majority of the square's houses, built in the nineteenth century, remain outwardly unchanged although remodeled into apartments. On Gramercy Park West is an old row of prim red-brick houses enlivened by some lacy wrought-iron entrance porches, and on the south, a group of staid brownstone and brick dwellings stands firmly against time. The rooms are spacious; windows often reach from floor to ceiling. In many of the cellars the silver and plate vaults—felt-lined rooms with ponderous iron doors—remain intact.

Well-known families lived in Gramercy Park and they entertained notable visitors. At 1 Gramercy Park West, Dr. Valentine Mott, a distinguished physician, played host to the Comte de Paris during the Civil War. (House numbers begin at Gramercy Park West and East Twenty-first Street and run from 1-61 in a counterclockwise direction.) Two houses of

---

BEEKMAN PLACE AND SUTTON PLACE

121. Riverview Terrace
122. East Fifty-third Street Dock
     (Dead End)
123. River House
124. Hale House

125. One Beekman Place
126. Beekman Tower Hotel
127. Site of Beekman House (P.S. 135)

KIP'S BAY AND TURTLE BAY

128. Kip's Bay Boys Club
129. New York Cancer Institute Clinic
130. Turtle Bay Music School
131. Morris Sanders' House
132. Michael Hare's House
133. William Lescaze's House
134. Abattoir Center
135. Nathan Hale Commemorative Tablet
136. Beaux Arts Apartments

137. Tudor City
138. Consolidated Edison Company Waterside Station
139. Daily News Building
140. Queens Midtown Tunnel
141. Site of St. Gabriel's Church
142. St. Gabriel's Park
143. New York Steam Corporation Station
144. Bellevue Hospital

Greek Revival style, No. 3 and 4, are joined architecturally by an exquisite cast-iron balcony that runs across both red-brick fronts. No. 3 is occupied by the NETHERLAND CLUB, whose members are descendants of the Dutch settlers. A pair of iron mounted lamps at the entrance of No. 4 was placed there by the city in honor of James Harper, the occupant who was mayor in 1844–5. (At the mayor's request such lamps are placed near the entrance of his home. This custom arose because the early chief executives wished to be immediately available for nocturnal emergencies.) Mayor Harper was one of the founders of Harper and Brothers, publishers.

Two distinguished clubs, the NATIONAL ARTS CLUB at 15 Gramercy Park South, and THE PLAYERS at No. 16 are on the south side. Samuel J. Tilden, who lived at No. 15, constructed an underground passageway to an exit on Nineteenth Street, so that he might escape boors and political enemies. The Players, an actors' club, was founded in 1888 by Edwin Booth who employed Stanford White to remodel the building. Booth lived here for many years; the furnishings in his room remain intact, and his portrait by Sargent hangs over the fireplace in the main room. A bronze STATUE OF BOOTH in his role as "Hamlet" is in Gramercy Park. It was designed by Edmond T. Quinn and erected by the club. Each year, on the actor's birthday, November 13, a memorial wreath is placed on the statue by the members.

Number 19 was the home of Mrs. Stuyvesant Fish in the 1890's, when she ruled the "Four Hundred" and society watched the antics of Harry Lehr, its bad boy. David Lamar, the "Wolf of Wall Street," Edward Sheldon, the playwright, and William C. Bullitt, ambassador to France in 1939, were later occupants. A descendant of Samuel Ruggles, Mrs. John A. Vanderpoel, lives at No. 22. Stanford White, Robert Ingersoll, and John Bigelow once had homes on the park. Cyrus Fields' old house stood on the northeast corner of Lexington Avenue and Gramercy Park North. Richard Watson Gilder died at No. 24.

The FRIENDS' MEETING HOUSE, Nos. 27-30 (144 East Twentieth Street), houses one of the oldest active Quaker groups. The simple one-story building was erected in 1859. Its austere interior is still illuminated with gas lamps. A service for distressed travelers, established by the congregation, led to the formation of the Travelers' Aid Society in 1905.

Two studio apartment buildings are on the east side of the park: No. 34 AND No. 36 GRAMERCY PARK EAST. The design of No. 34—the arabesque panels of foliated details, the bay windows, and the octagonal turret, roofed with a conical cap—follows Richard M. Hunt's adaptation of the French Empire style. The façade of the adjoining building, No. 36, is a veritable gallery of decorative detail: terra cotta with elaborate Gothic motifs, bay windows, traceried heads, and balustrades. Cast stone figures of armored knights holding spears and flame lamps guard the entrance court of the building.

In a group of remodeled houses in East Nineteenth Street, a block south of the park, lives a small colony of artists and writers, including Ida Tarbell, writer, Cecilia Beaux, painter, Clara Fargo Thomas, muralist, and George Julian Zolnay, sculptor.

The office building at 112 East Nineteenth Street houses many liberal organizations; among them are the American Student Union, City Affairs Committee, International Labor Defense, League for Industrial Democracy, and American League for Peace and Democracy.

At Fourth Avenue and Twenty-first Street, a block west of the park, is the CALVARY EPISCOPAL CHURCH. The congregation was organized in 1836, and communicants have included members of the Roosevelt, Astor, and Vanderbilt families. The pastor, Dr. Samuel M. Shoemaker, is a prominent leader of the Oxford Group, and the nine-story Calvary House is accepted as Group headquarters in America.

North of the park, at 9 Lexington Avenue, was the HOME OF PETER COOPER, founder of Cooper Union (*see page 121*), well-known engineering and arts school. Like the Harper home, the residence has two lamps in front of the doorway, mementoes of the administration of Mayor Abram S. Hewitt, a son-in-law of Cooper. The building was occupied by Cooper's descendants until 1938.

On the southwest corner of Lexington Avenue and Twenty-second Street is the BUILDING OF THE RUSSELL SAGE FOUNDATION, a dignified edifice suggesting a Florentine Renaissance palace, where the diversified sociological research and educational activities financed by the Sage bequests and endowments are administered. The Foundation has one of the largest social welfare libraries in the world. The NEW YORK SCHOOL OF SOCIAL WORK, a Foundation-sponsored group, has its quarters in the building. It is the oldest and one of the outstanding institutions of its kind in the country.

The CHILDREN'S COURT, a part of the Domestic Relations Court, is at 137 East Twenty-second Street. The work of the Court, and its adjunct, the Probation Bureau, is primarily with delinquent and neglected children and has effectively reduced the number of child offenders. A block west, at 105 East Twenty-second Street, is the UNITED CHARITIES BUILDING, the headquarters of more than forty-five social welfare agencies.

The SCHOOL OF CIVIC ADMINISTRATION AND BUSINESS, a co-educational division of City College (*see page 294*), occupies the seventeen-story building on the southeast corner of Twenty-third Street and Lexington Avenue, the original site of the college.

The MADISON SQUARE STATION, NEW YORK POST OFFICE, 149 East Twenty-third Street, opposite the school, is a significant example of an evolving American style, a new classicism free of dependence on the works of antiquity. It was built in 1937 after plans by Lorimer Rich.

UNION SQUARE DISTRICT

Area. 14th St. on the south to 18th St. on the north; from 3d Ave. west to 6th Ave. Map on page 193.

Union Square district belongs to the working people of New York. It is an amusement center, but its ornate moving-picture theaters, glittering marquees, and gaily lighted buffets are fewer in number and less persuasive than those of Times Square. It is a shopping mart, but few of its stores have the fine goods and appointments of the Fifth Avenue fashion center: instead, their bare floors may be filled with racks holding scores of garments, many models of a kind, and their show windows, in many cases, are packed with cheap merchandise. The movie houses, likewise, offer the most for the money—double features and "screeno"; the dining places are cafeterias and lunchrooms, where large portions of plain food are dispensed for nickels, dimes, and quarters.

Before these cheap stores, cheap movies, cheap restaurants passes a ceaselessly moving crowd of men, women, and many children, of all nationalities. Hawkers and pitchmen find this street easy pickings among customers who can afford the little luxuries of Union Square—pretzels, sliced cocoanut, gloves, scarves, neckties, and popular song sheets. They buy magic "roots" which sprout fullblown artificial gladiolas, peonies, or regal lilies; prophecies from a turbaned seer; risqué cartoons; or a dozen low-quality socks for fifty cents. Many beggars—legless beggars on rollerskate platforms, footless, handless, or blind beggars; playing the saxophone, the guitar, singing—move slower-paced through the crowd. The poor, they know, give to the poor. Passers-by stop at the busy newsstands for political literature, and along the curb newsboys hawk the *Daily Worker* and other radical newspapers of every shade. Youths and girls rattle collection boxes for the benefit of many causes—the Chinese people, Jewish refugees, political prisoners, or workers on strike.

Touched with a bit of Coney Island, democratic, with a robust and loquacious vitality, Union Square derives its peculiar identity from its international reputation as the center of America's radical movement. The tradition of Union Square as a forum for mass protest was not born until the first decade of the present century. The Flour Riots of 1837 centered about City Hall; in the 1870's the battleground moved north to Tompkins Square. During the Civil War, Union Square took on significance when the Union cause was commemorated in meetings, reviews, and parades of departing troops and in the torchlight processions of the pro-Lincoln "Wide Awakes," the Young Republicans of that day. In 1873 unemployment protests were staged, but it was not until the numerous meetings of Anarchists, Socialists, and "Wobblies" (members of the Industrial Workers of the World) were held there during the years preceding the World War, that the square began to assume its importance as a gathering place.

Meetings and occasional clashes with the police continued with increasing frequency. On August 22, 1927, the night set for the execution in Boston of the anarchists, Nicola Sacco and Bartolomeo Vanzetti, a shoemaker and a fish peddler, machine guns were mounted on the roof of the six-story building now occupied by Klein's famous dress emporium, at 28-30 Union Square East, and were trained on a compact mass of more than five thousand tense, silent men and women, part of the angry crowd that had packed the square throughout the day. A little after midnight a sign was thrust outside the *Daily Worker* windows: "Sacco Murdered." Some minutes later another sign appeared: "Vanzetti Murdered." A throaty wail of anguish arose. A small procession that immediately formed was dispersed by police, and several marchers were injured.

On May 18, 1929, the Communist Party led an "anti-police brutality" demonstration and again the police charged. Many heads were broken and twenty-seven demonstrators, including nine children, were arrested.

With the mass unemployment that followed the financial crisis of October, 1929, the square became the gathering place for the jobless. On March 6, 1930, the largest gathering ever held in Union Square occurred: more than thirty-five thousand unemployed workers and sympathizers crowded around a number of speakers' stands. When the demonstrators started to march toward City Hall, the police broke up the parade. A hundred persons were injured and thirteen arrested.

This mass meeting ushered in a new period in the history of labor demonstrations in Union Square. Public reaction against police interference won the right of assembly in this park. It became accepted in New York City that the May Day Parade was privileged to be reviewed at the north end of the square.

Recent years have seen the development of many protest centers throughout the city, diminishing the former concentration of such activities in Union Square. The soapbox speaker's old stamping grounds, the traffic triangles at the corners of the square, are now islands of verdure. Nonetheless, Union Square is likely to continue as the heart of the city's radical activities, for in its neighborhood are headquarters of many of New York's radical and progressive groups and labor organizations: the Socialist Party and its newspaper, the *Socialist Call,* the Communist Party and its newspaper, the *Daily Worker,* the Rand School of Social Science, the International Workers Order, the International Labor Defense, the American Civil Liberties Union, the American League for Peace and Democracy, the League for Mutual Aid, the International Ladies Garment Workers Union, the Amalgamated Clothing Workers of America and a host of others.

It would seem that Union Square was appropriately named; the aptness of the title, however, was accidental. The square was laid out in 1811 as Union Place, the name deriving from the connection of the extended Bloomingdale Road (now Broadway) and Bowery Road (now Fourth Avenue). Shortly after the neighborhood became one of New York's most sedate and exclusive suburbs, inhabited by the city's wealthiest citizens. Among its residents were James Roosevelt, Robert Goelet, and Daniel Drew. The small park was surrounded by a heavy iron fence, the gates of which were locked at sundown. The fence was not removed until the 1870's when Union Place had become Union Square.

Union Square as a theatrical district had its beginning in 1854, when the Academy of Music was audaciously opened as the home of grand opera on the north side of Fourteenth Street near Irving Place. The land between Second and Third Avenues on Fourteenth Street was at that time occupied by a truck farm. Seven years later, when James Wallack built his theater at Thirteenth Street and Broadway, his friends considered him a madman for moving so far uptown from the Bowery. Irving Hall, erected at Irving Place and Fifteenth Street in 1859, is now known as the IRVING PLACE THEATRE. Subsequently, the Union Square Theatre was built on Fourteenth Street and Broadway, and Tony Pastor's opened on Fourteenth Street near Third Avenue, next to the old headquarters of Tammany Hall.

During the 1870's theaters, hotels, and fine restaurants, reflecting the exuberance of the growing city, made this neighborhood the center of good living and gaiety. In the late 1860's Delmonico's restaurant moved from the City Hall section to Fourteenth Street and Fifth Avenue. LUCHOW's, still one of the most famous eating places in New York, was established in 1882 in its present quarters on Fourteenth Street near Irving

Place. Italian, French, Hungarian, and English restaurants were available to the gourmet.

On the west side of Union Square, at Fifteenth Street, stood Tiffany's great jewelry shop in the building which now houses the AMALGAMATED BANK, the first labor bank in New York and the largest institution of its kind in the United States. Between Sixteenth and Seventeenth Streets Brentano's Literary Emporium sedately served the elite. Farther west and north toward Sixth Avenue, the shopping center included Hearn's, B. Altman's, Siegel-Cooper, and farther south on Broadway, Stewart's (now Wanamaker's), and Daniel's.

By 1900, with the city's steady growth northward, the character of the district had definitely changed. Some of the restaurants and theaters had moved to Madison Square; the business center had shifted, or rather split, leaving a great gap between uptown and downtown New York, into which, during the next decade, the young needle trades rushed like a tide. Besides cheap rents—real-estate values had fallen rapidly—the neighborhood offered two great advantages to the industry: it was on the outskirts of the fashionable shopping center, and it was near a plentiful and cheap labor supply—the immigrant families of the Lower East Side. The old Union Square homes were soon converted into tenements to house thousands of needle trade workers.

Artists made studios of the great attic rooms in the few mansions still standing, and the south side of Fourteenth Street became virtually an extension of Greenwich Village. Such men as Max Weber, Walt Kuhn, Reginald Marsh, Emil Ganzo, Joseph Stella, Ernest Fiene, Walter Pach, Alfred Dehn, and Art Young made their homes here. In the 1920's came Raphael Soyer, Morris Kantor, Louis Lozowick, and Yasuo Kuniyoshi; and in the 1930's, William Gropper, Arnold Blanch, William Zorach, and Doris Lee. Ambrose Bierce wrote some of his famous short stories on Fourteenth Street. Later Michael Gold, Joseph Freeman, and Albert Halper, author of *Union Square,* came there to live and write.

The years 1910 to 1921 saw this district at its most depressed level. It was an area of burlesque houses, shooting galleries, and shoddy businesses. Real-estate values sank to a new low and in 1921 many parcels of property were sold at foreclosure. S. Klein, operator of a dress establishment, bought three of these dilapidated buildings on the east side of the square and began a program of expansion. (The ground floor of the one at the Fourteenth Street corner had been occupied by Joe's, a saloon that was used by Hugh A. D'Arcy as the setting for his sentimental poem, *The Face on the Barroom Floor.* The verse first appeared in the New York *Dispatch,*

August 7, 1887.) OHRBACH'S followed suit and these two establishments, dealing in women's apparel, gave the impetus from which developed today's substantial shopping center.

As a retail district Union Square, more strictly Fourteenth Street, is perhaps the city's largest outlet for low-priced women's merchandise. KLEIN'S, doing a tremendous business in women's apparel, employs a minimum of sales people, and customers help themselves in cafeteria fashion. The presence of store detectives inhibits shoplifting. HEARN'S DEPARTMENT STORE, between Fifth and Sixth Avenues on Fourteenth Street, has shared in the general retail rejuvenation of the section. The stores of Fourteenth Street no longer draw their clientele exclusively from the East Side. Women from near-by cities, from the suburbs, and from every part of New York come bargain hunting here. In line with the district's labor character, most of its business houses are either unionized or in process of becoming so. The shoppers here are probably the most union-conscious consumers in the country. An everyday sight on Union Square is the picket line, whether it be in front of a restaurant, an orange-drink stand, or a shoe shop.

UNION SQUARE PARK, after years of neglect, was landscaped in 1935–6. The level of the ground was raised several feet above the street in order to allow for the construction of an underground concourse connecting the various subway routes below. At the north end a colonnaded bandstand was constructed, overlooking a large plaza where automobiles are parked unless a mass meeting is scheduled.

A number of monuments and pieces of sculpture of high merit are in the square. The most commanding of these is a bronze equestrian STATUE OF WASHINGTON near the southern end of the park facing Fourteenth Street. The work of Henry Kirke Brown, it was one of the earliest equestrian statues in America. J. Q. A. Ward designed the base. The statue, dedicated on July 4, 1856, was originally placed at the southeast corner of the square, where Washington was said to have been received by the citizens of New York following the evacuation of the city by the British on November 25, 1783.

Other monuments include a heroic bronze STATUE OF LINCOLN, also by Brown, and a bronze FIGURE OF LAFAYETTE by Frédéric Auguste Bartholdi, designer of the Statue of Liberty. From the center of the square rises an eighty-foot LIBERTY POLE, erected in 1924. It commemorates the Declaration of Independence and honors the Tammany leader, Charles Francis Murphy. In the sculptured, drum-shaped base, designed by Anthony de Fransisci, are engraved Jefferson's words: "How little my countrymen know what precious blessings they are in possession of and which no other people on earth enjoy."

The diverse architecture of the buildings surrounding Union Square does not supply the unified feeling of enclosure implied by the word "square," but it does offer an interesting record of architectural styles that have been popular in past years. The LINCOLN BUILDING, erected at 1 Union Square in 1889, is an example adapted from Romanesque work; at No. 33 the Union Building, built in 1893, has richly framed windows inspired by Spanish Moorish design. The cast-iron front widely popular in the last quarter of the nineteenth century is exemplified by the AMAL-GAMATED BANK BUILDING at 11-15 Union Square, erected in 1870–71.

Most of the recent buildings, however, are faced with stone. Three divisions of each façade are clearly marked: a base ornamented with classical details, an intermediate portion of undecorated masonry pierced by regular windows, and a crowning element at the top consisting of arched windows and an elaborate cornice. The BANK OF THE MANHATTAN COMPANY at 31 Union Square and the HARTFORD BUILDING at No. 41 are typical.

The decreased demand for industrial floor area and the increased number of vacancies, in the years following the financial crisis of 1929, led to the popularity of a new type of structure—the taxpayer. This was designed to yield rent that was sufficient to pay the real-estate taxes; it could be replaced by a larger building during a more prosperous period. Such an example is at 31 EAST SEVENTEENTH STREET, a two-story structure of light-cream brick and panels.

In the northeast corner of the square—Seventeenth Street and Fourth Avenue—is TAMMANY HALL, the headquarters of the city-wide system of Democratic political clubs. Here the inner council of sachems meets to set Tammany's policies and to plan campaigns. When the organization wins at the polls, club leaders and district workers swarm to the Hall for a rousing election night celebration, but such joyful gatherings have been infrequent in recent years. The building, erected in 1929, has some resemblance to the old Federal Hall that stood at Broad and Wall Streets.

Although the CONSOLIDATED EDISON BUILDING is one block east of the square—Fourteenth Street and Irving Place—it is already part of the square's tradition. The building, completed in sections between 1915 and 1929, occupies the site of the old Academy of Music. The mausoleum-like tower rises 531 feet above the square; its bright lights, visible for miles, and the illuminated dial of the great clock below, are welcome landmarks.

MADISON SQUARE DISTRICT

Area: 18th St. on the south to 27th St. on the north; from 6th Ave. east to 4th Ave. Map on page 193.

The "Flatiron" Building, whose very name has to be explained to a younger generation, is the only tangible evidence that there ever was a Madison Square—a glamorous Madison Square. Here Ward McAllister's "Four Hundred" dined and danced at Delmonico's, and the old aristocracy, including the Roosevelts, lived in brownstone mansions following a pattern of life preserved only in the pages of novels about "little old New York."

Here, too, were some of Stanford White's most beautiful buildings: the Madison Square Presbyterian Church, with its pillared portico, columns of green granite, and Pantheon-like dome; old Madison Square Garden *(see page 331)*, with its copy of the Giralda tower of Seville surmounted by Augustus Saint-Gaudens' statue of the glorious Diana.

On the site of the old Garden, at Madison Avenue and 26th Street, rises the New York Life Insurance Building. Two blocks south, on the east side of the park, is the Metropolitan Life Insurance Building. The paths that crisscross the park seem to have been expressly laid out for the convenience of the thousands of office workers hurrying from subways and busses to these great skyscrapers. Lesser buildings flank the Broadway side. Factories and sales rooms of the toy, novelty, silk, woolen, and men's clothing industries and headquarters of benevolent and welfare organizations are scrambled throughout the Madison Square district; on Fourth Avenue, a block east of the park, many of the nation's well-known publishers have their offices.

In the acute-angled triangle made by the scissors-like intersection of Broadway and Fifth Avenue, at Twenty-third Street, is the old twenty-one-story FLATIRON BUILDING, completed in 1902 from plans by D. H. Burnham and Company. Its exterior walls as well as floors are supported at each story by the steel frame. This was a logical advance over the structural system used in the World Building on Park Row. Previously, the area of the base and the thickness of the exterior walls were the main technical factors in determining the height of a building; the development of the new principle made possible greater heights.

It was christened the Fuller Building, but because of its shape became known as the "Flatiron." Pictured on postcards, stamped on souvenirs, its image was familiar to American minds, young and old. Standing on what was traditionally the windiest corner of the city, it was facetiously considered a good vantage point for the glimpse of a trim ankle, in the long-skirted, prewar era; policemen used to shoo loungers away from the Twenty-third Street corner, and the expression "twenty-three skidoo" is supposed to have originated from this association.

Completion of the Fuller Building presaged the end of Madison Square as a social center. Within less than a decade (1908), "the skyscraper" was outclassed by a neighbor, the METROPOLITAN LIFE INSURANCE BUILDING. Designed by Le Brun and Sons, it fronts the park on Madison Avenue, between Twenty-third and Twenty-fourth Streets and rises seven hundred feet (fifty stories) above street level. While the bold simplicity of the design gives the tower great strength, the faulty scale of the details make it look much smaller than it actually is. The tower clock has four faces— each twenty-six and a half feet in diameter—with minute hands weighing a thousand pounds each and hour hands seven hundred pounds. The four enormous chimes, the largest of which weighs seven thousand pounds, sound a measure by Handel every quarter-hour from seven in the morning until ten at night, when a beacon light takes over the watch, flashing red for the quarter-hours and white for the hours. The building is connected to a smaller annex by a covered bridge high above Twenty-fourth Street.

In the shadow of the Metropolitan Life, at the north corner of Twenty-fifth Street and Madison Avenue, is the marble BUILDING OF THE APPELLATE DIVISION OF THE SUPREME COURT, a work of considerable harmony and delicacy. It was designed by James Brown Lord and erected in 1900. Above the roof balustrade is a galaxy of statuary, including allegorical representations of Justice and Peace, together with figures of famous lawgivers. Sculptors represented include Philip Martiny, Karl Bitter, Herbert Adams, and Edward C. Potter. The interior, profuse with veined yellow marble, gilt plaster relief, carved woodwork, and murals, recalls High Renaissance decoration.

The NEW YORK LIFE INSURANCE BUILDING occupies the block from Twenty-sixth to Twenty-seventh Street, from Madison to Fourth Avenue. This 617-foot structure was completed in 1928 from plans by Cass Gilbert, designer of the Woolworth Building. Although the Gothic ornament is similar to that of the Woolworth Building, it lacks the powerful upward movement embodied in the latter. From the 1830's to the early 1870's the site was occupied by the New York and Harlem (Railroad) Union Depot.

At the northwest corner of Madison Avenue and Twenty-sixth Street is the home of the AMERICAN SOCIETY FOR THE PREVENTION OF CRUELTY

TO ANIMALS, founded in 1866 by the humanitarian Henry Bergh. It also houses a dispensary and hospital. The MANHATTAN CLUB, at the southeast corner, was prominent in the late nineteenth century as headquarters of Democratic leaders. The Manhattan cocktail is said to have originated there.

The Fifth Avenue Building, northwest corner of Fifth Avenue and Twenty-third Street, occupies the SITE OF THE OLD FIFTH AVENUE HOTEL, a center of the city's social and political life in the Gilded Age. When it was completed in 1859, the Fifth Avenue Hotel was dubbed "Eno's Folly," because people doubted a hotel so far uptown could succeed. It prospered, however, and became a meeting place for Republican politicians. In one of the downstairs sitting rooms of the hotel was the "Amen Corner," so named because Senator Thomas Platt, Republican boss, there gave orders to his henchmen. Around the corner from the Fifth Avenue Building, at 55 West Twenty-third Street, was the Eden Musee with its Chamber of Horrors, containing waxwork representations of notorious crimes. It remained here from 1884 until 1915, when the wax figures were sent to Coney Island.

Delmonico's, one of New York's most famous restaurants, moved to Fifth Avenue and Twenty-sixth Street in 1876. It reached the peak of its glory at this location: the great dining salon was a favorite haunt of such notables as Berry Wall (King of the Dudes), John Drew, Richard Mansfield, Charles and Daniel Frohman, and a host of other prominent actors, sportsmen, financiers, and social leaders. Then O. Henry could say of this district, "Here is the fly-eye of New York. Spin it on a pivot and you would see the world."

Fifty years later (1939) a new generation got an inkling of the district's former glory when one of its grimy buildings, an office BUILDING AT 900 BROADWAY, emerged from a scrubbing as an architectural challenge to the modernists. The structure, which was built in 1887 after plans by Stanford White, was far ahead of its time in its subtle use of brick and terra-cotta color and in the originality of its structurally expressive design. Four stories have been added to the original six.

Madison Square has changed with the growth of the city, but the six-acre park, the only break in the wall of Fifth Avenue blocks between Washington Square and Fortieth Street, has kept its shady walks and its statues. The FARRAGUT STATUE, in the park, was designed by Augustus Saint-Gaudens; its base by White. It was unveiled in 1881 by John H. Knowles, the sailor who had lashed Farragut to the mast in the historic naval engagement of the Civil War in Mobile Bay. An obelisk-shaped monument west of the park is a MEMORIAL TO GENERAL WILLIAM JEN-

KINS WORTH, Mexican War hero whose body lies under the shaft. The ETERNAL LIGHT, an ever burning star atop a lofty flagpole on the Fifth Avenue side, commemorates the valor of the American Expeditionary Forces in France during the World War. At Christmas a great evergreen, brilliant with colored lights—probably the first community Christmas tree in the city—sheds a glow over the park. Carols are sung and "good will toward men" rings out in the usually workaday atmosphere. The tree celebration, conceived by Orlando Rouland, artist, and his wife, has been held in the square every Christmas since 1911.

The early days of this section are recalled by the ROOSEVELT HOUSE, 28 East Twentieth Street, birthplace and boyhood home of Theodore Roosevelt. *(Open weekdays, except Monday, 9 a.m. to 5 p.m.; Sunday and holidays 1 to 5 p.m.; admission 25¢ Wednesday and Friday, other days free.)* It is furnished in the style of the 1870's and contains a collection of diaries, letters, manuscripts, cartoons, and other mementos of the President.

The square was named, indirectly, for President Madison. Early in its history the park site was a pauper's burying ground. The area accommodated, successively, an arsenal and the House of Refuge. The latter, said to be the first such institution in the country, was opened in 1825 under the auspices of the Society for the Reformation of Youthful Delinquents. It was destroyed by fire in 1839.

When the land around the arsenal was used as a parade ground in the first half of the nineteenth century, a Corporal Thompson operated a tavern here which was a rendezvous for the sporting crowd. The inn was known as both Corporal Thompson's Roadhouse and Madison Cottage. It was razed in 1852 and on its site was built Franconi's Hippodrome, a circus, and later the Fifth Avenue Hotel. Madison Square Park was officially opened in 1847. It was here that baseball as a national sport was given its original impetus. In 1845, a group of "gentlemen who had been playing the game since 1842 as a means of exercise" organized the Knickerbocker Club and drew up the elementary rules of the game. The improved sport spread rapidly through the country, becoming known as the "New York Game." During the next decades, the sportsmen who gathered in the near-by inns were supplanted by the aristocrats who wined and dined at the many restaurants and hotels that were established around the square—the Café Martin, the Holland House, the Albemarle, St. James, Victoria, Brunswick, Hoffman House, and others. (The bar in the Hoffman House was the most popular on Broadway, owing perhaps to the scandalous painting by Bouguereau of a nude nymph surrounded by satyrs.) These establishments flourished until comparatively recent times.

KIP'S BAY AND TURTLE BAY

Area: 27th St. on the south to 59th St. on the north; from 3d Ave. east to East River (excluding Beekman and Sutton Places). Map on page 193.

Kip's Bay-Turtle Bay neighborhood, sometimes known as the mid-town East Side, is a riverside back yard for the more imposing mid-town section west of it. Huge industrial enterprises—breweries, laundries, abattoirs, power plants—along the water front face squalid tenements not far away from new apartment dwellings attracted to the section by its river view and its central position. The numerous plants shower this district with the heaviest sootfall in the city—150 tons to the square mile annually.

The area near Second Avenue and East Thirty-fifth Street was the site of Jacobus Kip's farm, "a goodly estate, covering one hundred and fifty acres, and comprising meadow, woodland and stream." It extended eastward to a bay subsequently named for Kip. In 1655 he built a mansion of imported brick for his young bride, Marie de la Montagne; the house stood on the farm for almost two hundred years. A sixty-acre tract, one mile north, was settled in 1677 by the De Voors who called it the Spring Valley Farm. Through it ran the Saw Kill to a rocky indentation of the East River. Because of its shape, the indentation was called Turtle Bay.

Important events of the American Revolution took place in this district. A British military storehouse at the foot of East Forty-fifth Street was stormed by the Liberty Boys in a midnight raid in 1773. It was in Kip's Bay that British men-of-war anchored September 15, 1776, to take over Manhattan Island. The Revolutionary army, wearied and disheartened after the disastrous defeat on Long Island, broke before broadsides from these vessels and fled toward Harlem Heights. George Washington tried to stem the rout. "It was said that he drew his sword and threatened to run the cowards through," wrote Rupert Hughes in his biography of Washington, "he used the cane whip he carried, and he beat his people over the shoulders in an insane hatred of their shameless cowardice. He flogged not only private soldiers but officers as well. He lashed colonels across the shoulder blades . . . He flailed a brigadier general." The next day Washington succeeded in rallying his troops and defeated the enemy at Harlem Heights. Before the Battle of Long Island the Americans had thrown up redoubts at Kip's and Turtle bays, which were subsequently captured, and for the duration of the war British frigates were stationed there. During the War of 1812 the shores were again fortified.

Early in the nineteenth century this region was the site of the country estates of many prominent New Yorkers, among them Horace Greeley, the editor, and Francis Bayard Winthrop, bank director and poet. By the 1880's, however, the estates had been broken up into lots upon which rows of brownstones were built. Today much of the district is a slum. El trains of the Second and Third Avenue lines thunder by constantly, and First Avenue, an important commercial traffic artery, brings an endless, noisy procession of trucks. Kip's and Turtle bays have long been filled in, and their names have vanished from maps. A scrawny ledge of rock at the foot of Forty-fifth Street marks the approximate location of Turtle Bay, while of Kip's Bay nothing remains but the name, used by a few local organizations and business firms. For convenience, Forty-second Street may be taken as the dividing line between the two sections.

Bellevue Hospital *(see page 316)*, one of the oldest in the country, occupies the blocks between Twenty-sixth and Thirtieth Streets, east of First Avenue to the river.

On the site of the old bay is the KIP'S BAY STATION OF THE NEW YORK STEAM CORPORATION, First Avenue and Thirty-fifth Street, which supplies steam to midtown skyscrapers, such as the New York Central, Chrysler, Lincoln, Chanin, and Empire State buildings. This service has made possible in large buildings the elimination of heating equipment and the utilization of additional rentable floor area. The steam is forced through underground conduits at a speed of two hundred miles an hour. The huge WATERSIDE STATION OF THE CONSOLIDATED EDISON COMPANY at Thirty-eighth Street and the East River, near the load center of the city, can generate 367,000 kilowatts of electricity. *(Visitors admitted.)*

ST. GABRIEL'S PARK, on First Avenue, opposite the steam plant, is one of the few recreational areas in the neighborhood. The near-by St. Gabriel's Church, at 310 East Thirty-seventh Street, is distinguished for having provided two of the seven American cardinals in the history of the Roman Catholic Church: the late Archbishop of New York, Patrick Cardinal Hayes, and his predecessor, James Cardinal Farley.

The entire block on which the church stands is scheduled (1939) to be razed to make way for an approach to the QUEENS MIDTOWN TUNNEL, construction of which commenced in October, 1936. The vehicular tunnel's twin tubes will extend 7,750 feet from Second Avenue at Thirty-seventh Street to Borden Avenue near Vernon Avenue in Long Island City. The tube for westbound traffic will be 7,785 feet long, and the one for eastbound traffic, 7,500 feet. These are being constructed by the New York City Tunnel Authority with the aid of a PWA loan and grant of more than $58,000,000. By the time the tunnel is completed in 1940, about two

whole blocks of substandard dwellings and small parts of ten others will
have been demolished, and more will go as the East River Drive is extended through the neighborhood. Eventually, a passageway will be burrowed underneath Manhattan, connecting the Queens Midtown Tunnel
with the Lincoln Tunnel *(see page 156)*.

Dominating the entire district from a high bluff over First Avenue is
TUDOR CITY, a $25,000,000 group of apartment houses built in the
1920's. It stretches east of Second Avenue from Fortieth to Forty-fourth
Street. Forty-second Street runs through a tunnel under the development.
The twelve buildings, decorated with details of English Cottage design,
vary in height from ten to thirty-two stories and contain some three thousand apartments. A private park, which the main buildings face, is
reserved for the use of Tudor City residents. Part of this rocky site was
known as Corcoran's Roost in the 1880's, when it was the lair of the Rag
Gang and was ruled by Paddy Corcoran and his sons.

A block west rises the thirty-six-story NEWS BUILDING, 220 East Forty-
second Street, one of the city's most distinctive skyscrapers. The lucid expression of its unbroken vertical stripes distinguishes the building from the
surrounding humdrum architecture. The stripes, which begin as alternat-
ing bands of white piers, and dark window and spandrel, end abruptly at
the top of a forty-foot blank wall. The parapet hides from view roof
tanks, elevator bulkheads, and stair towers. The structure was designed by
John Mead Howells and Raymond Hood and cost $10,700,000, including
printing machinery. Since their completion in 1930, the building and the
adjoining nine-story annex on Forty-first Street have housed the various
departments of the New York *Daily News,* the tabloid that has a larger
circulation than any other newspaper in the country. The News Information Bureau, a general service covering a great variety of subjects, served
about 625,000 persons in 1938; the same year more than 81,000 visitors
inspected the ultramodern printing plant. *(Guide service daily at 2, 3, 4, 5,
7:45 and 8:45 p.m.)*

Another striking design by Raymond Hood is that of the near-by BEAUX
ARTS APARTMENTS, two expensive residence buildings at 307 and 310
East Forty-fourth Street. Built in 1929, the houses face each other and are
slightly set back to suggest a court. To some critics the use of dark brick
between windows achieves an effect of horizontality that appears forced.

The NEW YORK MIRROR, a Hearst tabloid, is published at 235 East
Forty-fifth Street. The ABATTOIR CENTER extends along First Avenue
from Forty-second to Forty-sixth Street. In order to reach these eastern plants of the large meat packers, cattle and sheep are detrained at

New Jersey terminals on the Hudson River and transported in livestock barges to unloading piers on the East River. Here they are rested and fed for twenty-four hours before slaughter. The entire output of these plants is consumed by inhabitants in the metropolitan area.

With the development of modern sanitation, many of the most objectionable aspects of the slaughterhouse neighborhood disappeared. To the past belong such features as dilapidated shacks, runaway livestock, and strong, unpleasant odors. Still employed, however, is the Judas bellwether, the sheep that leads a flock to slaughter. At the turn of the century the slaughterhouses played an important role in the life of the city's immigrants. They strongly believed in the medicinal value of blood, and when illness came they went to the abattoirs and bought blood for five cents a glass.

On the wall of the Wilson meat-packing plant, on the southeast corner of First Avenue and Forty-sixth Street, is a TABLET commemorating the execution of Nathan Hale (September 22, 1776), which is supposed to have occurred near here.

The combined residence-and-office of three architects in Turtle Bay area represent interesting developments in building design. WILLIAM LES-CAZE'S HOUSE, 211 East Forty-eighth Street, is air-conditioned and insulated with glass brick to keep out noise of the street and near-by els. The exterior is designed so as to lead the client into the office and the social visitor into the home. The brownstone treatment of MICHAEL HARE'S HOUSE, 212 East Forty-ninth Street, agrees admirably with that of neighboring buildings. The facade is set back slightly between party walls. MORRIS SANDERS' HOUSE, 219 East Forty-ninth Street, excites interest because of its vertical alternation of windows and open porches. The interiors of the three buildings achieve striking effects through the imaginative use of color, texture of materials, and the sequences of well-related spaces.

Two of the many alert social agencies in the neighborhood maintain headquarters on Fifty-second Street. At No. 244, the TURTLE BAY MUSIC SCHOOL, established in 1924, provides free music instruction for talented children of the poor, while at No. 301, the KIP'S BAY BOYS CLUB, founded in 1913, conducts organized educational and recreational activities.

The northern part of the district, sandwiched between Park Avenue and Sutton Place, borrows a little of the character of those wealthy neighborhoods. Many better-class dwellings occupy the side streets, and on Third Avenue are a great many antique shops.

Fifty-ninth Street, the northern boundary of this district, leads to the entrance of the QUEENSBORO BRIDGE at Second Avenue. The crossing, a balanced cantilever structure with a marked angular appearance, lacks the graceful continuity and flow of line of the East River suspension bridges. It was designed by the municipal department of bridges and completed in 1909 at a cost of about $20,800,000, including land and construction. The bridge crosses Welfare Island (reached by elevators descending from the bridge's roadway) to Long Island City. About 7,450 feet long (including approaches), it has a west channel span of 1,182 feet, a Welfare Island span of 630 feet, and an east channel span of 984 feet.

The New York Cancer Institute of Welfare Island *(see page 423)* maintains a clinic at 124 East Fifty-ninth Street.

MURRAY HILL

Area: 27th St. on the south to 42d St. on the north; from 6th Ave. east to 3d Ave. (excluding 5th Ave.). Map on page 193.

The district known as Murray Hill, now bordered by many of the world's tallest buildings, recalls to the sentimental New Yorker a vision of baroque brownstone mansions, crinoline and lavender, hoop skirts and trailing gowns, hansom cabs and four-in-hands. In the last decades of the nineteenth century Murray Hill harbored the ample dwellings of many of New York's "Four Hundred." A few of these remain and reinforce the contrast between the leisurely magnificence of Victorian days and the dynamic austerity of twentieth-century New York—a contrast which, as time passes, will be found chiefly in old prints or such novels as those of Edith Wharton, who so scrupulously evoked the flavor of Murray Hill's opulent past.

At the southern edge of this locality stands the PROTESTANT EPISCOPAL CHURCH OF THE TRANSFIGURATION, 1 East Twenty-ninth Street, better known as the "Little Church Around the Corner." More marriage ceremonies are performed here, perhaps, than in any other church in the city. The edifice gained its more popular name in 1870 when the pastor of a fashionable Madison Avenue congregation refused burial services to George Holland, an actor, and suggested to Joseph Jefferson, a friend of the deceased, that he "try the little church around the corner." The ensuing publicity made the church a shrine for theater people. The EPISCOPAL ACTORS GUILD OF AMERICA, of which Otis Skinner is head, has headquarters in the church building.

The grouping of small stone buildings around a garden dominated by a magnificent English elm is exceedingly picturesque, and without doubt the church is one of the most painted and etched religious edifices in America. Among the notable features of the interior are the fine use of wood in vaulting, arches, and screens; the Bride's Altar, with carved oak reredos incorporating old Scottish panels; the St. Faith window, partly of fourteenth-century Belgian glass; the old paintings used as stations of the cross; and Saint Mary's Chapel.

The area from Twenty-ninth to Thirty-fourth Street and Third to Fifth Avenue, with Lexington Avenue as the main artery, is devoted chiefly to the wholesale furniture and allied trades. At 206 Lexington Avenue is the FURNITURE EXCHANGE, erected in 1926, owned co-operatively by the tenants and operated for the trade. Performing a similar function for the rug and carpet industry is the TEXTILE BUILDING at 295 Fifth Avenue, erected in 1921.

South of Thirty-second Street, Fourth Avenue is lined with large office buildings, many of which are occupied by publishing firms, notably those at Nos. 432 and 386. The design of the 2 PARK AVENUE BUILDING represents a considerable break with past styles. The ornamental detail consists of geometric patterns formed by variations in wall surfaces and by the colored terra cotta at the top of the building. The structure was designed by Ely Jacques Kahn and erected in 1927.

On the southeast corner of Park Avenue and Thirty-fourth Street stands one of New York's most impressive armories, used as headquarters for three National Guard (New York) units: the 87th Infantry Brigade, the 71st Infantry Regiment, and the 101st Signal Battalion. The building was completed in 1904 from a design by Clinton and Russell. Its lofty tower was copied from that of the town hall in Siena, Italy. The main drill hall, 190 by 205 feet, is used for drills, reviews, social events, and exhibitions.

Opposite the armory, on the southwest corner, is the VANDERBILT HOTEL, built in 1912 after plans by Warren and Wetmore. The structure is an example of the eclectic use of Italian Renaissance, Mexican, and Adam influences. The Caen stone walls of the main lobby bear sculptured panels by Beatrice Chandler; the Della Robbia Room in the basement has decorations by Smeraldi in the spirit of French eighteenth-century *chinoiseries*.

The northeast corner of the same intersection, formerly known as One Park Avenue, is occupied by the mid-Victorian RESIDENCE OF MRS. ROBERT BACON, widow of an ambassador to France. When Park Avenue was extended two blocks south to Thirty-second Street, Mrs. Bacon sued the city, asking to retain the original address. Despite the fact that she lost the

suit, and that the office building at the northeast corner of Park Avenue
and Thirty-second Street is now known as One Park Avenue, her residence
is listed in the telephone directory as "1 Park Avenue."

Business has almost completely usurped the once exclusive Murray Hill
section of Madison Avenue. The last remaining residence of importance
is the J. P. MORGAN HOME at 231 Madison Avenue, a large brownstone
edifice bearing in its exterior details a slight suggestion of French Renaissance influence. The two buildings of the MORGAN LIBRARY on East
Thirty-sixth Street—creation of J. P. Morgan the elder and his son, the
present J. P. Morgan—are among the most luxuriously appointed private
museums in the world. The main building at 33 East Thirty-sixth Street, a
fine example of early sixteenth-century Italian Renaissance style, was designed by McKim, Mead, and White and erected in 1913, on principles
associated with the Acropolis, the unpierced white marble walls being
built without the use of mortar. The annex at No. 29, completed in 1928
by the younger Morgan on the site of the elder's home, was intentionally
subordinated to the main building by the architect, Benjamin W. Morris,
and while the most expensive materials have been used throughout, the
impression is one of simplicity and severity. Although both edifices are
outstanding architectural monuments in themselves, they are hardly suited
to the display of the treasures they house because of their basically poor
lighting.

The library, established in 1924, contains a valuable collection of sculpture, paintings, prints, *objets d'art,* and rare manuscripts and books. Among
the most notable items in the art collection are the *Infant Hercules,* ascribed to Michelangelo; a sixteenth-century *Madonna and Saints* of the
school of Giovanni Bellini; a fifteenth-century mantel sculptured by the
Florentine, Desiderio Settignano; a Donatello terra-cotta bas-relief of a
Madonna and Child; a seventeenth-century Chinese vase once the possession of Emperor K'ang Hsi; and the Morgan ruby. The collection of
manuscripts and books includes the Mainz Psalter of 1465 and the Ash-
burnham Gospels of the ninth century, two of the rarest volumes in the
world, and the first printed editions of Caesar, Virgil, Plutarch, Dante,
Cicero, Tasso, and many others.

The buildings are open to sightseers *(Main: Tuesday and Thursday
11 a.m. to 4 p.m., Saturday 10 a.m. to 1 p.m. Annex: weekdays 10
a.m. to 5 p.m.; closed Sunday and legal holidays).* To make use of the
library one must have a card, obtained by writing to the director.

Of the many professional, political, and social clubs in this section,
the most famous is the UNION LEAGUE CLUB, which occupies spacious

quarters in a modern building at 38 East Thirty-seventh Street. Stronghold of Republican conservatism, the club was organized in 1863 by Professor Wolcott Gibbs as the Union League of America to combat secession sentiment then rife in the city; together with similar organizations in Philadelphia and Baltimore, it aided in recruiting and equipping a regiment of Negroes in 1864. During Theodore Roosevelt's Bull Moose insurgency the club signified its displeasure by banishing his portrait from the library, but after his defeat restored it to its original place.

Business and professional associations in the vicinity include the ADVERTISING CLUB at 23 Park Avenue; the AMHERST CLUB at 273 Lexington Avenue; the ARCHITECTURAL LEAGUE OF NEW YORK at 115 East Fortieth Street; the ENGINEERS' CLUB, 32 West Fortieth Street; the CHEMISTS' CLUB, 52 East Forty-first Street; and the TECHNOLOGY CLUB, 22 East Thirty-eighth Street. Midston House, on Madison Avenue between Thirty-seventh and Thirty-eighth Streets, houses the UNIVERSITY OF PENNSYLVANIA CLUB, MILLS COLLEGE CLUB, and the AMERICAN ASSOCIATION OF UNIVERSITY WOMEN. The DARTMOUTH COLLEGE CLUB is at 30 East Thirty-seventh Street, the WILLIAMS CLUB at No. 24, and the PRINCETON CLUB at 39 East Thirty-ninth Street.

Spreading northward from Thirty-sixth Street, Murray Hill encompasses a number of houses belonging to New York's aristocracy. Several of these brownstones with their elaborately carved detail, enormous bays, and impressive vestibules, date from the post-Civil War era. From 1870 through the 1890's, the Hill, restricted since about 1850 to residential purposes, attracted many of New York's leading families, among them the Belmonts, Rhinelanders, Tiffanys, and Havemeyers. Around the turn of the century the neighborhood gradually began to lose ground in its effort to restrict commercial establishments, and with the opening of Grand Central Terminal in 1913 it could no longer remain exclusively residential.

From the 1830's to the 1890's, what is now Park Avenue and its southern extension, Fourth Avenue, held the tracks of the New York and Harlem Railroad. After 1842 the use of steam-power was forbidden below Thirty-second Street, and horsecars of the New York and Harlem Railroad and later of the New York and New Haven, supplanted the downtown trains. As early as 1833 a cut was made through Murray Hill between Thirty-second and Forty-second Streets, and in 1846 the Common Council ordered the cut to be bridged; subsequently it was converted into an arched brick tunnel. A group of young hoodlums, known as the Fourth Avenue Tunnel Gang, made their headquarters here about the time of the

Civil War. Richard Croker, later Tammany chief, was said to have been one of the leaders.

In 1854 an order of the Common Council further restricted the use of steam-power, and the horsecar lines were extended to Forty-second Street. Here, in 1871, the Harlem Railroad Company opened the Grand Central Depot. Horsecars were replaced in the late 1880's by cable cars and in 1896 the Harlem road leased the lines below Forty-second Street to the Metropolitan Street Railroad Company. Streetcars were replaced by motor busses in 1933 and the use of the old Fourth Avenue tunnel was limited to private motor vehicles. At Fortieth Street the tunnel gives access to the ramp around the new Grand Central Terminal.

The venerable MURRAY HILL HOTEL, crowning glory of the elegant 1890's, fronts Park Avenue between Fortieth and Forty-first Streets. This hostelry was patronized by such diverse celebrities as Mark Twain, Senator George Hearst, Jay Gould, "Diamond Jim" Brady, and Presidents Cleveland and McKinley. Completed in 1884 after plans by Stephen Hatch, the hotel with its red and white marble floors, carmine plush, gilt-framed mirrors, and rococo walls and ceilings, has been little changed. It is eight stories in height, and has six hundred rooms, many of which retain the original furniture. The exterior is faced with a conglomeration of granite, brownstone, and red brick that was considered in its day the acme of architectural raiment. Fine circular fire escapes of wrought iron grace the bays of the Fortieth Street façade. The lobby, entered from Park Avenue by a double stairway, is decorated in red and gold in the best Victorian tradition. At the southwest corner of Forty-second Street and Park Avenue formerly stood the Hotel Belmont, famous for the magnificence of its bar and the cuisine of its French chefs; and at the southeast corner the popular Grand Union Hotel, headquarters for visting officers during the Civil War. The latter's host for many years was Simeon Ford, *bon vivant* and prince of after-dinner speakers.

FIFTH AVENUE SHOPPING DISTRICT

Area: 34th to 57th St. Map on page 193.

At Thirty-fourth Street, Fifth Avenue abruptly emerges from a street of buildings housing wholesale clothing, textile, and bric-a-brac concerns to become the aristocrat of shopping thoroughfares. Some of New York's most exclusive hotels and clubs and fashionable churches as well as many nationally known retail establishments front its broad sidewalks. The top of a Fifth Avenue bus provides one of the best views of the avenue, with its endless flow of well-dressed pedestrians and its conglomeration of architectural styles and signless show windows.

In the last quarter of the nineteenth century Fifth Avenue was a street of fine residences. Its transformation into a retail center in the 1900's aroused such opposition that echoes of protest are still audible. One of those mainly responsible for the invasion of trade was Benjamin Altman, whose store stands on the northeast corner of Fifth Avenue and Thirty-fourth Street, diagonally opposite the Empire State Building *(see page 319)*. Like many merchant princes who elevated counter trade to a major business, Altman originally opened shop in modest quarters on Third Avenue near Tenth Street and moved on as the flood of population swept gradually northward; in 1906 he came to the present address. Opposite stood the old Waldorf-Astoria Hotel (the site of the Empire State Building) ; to the north marched a double file of baronial homes, citadels of the social peerage.

In order to appease protesting residents, Altman erected a building whose mundane function was decorously hidden by a façade resembling a Florentine palace; until recently not even the owner's name appeared on the exterior. As commerce—having thus crept in disguise into the avenue —appropriated most of the district, residents moved farther up the avenue.

Within about a decade ALTMAN'S was joined by OPPENHEIM COLLINS (1907) and McCREERY'S (1913), both on West Thirty-fourth Street, and BEST AND COMPANY (1910), Fifth Avenue and Thirty-fifth Street. Charles Tiffany commissioned McKim, Mead, and White to build his great jewelry store at 409 Fifth Avenue in the style of the Palazzo Vendramini in Venice, while opposite, at Thirty-sixth Street, rose another palatial shop—designed by the same architects—for the Gorham Company, silversmiths, jewelers, and stationers. The latter building is now occupied by RUSSEKS (women's apparel). The construction of LORD AND TAYLOR in 1914 at Thirty-eighth Street marked a break with tradition (Starrett and Van Vleck were the architects) ; the avenue now had a building that was frankly commercial as well as dignified. Many of the smaller stores, eclipsed as show places by the graceful candor of the Lord and Taylor edifice, hastily incorporated large display windows and arched entrances. When FRANKLIN SIMON'S (1922) arose at Thirty-eighth Street, a new trend in department store architecture, which was to exert considerable influence on American main streets, was definitely established.

About the time of the World War, Fifth Avenue became the country's leading fashion center: the Fifth Avenue label represented the best in

American taste. Real-estate values and rents on the avenue reached astronomical figures, and under merciless competition only the wealthiest and most firmly entrenched establishments survived. The avenue catered exclusively to the wealthy until the 1930's, when medium- and low-price stores gradually appeared. The Fifth Avenue hallmark, however, has lost little of its aura.

Symbolic of the newer trend is the granite-faced home (opened in 1935) of S. H. KRESS AND COMPANY, at the northwest corner of Thirty-ninth Street, which boldly faces the terra-cotta edifice of its competitor, F. W. WOOLWORTH AND COMPANY (1939). The simple lines of these buildings, two of the most sumptuous dime stores in America, undoubtedly will influence future fronts along the avenue. At the southeast corner of Fortieth Street is the store of ARNOLD CONSTABLE AND COMPANY, an organization founded in 1825.

From Fortieth to Forty-second Street, on the west side of Fifth Avenue, where the Croton Reservoir was once located, is the Central Building of the New York Public Library (see page 325). Behind it are the 9.603 acres of BRYANT PARK, the site from 1822 to 1825 of Potter's Field, and of the 1853 World's Fair. The huge Crystal Palace (an inferior copy of the London structure), which dominated that fair, was gutted by fire in 1856. In 1871 the land, which had been acquired by the city in 1822, was reserved for a park and called Reservoir Park. Thirteen years later it was renamed for the New York editor and poet, William Cullen Bryant, but not until 1933, after the park had been torn up many times, was the present landscape plan adopted. One of its interesting features is the library's outdoor "reading room," maintained in summer under the trees.

Across West Fortieth Street, at No. 40, are the black and gold peaks of the AMERICAN RADIATOR BUILDING. The structure, designed by Raymond Hood and built in 1924, was an early attempt to clothe a skyscraper in bold colors. The unusual tower design of the building permits window light on all sides, the tall shaft merging at the top into a complexity of setback forms. The NATIONAL REPUBLICAN CLUB and the ENGINEERS' CLUB have quarters at 54 and 32 West Fortieth Street, respectively. Around the block, at 1 West Thirty-ninth Street, is the gown shop of LANE BRYANT, INC., noted for its maternity-clothing department; the ENGINEERING SOCIETIES BUILDING, with its library and auditorium, is at No. 29.

At the intersection of Forty-second Street and Fifth Avenue stands the 699-foot building known as 500 FIFTH AVENUE, designed by Shreve, Lamb, and Harmon, architects of the Empire State Building. The architecture of the RUPPERT BUILDING, 535 Fifth Avenue, was the cause of a publicized controversy. H. Craig Severance, its designer, sued the *New Yorker* for stating that "the central tower . . . has the grace of an overgrown grain elevator." The suit was settled by publication of a satisfactory retraction. Nevertheless for about a decade it put a damper on architectural criticism. In retrospect the magazine's comments seem more unusual than the design of the building. The FIFTH AVENUE BANK on the northwest corner is an interesting landmark made of three brownstone residences. The bank has occupied the premises since 1890.

The thirty-eight-story FRENCH BUILDING, 551 Fifth Avenue, was erected in 1927 by the Fred F. French Company, who were also the architects. The use of the maximum volume permitted by setback laws resulted in an awkward massing of the tower in comparison with the lower part of the building. An unusual element in the design is the somewhat questionable faïence polychromy.

The building at 575 Fifth Avenue is occupied by the firm of W. AND J. SLOANE, a furniture house of note. The FINLEY J. SHEPARD RESIDENCE at the northeast corner of Forty-seventh Street, and the HOME OF ROBERT W. GOELET at the southeast corner of Forty-eighth, brownstone houses typical of the old Fifth Avenue, are two of the very few remaining residences on Fifth Avenue south of Sixtieth Street. Opposite the Goelet home is the nationally known jewelry establishment of BLACK, STARR, AND FROST-GORHAM, INC.

The brownstone edifice on the northwest corner of Forty-eighth Street houses the COLLEGIATE CHURCH OF ST. NICHOLAS, the oldest congregation in Manhattan, dating from 1628. Theodore Roosevelt was a member of this church, and his pew is marked by a tablet. The first Collegiate church to bear the name St. Nicholas was built in 1642 inside Fort Amsterdam. The present building, erected in 1872, was designed by W. Wheeler Smith. The dark silhouette of its sharp spire is in dramatic contrast to the flat gray walls of the massive RCA Building in Rockefeller Center beyond.

SAKS FIFTH AVENUE, Forty-ninth to Fiftieth Street, was the first of the larger stores to be built on the upper avenue. Saks, Bergdorf-Goodman, Bonwit Teller, and a few other avenue shops are widely known for their striking window displays, mounted with the care of a Belasco stage-set. Rockefeller Center *(see page 333),* across the street, supplies an effect of rare architectural unity to this section of the avenue. In the RCA Building of the Center is the popular New York Museum of Science and Industry *(see page 342).*

Across the street, Fiftieth to Fifty-first Street, the needle-pointed Gothic towers of St. Patrick's Cathedral *(see page 344)* rise 330 feet above the surging traffic of the avenue. Two blocks away, on the northwest corner of Fifty-third Street, stands ST. THOMAS CHURCH (Protestant Episcopal), founded in 1823. The present edifice, the work of Cram, Goodhue, and Ferguson, was completed in 1913, and replaces one on the same site destroyed by fire in 1905. The symmetrical main portal appears to call for twin towers, although the building has but one. Consequently the structure lacks the sense of balance of a frankly unsymmetrical design. The interior, of soft yellow sandstone, has great distinction. The beautifully ordered mass of statuary in the great reredos over the altar is the work of Lee Lawrie; and the delicate wood carvings on the pulpit, choir stalls, lectern, and organ case, representing both historical and contemporary subjects, were executed under the supervision of the late Bertram G. Goodhue.

For several generations St. Thomas Church has been noted for its fashionable weddings, and in the ornamental work above the Bride's Door—the entrance to the south of the main portal—the sculptor chiseled a dollar sign next to a "true-lover's-knot," a comment that has been left unmolested. From St. Thomas, as from the other churches in the neighborhood, come the worshippers who form the Fifth Avenue Easter parade, an event that has attracted thousands of sight-seers since the days of bonnets and bustles. Directly behind the church is the new home of the Museum of Modern Art *(see page 347)*, 11 West Fifty-third Street.

Another great city house of the 1880's surviving in this neighborhood is the brownstone RESIDENCE OF CORNELIUS VANDERBILT III, near the northwest corner of Fifth Avenue and Fifty-first Street. Adjoining it on the north was a more famous dwelling—designed by Richard M. Hunt—which was razed in 1926. Both were built by W. H. Vanderbilt, and were known as the "twin mansions." The former home of the patrician Union Club on the northeast corner of Fifty-first Street now houses the GRAND CENTRAL GALLERIES, sponsors of the more academic tradition in American art. *(Open weekdays 9 a.m. to 5:30 p.m.; admission free.)*

The building occupied by the UNIVERSITY CLUB, northwest corner of Fifty-fourth Street, was completed in 1900, the work of McKim, Mead, and White. Reminiscent of a fifteenth-century Italian palazzo, it is one of the handsomest structures on the avenue. Decorating the exterior are eighteen college shields carved in marble. The interior has colorful Renaissance frescoes, and murals by H. Siddons Mowbray.

The HOTEL ST. REGIS on the southeast corner of Fifth Avenue and Fifty-fifth Street, and the GOTHAM HOTEL on the southwest corner, are the first of the group of luxurious hotels clustering around the southern end of Central Park and the Grand Army Plaza *(see page 229)*. Both were built at the beginning of the century. In the bar of the St. Regis is Maxfield Parrish's well-known painting, *Old King Cole*. The Gotham has for years been popular with foreign (particularly English) visitors, and is notable for its cuisine. The press of the expanding Fifth Avenue shopping trade is evident in the installation of stores on its Fifth Avenue abutment, space formerly occupied by a large dining room.

ELIZABETH ARDEN'S at No. 691 and HELENA RUBINSTEIN'S at No. 715, are among the most luxurious beauty salons in the country. The façades exemplify the current trend toward simplicity in retail shop design.

Two of America's best-known jewelry firms are CARTIER'S at the southeast corner of Fifty-second and MARCUS AND COMPANY at No. 681. These establishments, together with Black, Starr, and Frost-Gorham, carry on the avenue's luxury-trade tradition that was started by Tiffany.

On the southwest corner of Fifty-sixth Street, fine crystal ware is displayed in the five-story HOME OF THE STEUBEN GLASS COMPANY, a division of Corning Glass Works. The building, designed by John Gates, has walls chiefly built of glass bricks. The BONWIT TELLER store, dealing exclusively in women's apparel, on the northeast corner of Fifty-sixth Street, has the distinction of being headed by a woman, Mrs. Hortense Odlum. Another fashionable store is Bergdorf-Goodman *(see page 230)*, on the southwest corner of Fifty-eighth Street.

GRAND CENTRAL DISTRICT

Area: 42d St. on the south to 47th St. on the north; from 3d Ave. west to 5th Ave. Map on page 193.

Huge GRAND CENTRAL TERMINAL, set squarely athwart Park Avenue on the north side of Forty-second Street, is one of the great railway passenger terminals of the world. Around it, inevitably, have gathered skyscraper office buildings, large hotels, clubs, stores, and restaurants, until the Grand Central zone has become one of those inner cities that characterize a metropolis.

As the New York end of two important railroads—the vast New York Central system, which reaches to the Mississippi, and the New York, New Haven, and Hartford, which serves Boston and New England—the terminal is one of the city's two principal gateways, the other being Pennsylvania Station *(see page 165)*. Not only long-distance travelers use the terminal; many of the more than five hundred trains that enter and leave daily carry commuters who live north and northeast of the city, while on an average of every four seconds during the day three IRT subway lines (Lexington Avenue, the Times Square-Grand Central shuttle, and Queens) discharge and receive passengers in stations connected with the terminal. The number of people who pass through Grand Central in a year approximates the total population of the United States. Considerable numbers of these, however, use the building as a "short cut," as a refuge from bad weather, or for other purposes not connected with travel.

The terminal covers three blocks between Forty-second and Forty-fifth Streets, but the double-deck railroad yard extends under Park Avenue to a point near Fifty-ninth Street. There the forty-one tracks on the upper level and the twenty-six on the lower level finally narrow to the single-level, four-track line that stays underground until it reaches Ninety-sixth Street. Through trains use the upper level; most suburban trains, the lower; it is only by using two levels that the tremendous volume of traffic can be handled on the forty-eight acres of available land. Trains must be moved out, in most cases, almost as soon as they are unloaded, for Grand Central is a dead end with limited space. Deep under the thirty-four miles of yard track is a power plant.

The monumental Forty-second Street front of the terminal is surmounted by Jules Coutan's massive statuary group, forty-eight feet high, in which figures representing Mercury, Hercules, and Minerva are arranged about a clock thirteen feet in diameter. Park Avenue, blocked by the building, mounts to the second-story level by a bridge over Forty-second Street, divides right and left near the heroic bronze figure of Commodore Cornelius Vanderbilt, to encircle Grand Central, then tunnels through the New York Central Building immediately to the north, and returns to grade at Forty-sixth Street. This highway is an integral part of the terminal's structure. The space beneath it on the Forty-second Street and Vanderbilt Avenue sides is occupied by stores. The area beneath the highway bridge over Forty-second Street is named Pershing Square in honor of General John J. Pershing. Free information about the city is provided by a municipal office in a building that runs from Forty-first to Forty-second Street beneath the viaduct. This steel and glass-brick structure was built by the city in 1939 to serve visitors to New York.

Although the main entrance is the one directly facing Pershing Square, the corner entrance at Forty-second Street and Vanderbilt Avenue is probably used by most people. Indoor ramps lead from both entrances to the impressive main concourse, 125 feet wide and 385 feet long, that is depressed more than a story below street level. Around the sides, great square piers rise 125 feet to support a vaulted blue ceiling in which illuminated constellations of the zodiac twinkle. The ecliptic of the zodiac, by an error in painting, runs the wrong way. The enormous size and lavish use of marble on floors as well as walls give the concourse an aspect of grandeur that is emphasized by shafts of sunlight pouring through the seventy-five-foot windows. The effect is heightened at Christmas and Easter by soft organ music from one of the surrounding balconies.

Ticket windows line the south wall, while directly opposite are the gates to the track platforms. The circular information booth in the middle of the open floor is one of New York's most popular meeting places.

During the nine o'clock and five o'clock rush hours, this great hall swarms with scurrying crowds in which the red caps of the porters—there are 495 of them—stand out. Shortly before the Twentieth Century Limited leaves for Chicago at six in the evening, a gray and red carpet is unrolled between the gate and the platform.

The lower level concourse is similar to the upper in floor plan, but is prevented by its necessarily lower ceiling from achieving a like grandeur. The two are connected by stairways and broad ramps, and are surrounded on three sides by interconnected passages along which run rows of stores: food, liquor, flower, apparel, book-, and barbershops; restaurants; newspaper and magazine stands; telegraph and theater ticket agencies; lunch and milk bars. A newsreel theater, an art gallery, Travelers' Aid service, and recreational exhibits are available in the building. All these facilities, reached by underground corridors from adjacent hotels and office buildings, make Grand Central also a neighborhood shopping center.

The terminal was opened by the New York Central Railroad in 1913 to replace the old depot on the same site. The architects, Warren and Wetmore, Reed and Stem, used the available space with such economy that Grand Central is rightly considered an engineering marvel. A plan considered at one time provided for the addition of a third concourse, at street level, to accommodate casual pedestrian traffic; but this has never been built.

The NEW YORK CENTRAL BUILDING, directly north between Forty-fifth and Forty-sixth Streets, houses offices of the railroads using the station. Its ornate dormer-studded peak, overlooking Park Avenue, is an architectural curiosity. Applied columns that support inverted brackets, and are themselves supported by brackets—a questionable use of architectural motifs as sculptural decoration—appear below the roof.

The din of motor and streetcar traffic on Forty-second Street, the shunt and shuffle of pedestrians, the upward thrust of the buff and yellow sky-scrapers around the terminal, produce an impact not easily forgotten. Among the towering buildings in this area is the thirty-story GRAYBAR, facing Lexington Avenue between Forty-third and Forty-fourth Streets, and connected with the terminal by a broad passageway. Designed by Sloan and Robertson, it contains more than a million square feet of rentable floor space and when constructed in 1927 was rated as the largest office structure above ground in the world. It houses many nationally prominent advertising agencies.

North of the Graybar is the GRAND CENTRAL POST OFFICE, which, except for the General Post Office and the Church Street Annex, handles a greater volume of mail than any station in the city.

Most conspicuous of the Forty-second Street towers is the CHRYSLER BUILDING, completed in 1929 at the northeast corner of Lexington Avenue. This building's seventy-seven stories, terminating in a needle-like spire, make it the second tallest structure in the world. It was one of the first skyscrapers to use exposed metal as an integral part of its design. At the fourth setback the building corners flare outward, projecting great metal discs resembling 1929 Chrysler radiator caps.

The building represents a "modernistic" movement in architecture to avoid historical precedent in an effort to achieve freshness, originality, and a striking effect. Sharp contrasts of color and line appear in the tower treatment. The lower portion of the wall is noteworthy for the basket pattern of the stone veneer.

William Van Alen, architect of the Chrysler Building, and his former partner, H. Craig Severance, became rivals when each was commissioned to design the world's tallest building. When the Chrysler tower seemed likely to terminate at 925 feet, the builders of the Bank of the Manhattan Company (see page 88) structure at 40 Wall Street (designed by Severance and Yasuo Matsui) decided to halt their operations at 927 feet. Meanwhile, steel workers were secretly assembling the rustless steel sections of the Chrysler spire which, when lifted through the dome and bolted into place, brought the building to its triumphant height of 1,048 feet. Subsequently the Empire State Building (see page 319) stole the laurels.

The angular Chrysler lobby is finished in sumptuous African marble. On the ground floor, a revolving motorcar display can be seen from the street through reflectionless windows. In the building are located many advertising agencies, the eastern headquarters of the Chrysler Company, and the "Cloud Club," composed of advertising, aviation, steel, and railroad executives. There is an Observation Room at the base of the metal spire. *(Open daily 9 a.m. to 6 p.m.; admission 55¢.)* The view during clear visibility encompasses a fifty-mile radius.

Diagonally opposite the Chrysler Building at 122 East Forty-second Street is the fifty-six-story CHANIN BUILDING, designed by Sloan and Robertson and built in 1929. A wide bronze band decorated with figures of birds and fishes runs along the entire front above the first story windows. On the fiftieth floor is a completely equipped little theater, designed by Jacques Delamarre.

The largest of the Grand Central hotels is the COMMODORE, Forty-second Street and Lexington Avenue, with two thousand rooms. Although only twenty-eight stories high, the Commodore has five additional stories underground, through two of which run railway and subway tracks, insulated from the foundation columns to prevent vibration.

The BOWERY SAVINGS BANK BUILDING, 110 East Forty-second Street, is well known for its cast-bronze doors, made by William H. Jackson and Company, and for its great banking hall, lavishly finished in mosaic and marble. Among the symbols represented in the rich architectural detail of the building are the bull and bear of Wall Street, the lion for power, rooster for punctuality, and the squirrel for thrift. The structure was completed in 1923 and is considered the masterpiece of York and Sawyer, architects.

The fifty-three-story LINCOLN BUILDING, 60 East Forty-second Street, with nine hundred thousand square feet of rentable area, was erected in 1930.

Within the immediate vicinity of Grand Central are the ticket offices of eleven air lines serving the entire country. Their sleek, elongated, black limousines convey passengers almost hourly from ticket offices to Long Island and New Jersey airports.

Narrow Vanderbilt Avenue, extending along the west side of the terminal from Forty-second to Forty-seventh Street, is fronted by the YALE CLUB at Forty-fourth Street. Charles and Company, for ninety years dealers in fine domestic and exotic foods, occupied a store at 48 East Forty-third Street, near Vanderbilt Avenue, until 1938.

Along Madison Avenue, the Bond Street of America, are many of the outstanding men's shops in the city. The avenue is also a street of hotels: the BILTMORE, at Forty-third Street, national headquarters of the Democratic Party; the ROOSEVELT at Forty-fifth Street, named for Theodore Roosevelt; and the RITZ-CARLTON at Forty-sixth Street, one of an international chain of hostelries whose name has become a slang term connoting exclusiveness.

(The cost of the food and drink for an average debutante supper for some six hundred guests at the Ritz was about $4,750 in 1938.)

To the east, on Lexington Avenue between Forty-sixth and Forty-seventh Streets, is somber GRAND CENTRAL PALACE, where annual automobile, flower, and motorboat shows, and numerous industrial exhibitions are held. It was built in 1912 from designs by Warren and Wetmore.

On the northeast fringe of the Grand Central area, along Lexington Avenue, is another group of hotels, including the LEXINGTON at No. 511, the SHELTON at No. 527, the BARCLAY at No. 530, and the BELMONT PLAZA at No. 541.

The thirty-four-story Shelton, when completed in 1924, was one of the earliest setback structures in the city. The architect, Arthur Loomis Harmon, sensed the great aesthetic possibilities inherent in a studied proportioning of the huge masses of the modern skyscraper, and created a composition of forms which exerted a profound influence on later buildings. It is unique among tall buildings in that the walls slope in toward the top to avoid the optical illusion of overhanging. Italian Romanesque details are placed where they tend to accentuate the main forms. The structure was a favorite subject of Georgia O'Keeffe, noted New York artist, whose paintings helped make it one of the best-known buildings of the 1920's. Both the Architectural League of New York and the American Institute of Architects awarded medals for its design.

BEEKMAN PLACE AND SUTTON PLACE

Area: 48th St. on south to 59th St. on north; from 1st Ave. east to East River. Map on page 193.

The small area centering around Beekman and Sutton Places offers an extreme example of New York's flair for making Mrs. O'Grady and the Colonel's Lady close if uncommunicative neighbors. Here drying winter flannels are within fishpole reach of a Wall Street tycoon's windows, and the society woman in her boudoir may be separated only by a wall from the family on relief in a cold-water flat.

The neighborhood extends for eleven blocks along two East River bluffs grooved by dead-end streets. The narrow channel between Welfare Island and the bluff brings freighters within hailing distance. Millionaires' yachts dock close to gravel barges. Gulls skimming the surface mark the sewage outlets into the river; but from a penthouse window, at night, there is only the impressive stretch of dark water and the lights of the metropolis.

Beekman Place, which runs for two blocks along the south bluff (from Mitchell Place, the north side of East Forty-ninth Street, to East Fifty-first Street), was named for a descendant of William Beekman, who came from Holland with Peter Stuyvesant. Sutton Place, which extends from East Fifty-seventh to Sixtieth Street along a similar high, rocky formation over the river, was named in 1880 for a family owning a line of clipper ships. In 1875, Effingham Sutton and James Stokes had purchased property in the vicinity for a real-estate development. Sutton Place South, a later extension, runs from Sutton Place to East Fifty-fourth Street, and is separated from the Beekman Place neighborhood by the blocks in the valley between East Fifty-fourth and Fifty-second Streets.

In the brownstone decades of the last century the district was the home of the well-to-do, but as the slums moved northward, tenements were erected and most of the brownstones were abandoned to the poor, many of whom worked in the packing and slaughterhouses and coalyards along the river. The wealthy, drawn by the river setting, began to reclaim the neighborhood in the 1920's, in large part through the initiative of the late Elisabeth Marbury, internationally famous literary agent, Miss Anne Morgan, and Mrs. W. K. Vanderbilt.

Mitchell Place climbs from First Avenue to Beekman Place on a cut-stone ramp. The twenty-six-story BEEKMAN TOWER HOTEL, at No. 3, formerly the Panhellenic Hotel, was built in 1928 as a residence and meeting place for women belonging to national Greek-letter college sororities; it is now a hotel for men and women. The structure's distinction is attained through its purity of form. The tower walls are of tan brick and tan mortar. The four corners are beveled, and their deep-set windows accent the verticality inherent in the shaft. The architect was John Mead Howells.

The docks at East Forty-ninth and East Fifty-third Streets offer a comprehensive view of the rear of Beekman Place as well as the hospitals on Welfare Island. ONE BEEKMAN PLACE, a huge apartment building with a series of terrace gardens on its river side, is occupied by many families prominent in society and the theater.

A plaque sundial is set in the house wall on the north side of the dead end of East Fiftieth Street. Since the sun strikes here only between seven and two, other hour markings are omitted; but the time it marks is about two hours late because the gnomon is bent. Behind a terrace on East Fifty-first Street is a building called the HALE HOUSE. The East Fifty-first Street wall of this residence has two faded frescoes: one depicts the trial and execution of Nathan Hale; the other, a "kissing bridge" of old Manhattan. A stone wall, topped with broken, multicolored glass embedded in cement, encloses the terrace.

On the northwest corner of East Fifty-first Street and First Avenue, Public School 135, erected more than fifty years ago but still in use, occupies the SITE OF BEEKMAN HOUSE (1763–1874), headquarters of General Charles Clinton and Sir William Howe during the Revolution. Major André slept there one night and the next morning "passed out to dishonor"; the drawing room was another of the numerous places where Nathan Hale is alleged to have been tried and sentenced. An original mantel of this room is in the galleries of the New York Historical Society, 170 Central Park West.

The dock off East Fifty-third Street is said to have inspired Sidney Kingsley's play, *Dead End,* which dramatizes the contrast of wealth and poverty in a single district. Rising sheer from the river shore between East Fifty-second and Fifty-third Streets is RIVER HOUSE, one of the most palatial structures in the city. It was designed by Bottomley, Wagner, and White as a co-operative dwelling. The building's towers and the general mass of its twenty-six stories impose a conspicuous design on the sky line of the Middle East Side. The RIVER CLUB occupies the lower floors. It has squash and tennis courts, a swimming pool, ballroom, and floating dock for pleasure craft. Vincent Astor's white *Nourmahal* frequently drops anchor off East Fifty-second Street.

Near the shore at Fifty-third Street a man named Youle in 1821 built a tall shot tower that toppled during construction, but was replaced and served as a landmark until the Civil War. The rocky land that juts into the river at the end of East Fifty-fifth Street used to be known as Cannon Point.

On the east side of Sutton Place South, between East Fifty-fifth and Fifty-sixth Streets, is a renovated apartment unit. Ten years ago it was known as the "Ark" and housed a colony of writers and artists paying minimum monthly rentals of eleven dollars. An enterprising real-estate firm acquired the property; the interiors were remodeled, the old brick exteriors were painted black, trimmed in white, with scarlet, green, and canary-yellow doors—and rentals rose. Most of the block to the west is occupied by the abandoned red-brick buildings of the Peter Doelger Brewery. Attached to the old brewery is the more recently vacated Brewery Restaurant, well-known speak-easy during Prohibition.

New apartment buildings line East Fifty-seventh Street, "front entrance" to Sutton Place. East Fifty-eighth Street ends at Sutton Square, so named in 1920 when the surrounding houses were remodeled. North of the square, facing the river, is RIVERVIEW TERRACE, a single row of brown-stones occupied by old residents of the neighborhood. An iron fence, fronted with shrubbery, flowers, and ten evenly spaced maple trees, extends along the edge of the bluff. The imperturbable atmosphere of this small court is unrivaled by the synthetic environment of larger, more carefully planned real-estate developments. On stormy days the waves breaking against the rocks on the river shore can be heard above the rumble of traffic crossing the great Queensboro Bridge overhead.

The scene changes abruptly to the north. The huge smokestack of a New York Steam Corporation plant adjoins Riverview Terrace. At Sixtieth Street Sutton Place passes under the Queensboro Bridge and into the more plebeian world of York Avenue.

CENTRAL PARK SOUTH, THE PLAZA, AND FIFTY-SEVENTH STREET

Area: 57th St. on the south to Central Park South on the north; from Broadway east to Fifth Ave. Map on page 277.

From Columbus Circle's whirlpool of noisy workaday confusion, pre-sided over by a statue of Isabella's adventuresome ambassador, Central Park South emerges as a resplendent thoroughfare. Terminating at Grand Army Plaza and Fifth Avenue, it traverses three long blocks from the Circle to Fifth Avenue, with smart hotels—some of them more than forty stories high—on one side, and the two-and-a-half-mile vista of the park on the other *(see page 350).* Central Park South's sister-street in impor-tance, Fifty-seventh, is one of opulent shops and stores, concert halls and schools of art, dancing, and music. Fifty-eighth Street is the comparatively poor relation.

The plaza from Fifty-eighth to Sixtieth Street provides a formalized entrance to the park; it also serves as an impressive forecourt for the stately hotels surrounding it. The official name, seldom used, is Grand Army Plaza. In the northern half is the STATUE OF GENERAL WILLIAM TECUMSEH SHERMAN, and in the southern half, the PULITZER MEMORIAL FOUNTAIN. The Sherman statue, which brought fame to Augustus Saint-Gaudens when it was unveiled at the Paris exposition in 1900, was placed in the plaza in 1903. Modeled with fine precision, this bronze and gilt equestrian statue is one of the city's most impressive monuments. The Pulitzer Memorial, called the *Fountain of Abundance,* consists of two shallow pools and four basins rising in steps to a height of more than twenty feet. In the top basin is a pedestal that supports the bronze figure of a young woman holding a basket of fruit. The symbolism of abundance is further carried out by two marble cornucopias at the base. The sculptor was Karl Bitter, and the architects were Carrère and Hastings. Funds were provided by the will of Joseph Pulitzer.

The buildings around and near the plaza display an extraordinary unity, growing out of a harmony of color, material, and scale. Their roofs are picturesque, some tiled, others copper, but nearly all in various shades of green. This harmony extends to architectural treatments. The PLAZA HOTEL (opened in 1907) on the west side was designed by Henry J. Hardenbergh in French Renaissance style, and the later buildings, east and south of the plaza, were carefully related to it: the HECKSCHER BUILDING (1921) by Warren and Wetmore; the SHERRY-NETHERLAND HOTEL (1927) by Schultze and Weaver; the SAVOY-PLAZA HOTEL (1928) by McKim, Mead, and White; the HOTEL PIERRE (1930) by Schultze and Weaver; the BERGDORF-GOODMAN and DOBBS BUILDINGS (1928) by Buchman and Kahn; the SQUIBB BUILDING (1930) by Ely Jacques Kahn; and the NEW YORK TRUST COMPANY BUILDING (1930) by Cross and Cross.

All the hotels of the plaza group are alike in their luxurious appointments, yet each attracts a special clientele. The Plaza Hotel is patronized by the well-established older groups of society, though to a war generation it was a rendezvous of youth, as recorded in F. Scott Fitzgerald's novel, *The Great Gatsby*. The Hotel Pierre has become popular with the Park Avenue crowd for coming-out parties. The Savoy-Plaza and Sherry-Netherland are residential hotels. In the walls of the entrance of the latter are two sculptured panels from the W. H. Vanderbilt mansion. They were designed by Richard M. Hunt.

At Sixtieth Street and Fifth Avenue, the METROPOLITAN CLUB, a stronghold of late nineteenth-century exclusiveness, occupies a dignified Florentine palazzo that was designed by McKim, Mead, and White and was completed in 1893.

Central Park South, in character, is an extension of the plaza. Its skyscraper hotels, seen from the park, have a magnificent quality as a group. The ST. MORITZ, at No. 50, is noted for its continental atmosphere, and its Café de la Paix, a sidewalk restaurant, is reminiscent of its Parisian prototype. The BARBIZON PLAZA, on the northwest corner of Fifty-eighth Street and Sixth Avenue, extends to Central Park South. Another of the street's leading hotels, HAMPSHIRE HOUSE, at No. 150, was opened in 1937. When three-quarters finished, its construction was halted by the depression of the early 1930's, and for six years the thirty-seven-story building was a derelict with boarded-up windows. ESSEX HOUSE, at No. 160, is an imposing structure forty-three stories high. Like other hotels in this neighborhood, it is patronized by Hollywood stars.

On the southeast corner of Central Park South and Seventh Avenue is the NEW YORK ATHLETIC CLUB. The building was completed in 1928 from designs by York and Sawyer. Cold formality characterizes both the exterior and the public rooms of this twenty-one-story structure. Founded in 1868, the club has 4,700 members, including many prominent social and political figures. Its teams frequently have been the leading point-winners for the United States at the Olympic games.

The GAINSBOROUGH STUDIOS, at No. 222, is one of the oldest studio apartment buildings in the city. A frieze, extending across the second story, represents a festival procession and in its center is a bust of Gainsborough. Along Fifty-eighth Street, one block south of the park, are small but exclusive hotels, studios in old brownstone houses, a theater, art shops, and garages. The rooming houses on this street are patronized by career-bent girls of genteel background and slender purses—the type depicted in the play *Stage Door,* by Edna Ferber and George S. Kaufman.

Fifty-seventh Street is America's Rue de la Paix. The names of some of the shops are in letters so small as to seem merely a grudging identification. Here, amid fashionable women's specialty shops, are some of the city's oldest galleries and probably the greatest concentration of art dealers in America. The Fifty-seventh Street establishments exhibit works of virtually every period and phase in the history of art as well as examples of all contemporary movements.

CARNEGIE HALL, at Seventh Avenue and Fifty-seventh Street, extending through to Fifty-sixth Street, is a six-story building, reminiscent of Italian Renaissance architecture, with a fifteen-story tower in which are studio apartments. The auditorium, with a seating capacity of 2,760, is unusually plain, the only relief being provided by the rose and gilt furnishings of the two tiers of boxes around three sides. Although it was constructed in the early days of acoustical engineering, few auditoriums have such excellent acoustics. It was designed by William B. Tuthill, assisted by several consultants, including Messrs. Hunt, Adler, and Sullivan. The hall was built as a new home for the Oratorio Society and was opened May 5, 1891, with a five-day music festival, at which Tchaikovsky conducted several of his own works. That same season Paderewski gave his first American performance. Subsequently Joseph Lhevinne and Mischa Elman made their American debuts here, and Efrem Zimbalist his

New York debut. The Philharmonic Orchestra made its first appearance in the Hall in 1892, with Anton Seidl as conductor. Toscanini came as guest conductor of the orchestra in 1926 and 1927, and as regular conductor thereafter until his farewell performance April 29, 1936. One evening in 1938, "jitterbugs" crowded the auditorium to hear Benny Goodman's swing orchestra. Many notables in fields other than music have appeared on the Carnegie stage.

When Andrew Carnegie was persuaded by Walter Damrosch to invest two million dollars in the enterprise, he did so in the belief that a patron of the arts could profit financially. Continuing operating deficits dispelled his hope of profit. Despite crowded houses, the hall never paid its way and had to depend upon private subsidization in order to survive until, in 1925, a syndicate purchased the property and made extensive alterations. Among other changes, a banquet hall was converted into an art gallery for the use of the tenants of the 150 studios in the building.

The completion of Carnegie Hall in 1891 established the district as the foremost musical center of the country. Manufacturers of musical instruments, especially pianos, opened impressive showrooms along Fifty-seventh Street. In 1925 STEINWAY HALL, No. 113, was built. Its lower stories are devoted to displays; the remainder house sales offices, headquarters of musical organizations, shops of specialized instrument manufacturers, studios, and a concert hall. The dignified sixteen-story structure with its limestone front was designed by Warren and Wetmore.

Complementing the section's national importance as an art center are its influential art schools. Among these is the ART STUDENTS LEAGUE, in the FINE ARTS BUILDING, 215 West Fifty-seventh Street. Designed by Hardenbergh and built in 1898, it is an excellent imitation of the graceful style of architecture of Francis I's reign. The annual shows of the National Academy are held here. Near by, at No. 225, the FEDERAL ART PROJECT GALLERY exhibits the mural and easel paintings and sculpture of WPA artists.

One sentimental detail of this area is unique in New York. Near the plaza, along the north side of Central Park South, hansom cabs, gracious relics of a more leisurely epoch, wait for revelers who finish off the night with a ride around Central Park.

UPPER FIFTH, MADISON, AND PARK AVENUES

Area: 47th St. on the south to 110th St. on the north; from 5th Ave. east to Lexington Ave. (excluding area east of 5th Ave. between 96th and 110th Sts., and 5th Ave. between 47th and 60th Sts.). Maps on pages 237 and 277.

Elegant bluebloods and solid burghers, tycoons and ne'er-do-wells, social *arrivistes* and just plain people (or New Yorkers a little more affluent than the average)—these are the residents of this district. It is a quarter of old mansions, air-conditioned apartments, exclusive clubs, luxurious hotels, fabulous penthouses; of great churches and museums; of art galleries, antique shops, and specialty stores; of high-priced cafés, cocktail lounges, night clubs.

In the face of an advancing business district the core of the city's fashionable residential section moved northward from Washington Square in the 1860's. It retreated steadily up Fifth Avenue until the startling development of Park Avenue in the 1920's deflected its course eastward. About ten years ago the exact geographical center of the addresses contained in the *Social Register* was determined painstakingly by realtors: it was near Sixty-eighth Street on Madison Avenue. It remains near the same spot to-day.

By 1872 Fifth Avenue was lined with residences as far as Fifty-ninth Street. Edith Wharton in "A Little Girl's New York," a posthumous magazine article, recalls that "the little brownstone houses, all with Dutch 'stoops' . . . and all not more than three stories high, marched Parkward in an orderly procession, like a young ladies' boarding school taking its daily exercise." She remembers when Fifty-seventh Street was a "desert" and new construction on Fifty-ninth Street was regarded as a "bold move which surprised and scandalized society." When Central Park was completed (1876) the movement northward continued and the dwellings erected were pretentious and rococo, with limestone supplanting the brownstone fronts. Not until the twentieth century, however, did the long stretch of the avenue facing the park achieve its fame as "Millionaires' Row."

When, in 1905, Andrew Carnegie built his mansion at Ninety-first Street his nearest neighbors were inhabitants of a shanty. Soon one commodity king after another—in the company of the Astors, Vanderbilts, Whitneys, Belmonts, and Fishes—erected sumptuous dwellings on the avenue. Among these industrialists were Henry Phipps (iron), Daniel G. Reid (tin plate), Charles T. Yerkes (rapid transit), James B. Duke (tobacco), O. H. Havemeyer (sugar), Edward S. Harkness (oil), Sir Roderick Cameron (ships), and F. W. Woolworth. Senator William A. Clark of Montana, a copper magnate, erected at Seventy-seventh Street one of the costliest private homes ever built in New York, with material brought from every country in the world.

Charles A. Beard, in *The Rise of American Civilization,* described the dwellings of millionaires as "chateaux of French design, mansions of the Italian renaissance, English castles of authoritative mien—a riot of periods and tastes—with occasionally a noble monument to the derivative genius of some American architect trained in Europe and given freedom to create." This description of the architecture of the Gilded Age (the late nineteenth century) was equally true of the 1900's. Today, as in the past, heavily curtained windows and drawn blinds contribute to the museumlike atmosphere of Millionaires' Row.

Fifth Avenue, as well as the other streets on the upper East Side, has been affected greatly by the postwar trend toward apartments. Its doom as Manhattan's last stronghold of single-family homes seems certain. Some of the wealthiest families have closed or sold their homes and moved into apartments; many have their mansions on Long Island or elsewhere and maintain more modest quarters in the city.

The growth of Madison Avenue and the cross streets followed that of Fifth Avenue. Park Avenue, as the railroad back yard to the sector, lagged far behind. Between 1890 and 1910 old twenty-foot flats were replaced by seven- and nine-story elevator apartments, but it was not until after the World War, when it was demonstrated that skyscraper apartments could be constructed on stilts free from the vibration of the New York Central Railroad yards hidden below, that Park Avenue became fashionable. To-day a double row of tall apartments, broken by an occasional church or single-family dwelling, stretches from the Grand Central Terminal at Forty-sixth Street to the uncovered railroad tracks at Ninety-sixth Street, where the avenue abruptly changes into a slum tenement area—Spanish Harlem.

One of the broadest of New York's thoroughfares, Park Avenue is divided by a fenced-in parking of well-tended grass, flower beds, and shrubbery. As the main artery of this locality, it is constantly filled with fast noncommercial traffic—busses, drays, and trucks being banned. On the scrubbed sidewalks sedate housemen exercise dogs; under the marquees uniformed doormen stand guard, ready to aid top-hatted men and be-gowned women in their journey from foyer to car, car to foyer.

No other street in the world approaches Park Avenue in its residential concentration of wealth. Apartment rentals average as much as $1,500 per room annually, yet it has been termed a "super-slum" by authorities on modern housing and city planning. Its architecture is noteworthy for its lack of imagination, one building resembling another like peas in a pod. Although the apartments have all modern conveniences and luxuries, adequate provision for light and air and view was generally neglected.

Madison Avenue is one of the world's most opulent marts. Its recent development as a smart shopping center is due largely to its situation between wealthy Fifth and Park Avenues. Below Fifty-ninth Street, among the hotels and office buildings, the shops—more intimate than those on Fifth Avenue—feature one or two specialties, domestic or imported: period furniture, luggage, millinery, pets, flowers, paintings, perfumes. Lexington Avenue, while still serving the tenement district to the east, is becoming another street of fine shops.

The HOTEL MARGUERY, a luxurious apartment hotel, occupies the west side of Park Avenue between Forty-seventh and Forty-eighth Streets.

The WALDORF-ASTORIA, on the block between Forty-ninth and Fiftieth Streets, Park and Lexington Avenues, is successor to the old Waldorf-Astoria that stood on the site of the present Empire State Building *(see page 319)*. Opened in 1931, it continues the traditions of the old hotel: the celebrated Oscar is still host, and it still maintains the Peacock Alley, the Empire Room, and Astor Gallery. So many of the city's important social functions take place in the Waldorf-Astoria that it has been called New York's unofficial palace. Flags denoting the visit of foreign dignitaries are flown frequently.

The massive building, designed by Schultze and Weaver, is of limestone and light-colored brick, with a granite base. Above the first eighteen stories, which rise sheer, a well-proportioned series of setbacks is surmounted by twin chrome-capped towers that bring the building's height to 625 feet (forty-seven stories). The figure over the main entrance on Park Avenue, designed by Nina Saemundsson, represents the Spirit of Achievement.

In the interior, rare marbles, matched woods, selected stones, and nickel-bronzes are employed with exceptional skill. The furniture is eighteenth-century English and early American in design. Decorations were executed by noted artists: the murals in the Sert Room are by José Maria Sert; the rug *(The Wheel of Life)* and the paintings in the main foyer, by Louis Rigal; the murals in the Starlight Roof Garden, by Victor White. Tony Sarg decorated the Oasis, a popular rendezvous at the cocktail hour.

There are more than 2,200 rooms in this hotel in which more than forty million dollars was invested. About two thousand people are on its staff. The towers are reserved for residential suites, some of which have garden terraces. Eighty per cent of the building is over the tracks of the New York Central, and private railroad cars may be shunted to a special entrance.

Just south of the Waldorf, at 299 Park Avenue, is the PARK LANE HOTEL, completed in 1924 from plans by Schultze and Weaver. LOUIS SHERRY'S at 300 Park Avenue, is one of the most select restaurants in the upper East Side.

ST. BARTHOLOMEW'S CHURCH, on the east side of Park Avenue between Fiftieth and Fifty-first Streets, has had since its founding in 1835 one of the city's wealthiest congregations. The monumental mass of the Waldorf-Astoria Hotel and the slender tower of the General Electric Building provide an impressive setting for this elegant church. The present building, of Byzantine architecture, completed in 1930, cost $5,400,000 and is on a site valued at approximately $1,500,000. The original architect was Bertram G.

KEY TO UPPER EAST SIDE MAP

UPPER MADISON AND PARK AVENUES
(For Upper Fifth Avenue see map on page 277.)

1. Waldorf-Astoria Hotel
2. Park Lane Hotel
3. Hotel Marguery
4. Louis Sherry's
5. Villard House
6. St. Bartholomew's Church
7. Hotel Ambassador
   Dutch Treat Club
8. Columbia Broadcasting System
9. Racquet and Tennis Club

10. Ritz Tower (Hotel)
11. Grolier Club
12. Home of Mrs. James Roosevelt
13. Church of St. Vincent Ferrer
14. Hunter College
15. Union Club
16. Residence of Former Senator Arthur Curtiss James
17. Residence of George Blumenthal
18. New York Society Library

YORKVILLE

19. New York Labor Temple
20. Yorkville Casino
21. Gracie Mansion
22. Doctors' Hospital
23. Welfare Island Ferry Slip
24. New York Public Library, Webster Branch
25. Parsonage of the Jan Hus Presbyterian Church
26. Bohemian National Hall
27. Kip's Bay-Yorkville Health and Teaching Center
28. Church of St. Catherine of Siena
29. German Reformed Church

30. St. Catherine's Park
31. Memorial Hospital for the Treatment of Cancer
32. New York Hospital and Cornell University Medical College
33. Rockefeller Institute for Medical Research
34. Model Tenements
35. Smith's Folly
36. L'Église Française du Saint-Esprit Sixty-first Street Methodist Episcopal Church
37. First Swedish Baptist Church

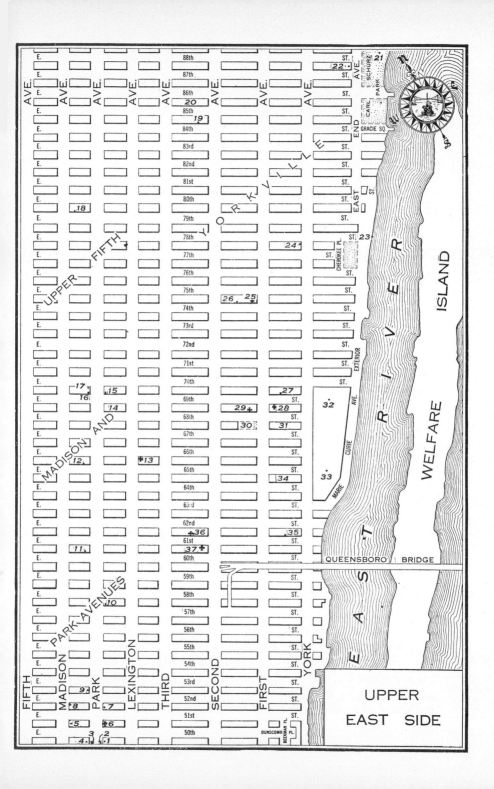

UPPER

EAST SIDE

Goodhue; his designs were later revised by Mayers, Murray, and Phillips, his associates, to include the terraced community house and the much-discussed dome. The whole group is built of salmon-colored brick and Indiana limestone, with tile and marble of various colors.

Outstanding, on the exterior, is the famous portico by McKim, Mead, and White, an academic copy of Southern French Romanesque work. With its three bronze doors, it is a memorial gift of the family of Cornelius Vanderbilt, which was part of the earlier edifice at Madison Avenue and Forty-fourth Street. The doors are decorated with elaborate bas-reliefs by Andrew O'Connor, associated with Daniel C. French (main door), Philip Martiny (north door), and Herbert Adams (south door), depicting scenes from the Old and New Testaments. The interior of the entrance portico, rich in marbles and mosaic, sets the color tone for the church— a golden brown. The unrelieved brilliance of the décor prevents it from achieving full effectiveness.

St. Bartholomew's has always been famous for the dignity and beauty of its service, for its preaching and its music. Among its art treasures is the Angel Font by the Scandinavian sculptor, Thorwaldsen.

The Hotel Ambassador, on the east side of Park Avenue between Fifty-first and Fifty-second Streets, was designed by Warren and Wetmore, and erected in 1921. A residential hotel, it is popular in diplomatic circles and has been called the "social embassy of two continents." The Dutch Treat Club, membership in which is limited to those prominent in the creative arts, holds its meetings here.

The clubrooms and athletic facilities of the Racquet and Tennis Club, 370 Park Avenue, are housed in a building erected in 1918, designed in the Italian Renaissance style by McKim, Mead, and White. The club, one of the most fashionable sports associations in the city, has two tennis courts built of a special composition on slate foundations, each costing about $250,000.

Villard House, a group of mansions surrounding a court, occupies the east side of Madison Avenue between Fiftieth and Fifty-first Streets. Built in 1885—McKim, Mead, and White, architects—these houses were among the first American buildings to follow a style derived from the Italian Renaissance palaces. Their masonry is a mellow brown sandstone. Cornices, windows, court arcade, and general scale are reminiscent of Italian prototypes. One of the first owners was Henry Villard, German-American railroad magnate, whose wife was the daughter of William Lloyd Garrison; a son, Oswald Garrison Villard, was formerly publisher and editor of the *Nation*. The largest house of the group, formerly occupied by the

Villards, and later purchased by Whitelaw Reid, former ambassador to England, costs about $750,000. It contains works of Saint-Gaudens, La Farge, and Abbey. At present only two houses of the group are tenanted. The court, in recent years, has been dubbed New York's most exclusive parking space. The block to the south, where the New Weston Hotel now stands, was the site of Columbia University from 1857 to 1897.

At 485 Madison Avenue are the HEADQUARTERS AND STUDIOS OF THE COLUMBIA BROADCASTING SYSTEM, the second leading national network.

A belt of night clubs stretches across the upper East Side in the Fifties. Among the most noted are the STORK CLUB, 3 East Fifty-third Street, and EL MOROCCO, 154 East Fifty-fourth Street, where café society idles away the night and newspaper columnists gather much of their material.

Fifty-seventh Street is celebrated for its women's style shops, as well as for shops dealing in art work of all kinds. The forty-two-story RITZ TOWER, Park Avenue and Fifty-seventh Street, was erected in 1925 as part of the Hearst apartment hotel chain from plans by Emery Roth, architect, Carrère and Hastings, associates. Arthur Brisbane, popular columnist for Hearst newspapers, had a duplex apartment in the tower.

On congested, narrow East Fifty-ninth Street there are a few second-hand bookstores and -stalls. The GROLIER CLUB, 47 East Sixtieth Street, named for the sixteenth-century French bibliophile, Jean Grolier, was established in 1884 for the promotion of bibliophily and the bookmaking craft. *(Visitors may examine its collection upon application to the librarian.)*

The small but very valuable BACHE COLLECTION, housed in the five-story former residence of Jules S. Bache, at 814 Fifth Avenue (Sixty-second Street), was opened to the public in 1937. *(Open Tuesday, Wednesday, Thursday, and Saturday 11 a.m. to 4 p.m., closed from June through September; admission by ticket, obtained by telephoning or writing the custodian.)* The collection contains no American pieces and no works later than the eighteenth century. There are paintings by Rembrandt, Titian, Botticelli, Petrus Christus, Watteau, Goya, Velásquez, Raphael, Gainsborough, Romney, Reynolds, and Holbein. Also in the collection are reliefs by Luca della Robbia, sculpture by Donatello, Flemish and French tapestries, early Italian and English furniture.

The entrance hall contains the works of Italian masters, while in the dining room are English paintings. French paneling in the salon at the front of the second floor provides a background for works of that country. In a richly decorated room in the rear are the Dutch masterpieces. Watteau's *The French Comedians* is historically one of the most interesting items of the Bache Collection. Voltaire presented this picture to Frederick the Great and it was claimed as personal property by the former Kaiser at the time of his abdication. Perhaps the painting that is best known to the public is Raphael's portrait of the son of Lorenzo the Magnificent, the *Duke of Nemours,* once owned by the Grand Duchess Marie of Russia.

Temple Emanu-El is at 1 East Sixty-fifth Street *(see page 356).* The COLONY CLUB, a rendezvous for women in the *Social Register,* is housed in a six-story Georgian building of red brick, at 564 Park Avenue (Sixty-second Street), designed by Delano and Aldrich, and erected about 1915. The RESIDENCE OF MRS. JAMES ROOSEVELT, 47 East Sixty-fifth Street, is used by the President on his visits to New York City.

HUNTER COLLEGE, the women's branch of the College of the City of New York, occupies the block between Sixty-eighth and Sixty-ninth Streets, Park and Lexington Avenues. A new five-million-dollar building (under construction 1939), replacing one on Park Avenue burned in 1936, will be of limestone and brick, sixteen stories in height. The architects are Shreve, Lamb, and Harmon, and Harrison and Fouilhoux. The building will accommodate more than five thousand students. Meanwhile classes are held in the six-story stone building on Lexington Avenue. The college was established in 1870 as the Normal College of the City of New York, the name being changed in 1914 in honor of Thomas Hunter, the founder. The institution, which has annexes in other parts of the city, offers a four-year course leading to an A.B. degree. Since 1934, emphasis has been shifted from pedagogical training to a general liberal arts education.

The old and fashionable UNION CLUB occupies a handsome building, completed in 1933, on the northeast corner of Park Avenue and Sixty-ninth Street. Across the avenue is the RESIDENCE OF FORMER SENATOR ARTHUR CURTISS JAMES, copper and railroad magnate. On the southwest corner of Seventieth Street and Park Avenue is the RESIDENCE OF GEORGE BLUMENTHAL, financier and president of the Metropolitan Museum of Art.

The FRICK COLLECTION, consisting of fourteenth- to nineteenth-century paintings and other works of art housed in the former home of Henry C. Frick, at 1 East Seventieth Street, was opened as a museum in 1935. *(Open weekdays, except Monday, 10 a.m. to 5 p.m.; Sunday and holidays 1 to 5 p.m.; closed August; admission free.)* The mansion, completed in 1914 on the site of the Lenox Library, was designed by Carrère and Hastings in the Louis XVI manner. The sculptured lunettes over the front door and the Fifth Avenue portico are by Attilio Piccirilli. The steel industrialist left the house in trust, stipulating that his wife should enjoy the right of residence for life. After Mrs. Frick's death in 1931 the house was remodeled and enlarged under the architectural supervision of John Russell Pope.

The lobby leads to a glass-roofed court of greenery and splashing water. The Oval Room (between two galleries on the north side of the house), entered from the court, contains Velásquez' magnificent *Philip IV*. In the new East Gallery—where chairs of Beauvais tapestry stand against old-rose walls—paintings by Piero della Francesca, Tintoretto, Vermeer, Ingres, and Cézanne constitute a harmonious group. The dull green velvet of the West Gallery forms an unobtrusive background for Renaissance furniture and bronzes as well as for pictures. The painters represented include Bronzino, Veronese, El Greco, Goya, Hals, and Rembrandt. The primitives of the collection are in the small room at the end of this long suite, with Limoges enamels and French Renaissance furniture.

Not the least distinguished of the front rooms is the central one, where a vibrant El Greco and two Holbeins face a Giovanni Bellini and two Titians. The remainder exhibit largely eighteenth-century works. In the library and the dining room, together with French and Italian sculpture, Chinese porcelains, and some Georgian silver, are most of the English pictures of the collection. Two small rooms overlooking Seventieth Street contain a group of fanciful Bouchers. The Fragonard Room owes its name and its character to four panels painted for Madame Du Barry which she rejected but which are now considered masterpieces. Seven smaller panels by Fragonard are there also, with a lovely marble by Houdon, and furniture by famous French cabinetmakers of the period.

The neighboring halls contain several of the most notable pieces of furniture, a rare early portrait by Boucher of his wife, and nineteenth-century pictures by Corot, Daubigny, Turner, and Whistler. On the main stair landing is an organ designed by Eugene W. Mason. Chamber music concerts and frequent lectures by members of the staff and well-known critics of the fine arts are given in the circular music and lecture rooms which adjoin the court and are hung with Italian brocade.

The remodeled residence at 53 East Seventy-ninth Street has been since 1937 the home of the NEW YORK SOCIETY LIBRARY. Founded in 1754 with 650 volumes—many of them having been sent to New York by the Society for the Propagation of the Gospel in Foreign Parts—the library received a charter in 1772 from George III. For a time it occupied part of the old City Hall on Wall Street, and from 1856 to 1937 it was located at 109 University Place. Members have included Aaron Burr, Alexander Hamilton, Washington Irving, George Bancroft, and many figures famous in the arts. At present the library has more than 150,000 volumes and is rich in Americana and belles-lettres. The library is open to the public for serious research, but circulation of books is limited to members.

The Metropolitan Museum of Art *(see page 368)* fronts Fifth Avenue between Eightieth and Eighty-fourth Streets, and just across the avenue, at 3 East Eighty-third Street, amid a row of mansions, is an incongruous, two-story frame house, with a horseshoe nailed above its door. The ANDREW CARNEGIE MANSION at Fifth Avenue and Ninety-first Street is a red-brick Georgian structure of four stories, with limestone base and trim and a copper mansard roof. Babb, Cook, and Willard were the architects. The HOME OF THE LATE FELIX N. WARBURG, banker, an ornate structure in French Renaissance style, occupies the northeast corner of the avenue and Ninety-second Street.

A number of institutions cluster at the end of Millionaire's Row. MOUNT SINAI HOSPITAL with its many buildings occupies the blocks between 99th and 101st Streets, Fifth and Madison Avenues. At the southeast corner of 103d Street stands the imposing new building of the NEW YORK ACADEMY OF MEDICINE, which was organized in 1847 to raise the standards of the medical profession, and which has since admirably devoted itself to the public weal. One block farther to the north is the pleasing Museum of the City of New York *(see page 377)*. Between 104th and 105th Streets is the building which houses the HECKSCHER FOUNDATION FOR CHILDREN and the NEW YORK SOCIETY FOR THE PREVENTION OF CRUELTY TO CHILDREN; the former is devoted to recreational work for underprivileged children, the latter to the care and education of abused and delinquent children. The NEW YORK MEDICAL COLLEGE, FLOWER, and FIFTH AVENUE HOSPITALS group occupies the block between 105th and 106th Streets. The hospital structures are built in the form of a St. Andrew's Cross.

North of 106th Street the character of Fifth Avenue changes, but not as suddenly as does the rest of the upper East Side, which merges with Spanish and Italian Harlems at 96th Street. In the top floor of the unpretentious apartment house at 1274 Fifth Avenue lives Fiorello H. La-Guardia, mayor of the city of New York.

YORKVILLE

Area: 59th St. on the south to 96th St. on the north; from Lexington Ave. east to East River. Map on page 237.

Popularly synonymous with the German quarter, Yorkville in reality is a much more inclusive section. The names on newsstands, shop windows, restaurants, bars, and many travel bureaus indicate that Czechs, Slovaks, Hungarians, and Irish also live in this locality. However, in the vicinity of East Eighty-sixth Street, Yorkville's Broadway, Germans and Austrians overwhelmingly predominate.

German families have settled in Yorkville since the original hamlet was established in the 1790's. The village centered around the old Boston Post Road (Third Avenue) between what is now Eighty-third and Eighty-ninth Streets. In the vicinity were the river and country estates of Manhattan's early aristocrats—the Astors, Primes, Rhinelanders. In 1834 the New York and Harlem Railroad was extended to the village; a year later a stagecoach line was established. These two events signalized the breaking up of the old homesteads and accelerated the hamlet's development as a suburban community. During the 1880's and 1890's solid blocks of stereotyped brownstones were constructed as homes for the well-to-do; but they were rapidly taken over by families who had moved away from the congested "Little Germany" in Tompkins Square. In the years following, the Germans, unlike many other foreign-born groups, adopted American mores, and Yorkville began to lose its Germanic quality. During the 1920's, however, the postwar poverty of Germany together with the comparatively high German immigration quota of the United States gave impetus to a new influx. The district again became the home of New York's German colony.

First Avenue is the most central route through Yorkville. Marie Curie Avenue and its extension, East End Avenue, skirt the district's water front. Behind the Rockefeller Institute and the New York Hospital, Marie Curie Avenue has a pleasant park-promenade to Seventieth Street, furnishing a good view of the East River and Welfare Island. East End Avenue leads to the charming Carl Schurz Park on the river bank between Eighty-fourth and Eighty-ninth Streets. Beginning in the northern part of this district is the East River Drive, which also has a walk along the water's edge.

The FIRST SWEDISH BAPTIST CHURCH, a block and a half west of First Avenue at 250 East Sixty-first Street, is an interesting modern building developed from Swedish architecture. Cornerstones of black granite contrast with the light brick façade. Doors, set at an angle to the street line, are placed next to the cornerstones in an arrangement similar to that used in old churches in Sweden. The two steeples are reproductions of towers in Sweden. The warm interior represents an outstandingly successful integration of decoration and architectural design. Martin Hedmark was the architect. The church, which was built in 1930, is attended by Swedes from all parts of the city.

Diagonally across East Sixty-first Street, at No. 229, L'ÉGLISE FRANÇAISE DU SAINT-ESPRIT, a Huguenot (French Protestant) church, shares its quarters with the SIXTY-FIRST STREET METHODIST EPISCOPAL CHURCH.

A half-block east of First Avenue, at 421 East Sixty-first Street, is SMITH'S FOLLY, one of Yorkville's few remaining historic houses. This simple Colonial stone structure, enclosed by a white picket fence and with a well-kept lawn and garden, nestles close to a garage and three gas tanks in the shadow of the huge cantilever Queensboro Bridge. It was built in 1799 by Colonel William S. Smith, son-in-law of President John Adams, and was originally the stable on his estate. He lost the property, allegedly through gambling, before his ambitious "Mount Vernon on the East River" was completed. The house burned down in 1826 and was not rebuilt. The stable later became a tavern. In 1830 it was sold to Jeremiah Towle, city surveyor, whose family occupied it until 1908. Since 1924 it has been the clubhouse of the Colonial Dames of America. The interior is furnished in typical Colonial style but has no museum pieces. *(Permission to visit must be obtained from the Colonial Dames of America.)*

The block between First and York Avenues, and Sixty-fourth and Sixty-fifth Streets, is occupied by MODEL TENEMENTS erected (1900–1915) by the City and Suburban Homes Company, a limited-dividend housing enterprise organized in 1896 with the object of providing sanitary homes for wage earners. Thirteen of the buildings, on First Avenue and Sixty-fourth Street, constructed in 1900, constituted the second modern model tenements built in Manhattan. (The first was erected two years earlier on the West Side by the same firm.) The company still operates these and other tenements it built in Yorkville. The average rent is $6.50 a week for two rooms with bath.

Annually on the first Sunday afternoon in October the CHURCH OF ST. VINCENT FERRER, 869 Lexington Avenue near Sixty-sixth Street, holds the Rosary Procession which ends with the blessing of roses and their distribution among the congregation. Father Tom Burke, one of the greatest nineteenth-century Roman Catholic pulpit orators and one of the best-known members of the Order of Preachers, delivered sermons at this church.

The present building, erected in 1917, was designed by Bertram G. Goodhue. It reveals Goodhue's deep understanding of Gothic architecture, and in the handling of materials, the preciseness of proportions, and the religious feeling embodied, it ranks as a masterpiece. The church is the earliest example in New York City of the architect's characteristic treatment of molding and sculpture: they seem to grow directly out of the structural stone without the use of brackets and bases. Lee Lawrie, who did the sculpture, subsequently collaborated with Goodhue on many other buildings.

The monumental, yellow and gray buildings overlooking the East River from a cliff between York and Marie Curie Avenues, Sixty-fourth and Sixty-eighth Streets, belong to the ROCKEFELLER INSTITUTE FOR MEDICAL RESEARCH. The principal structures, beginning with the powerhouse at the southern end of the row and proceeding north, are the sixty-bed hospital, the nine-bed isolation pavilion, Central Laboratory, Middle Laboratory, and North Laboratory. The smaller buildings are the library and animal houses. Service tunnels connect all these units.

Well over a hundred scientists, including many with international reputations, devote their time to research. Two research divisions are housed here: the Department of Laboratories and the Department of the Hospital. The Department of Animal and Plant Pathology has its own establishment near Princeton, New Jersey. Only patients suffering from diseases under investigation are accepted by the hospital; they are given treatment free.

The institute was founded in 1901 by John D. Rockefeller. Three years later the first laboratory was opened in a small building at 127 East Fiftieth Street with a scientific staff consisting of Simon Flexner, pathologist and director; Hideyo Noguchi, Eugene L. Opie, and J. E. Sweet, pathologists; Samuel J. Meltzer, physiologist and pharmacologist; and P. A. Levene, biological chemist. In 1906 the present Central Laboratory was opened. The hospital was completed in 1910, and in the same year Mr. Rockefeller provided an endowment. The institute also administers a legacy from Henry Rutherford for the promotion of cancer research.

The value of the institute's research is indicated by the work of Dr. Noguchi, who obtained the first pure cultures of spirochete, established the syphilitic nature of general paralysis, and discovered the parasite of yellow fever.

The Rockefeller Institute was built on ground belonging to the Schermerhorn family. Their imposing farmhouse, once the summer home of Governor George Clinton, was intact at the time the Rockefellers purchased the property. The Schermerhorns' neighbors were the Joneses, Winthrops,

Dunscombs, Kings, and Hoffmans. Jones' Wood was north of Seventieth Street, part of a ninety-acre farm owned before 1803 by the Provoost family. Samuel Provoost was the first Protestant Episcopal bishop of New York, while his cousin, David, was a famous smuggler. Near his landing place, now occupied by the New York Hospital, David Provoost hid his contraband in what came to be known as Smugglers' Cave. Jones' Wood subsequently became a popular picnic resort; its purchase for a municipal park was considered in the 1850's, but the site of Central Park was chosen instead.

The MEMORIAL HOSPITAL FOR THE TREATMENT OF CANCER occupies the block bounded by Sixty-seventh and Sixty-eighth Streets, York and First Avenues. When completed, the hospital will be one of the finest cancer research centers in the world. The construction was partly financed by John D. Rockefeller, Jr. The twelve-story main structure, with a penthouse, facing Sixty-eighth Street, was designed by James Gamble Rogers and Henry C. Pelton. The ornamental treatment is based on the use of applied modern details: long horizontal lines suggest balconies; color designs imitate corner windows.

Across Sixty-eighth Street is the CHURCH OF ST. CATHERINE OF SIENA, erected in 1930–31, whose interior as well as the exterior is of brick. Wilfrid E. Anthony was the architect. On the same side of the street, just west of First Avenue, is the GERMAN REFORMED CHURCH, facing small St. Catherine's Park. A monument within the church honors an active member of the congregation, Friedrich Wilhelm von Steuben, the doughty baron who drilled the Continental Army. About 1800 John Jacob Astor was clerk and elder as well as treasurer of the church. The present edifice, a combination of Romanesque and early Gothic styles distinguished by its simplicity, was erected in 1897. Its bell was presented in 1908 by Kaiser Wilhelm II, in honor of the church's 150th anniversary.

Just east of First Avenue, at 411 East Sixty-ninth Street, is the KIP'S BAY-YORKVILLE HEALTH AND TEACHING CENTER opened in 1938. The center, associated with the Cornell University Medical College, is used to train students in preventive medicine and public health administration. The building houses a number of public health services and clinics.

New York Hospital and Cornell University Medical College
Covering the three blocks (ten and a half acres) between Sixty-eighth and Seventy-first Streets, York and Marie Curie Avenues, the glazed white-brick buildings of the NEW YORK HOSPITAL AND THE CORNELL UNIVER-

SITY MEDICAL COLLEGE form one of Manhattan's most striking architectural groups. *(Guide service available to visitors Monday, Wednesday, and Friday 2 to 3:30 p.m.; Tuesday and Thursday to 3:15 p.m.)* For the design, the architects, Coolidge, Shepley, Bulfinch, and Abbott, of Boston, received the 1933 gold medal of the New York Architectural League. The fifteen buildings, which cost more than thirty million dollars, are so placed and subordinated to the main tower that they give the effect of a single vast structure. At first glance the mass of this powerful group is reminiscent of the Palace of the Popes at Avignon. Pointed arch windows that rise to the full height of the eight-story pavilions flanking the main entrance establish a Gothic motif; yet actually the group is an outstanding example of modern architecture, for its beauty grows out of its functional organization and the aesthetic counterplay of its parts. In contrast to the Columbia Presbyterian Medical Center, the windows here are skillfully used to express the function of each division of the hospital. The interior lacks the forbidding features associated with older hospitals and is, instead, filled with sunshine and decorated in color.

The second to the ninth floors are given over to pavilions patterned after the wards in the Royal Hospital in Copenhagen. The largest pavilions have no more than sixteen beds and even these are divided into four-bed sections by glass partitions. Each pavilion has a spacious lounge overlooking the East River with Vitaglass windows on three sides.

The adjoining buildings house the Women's Clinic (which includes the Lying-in Hospital), the Children's Clinic, the Psychiatric Clinic, the Out-Patient Building, Cornell University Medical College, staff quarters, a 250-car garage, and a nurses' residence with a capacity of five hundred. The Lying-in Hospital, now the maternity division of the New York Hospital, was organized in 1789 following an epidemic of yellow fever that brought the plight of widowed expectant mothers to the public attention. After many vicissitudes, in 1892 the hospital society joined forces with a Midwifery Dispensary serving the tenements. Through the interest of J. P. Morgan, the society acquired its own hospital in 1899 in the Stuyvesant Square neighborhood, which it occupied until the move uptown was made.

This newest of Manhattan's medical centers (completed in 1932) shelters the city's oldest hospital. In 1769 Dr. Samuel Bard of King's College (now Columbia University) pleaded for "an hospital for the sick poor of the colony," which incidentally would serve as a medical training school. King George III granted the charter in 1771. While anatomical instruc-

248   MANHATTAN: MIDDLE AND UPPER EAST SIDE

tion was given during the early years and the building was used as an
army hospital during the Revolution, the hospital was not opened for
civilian service until 1791.

Many prominent men have served as governors of the institution.
Among them have been John Watts, John Jay, Robert Livingston, Philip
Hone, Aaron Burr, Lindley Murray, John Jacob Astor, Joseph H. Choate,
and Isaac Roosevelt.

Cornell University Medical College, founded in 1898, first occupied a
building at Twenty-eighth Street and First Avenue. After 1912 the college
co-operated with the New York Hospital, and in 1927 the New York
Hospital-Cornell Medical College Association was formed. At that time
both institutions obtained additional funds, including a gift of more than
twenty million dollars from Payne Whitney, two million dollars each
from J. Pierpont Morgan and the Laura Spelman Rockefeller Memorial,
and one million dollars each from George F. Baker and George F. Baker,
Jr. The hospital, with eleven hundred beds, is one of the largest in the
city; the college is one of the smallest in number of students. Both exemplify the highest standards of the medical profession.

The New York Hospital annually treats more than twenty thousand
bed-patients and more than forty thousand out-patients, accepting, as it
has since 1791, "patients who need its help, without regard to race, creed,
or ability to pay." Sixty-five per cent are pavilion patients. Modern equipment and a distinguished medical staff have given the hospital one of the
lowest surgical mortality rates in the country.

Unlike many general hospitals, the New York Hospital has always
treated mental disorders. As early as 1821 Bloomingdale Asylum was
established by the hospital on the site of the present library of Columbia
University. It moved to White Plains in 1894 and is now known as the
New York Hospital—Westchester Division. The Payne Whitney Clinic, an
important unit of the center itself, treats only psychiatric cases.

Public interest in the hospital found expression in an unusual way in
1938 when more than one hundred anonymous donors of all denominations contributed a total of one thousand dollars for the removal of swastika designs from the 325-foot chimney. The ancient symbol that had been
given a new significance by Chancellor Hitler's rise to power in Germany
was replaced by Greek crosses.

"Little Bohemia"

In addition to the great New York dailies, the newsstands along First
Avenue in the lower Seventies carry the two dailies, *New Yorkske Listy*

YORKVILLE 249

(Czech), and *New Yorksky Dennik* (Slovak), for here between Seventy-first and Seventy-fifth Streets east of Second Avenue is New York's "Little Bohemia." After Czechoslovakia became an independent nation in 1918 many Slovaks from downtown moved up into the Czech quarter, and the two groups have combined many of their interests. Pride in their languages and traditions, however, has prompted them to maintain separate *sokols* where after public-school hours the children can be taught their native speech and history. Their societies present native dramas, folk songs, and dances. On Decoration Day the Czechoslovaks parade in colorful native costume. The largest meeting place is BOHEMIAN NATIONAL HALL, between First and Second Avenues at 319 East Seventy-fourth Street, where nearly a half hundred organizations, the oldest having been formed by the Czechs in 1863, meet regularly. In the PARSONAGE OF THE JAN HUS PRESBYTERIAN CHURCH, 351 East Seventy-fourth, are fourteen rooms appointed in typical Czechoslovak peasant style. Excellent restaurants in the neighborhood serve tripe soup, stuffed cabbage *(zeli* or *kapusta),* and roast goose, Bohemian style.

The Hungarians, in the upper Seventies, aid in giving Yorkville its Central European atmosphere. The Hungarian daily, *Amerikai Magyar Nepszava,* is found on the newsstands in this vicinity; Tokay wine is featured in the liquor stores; and in the delicatessens are sold goose livers and the famed Hercz, Pick, and Drossy salamis from Budapest. The Hungarian cuisine is noted for its variety and savory sauces; in this neighborhood, particularly on East Seventy-ninth Street between First and Second Avenues, are many restaurants whose specialties are chicken *paprikas, rostbraten,* and *strudel.* On Hungarian Independence Day, March 15, the Hungarians hold a celebration; they usually parade to the statue of Louis Kossuth, hero of the 1848 revolution in Hungary, on Riverside Drive.

The WEBSTER BRANCH OF THE NEW YORK PUBLIC LIBRARY, 1465 York Avenue near Seventy-eighth Street, is popularly known as the "Czech Library" and has a Czechoslovak collection of about 15,000 volumes. A group of MODEL TENEMENTS erected by the City and Suburban Homes Company, between York and Marie Curie Avenues, Seventy-eighth and Seventy-ninth Streets, represents one of the most significant Manhattan housing developments prior to the building of the Amalgamated Dwellings on the Lower East Side. At the foot of East Seventy-eighth Street is a WELFARE ISLAND FERRY SLIP. Contributions from 180 of New York's richest families helped to finance the construction of the DOCTORS' HOSPITAL at Eighty-seventh Street and East End Avenue. Its elegant furnishings match those of a Park Avenue hotel.

Beautiful CARL SCHURZ PARK extends along the river from Gracie Square (East Eighty-fourth Street) to East Eighty-ninth Street. Adjoining it on the south and west is a fashionable residential section, with tall new apartment buildings and renovated old homes and tenements. Built on two hills and pleasingly landscaped, the park affords an excellent view of the river and its traffic.

The white frame Colonial house on the northern and highest ground of the park is the GRACIE MANSION, built in 1799 by Archibald Gracie and carefully restored by the Park Department in 1927. The house is furnished in the style of the late eighteenth century with furniture lent by museums and private collectors. *(Open daily, except Monday, from 11 a.m. to 5 p.m.; admission free.)*

This hook of land on the East River has played an important part in the social and political history of New York. The first known owner named it "Horn's (Hoorn's) Hook" for his native Hoorn on the Zuyder Zee. The first house to occupy the site was built by Jacob Walton a few years before the Revolution. The house and grounds were appropriated by the American Army in 1776 and a fort mounting nine guns was set up. On September 15, 1776, a bombardment by the English battleships completely destroyed the house, and the Americans abandoned the fort. It was used by the English as an army camp until November, 1783. At the turn of the century Gracie, a wealthy merchant of Scottish birth, purchased the property, leveled the military works, and built his home and gardens. About 1811 he enlarged the house.

Many famous men were guests at the Gracie Mansion, including Louis Phillipe, later King of France; President John Quincy Adams, James Fenimore Cooper, and Washington Irving. Neighbors, as well as guests, were John Jacob Astor and Alexander Hamilton. The Gracies occupied the house until 1823, when Joseph Foulke purchased the estate.

In 1891 the city acquired that part of the present park lying north of Eighty-sixth Street and added it to the southern part which had been a picnic ground. The easternmost block of Eighty-sixth Street was added recently to the park. Formerly called the East End Park, it was renamed (1911) in honor of Carl Schurz (1829-1906), German revolutionary, who soon after his arrival in America in 1856 became a leader of the newly formed Republican Party. A close friend and adviser of Lincoln, he served during the Civil War first as Minister to Spain and then as major general in the Union Army. In later years he was a senator from Missouri, Secretary of Interior under President Hayes, editor of the New York

Evening Post and *Harper's Weekly,* and a leader in the civil service reform movement. He lived in New York from 1881 until his death.

West of the park is the German section of Yorkville. East Eighty-sixth Street is lined with restaurants, cabarets, theaters; beer, meeting, and dance halls; and delicatessen and pastry shops. Adjacent streets and avenues have an unmistakable German character.

Restaurants offer such favorite dishes as *wiener schnitzel,* a Viennese cutlet of veal, sautéd, garnished with string beans, beets, tomatoes, and capers, and *gehacktes hirsch-steaks.* Some cafés are typically Viennese in appearance, quiet family resorts; others feature singing waiters and Bavarian atmosphere. The doormen of several of the restaurants are barkers garbed in long socks, brief leather pants held by suspenders, and plumed Tyrolean hats.

The pastry shops—*Konditoreien*—not only serve coffee and pastry and meals, but are rendezvous where guests transact business, discuss politics, play cards, further their romances—or read the newspapers. The larger shops, on Eighty-sixth Street east of Third Avenue, have afternoon and evening concerts. At frequent intervals a vendor makes the round of the tables proffering propaganda periodicals or the more conservative *Staats-Zeitung und Herold.* The delicatessen shops sell sausages that are as various as the spices in Levantine foods. There are *plockwurst, cervelatwurst, mettwurst, streichwurst, bauernwurst, leber-, rot-,* and *knackwurst,* and many others.

The YORKVILLE CASINO, 210 East Eighty-sixth Street, is the meeting place of many German organizations. Here also is one of the several theaters in the neighborhood which show German motion pictures.

Several Nazi propaganda agencies maintained headquarters in Yorkville. The GERMAN-AMERICAN BUND and its official paper, *Deutscher Weckruf und Beobachter,* which under the leadership of Fritz Kuhn directed Nazi work throughout the country, had their national offices at 178 East Eighty-fifth Street. The GERMAN-AMERICAN BUSINESS LEAGUE, in the same building, published directories of firms to be patronized by Nazi adherents. The Nazis occasionally paraded through Yorkville in their uniforms, which were of three kinds: black trousers, white shirts with swastika armbands, and black caps, for the rank and file members; olive-drab military uniforms, for the guards; and imported regulation German uniforms for the storm troops. In the spring of 1938 the Yorkville Casino was the arena of a bloody fight between Nazi sympathizers and a group of people who were members of the American Legion.

Anti-Nazi centers in Yorkville were the GERMAN WORKERS CLUB at 1501 Third Avenue, and the GERMAN CENTRAL BOOK STORE, 218 East Eighty-fourth Street, which was stocked with German books banned by Hitler. At 243 East Eighty-fourth Street was the NEW YORK LABOR TEMPLE, erected by German workers in the early part of the century. It was a meeting place for numerous unions, singing groups, and *Turnvereine* (athletic associations). The temple was operated on a nonprofit basis by the Workmen's Educational Association. The German anti-Nazi newspaper, the *Deutsches Volksecho,* had a wide circulation in Yorkville.

TIMES SQUARE

MIDTOWN MANHATTAN

MAY DAY, UNION SQUARE

RUTHERFORD PLACE, STUYVESANT SQUARE

LITTLE CHURCH AROUND THE CORNER

FIFTH AVENUE SHOPS

FIFTH AVENUE HOMES

EAST FORTY-FIRST STREET AND THE PARK AVENUE RAMP

GRAND CENTRAL TERMINAL

MCGRAW-HILL BUILDING

D. Spiegel

The Harlems

NEGRO HARLEM—SPANISH HARLEM—
ITALIAN HARLEM

Area: E. 96th St. and W. 110th St. on the south to W. 155th St. on the north;
from 5th Ave. (96th to 110th St.), Morningside Ave., and St. Nicholas Ave. (125th
to 155th St.) east to East and Harlem rivers. Maps on pages 54-55 and 255.
Principal north-south streets: 1st, 5th, Lenox, 7th, St. Nicholas, and Edgecombe Aves.
Principal cross streets: 116th, 125th, 135th, and 145th Sts.
Transportation: IRT Lenox Ave. subway; 110th to 145th St. stations; IRT Lexington Ave. subway (local), 96th to 125th St. stations; 8th Ave. (Independent)
Washington Heights or Grand Concourse subway (local), 110th to 145th St. stations;
3d Ave. el, 96th to 129th St. stations; bus lines on all principal north-south
streets.

HARLEM IS blocked in by the high ridges of Morningside Heights and
St. Nicholas Terrace, by the East and Harlem rivers, and by Ceneral Park.
Along the East River is the Italian section; north and east of Central Park,
the Spanish; and farther north, the Negro district, its boundaries extending into the Italian and Spanish neighborhoods and creeping northward
into Washington Heights.

Built up solidly with tenements, old apartment houses, brownstones
converted into flats, and occasional small frame residences, Harlem is a
poor man's land. Half a million persons are crowded into its three square
miles—the largest single slum area in New York. The nondescript drabness
of the streets is relieved by a chain of three "ribbon parks"—Morningside,

St. Nicholas, and Colonial—along the ridge, two smaller parks within the district itself, and Harlem River Houses and the East River Drive. But the distinguishing features of the district are derived from its vivid population groups, with their national and racial cultures.

Nieuw Haarlem was established in 1658 by Director Peter Stuyvesant in the lush bottomland between Harlem River and Morningside Heights. The village was named for the old Dutch city, in all probability by the director himself. A few Hollanders, French Huguenots, Danes, Swedes, and Germans developed rich farms there and gave them such idyllic names as Quiet Vale and Happy Valley. New Harlem was about ten miles from the little town of New Amsterdam on the island's southern tip, and was connected with it by a road built "by the [Dutch West India] Company's negroes" on an Indian trail, now part of Broadway. During the next two centuries it retained its pastoral charm and separateness—the British even

---

KEY TO MAP OF THE HARLEMS

SPANISH HARLEM

1. Church of St. Francis de Sales
2. Church of St. Cecilia
3. Iglesia Metodista Episcopal
4. Teatro Latino

5. Church of Our Lady of the Miraculous Medal
6. Teatro Hispano
7. Public Market Place

ITALIAN HARLEM

8. Thomas Jefferson Park
9. Our Lady of Mt. Carmel Church

10. Haarlem House

NEGRO HARLEM

11. Finnish Hall
12. Harlem Community Art Center
13. Kingdom of Father Divine
14. Apollo Theater
15. Metropolitan Baptist Church
16. Commandment Keepers' Congregation
   Order of Ethiopian Hebrews
17. Kings Chapel Assembly
18. Tree of Hope
19. Lafayette Theatre
20. Offices of the Amsterdam News
21. St. Philip's Protestant Episcopal Church
22. Offices of the New York Age

23. National Association for the Advancement of Colored People
24. Y.M.C.A., Harlem Branch
25. New York Public Library, 135th Street Branch
26. Central Harlem Health Center
27. Harlem Hospital
28. Offices of the New York Urban League
29. Abyssinian Baptist Church
30. Strivers' Row
31. Savoy Ballroom
32. 369th Regiment Armory
33. Dunbar Apartments
34. Harlem River Houses

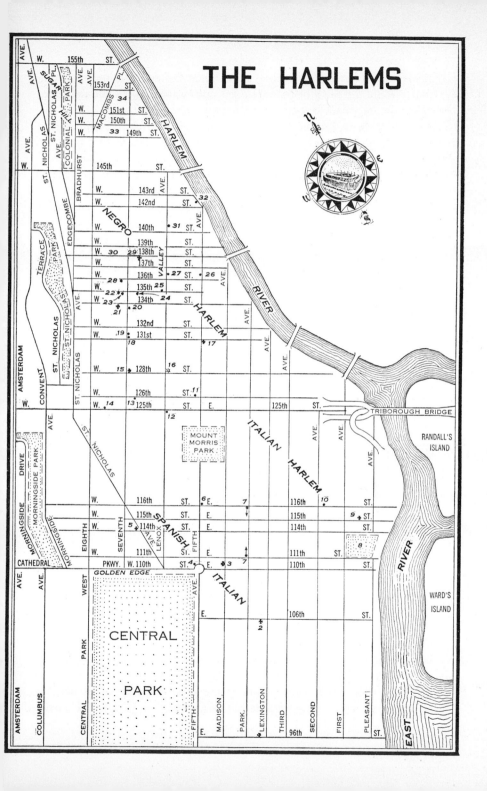

THE HARLEMS

permitted it to retain the name of New Harlem after capturing the city in 1664—while the town below expanded northward and became the country's most important commercial center.

At the turn of the nineteenth century the western half of the region was occupied by country estates along the heights. The eastern part, between present-day 110th and 125th Streets (east of Fifth Avenue), was purchased by James Roosevelt, great-grandfather of Franklin Delano Roosevelt, and cultivated by him as farm land. He sold the property about 1825 for $25,000. In the 1830's the Harlem Railroad was built, and what had been a charming rural area became a rapidly growing suburb. The Third Avenue horse railroad was chartered in 1853. The journey from Manhattan still required, however, an hour and twenty minutes, providing "no horse balked or fell dead across the tracks." The most efficient method of travel was by steamer of the Harlem Navigation Line on the Hudson River, which made the trip from Peck Slip to 125th Street in an hour and a half.

With the extension of the elevated rapid transit lines to Harlem in 1880, the section took its place as a fashionable neighborhood of New York City. The blocks were filled with aristocratic apartment houses and the popular brownstones. Fine horses were shown off on Lenox and Eighth Avenues, and polo was played at the near-by Polo Grounds. The peak of this phase of Harlem's development was reached with the opening of the Harlem Opera House at 209 West 125th Street in 1889, an enterprise undertaken by Oscar Hammerstein. At that time, and for two succeeding decades, Germans were the dominant element in the well-populated community, with the Irish ranking second in number. During the great immigration waves of the 1880's and 1890's many Jews and Italians settled in Harlem. The white groups began to move out of middle Harlem in the early 1910's when Negroes from lower Manhattan succeeded in renting apartments there. The great influx of Negroes from the South and the West Indies, however, started in the World War period while Puerto Ricans and other Latin-American groups flocked to Harlem after the war.

Harlem's racial groups introduced their native flavors into the aging buildings of the district. The old-world customs which the Italians brought with them from Sicily and Italy have succeeded in varying degrees in resisting assimilation into the new ways of life. Negroes blended into their New York environment habits and qualities carried from the southern states, Africa, and the West Indies. The Spanish Harlemites reflect in their recreation, their public markets, and their changing social life, the traditions in which they were reared. Unfortunately, this native picturesqueness has in large part been preserved by extreme poverty, with its overcrowding, illiteracy, malnutrition, disease, and social dislocation. Several health centers have striven to alleviate the distress from disease. The Negro district's Central Harlem Health Center, the Puerto Rican Service Center, and Little Italy's East Harlem Health Center serve thousands of persons daily. The centers direct their work along the lines of preventive as well as therapeutic medicine.

Crime and juvenile delinquency have germinated in the tenements despite periodic police cleanups. Especially during the Prohibition years, the Harlems became the headquarters of several notorious gang leaders, who gathered recruits among the youth of the slums. Harlem's church groups and settlement houses, such as the Haarlem House, have done their utmost to improve the morale of the locality.

The Works Progress Administration has made a significant contribution to the cultural life and social welfare of Harlem. It provides assistance to the health centers, operates the Lower Harlem Chest Clinic for tuberculosis diagnoses, and assigns teachers and recreational directors to church community centers. The WPA Federal Arts Projects conduct varied cultural activities: the Music division maintains three schools (Central Manhattan, Harlem, and Hamilton branches), the Art unit supervises the Harlem Community Art Center, the Negro Theater presents productions at the Lafayette Theater.

NEGRO HARLEM

Area: W. 110th, 120th, and E. 125th Sts. on the south to 155th St. on the north; from Morningside Ave. and St. Nicholas Ave. (125th to 155th St.) east to Lenox Ave. (110th to 120th St.), Madison Ave. (120th to 125th St.), and the Harlem River. Map on page 255.

Negro Harlem, into which are crowded more than a quarter of a million Negroes from southern states, the West Indies, and Africa, has many different aspects. To whites seeking amusement, it is an exuberant, original, and unconventional entertainment center; to Negro college graduates it is an opportunity to practice a profession among their own people; to those aspiring to racial leadership it is a domain where they may advocate their theories unmolested; to artists, writers, and sociologists it is a mine of rich material; to the mass of Negro people it is the spiritual capital of Black America.

Negroes began to move into Harlem in 1901 as a result of a deflated boom in real estate there. Because of the lack of adequate transportation facilities, fine apartments erected by speculative real-estate promoters were left tenantless. A Negro agent, Philip A. Payton, persuaded landlords to accept Negro tenants, and hundreds of families soon deserted old tenements in the crowded West Fifty-third Street and San Juan Hill (west of Columbus Circle) sections and poured into Harlem. Their infiltration was at first bitterly resisted by white tenants, landlords, and bankers.

During the World War Negroes from the South, from the British West Indies, and even from the neighboring Spanish- and French-speaking islands flocked to the North spurred by promises of highly paid industrial jobs. By 1919 the Negro population of Harlem had quadrupled. Race riots in southern cities in the postwar period caused a further large migration to the North. Though they did not succeed in escaping economic insecurity and race discrimination, the Negroes were able to build within the metropolis a city of their own, a cosmopolitan Negro capital which exerts an influence over Negroes everywhere.

Although the community possesses fine residences and wealthy churches, wide boulevards, theaters, hotels, and cafés, its dreadful slums are among the most notorious in New York. Barred from most residential areas in the city, Negroes pay rents 50 per cent higher than those charged for comparable living quarters elsewhere.

Under these circumstances social and health conditions are, of course, extremely poor. In 1934 a survey of Negro Harlem showed that among twenty thousand persons chiefly from the relief rolls, 3 per cent suffered from pulmonary tuberculosis. One block in particular, from Lenox to Seventh Avenue between 142d and 143d Streets, was referred to because of its congestion as the "lung block," the rate of death from tuberculosis being twice that of white Manhattan. Maternal and infant mortality rates are more than double those of the city. A mayor's commission appointed to study the causes of a riot there in 1935 revealed that tuberculosis and other diseases were widespread, and that medical and clinical care were dangerously inadequate.

Those who live in Harlem know it as a number of little worlds, represented by such titles as the "Valley," the "Golden Edge," "Sugar Hill," and the "Market." Each is descriptive of a different stratum of the community. The Valley is the slum area, extending from 130th to 140th Street, east of Seventh Avenue. Apartments along the Golden Edge, the part of the neighborhood facing Central Park, house the professional class. On Sugar Hill, the affluent live in dignity and comparative splendor. The

Market is the name given with ironic accuracy to the stretch from 110th to 115th Street on Seventh Avenue, which is frequented by streetwalkers. Sharp divisions exist between the dwellers in these various sections.

Two main thoroughfares cut through the district. Seventh Avenue, Harlem's widest street, with islands in its center, runs from West 110th to West 155th Street, and is one of the chief bus routes through Harlem and to Washington Heights. This avenue is lined with apartment houses, retail stores, beauty parlors, restaurants, and corner saloons. Lenox Avenue, a block to the east, is generally regarded as Harlem's principal boulevard. It is a wide, shabby avenue, flanked by cheap shops, bars, lunchrooms, pool parlors, and "gin mills." Peculiar to the avenue are the mobile lunch-stands which appear in the afternoon and early evening. These are usually operated by elderly men and women, and serve popcorn, baked sweet potatoes, peanuts, jam, sausages, and other popular tidbits. Most of these carts are old and rickety and the food is heated over kerosene lamps.

One Hundred and Twenty-fifth Street, a key crosstown traffic artery leading directly to the entrance of the Triborough Bridge *(see page 390)* at Second Avenue, is Harlem's chief business thoroughfare. Although Negroes live along the streets north and south of it, West 125th Street is not predominantly a Negro center; white residents of Morningside Heights and Manhattanville have used it as a shopping center for years. Two 125th Street hotels—the THERESA, at Seventh Avenue, and the TRI-BORO, at Fifth Avenue—still have white managements and clienteles. From Third Avenue to St. Nicholas Avenue are many stores, movie houses, real-estate offices, banks, and eating places, the overwhelming majority being owned and operated by whites. That no Negroes were employed in these businesses was always resented by Harlemites, who are the majority of customers. In 1935 an incident in one of these shops developed into a riot of alarming proportions. In recent years picketing and pressure by labor unions and citizens' groups have compelled the larger 125th Street stores to employ Negro help.

At 253 West 125th Street, near Eighth Avenue, is the APOLLO THEATRE, known as Harlem's "opera house." Opened in 1913 as a burlesque house, it became in 1934 a vaudeville theater. Weekly all-Negro revues, with outstanding dance orchestras and musical comedy favorites, are presented to mixed audiences. The theater is owned and managed by whites, but the actors, actresses, and other employees are Negro.

The HARLEM COMMUNITY ART CENTER, 290 Lenox Avenue, established in 1937, provides free instruction in the arts and crafts for adults and children. The quarters, equipment, and teaching staff are supplied by the WPA Federal Art Project, and the working materials are purchased from funds contributed by residents of the community.

FINNISH HALL, 13 West 126th Street, is an important social, educational, and recreational center for the large group of Finnish people living in the area east of Lenox Avenue between 120th and 128th Streets.

At 152 West 126th Street is the most important KINGDOM OF FATHER DIVINE in Harlem. Father Divine, Negro religious leader of the "Righteous Government," has thousands of followers who call him "God" and who believe him to be God in the flesh. One of their chants holds: "He has the world in a jug and the stopper in his hand." His adherents are called "angels" and assume such names as Glorious Illumination, Heavenly Dove, and Pleasing Joy. Since Marcus Garvey's time no Negro has achieved a larger following among the masses of Harlem. Father Divine, a stocky baldheaded man with an intimate rhythmical style of Bible oratory, preaches a simple Christian theology emphasizing the principles of righteousness, truth, and justice. The slogan of his cult is "Peace," the word being used as a salutation and an interjection, sometimes coupled with "Thank you, Father." He exacts celibacy from his followers. Assistance from public relief agencies is prohibited.

A kingdom serves as meeting hall, restaurant, and rooming house. No regular prayer meetings are held there but throughout the day hymns and songs praising Father Divine are spontaneously sung and music in dance tempo is played. Usually, Father Divine delivers an address at eleven o'clock in the evening at the 126th Street kingdom *(open to the public)*. He also presides at private "banquets" for sect members only, at which he delivers "messages." A popular feature of the kingdoms are the low-cost meals served to all comers. Priced at fifteen cents, they consist of a meat dish—veal, chicken, or turkey—vegetables, bread and butter, and tea or coffee. Thousands of such meals are served daily in the various kingdoms, where lodgings are also available in dormitories at two dollars a week. Father Divine's followers have accumulated much city and country property, including the "Krum Elbow" five-hundred-acre estate opposite President Roosevelt's family seat at Hyde Park on the Hudson River; they also maintain an undisclosed number of missions, farms, gasoline stations, grocery stores, and other enterprises, all under the immediate directorship of the evangelist. These holdings are in the names of "angels," but the actual financing of the purchases is shrouded in mystery. Thus far, all attempts to probe the finances of Father Divine and his sect have been unsuccessful. A former Divine kingdom at 20 West

115th Street was bought in 1938 by Bishop "Daddy" Grace, evangelist, who aspires to the popularity achieved by Father Divine.

The METROPOLITAN BAPTIST CHURCH, 151 West 128th Street, one of the larger and more influential Harlem churches, was founded in 1896 by a former slave, the Rev. Dr. Willis W. Brown, whose son is the present pastor. The church is the headquarters of the Negro Baptist Ministers Conference.

One of the city's two synagogues for black Jews is the COMMANDMENT KEEPERS' CONGREGATION, 87 West 128th Street. Founded in 1919, it serves 800 of Negro Harlem's 3,500 members of that faith. Eighty per cent of the congregation are Ethiopians, the others being American-born Negro converts. The synagogue is also the HEADQUARTERS OF THE ROYAL ORDER OF ETHIOPIAN HEBREWS, INC., a fraternal religious group dedicated to the study of the laws and culture of Israel. The congregation is orthodox; services are conducted in both Hebrew and English. Its members are not to be confused with the Falashas, Ethiopian Jews, a few of whom live in New York but keep themselves apart from both white and Negro Jews, maintaining that they are the only real Jews. The Falashas claim descent from King Solomon and the Queen of Sheba; the Ethiopians of the synagogue trace their descent from Judah and Benjamin.

KINGS CHAPEL PENTECOSTAL ASSEMBLY, 2143 Fifth Avenue, is one of New York's few buildings in the "New International" style. A starkly simple structure, it was designed by Vertner W. Tandy and contains parts of two former dwellings on the site.

On Seventh Avenue, near 131st Street, is Harlem's LAFAYETTE THEATER in whose wings the Negro theater tradition in America has been made. On its stage have appeared in the last quarter of a century such famed Negro actors and actresses as Andrew Bishop, Frank Wilson, Rex Ingram, Inez Clough, Rose McClendon, Anita Bush, Laura Bowman, Leigh Whipper, "Black Patti" (Siseretta Jones), and many others. Since 1935 the Lafayette has housed the WPA Federal Negro Theater. In 1937 it presented Orson Welles' unusual and notable version of Shakespeare's *Macbeth,* played with an all-Negro cast.

On the sidewalk in front of the Lafayette stands the stump of the original TREE OF HOPE, a Harlem landmark for many years. Out-of-work Negro actors and actresses used to stand around the tree and exchange information about jobs. When one of them got work he ascribed his good luck to the tree and would kiss it in gratitude. From this custom the tree acquired its name. When it had to be cut down because of age it was replaced by another that stands a few feet away. The new one was dedicated by Bill "Bojangles" Robinson, famed dancer and Harlem's leading stage luminary. One of the community's wealthiest and most active citizens, Robinson is also the locality mayor of Harlem. (A locality mayoralty is an unofficial position that is given to a popular citizen by other members of the community.)

Beale Street is the name applied to 133d Street, between Seventh and Lenox Avenues because of its similarity to the Memphis thoroughfare. In the 1920's the street was called "Jungle Alley" and was publicized as the primitive essence of Harlem life. Actually, however, Jungle Alley was a deliberately arranged show place for those willing to pay, and it succeeded in drawing visitors from many parts of the world. The depression ended its popularity in the early 1930's, and of the many gay spots that lined the street—the Nest, Pod's and Jerry's, Mexico's—only Dickie Wells' place remains.

At 87 West 133d Street, Philip A. Payton, the Negro realtor instrumental in bringing the Negro to Harlem, operated a real-estate office. The houses in this area were referred to in those days as "oatmeal flats," because the Negroes who lived in them, forced to pay disproportionately high rents, were left without sufficient money for food.

St. Philip's P. E. Church, 214 West 134th Street, is said to be the wealthiest Negro church in America. It owns a great deal of real estate, and by purchasing apartment buildings and renting them to Negroes the church was an important factor in the settlement of Harlem. The church structure, a plain edifice in red brick, completed in 1911, was designed by Vertner W. Tandy and George W. Foster, Negro architects, and cost $250,000.

On or near 135th Street, especially where it crosses Seventh and Lenox Avenues, are many of the community's leading institutions: the Harlem Branch of the Young Men's Christian Association in a building at 180 West 135th Street (opened in 1933 at a cost of more than a million dollars), an important cultural and recreational center, and one of the few neighborhood places with hotel accommodations for Negroes; a Branch of the New York Public Library, 103 West 135th Street, which houses the Schomburg Collection of four thousand books on the Negro; the local Offices of the National Association for the Advancement of Colored People, 224 West 135th Street, and the New York Urban League, 202 West 136th Street; two New York Negro newspapers: the *Amsterdam News,* 2271 Seventh Avenue, and the New York *Age,* 230 West 135th Street; and the many offices of Negro lawyers and doctors.

In this vicinity numerous fraternal and political organizations parade and demonstrate, and here the Negroes gather when there is occasion for a celebration: a Joe Louis victory in the fight ring packs the streets. In summer the sidewalks are crowded with loiterers and strollers; the unemployed move chairs to the pavement and set up cracker boxes for checker games. On Lenox Avenue soapbox orators draw crowds nightly with lectures on everything from occultism to communism, one of the speakers being, inevitably, a disciple of Marcus Garvey, leader of the back-to-Africa movement, now an exile in England.

SMALL'S PARADISE, 2294½ Seventh Avenue, one of the three night clubs for which Harlem was famous in the 1920's, still functions on Seventh Avenue; of the other two—Connie's Inn and the Cotton Club— the former went out of business and the latter is now in Times Square. Small's, under the name of the Black Venus, was described in *Nigger Heaven*, a widely read novel by Carl Van Vechten, the first white novelist to discover "Hot Harlem." Within a few blocks of Small's are two other well-frequented night clubs with regular floor shows with Negro casts: the PLANTATION CLUB, 644 Lenox Avenue, and YEAH MAN, 2350 Seventh Avenue; also, two of Harlem's best-known eating places, the MONTEREY, 2339 Seventh Avenue, and the LITTLE GRAY SHOP, 2465 Seventh Avenue.

The question of employment for Negroes in Negro-patronized institutions has been the subject of a long controversy at HARLEM HOSPITAL, 136th Street and Lenox Avenue, a 365-bed municipal hospital. Though Negroes have been added to the medical staff from time to time, the majority of the staff are white; only one executive post, that of surgical director, is held by a Negro. The hospital, founded in 1887, has a training school for Negro nurses.

A block from the hospital, on Fifth Avenue between 136th and 137th Streets, is the CENTRAL HARLEM HEALTH CENTER, a place of vital importance to this city-within-a-city. The center's chief work is preventive medicine, with emphasis on child care and on the checking of communicable diseases. The center, the only place of its kind for the district's quarter-million population, is a three-story brick and stone building of Georgian Colonial design. It was opened in 1937, at a cosᴜ of $270,000 and financed by Federal Government loans.

The most popular religious denomination in Harlem is the Baptist, and Harlem has the world's largest church of that denomination, Negro or white—the ABYSSINIAN BAPTIST CHURCH, 132 West 138th Street. Founded in 1808, it is the largest, oldest, and most influential Negro church in New York. It has a membership of more than 13,000, and more than thirty auxiliaries of the church are actively engaged in religious and community services, including a forum where Negro and white men and women of national prominence speak. Its pastor is the Reverend A. Clayton Powell, Jr., outstanding civic leader. The building, erected in 1923 at a cost of $334,000, is an imposing structure of New York blue stone. Of combined Gothic and Tudor styles, it was designed by a Negro architect, Charles W. Bolton, and has served as a model for other churches in New York and elsewhere.

In contrast with such imposing edifices as the Abyssinian Baptist Church, are the numerous "storefront" churches in almost every street. These are stores which have been converted into churches by installing rows of benches and a pulpit. They are usually bare of decoration, except for window curtains.

West 138th and 139th Streets, between Seventh and Eighth Avenues, are known in Harlem as STRIVERS' ROW because so many Negroes aspire to live in the attractive, tan-brick houses on these two tree-shaded streets. The residents are mostly of the better-paid, white-collar and professional class; some rent furnished rooms in order to meet the comparatively high rental. The 130 dwellings were designed by Stanford White and erected shortly before the Negroes came to Harlem. The most interesting section of the row is the north side of 139th Street. Here dark brick and terra-cotta façades, enriched with wrought-iron balconies and delicate entry porch roofs, were designed with considerable artistry in the spirit of the Florentine Renaissance.

Probably Harlem's best-known dance hall is the SAVOY BALLROOM, Lenox Avenue and 140th Street. Although patronized by many white persons it is the Negroes' own place. Many popular dances of the more energetic type have originated at the Savoy, including the Lindy Hop, Truckin', the Susie Q, and the Shag. The Negro orchestras that have played at the Savoy are among the leaders in the world of swing music and include those of Duke Ellington, Louis Armstrong, Cab Calloway, Noble Sissle, Jimmie Lunceford, Chick Webb, Claude Hopkins, Willie Bryant, and Fletcher Henderson.

A Negro unit of the New York State National Guard is housed at the 369TH REGIMENT INFANTRY ARMORY, Fifth Avenue and 143d Street. During the World War, this regiment (then the Fifteenth) received from the French Government a collective citation for conspicuous valor and the Croix de Guerre was pinned to the regimental colors. The regiment is headed (1939) by Colonel Benjamin O. Davis; he and his son are the only Negro line officers in the United States Army.

Sugar Hill, Harlem's finest residential section, is the neighborhood west of Eighth Avenue, from about 138th to 155th Street. Here, along Edgecombe, St. Nicholas, and Convent Avenues, are elaborately decorated apartment houses tenanted by Harlem's most successful citizens. Bill Robinson, Jack Johnson, Duke Ellington, Cab Calloway, Harry Wills, George Schuyler, and Walter White are among those who live or have lived on Sugar Hill. One of the dwellings is the Florence Mills Apartments, Edgecombe Avenue and 153d Street, named in honor of the internationally famous Negro musical comedy star, who died in 1927.

At the extreme northeastern end of Harlem, where Seventh Avenue and the Harlem River meet, are two of the locality's most important housing developments. At Seventh Avenue and 150th Street are the PAUL LAURENCE DUNBAR APARTMENTS, occupying an entire city block. The six separate buildings, six stories high and of variegated red Holland brick, are grouped around a central garden, with a playground for the smaller children. The development, named for the noted Negro poet, was financed by John D. Rockefeller, Jr., and designed by Andrew J. Thomas. It was completed in 1928 and conducted on a co-operative basis until 1936 when, as a result of many defaults in payment, Mr. Rockefeller foreclosed; the Dunbar National Bank, in the building, the only bank in Harlem operated by Negroes, was subsequently liquidated. He reimbursed the former tenant-owners for their capital payments and operated the apartments on a rental basis, maintaining the same management and social activities. A block north, from 151st to 153d Street, are the Harlem River Houses *(see page 392)*, the first example of large-scale public housing in Manhattan.

SPANISH HARLEM

Area: E. 96th and W. 110th Sts. on the south to E. 116th and 120th Sts. on the north; from Lexington Ave. (96th to 116th St.) and Madison Ave. (116th to 120th St.) west to 5th Ave. (96th to 110th St.) and Lenox Ave. (110th to 120th St.). Map on page 255.

Though called Spanish Harlem, this district is not the home of Spaniards but of Latin-Americans. European Spaniards have their own small colonies on West Fourteenth Street and in the vicinity of Cherry Street. Living in the Harlem quarter side by side are Puerto Ricans, Cubans,

American Negroes, West Indian Negroes, South Americans, and Mexicans. Puerto Ricans are in the overwhelming majority, numbering about one hundred thousand persons, or 85 per cent of the area's population.

Spanish Harlem first acquired its present character after the World War, when thousands of Puerto Ricans and Latin-Americans came to New York. Poverty, famine, or successive political upheavals in their native countries drove these people to the United States. They settled in Harlem because of the cheap rents and the sympathetic environment. Sixty per cent of the residents, however, have not been able to obtain regular employment since their arrival. The section around the 110th Street station of the Lexington Avenue subway, with its clutter of shops, tenements, and dime movie houses, is typical of the community.

The neighborhood's more important business places are on Fifth and Madison Avenues, between 110th and 116th Streets, and on 116th Street, east and west of Fifth Avenue. These range from small well-kept shops to fairly large and prosperous establishments. Numerous restaurants offer such typically Spanish food as *arroz con pollo* (rice with chicken) and *gazpacho* (Andalusian stew). Much of their patronage is drawn from visitors, who have more money to spend than the local residents. Noticeable, too, is the number of music shops with large assortments of mandolins, Spanish guitars, lutes, and *bandurrias,* phonograph records, and such sheet music as *La Violetera* (The Violet Seller), *La Partida* (The Parting), the universally popular *La Paloma* (The Dove), and other old favorites.

The near-by side streets are crowded with lightly stocked drygoods stores, *bodegas* (grocery stores), and *canicerías* (meat stores) and with blocks of old, broken-down houses, their stoops alive with people.

It is perhaps the PUBLIC MARKET PLACE that expresses most vividly the Latin-American character of the locality. The market, owned by the city, extends along Park Avenue under the New York Central viaduct, from 111th to 116th Street. Its block-long, steel-and-glass sheds, replace an old pushcart market. Besides little green limes, tangerines, oranges, bananas, and lemons, many tropical fruits grown in the various homelands of the inhabitants of Spanish Harlem are in season displayed here. Piled high in the racks are avocados (sometimes called alligator pears), mangoes with their strong flavor of turpentine, guavas from Cuba, and melon-like papayas, the leaves of which the Puerto Rican wraps around tough meat to make it tender. Tamarinds are sold to make a lemonade-like drink called *tamarindo;* and the long brown roots of the tropical cassava swing overhead.

Garbanzos (chick-peas), red kidney beans, dried peas, and lentils are in open sacks. Strings of fiery red peppers hang above their sweet-flavored kin, the pimientos. From the spice stalls women pick twenty or thirty different varieties which are mixed and stuffed into one bag. Fish of all kinds are on display, including huge tuna sold in slices.

The women shoppers move about with dignity: fair-skinned Creoles with dark eyes, lean-faced, copper-complexioned Spanish Indians, sensitive-looking West Indian Negroes. Voices are musical, and bargaining is done in a friendly spirit. The first price asked is always more than the Puerto Rican vendor expects to receive: *regatear* (to bargain) is the custom in his country.

To Spanish Harlemites bargaining is more than a tradition; to save a few pennies is a necessity. Those who succeed in finding employment work as poorly paid domestics or at menial occupations in hotels, laundries, cigar factories, or on Works Progress Administration projects; women and girls earn meager wages in local embroidery shops. Racial discrimination and lack of opportunity to learn skilled trades have kept both sexes from better-paid jobs.

Many Puerto Ricans suffer from malnutrition and are physically so underdeveloped that they are rejected for manual labor. Their diet in New York, except for the addition of a few vegetables, remains much the same as in their native land: a roll and black coffee for breakfast; for the other meals canned tomatoes, white rice, dried fish, and meat about twice a month.

In Spanish Harlem, the death rate from tuberculosis is high compared to the 52 per 100,000 for white persons in New York as a whole: among white Puerto Ricans the rate is 200 per 100,000; for colored groups, 553 per 100,000. The district's infant mortality rate is the highest in New York.

With little money to spend, the residents of this neighborhood have few and simple amusements. They attend the cheap movie houses, and the TEATRO LATINO, at Fifth Avenue and 110th Street, and the TEATRO HISPANO, at Fifth Avenue and 116th Street, which show Spanish-language films, many of them made in South America and Mexico. (The Hispano also presents Spanish vaudeville.) They gather in the evening at each other's homes to talk and entertain themselves over cups of black coffee. The different national groups have their favorites among the inexpensive restaurants and cabarets, where there is much music and festivity on Saturday nights. Several cafés and night clubs, featuring Cuban music, draw their patronage from the wealthier Spanish-speaking element and from visitors.

Cock-fighting, a sport that is legal in Puerto Rico but illegal in New

York, goes on now and then in Spanish Harlem. The place and time are carefully guarded; the audience gathers surreptitiously in a basement or empty room, where a small shallow wooden "ring" has been laid with dirt and sand. The cocks' steel-tipped talons are examined carefully by their sponsors. The birds are brushed, caressed, huskily exhorted, and then let loose amid excited betting and low-pitched cheering. Not till one of the cocks lies dead is the fight finished. Then the winner is embraced, washed, and hurried into hiding.

Most of the Latin-Americans in Spanish Harlem are of peasant or peon stock. The majority are American citizens. (All Puerto Ricans are.) They have an intense love of their homelands, and despite an occasional flurry of nationalist jealousy, a warm sense of neighborhood solidarity. Almost all are propertyless working people. They have their own political clubs, and during the past few years some organizations that were once interested primarily in the politics of the homelands, have become powerful pressure groups fighting for improved conditions in Spanish Harlem. As a result, their influence in city politics has increased. In 1937 this district elected O. Garcia-Rivera, a Puerto Rican lawyer, to the New York State Assembly.

The majority of Spanish Harlemites are Roman Catholics. The neighborhood Catholic churches include ST. FRANCIS DE SALES, 137 East 96th Street; ST. CECILIA, 220 East 106th Street; and OUR LADY OF THE MIRACULOUS MEDAL, 77 St. Nicholas Avenue. The IGLESIA METODISTA EPISCOPAL, 1664 Madison Avenue, where services are held in Spanish, is an outgrowth of a Methodist mission among Puerto Ricans and other Spanish-speaking people in New York.

The most important holiday observed in Spanish Harlem is *Día de la Raza* (Day of the Spanish Race), celebrated on Columbus Day by all Spanish-speaking people. They hold a ceremony in front of the statue of Columbus—a copy of the one in Madrid by Suñol, the Spanish sculptor—at the south end of the Central Park mall.

ITALIAN HARLEM

Area: 96th St. on the south to 125th St. on the north; from Lexington Ave. (96th to 116th St.) and Madison Ave. (116th to 125th St.) east to East River. Map on page 255.

Italian Harlem comprises a district which borders on the East River and overlooks Ward's *(see page 425)* and Randall's Islands *(see page 424)* and the Triborough Bridge *(see page 390)*. The Second and Third Avenue els run through the neighborhood, adding their noise to the rumble of trucks that pass ceaselessly along First Avenue. Near the river are bulky gas tanks—brown, massive, ugly, yet no more ugly than the houses huddled in their shadow.

Of the present Harlem communities Italian Harlem was formed the earliest, drawing upon immigration from the 1880's through the 1910's. The Sicilian and southern Italians who crowded into Harlem's five-story tenements had left farm and village behind. Those from the same village clustered together, so that, like a jig-saw map, Italy fell town by town along the streets of Harlem. The new generation grew up in closely packed tenements, and its children now play about the dark cavernous doorways of these same buildings. By force of numbers the Italians stamped their imprint upon the neighborhood, although a score of nationalities live in adjoining streets. The 150,000 persons in this area of one square mile make it the most densely populated section of Manhattan and the largest colony of Italian-Americans in the country.

The traditionally carefree singing spirit of Italians pervades the crowded sidewalks of First Avenue, from 107th to 116th Streets. As in the market place of a Neapolitan village, the Italian housewives, and often the men themselves, haggle for greens, oils, and olives; cheese and macaroni; sea urchins, devilfish, and razor clams which might have come directly from the Aegean Sea. The delicious and curiously shaped bread of Italy is displayed alongside children's underwear and men's work gloves. Finochio and pomegranates lie in bins next to those containing potatoes and the garlic-onions so relished by Sicilians.

Along the market street are many cafés and restaurants—small, modest places which preserve the air of their prototypes in Palermo, Naples, or Rome. The menu consists of native dishes—spaghetti, *minestrone, scallopine,* chicken *alla cacciatore, pizza.* The coffee houses, neighborhood meeting places usually filled with sprightly conversation and cigar smoke, serve *caffè espresso* (Italian coffee made to order), and a wide variety of gaudy pastries.

THOMAS JEFFERSON PARK, between First Avenue and the river, from 111th to 114th Street, is known as the Italian park. This is no vast landscaped stretch of green, but its area of six square blocks is a retreat for the teeming section. It includes a swimming pool, a baseball diamond, handball and basketball courts, a children's playground, and alleys for *boccie* (the Italian version of bowling). In winter the bathhouse is used as a children's game room.

The center of the religious life of the district is the CHURCH OF OUR LADY OF MOUNT CARMEL, 449 East 115th Street. Overhead, from the rectory windows, two large Italian flags flap briskly. Inside the church is the shrine of Our Lady, enriched with precious jewels. The fiesta of Our Lady of Mount Carmel, the great religious and social event of the community, takes place on July 15, 16, and 17. It is suggestive of an old-world spectacle: the ritual procession, headed by a brass band and followed by clergy and the statue of the Virgin borne by the beneficiaries of "miracles," winds slowly through the bedecked streets. Donations, fluttering from the tenement windows, are caught and tossed into an outspread cloth or pinned to ornate banners. Many pilgrims walk barefooted. Occasionally the procession halts under the window of a particularly generous donor and the priest recites the *Dispensorio* while firecrackers explode and the throng stands with bowed heads.

HAARLEM HOUSE, the oldest (1898) and most notable of Harlem's settlements, maintains headquarters at 311 East 116th Street. In addition to Americanization services and assistance to immigrants, the institution conducts a varied program of activities for the benefit of the poor—classes in vocational and cultural subjects, clubs, games, debates, and forums—and participates in progressive municipal campaigns.

A radical change in the character of the district's river front was brought about by the construction of the East River Drive approach to the Triborough Bridge. The Drive borders the river from Ninety-second to 125th Streets, its clean wide sweep of roadway and adjoining landscaped mall replacing the dumps, tenements, and shanties that had made an ugly stretch along the water front. Benches placed beneath trees on both sides of the Drive make it useful and attractive to residents of the neighborhood as well as to motorists. Because of the Drive the bordering avenue has become a likely place for real-estate development, and it is probable that luxurious apartment houses, like those on Sutton Place, Gracie Square, and East End Avenue, will soon rise here.

D. Spiegel

Upper West Side and Northern Manhattan

CENTRAL PARK WEST DISTRICT—RIVER-
SIDE DRIVE—MORNINGSIDE HEIGHTS AND
MANHATTANVILLE—WASHINGTON HEIGHTS
—INWOOD—MARBLE HILL

Area: 59th St. on the south to Harlem River Ship Canal (and Marble Hill) on the north; from the Hudson River east to Central Park, Morningside Ave., St. Nicholas Ave. (125th to 155th St.), and the Harlem River. Maps on pages 54-55 and 293.
Principal north-south streets: Broadway, Amsterdam Ave., Riverside Drive, and Henry Hudson Parkway.
Principal cross streets: 72d, 86th, 96th, 110th, 125th, 145th, 155th, 181st, and Dyck-man Sts.
Transportation: IRT Broadway-7th Ave. subway (local), 59th to 225th St. stations; 8th Ave. (Independent) Washington Heights subway (local), 59th to 207th St. stations; Fifth Ave. buses Nos. 4, 5, 8, and 19; Broadway surface car.

A ROCKY ridge rises gently on the west side of the city, between 59th Street and 110th Street, and attains commanding elevations in the neighborhood of Washington Heights, where many fine residences and institutions have found an advantageous natural setting. Along the Hudson are Riverside, Fort Washington, Fort Tryon, and Inwood Hill parks. Above

110th Street, Morningside, St. Nicholas, Colonial, and High Bridge parks have been developed along the precipitous eastern edge of the ridge.

The area west of Central Park is almost level except along the river; but at 110th Street the terrain ascends abruptly to form Morningside Heights, on which stand the Cathedral of St. John the Divine, Columbia University, and other well-known institutions. At West 125th Street a broad and slanting ravine cuts across the ridge from Harlem Flats to the Hudson, forming the Manhattanville neighborhood. North of the ravine is St. Nicholas Heights, part of the eastern border of the Upper West Side. West and north, where the elevation is known as lower Washington Heights (or Hamilton Heights), the cross streets slope, often very steeply, toward the river, giving glimpses of the water and the wooded Jersey shore. Washington Heights proper extends from 155th to 176th Street.

The ridge forks at 176th Street, one spur (Laurel Hill) bordering the Harlem River and the other (Long Hill) the Hudson, with Broadway descending the narrow valley between them to the Inwood plain. Across the Harlem and northeast of Inwood Hill Park is the Marble Hill section, a part of the borough of the Bronx geographically, but still under the jurisdiction of the borough of Manhattan.

Broadway runs through this section, crossing 230th Street, Manhattan's northern boundary line. From Columbus Circle to 181st Street it is simply the main street of a large and prosperous residential district. Hundreds of thousands of shoppers, movie-goers, diners, and strollers, whose homes are in the phalanxed apartment buildings and hotels near by, crowd this wide thoroughfare. Yet the promenades and benches of the central parking retain for the street a suburban atmosphere of neighborliness and leisure.

St. Nicholas Avenue cuts into the section at about 125th Street, and the Harlem River Driveway begins west of the Polo Grounds at 155th Street, below Coogan's Bluff.

Riverside Drive, beginning at Seventy-second Street and ending at Dyckman Street, precariously follows the western edge of the ridge. The Riverside Church, Grant's Tomb, the Columbia Presbyterian Medical Center, and the Cloisters are visible from the Drive. On the lowlands between the ridge and the Hudson River runs the Henry Hudson Parkway—a through highway connecting with the Westchester County Parkway system—and the newly built river terraces.

The area between Broadway and the Hudson River from Fifty-ninth to Seventieth Street is a plebeian district. Above Fifty-ninth Street several avenues change their names: Eighth Avenue to Central Park West; Ninth

Avenue to Columbus Avenue, which ends at Cathedral Parkway (110th Street); Tenth Avenue to Amsterdam Avenue; Eleventh Avenue to West End Avenue. Despite its change of name, Columbus Avenue, burdened with the el, remains a shabby back street of Central Park West.

The area from what is now 59th to 135th Street was part of the region called *Bloemendael* (vale of flowers) by the Dutch in patriotic remembrance of a town near Haarlem in the old country. In the vicinity of 100th Street was Bloomingdale Village; well into the last century the tract of farms and country estates on the Upper West Side was known as the Bloomingdale district. Washington Irving in his *Knickerbocker's History of New York* described this section as "a sweet rural valley, beautiful with many a bright flower, refreshed by many a pure streamlet, and enlivened here and there by a delectable little Dutch cottage, sheltered under some sloping hill; and almost buried in embowering trees."

During the period of Dutch settlement a road led through the 125th Street ravine, called the Widow David's Meadow, to the Hudson River, where, as now, a ferry plied to Jersey. The tribes who occupied Manhattan north of the ravine were not parties to the Minuit purchase and treaty, and their resentment of Dutch encroachment upon their territory led to sporadic warfare. In the 1640's Governor Kieft added to the natives' indignation by apportioning their land to various grantees and finally in 1655 the Indians raided and destroyed a village in the Marble Hill region, ending further Dutch settlement. Under English rule in the 1680's farmers began to develop the "Great Maize Land"—the fertile Inwood valley— through which an Indian trail ran. In 1693 Frederick Philipse built a bridge—the King's Bridge—over Spuyten Duyvil ("in spite of the Devil") Creek, near what is now the junction of West 230th Street and Marble Hill Avenue. Later, the trail leading to the bridge became the Kingsbridge Road, which, across the Harlem, divides into the Boston and the Albany Post Roads.

Bloomingdale Road was opened in 1703, running from what is now Twenty-third Street to 114th Street; in 1795 it was extended to 147th Street where it joined Kingsbridge Road. Following the opening of the highway, more of the land on the Upper West Side was brought under cultivation, and the establishment of country estates there and farther north was begun in the pre-Revolutionary period.

The development of the region was accelerated during the Federal period. Under the gridiron plan of 1811 the city was laid out in broad avenues and narrow cross streets as far north as 145th Street. In the first decade of the nineteenth century the village of Manhattanville grew up in the valley known in Revolutionary days as the Hollow Way; the village occupied the area between West 125th and 135th Streets.

In 1851 the Hudson River Railroad from New York to Albany was opened, with several local stations in upper Manhattan; but it was not until the opening of the Western Boulevard in 1869 that the rural character of the section began to change. This thoroughfare, known simply as the Boulevard and becoming a part of Broadway in 1899, started at Fifty-ninth Street and followed the general direction of the old Bloomingdale Road. During the 1890's it was a favorite route of bicycle riders. The Ninth Avenue el was extended through the Upper West Side in 1879; and in 1891 the first part of Riverside Drive was completed. Mansions, hotels, and apartments, many of them still standing, were built in the area west of Central Park. Trolley and subway services to the northern localities were established in the first years of the century, and with a building boom in the 1920's this part of the neighborhood acquired its present middle-class aspect.

The entire region is rich in historic memorials. The house built by Roger Morris in 1765, now known as the Jumel Mansion, stands at Edgecombe Avenue and 160th Street. During the Revolution the Morris home served as a headquarters for both American and British forces. The home of the first Secretary of the Treasury, Hamilton Grange (on Convent Avenue north of 141st Street), is typical of the country homes of the post-Revolutionary period.

Two important battles, fought in 1776, are recalled by markers throughout this upper portion of Manhattan: the Battle of Harlem Heights and the Battle of Fort Washington. Following the defeat of the New York City defenders in the Battle of Long Island, August 27, the city itself was easily captured by the British on September 15, the defenders hastily retreating to their fortified heights north of the 125th Street ravine to the Spuyten Duyvil. The Battle of Harlem Heights occurred September 16. A detachment of Americans, descending into the Hollow Way, succeeded in drawing a British advance force down into the valley and into an attack. The British retreated and entrenched themselves until, on being reinforced shortly afterward, they took a stand in a buckwheat field (now the site of Barnard College). The Americans, also receiving further support, drove the British back to the neighborhood of what is now 105th Street, where the fighting ceased on the appearance of more British and Hessian troops sent up by General Howe. Called an "affair of outposts" by General Howe, the Battle of Harlem Heights was important in that it raised the morale of Washington's hard pressed militia.

In October General Howe, with the aid of the British fleet, attempted to attack the rear guard of Washington's army. To thwart the British plans, Washington led his divisions across King's Bridge and into Westchester, leaving behind a garrison at Fort Washington under Colonel Robert Magaw. The fort was a five-bastioned earthwork west of what is now Fort Washington Avenue and about in the line of 183d Street.

On November 16 a battle took place. The Americans were completely surrounded: two columns of Hessians under General von Knyphausen assaulted the outworks on Long Hill, one scaling the hill from the north, the other from the east. Under a bombardment from the east bank of the Harlem (Fordham Heights), General Cornwallis crossed the river at 201st Street. Lower down, the Forty-second Highlanders crossed the river at about High Bridge. British troops under Lord Percy advanced from the south, and warships fired from the Hudson.

The defenders of the outworks were killed, captured, or driven within the untenable fort; and Colonel Magaw surrendered. The defense of Fort Washington had been a mistake, and the loss of many of Washington's best-equipped men—54 killed and 2,634 captured—was disastrous. Until the close of the war British and Hessian troops were encamped within the repaired fortifications of the heights. The outwork on Long Hill was renamed Fort Tryon, after William Tryon, last English civil governor of New York, and the present Fort Tryon Park includes the site.

CENTRAL PARK WEST DISTRICT

Area: 59th St. on the south to 110th St. (Cathedral Parkway) on the north; from Central Park West to the West Side Highway and Riverside Drive. Map on page 277.

This district, encroached upon by two run-down areas—Middle West Side on the south and Harlem on the northeast—is bordered by three of Manhattan's aristocratic thoroughfares, West End Avenue, Riverside Drive *(see page 284),* and Central Park West. The last-named street, a continuation of Eighth Avenue, has one of the most distinctive sky lines in the city, which can be seen to better advantage from various points in Central Park than from the street itself. Dominating the sky line are the towers of five apartment buildings, set between Sixty-second and Ninety-second Streets.

The CENTURY APARTMENTS, designed by the office of Irwin S. Chanin, architects, and constructed in 1931, fronts Central Park West from Sixty-

KEY TO MAP OF UPPER FIFTH AVENUE, CENTRAL PARK SOUTH, CENTRAL PARK WEST DISTRICT, AND RIVERSIDE DRIVE

CENTRAL PARK SOUTH, THE PLAZA, AND FIFTY-SEVENTH STREET

1. Hotel Pierre
2. Metropolitan Club
3. Sherry-Netherland Hotel
4. Savoy-Plaza Hotel
5. Squibb Building
6. Heckscher Building
7. Dobbs Building
8. Pulitzer Memorial Fountain
9. Statue of General Sherman
10. Hotel Plaza
11. Hotel St. Moritz
12. Barbizon Plaza Hotel
13. Hampshire House
14. Essex House Hotel
15. New York Athletic Club
16. Steinway Hall
17. Carnegie Hall
18. Gainsborough Studios
19. Fine Arts Building
    Art Students League
20. Federal Art Project Gallery

CENTRAL PARK WEST DISTRICT

21. Church of St. Paul the Apostle
22. Columbus Circle Garage
23. Twelfth Regiment Armory
24. New York WPA Headquarters
25. Statue of Dante
26. Empire Hotel
27. Site of the Century Theater
    Century Apartments
28. Y.M.C.A., West Side Branch
29. Society for Ethical Culture
    Ethical Culture School
30. Free Synagogue
31. Congregation Shearith Israel
32. Majestic Apartments
    Explorers Club
33. Dakota Apartments
34. Sherman Square
35. Verdi Square
    Statue of Giuseppe Verdi
36. Ansonia Hotel
37. West End Collegiate Church
38. Collegiate School
39. Apthorp Apartments
40. First Baptist Church
41. New York School of Fine and Applied Art
42. New York Historical Society
43. Museum of Natural History
44. Roosevelt Memorial Building
45. Hayden Planetarium
46. Congregation B'nai Jeshurun
47. Walden School
48. Trinity School
49. Pomander Walk
50. First Church of Christ Scientist
51. Straus Park
    Straus Memorial Fountain
52. National Academy of Design
53. Sixtieth Street Yards of the New York Central Railroad

RIVERSIDE DRIVE
(Also see map on page 293)

54. Monument to Henry Hudson
55. Charles M. Schwab Mansion
56. Mount Tom
57. Soldiers' and Sailors' Monument
58. Statue of Joan of Arc
59. Firemen's Memorial
60. Bust of Orestes A. Brownson
61. Master Institute of United Arts

Continued on Page 278

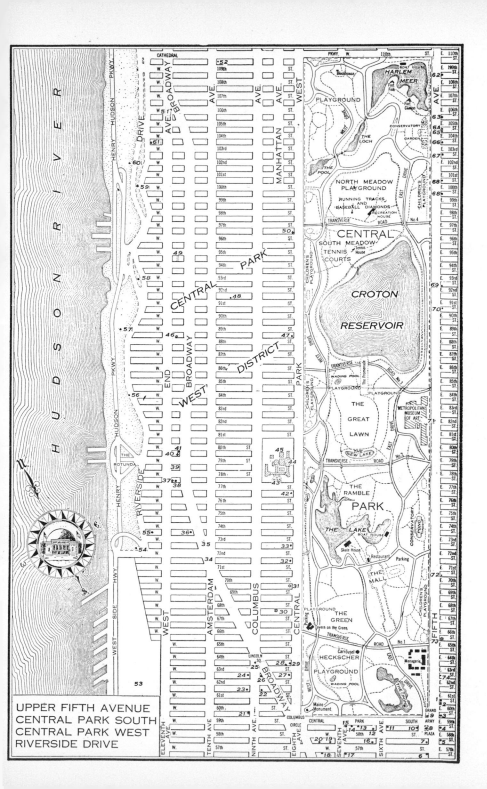

UPPER FIFTH AVENUE
CENTRAL PARK SOUTH
CENTRAL PARK WEST
RIVERSIDE DRIVE

second to Sixty-third Street. It occupies the site of New York's most spectacularly unsuccessful theater. The playhouse, which had been erected in
1909 at a cost of three million dollars, was intended for a national theater
free of commercialism. It had a prominent horseshoe of boxes for the use
of its many wealthy backers. After two years of epic striving the New
Theater, as it was called, had netted a deficit of $400,000 and the charge
of being a "Shrine of Snobbery." It was rechristened the Century Theater
in 1911; the Century Opera House in 1913; the Century again in 1915,
with Ziegfeld presenting musical shows. But despite a magnificent interior, no change in name, management, or type of performance seemed able
to overcome the handicap of the out-of-the-way location.

At 5 West Sixty-third Street is the West Side branch of the YOUNG
MEN'S CHRISTIAN ASSOCIATION. Besides a dormitory and a gymnasium,
the West Side "Y" operates trade schools that enroll some two thousand
students annually. The immense building, architecturally reminiscent of
North Italian Romanesque brickwork, is the work of James Dwight Baum.

The two buildings on Central Park West between Sixty-third and Sixty-
fourth Streets house the SOCIETY FOR ETHICAL CULTURE and the mid-
town ETHICAL CULTURE SCHOOL. Founded in 1876 by Dr. Felix Adler,
the society emphasizes direct moral teachings without alliance to creed or
sect. It is perhaps best known for its experiments in advanced educational
methods among children, which are studied by educators from all parts
of the world. The Ethical Culture School System developed from the first
free kindergarten in New York, established by the society in 1878, and
from the Working Man's School of the United Relief Works, opened
by the society shortly thereafter. Classes in the Ethical Culture Schools
range from the pre-kindergarten to the graduate school for women.
Fieldston, a junior high and college preparatory school, is at Riverdale,

---

Continued from Page 276

UPPER FIFTH AVENUE

the Bronx. Robert D. Kohn, architect and president of the society, designed the society building, 2 West Sixty-fourth Street, in which the Sunday meetings are held. The building deviates considerably from the classic tradition and is characterized by originality in its details. The auditorium, well suited to the community character of the Sunday services, has fine wood carving and simple vaulting that are noteworthy.

At 40 West Sixty-eighth Street is the FREE SYNAGOGUE. (Carnegie Hall is used by the congregation on major holidays and on Sunday mornings.) It was founded in 1907 by Rabbi Stephen S. Wise as a free pulpit that could be used not only to convey a religious message, but could serve also as a public forum. Rabbi Wise has been prominent in civic reform movements and is an ardent Zionist and eloquent leader of American Jewry. He is founder and president of the Jewish Institute of Religion, a rabbinical training school which is unusual in that preparation is offered for leadership in conservative, reformed, or orthodox synagogues. It has headquarters in the Free Synagogue building.

CONGREGATION SHEARITH ISRAEL, Central Park West and Seventieth Street, is the oldest Jewish congregation in America. It was founded in 1655 by Spanish and Portuguese Jews who had fled the Inquisition, first to Brazil and then to New Amsterdam. Their first synagogue was a mill loft; after several moves the congregation occupied the present quarters in 1897. Designed by Bruner and Tryon, the synagogue is late Italian Renaissance in style. One of the rooms, used as a chapel, is furnished with fixtures and religious ornaments from the first synagogue built by the Congregation in 1730. Numerous photographs and paintings of historical interest are in other rooms. Commodore Uriah P. Levy, who was responsible for the abolition of corporal punishment in the United States Navy; Emma Lazarus, one of whose poems is inscribed on the Statue of Liberty; and U.S. Supreme Court Justice Benjamin N. Cardozo were members of Congregation Shearith Israel.

The twin-towered MAJESTIC APARTMENTS, 115 Central Park West, was, like the Century, built by Irwin S. Chanin. Within, are the quarters of the exclusively masculine EXPLORERS CLUB, founded in 1904. Dr. Vilhjalmur Stefansson is president, and the membership of about six hundred includes most of the noted American explorers. The quarters contain a Museum of Exploration (not open to the public) displaying materials used by famous explorers, among them Stefansson, Peary, and Bartlett; the club owns a number of manuscripts of historic value.

The browned and mellowed yellow-brick building on Central Park West between Seventy-second and Seventy-third Streets is the DAKOTA APART-

MENTS, whose gables, oriel windows, cupolas, and pinnacled dormers recall the elegant 1880's. The entrance is through an arched gateway on Seventy-second Street (closed at midnight) which gives access to an interior court, decorated by two fountains. The building, which dates from 1881, still uses its original elevators powered by steam pumps.

The NEW YORK HISTORICAL SOCIETY is on Central Park West between Seventy-sixth and Seventy-seventh Streets. The society, founded in 1804, is the second oldest of its kind in America. The central section of the present building was erected in 1908 from plans by York and Sawyer. In 1937–8 two wings were added and alterations made from plans by Walker and Gillette.

In addition to a library and art galleries, the building features a museum of Americana containing sleighs, waistcoats, war feathers, bows and arrows; souvenirs of the New York Volunteer Fire Department; and the lead remains of the Bowling Green statue of King George III that was torn down and used for bullets by the Liberty Boys during the Revolutionary War. *(Museum open weekdays 10 a.m. to 5 p.m., Sunday and holidays 1 to 5 p.m.; library open daily except Sunday 10 a.m. to 5 p.m.)* Among the collections are the Schuyler and De Peyster family silver; the sculptures of Charles Allen Munn and John Rogers; 460 original Audubon water-color drawings for *Birds of America;* and a wealth of documents and maps pertaining to the port of New York. The American portrait gallery has works of such artists as Gilbert Stuart, John Trumbull, Benjamin West, and Daniel Huntington. Included among the European paintings are groups representing various schools of the Italian Renaissance. The society's collection of Egyptian Antiquities is now in the Brooklyn Museum *(see page 488).*

The American Museum of Natural History and the Hayden Planetarium *(see page 358)* are between Seventy-seventh and Eighty-first Streets, Columbus Avenue and Central Park West. At 1 West Eighty-eighth Street are the buildings of the WALDEN SCHOOL, established in 1914, a pioneer in progressive education. Classes run from nursery through high school. The building is decorated with friezes and murals by the children.

TRINITY SCHOOL, a preparatory day school for boys, at 139 West Ninety-first Street, was established in 1709 by the English Venerable Society for the Propagation of the Gospel in Foreign Parts. For 125 years it gave virtually all the free instruction in the city; today it operates as a private school charging tuition fees. College preparatory courses are supplemented by instruction in the doctrines of the Episcopal Church.

The FIRST CHURCH OF CHRIST SCIENTIST occupies the north corner at Ninety-sixth Street and Central Park West. The design of the building, by Carrère and Hastings, is eclectic. The granite exterior shows English Renaissance characteristics, while the handsome interior, with its rich marbles and gracefully curving stairways, recalls the style of the French Renaissance. The church was erected in 1903.

Ninety-ninth Street between Central Park West and Columbus Avenue is occupied by a Negro colony, an outpost of Harlem.

The Broadway Section

On the southwest corner of Sixtieth Street and Columbus Avenue, a block west of Broadway, is the CHURCH OF ST. PAUL THE APOSTLE, home of the Paulist Fathers, an indigenous Catholic order, founded in 1858.

A dozen of the most typically American artists of the 1880's contributed to the interior design of this church but the structure was largely planned by the Paulist Fathers themselves. The massive ruggedness of the sparsely ornamented granite exterior contrasts strongly with the richness of the interior, which contains work by the sculptors Augustus Saint-Gaudens, Bela Pratt, Frederick MacMonnies, and Philip Martiny; the painters John La Farge, William Laurel Harris, Marquis Wentworth, and Robert Reid; and Stanford White and Bertram Goodhue. The architect was Jeremiah O'Rourke. The original plans of the church were considerably modified by Father George Deshon, a West Point graduate, and this fact, together with the simplicity of the exterior, once gave the building the sobriquet of "Father Deshon's fort." Construction was begun in 1876.

The TWELFTH REGIMENT ARMORY, the headquarters of the 212th Coast Artillery and the Coast Artillery Brigade, fronts Columbus Avenue from Sixty-first to Sixty-second Street. Built in 1887 by army engineers, it is a castellated structure of red brick with granite trim, which has served as a background for motion-picture shots representing medieval forts.

A very different type of architectural achievement is the COLUMBUS CIRCLE AUTOMATIC GARAGE at Sixty-first Street and Columbus Avenue, whose almost windowless orange-colored walls rise simply and directly for twenty-seven stories. The design by Jardine, Hill, and Murdock suggests the simplicity and functionalism of an American grain elevator.

At Sixty-fourth Street, Broadway intersects Columbus Avenue, forming LINCOLN SQUARE. Here, flanked on the south by the towering Empire Hotel (44 West Sixty-third Street) and the huge loft building (70 Columbus Avenue) that serves as headquarters for all New York City WPA projects except the Arts group, is the small DANTE PARK with a bronze statue of the author of the *Divina Commedia*. The architects, Warren and Wetmore, and the sculptor, Ettore Ximenes, have adhered to the traditional conception of Dante as a figure of quiet austerity.

Where Broadway crosses Amsterdam Avenue at West Seventy-second Street, two blocks west of Central Park West, are VERDI SQUARE, to the north, and SHERMAN SQUARE, to the south, irregular spaces left over from the unfortunate intersection of too many streets. Within the former, a heroic bronze STATUE OF GIUSEPPE VERDI stands on a fifteen-foot granite pedestal. Grouped around the pedestal are four life-size figures depicting characters in the composer's operas. The monument, sculptured by Pasquale Civiletti, was erected in 1906 by the Italian community.

The neighborhood was built up in the 1890's when brownstone, an easily worked stone available in the vicinity of New York, was adapted to prevailing architectural fashions. The rows of buildings that survive in the cross streets cut by Broadway present a picture of the changing tastes of the final years of the nineteenth century. Many of them, particularly those in the lower Seventies, were built for speculative purposes in block-long rows of identical houses. Others, particularly in the Eighties, were built singly, each house, though limited by a twenty- or twenty-five foot frontage, attempting to outdo architecturally its many neighbors. The result was frequently a brown "wedding cake" façade with overrich ornamentations, cornices, gables, dormers, and bay windows.

Many hotels are near the two squares. Those built in the early years of this century are recognizable by their rococo exteriors. In their day this excessive ornamentation was an admired importation, representing as it did the influence of the École des Beaux-Arts upon American architects who studied in Paris. Perhaps the most distinguished survivor of the buildings of that time is the sixteen-story ANSONIA, 2107 Broadway, designed by H. J. Hardenbergh, and built in 1900. The interior has been modernized. Many celebrities have made their homes here, including Florenz Ziegfeld, Babe Ruth, Giovanni Martinelli, Mischa Elman, and Theodore Dreiser.

At 241 West Seventy-seventh Street, near West End Avenue, is the COLLEGIATE SCHOOL, established by the Dutch in 1637, and in continuous operation since, except for a brief suspension during the British occupation. Adjoining the school is the WEST END COLLEGIATE CHURCH (Dutch Reformed). This group of buildings, designed by R. W. Gibson and erected in 1892, is an excellent example of Dutch architecture. The school building is a close copy of the *Vleeschhuis*—the market building of Haarlem, Holland—but the group as a whole shows a highly creative use of historic Flemish forms. Peculiarly Dutch are the stepped gables, the fine modeling of terra-cotta ornament, and the skillful handling of long bricks.

Occupying the block between Seventy-eighth and Seventy-ninth Streets, Broadway and West End Avenue, is the massive APTHORP APARTMENTS, a twelve-story building surrounding a court. Large archways mark the entrances to the court, on both Broadway and West End Avenue. At Broadway and Seventy-ninth Street is the FIRST BAPTIST CHURCH, referred to as the "Mother of Churches" by the Baptists for its role in founding other churches of this denomination in America. The congregation had its origin in 1728 in group meetings of the Baptists; their first church, on Gold Street, was not built until 1745. The present structure was erected during 1891–2.

The NEW YORK SCHOOL OF FINE AND APPLIED ART, a block north at 2237 Broadway, was founded in 1896 by Frank A. Parsons and inaugurated in 1904 the first course in interior decoration taught in any American art school. Its reference library contains more than ten thousand photographic plates of interiors and other material on the decorative arts. The school has branches in Paris and Italy.

At 257 West Eighty-eighth Street, west of Broadway, is the synagogue of CONGREGATION B'NAI JESHURUN (Conservative). The building was designed by Henry Beaumont Herts and Walker Schneider and was built in 1918. Its façade is a striking composition featuring a tall Romanesque portal; the interior, which is pleasantly arranged, is decorated with intense polychrome ornament.

Between Broadway and West End Avenue, and running from Ninety-fourth Street to Ninety-fifth Street, is POMANDER WALK, a double row of small English-style houses, built in 1921, intended for and first occupied by theatrical people. The houses took their name from a little street of the London suburb, Chiswick, publicized in 1911 in the play *Pomander Walk*, produced in New York and London. At 106th Street, where West End Avenue terminates in Broadway, is a triangular park containing a FOUNTAIN IN MEMORY OF ISIDOR AND IDA STRAUS, philanthropists who lost their lives in the *Titanic* disaster. The monument, designed by Evarts Tracy, is the work of the sculptor, Augustus Lukeman.

The NATIONAL ACADEMY OF DESIGN, established in 1825 by a group of rebel students from the American Academy of the Fine Arts, is at 109th Street and Amsterdam Avenue. It offers free day and evening courses in nearly all branches of the fine arts. Samuel F. B. Morse, inventor and portrait painter, was its first president, and the present one, Jonas Lie, is well known as a painter of sea subjects.

The respectable calm of this Central Park West District has been occasionally ruffled. In one block of West Seventies, for example, showgirl Dot King and Joseph P. Elwell were both murdered. In 1931, more than 10,000 spectators lined West Ninetieth Street while 150 policemen besieged notorious "Two-gun" Crowley and captured him after a rattling small-arms battle. These events, however, are no more typical of the normal life of the neighborhood than is the Explorers Club.

RIVERSIDE DRIVE

Area: 72d Street to Dyckman Street bordering the Hudson River. Maps on pages 277 and 293.

Riverside Drive, like Wall Street, is a national symbol of wealth, but unlike Wall Street it has never quite deserved its reputation. From the 1890's until after the World War, to be sure, it was popular with the newly rich, whose ornate gray and brownstone battlemented houses bore witness to economic success; yet, lacking an old-family tradition, it never rivaled streets like Fifth Avenue in the esteem of fashionable society. In its location, however, with its fine parks, and impressive buildings and monuments, Riverside Drive is unsurpassed by any street in New York.

The Drive rides the precipitous western escarpment of the island from Seventy-second Street to Dyckman Street, winding, rising, dipping, for almost seven miles, yet always maintaining an elevation that permits a spreading view of the Hudson River, the Palisades, and the George Washington Bridge. The Drive is walled off on the east by apartment houses, old and new, a few mansions, some notable institutions, and occasional blocks of converted dwellings where a twenty-dollar-a-week clerk may rent a small room and write the folks back home that he is living on the Drive.

Along the slope between the high roadway and the river, a narrow park borders the Drive for most of its length; this strip of greenery is named RIVERSIDE PARK up to 158th Street where it becomes FORT WASHINGTON PARK. At the very edge of the river, and superseding the Drive as a through automobile route, run the twin lanes of the new HENRY HUDSON PARKWAY, which connects with the West Side highway below Seventy-second Street and empties into the Saw Mill River Parkway at the Westchester County line. This road is intended eventually to form part of a continuous express route around Manhattan's rim.

But the roadway is only one feature of a $24,000,000 development planned for the area between the river and Riverside and Fort Washington parks. An extensive system of public playgrounds, nearing completion in 1939, includes tennis, basketball, handball, and horseshoe courts, softball and baseball diamonds, football and athletic fields, roller-skating rinks, cycle paths, playgrounds for small children, and additional facilities for shuffleboard, paddle tennis, and dancing. At Seventy-ninth Street, looking out over the river, is a handsome granite structure, the center of a recreation area that includes a wading pool and sports fields. In the technical language of the Henry Hudson Parkway Authority, however, it is known as a grade elimination structure. The roadway on its roof is one petal of a cloverleaf which sorts traffic to and from the Drive. A circular opening in the center of the petal permits a passing view of a huge fountain far below. On the river side a colonnade and a porch esplanade overlook a small yacht basin. The basement is a two-hundred-car garage.

That part of the park not devoted to playgrounds is being landscaped. First, the ugly New York Central Railroad tracks, whose presence here has been a point of controversy in the State Legislature, have been covered by a concrete roof as far as 124th Street. This roof, in turn, has been transformed into a wide pedestrian promenade with flower beds running down the center. One hundred and thirty-two acres have been added to the park by this improvement and by filling in and straightening the jagged edge of the foreshore. The parkway runs on parts of this made land. The landscaping scheme provides for the planting of large shade trees at the outskirts to furnish a towering green background for masses of colorful flowering shrubs.

The terraces breaking the sharp slope leading down to the river wind along the water front, sometimes as a narrow strip of green and sometimes jutting out surprisingly into a wide space of well-kept mall or wooded park. Auto parkway and pedestrian footways curl around and over hills and up and down the difficult ascent. Opposite Fort Washington Park, changing sunlight plays against the reddish-ochre fluted cliffs of the Palisades on the New Jersey shore, reached by way of George Washington Bridge or Dyckman Street Ferry.

When "the fleet's in," battleships line the Hudson from the Battery to Spuyten Duyvil. At night the crisscrossing beams of their searchlights fill the sky over the whole city with a strange and shifting brilliance, while sailors on leave and their friends congregate in the park.

Early in the nineteenth century this western shore line was occupied principally by squatters and their goats. In 1872, after the introduction of a bill in the 1866 Legislature, the property was acquired by the city. Designed by Frederick Law Olmsted, the landscape architect who revolutionized America's ideas on park planning, the Drive was completed from Seventy-second Street to 129th Street by 1885; the year 1902 saw the opening of the viaduct that crosses 96th Street. Not until the end of 1908 was the next stretch built as far as 145th Street, and several years later another ten-block jump joined the Drive with another road, between 155th and Dyckman Streets, which had been in use since 1896. In its early days, the Drive was the favorite place to show off a fashionable equipage.

Where the Drive begins at Seventy-second Street is a weather-beaten bronze MONUMENT TO HENRY HUDSON, erected in 1909 by the Colonial Dames of America to commemorate the tercentenary of Hudson's discovery of the river. For most visitors, however, the Drive begins at the CHARLES M. SCHWAB MANSION, which lords over the square block from Seventy-third to Seventy-fourth Street. It was designed by Maurice Ebert and is said to have cost more than $2,500,000. The central façade is reminiscent of the chateau of Chenonceaux, and the sides, of the castles of Blois and Azay-le-Rideau.

A rocky knob at Eighty-fourth Street and the Drive, its outline barely softened by trees and bushes, is known as MOUNT TOM. Here Edgar Allan Poe, living in the neighborhood in the summers of 1843 and 1844, used to sit alone for hours gazing at the Hudson.

At Eighty-ninth Street, on a magnificent site, the SOLDIERS' AND SAILORS' MONUMENT, completed in 1902 at a cost of a quarter of a million dollars, honors the Union fighters in the Civil War. The monument, more sculpture than architecture to many, lacks the clarity of form and simplicity of some of the better American memorials. The architects were Charles W. and Arthur A. Stoughton and Paul E. Duboy. Near the monument, cannon have been mounted on rough-hewn granite boulders.

At Ninety-third Street a bronze equestrian STATUE OF JOAN OF ARC, cast from a model by Anna Hyatt Huntington, is mounted on a base containing fragments from Rheims Cathedral, scene of the Maid's greatest triumph, and stones from the Tower of Rouen, where she awaited trial and death. The FIREMEN'S MEMORIAL at 100th Street is a colossal tablet flanked on both sides by heroic figures representing Courage and Duty. The sculptor was Attilio Piccirilli. A bas-relief on the tablet depicts one of the colorful horse-drawn engines which constituted New York's fire-fighting equipment in 1913, when the memorial was erected.

In Riverside Park, near 102d Street, is a BUST OF ORESTES AUGUSTUS BROWNSON (1803–1876), cast after a model by Samuel Kitson. Brownson was a dynamic if somewhat unstable element in the early American labor movement. In religious belief he went from Presbyterianism to Universalism to Unitarianism, and finally joined the Roman Catholic Church. He was also a writer on social reforms, and his point of view was associated with the transcendentalist movement of his time.

At 103d Street a twenty-eight-story apartment building houses the MASTER INSTITUTE OF UNITED ARTS, formerly the Roerich Museum, named for that extraordinary Russian painter, author, mystic, and explorer, Nicholas Roerich. It was founded in 1922 for the purpose of promoting the unity of arts and cultures. The present building, erected in 1929 with the co-operation of the International Art Center and designed by Harvey Wiley Corbett and Sugarman and Berger, was the first in the locality to employ stepped setbacks affording a number of apartment terraces, corner windows that command the view, and other modern architectural features. The first three floors are occupied by an educational center, comprising a museum of modern art, with especial attention to living American artists *(open daily, except Monday, 1 to 5 p.m.; admission free);* a school offering courses in music, art, literature, and related subjects; two libraries, one containing many rare Tibetan manuscripts; and an auditorium used for lectures, recitals, plays, and motion pictures. Apartments occupy the remainder of the building. The Master Institute's most ambitious move was the sponsoring of a treaty for the protection of cultural institutions in wartime, signed in 1935 in the presence of President Roosevelt by the representatives of twenty-one American republics. The proposal, however, was not furthered by the League of Nations.

A nine-foot STATUE OF SAMUEL J. TILDEN, governor of New York State and Democratic nominee for President in 1876, stands on a granite pedestal at 112th Street. It is the work of William O. Partridge. A block north is John Horvay's STATUE OF LOUIS KOSSUTH, the Magyar patriot.

INTERNATIONAL HOUSE, facing the Riverside Church *(see page 387)* across a formal little park, is a residential and cultural center. It was built in 1924; the land, building, and equipment were donated by John D. Rockefeller, Jr. Admission is limited to students—40 per cent of whom come from foreign countries—taking at least eight points of work in local schools or devoting an equivalent amount of time to academic research. Murals in the main reception room, painted by Arthur B. Davies, present the conception of the unity of all peoples.

The Drive forks here to form an oval enclosing the Claremont Inn and the famous GRANT'S TOMB. *(Tomb open 9 a.m. to 5 p.m. June 21 to Sept. 21, 9 a.m. to 4:30 p.m. Sept. 21 to June 21; admission free.)* It is said that few New Yorkers have ever visited the tomb, and no visitor has ever missed it. Set on a hill overlooking the river, the massive granite sepulcher, designed by J. H. Duncan, is imposing in scale. "A great democratic demonstration caught in the fact," Henry James called it, "unguarded and unenclosed . . . as open as an hotel or a railway station to any coming and going." The high conical roof slopes downward to a circular colonnade atop the cube of the main hall; the difficult problem of uniting the three forms harmoniously remains unsolved. Between two carved allegorical figures on the parapet wall is inscribed Grant's well-known exclamation, "Let us have peace." Within the massive bronze doors the dim light of purple stained-glass windows, reflected on white marble, produces a feeling of solemnity. Sunk in the center of the floor is the round well of the crypt, holding twin sarcophagi that contain the remains of General and Mrs. Grant.

The marble walls of the tomb's cruciform room rise in a dignified design of arches to a rotunda. Four figures, carved in relief, represent the four epochs in the General's life—Youth, Military, Civil Life, and Death. In the north end are two reliquary rooms containing Civil War battle flags and memorials. The tomb cost $600,000, raised through contributions from ninety thousand subscribers; it was completed in 1897. From 150,000 to 200,000 people visit the memorial annually.

COMMEMORATION TREE, directly north and in the rear of the tomb, is a ginkgo tree. It and a Chinese cork tree nearby were planted in 1897 by Li Hung Chang, Grand Secretary of State, and Yang Yu, Envoy Extraordinary and Minister Plenipotentiary, of China.

At the north end of the oval is CLAREMONT INN, a green-trimmed. white frame manor house said to have been built in 1783 by George Pollock, a wealthy linen merchant. It was named, as was the hill on which it stands, for Claremont in Surrey, England. Among the manor's tenants were Joseph Alston, husband of Aaron Burr's daughter, Theodosia; Michael Hogan, British consul at Havana; and Joseph Bonaparte. The Claremont, established as a restaurant in the years preceding the Civil War, is attractive in summertime with dancing and outdoor service under colorful awnings.

Down the slope toward the river, and a few steps south of the Inn, a stone urn "Erected to the Memory of an Amiable Child" and dated July 15, 1797, marks the GRAVE OF ST. CLAIRE POLLOCK, aged five, who fell to his death on the rocks below the Claremont. When George Pollock, the child's uncle, sold the property he requested that this grave be kept inviolate.

Two viaducts, one for the Drive, executed in the graceful, decorative manner which marks the steel-work of the turn of the century, and a longer one for the Henry Hudson Parkway, cross the Manhattanville valley. A bronze TABLET at the south end of the Drive viaduct commemorates the Battle of Harlem Heights.

The U.S.S. *Illinois,* a decommissioned battleship, is anchored at the foot of 136th Street. Dismantled and fitted with a wooden enclosure, it serves the U.S. Naval Militia and the U.S. Naval Reserve for recreation and drill.

The charm of the Drive fades somewhat above 135th Street; not until 153d Street, at Trinity Cemetery *(see page 297),* does it regain its beauty. Northward from 153d Street many small craft anchor at private boat-club landings.

From 153d to 158th Street the Drive skirts the western end of what was the estate of John James Audubon, the painter-naturalist, who lived here from 1841 to 1851, when the district was still comparatively wild. Later the estate, "Minnie's land," passed into other hands, and Audubon's house, which stood at 156th Street, was demolished in 1930. A PLAQUE on a large apartment house at 765 Riverside Drive designates the site and reminds the passerby that Samuel F. B. Morse, while a guest of the Audubons, conducted many of his experiments there, and received the first telegraphic message from Philadelphia.

Between 165th and 168th Streets, the tall buildings of Columbia Presbyterian Medical Center *(see page 298)* are visible. The area between the Drive and the river for a considerable distance north of 165th Street is a very steep grade. Playgrounds are planned for the new land on the water front.

The stretch between the George Washington Bridge *(see page 399),* 179th Street, and Dyckman (200th) Street is perhaps the most satisfying to the eye. The Drive joins the northbound lane of the Parkway at the bridge. The southbound lane runs on a ledge below. A footpath at 192d Street leads to the rock gardens of Fort Tryon Park *(see page 302)* and the Cloisters *(see page 303).* Beyond the park, at Dyckman Street, Riverside Drive terminates, and Henry Hudson Parkway crosses a viaduct to enter Inwood Hill Park *(see page 305).*

MORNINGSIDE HEIGHTS AND MANHATTANVILLE

Area: 110th St. on the south to 135th St. on the north; from Riverside Drive east to Morningside Ave. and St. Nicholas Ave. (125th to 135th St.). Map on page 293.

The neighborhood of Morningside Heights is distinguished by many beautiful buildings devoted to learning or to religious worship. Columbia University, with the affiliated Barnard College, is here; the Union Theological Seminary, the Jewish Theological Seminary, the Juilliard School of Music, and several other noted institutions. To the west is the tower of the Riverside Church *(see page 387)*, Riverside Drive and West 122d Street, and the elevation on the southeast is crowned by the Cathedral of St. John the Divine *(see page 380)*, Amsterdam Avenue and West 112th Street.

North of the cathedral is the CHURCH OF NOTRE DAME DE LOURDES, Morningside Drive at 114th Street, where sermons are delivered in French. Its services are attended regularly by language students from Columbia. The church building, French Renaissance in style, was dedicated in 1915. A striking feature of the interior is a beautifully lighted grotto, in the apse, so constructed that the grotto appears to have been hollowed from the rock of the Morningside cliff. Mrs. Geraldine Redmond, who donated the property, had the grotto built as an expression of faith, after her son's cure at the famous church in Lourdes, France.

MORNINGSIDE PARK, extending from Cathedral Parkway (110th Street) to 123d Street, east of the cathedral, includes the narrow strip of ground formed by the rocky cliff that falls sharply from Morningside Drive, the eastern edge of the Heights proper, to Morningside Avenue, a block farther east on the plain below. Some of the exposed rocks in the park date from the pre-Cambrian period. Stone steps zigzag up the side of the rock at 116th Street. At its top, within a semicircle of polished stone benches, facing the Drive, is a bronze STATUE OF CARL SCHURZ *(see page 250)*, by Karl Bitter, sculptor, and Henry Bacon, architect, erected in 1912. Continuing west, 116th Street passes through the campus of Columbia University *(see page 383)*, whose buildings occupy the area from 114th to 121st Street, from Broadway to Amsterdam Avenue. The buildings of Barnard College for women, a part of Columbia University, are west of Broadway from 116th Street north to 120th Street.

Directly north of Barnard College, the UNION THEOLOGICAL SEMINARY occupies the blocks running from 120th to 122d Street, and from Claremont Avenue east to Broadway. The intimate grouping of the seminary buildings recalls an English college quadrangle. Designed by Allen and Collens, and completed in 1910, the buildings include a library, dormitories, gymnasium, and refectory, residences for the president and faculty, as well as a fine chapel in English perpendicular style.

Union Theological Seminary, founded in 1836, has graduated thousands of ministers, missionaries, and scholars of all Protestant denominations. It has stood for freedom in inquiry and thinking, and its professors have made many notable contributions to theological literature. The works of Arthur McGiffert, historian of the Christian Church, and James Moffett, biblical scholar and translator, have been outstanding. Distinguished alumni include Harry Emerson Fosdick, pastor of the Riverside Church; Ralph W. Sockman, minister of New York's Christ Church (Methodist Episcopal); and Norman Thomas, Socialist leader. On the present faculty are scholars from all the largest Protestant communions, and the student body of more than three hundred is drawn from all parts of the United States and from many foreign lands. Faculty members Harry F. Ward and Reinhold Neibuhr are widely known for their activity in liberal and progressive movements. The seminary is academically affiliated with Columbia University, but is an independently administered institution. Its School of Sacred Music is one of the few of its kind in the country. The president of the seminary is Henry Sloane Coffin.

Across Broadway, on the east side between 122d and 123d Streets, is the JEWISH THEOLOGICAL SEMINARY OF AMERICA, one of the nation's foremost institutions of Jewish education. It was designed by William Gehron and completed in 1930. An adaptation of Colonial Georgian architecture, it lacks the warmth and expressiveness of its prototype. The seminary houses a 115,000-volume library that includes many rare books and manuscripts, and a museum that contains ancient Palestinian coins and amulets, fragments of the Hebrew original of Ecclesiasticus, and oil lamps used more than two thousand years ago by the Maccabees in Palestine. *(Open daily 9 a.m. to 5 p.m., except Friday and Saturday; admission free.)* In addition to its graduate courses, open only to candidates for the rabbinate who possess collegiate degrees, the school has a teachers' institute and a college of Jewish studies, and conducts classes for young Jewish laymen.

North of the Union Theological Seminary, at 120-130 Claremont Avenue, is the JUILLIARD SCHOOL OF MUSIC, considered among the leading schools of its kind in the country. Of restrained classical-modern lines, the buildings include the Institute of Musical Art, the original structure, designed by Donn Barber and completed in 1910, and the contiguous, larger

Graduate School and Auditorium, by Shreve, Lamb, and Harmon, completed in 1931. The school is endowed by the Juilliard Musical Foundation, created in 1920 by the terms of the will of Augustus D. Juilliard, merchant and philanthropist. Operated as a nonprofit-making organization, it provides training in all branches of music to more than a thousand enrolled students annually. Ernest Hutcheson, pianist, is the president of the school, and Oscar Wagner, pianist, the dean.

At 122d Street the Broadway subway emerges and becomes an elevated structure, swings out over the valley of West 125th Street and Manhattanville to a height of about fifty-two feet above street level, and then disappears underground again on meeting higher ground at 135th Street. The red-brick building of Manhattanville's ST. MARY'S CHURCH (Protestant Episcopal), West 126th Street between Old Broadway and Amsterdam Avenue, contains a plaque in memory of James Cook Richmond, who was one of its rectors and fought in Greece with Lord Byron in the cause of Greek independence.

The most conspicuous landmark in the northeast section of the area is formed by the ten school buildings of the SOCIETY OF THE SACRED HEART, a Roman Catholic order, whose grounds extend from Convent Avenue to St. Nicholas Terrace, and from West 130th to West 135th Street. The schools include the Annunciation Girls' School, the Father Young Memorial High School, and the Manhattanville College of the Sacred Heart. The last-named, established in 1841, is a liberal arts college for women with an enrollment of some three hundred students (1939). The Pius X School of Liturgical Music of the college, organized in 1916, provides instruction for students and teachers of church music. The first of the ten buildings on the campus was erected in 1847.

During Christmas week elaborately costumed productions of classical drama or mystery plays are staged in the upper auditorium of the CHURCH OF THE ANNUNCIATION, Convent Avenue and 131st Street. The building was erected in 1906. Its predecessor, built in 1853, occupied a site two blocks to the west, on Old Broadway.

From St. Nicholas Terrace, along the summit of St. Nicholas Heights, stone steps cut into the side of the rocky bluff lead down into the strip of park land below and thence east to St. Nicholas Avenue and the plain of Harlem.

NORTHERN MANHATTAN

KEY

MORNINGSIDE HEIGHTS AND MANHATTANVILLE

1. Statue of Samuel J. Tilden
2. Statue of Louis Kossuth
3. Cathedral of St. John the Divine
4. Church of Notre Dame de Lourdes
5. Statue of Carl Schurz
6. Columbia University
7. Barnard College
   Site of Battle of Harlem Heights
8. Union Theological Seminary
9. Riverside Church
10. Jewish Theological Seminary
11. Juilliard School of Music
12. Grant's Tomb
13. Commemoration Tree
14. International House
15. Grave of St. Claire Pollock
16. Claremont Inn
17. St. Mary's Church
18. Church of the Annunciation
19. Society of the Sacred Heart
    Manhattanville College of the Sacred Heart
20. U.S.S. Illinois

WASHINGTON HEIGHTS

21. Hebrew Orphan Asylum of the City of New York
22. Lewisohn Stadium
23. City College
24. St. Luke's Church
25. Hamilton Grange
    Statue of Alexander Hamilton
26. St. Ann's Church for Deaf-Mutes
27. Trinity Church Cemetery
28. Chapel of the Intercession
29. Museum of the American Indian
30. Hispanic Society of America
31. American Numismatic Society
32. American Academy of Arts and Letters
33. Church of Our Lady of Esperanza
34. American Geographical Society
35. Polo Grounds
36. Roger Morris Park
37. Jumel Mansion

Columbia-Presbyterian Medical Center

38. Institute of Ophthalmology
39. Babies Hospital of the City of New York
40. College of Physicians and Surgeons
    School of Dental and Oral Surgery
41. Presbyterian Hospital
42. School of Nursing
43. Neurological Institute
44. New York State Psychiatric Institute and Hospital
45. High Bridge Water Tower
46. Bennett Park
47. Yeshiva College
48. George Washington High School
49. Mother Cabrini High School

INWOOD

50. Site of Fort Tryon
51. Jewish Memorial Hospital
52. The Cloisters
53. Dyckman House
54. Baker Field

WASHINGTON HEIGHTS

Area: 135th St. on the south to 193d St., Hillside Ave., and Dyckman St. (to Harlem River) on the north; from Riverside Drive east to St. Nicholas Ave. (135th to 155th St.) and Harlem River (155th St. to Dyckman St.). Map on page 293.

Hamilton Place runs diagonally from Broadway at 136th Street to a square at Amsterdam Avenue and 143d Street that also bears the name of the first Secretary of the Treasury and most distinguished resident of the region that became known as Washington Heights. This southern portion of Washington Heights is often called Hamilton Heights. On a bluff above Hamilton Place, between 136th and 138th Streets, is the bulky red-brick HEBREW ORPHAN ASYLUM OF THE CITY OF NEW YORK. The buildings were erected in 1884. The stolid main structure at 1560 Amsterdam Avenue has a tall tower and a steep-pitched dormered roof. The orphanage, one of the largest in the city, was established in 1832.

The campus of the MAIN CENTER OF CITY COLLEGE extends along Amsterdam Avenue from 136th to 140th Street. Occupying the two blocks opposite the orphanage is LEWISOHN STADIUM, an athletic arena given to City College by Adolph Lewisohn in 1915. The stadium is known to the public less for its sports events than for the summer-night concerts given there since 1918 by the Philharmonic Symphony Society *(concerts from the last week in June to the end of August; admission 25¢ to $1.50).* Low admission fees permitted a wide New York audience to enjoy symphonic music at the stadium long before this music was made available by radio. Willem van Hoogstraten, José Iturbi, Albert Coates, and Alexander Smallens are among those who have conducted these concerts. Soloists and dancing and choral groups are featured. With the temporary chairs in the field or "orchestra," the stadium has a seating capacity of about fifteen thousand. Built of concrete on the grade sloping east from Amsterdam Avenue, with tiers of stepped seats and a Doric colonnade, the structure, designed by Arnold W. Brunner, is a simplified version of the ancient Greek hillside amphitheater. Its classicism is in marked contrast to the medievalism of the college buildings proper, to the north.

The group of City College buildings crowning the ridge between St. Nicholas Terrace and Amsterdam Avenue, 138th and 140th Streets, was built in 1903–7 at a cost of four million dollars from plans by George B. Post. Its units form an imperfect quadrangle split by Convent Avenue. The Library Building, erected in 1929 and designed by Crow, Lewis, and Wich, is on St. Nicholas Terrace at 140th Street; a new wing is being constructed with the assistance of the WPA (1939). The massive Main Building—the eastern side of the quadrangle—follows closely the curve of the rocky bluff above St. Nicholas Park. The Gymnasium Building and the Townsend Harris Hall are on the south side, and the Chemistry, Mechanical Arts, and Technology buildings are on the north. The placement of these buildings around a court, gives an impression of spaciousness despite the limited area. All the buildings are late English Gothic in style. They are built of Manhattan schist—quarried from a near-by subway excavation—a rock rarely used in construction, and are trimmed with an unusually white terra cotta. The schist has aged and blackened, but the terra cotta remains a pristine white.

City College, one of the four units of the College of the City of New York, has an enrollment of some thirty thousand students. (Since 1917 women have been admitted to evening sessions.) Its College of Liberal Arts and Sciences, School of Technology, and School of Education occupy the Washington Heights buildings; its School of Business and Civic Administration, a co-educational division, is housed at the original site of the college, Lexington Avenue and Twenty-third Street. Free to residents of the city, admission is competitive and the number of applicants far exceeds the classroom capacity. Its students have a reputation for an interest in economics and political science that extends beyond the curricula.

The college was founded in 1849. A bill enacted by the State Legislature two years before, despite strong opposition by the press, authorized the Board of Education for the city and county of New York to establish a "Free Academy" for pupils who had attended the common schools and could pass the entrance examinations. Fifty thousand dollars were allotted for the buildings and twenty thousand dollars annually for maintenance. The Free Academy's first class of 143 students entered on January 15, 1849, and the first faculty consisted of a principal—Dr. Horace Webster—and five professors. In 1866 the institution was rechartered as a body corporate under the present name.

North of 141st Street, at 287 Convent Avenue, is the HAMILTON GRANGE. The two-story frame structure, built by Alexander Hamilton in 1802 as a country home, was moved in 1899 from its original location, two blocks farther north, and is now wedged in between an apartment house and St. Luke's Church. The grange is a good example of late post-Colonial architecture common in the early years of the Republic, and is noted for its woodwork. The house was designed by McComb, the architect who is better known for his work on City Hall. It is maintained as a museum by the American Scenic and Historic Preservation Society. *(Open*

Monday to Friday 10 a.m. to 5 p.m., Saturday 10 a.m. to 1 p.m., closed Sunday and holidays; admission free.) Displayed within are memorabilia of the Hamilton family and furniture of the post-Colonial period. Near the sidewalk is a STATUE OF ALEXANDER HAMILTON, sculptured by William Ordway Partridge, and erected by the Daughters of the American Revolution. ST. LUKE'S, erected in 1891, is a fine Richardson Romanesque building.

At 511 West 148th Street is ST. ANN'S CHURCH FOR DEAF-MUTES (a chapel of the Episcopal Church of St. Matthew and St. Timothy). The church, the first of its kind in the world, was founded in 1852 and the present building was erected in 1898. In a chapel flooded with light for those who must depend upon sight alone, the pastor delivers his sermons in sign language and the choir "sings" with its hands.

The lower Washington Heights section overlooking Harlem, particularly between 145th and 155th Streets and Edgecombe and Amsterdam Avenues, has in recent years been populated largely by well-to-do Negroes, who live in costly private homes and in apartment buildings such as the thirteen-story Colonial Parkway Apartments at 409 Edgecombe Avenue, which has eighteen penthouses.

In Washington Heights there are numerous MEMORIALS OF THE BATTLE OF FORT WASHINGTON. Three tablets along Broadway mark the successive lines of entrenchments used by the American defenders. The first is on a boulder in the park area between 147th and 148th Streets, the second on the northwest corner at 153d Street, and the third on the southeast corner at 159th Street.

TRINITY CHURCH CEMETERY, now divided by Broadway, extends from Riverside Drive to Amsterdam Avenue between 153d and 155th Streets, with the beautiful CHAPEL OF THE INTERCESSION on the southeast corner of Broadway and 155th Street. Both the cemetery, laid out in 1843, and the chapel, completed in 1915, belong to Trinity Corporation, and the chapel's congregation is one of the eight in Trinity Parish. The distinctly American Gothic buildings forming the church—the chapel proper, bell tower, vicarage, and parish house—are all constructed of vigorously designed random ashlar masonry with limestone trim and tracery. All may be entered from a square open court surrounded by a vaulted arcade. The group as a whole has a splendidly organized site plan. In the interior of the chapel, pleasing use has been made of carved and richly painted wood. An unusual timber ceiling in bright colors enlivens the dark-brown walls. The high altar is inlaid with 1,563 stones collected from the Holy Land and other places of early Christian worship. The chapel, with its chaste structural lines and the majestic height of its columns and ceiling, seems of cathedral stature. The architect of the buildings, Bertram Grosvenor Goodhue, whose ashes are contained in a memorial wall tomb of Champville marble in the north transept of the chapel, was a master of the free, creative use of the Gothic style.

The wooded, hummocky cemetery is much more isolated and tranquil— much more like a graveyard, in short—than the famous one attached to Trinity Church at Wall Street and Broadway *(see page 310)*. It is the largest cemetery in Manhattan, and burials are still being made there. Tombstones bear names of historic New York families, including the Bleeckers, Remsens, Van Burens, Schermerhorns, and Astors. A vault bearing the name Monroe is sometimes mistakenly designated as the burial place of President James Monroe, who actually was buried first in the Marble Cemetery on East Second Street and later in Richmond, Virginia. Among the notable persons buried here are Alfred Tennyson Dickens, son of Charles Dickens; Philip Livingston, a signer of the Declaration of Independence; Morgan Dix, rector of Trinity Church; Madame Jumel; Robert Chanler, the artist; and Clement C. Moore, author of the famous poem commencing, " 'Twas the night before Christmas." The tomb of John James Audubon, the naturalist, is marked by a sixteen-foot runic cross. An avenue and a theater in the neighborhood bear his name.

Grouped about a court opening westward on Broadway between 155th and 156th Streets are five nationally known institutions *(see page 395)*, the Museum of the American Indian, the Hispanic Society, the Numismatic Society, the Geographical Society, and the American Academy of Arts and Letters. The CHURCH OF OUR LADY OF ESPERANZA, 624 West 156th Street, is a mission for Spanish-speaking residents of the city. At 157th Street, Broadway starts its climb through Washington Heights proper, and Fort Washington Avenue begins at 159th Street, extending to Fort Tryon Park at 191st Street.

North of 155th Street, near the Harlem River, is the POLO GROUNDS, home of the New York Giants, National League baseball team. This stadium, built in 1912, seats about sixty thousand spectators for baseball or football games. Immediately west of the Polo Grounds Edgecombe Avenue climbs the crest of Coogan's Bluff and affords a view, across the Harlem River, of Queens and the Bronx. The vista is most sweeping from ROGER MORRIS PARK, on a rise above Edgecombe Avenue between 160th and 162d Streets. The entrance to the park is on Jumel Terrace near 160th Street.

The JUMEL MANSION—in Roger Morris Park—one of the most interesting Georgian Colonial houses in New York City, was built by Roger Morris, a Royalist sympathizer, about 1765, and occupied by him until 1775, when he left for England. His wife's name, before her marriage, was linked romantically with that of Washington. The estate stretched from river to river with "Fishing, Oystering and Claming at either end." The house was used as headquarters successively by General Washington (September 14–October 18, 1776) and Colonel Magaw, and after the defeat of the American forces, by the British command. After 1783 the house passed through various hands, becoming a tavern in 1796. Stephen Jumel, a wealthy French merchant, purchased the property in 1810 and restored it. In 1832 Stephen Jumel died and in the following year Aaron Burr, then almost eighty, came to live in the mansion as the husband of Madame Jumel. The marriage lasted but a year; Burr died in 1836, Madame Jumel in 1865. The city acquired the property in 1903, and in 1907 the house was opened as a museum under the auspices of the Daughters of the American Revolution and the Washington Headquarters Association. *(Open daily, except Monday, from 11 a.m. to 5 p.m.; admission free.)*

The mansion is a Georgian Colonial wood structure with some details, such as corner quoins, in imitation of stone construction. A two-story portico is a feature that is rare in New York. The slim columns and the fineness of execution of the iron balcony and of the railing atop the hipped roof give an effect of unusual elegance. An example of the economy employed by Colonial builders is revealed on the northeast side of the house, the side that was least likely to be seen by important visitors; the wall here was built of shingles, less expensive than boards. The interior is thoroughly Georgian Colonial in character. The moldings are strong and simple in treatment, and the hallways are decorated with semielliptical archways. The furnishings preserved by Madame Jumel during her long lifetime, as well as such pieces as Aaron Burr's desk, are on display.

Sylvan Terrace, a short private street that approaches the Jumel Mansion from the west, is still lined with old frame houses.

The COLUMBIA PRESBYTERIAN MEDICAL CENTER, along Broadway from 165th to 168th Street, one of the largest, most comprehensive and fully equipped in America, occupies a twenty-acre site directly overlooking Riverside Drive and the Hudson River and facing the Fort Lee cliffs of the Palisades. The magnificence of its commanding site is best appreciated from Riverside Drive or Henry Hudson Parkway. The massive tan structures rise in an impressive, quasi-pyramidal pile to a height of 496 feet above the river. The architecture is simple, and to many, rather uninspired.

Several affiliated hospitals, a medical school, clinics, and research laboratories—all pool their resources to provide the Center's wealth of medical facilities. It comprises four major corporate units: the Columbia University medical and dental group, namely, the College of Physicians and Surgeons and the School of Dental and Oral Surgery; the Presbyterian Hospital group, including the Squier Urological Clinic, the Sloane Hospital for Women, the School of Nursing, the Harkness Pavilion for private patients, and the Institute of Ophthalmology, or the eye hospital; the Babies Hospital of the City of New York; and the Neurological Institute. Not affiliated but adjoining the group is the NEW YORK STATE PSYCHIATRIC INSTITUTE AND HOSPITAL. Construction of the Center began in 1925, and cost thirty million dollars; most of the present buildings were opened at a public dedication on October 12, 1928. A few, notably the Institute of Ophthalmology, have been added since.

Architecturally, the Center takes its place among the pioneering structures of the late 1920's when traditional styles were being abandoned in favor of a utilitarian approach. The buildings are strikingly free of external ornament. Walls, piers, and spandrels are sheer; wings and setbacks have no cornices; chimneys are treated as pylons, and the large windows are in flat reveal to admit a maximum of light. The entire group was designed by James Gamble Rogers, Inc., architects, except for the Psychiatric Institute, which was the work of Sullivan W. Jones, State architect.

The main building of the Presbyterian Hospital (twenty-two stories, three below street level) forms the nucleus of a group of buildings south of 167th Street. It adjoins the College of Physicians and Surgeons, an eighteen-story building, the center of a group on West 168th Street near Broadway. The two institutions have been associated since 1911, when the hospital became the training school for the college, a relationship that eventually led to the formation of the Center. The college was founded in 1807; the hospital in 1868. Noted for its medical research activities, the school pursues such representative lines of inquiry as the study of the structure and functions of the reproductive system and endocrine glands and of tissues grafting techniques. (Late in 1938 the Presbyterian Hospital took possession of seven and a half acres of land and eight old brick buildings, formerly occupied by the New York School for the Deaf, at Riverside Drive and 165th Street.)

The nine-story Institute of Ophthalmology, or the eye hospital, built in 1933, is the first of a projected series of buildings along the 165th Street frontage. In 1931 a member of the staff removed a cataract from the eye of the King of Siam, who had traveled to New York to obtain his services. South of the Presbyterian Hospital, on Broadway, is the twelve-story Babies Hospital, which has, as an unusual feature, a special-temperatures ward for the benefit of premature "incubator" babies. The thirteen-story Neurological Institute, on the west side of Fort Washington Avenue at 168th Street, is noted especially for its studies of conditioned reflexes of children. An experiment of international interest in human behavior is being conducted with the "scientific" twins, Jimmy and Johnny, whose social development is being charted by the hospital staff. One of the boys is being "conditioned," that is, his behavior is guided by specialists; the other is allowed to mature without interference.

Near by, at Amsterdam Avenue and 173d Street, is the entrance to HIGH BRIDGE, the oldest of New York's great bridges. It was built (1837–48) as part of the Croton Aqueduct System. About 24,000,000 gallons of water a day flow across the bridge to Manhattan. A pedestrian walk affords a fine view of the Harlem. Edgar Allan Poe frequently came here when he lived in near-by Fordham, the Bronx (1846–9). Built long before modern bridge-building principles were practiced, the original High Bridge was Roman in architectural conception, and its procession of massive stone arches over both the land and water areas was a favorite subject for artists. In the early 1920's a single span of steel replaced the stone piers in the bed of the river because they interfered with navigation. Though it is not now the "old High Bridge" of song and story, of art students and of lovers, much of the bridge's charm remains, along with a few of the old arches. The HIGH BRIDGE WATER TOWER, standing at the Manhattan side of the bridge and resembling a medieval watch-tower, is a landmark.

The HARLEM BRIDGE at 181st Street and Amsterdam Avenue, formerly the Washington Bridge, was opened to traffic in 1888; its construction is similar to the present High Bridge. It is part of the US 1 highway system that fringes, in most part, the Atlantic Coast from Maine to Key West; highway traffic flows across the bridge to and from the George Washing-ton Bridge (see page 399), another link of the system, at 179th Street and Fort Washington Avenue. The Harlem, too, has been sketched frequently by artists; its great span is strikingly silhouetted against the Manhattan bluffs. Both the Harlem and High bridges are excellent "grandstands" for viewing the water sports on the river, which from about Dyckman Street to the Polo Grounds is the scene of intercollegiate rowing contests and regattas. Columbia University and Manhattan College maintain boat-houses on the river banks.

The highest natural elevation in Manhattan (267.75 feet) is attained at a point near the intersection of Fort Washington Avenue and 183d Street.

The RABBI ISAAC ELCHANAN THEOLOGICAL SEMINARY AND YESHIVA COLLEGE, 187th Street and Amsterdam Avenue, was founded in 1887, the first Jewish parochial school in North America. The present five-story building was opened in 1929. Besides regular high school and college courses, the institution provides Hebrew training and prepares students for the Orthodox Rabbinate. In 1938 there were 578 students.

The GEORGE WASHINGTON HIGH SCHOOL, Audubon Avenue and 192d Street, is one of the largest and best-equipped schools in the city. The building and grounds are on the site of the outpost held by Colonel Baxter and his several hundred Pennsylvanians during the Battle of Fort Washington. By 1863 all trace of the exact location of the fortifications erected by the Americans had been lost, but investigations in 1935 by the History Department of the high school identified one of the redoubts by the mortared wall of boulders between Fort George Avenue and the school grounds. The wall is more than two hundred feet long and in some places ten feet high.

Half of the land on which Fort Washington was located is now BENNETT PARK, Fort Washington Avenue and 183d Street. Within the park is a wall three to six feet in height, a reproduction of part of the fort. The site was part of the estate of James Gordon Bennett, Jr., who presented it to the city in 1903 in memory of his father, founder of the New York *Herald*.

MOTHER CABRINI HIGH SCHOOL, a modern four-story brick building at 701 Fort Washington Avenue, is named for Mother Francesca Saverio Cabrini, the first United States citizen to attain beatification by the Roman Catholic Church. When her beatification was proclaimed in November, 1938, her body was removed from the anteroom and entombed beneath the altar in the school's chapel, which is maintained by the order Mother Cabrini founded, the Missionary Sisters of the Sacred Heart. The name of the thoroughfare one block west of Fort Washington Avenue was changed in 1939 from Northern Avenue to Cabrini Boulevard.

INWOOD

Area: 193d St., Hillside Ave. and Dyckman St. (east to Harlem River) on the south to Harlem River Ship Canal on the north; from the Hudson River east to the Harlem River. Map on page 293.

In 1876 Frederick Law Olmsted—who with Calvert Vaux had designed Central Park nineteen years earlier—and J. James R. Croes suggested to the Department of Parks that the Inwood section be developed as a residential area and submitted a tracing proposing "what the English call a terrace . . . the crescent-shaped intermediate space being either a quiet slope of turf, a parterre of flowers, a playground, a picturesque rocky declivity treated perhaps as a fernery or alpine garden." While the Olmsted-Croes plan was not carried out in detail, it did prompt the city government and private citizens to co-operate in preserving the beauty of Inwood's topography, and it greatly influenced the present character of the district.

About two-fifths of Inwood, virtually all the western portion, is park land. Exquisite Fort Tryon Park, a cliff-sided plateau, intrudes its rocky bulk between Broadway and Riverside Drive from 192d Street to Dyckman Street, then Inwood Hill Park rises somewhat less abruptly and, together with the low-lying Isham Park, fills the nub of land that separates the Hudson from the Harlem River.

These rivers and wooded hills insulate a suburban community that is as separate an entity as any in Manhattan. Its inhabitants, most of whom have moderate incomes and can afford thirty to fifty dollars a month for rent, do most of their shopping along Broadway and St. Nicholas Avenue, the two principal north-south streets, and Dyckman Street, which slants transversely across the island.

FORT TRYON PARK is one of the most beautiful public parks of America —landscaped with trees, lawns, terraces, rock gardens, paved walks, and many benches, all cleverly ordered in harmonious composition. The precision of its design is explicitly urban. The views from its heights are perhaps the finest Manhattan offers, for they sweep mile after mile of the Hudson and the Palisades, and, to the east, range across the lowlands of Inwood. At the southern entrance to the park, near Fort Washington Avenue, a large sloping rock garden forms an approach to the stone ramparts marking the site of old Fort Tryon, built in the summer of 1776 and taken in the fall of the same year by the Hessians. The landscaping was done, appropriately, by Frederick Law Olmsted, son of the proposer of the park plan for Inwood.

The park's sixty-two acres include the grounds of the former C. K. G. Billings estate. John D. Rockefeller, Jr., bought the property in 1909 for $1,700,000, gave it to the city in 1930, and spent $3,600,000 improving it. The gift was in accordance with an agreement between Mr. Rockefeller and the city whereby the eastern ends of Sixty-fourth and Sixty-eighth Streets were closed and conveyed to Rockefeller Institute *(see page 245)*.

Automobiles enter Fort Tryon Park from Riverside Drive through a cut in the solid rock that leads circuitously to parking spaces and to an observation terrace overlooking the Hudson. An unconsciously metropolitan touch is added by the sign, "Park here only while enjoying view from car." Another motor road enters from the end of Fort Washington Avenue. The Eighth Avenue (Independent) subway station at 190th Street is carved out of the side of the east cliff; from it passengers are delivered by elevator to the promenade at the southern entrance. East of the station a playground for adults will be constructed.

The colored granite, tile-roofed building that stands in impressive isolation on the northern crest of the park is the CLOISTERS, branch of the Metropolitan Museum of Art *(see page 368)*, sheltering a collection of medieval art. *(Open daily 10 a.m. to 5 p.m., Sunday 1 to 6 p.m., Christmas 1 to 5 p.m.; admission 25¢ Monday and Friday, other days free.)* The building includes four cloisters and an arcade of a fifth, a chapel incorporating the remains of a Romanesque twelfth-century church, an original chapter house, and nine other exhibition areas, all chronologically arranged and so constructed as to include original structural or decorative members. A simple square tower surmounts the entrance. The central and largest cloister is that of St. Michel de Cuxa. Open to the sun, and surrounded by pink marble arches and columns, it dates from the twelfth century. Other cloisters are those of St. Guilhem-le-Désert (late twelfth to early thirteenth century), Bonnefont-en-Comminges (thirteenth to fourteenth century), and Trie (second half of the fifteenth century). The latter two overlook the park to the south and the Hudson River.

The halls and chapels contain such notable sculptures as the tomb effigy of Jean d'Alluye, who died about 1248, a Romanesque torso of Christ, a fourteenth-century sainted deacon, and many superb statues of the Virgin, particularly from the Ile de France and Lorraine. A set of six handwoven, fifteenth-century tapestries depicting the *Hunt of the Unicorn* was given by Mr. Rockefeller in 1935; they are displayed in a special room. These textiles, on which is portrayed an allegory of the Incarnation, with Christ represented by the fabulous unicorn, symbol of purity, are remarkable for their beauty of color and design and the intensity and vitality of their pictorial realism. While these tapestries have many Flemish characteristics, it has not been possible to establish their origin.

The Cloisters collection was started by the late George Grey Barnard, the sculptor, who spent many years in France gathering examples of medieval art; a few of them were found in barns and pigsties near ruined churches and monasteries. In December, 1914, the artist placed the collection on display in a building specially built for it on Fort Washington Avenue. The Metropolitan Museum bought the collection in 1925 with funds provided by Mr. Rockefeller. When the Fort Tryon property was given to the city by Mr. Rockefeller in 1930, four and a half acres were reserved as a site for a museum building to be devoted exclusively to the collection. Land along the Palisades on the opposite side of the Hudson was acquired by the patron to insure the view.

Plans were drawn by Charles Collens of the Boston firm of architects, Allen, Collens, and Willis, in collaboration with officials of the Metropolitan Museum. The building was opened in the spring of 1938.

The ten-story JEWISH MEMORIAL HOSPITAL, at Broadway and 196th Street near the southeast corner of Fort Tryon Park, is a modern design in dull red brick and stone. A nonsectarian institution, it was organized in 1905. The present structure, dedicated to Jewish soldiers, sailors, and marines who died in the World War, was completed in October, 1937.

Dyckman Street runs along the bottom of the valley that separates Fort Tryon Park from Inwood Hill Park. Week-end hikers on their way to Palisades Interstate Park cross the Hudson on the ferries that work between the western end of Dyckman Street and Englewood, New Jersey. Immediately south of the ferry slips the river shore is fringed with yacht and canoe club landings.

The only eighteenth-century farmhouse in Manhattan is the DYCKMAN HOUSE at 204th Street and Broadway. It is a two-story white building with an older small south wing; the lower walls are of fieldstone, brick, and wood, and the upper story of clapboard. Typically Dutch Colonial are the high basement, and the low-pitched gambrel roof, curved to swing over a full-length porch. William Dyckman, who inherited the estate from his grandfather, built the first house here in 1748. During the Revolution the contesting armies ravaged the district and the British burned the house, but after the war, in 1783, Dyckman rebuilt it. Descendants purchased and reconditioned the building and in 1915 presented it to the city as a museum of Dutch and English Colonial furniture and curios. The household wares are authentic, although they were not used in this house. *(Open daily 11 a.m. to 5 p.m., closed Monday; admission free.)*

Two blocks west of the Dyckman House, at Payson Avenue, is an entrance
to INWOOD HILL PARK. Until 1938, save for dirt paths, drinking fountains, and open-air fireplaces, little had been added to the pristine woods.
Shrubs such as lilac, hackberry, and blueberry, and countless trees, including many varieties of maple, Chinese white ash, and oriental pine, are
spread through the park. With the extensive reclamation of the Hudson
River water-front area from Seventy-second Street to Spuyten Duyvil, the
Department of Parks announced plans for landscaping the 167 wildest
acres in Manhattan.

This was once an Algonquin Indian settlement, Shora-Kap-Kok, meaning "in between the hills." (The Spuyten Duyvil section, across the Harlem River, has a Kappock Street.) Algonquin weapons and utensils have
been found on the site of the village in the park's eastern valley. The
gaunt stump of a huge tulip tree that stands near an indentation of the
Harlem River Ship Canal marks, according to legend, the site of a meeting between Henry Hudson and the Indians, and is said to have been
planted by the Indians to commemorate that occasion. Army equipment
left by British and American Revolutionary forces has also been uncovered
in the park.

In the western section of the park, the Henry Hudson Parkway, on its
way to the Westchester County Parkway System, ascends a steep grade to
the HENRY HUDSON BRIDGE. Forming a graceful gateway to the Harlem
River Ship Canal, the daring single arch of the handsome steel bridge
bears the unusual double-deck roadway above. The bridge has an over-all
length of 2,000 feet and a clearance, at its center, of 142.5 feet above high
water. It was completed in 1938 and cost more than two million dollars.
Emil H. Praeger, chief engineer, and Clinton F. Loyd, chief architect, of
the firm of Madigan-Hyland, designed the structure, which is owned
and operated by the Henry Hudson Parkway Authority.

Adjoining Inwood Hill Park on the east and also fronting on the Harlem, is little twenty-acre ISHAM PARK, presented by the descendants of
William B. Isham. Its Cooper Street entrance is guarded by World War
cannon. Rough-hewn stone steps ascend to a semicircular terrace where
one of several stone benches bears an inscription attesting to the hospitality
of the old Isham homestead. The mansion stands at the summit of the hill.
In 1938 the Harlem River Ship Canal here was straightened by cutting a
channel through the Spuyten Duyvil peninsula, and the Department of
Parks began the improvement of Inwood Hill and Isham parks. Part of
the old course of the canal will be filled in and, together with the southerly
tip of the peninsula, will form a strip of man-made land paralleling the

canal to the eastern shore of the park. A boat basin and large playfield will be constructed and the entire park landscaped.

To the west, between 218th Street, Broadway, and the Harlem River, lies Columbia University's BAKER FIELD. It has baseball and football fields, a stadium, a cinder track, and boathouses.

For all Inwood's considerable age, there is a newness to much of the district. The apartment houses and the spectacular improvements in parks, bridges, and highways are, for the most part, recent achievements. These late changes have only helped Inwood to become very nearly what Olmsted and Croes envisioned in 1876—a residential neighborhood "for fairly comfortable people."

MARBLE HILL

Area: Harlem River Ship Canal on the south to 230th St. on the north; from Ewen St. east to Exterior St. Map on page 293.

Marble Hill, Inwood's little neighbor to the northeast, is tied to Manhattan Island by the bridge over which Broadway crosses the Harlem. The hill was called Papirinemen by the Indians, meaning "a place parcelled out." Old marble quarries gave it the name most commonly used, but occasionally it is referred to as Kingsbridge, a name derived from a bridge, the first across the river, that Frederick Philipse built in 1693. Indignant farmers resented paying toll to Philipse, a wealthy Dutch Colonial, and erected the free Farmers' Bridge. General Washington's troops used both crossings in their retreat to White Plains after the battle on Harlem Heights.

Like Inwood, Marble Hill is a relatively quiet neighborhood. Modest apartment houses look out across the New York Central tracks and the Harlem River, but many of the residences along its hilly streets are two-story frame cottages.

D. Spiegel

Major Points of Interest

NEW YORK AQUARIUM

(NOTE: The Aquarium was demolished in 1942 but the following account is of historical interest.)

THE New York Aquarium is set in the marine atmosphere of Battery Park. Housed in a circular three-story building, a converted fort, in the northwest section of the park, it is second in size among the world's forty or more great public aquaria, but first in variety and number of specimens. In the thirty-six years ending December, 1938, more than seventy-six million visitors passed under the two gilded figures of sea horses carved above the main doorway. The average attendance is about seven thousand a day. On certain days, however, when the fleet has been anchored in the harbor, sailors on shore leave have brought the daily attendance to more than fifty thousand.

According to a recent census the exhibition comprises some 8,877 fishes, 872 invertebrates, 198 reptiles, 65 amphibians, and 12 birds. The stock, subject to frequent change and replacement, is housed in 7 large floor pools, 88 large glass-fronted wall tanks, 83 small tanks, and 29 large reserve tanks containing specimens not on exhibition.

A casual inspection of the aquarium building is sufficient to recognize its original military character and its resemblance to Castle Williams on Governors Island to the south of Battery Park. Built by the Federal Government about 1807, it was known at first as the West Battery and stood on the Capske, a cluster of rocks a short distance from the shore line of that time. It was renamed Castle Clinton after the War of 1812. When it became evident that its worth as a harbor fort was dubious, it was ceded to the city of New York. As Castle Garden it was the scene of notable public and social events. Lafayette was welcomed here in 1824, Louis Kossuth in 1851, and Edward VII—then Prince of Wales—in 1860. Here Professor Morse demonstrated the telegraph in 1835, and in 1850, under the sponsorship of P. T. Barnum, Jenny Lind, the "Swedish Nightingale," made her American debut. An undistinguished bust to the right of the entrance commemorates her success.

In 1855 Castle Garden became the country's chief immigrant station. Here raw Irish were recruited to fill the ranks of Meagher's brigade during the Civil War, and here landed the Italians who swarmed into Mulberry Bend and the Jews who supplied labor power for the garment and cigar lofts of the East Side. From 1855 to 1890, 7,690,606 aliens entered the United States through the Castle Garden station. In the latter year an investigation under Governor Cleveland resulted in the transfer of immigrant reception and care to a commissioner at Ellis Island, and Castle Garden was closed, to be opened six years later as the Aquarium of the City of New York.

In 1902, the operation of the aquarium was assigned to the New York Zoological Society, with the city supplying the funds. Although plans for remodeling were drawn that same year by the famous firm of architects, McKim, Mead, and White, the changes recommended were not made until the 1920's.

The original eight-foot-thick walls, massive bolt-studded doors, and gun embrasures of Castle Clinton remain. The chief change in the exterior has been the addition of a white square-fronted administration and laboratory annex, with an ornamented main entrance, which forms the east façade. The interior of the building has been converted into a gay and pleasant exhibition hall. The rotunda, aisle, and two-level ring of tanks, which follow the old circular walls, unite to form an interesting play of spaces and shapes. Even the radiators have been used decoratively as bases for the columns. The walls are decorated with Charlotte Anne Case's bright marine murals.

For thirty-five years Dr. Charles Haskins Townsend served as director of the aquarium. He was succeeded upon his retirement in November, 1937, by Charles M. Breder, Jr., an ichthyologist of note who had served for fourteen years as assistant director and aquarist. Breder introduced important improvements in the complex system of water circulation, aeration, and temperature maintenance necessary to the well-being of the aquarium's ten thousand-odd specimens. Behind the tanks a system of catwalks enables attendants to patrol the building, unseen by the visitor. Three circulatory systems carry 300,000 gallons daily of pure sea water, harbor water, or New York City water to the creatures, according to their various needs. Certain rare tropical varieties are brought to the aquarium in their native water, which is carefully guarded, filtered, and maintained at the temperature to which the fish are accustomed. Temperatures range from 40°F. to 90°F., the brook trout taking the coldest and the lungfish the warmest.

School children, inquiring laymen, and amateur and professional scientists come in throngs to see varieties of fish ranging from the common fresh-water specimens to strange deep-sea monsters, from delicate minnows to frighteningly ugly 300-pound groupers. The electric eels, which generate enough current to light a bulb above the tank, are first in popular acclaim; runners-up are the lacy Siamese fighting fish, hideous green and spotted morays, and grotesque toadfish. In the large pools on the ground floor graceful California sea lions bark and disport themselves before a gallery of enthusiasts. Here also are the enormous sea turtles, penguins from South Africa, seals, turtles, alligators, and crabs. In the many smaller tanks around the balcony perpetual submarine ballets are staged by minute and delicately colored tropical fishes—silvery moonfish, blue or green parrot fish, fringe-tailed goldfish, and angel and butterfly fish.

The aquarium operates a fish hatchery that produces millions of tiny food and game fishes, which are deposited in the various waters of the State to grow and breed. Research is carried on in the laboratory and the thousand-volume library. The aquarium is the first stop of visiting ichthyologists from such distant points as London, Paris, and Göteborg, the marine institute at Tel Aviv, and the Australian Museum at Sydney. Director Breder is always on the alert for an advantageous swap, trading, for example, a batch of common horseshoe crabs for some exotic specimens.

The aquarium operates on an annual budget of about eighty-seven thousand dollars, with approximately sixty-seven thousand dollars provided by the city of New York and the balance by the New York Zoological Society. After the salaries of a staff of thirty-eight, and maintenance, heating, and repairing costs have been deducted, there is nothing left for the purchase of new specimens. The only funds available for this purpose come from the sale of booklets, post cards, and souvenirs—something less than two thousand dollars a year. Wireless operators on ocean freighters obligingly carry to far-off corners of the world castoff clothes, whisky, and other goods given them by the aquarium, and barter them for rare fish to add to the aquarium's collection.

TRINITY CHURCH

Broadway and Wall St. IRT Lexington Ave. subway to Wall St.; or BMT subway (local) to Rector St.; or 9th Ave. el to Rector St.; or Broadway bus to Rector St.

The good Queen Anne, in 1705, gave to the young parish of Trinity Church a grant of land to be used "for the benefit of said Church and other pious uses." The yearly rent stipulated was thirty pounds, "a reasonable request." The farm lay west of Broadway, extending from Fulton to Christopher Street.

Thus Trinity, the first Protestant Episcopal church established in New York, came into ownership of a good section of lower Manhattan and, as a consequence, became possibly the world's wealthiest parish of that denomination.

Compared to the great cathedrals subsequently erected in New York, there is little about the century-old structure, fronting on Broadway and facing into Wall Street, that in any way suggests this great wealth. Yet, for its day—it was completed in 1846—the church, designed by Richard Upjohn, one of the famous architects of the period and sponsor of the Gothic Revival mode, doubtless was considered duly impressive. The church is constructed of dark brownstone in a free rendering of perpendicular English Gothic. Although only 79 feet wide and 166 feet long, the building is so beautifully proportioned that it holds the attention, even in its present setting, enclosed as it is by high office buildings that would dwarf any less inspired structure. Graceful porches project beyond its side entrances. The main entrance, at the foot of Wall Street, is in the base of the rectangular tower fronting the nave. The tower is surmounted by an octagonal spire with a cross at the top. For years, the spire, attaining a height of 280 feet above the steps, served as a landmark. Both the tower and the spire are of brownstone ashlar, and are exceptionally fine in work manship. The first "Ring of Bells," a gift from London, was received in 1797, and is the oldest in the city. Others were added and today the chimes of Trinity include ten bells. They were originally intended to be swung, but the difficulty of obtaining competent ringers, and the fact that the public preferred tunes to changes, resulted in their being made stationary. The clappers are connected to a ringing case in the room below the belfry.

Three pairs of bronze doors, at the base of the tower, to the east, north, and south, designed by Richard M. Hunt, the architect, are the gift of William Waldorf Astor as a memorial to his father, the second John Jacob Astor. They are designed with bas-relief decorations in the manner of Ghiberti's doors for the Baptistery in Florence. The main entrance panels were executed in bas-relief by Karl Bitter, and represent symbolic scenes from the Bible, as do the north doors, the work of J. Massey Rhind. The panels in the south door, designed by G. M. Niehaus, depict Dr. Henry Barclay, second rector of the church, preaching to the Indians in 1739, the consecration of Trinity Church in 1846, and George Washington in St. Paul's Chapel following his inauguration in 1789.

Double rows of carved columns support the groined nave vaulting. Seven white marble panels above the high altar depict scenes from the life of Christ, particularly associated with the Last Supper. The reredos of Caen stone, perpendicular Gothic in style, is divided by buttress forms into three bays, in which are figures of the Twelve Apostles. The stone floor, walls, pillars, pews, and even the glass of the windows almost completely filling both walls, are, uniformly, of an even and mellow tone of soft yellow-brown. They have the worn, but unsoiled tint of a well-kept ancient vellum manuscript. In striking contrast to this color scheme, yet not garish, is the brilliant stained-glass window (above and behind the reredos) of burning blue and ruby. Blending harmoniously with these two effects is the warm ivory of the marble in the altar.

All Saint's Chapel, at the west end of the north aisle, is a fine example of the English Gothic style that flourished during the latter half of the fourteenth century. It was designed by Thomas Nash, who also designed the baptistery (near the northeast corner of the chancel). In the latter is a fourteenth-century altarpiece.

The parish came into existence during the reign of King William III, when on May 6, 1697, the charter was signed by Governor Fletcher. Episcopalians in the colony, however, had been holding religious services since the English acquisition of New Amsterdam in 1664, worshiping in a chapel of the fort that stood near the Battery.

The first church, opened in 1698, was destroyed in the fire of 1776. It lay in ruins until 1787, when the church was reconstructed. More than a half century later it was replaced.

From the beginning Trinity numbered among its parishioners the city's most distinguished personages, some of whose descendants still worship there. Many of those early parishioners lie buried in the churchyard which surrounds the building on the north, west, and south sides. Carved in the weathered slabs are inscriptions naming such honored dead as Alexander Hamilton, Robert Fulton, Captain James ("Don't Give Up The Ship") Laurence, Albert Gallatin, William Bradford, founder of the city's first newspaper, the *Gazette,* and earliest champion of the freedom of the press, and John Watts. The Martyr's Monument, a tall memorial to American patriots who died while imprisoned by the British in New York, stands near the Broadway-Thames Street corner.

Near the iron railing along Broadway on a sunken granite stone is carved the name, Charlotte Temple. Charlotte, said to have been the granddaughter of the Earl of Derby, eloped with an English officer, who brought her to America and abandoned her after the birth of her child. A popular novelist of the day (1790), Sarah Haswell Rowsan, used her story in *Charlotte Temple,* one of the most widely read novels in the English language.

At noon the cemetery is a retreat for workers from the office buildings of the financial district. During their lunch hour, they sun themselves on the benches along the paths, or on the steps and railings of the porticos.

Trinity is the parent of seven subsidiary chapels: these are not small annexes of the mother church, but rather they include some of the largest and most beautiful church structures in New York. One is old St. Paul's Chapel *(see page 98),* north of Trinity on Broadway; and another, the one most recently built, is the Chapel of the Intercession, in Trinity Cemetery *(see page 296).*

The controlling corporation still owns about one-fifth of the original grant, estimated to be worth about ten million dollars. The remainder was given to church and educational institutions. The acquisition of these vast holdings has furnished a classic example, for reformists and economists, of the social evil of land speculation. As recently as 1938, in the Federal Theater production, *". . . one third of a nation . . .,"* a play dealing with housing conditions, the church's history was recalled, from the granting of land to the young parish in 1705 to the municipal investigation of 1894. In the latter year it was revealed that tenement property acquired by the church corporation at the expiration of long term leases comprised a portion of the city's worst slums. The church has since divested itself of its tenement holdings.

BROOKLYN BRIDGE

Park Row east of City Hall Park, Manhattan, across East River to Sands and Washington Sts., Brooklyn. IRT Lexington Ave. subway to Brooklyn Bridge; or BMT subway (local) to City Hall; or 2d or 3d Ave. el to City Hall; or Broadway or 4th Ave. bus to City Hall Park.

Brooklyn Bridge, soaring over the East River, is the subject of more paintings, etchings, photographs, writings, and conversations than any other suspension bridge in the world. Uniting the maze of the nineteenth-century brick and frame residences, factories, and warehouses of the Brooklyn shore and the modern skyscraper district of lower Manhattan, the majestic highway has supplied an extravagant theme to romantic and symbolic fancies. Native artists, including the noted water-colorist John Marin and the abstractionist Joseph Stella, have played many variations upon its graceful catenaries, suspenders, and granite towers; while the poet Hart Crane conceived it in his *The Bridge* as the dynamic emblem of America's westward march.

During more than half a century of continuous use, the bridge has retained its place as the most picturesque of the sixty-one spans that bind Greater New York into a world metropolis. It was designed in 1867 by John A. Roebling, who had built the bridge at Niagara Falls and the more remarkable one over the Ohio River at Cincinnati. While engaged in drawing the plans for Brooklyn Bridge, Roebling sustained an injury which resulted in his death from tetanus a year before construction began. His son, Washington A. Roebling, became construction engineer, but he too was injured. From a window of a Brooklyn Heights residence he supervised the construction of the bridge, watching its progress through a telescope.

The bridge was opened to traffic on May 24, 1883, pedestrians being charged a toll of one cent. Six days later a tragedy occurred on the crowded walk. A woman fell down the wooden steps at the Manhattan approach to the promenade, and her screams resulted in a panic in which twelve persons lost their lives and scores were injured.

Unlike the steel towers of the East River bridges that followed, the buttressed towers of this bridge, rising 272 feet above mean high water, are constructed entirely of granite. Expressing the increasing load, they become thicker as they extend downward; and the segmental arches that tie the piers together are buttressed against lateral thrust. The whole design is a superbly clear statement of the contrast between the ponderous compression in the towers and the tight-strung tension of the steel members. The roadway platform, eighty-six feet in width, is hung on two-inch diameter steel suspenders strung from two pairs of cables—the catenaries—sixteen inches in diameter. Each cable is composed of 5,296 galvanized steel wires. (The total length of wire used is 14,357 miles, a distance more than half the circumference of the earth.) Each is capable of sustaining a live load of 12,000 tons, or a total live load equal to 48,000 tons, the weight of the structural steel in the Empire State Building.

The bridge has an over-all length of 6,016 feet, and the center of the 1,595.5-foot channel span is 133 feet above the river at mean high water. Until the Williamsburg Bridge was completed in 1903, with an over-all length of 7,308 feet, Brooklyn Bridge was the world's longest suspension span.

Among the ingenious methods introduced by the younger Roebling in the construction of the bridge—methods which have since exerted considerable influence on engineering technic—were the pulley-and-reel system for spinning the cables of the catenaries, the use of semi-flexible saddles as cable rests to provide for expansion and contraction owing to temperature changes, the employment of chains of eyebars in the anchorages and wire wrapping as protective covering for the finished cables, and the cross-lacing of suspenders with stay cables that act as bracers.

The center promenade, a board footwalk twelve feet above the floor of the bridge, is flanked on each side by elevated tracks and one-way, double-lane driveways, which accommodate both trolley and vehicular traffic. The Manhattan approach to the footwalk slopes upward from the damp, gloomy Park Row floor of the BMT terminal opposite City Hall Park. In this dark and rather vague spread, where the streetcar lines crossing the bridge curve into their terminals, are news venders, frankfurter stands, and iron gates, usually closed, leading to the elevated lines overhead. This almost subterranean atmosphere is also characteristic of the Brooklyn approach, which is graded to the Sands Street level of the sprawling BMT terminal structure.

In the Manhattan abutment are wine vaults, suggestive of Roman catacombs. Built in 1876, seven years before the bridge was opened, they were used until recently by a New York department store as a storage place for European liquors. The cellars, entered from 209 William Street, were sealed during Prohibition.

The bridge quickly became popular as a Sunday promenade. Here strolled women in Sunday ruffles, hourglass stays, bustles fringed with everything but bells, and shoes laced up to the kneecap; gentlemen trussed in broadcloth to the Adam's apple, inquisition collars to the ears, and trousers to the toes. Foot traffic gradually waned, however, with the installation of surface cars on the bridge and with the building of the larger Williamsburg, Manhattan, and Queensboro bridges. The elevated line began operating over the bridge in September, 1883, the surface cars in 1898. The present workday traffic averages about twenty-six thousand vehicles.

The bridge affords a magnificent view of the East River, the harbor, and downtown Manhattan—the buildings of the financial district changing their hues during the different hours of the day. Down below, seen from the Manhattan grade, lies the darkness of the old city—markets and gloomy warehouses to the south; and on the north, slums, elevated lines, and crooked streets, where one notices horse-drawn vehicles and an old mission with JESUS SAVES painted on the walls in large white block-lettering. Knickerbocker Village, a housing development *(see page 115)*, is set among these slums spreading north from the foot of the bridge.

The apocrypha of Steve Brodie belong among the bridge's more distinctive legends. There are men living who claim they saw Brodie's leap from the bridge in July, 1886, the rescue skiff tossing on the East River, the hero-worshipers who cheered as he climbed to the dock; on the other hand, mention of his name causes many old-time barkeepers to put their tongues in their cheeks. In any event, Brodie has entered the American idiom: to "pull" or "do a Brodie" has come to serve as a synonym for taking a high dive, whether on the stock market, in a love affair, or in the prize ring.

The promenade still draws its visitors, lyrical, noisy, or inarticulate. In the famous "view" of the bay and sky line, tourists encounter the original of a long-familiar picture post-card panorama; while the high arched towers and vast curving cables of the bridge itself are rediscovered daily by amateur camera artists. On summer days old ladies, invalids, Sunday morning strollers, unemployed men, and wandering boys and girls absorb here the indolence of space, sun, and water. Employees of downtown office buildings seek at the bridge during lunch time and after work a session with the outer world. At twilight, the conventional beauty of the setting attains such intensity that even the wisecracks of up-to-date lovers are sublimated. And in the wastes of night, so passionate is the contrast between the deserted and melancholy bridge entrances and the moonlit

altitude of the passage itself, that the solitary pedestrian feels himself
drawn into association with all the extravagances of the poets.

BELLEVUE HOSPITAL

1st Ave. to East River, 26th to 30th St. IRT Lexington Ave. subway (local) to
28th St.; or 3d Ave. el to 28th St.; or 2d Ave. el to 23d St.; or 1st Ave. bus to
26th St.

One of the twenty-six municipal institutions under the supervision of
the Department of Hospitals, Bellevue is the oldest general hospital on
the North American continent. Probably no other hospital in the world
admits so many patients and treats such a diversity of ailments. Contagious
cases, however, are transferred to the near-by Willard Parker Hospital. The
number of cases for 1938 totaled more than the population of San Francisco: 65,352 admissions and births, 634,242 outpatient visits, and 28,253
ambulance calls.

A city complete in itself, Bellevue covers approximately twelve square
city blocks. Its twenty-five buildings contain 102 wards and cost more than
twenty-three million dollars. The massive eight-story Psychiatric Hospital
at the northwest corner, of clean red brick trimmed with natural gray
stone, exemplifies the hospital's program of modernization. A new Administration Building with three chapels is under construction (1939).

Bellevue serves a heavily populated area of the East Side between East
Houston and Forty-second Streets, east of Sixth Avenue. Hospitalization,
medical care, and clinical treatment are provided without cost to anyone
who is unable to pay for them, investigation as to ability to pay being
made after, and not before, admission is granted and treatment begun.
Bellevue is a free, not a charity, hospital, and according to a city law, it
must accept any applicant who resides in its district and requires medical
treatment.

The ambulance service operates on a twenty-four-hour basis, and an ambulance and doctor can be dispatched within thirty seconds after a call for
aid has been received. Bellevue's morgue, the official mortuary for New
York County, is in the Pathological Building on Twenty-ninth Street. The
same building also houses the Medical Examiner's office, where New
York's official autopsies are performed, and the headquarters of the Mortuary Division of the city Department of Hospitals. About twenty thousand
bodies pass each year through Bellevue's morgue, eighty-five hundred of
which are never claimed. All unclaimed bodies are photographed and de-

ST. BARTHOLOMEW'S CHURCH AND GENERAL ELECTRIC BUILDING

ST. PATRICK'S CATHEDRAL

HOTEL SAVOY-PLAZA

DEAD END NEAR SUTTON PLACE

PARK AVENUE AND THE WALDORF-ASTORIA TOWERS

TEMPLE EMANU-EL

RCA BUILDING, ROCKEFELLER CENTER

NEW YORK HOSPITAL — CORNELL UNIVERSITY MEDICAL COLLEGE

scribed, and a docket entered for them at the Police Department's Bureau of Missing Persons. After reposing for two weeks or more in refrigerated vaults of the morgue, some of the cadavers are given to private embalming schools whose students practice in a room adjoining the vaults, and a certain number are allotted to medical schools for dissection. The remainder, about 170 a week, are placed in plain, wooden coffins and carried on a barge, up the East River to Potter's Field on Hart's Island *(see page 551)*.

In the new Psychiatric Hospital, the alcoholics, the sexually unbalanced, the hysterical, and the alleged insane are under care. The Psychiatric Division of Bellevue has become a laboratory for the medical and social-service professions in the United States. The "disturbed," or violent, wards utilize none of the old-fashioned, inhumane methods that some hospitals still employ for pacifying psychotics. Though overcrowding detracts from the desired effect, the new building, with its pleasant murals, minimizes the sense of confinement. The Psychiatric Hospital, originally planned to care for 630 patients, was pathetically overcrowded only six months after it was opened in 1936.

The medical departments of three outstanding universities are affiliated with Bellevue: Columbia, Cornell, and New York. A fourth group of doctors and internes not connected with these particular schools is included in an open division. Bellevue's 550 staff doctors, 200 internes, and 400 clinic physicians are, for the most part, either faculty members of these schools or regular hospital employees who are selected by the schools. New York Training School for Nursing, established in 1873 by Bellevue, was the first of its kind in the United States. Its standards have since served as a norm for other schools. The hospital also maintains the Mills Training School for Male Nurses.

Bellevue's list of contributions to medicine is a long and notable one. Its ambulance service, inaugurated on a horse-and-buggy basis in 1869, was the first in the world. Doctors Valentine Mott, James R. Wood, William H. Van Buren and F. H. Hamilton brought the hospital fame through their medical and surgical discoveries. At Bellevue, Dr. Herman Biggs founded the first bacteriological laboratory in the United States, Dr. Lewis A. Sayre pioneered in orthopedics, and Dr. William H. Welch established America's first pathological laboratory. Noted graduates include Dr. William S. Halstead, who first used cocaine as an anesthetic; Dr. Frank Harley, inventor of the electrical surgical saw; Dr. William H. Gorgas and Dr. Jesse W. Lazear who, with Dr. Walter Reed and others, discovered how yellow fever was transmitted, and eradicated the disease from Cuba and Panama.

Bellevue's history goes back to British New York in 1736, when the city corporation ordered the construction of a "Publick Workhouse and House of Correction" on the site of the present City Hall Park. Infirmary activities were confined to a single room with six beds. To accommodate ever increasing numbers of the needy, new buildings were erected, until by 1811 the hospital section of the workhouse had become its largest department. When further expansion became imperative, Belle Vue Farm, the present site of the hospital, was purchased (1816), and the new group of buildings became known as Bellevue Establishment. Constant increase in population and resultant clinical demands on the hospital during the nineteenth century necessitated frequent additions to and renovations of the plant. Modern Bellevue began in 1908, when it became a part of the "Bellevue and Allied Hospitals." In 1929 the Department of Hospitals of the City of New York was created, with Bellevue as one of its units.

Under the spur of PWA and WPA grants, added to city appropriations, the old Bellevue, with its maze of mid-Victorian buildings of ominous gray, has given place to the group of eight-story structures of brick and stone with granite foundations. The firm of McKim, Mead, and White designed these new buildings with the exception of the Psychiatric Hospital; the architects of the latter were C. B. Meyers and Thompson, Holmes, and Converse. In February, 1938, the C & D Building was opened as a model unit for the treatment of pulmonary diseases. When the new Administration Building is erected, it will complete the group of seven great units making up the new Bellevue.

Architecturally, there is a deliberate suppression, on the exterior, of the functional differences between the various elements and parts of the buildings. The interiors, in contrast, are designed as frank expressions of their uses and of the materials employed, with reliance for effect placed upon tasteful proportioning and choice of color. The walls of the buildings have been decorated with the murals executed under the auspices of the WPA Federal Art Project.

Bellevue, like all large municipal hospitals, is still to some extent the object of fear and rumor, for in handling vast numbers of humanity's underprivileged it naturally has a high death rate. Almost vanished, however, are such once popular superstitions among the poor as that of the "Black Bottle," used to do away with troublesome patients. In the past, charges of unsanitary conditions, a depleted commissary, political graft, and inadequate care by nurses and orderlies had considerable basis in fact. Scandalous conditions at the hospital—lack of supplies and often food, vicious surroundings, and untrained female prisoners acting as nurses—contributed to a frightful mortality during the cholera plague of 1832, when more than thirty-five hundred New Yorkers died of the disease and a very few who entered Bellevue recovered. Again, the Civil War all but demoralized the work of the hospital. The school for nurses was established after an investigation by public-spirited women disclosed that the nurses "were nearly without exception to the last degree incompetent. . . ."

The pesthouse and prison atmosphere of Bellevue's past has been obliterated. Through the years the hospital has steadily improved, and today it ranks as one of the best medical centers in the world. To the average New Yorker, Bellevue Hospital is a reassuring symbol of man's humanity to man. To the poor of the East Side, admission to the hospital often represents a dividing line between illness and good health, life and death. Overcrowding and understaffing continue to be the chief difficulties. The new buildings have done much to remedy crowding, but it remains a vital problem to the hospital, which must receive all comers even though it is forced to put up cots in the corridors. Understaffing has been mitigated by substantial additions to the staff in 1938, bringing the total to 3,200 employees—nurses, orderlies, attendants, and others; at the same time, the old twelve-hour shift was cut to eight. Some six hundred WPA workers are assisting in the children's, clerical, and other departments.

EMPIRE STATE BUILDING

5th Ave., 33d to 34th St. IRT Lexington Ave. subway (local) to 33d St.; or IRT Broadway-7th Ave. subway to Pennsylvania Station (34th St.); or BMT subway to 34th St.; or 5th Ave. bus to 34th St. Observatories on 86th and 102d floors; hours, 8 A.M. to 1 A.M.; admission: adults $1.10, children 25¢.

The Empire State Building, 1,250 feet high, is the tallest structure in the world. Seen from a distance it emerges above New York like a great inland lighthouse. The Chrysler Building, second in height, measures 1,046 feet to the tip of the lance; the Woolworth Building, for many years the tallest tower of Manhattan, is only 792 feet. The Eiffel Tower in Paris is 1,024½ feet to the top of the flagpole.

The great limestone and steel structure has been called a monument to an epoch—the boom years from 1924 to 1929. The building became, as those who envisioned it promised, an internationally known address.

The superb main shaft of the Empire State rises in an almost unbroken line out of the broad five-story base that covers approximately two acres adjoining Fifth Avenue. Atop the shaft, at the eighty-sixth floor level, is the 200-foot observation tower—a sixteen-story glass and metal extension shaped like an inverted test tube buttressed by great flaring corner piers. Though the design of the tower is pleasing in itself, it has been widely criticized for a lack of unity in its relation to the shaft.

Its architectural importance far transcends the matter of height alone. The design, for which Shreve, Lamb, and Harmon won the gold medal of the Architectural League in 1931, is essentially modern. The great tower walls are composed almost entirely of standardized machine-made parts. Not only the windows but the cast aluminum panels or "spandrels" under them, even the stone column facings and the steel strips that enclose them, are standardized units. The pattern—window, spandrel, window, spandrel —is repeated without a break for 725 feet. Such a wall treatment is the direct opposite in conception of such early skyscraper buildings as the Flatiron, where each story is adorned with a minor horizontal terra-cotta cornice.

A peculiarity of the Empire State Building is that the windows, instead of being set back into the wall, appear to be flush so that the effect is one of a continuous wall. By this expedient the architects not only avoided gouging the wall into something resembling an immense waffle iron, they also eliminated the need to trim the stone around the openings, thus saving much time and money in construction.

The color scheme of the building, though losing its remarkable first "blond" tone through weathering, is spectacular in early and late sunlight. The aluminum spandrels and the soft-textured limestone are tinged with gray and lavender, and the silvery sheen of metal on the walls creates an effect of airy lightness.

On Fifth Avenue a monumental but somewhat dull entrance, flanked by heavy stone pylons the full height of the five-story base, opens into a long hall, three stories high and lined with Rellante and Rose Famosa marbles. The high silver-leaf ceiling is painted in metallic colors with geometric patterns suggesting stars, sunbursts, and snowflakes. On the wall opposite the Fifth Avenue entrance is a great brass and aluminum plaque depicting the Empire State under a blazing sun. Subsidiary entrances give access to the building from both Thirty-third and Thirty-fourth Streets.

The entire building is planned around a central core roughly pyramid-shaped, containing the utilities and the sixty-seven elevators. Though run at a lesser speed, the self-leveling elevators can rise 1,200 feet a minute. Because of its height, nearly one-third of the whole must be devoted to elevators and utilities. In rentable floor space, the Empire State, with 2,158,000 square feet, ranks among the three largest office buildings in the United States, the others being the Merchandise Mart in Chicago and the RCA Building at Rockefeller Center.

The speed with which the Empire State was built set a new mark in construction efficiency. On October 1, 1929, the first truck rolled into the former Waldorf-Astoria Hotel to begin demolition; May 1, 1931, the completed Empire State Building was formally opened by Alfred E. Smith, its president. When construction (by Starrett Brothers and Eken) was in full swing, an average of four and a half stories were erected every week, and at top speed, fourteen and a half stories in ten working days. Because of lack of sidewalk storage space, the supplying of building materials had to be synchronized exactly with construction speed. The land cost sixteen million dollars, the purchase including the magnificent old Waldorf, which had occupied the site some thirty-five years and had itself cost thirteen million dollars.

In the first five years of its existence, more than four million visited the building's observatories on the 86th and 102d floors, whence, on clear days, a fifty-mile panorama is visible. The city, with its waterways and suburbs, spreads like a relief map a quarter of a mile below; and directions for identifying the various points are marked on the observation terrace. To the south, near the tip of Manhattan, is the Wall Street district. To the southeast lies Brooklyn, and crossing the East River are the Williamsburg, Manhattan, and Brooklyn bridges, from north to south. In the southwest, the Statue of Liberty is outlined, and beyond it lies Staten Island.

To the west are the docks of the Hudson (North) River where ocean liners are berthed; on the other side of the water is the ridge of the Palisades; and beyond, the flatlands of New Jersey. In the northwest the Orange Mountains dim the horizon far beyond the Palisades; in the immediate foreground is Broadway, cutting diagonally through the Garment Center and Times Square, and then swerving west and continuing north to Yonkers. The sheer white wall of the RCA Building of Rockefeller Center dominates the foreground directly north; beyond it lies rectangular Central Park. In the vague distance across the snake-like Harlem River, extends the Bronx.

To the northeast, Fifth Avenue cuts straight through the vista that comprises the skyscrapers of the mid-town section: the view moves clockwise from the hotels of Central Park South and the Plaza to the twin towers of the Waldorf-Astoria Hotel, then to the gold-leafed tower of the New York Central Building. The Chanin, Chrysler, Daily News buildings and the mass of Tudor City mark the Forty-second Street line to the

East River. Welfare Island, with its hospitals, lies under Queensboro Bridge to the northeast, and past the river stretches the borough of Queens, the World's Fair Grounds lying near the north shore. Directly east, the most conspicuous landmark is Bellevue Hospital on the west bank of the river. Initiates visit the tower in the late afternoon, dine in the café on the eighty-sixth floor, and stay until the lights of the city come on.

METROPOLITAN OPERA HOUSE

Broadway, 39th to 40th St.   IRT Broadway-7th Ave. subway to Times Square; or 8th Ave. (Independent) subway to 42d St.; or BMT subway to Times Square; or Broadway bus to 40th St.   Season: November to March. Admission: $1 to $7.

Efforts to provide a new building for the Metropolitan Opera House are made perennially—indeed, Rockefeller Center is a by-product of this movement. Yet, the warehouse-like yellow-brick structure that occupies an entire block on the edge of the garment district, remains the home of the world's foremost opera company: and within its original domicile the opera continues to expand its activities and enlarge its functions.

The opening of the Metropolitan Opera House in 1883 was part of the great wave of artistic endeavor which arose in America in post-Civil War days. The new moneyed aristocracy, assuming in the last decades of the nineteenth century the role of art patron, depended for its aesthetic tutelage on the taste of contemporary European capitals. Immense numbers of paintings, sculptures, and architectural models, both good and bad, were imported. New museums appeared in American cities, and great private collections were initiated.

With all this grandiose expansion of artistic enterprise, there were, however, certain misgivings when the ambitious plans for opera in America were announced. The New York *Times* wrote that the auditorium envisioned for the presentation of Italian opera was "on a scale of *possibly* too great magnitude." Its interior would "dazzle the eyes" of an assemblage accustomed to "the primitive surroundings" of the old Academy of Music, its predecessor on Fourteenth Street.

The opera house was designed by J. C. Cady, a prominent architect of the day. That Mr. Cady was without experience in theater construction seemed to matter little; audiences ever since have paid for his mistakes, as but half the stage can be seen from the side seats of the balcony and family circle. What did matter at the time, especially to the press and to readers of its society columns, was that the opera house had a "Golden Horseshoe"—two tiers of boxes and a row of *baignoires*—occupied by the seventy original stockholders, among them the Vanderbilts, the Morgans, and the Goulds.

Henry E. Abbey directed the opera during the first season. At the opening performance Vianesi conducted and Christine Nilsson sang the role of Marguerite in *Faust*. The Horseshoe was crowded with patrons whose total wealth was estimated at more than five hundred million dollars. Socially the first season was successful, but financially it showed an estimated loss of six hundred thousand dollars, a deficit underwritten by patrons who thus established a precedent.

The following year Dr. Leopold Damrosch, German-American musician (1832–85), became the director. He suggested the introduction of the music of Wagner, then hardly known in New York and considered extremely radical. Wagner's works filled the house with delighted audiences, and incidentally reduced the deficit.

Fire gutted the supposedly fireproof structure in August, 1892. It was quickly rebuilt, and reopened in November, 1893. Ten years later, it was redesigned by Carrère and Hastings, who eliminated the *baignoires* of the Golden Horseshoe and retained the two tiers of boxes which came to be known as the Diamond Horseshoe. Because of limited funds, the architects chose to treat the entrances and corridors simply and to splurge in the auditorium itself, which was fashioned into a magnificent, spacious hall. The tiers sweep around in great horizontal arcs from the proscenium. Vigorous carved decorations impart a sense of richness to the generous and handsome proportions of the auditorium.

Opera continued to appeal to a large number of opera goers as a spectacle rather than as music. Audiences demanded familiar works—*Aïda, Il Trovatore, Faust*—and, because this exotic business was associated with foreigners in the popular mind, native singers often masqueraded under alien names. (Precedent for this custom was set the first season, when Alwina Valleria [Schoening] sang the role of Leonora in *Il Trovatore*.) Meanwhile the star system, abandoned to some extent through the Wagnerian period, was resumed in 1898 under the directorship of Maurice Grau. During the "golden age of song," names, world-famous then, and still well-remembered, headed the bills: the De Reszkés, Nordica, Scotti, Sembrich, Lehmann, Eames, Calvé, Schumann-Heink. Caruso, under the directorship of Heinrich Conried, made a nervous debut in *Rigoletto*, November 23, 1903. The next year he opened the season in *Aïda*, the first of sixteen consecutive "Caruso opening nights." His last appearance was in

Elisir d'Amore; although he suffered from a hemorrhage he insisted on singing and was able to finish an entire act. He died in 1921.

Arturo Toscanini during his tenure as conductor, from 1908 until 1915, established the highest musical standards the Metropolitan has known, and his departure, after disagreements with the management, was a severe loss to American opera. But the man who probably influenced the Metropolitan more than any other was Gatti-Casazza, who became director in 1908 and remained in charge until 1935. He widened the Opera's repertory to include new and varied works: *Pelléas et Mélisande* by Debussy; *Boris Godounoff* by Moussorgsky (the title role played by Chaliapin); the neglected classics of Gluck and Mozart; and recent compositions, including Walter Damrosch's *Cyrano de Bergerac,* and Deems Taylor's *Peter Ibbetson* and *The King's Henchman* for which Edna St. Vincent Millay wrote the libretto. He introduced to Metropolitan audiences such singers as Giovanni Martinelli, Amelia Galli-Curci, and Kirsten Flagstad. *Salome* was first produced by the Metropolitan, January 22, 1907, with Olive Fremstad in the leading role, but the Dance of the Seven Veils aroused protest, and the management did not offer the opera again until January 13, 1934. Two outstanding events of the Gatti-Casazza tenure were the world premières of Puccini's *Girl of the Golden West* and Humperdinck's *Goose Girl.*

From 1910 to 1929, the management not only succeeded in operating the Metropolitan on a sound financial basis but also accumulated a surplus. With the depression, however, the contributions of stockholders fell off, and although crowds might stand in line for seats in the family circle or for standing room, the balconies might be packed by the time the late arrivals reached their places in box and orchestra, bravos might thunder from under the roof, there was always a deficit at the end of the season. The Metropolitan faced ruin.

Then, in 1935, a reorganization was effected. The Metropolitan Opera Association was formed, with a management committee that included John Erskine as chairman, Lucrezia Bori, Cornelius Bliss, and Allen Wardwell. Public contributions were solicited, and a subsidy was obtained from the Juilliard Musical Foundation. The association sold radio rights for Saturday matinee broadcasts, receiving as much as ninety thousand dollars a season. Edward Johnson, for many years a Metropolitan tenor, was made director. Thus the Metropolitan was saved, and as a result of the radio broadcasts it had achieved a great popular audience. Appreciative letters were received from farmers, filling-station attendants, cowpunchers. The institution had definitely altered its relation to society.

In other directions as well, it was on its way toward becoming a national institution. American ballets were presented during three successive seasons (1935-8). To encourage American singers several hundred young voices from all parts of the Nation are heard each season by a committee of musicians; the best are given an opportunity to sing on radio programs, and some are selected for the spring opera season. Those who distinguish themselves participate in the regular winter performances. Together with regular broadcasts of the best symphony music, the free concerts given in museums and other public buildings, and the Federal music theaters, the Metropolitan Opera of today is a significant part of a tendency toward the broad dissemination of musical culture.

THE NEW YORK PUBLIC LIBRARY: THE CENTRAL BUILDING

5th Ave. and 42d St. IRT Lexington Ave. subway to Grand Central (E. 42d St.), or IRT Broadway-7th Ave. subway to Times Square (W. 42d St.), then Queens line to Fifth Ave.; or 8th Ave. (Independent) subway to 42d St.; or BMT subway to Times Square; or 5th Ave. bus to 42d St. Hours: weekdays 9 A.M. to 10 P.M., Sunday 1 to 10 P.M.

Eleven thousand readers and visitors, on an average day, enter the Fifth Avenue building of the New York Public Library. Here is the center of a library system which, exclusive of separate systems in Brooklyn and Queens, is second in size in America only to the Library of Congress. In the reference department, which occupies the greater part of this building, eighty miles of shelves are crowded with more than two and one-half million books. Approximately a million and one-half books more are available through the Circulation Department, which comprises fifty-one branches and eleven subbranches in Manhattan, Richmond, and the Bronx. The library's collections are strong in history and biography, especially in relation to America; supplementing tens of thousands of books in the Americana collections are thousands of prints and etchings, and scores of valuable documents and maps dealing with the nation's history.

The building, which occupies the site of the old Croton Reservoir, was designed by the firm of Carrère and Hastings, architects, and completed in 1911. It cost $9,000,000. Architecturally, it is an outstanding example of the eclectic neoclassic style that was popular following the Chicago Columbian Exposition of 1893. The building has been much criticized for lack of functional expression, overabundant detail, and the sacrifice of utilitarian values for the sake of appearance. Nonetheless, it fully justifies the pride of its generation, for it was and still is a magnificent civic monument. Its huge substantial bulk of white Vermont marble, ornately decorated, darkened by the weathering of time and thereby made to seem more massive, commands attention even on Fifth Avenue, bordered as it now is with new, spectacular architecture.

Thomas Hastings, of the firm of Carrère and Hastings, was never completely satisfied with the Fifth Avenue front, and made numerous studies for its alteration. His widow provided in her will a sum of money which might be applied to the cost of alterations. The west, or rear, elevation is artistically beyond criticism even from the functionalist standpoint; tall narrow windows, lighting the seven floors of stacks within, extend all the way to the large windows of the reading rooms in the attic story, forming a façade that is truthfully and skillfully handled.

A long forecourt, extending the full length of the Fifth Avenue side, has become familiar throughout the nation as a meeting place for all classes. A few broad steps flanked by E. C. Potter's famous couchant lions lead to a raised, pigeon-inhabited walk, separated from the street by a stone parapet. For more than a generation this place has attracted tourists, eccentrics, lovers, visiting celebrities, and itinerant intellectuals from the farthest corners of the country.

The façade is dominated by a central pavilion with a triple-arched deepset portico and coupled Corinthian columns. Surmounting the colonnade is an attic parapet embellished with six vigorously modeled figures, by Paul W. Bartlett, representing History, Drama, Poetry, Religion, Romance, and Philosophy. The fountain figures in wall niches on either side of the portico, by Frederick MacMonnies, represent Truth and Beauty. The grotesque sculptural groups in the pedimented end pavilions, by George Gray Barnard, represent History and Art.

The entrance from Fifth Avenue leads into a two-story vestibule with a vaulted ceiling of veined white Vermont marble and wide stairways on opposite sides of the hall. The effect is impressive and cold, but the scene is humanized by the busy information desk facing the entrance, and by the activities of those who use the hall (with its four marble benches) as a meeting place.

The immense size of the entrance hall, the elaborate series of stairways, the wide corridors, the vistas of columns and vaulting, may seem improvident in view of a relative shortage of actual library space. But the library is more than a place for the study of books; in effect it is a center of the city's intellectual life, and the monumental character of its design is, therefore, appropriate.

An elaborate classification and shelving system, by which any book in the Forty-second Street collection can be brought to the delivery desk in six and one-half minutes, is entirely modern in character. Delivery centers about Room 315, which houses three units: the Public Catalogue Room and the adjoining North and South Main Reading Rooms. The reading rooms constitute, in effect, a single hall of vast scale with an elaborately decorated ceiling. Every item of the immense reference collection is indexed and cross-indexed in the catalogue—six million entries in all.

In the American History Room (300) are books from the libraries of George Bancroft, James Lenox, Gordon Lester Ford, Thomas Addis Emmet, and Theodore Bailey Myers; and dictionaries and grammars of the Indian languages. The Economics Division (Room 228) possesses the Dugdale Collection of books on pauperism and criminology, the Henry George Collection on single tax, and a comprehensive collection of mid-nineteenth-century works on socialism. More than 3,000 languages and dialects are represented in the library's collection. Of these, more than 50,000 volumes, some of them purchased with the Jacob H. Schiff Fund, are to be found in the Jewish Division (Room 216). Mr. Schiff also gave the library 317 water-color paintings, by James Tissot, illustrating the Old Testament. Other separate language collections are the Slavonic, in Room 216, and the Oriental, in Room 219. In the Music Room (324) are more than 75,000 catalogued items: books, pamphlets, orchestra scores, sheet music, and phonograph recordings.

The Rare Book Room (303), entered only by special permission, contains 50,000 treasures, including the Lenox copy of the Gutenberg Bible, in two volumes; the only known existing copy of the original folio edition in Spanish (printed in Barcelona in April, 1493) of Christopher Columbus' letter concerning his discoveries in America; the full first folio edition of Shakespeare (1623); and the Bay Psalm Book, printed in Cambridge, Massachusetts, in 1640, the first English book published in America. The final draft of Washington's "Farewell Address," in his own handwriting, and other American and British documents of historical importance are in the Manuscript Room (319). Here, and in the Spencer Collection (Room 322), are more than 100 illuminated manuscripts produced in Europe from the ninth to the sixteenth centuries. In the Spencer Room rare illuminated manuscripts from the Spencer Collection and superbly illustrated and finely bound books are displayed. Among the noteworthy items is the early fourteenth-century Tickhill Psalter.

The Newspaper Room, near the Forty-second Street entrance, attracts a cosmopolitan group of readers. It has current newspapers from all parts of the world, and files of New York City newspapers of the nineteenth and twentieth centuries. Some papers are now available on rolls of motion-picture film, a single one reproducing, by means of microphotography, an entire month's output of a metropolitan daily.

Special art or bibliographic exhibitions are generally on view in Rooms 112, 113, 316, 321, and 322. Along the walls of the third-floor corridors are old Dutch, English, French, and Italian maps of the New World, as well as early American prints of both documentary and artistic value. These are part of the Phelps Stokes Collection of American Historical Prints, presented to the library in 1930. Among them is Paul Revere's engraving of the British landing in Boston in 1768.

In the Lenox Gallery (Room 318) are three portraits of Washington: two by Gilbert Stuart, and a copy by Rembrandt Peale of Stuart's first portrait. Munkacsy's *Blind Milton Dictating to His Daughters* typifies the narrative painting popular in the last century. There are portraits by Gainsborough and Reynolds, landscapes by Landseer and Morland, and Copley's distinguished *Lady Frances Wentworth*.

The Stuart Gallery, opposite the Main Catalogue Room, contains additional examples of the anecdotal painting of the middle-nineteenth century, when works entitled *Hope and Faith* and *Pilgrims Going to Church* were admired. It has some fine examples of the Hudson River school. Sunday visitors will find this collection closed, as its donor, Mrs. Robert L. Stuart, stipulated.

The Print Room (308) contains more than 100,000 items, including full sets of Whistler and Haden, an excellent selection of English engravings and Japanese prints, and innumerable American historical prints. Dürer is well represented, and there are 800 prints by Daumier, including the only etching he ever made, 900 lithographs by Joseph Pennell, and a complete set of Mielatz's views of New York City. Another group comprises eighty engravings of Turner's work, etched by the painter himself. The library possesses one of the best contemporary collections in the city, purchased with moneys from the Samuel P. Avery Fund.

Operating expenses of the central building are paid from the interest of the nearly $44,000,000 principal fund of the library. The branches and the Circulation Department are maintained through municipal appropriations. The library is administered by the staff officers and a board of trustees, including the mayor, the comptroller, and the president of the City Council as ex-officio members.

The library developed from the consolidation of the Astor and Lenox libraries and the Tilden Trust, effected in 1895. This great institution was built as much by the devotion of the people who fought for free libraries in the face of general indifference as by generous gifts. James Green Cogswell, a teacher, persuaded the first John Jacob Astor that a "fitting testimonial to his adopted country by its richest citizen" should be a library. (A huge monument to Washington had been favored for a time.) In 1848 the schoolmaster who "had stayed at the old gentleman's elbow to push him on" had his reward. Astor, in his will, gave $400,000 and a plot of land to the city for a library, and accordingly a reference library was opened in 1854 on Lafayette Place. Together with books and bequests by members of the Astor family, it represents a total of $1,000,000. The Lenox Library, opened in 1875, was founded by James Lenox, book lover and scholar; at the time of consolidation, it contained 85,000 volumes and had an endowment fund of $505,000. Samuel J. Tilden, governor of New York in 1874 and Democratic candidate for President in 1876, died in 1886 and left his money for a free library and reading room. The Tildren Trust brought an endowment of $2,000,000, after the original bequest of about $4,000,000 had been reduced by a successful contesting of the Tilden will.

The Lenox Library had been intended for scholars rather than for popular use. In the 1880's the experience of the Astor and Lenox libraries made it seem foolhardy to expect that public libraries would be supported, and with the establishment of the Tilden Fund a consolidation with the Astor and Lenox libraries was sought. Meanwhile, women of the Grace Episcopal Church, adopting a different approach, had collected 500 books and obtained a room on Thirteenth Street for a popular library. Readers, no longer overawed by the magnificence of the earlier institutions—the Astor Library, for instance, had liveried doormen—came in such numbers that the sidewalks were blocked during the two hours once a week when the library was open. Such libraries soon were established in other neighborhoods, and in 1887 they were united as the New York Free Circulating Library, and financial help was given by the city. In order to benefit from a $5,200,000 gift made by Andrew Carnegie to the city for library buildings, the New York Free Circulating Library with eleven branches joined the Astor-Lenox-Tilden consolidation in 1900, and still later, nine other independent libraries were united with it. Thus began the New York Public Library's Circulation Department.

Today, the offices of the Circulation Department, the Department's Union Catalogue, the Picture Collection, Central Children's Room, and the Central Circulation Branch are in the Central Building.

Notable among the branches are the Music Library, 121 East Fifty-eighth Street, the Municipal Reference Library, Municipal Building, and the Library for the Blind, 137 West Twenty-fifth Street. More than 10,000,000 books are lent to readers annually by the Circulation Department, and the Picture Collection, with a classified stock of more than 800,000, makes nearly 900,000 loans a year.

MADISON SQUARE GARDEN

8th Ave., 49th to 50th St. IRT Broadway-7th Ave. subway (local) to 50th St.; or 8th Ave. (Independent) subway (local) to 50th St.; or BMT subway (local) to 49th St.; or 9th Ave. el to 50th St.; or 8th Ave., 9th Ave., Broadway or 7th Ave. bus to 50th St.

New Yorkers think only of what happens inside of Madison Square Garden. The rare individual who wanders down Forty-ninth or Fiftieth Street for a view of the building itself sees nothing but blank brick walls and fire escapes. The main entrance opens on Eighth Avenue through an arcade, but the Garden proper is concealed behind a smaller structure and runs back toward Ninth Avenue.

This plain building is, however, already famous as America's chief indoor arena. Charity benefits, national political conventions, championship prize fights, cowboy rodeos—all draw throngs to Madison Square Garden. The composition of the crowd on one night contrasts sharply with that of another. From the vantage of a $315 box, the aristocracy, in evening attire, politely applauds the horse show. Twenty-five cents is the price of admission to a Communist rally at which 20,000 people rock the Garden with cheers. Politicians, sportsmen, and socially prominent personalities occupy $16.50 ringside seats to watch a pair of heavyweights in action for an hour or less, while *hoi polloi* sit in cheap seats under the roof. On a good night patrons eat 12,000 hot dogs, washed down with 1,000 gallons of beer and soda pop, while sixty private policemen, unarmed, are stationed there to prevent disorder.

From the top balcony at the Ninth Avenue end, an Olympic ski jumper darts down a slide, hangs momentarily in the air, lands on a snow mound, and stops near the Eighth Avenue end of the arena. Children crowd under the big top for circus matinees. For seventy-five cents a sleepless night is spent at the six-day bicycle races. Three thousand carefully reared and pedigreed pets compete in a dog show. The President makes a speech at a political meeting. A world champion figure skater dances the tango under a spotlight. A professional hockey game is halted by a brawl while fans add to the racket with cowbells and jeers. Tennis matches, basketball games, track meets, and trade exhibitions are among the events staged regularly in the arena. A $34,000 mineral-wool ceiling was especially provided to improve the acoustics when Paderewski played for charity.

Madison Square Garden is a successor to two earlier Gardens that were actually on Madison Square, at Madison Avenue and East Twenty-sixth Street. The first of these occupied the abandoned New York and Harlem (Railroad) Union Depot that had housed Barnum's Hippodrome and then Gilmore's Garden before acquiring the name Madison Square Garden in 1879. It was replaced in 1890 by the building later known as the "old Garden." P. T. Barnum, J. P. Morgan, and Darius Mills were among its directors. Stanford White designed the structure—one of the most impressive of its day. Its beautiful tower, copied from the Giralda in Seville, was surmounted by Augustus Saint-Gaudens' statue of Diana. In the roof garden White was killed in 1906 by Harry K. Thaw, and the murder developed into one of the outstanding scandals of the era.

Saint-Gaudens had clothed Diana in a drapery but this was soon torn away by the winds. The graceful figure was a welcome and familiar sight for many years. It was only when the building was demolished that those who concerned themselves with the fate of the lovely lady discovered that she was put together with rivets as large as those in a battleship. Saint-Gaudens' *Diana* is today a New York legend. The Pennsylvania Museum of Art owns her in what might be called the flesh. A working model stands in a niche in the Museum of the City of New York.

The old Garden became a national show place, scene of a bewildering variety of events. There William Jennings Bryan accepted the Democratic nomination for President, Adelina Patti sang, and Jack Dempsey knocked out Bill Brennan in defense of the heavyweight title. Six-day go-as-you-please (walk, run, or crawl) races, the Wild West Show, aquatic exhibitions in the mammoth pool, the first American automobile shows, and mass meetings of the Christian Endeavor Society drew large audiences.

Two master showmen—Tex Rickard, gambler, promoter, and cattleman, and John Ringling, circus magnate—were responsible for the success of the old Garden. Rickard's first local enterprise, the Willard-Moran fight, grossed $250,000. His spectacular methods were so effective that, when the Garden was razed to make room for the New York Life Insurance Company Building, he was able to interest a group of financiers in the construction of a new and greater Garden, a project he directed until his death in 1929.

The present Garden was designed by Thomas W. Lamb, theater architect, and constructed in 1925. It has a seating capacity of 18,903 for boxing bouts, 15,500 for hockey games, and 14,500 for bicycle races. The building can be emptied of a capacity crowd in five minutes. The roof of the structure is carried by steel trusses that make columns largely unnecessary, thus permitting a clear view of the arena from almost any seat. The main seating section, comprising whorls of seats on an incline, rims the elliptical arena floor. Two balconies, similar to the main section, are cantilevered from the walls. When only part of the arena floor is used for staging events, the remainder is filled with rows of seats. The land and building cost $5,600,000.

The different uses to which the arena is put requires flexibility in its plant operation and extraordinary efficiency on the part of the Garden staff. Within three or four hours after a hockey game, for instance, two tractors clear the rink of ice and a gang of thirty men cleans house and prepares the arena with a ring and 4,200 additional seats for a championship boxing bout the next evening. Brine flowing through thirteen miles of pipe under the concrete floor freezes the rink for hockey again in eight hours. In six or seven hours two pulverizers driven by internal combustion motors change 500 tons of ice into snow for the annual Winter Sports Show. Since no satisfactory sectional track has as yet been designed, 300 men build a new track for each six-day bicycle race, completing it in eight hours at a cost of about five thousand dollars. During the horse show, the circus, and the rodeo, the animals are quartered in the basement: a contractor, on such occasions, "rents" 690 tons of earth to the Garden for $2,500.

The Garden is operated by the Madison Square Garden Corporation, of which Colonel John Reed Kilpatrick is president. Its income is derived from the promotion of sports events and from rentals. Among the annual spectacles are the Six-Day Bicycle Race, the Winter Sports Show, the Skating Carnival, and the New York Police and Firemen's Shows. The arena has been rented to the Ringling Brothers-Barnum and Bailey Circus for twenty-seven days each spring at the flat rate of $100,000; the price for most public meetings is $3,500 a night on weekdays and $5,000 a night on Saturdays and Sundays. Professional hockey, which the Garden controls in New York, is perhaps the most consistently profitable venture, with the gate running well over $700,000 a year. The Garden owns the New York Rangers, and receives 40 per cent of the receipts from the games of the New York Americans. The amateur Rovers, who play Sunday afternoons, provide a "farm" for the Rangers.

With the economic depression and the passing of the million-dollar gate, the Garden's income dwindled. But in 1932, despite the adverse business situation, the Garden spent $160,000 to build the Madison Square Garden Bowl, seating 80,000 people, in Long Island City. Though the Bowl proved of little or no profit (having been used only for an occasional prize fight and in 1936 for midget auto racing on a specially constructed asphalt track), the Garden has recovered from the lean days of the early 1930's.

The Garden is still said to be "the largest and most prosperous sports organization in the world." From early October until late May the arena is rarely empty. But when the thirty-six circus elephants lumber from the building, signaling the close of the season, the Garden goes dark. Then, for four months, New York is quieter and less colorful.

ROCKEFELLER CENTER

5th Ave. to 6th Ave., 48th to 51st St. IRT Broadway-7th Ave. subway (local) to 50th St.; or IRT Lexington Ave. subway (local) to 51st St.; or 8th Ave. (Independent) Queens subway to 5th Ave. (53d St.); or BMT subway (local) to 49th St.; or 5th or 6th Ave. bus to 50th St.
Guided Tours. Rockefeller Center: adults $1.00, children 50¢; 10 A.M. to 9 P.M. National Broadcasting Company Studios: studio tour 55¢, television tour 55¢, combination 90¢; 9 A.M. to 11 P.M. (does not include sponsored broadcasts). Sky Gardens: 50¢, 10 A.M. to 5 P.M. from May 1 to November 1.
Single Admissions. Radio City Music Hall: 40¢ to $1.65, performances begin about 11:30 A.M. Observatory (RCA Building, 70th floor): adults 40¢, children 20¢; 10 A.M. to midnight.

The twelve buildings of Rockefeller Center constitute not only a vast skyscraper group but an organized city. The group, said to be the largest ever undertaken by private enterprise, represents the belated culmination of the boom of the 1920's.

Covering twelve land acres in the fashionable mid-town shopping district, the project includes a vast skyscraper office center, a shopping center, an exhibition center, and a radio and amusement center. The western front, along Sixth Avenue, is made up of buildings devoted primarily to entertainment: the RKO Building and the adjoining Radio City Music Hall, the National Broadcasting Company's extension of the seventy-story RCA Building, and the Center Theater. The name "Radio City," which is often incorrectly applied to all of Rockefeller Center, properly designates only this western portion.

Sharing the eastern exposure, four lesser buildings serve as Fifth Avenue showcases for foreign nations: the British Empire Building, La Maison

Française, the Palazzo d'Italia, and the International Building East. Slightly behind the latter two rises the forty-one-story International Building. The Time and Life Building, the Associated Press Building, and 30 Rockefeller Plaza (RCA Building) tower about the plaza, as will Holland House, one of the two new buildings still to be constructed (1939).

In its architecture Rockefeller Center stands as distinctively for New York as the Louvre stands for Paris. Composed of the essential elements of New York skyscrapers—steel framing and curtain walls, encasing elevators and offices—the group relies for exterior decoration almost exclusively on the pattern of its windows, piers, spandrels, and wall surfaces. Its beauty derives from a significant play of forms, and light and shadow. Its character—abrupt, stark, jagged, and powerful—arises fundamentally from the spacing of the buildings, from their direct functionalism, their mass, their silhouette, and their grayish-tan color; not (as in the case of the buildings surrounding the nearby Grand Army Plaza) from ornamental roofs, reminiscent styles, or elaborate setbacks. The color tone of the Center is given by the warm tan limestone walls, the slate-gray cast aluminum spandrels under the windows, and especially by the light-blue window shades inside; the gray of the whole, blending into the surrounding atmosphere, adds to the apparent height of the group.

Noteworthy is the integration of architecture with such "allied arts" as mural painting, sculpture, metal work, mosaic, wood veneering, and the like. Where individual skyscrapers in the past have boasted of employing a single painter and sculptor in addition to the architect to direct the work, Rockefeller Center gave employment to painters, sculptors, and decorators by whole groups and schools. The three architectural firms sharing equally the credit are Reinhard and Hofmeister; Corbett, Harrison, and MacMurray; and Hood and Fouilhoux.

In terms of site planning, Rockefeller Center represents a complete departure from similar developments in New York and other large cities. It is the first group of tall buildings that does not simply face on the existing streets. Instead, the three blocks were freshly considered as a unit. The RCA Building, as the tallest, was placed close to the center of the plot. To reach it, a new private street, "Rockefeller Plaza," was established, running north and south between Forty-eight and Fifty-first Streets, and a pedestrian walk was cut through to Fifth Avenue. All the other chief buildings are staggered both as to height and location, in order to shade one another as little as possible and to build an interesting composition of forms. Two of the twelve acres of the Center's site are open areas. The tower-like shapes of such structures as the Empire State Building result from the application of setback regulations to buildings on relatively small plots; the large scope of the site planning of the Center, on the other hand, made possible the characteristically slab-like main buildings with long, narrow, and efficient floor areas, easily penetrated by sunlight and fresh air.

The most impressive entrance to the Center is from Fifth Avenue through the Channel, a pedestrian passage 60 feet wide and 200 feet long

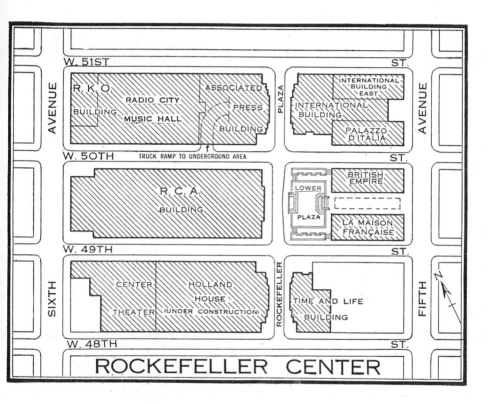

that separates the British Empire Building from La Maison Française. Six shallow pools bordered with yew hedges, in the center of this esplanade, are fed by bronze fountainheads designed by Rene P. Chambellan to represent rollicking tritons and nereids. The Channel slopes from Fifth Avenue down to a flight of stone steps that lead to the lower plaza, eighteen feet below street level. The plaza, 125 feet long and 95 feet wide, may be flooded for winter ice skating, or embellished with hedges and flower beds for summer use as an outdoor café. Against its west wall, Paul Manship's huge bronze figure of *Prometheus* rises above spouting streams of water. *Prometheus* has been the target of caustic criticism; his detractors have nicknamed him "Leaping Looie." From the top of the stairway, walks diverge, following the rim of the lower plaza past a series of fountains set in greenery to Rockefeller Plaza. Across this street is the entrance to the RCA Building.

Several doorways leading from the lower plaza to an underground concourse hint at Rockefeller Center's subterranean activity. A great underground shipping center and three-quarters of a mile of passages are entered through a 400-foot truck ramp just east of the Music Hall. A branch ramp turns off to a shipping room beneath the International Building, then enters the main truck area at a point directly beneath the lower plaza. This system handles all freight deliveries except those to the theaters and the RKO Building.

The 850-foot RCA (Radio Corporation of America) Building, the central member of the group, is one of New York's tallest structures and, in gross area, the largest office building in the world (1939). Its huge, broad, flat north and south façades, its almost unbroken mass, and its thinness are the features that impelled observers to nickname it the "Slab." The entrance is presided over by a rather astonishing bearded giant floating over a compass, in token of "the genius which interprets the laws and cycles of the cosmic forces of the universe to mankind." The side panels represent two of the "cosmic forces": Light and Sound. The whole was sculptured by Lee Lawrie. The screen below, with the appearance of crumpled cellophane, is made of square blocks of pyrex glass.

The walls of the elevator banks in the middle of the two-story lobby are covered by large murals. Those on the south wall are by José Maria Sert and represent "man's intellectual mastery of the material universe"; they deal with the evolution of machinery, the eradication of disease, the abolition of slavery, and the suppression of war. Those on the north, by Frank Brangwyn, depict "man's conquest of the physical world," portraying respectively the cultivation of the soil, the development of machinery, and the hope of mankind's salvation—the lessons of the Sermon on the Mount. A mural, painted by Diego Rivera and originally in this lobby, caused an international controversy when the management first screened it and finally destroyed it, contending that the artist had departed from the approved preliminary sketch. Others held that the mural was destroyed because it included a likeness of Lenin. The case became a classic conflict between the artistic rights of a creator and the property rights of a purchaser. The space is now occupied by a Sert mural depicting the triumph of man's accomplishments through the union of physical and mental labor. The Museum of Science and Industry (see page 342) is entered from the lobby.

The Sixth Avenue entrance to the RCA Building is surmounted by a glass mosaic by Barry Faulkner. Industriously assembled of about a million pieces of glass in 250 shades of color, it represents "thought enlightening the world." About thirty feet above the mosaic, in the spaces between windows, are four sculptured panels by Gaston Lachaise, American sculptor of the modern school. They are titled *Genius Receiving the Light of the Sun, Conquest of Space, Gifts of Earth to Mankind,* and *Spirit of Progress.*

The most widely known tenants of the RCA Building are the National Broadcasting Company and its parent, the Radio Corporation of America. NBC's twenty-seven broadcasting studios, offices and other facilities occupy about four hundred thousand square feet of space on ten floors. These quarters, air-conditioned, sound-proofed, and equipped for television, are the home of WEAF and WJZ, the key stations of NBC's Red and Blue networks, respectively, and form the largest broadcasting establishment in the world.

In the eastern end of the sixty-fifth floor is the Rainbow Room, a night club, where a color organ throws shifting patterns on a reflecting dome and a crystal chandelier over a revolving dance floor. The Rainbow Grill, at the western end of the same floor, is less formal in decoration and atmosphere.

The seventieth-floor observatory promenade, 200 feet long and 20 feet wide, affords one of the finest views of New York. At the eleventh-floor level, directly over the NBC studios, is the largest of the seven roof gardens in the development. Visitors enter directly upon the International Rock Garden, where specimens from all over the world are arranged along a stream that cascades, winds, and twists for a distance of 125 feet along the terrace. There are a native American garden, with its old rail fence and shaded pool; typical Spanish, Italian, Japanese, Dutch, and aquatic gardens; and, perhaps the most successful of all, an English garden with a sundial from Donnington Castle and fine examples of yew planting.

Offices of many motion-picture producers and distributors are in the thirty-one story RKO (Radio-Keith-Orpheum) Building which faces Sixth Avenue above Fiftieth Street. Three large panels, carved by Robert Garrison, extend across the Sixth Avenue façade; their subject is "Radio Spreading the Inspiration of the Past and Present." A mural by Boardman Robinson hangs in the lobby. Its subject matter is concerned with the spiritual challenge of modern civilization.

Immediately adjoining the RKO Building is the largest indoor theater in the world, Radio City Music Hall. The Music Hall was opened in

December, 1932, as a variety house under the direction of Samuel L. ("Roxy") Rothafel. It proved to be an unprofitable white elephant. Soon after, Roxy's mammoth variety shows were abandoned and the present type of show—motion picture and variety—was instituted under the management of Rockefeller Center, Inc.

The majestic foyer, fifty feet high, sweeps to a grand stairway leading to three mezzanines. Brocatelle wall covering repeats the rich henna of Ezra Winter's large mural above the stairway. Gold wall mirrors extend from the floor to the gold-leaf ceiling.

The spectacular modern auditorium contracts in a series of narrowing arches to the proscenium. Lights, hidden in the telescoped joints of these arches, can suffuse the great curved interior with glowing colors. The unusual excellence of the planning affords a pleasing and efficient arrangement of the seats.

The smoking- and powder-rooms are decorated with the work of Yasuo Kuniyoshi, Henry Billings, Stuart Davis, Witold Gordon, Buk Ulreich, and other artists. In the main lounge is William Zorach's sculptured *Dancing Figure* and the black walls carry vignettes by Louis Bouche. Robert Laurent's *Goose Girl* is placed on the first mezzanine. Gwen Lux's sculpture, *Eve,* stands in the main foyer.

Three circular metal and enamel plaques, representing the Theater, Dance, and Song, designed by Hildreth Meiere and executed by Oscar Bach, are the only decorations on the long Fiftieth Street exterior wall of the Music Hall.

Nearly everything about the Music Hall is tremendous. It seats 6,200 patrons, the staff of 600 employees is paid some $35,000 weekly. The 300-ton steel truss that supports the immense golden proscenium arch, sixty feet high, is the heaviest yet used in theater construction. The orchestra is the world's largest theater orchestra, and the screen, seventy by forty feet, is the world's largest. The stage, which cost more than $400,000 to build, has three seventy-foot sections that can be raised forty feet from the subbasement·to a position fourteen feet above normal stage level. Another Music Hall superlative concerns the troupe of "Rockettes," whose claim to the title of "world's finest precision dancers" has never been challenged.

The Center Theater, also facing Sixth Avenue, is smaller than the Music Hall and is very different in *decor.* Its foyer, lighted by five large windows, etched in relief, has Bubinga mahogany walls whose soft tones are accented by vermilion doors leading to the auditorium. The auditorium, seating

3,700 people, has walls of mahogany, and from its decorative ceiling hangs a six-ton chandelier, twenty-five feet in diameter, that is reputed to be the largest in the world. A special ventilating system carries off the heat produced by the four hundred bulbs in the chandelier.

Arthur Crisp, Maurice Heaton, and Edward Steichen were among the artists who decorated the mezzanines and lounges. The Forty-ninth Street exterior wall bears another metal plaque, said to be the largest ever made. Designed by Hildreth Meiere and executed by Oscar Bach, it represents the transmission of electric energy by radio and television.

The Center Theater has been used for motion pictures, for musical spectacles and for popular-priced opera, but it has never established itself as a profitable enterprise. Reduction of its seating capacity has been proposed as a remedy.

The entire western façade of Rockefeller Center could not be seen properly as long as it was partly hidden by the disfiguring Sixth Avenue elevated. Such optimistic expedients as brightening the el structure with aluminum paint were of little help. Now the el is gone.

The Time and Life Building and the Center Theater were the only buildings completed by 1938 in the block between Forty-eighth and Forty-ninth Streets. The former opens on Rockefeller Plaza from the east and is named for the two Luce publications having offices there. It was the temporary home of the Museum of Modern Art *(see page 347)* in 1938, while a new museum building was being erected. Holland House, a new sixteen-story structure in this block, west of Rockefeller Plaza, was under construction early in 1939.

Because Rockefeller Center, Inc., does not control the Fifth Avenue end of the Forty-eighth to Forty-ninth Street block, the Center presents only a two-block frontage on the east which consists of La Maison Française and the British Empire Building, between Forty-ninth and Fiftieth Streets, and the twin six-story extensions of the International Building, called Palazzo d'Italia and International Building East, between Fiftieth and Fifty-first Streets. Architecturally, these four buildings are restrained in design and very similar, even in their formal roof gardens.

The main entrance of the seven-story structure named La Maison Francaise carries a sculptured panel designed by Alfred Janniot in gold-leafed bronze. It greatly flatters its host city by representing Paris and New York joining hands over the figures of Poetry, Beauty, and Elegance. Three sculptured panels by Carl Paul Jennewein decorate the Fifth Avenue entrance of the virtually identical British Empire Building across the prom-

enade, while above them is the British coat-of-arms. In the panels nine figures in gold leaf represent the major industries of the Empire. The north
and south entrances bear panels designed by Lee Lawrie. The façades of
both La Maison Française and the British Empire Building are topped
by carved limestone insets by Rene P. Chambellan. Those on the former
building symbolize four epochal events in French history—the sword, the
rise of Charlemagne's Empire; the clustered spears, the united effort of new
France; the shield, the absolute monarchy under Louis XIV; the fasces,
Phrygian cap and laurel, the birth of the Republic. Similarly, those on the
British Empire Building are of historical significance, their motifs being
the crests of the kingdoms: Wales, England, Scotland, and Ireland.

These two structures are "dedicated to the commerce, industry and art"
of their respective nations. Similarly, the Palazzo d'Italia is dedicated to
Italy. The treatment of its façade includes a panel in cast glass by Attilio
Piccirilli. The motto "Arte E Lavoro . . . Lavoro E Arte" means "Art is
Labor; Labor is Art." The other motto "Sempre Avanti Eterna Giovinezza"
means, "Advance Forever, Eternal Youth." Piccirilli designed a similar
panel for the International Building East. Between these two northern
structures a court, forty-five feet deep, leads to four huge stone piers that
connect the two low buildings and form the entrance to the splendid Great
Hall of the forty-one-story International Building proper. For decoration,
a clever use is made of the reflection, in the plate glass of the lobby, of St.
Patrick's Cathedral (located across the street). From the three-sided court,
Lee Lawrie's forty-five-foot bronze figure of Atlas beetles down on Fifth
Avenue.

The general proportions and treatment of the International Building are
like those of the RCA Building. The spaciousness of the lobby, four stories
high, sixty feet wide and eighty feet long, is remarkable in a purely commercial building. The design is considered by many to be the best in the
Center. The effect of restrained modernism is heightened by the brilliant
choice of contrasting materials and the imaginative use of four wide escalators in place of monumental stairways. It houses a United States passport
office and many travel agencies, and is particularly well equipped for exhibitions and large displays. The corridors leading from the lobby are
notable for the way lighting has been used as decoration.

In 1929 the Rockefeller Center site, most of which was owned by Columbia University, was covered by two-hundred-odd buildings, many of
them housing speakeasies. The leases to the land were about to expire and
the tract was proposed as a suitable setting for a magnificent new opera

house. John D. Rockefeller, Jr., was approached as the most likely backer; when his support was assured the Metropolitan Square Corporation was formed and a lease was negotiated at ten times the sum the university had been deriving from the property. The agreement ceded tenancy to the corporation for twenty-four years, with three renewal options extending to the year 2015, at an annual rental beginning at $3,000,000 and gradually increasing to $3,600,000 by 1952.

The opera house project was abandoned after the Wall Street crash of 1929. Rockefeller was left holding three blocks of non-paying property and staggering rent and tax bills. It was then that the plan was conceived of using the land for a co-ordinated building group as "an example of urban planning for the future."

Under Rockefeller Center, Inc., successor to the Metropolitan Square Corporation, the engineering firms of Todd, Robertson, and Todd, and Todd and Brown commenced work in 1930. One and a quarter million tons of debris were hauled away in wreckage of the old buildings and excavation for the new. Between 1932 and 1938, 88,000 tons of Portland cement and 39,000,000 bricks were joined to structural steel to complete eleven buildings. With the completion of the Associated Press Building in 1938 only two buildings remained to be constructed. Holland House was to go up behind the Center Theater at once, and an office structure is planned for the southwest corner of the project.

Long before a shovelful of dirt was turned, Rockefeller Center was severely criticized. The project was called "wasteful and useless," "undistinguished," and "inartistic" as the first buildings rose. Disagreements with artists added to the confusion. Yet, out of the clamor of disparaging voices, the development grew: Rockefeller Center's position among the city's institutions is now secure. Reproach has given way to respect. New York began to be proud of these strong new towers. Approximately 80,000 visitors appear every day as well as 20,000 permanent tenants. The NBC studios alone draw about 700,000 sightseers annually, while about 900,000 people attend broadcasts.

Not the least of the many Rockefeller Center features that merit the title "world's largest" is the mortgage, which is held by the Metropolitan Life Insurance Company. It amounts to $44,300,000.

NEW YORK MUSEUM OF SCIENCE AND INDUSTRY

RCA Building, Rockefeller Center, 30 Rockefeller Plaza. IRT Broadway-7th Ave. subway (local) to 50th St.; or 8th Ave. (Independent) Queens subway to 5th Ave. (53d St.); or BMT subway (local) to 49th St.; or 6th or 5th Ave. bus to 50th St. Hours: daily 10 A.M. to 10 P.M. Admission: adults 25¢; children 10¢. Frequent lectures and motion pictures.

Housed appropriately in a setting typical of twentieth-century ingenuity and accomplishment, the museum is a focal point of interest for scientifically curious adults and a wonderland for children. It is known also as the Hall of Motion because its thousands of models, replicas, dioramas, working demonstrations, and visitor-operated machines dramatize the scientific achievements and industrial developments of the machine age; motion pictures, lectures, and conducted tours supplement these graphic illustrations of simple and complex mechanisms of the past and the present. The museum is visited annually by half a million people.

Approximately twenty-five hundred permanent displays and a constantly changing series of exhibitions—lent by notable research laboratories, government agencies, and industrial organizations—inform the visitor of the latest inventions, discoveries, and scientific developments. Included in the series of temporary exhibits have been zoning models and unified city planning designs of the New York City Housing Authority, graphic surveys of the work of the Rural Electrification Administration and the Tennessee Valley Authority, a collection of X-ray plates and photographs indicating the progressive steps in a brain operation, "Better Things for Better Living Through Chemistry," "Modern Plastics," "Steels of Today and Tomorrow," and "The Story of Man."

Permanent exhibits are grouped under the general classifications of textiles, shelter, food industries, power, aviation, communication, machine tools, highway, railroad and marine transportation, and electro-technology. Several hundred machines both in model form and actual size are either in continuous operation or may be put in motion at will; the visitor may operate an electric generator, a telautograph, a model locomotive, a power plant, an ocean depth finder, or a radio direction finder. Especially attractive is the experience of handling the controls of an actual airplane.

The 112 examples of sectional machine parts, mounted on the semicircular wall of the main rotunda, are popular features of the museum, for they afford thrilling discovery of machine operations usually hidden from view. Put in operation by means of push buttons, the gears, pulleys, levers, cogs, shafts, pinions, and other parts, brightly colored in red, blue, or green, spin, mesh, revolve, bend, or twist. In a rear section on the same floor, models of an ancient windmill, steam and hydroelectric plants and turbines, and a generating station illustrate the modes of power production. One model reproduces a cross section of the plant of the Brooklyn Edison Company.

Operating demonstrations of epoch-making inventions and discoveries in the story of electrical science are on exhibit in the division devoted to electro-technology; other demonstrations make clear the fundamental principles involved. Here also are modern business-office machines, such as the punching, sorting, and tabulating devices, that "think like a man."

A collection of ship models arranged in historical sequence begins with an Egyptian boat of 3500 B.C. and features famous ships of different periods, including the liner *Normandie*. Near by a group of marine engines illustrates the various types that have been developed through the years. The push of a button operates a large model of a floating dock with a ship.

A genuine covered wagon, a sleigh of Colonial days, an Egyptian oxcart of a date prior to 200 B.C. and still in a fine state of preservation, and a Model T Ford (presented by the inventor) are favorites among the vehicles in the highway transportation exhibit.

A comprehensive series of model locomotives, most of which may be operated by button, show progress in railroad transportation, from the Salamanca engine of 1812, the De Witt Clinton, and other famous "characters" of early railroading days up to the electric locomotive of the present. Examples of coupling and air-brake systems, signaling devices, and switch sections illustrate technical developments.

Scale-model dwellings in appropriate historical settings depict the history of housing from the neolithic lake dweller's shelter to the ultramodern residence of structural glass and stainless steel. Plowing implements, a working demonstration of milk pasteurization, gas and electric refrigerators, models of a sugar refinery, and a modern cold storage plant are features of the food industries division.

The story of the textile industry is graphically told by spinning and weaving machines—from the Colonial spinning wheel to the modern headstock, and from hand to power loom—and in the samples of fabrics produced by the various processes. An exhibit of interest to many visitors displays several types of modern looms suitable for school or home and finished articles from these looms. Another popular exhibit is a demonstration of the manufacture of rayon from wood chips to finished product.

The museum, established in 1927 by a bequest of Henry Robinson Towne, was known originally as the Museum of Peaceful Arts and was housed in the Scientific American Building. Within three years, however, its rapid growth made larger quarters necessary, and in 1930 the museum moved to the Daily News Building. It was installed in its present quarters in Rockefeller Center in 1936.

ST. PATRICK'S CATHEDRAL

5th Ave., 50th to 51st St. IRT Lexington Ave. subway (local) to 51st St.; or IRT Broadway-7th Ave. (local) to 50th St.; or 8th Ave. (Independent) Queens subway to 5th Ave. (53d St.); or BMT subway (local) to 49th St.; or 5th or Madison Ave. bus to 50th St.

St. Patrick's, America's first major cathedral built in the Gothic Revival style, is the seat of the Archdiocese of the Ecclesiastical Province of New York, which includes the dioceses of Brooklyn, Buffalo, Albany, Rochester, Syracuse, and Ogdenburg. Begun in 1858, the nave was opened November 29, 1877, and the cathedral dedicated May 25, 1879. With the exception of the Lady Chapel and two smaller chapels the entire project was designed by James Renwick (1818–1895).

The cathedral with its dependencies occupies an entire block. Although its twin spires are dwarfed by the skyscrapers of Rockefeller Center and other near-by buildings, its granite and marble mass is still impressive.

The design is based upon that of the Cathedral of Cologne; the Fifth Avenue façade is composed of a steep central gable flanked by towers and traceried spires. Above the canopied central portal is a rose window, twenty-six feet in diameter. The exterior is constructed of granite. Owing to the nature of this material much of the delicacy and grace characteristic of Gothic architecture is lost in the detail of the tracery, molded profiles, and carved ornament of the exterior. A purist would be disturbed by the lack of flying buttresses where he would expect to find them; the pinnacles of the missing buttresses are present, however, though their function is a bit puzzling in view of the lack of stone vaulting inside the church.

The plan of the cathedral is cruciform, with nave, transepts, and choir. The interior is reminiscent of Amiens with a forest of magnificent clustered piers of white marble separating the central aisle from the two side aisles. The unusual height of the side aisles suggests St. Ouen at Rouen, while the clustered columns, with their richly ornamented capitals, and the elaborately vaulted ceiling follow such English examples as York, Exeter, and Westminster Abbey. The triforium above the side aisles affords a continuous passage fifty-six feet above the floor, around the interior, broken only by the walls of the transepts. The entire architectural composition is unusually open and delicate, partly due to the slenderness of the nave piers, which are only five feet in diameter above the base. The interior has dignity and spaciousness, combined with religious somberness.

Forty-five of the seventy stained-glass windows are from the studios of Nicholas Lorin at Chartres, and of Henry Ely at Nantes. Rich in tone— some dark, some of pastel lightness—and combined with elaborate tracery, they glow in the sunshine, but unfortunately, much of the detail in them is too delicate to be legible at a distance. They become simply patterns of red, yellow, green, blue, and purple against the framework of the stone walls which, in the dusky light, takes on a tone of deepest gray.

The nave extends east from the main portal on Fifth Avenue; at its eastern end is the glimmering High Altar. Shallow aisle chapels, on both sides of the nave, contain altars dedicated to the worship of various saints. Below the first window of the north wall is the baptistery. Its beautiful font, carved of dark wood, rests on a marble base. The adjoining chapel is dedicated to St. Bernard and St. Bridget. Its richly decorated background, a reproduction, in ecru-colored marble, of the doorway of St. Bernard's chapel in Mellefont, Ireland, is flanked by clustered green columns.

The fourteen Stations of the Cross, around the transept walls, were designed by Peter J. H. Cuypers and carved in Holland. On the west side of the south transept is a small window dedicated to St. Patrick, the cartoon for which was drawn by Renwick. In the lower panel the architect is shown discussing the plans of the cathedral with Archbishop Hughes.

The statue of St. Francis, in the north ambulatory, is a reproduction of one by Giovanni Dupré in the Church of St. Francis at Assisi. In the south ambulatory is a Pietà, by William Ordway Partridge. It resembles the famous work of Michelangelo, although differing in composition and pose. The Chapel of the Little Flower, adjoining, contains a statue of St. Theresa by Mario Korbel.

In the choir itself, the High Altar, designed by Renwick, has a reredos adorned with statues of St. Patrick and other saints. Its treatment lacks the imagination of the work of later neo-Gothic architects such as Cram and Goodhue; and the white marble of which it is constructed contrasts too sharply with the mellow texture of the semicircular apse. The Archbishop's throne, on the north side of the choir, is of carved French oak, overhung by a delicate Gothic canopy, supported by columns, and crowned by a richly ornamented octagonal lantern. The white marble pulpit, on the south side, is another work of art from the hand of Renwick; from a stem of short, clustered columns, it expands cupshape and hexagonal in form, and is overhung by a petal-like canopy of chastely decorated translucent marble.

Behind the apse is the Lady Chapel of white Vermont marble—more pleasing than the granite of the cathedral proper—and adjoining it are two smaller chapels. These were designed by Charles T. Mathews. The first mass in Lady Chapel was said on Christmas Day, 1906.

The residences of the archbishop and rector are, respectively, at the northwest and southwest corners of Madison Avenue and Fiftieth Street. On the block north of the cathedral, on Madison Avenue, is a building housing Cathedral College, and other Catholic societies. On the northeast corner of Fifty-first Street and Madison Avenue is the chancery, a large stone structure.

The present church is an outgrowth of the first St. Patrick's Cathedral, founded in 1809. Rebuilt after a fire in 1866, the latter still stands at Mott and Prince Streets. Its founder, the Very Reverend Anthony Kohlmann, Vicar General of the New York See, was the head of the New York Literary Institute, a Jesuit establishment on the present site of the cathedral, where later, in 1842, was erected the little Church of St. John the Evangelist. In 1852, however, the trustees of St. Patrick's Cathedral acquired the property; and razing of the smaller building was soon begun to make way for the great edifice.

Once an outpost of the town, St. Patrick's is today in the crowded heart of the city; once a landmark visible for miles, its spires now are surrounded by the loftier towers of secular buildings. Nevertheless, through the years, the cathedral takes on greater significance for the large Catholic population of the metropolis. During the regularly scheduled services, the rich formality of historic Catholic ritual fills the dim spaces with music and intoned prayer, but on such occasions as the celebration of Mass on Christmas Eve and Easter, and the great parade on March 17, in honor of St. Patrick himself, the ceremonial splendor of a pageant is invoked. On other days societies organized under the cathedral's direct supervision—Catholic organizations of every sort, many of them groups organized within secular institutions of business and the professions—meet in tribute to the patron saint or day especially sacred to them. To grasp the magnitude of the cathedral's influence in the city, it needs only to be realized that the Roman Catholics of the archdiocese number one million.

MUSEUM OF MODERN ART

11 W. 53d St.   IRT Broadway-7th Ave. subway (local) to 50th St.; or 8th Ave.
(Independent) Queens subway to 5th Ave. (53d St.); or 5th Ave. bus to 52d St.
Hours: weekdays 10 A.M. to 6 P.M., Sunday 12 to 6 P.M. Admission 25¢; free on
Monday.

The Museum of Modern Art is New York's permanent meeting place
for the contemporary artistic energies of Europe and America. About a
mile and a half uptown, the Metropolitan Museum of Art sedately displays
its accumulated masterpieces of the past, but here, amid brownstone fronts
and small sidewalk trees, the strikingly modern building of the Museum of
Modern Art has become a symbol of those technical and imaginative innovations that have transformed the character of art during the past seventy
years.

Before the establishment of the museum the more advanced forms of
modern art had made their appearance in the famous "Armory Show" of
1913, in Alfred Stieglitz' "291 Fifth Avenue" and in the exhibitions of
the *Société Anonyme*. These showings, with occasional purchases, infrequent exhibitions, and such private collections as that of John Quinn, had
given New Yorkers a hint of the strange aesthetic events taking place here
and across the Atlantic.

Today the Museum of Modern Art sponsors the more important forms
of aesthetic experiment. As a consequence New York has been treated for
the first time in its history to the spectacle of long lines of people waiting
on the street for a chance to look at paintings. The great Van Gogh exhibition of 1935 caused New York journalists suddenly to note that art can
attract as many people as a prize fight.

Founded in 1929 under the sponsorship of a group of prominent collectors, the museum set out to encourage the study and appreciation of
modern art. At that time it still remained to be seen whether there existed
enough public interest in the newer art to justify the eventual establishment
of a permanent institution of exhibition and education.

To carry out its purpose more effectively, the museum decided at the
start to renounce the conventional policy of a single permanent exhibition
occasionally increased by acquisitions or loans. Contact with new aesthetic
movements could be maintained only if works were kept constantly passing through the museum. Modern art also had to be presented in such a
way that its implications and antecedents would be clarified.

The manner in which this program has been accomplished may be illustrated by the retrospective exhibition of abstract and cubist art. Three hundred and eighty-three pieces were assembled from all available sources. Together with abstract art of the last twenty-five years, examples of primitive sculpture (which served as a source for modernist treatment) as well as such European antecedents as Cézanne, Rousseau, and Seurat were also shown. To complete the setting, the exhibition indicated certain social uses and influences of abstract art by including reproductions of architectural designs, interior decoration, typography, commercial art, films, and other practical applications of the style. Thus, one exhibition became virtually a study course in one of the principal phases of modern art.

In the course of its ten years' history (1939) the museum has shown eighty-five exhibitions in New York to more than one and a half million visitors. Some, such as the exhibition of Cubism and Abstract Art just described, or The American Film 1895-1937, have been carefully historical; others have presented a particular problem, such as book illustration, mural painting, design for college architecture, or art for subways; and still others have included large groups of paintings by important masters of the recent past, among them the French painters Cézanne, Corot, and Daumier, and the Americans, Winslow Homer, Thomas Eakins, Albert P. Ryder. One-man shows of living artists have included paintings by Henri Matisse, Diego Rivera, Edward Hopper, and John Marin; sculpture by Lachaise, prints by Rouault, architecture by Le Corbusier and Aalto, photographs by Walker Evans. Other exhibitions have emphasized national achievement, for instance, German Painting and Sculpture (1931), Modern English Architecture, Murals by American Painters and Photographers, New Horizons in American Art (the WPA Federal Art Project).

Sources that have stimulated the modern imagination, such as Paleolithic cave paintings, African Negro sculpture, Aztec, Incan, and Mayan art, and even the art of children and the psychopathic have also been placed on view. American folk art, for example, produced between 1750 and 1900 by artists unheralded and unsung in fine art circles, was set before the modern eye because this naïve and serious work bears a stylistic affiliation with certain phases of living contemporary art.

About half the museum's exhibitions have been sent on tour to more than three hundred different institutions. The Van Gogh show for instance was seen not only by 142,000 New Yorkers but also by 800,000 other Americans in museums as far west as San Francisco and as far north as Toronto. It is chiefly because of its circulating exhibitions and its excellent publications that the museum may be considered a national institution.

Many of the museum's exhibitions are fed from the permanent collection as well as by loans from all parts of the world. Because of lack of space prior to the erection of the present building the permanent collection has never been shown in its entirety; the museum, however, plans to exhibit the most important objects in this collection. Its nucleus is the Lillie P. Bliss Bequest of 235 works, together with the gift of 181 items from Mrs. John D. Rockefeller, Jr. These are constantly augmented by acquisitions of European and American paintings and sculpture. The collection already possesses excellent examples of work by the best of the moderns and their immediate forerunners. Cézanne, Degas, Gauguin, Redon, Henri Rousseau, Seurat, and Daumier are represented by a rich collection containing several acknowledged masterpieces. More recent painters and sculptors include the Europeans, Picasso, Derain, Matisse, Braque, Modigliani, Segonzac, Maillol, Despiau, Brancusi, Dufy, and Dali, and the Americans, Hopper, Karfiol, Walkowitz, Gropper, Burchfield, Marin, Benton, Epstein, Lachaise, and Calder.

It has been a policy of the museum not to confine its interest to painting and sculpture but to include in its program almost all the living visual arts. Photography and the theater arts have been presented in large exhibitions and will probably be established as integral divisions of the museum's work. Already there are permanent museum departments devoted to architecture, industrial design, and motion pictures.

The Department of Architecture and Industrial Art was founded in 1932, following the controversial exhibition of modern architecture, which helped to popularize the International Style developed by Walter Gropius, Le Corbusier, Mies van der Rohe, and J. J. P. Oud. The department has also emphasized the pioneer work of the Americans, Henry Hobson Richardson, Louis Sullivan, and Frank Lloyd Wright. In 1934 the Machine Art Exhibition inaugurated the department's work in industrial and commercial design, which now includes furniture and utensils, typography and posters. The department works through competitions as well as publications and exhibitions.

The Museum of Modern Art Film Library, founded in 1935 principally with a grant from the Rockefeller Foundation, comprises a collection of motion picture films marking distinct stages in the development of the cinema. Its scope includes the earliest motion picture, such historic American productions as Griffith's *Intolerance* and Cruze's *Covered Wagon,* the Keystone comedies, the early Mary Pickford and Charlie Chaplin pictures, together with such German experiments as the *Last Laugh,* the work of the Russians Eisenstein and Pudovkin and of the surrealist *fantaisistes.* Film programs, to which members of the museum are admitted free of charge, are presented each season and have been distributed to scores of educational institutions throughout the country. The film library maintains active research and information services and presents each year in conjunction with Columbia University a course in the history and technique of the motion picture.

The museum regularly conducts a number of other activities. Modern art committees have been established in thirty cities. Museum publications, issued at reasonable prices, supplement and perpetuate the current exhibitions. A bulletin is issued six times yearly. The museum also houses a fine working library of more than three thousand volumes on modern art, periodicals, and photographs; and a lending collection of slides, photographs, and half-tone cuts for printing service. Lectures on a variety of subjects are also included in the museum's service.

The museum building, five stories above ground with a theater below, is constructed of reinforced concrete and steel with contrasting surfaces of veined marble, glass brick, blue glazed tile, and plate glass. Its interior affords rich but simple settings for the display of art. The museum is planned as part of a design that includes the Rockefeller Apartments to the north, and Rockefeller Center (see page 333) to the south. Eventually, the southern façade with its strong horizontal lines will terminate a plaza leading from the Center. The rear façade forms one side of a garden court of the apartment house; its setbacks were designed to allow sunlight to enter the garden.

CENTRAL PARK

Boundaries: 5th Ave. to Central Park West; Central Park South (59th St.) to Cathedral Parkway (110th St.). IRT Broadway-7th Ave. subway (local) to Columbus Circle (59th St.); or 8th Ave. (Independent) Washington Heights or Grand Concourse subway (local), 59th to 110th St. stations; or BMT subway (local) to 5th Ave. (59th St.); or 9th Ave. el, 66th to 110th St. stations; or 5th or 8th Ave. bus, 59th to 110th St. Map on page 277.

From the upper floors of an apartment hotel on its southern border Central Park appears as a vast irregular terrain marked by outcropping rock formations, wooded areas, and many bodies of water. Deep green marks it, summer and spring, and fall brings to it a variety of color that changes day by day. The park is enclosed by stone walls, with entrance gates at frequent intervals. It has two longitudinal boulevards, East Drive and West Drive, and four transverses depressed below the park's level— East Sixty-fifth to West Sixty-sixth, East Seventy-ninth to West Eighty-first, East Eighty-fifth to West Eighty-sixth, and Ninety-seventh Street east to west. Intersecting roads for motor traffic, thirty-two miles of winding footpaths, and a four-mile bridle path make up an informal pattern. An 840-acre tract, two and one-half miles long and a half mile wide, Central Park extends from the solid border of hotels and apartment buildings of West Fifty-ninth Street to Harlem at 110th.

The park's setting is the result of more than eighty years of planning and effort. The purchase of the land in 1856 was preceded by ten years' agitation by the press and by such public-minded citizens as Washington Irving, George Bancroft, and William Cullen Bryant, who became members of the first Park Board. The section was then on the outskirts of the city, and scrubby trees and outcropping rock formations marked the land which barely afforded pasturage for the gaunt pigs and goats of impoverished squatters. Egbert L. Viele was commissioned to make a topographical survey. His difficulties consisted not only in problems arising from the irregularity of the terrain, but in the opposition of the squatters, who saw in his visit the threat of eviction; it is believed that Viele's first attempt was abruptly terminated when the squatters ejected him bodily.

The park was designed by Frederick Law Olmsted and Calvert Vaux, and their general plan has since been followed. Construction began as a relief project under the stress of the panic and depression of 1857. Changes and improvement have been made in the design through the years; yet it may safely be claimed that under Park Commissioner Moses, of the La-Guardia municipal administration, the park achieved the appearance of a place more carefully tended than at any time in its history. Besides widespread renovation there has been an unprecedented development of new facilities, most of this the work of such agencies as the Civil Works Administration and the Works Progress Administration.

There are entrances to the park convenient to subways, to residential neighborhoods, and to the museums that were originally part of the park plan. The Merchant's Gate at Columbus Circle is often used by visitors who wish easy access to the Heckscher playground—a venture in which philanthropy and the Works Progress Administration have combined to provide for the recreational needs of children. The playground's facilities include a wading pool and a drinking fountain, with sculpture by F. G. Roth showing "Alice in Wonderland" and the "Duchess." From a hillside just beyond comes the familiar music of the Carousel. A round stone terrace on a hilltop is all that is left of the Kinderberg—an arbor where children played before such recreational developments as the Heckscher playground existed.

The Green, also accessible from the Merchant's Gate, holds the Tavern-on-the-Green, erected in 1870 to house a flock of Southdown sheep. The building was converted into a restaurant in 1934. A flagstone terrace, dotted in summer with gaily colored umbrellas, looks out upon West Drive.

Since 1903 Augustus Saint-Gaudens' equestrian statue of General William T. Sherman has marked the Plaza entrance (Fifth Avenue and Fifty-ninth Street) to Central Park, although horse-drawn hacks and Karl Bitter's *Abundance,* a nude female figure whose gold leaf has been recently renewed, are also identified with this corner. The surrounding architecture has been photographed so often that few visitors fail to recognize the dignified mansard of the Plaza Hotel and the terraced setbacks of the new apartment hotels, towering above the formal arrangement of the Plaza entrance itself, and reflected in the Pond at the park's southeastern corner.

At the entrance to the first walk is Gustave Blaeser's bust of the scientist, F. H. Alexander von Humboldt. It was unveiled in 1869, the park's second sculpture acquisition, the first having been the bronze *Tigress and Cubs* which stands near the colored umbrellas of the Zoo cafeteria.

The Plaza entrance, the one most often used, offers a direct course to the Mall, following East Drive, and a visit to the Pond where wild fowl, pelicans, and swans decorate the natural lagoons. A third and popular route is a path, between East Drive and the Fifth Avenue wall, that leads to the Zoo, past the dirt track where children may ride on Shetland ponies. Zoo buildings line the approach to the neat brick structures of the quadrangle designed by Aymar Embury II, architect for the Triborough Bridge and the Henry Hudson Bridge. *(Zoo open daily 11 a.m. to 5 p.m.; admission free.)* Outdoor cages and the sea lion pool occupy the inner court. Zoo buildings surround it on three sides; the cafeteria and pavilion take up the west side of the court. The new Zoo is in striking contrast to the former grimy buildings, where the iron bars of the cages were so rusted that the keepers carried guns for self protection. The Arsenal, at the Fifth Avenue side of the quadrangle, is an example of Gothic Revival architecture striving with its octagonal turrets for a medieval effect. It was built as a state arsenal in 1848 and has since served as the first home of the American Museum of Natural History, a weather bureau, and a police precinct; today it is the headquarters for the city Park Department.

An underpass next to the Primates house veers leftward to the Mall. At an intersection close to East Drive is the bronze figure by F. G. Roth of the Alaskan dog, Balto, and a bas-relief of Balto as the lead dog of a team of seven "huskies." The sculpture bears the inscription, "Dedicated to the spirit of the sled dogs that relayed antitoxin over six hundred miles of rough ice, across treacherous waters, through Arctic blizzards, from Nenana to the relief of stricken Nome in the winter of 1925."

The Mall cuts a diagonal line across the park's rectangle, pointing due north across the Lake towards the Belvedere Tower, purposely kept small in order to increase, by forced perspective, the illusion of distance. The Mall was intended by Olmsted and Vaux as a grand promenade. At the entrance to the wide walk lined with trees are bronze sculptures of Columbus, Shakespeare, Robert Burns, and Sir Walter Scott. In the gas-light era this was a playground for children; for a dime they could ride the length of the Mall in barouches drawn by teams of goats.

At the north end of the Mall is the Concert Ground where popular programs of classical music are given by Edwin Franko Goldman's band and by WPA orchestras. Across the ground from the orchestra shell Henry Baerer's huge bust of Ludwig van Beethoven broods over a female figure, representing the spirit of music, that rises from the foot of the pedestal. On summer evenings dances are held here against the background of lights and electric signs along the park's southern border.

During the day parts of the near-by roadways are roped off for cycling and roller skating, while east from the orchestra shell, on the site of the Casino, whose high prices were something of a scandal a few years back, is the Rumsey playground for children. On the concert ground itself performances of folk dancing and similar exhibitions are held.

The northern end of the Mall terminates in a balustrade. Broad steps lead through an arched underpass down to a brick terrace that extends to the Lake. In the center of the Terrace is Bethesda Fountain, the only piece of statuary arranged for in the original plans. Like the ornamented pilasters and balustrades of the stairways and the arcade, the bronze Bethesda, wings outspread, was executed by Emma Stebbins after the design by architect J. Wrey Mould. Worn stone, gurgling fountain, and the wooded hillside of the Ramble across the Lake succeed more than any other spot in the park in fulfilling the intent of Olmsted to take the city dweller out of his urban surroundings. The sound of oars in their locks, the flapping wings of waterfowl blend with the cries of children across the Lake and the Ramble, the latter deep with autumn, heavy with winter's snow, or yellow-green with another spring.

Left from the terrace a path explores the hilly area of the Ramble through deep gorges and past banks of rhododendrons and azaleas. Another path leads right, to the house, where flatbottom boats are for rent at a moderate fee. Conservatory Pond, a pool of formal design where toy yacht regattas are held, may be reached by an underpass near the boat-house.

Continuing northwestward by the Lake and the Ramble—a country sense of direction is of value in a large park with few signs—a rocky ledge and a series of stone steps lead to the Belvedere, where a U.S. Government Weather Bureau is maintained. The building resembles a miniature old castle, but its tower contains the modern scientific instruments used in predicting the weather; in winter it extends its field of applied science, flying a banner with a red ball when the ice on New Lake, just to the north, is safe for skating. A bronze tablet to Dr. Daniel W. Draper, who established the first Meteorological Observatory in Central Park in 1868, is fixed to the wall of the tower.

Belvedere Terrace, cut from Vista rock, looks out upon the area between the Belvedere and the Receiving Reservoir. In the immediate foreground is New Lake, and beyond it the oval expanse of the Great Lawn. The pages of Robert Nathan's novel, *One More Spring,* recall one of the most bitter years of the park's history, when the bowl of the drained reservoir was used as a refuge by victims of the depression. After the hovels had been removed the area was landscaped and the reservoir basin filled in.

To the left is the Shakespeare Garden, with an oak from Stratford on Avon and flowers and small shrubs mentioned in the work of the poet; and, close by, the replica of a nineteenth-century Swedish schoolhouse, brought to the Philadelphia Exposition in 1876. Northwestward also is Summit Rock, crowned by Mrs. Sally Farnum's equestrian statue of Simon Bolivar, Venezuelan liberator. A network of paths on the left leads to these points and to the Lower Reservoir playground, the central Promenade between the Great Lawn and the Receiving Reservoir, and the play area to the right which includes a roller-skating rink.

To the right from the terrace across the green oval of the Lawn are the buildings of the Metropolitan Museum of Art *(see page 368),* and the Obelisk, quarried by Thothmes III in 1600 B.C. and brought to this country in 1880 with much difficulty: unloaded at Staten Island it was towed on pontoons up the Hudson to Ninety-sixth Street and then in a great cradle it was rolled on cannon balls to the "worst place within the city for getting an obelisk to." The path that leads over billowing landscape to the neighborhood of the museum is the best approach to the Obelisk's two hundred tons of granite, whose hieroglyphics tell of Thothmes III, Rameses II, and Osarkon I. In 500 B.C. Cambyses, the Persian, overturned the monument, and in 12 B.C. Romans brought the shaft to Alexandria, and placed it before a temple. Although it is widely known as

Cleopatra's Needle, the obelisk has no known historical connection with Cleopatra.

The original wing of the Metropolitan Museum of Art, red brick and steep mansard, forms a background for the Obelisk and is surrounded on three sides by the classical stone structures of the later additions. Northwest of the museum grounds is a granite statue of youthful Alexander Hamilton, completed by Carl Conrads in 1880.

The Receiving Reservoir, raised above the general level of the park, extends from Fifth Avenue to Central Park West, is encircled by a cinder path and a bridle path, and is flanked east and west by motor roadways and asphalt walks. The many recreational facilities located north of the reservoir include the South Meadow tennis courts, the North Meadow baseball diamonds, and toward the northwest corner beyond the Pool and the Loch, a play area similar to the one immediately below the reservoir. More open than the neighborhood of the Lake and the Ramble, the north section boasts small rugged sections and rolling landscapes.

Between Conservatory Garden, with its beds of hardy American flowers and rows of crab apple trees, and Harlem Mere, where rowboats are also available, is a Memorial Bench honoring Andrew Haswell Green, "directing genius of Central Park in its formative period." The bench also marks the site of "Widow McGown's Tavern," built 1746 in McGown's Pass. The site was for some time referred to as Mount St. Vincent after the Sisters of Charity of St. Vincent de Paul, whose convent was located here in the middle of the last century. Soldiers of the Colonial Army retreated through McGown's Pass September 15, 1776. Subsequently the British occupied and built breastworks along the northern ridge of the present park, evacuating them November 21, 1783.

Other relics in this section date from the War of 1812. Fort Clinton, named for Mayor DeWitt Clinton, is commemorated by a mortar, cannon, and tablet. It formed a series of defenses with Fort Fish, named for Nicholas Fish; Nutter's Battery; and Blockhouse No. 1, the only building still standing. The Blockhouse is located on the rugged crest of a hill, south of the entrance to the park at Seventh Avenue and Cathedral Parkway.

The visitor to Central Park will find about him innumerable features that elude detailed description: the bird sanctuaries near the Plaza entrance, the Ramble, the Harlem Mere, the arbors shaded with wistaria, and the sloping paths and sudden corners where the noise of the city has been put away for the casual gurgle of a brook. Besides the statues already mentioned there are Karl Illava's World War Memorial to the Seventh

Regiment at the east wall north of the Arsenal; J. Q. A. Ward's Civil War Monument to the Seventh Regiment, north of the Tavern-on-the-Green and facing West Drive; the statues to Schiller, Webster, Morse, Mazzini, and Thomas Moore; the *Indian Hunter;* the *Eagles;* the *Falconer;* and the Romanesque statue of Commerce that since 1864 has lingered near the Merchant's Gate for which it was originally intended. Sight and sound mingle in the inventory of a day in the park, gulls wheeling above the reservoir, the whir of motors on the Drive and the backs of couples walking arm in arm toward the subway.

Lakes and roadways today follow much the pattern laid out for them in the Greensward plan. Except for the substitution of the oval curve of the Great Lawn for the rectangle of the old reservoir, the significant changes in the park have come about through the addition of recreational areas, varying from the children's playgrounds bordering the park to roller-skating tracks and horseshoe pitching courts used for championship matches. This adaptation of the park to planned recreation emphasizes its traditional purpose, to serve the needs of an urban population. Such acts of political vandalism as that practiced by the Tweed Ring—which allowed park trees to be cut down because they impeded the view from Fifth Avenue mansions—have kept in the public consciousness the importance of protecting its original function, which Olmsted emphasized in his pamphlet, *Spoils of the Park.*

There is one tablet that might well be added to the sculptural inventory, a bronze replica of the Greensward plan with a quotation from Frederick Law Olmsted. It should be placed near the Plaza entrance, where it could rub elbows with Humboldt. Before going to the Zoo or taking the sloping walk to the Pond to photograph the most photographed pelicans of Manhattan the visitor should read:

"It is of great importance as the first real park made in this country—a democratic development of the highest significance and on the success of which, in my opinion, much of the progress of art and aesthetic culture in this country is dependent."

TEMPLE EMANU-EL

5th Ave. and 65th St. IRT Lexington Ave. subway (local) to 68th St.; or 5th, Madison, or Lexington Ave. bus to 64th St.   Guide service available at 1 East 65th St.

Congregation Emanu-El, the oldest Reformed synagogue in New York City, was founded in 1845 by German Jews who had rejected many of the traditional forms and tenets of Orthodox Judaism. In 1927 the congregation merged with Congregation Beth-El, a Reformed group established in 1874, and two years later moved from its house of worship at Seventy-sixth Street and Fifth Avenue to the present temple. It has at present (1939) 1,600 members, among whom are many of the leading Jewish families in America.

Temple Emanu-El, one of the most impressive houses of worship in New York, is reputed to be the largest synagogue built in modern times. It is a group of three buildings: the temple proper, facing Fifth Avenue, Beth-El Chapel adjoining the temple on the north, and the community house with its 185-foot tower rising inconspicuously on Sixty-fifth Street behind these. In the temple façade, the keynote of the entire design is apparent: large, plain surfaces offset by areas of rich, concentrated decoration. Recessed within a high arch is a great rose window, with a row of lancets above and below. Beneath these are three bronze doors ornamented with Hebrew symbols and rosettes. The exterior of the little chapel is noteworthy for the fineness of its proportions. The Sixty-fifth Street façade, owing to the imperfect correlation of the temple, the community house, and tower, is not as satisfying as the Fifth Avenue front. The group, completed in 1929 at a cost of more than three million dollars, is a modern adaptation of early Romanesque architecture as it was used in Syria and the East. The exterior walls, of limestone, are self-supporting; only the roof is supported by a steel skeleton frame. The decoration of the beautifully colored interior shows a strong Byzantine influence. Robert D. Kohn, Charles Butler, and Clarence Stein were the architects for the entire group; the firm of Mayers, Murray and Phillip, the consultants.

The auditorium, which consists of a single nave, is 77 feet wide, 150 feet long, and 103 feet high, and can seat more than two thousand worshipers. The great arch of the façade is duplicated in the interior over the west gallery and again over the sanctuary. Along the north and south galleries it is recalled by five smaller arches over which are groups of clerestory windows in brilliant, well-chosen colors. The plain walls are covered with buff acoustic tile that shades to darker tones toward the dimly lighted ceiling where the exposed roof trusses and the plaster are decorated in reds, greens, blues, and gold. The lighting is from concealed sources, so arranged that, while adequate light illuminates the floor, the strongest is on the sanctuary.

The sanctuary is raised three feet above the temple floor, under a splayed arch of colored glass mosaic designed by Hildreth Meiere. The stained-glass windows of the main nave, west rose window, and chapels are the work of Montague Castle, Nicolo d'Ascenzo, Owen Bonaurt, Powell of London, J. Gordon Guthrie, and Oliver Smith. The marble columns of the Ark vary in color from deep purple to orange, and through the pierced bronze Ark doors can be seen the red velvet coverings of the Scrolls of the Law. The lamp for the perpetual light, hanging from the top of the Ark, is bronze, as are the Menorah candlesticks.

On high holidays, when the attendance is approximately tripled, loud speakers enable worshipers in the chapel, basement banquet hall, and community house assembly room to participate in the temple services, which are in English. The temple occupies a leading place in Reformed Judaism.

THE AMERICAN MUSEUM OF NATURAL HISTORY: HAYDEN PLANETARIUM

Central Park West, 77th to 81st St. IRT Broadway-7th Ave. subway (local) to 79th St.; or 8th Ave. (Independent) Grand Concourse or Washington Heights subway (local) to 81st St.; or 9th Ave. el to 81st St.; or 8th Ave. bus to 79th or 81st St.
Museum. Main entrance on Central Park West and. 79th St. Hours: weekdays 10 A.M. to 5 P.M., Sunday and holidays 1 to 5 P.M. Admission free. Restaurant on second floor, cafeteria in basement; closed Sunday.
Planetarium. Main entrance on 81st St. Performances: Monday to Friday at 2, 3:30, and 8:30 P.M.; Saturday at 11 A.M. and 1, 2, 3, 4, 5, and 8:30 P.M.; Sunday and holidays at 2, 3, 4, 5, and 8:30 P.M. Admission: adults 25¢ and 50¢ matinees, 35¢ and 60¢ evenings; children 15¢ at all times.

Besides being one of the world's largest institutions devoted to natural science exhibits, the American Museum of Natural History is also a research laboratory, a school for advanced study, a publishing house for scientific manuscripts, and a sponsoring agency of field exploration expeditions.

The incorporation of the museum in 1869 was an expression of the surge of interest in natural science stimulated by great advances, such as the use of the spectroscope, Mendel's law of heredity, Darwin's theory of evolution, the law of the conservation of energy, and the identification of light as an electromagnetic phenomenon. Its first collections were housed in the old Arsenal building in Central Park. The cornerstone of the first among the present structures was laid in 1874 by President Grant, and the museum was formally opened by President Hayes in 1877. Since then, new buildings for exhibition and study have been added, including the Theodore Roosevelt Memorial and the Hayden Planetarium; the occupation of the whole area of Manhattan Square, between Seventy-seventh and Eighty-first Streets, from Central Park West to Columbus Avenue, is projected.

From the beginning noted scientists, educators, and civic leaders have been associated with the museum. Among them are Professor Albert S. Bickmore, who in 1880 was largely responsible for the inauguration of a system of popular education in conjunction with the schools of the city; Morris K. Jesup, philanthropist, who was president of the institution for more than a quarter of a century; Henry Fairfield Osborn, paleontologist and geologist, who was also its president for many years; and the present director, Dr. Roy Chapman Andrews, naturalist and explorer.

Founded by subscriptions from private individuals, the museum has been supported by additional bequests, income from endowments, sale of corporate stock, and a membership fund, as well as by contributions from the city. It is governed by a self-perpetuating board of thirty-five trustees, with the mayor, comptroller, and park commissioner as ex-officio members. It employs a staff of 554. In 1936, more than 250 WPA workers were added to various departments, indicating the scope of the museum's work and its needs.

The museum's architecture is unhappily marred by a gross disparity of styles. The first building, facing Seventy-seventh Street, designed by J. C. Cady and Company, is a good example of the robust use of stone as structural material, a use developed by Richardson and his followers in the years before the Chicago Fair of 1893. The entrance on this side is vigorously indicated by the expressive massing of the dark salmon granite masonry and by a great monumental carriage-way. It leads directly into the older Memorial Hall with its busts of early American scientists and temporary exhibits. Later wing additions by Trowbridge and Livingston are in general conformity with the older part, but flatter and less positive in treatment.

The Roosevelt Memorial building facing Central Park West, completed in 1936 from designs by John Russell Pope, has, however, occasioned much adverse comment for its lack of relation to the adjoining structure and its pretentious Roman style. Nor have the murals in the high-ceilinged Memorial Hall on the second floor, by William A. Mackay, been too well received, the general impression being that their design is weak, and that the depiction of incidents from the life of Theodore Roosevelt lacks imagination.

On the other hand, the Hayden Planetarium, which is connected by a corridor with the Roosevelt Memorial, is among the most interesting examples of modern functional architecture. The architects were Trowbridge and Livingston. Particularly notable is the imaginative design of the Hall of the Sun, on the first floor, where form, light, and color have been ably handled.

Akeley Memorial Hall

The most spectacular exhibit, perhaps, is that in the Akeley Memorial Hall of African Mammals, entered from Roosevelt Memorial Hall. It illustrates an interesting exhibition technique—the use of life-like habitat groups in place of mounted single figures. Few exhibits match the wild-life drama presented in this hall.

Animals, settings—plains, jungles, and mountains—the weather, the day and night of Africa are recreated not only with objective accuracy but with imaginative insight. The lion, gorilla, antelope, buffalo, giraffe, rhinoceros, wild dog, boar, and many other creatures are represented in characteristi actions that give an amazing impression of vitality and reveal something of their mental nature. The vegetation is excellently simulated; in some cases actual rocks and bushes have been brought from the place repre-sented. Paintings in perspective and curved skies give the illusion that the landscape extends into the far distance. Large-scale maps of Africa may also be studied here; and there are sculptures, by Malvina Hoffman, of native human types.

Mammals

South Asiatic mammals, chiefly from the Indian peninsula, are exhibited in Vernay-Faunthorpe Hall, second floor, east wing, to the left of Roose-velt Hall. Two large elephants stand in the center of the hall. Large and small game, tigers, deer, leopard, and gibbon are shown amid their native fields and forests. A new hall of North Asiatic mammals, featuring the Siberian tiger, the Marco Polo sheep, and the giant panda will adjoin this exhibit (1939).

North American mammals are at present displayed in Allen Hall, second floor, southeast wing. Many of these have been given naturalistic settings as in Akeley Hall, notably a group of timber wolves on the trail of deer, and a scene showing beavers at work. On the first floor of the African wing, a new hall is at present under construction (1939), which may be entered from New York Hall, the first floor of the Roosevelt Memorial building. In the New York Hall are four large habitat groups, the Dutch-Indian, Roosevelt Ranch, Conservation of Wild Life in the Adirondacks, and Bird Sanctuary.

The phylogenetic interrelationship of the highest order of mammals is presented in the Hall of Primates, third floor, south pavilion. Here are shown all the types from lemur to man in characteristic surroundings, posture, and activities. A series of skeletons permits a comparative study of structural changes in the process of man's evolution. There is also an excellent collection of wild animal photographs.

The presentation of the synoptic series of mammals, which adjoins the Hall of Primates, leads still deeper into the background of the evolutionary process. Here mammals have been arranged in the order of their development from the egg-laying platypus (the duckbill) to man. Especially emphasized is the fact that the internal structure, not the external appearance determines the position of an animal in the line of evolution. A family tree of the orders of animal life from which mammals stem is also shown. A life-size model of a sulphur-bottom whale, the world's largest mammal, hangs from the ceiling (this particular one is seventy-six feet long). There is also the skeleton of Jumbo, the largest elephant ever brought to this country, presented to the museum by Phineas T. Barnum, the circus promoter.

Darwin Hall of Evolution

A basic exhibit of evolutionary processes is in the Darwin Hall of Evolution, first floor, south pavilion. Devoted chiefly to the orders of invertebrates, animals without backbone, it is arranged to illustrate developments in structure and function from the lowest form of animal life, the single-celled protozoa, through the plant-like sponges and polyps; flatworms and roundworms; exquisite rotifers; sea mats and lamp shells; the sea stars; the ringed worms; arthropods, crustaceans, and insects; mollusks, to the first chordates, or animals with a central nervous system. There are synoptic charts, family trees, and wax and glass models many times magnified, of the inhabitants of the invisible society so vital to our existence. Even more picturesque are reproductions of animal and plant groups, one enlarged one hundred diameters, or cubically a million times, in their characteristic rocky sea cave, wharf pile, tide pool, bay bottom, and pond homes.

Other exhibits in the hall illustrate laws of natural science discovered by Darwin and other biologists Specimens of dogs, pigeons, and fowl show the variation under domestication; a collection of mollusks illustrates color variation; while the coat-color of a family of rats presents the simpler features of Mendel's law of heredity.

Aquatic Life

The Hall of Fishes on the first floor, east wing, with its models and mounted specimens, is a chart of evolution undersea. Lowly "cartilage fishes" such as sharks and rays are succeeded by those of a higher, vertebrate structure. Here also are the terrible hags and blood-sucking lampreys, skates and electric rays, fishes with lungs and flappers, and a multitude of finned creatures whose brilliant colors rival those of birds. In a darkened inner room is a startling reproduction of a habitat, where deep-sea fishes gleam with their own light under tons of water. The hall also exhibits fresh-water fish.

Big game fishes, tuna, tarpon, sailfish, swordfish, and devilfish—victims of hook or harpoon—adorn the walls. Some are posed in mid-air, as if leaping out of the water as they try desperately to tear the fatal hook out of their mouths.

Near by, in the southwest court, is the Hall of Ocean Life. Skeletons and models of dolphins, porpoises, and other marine animals are displayed, among them the giant squid, right whale and blackfish, the narwhal and the terrible killer whale, which causes even the great sperm whale to flee in terror. There are habitat groups of seals, manatee, sea lions, and walrus, and a reproduction of a Bahama coral reef, showing sky, land, sea surface, and multitudinous undersea life. The Lindberghs' exploration plane, *Tingmissartoq,* and Dr. Beebe's bathysphere, collections of shells, and large paintings of sperm whaling and undersea life are other temporary features of the hall.

Birds

A hall in the south pavilion on the second floor is devoted to a number of habitat groups showing the birds of the major faunal areas of the world. Scenes of bird life in the American tropics, the Antarctic, the Andean zone, North Temperate and Palaearctic Alpine zone, the Gobi Desert, and other regions are presented with the same dramatic beauty that distinguishes the collections of African and Asiatic mammals.

The general collection of birds is in the near-by Hall of Birds of the World in the south central wing. Suspended overhead is an exhibit of birds in flight: condor, eagle, brown pelicans, asprey, albatross, and ducks and geese in formation. Several cases contain a synoptic arrangement of birds, the 13,000 known species being represented by examples from the principal groups, according to their structural relationships. The other exhibits are grouped in relation to their geographic origin. Specimens of now extinct birds may be seen, such as the passenger pigeon, once bred in North America by the millions, and the dodo, represented by a skeleton and a life-size reproduction copied from an old Dutch painting. There are also collections of birds' eggs and plumage, as well as exhibits dealing with structural adaptation.

North American birds are housed on the third floor, south central wing. The habitat groups were prepared under the immediate direction of Dr. Frank M. Chapman, curator of ornithology, and are masterly evocations of the landscape, flora, and fauna of every region of the continent. Eagles, herons, pelicans, swans, flamingos, grouse, and duck hawks are only a few of the magnificent birds seen in habitat groups either perched on inaccessible icy heights, standing on river banks by the thousands, feeding their young, or sweeping down from the Palisades of the Hudson River to pounce on living prey.

Specimens of local birds, resident and migrant, found within fifty miles of New York City, are in the first floor corridor of the Roosevelt Memorial.

Amphibians and Reptiles

The Hall of Reptile Life is on the third floor, east wing. Habitat groups, including those of Gila monsters, iguanas, giant salamanders, and the common bullfrog, are displayed. Cases contain specimens of alligators, crocodiles, king cobras, and turtles. Various educational exhibits accompany these, dealing with the evolution and habits of amphibians and reptiles, as well as the treatment of snakebite.

Near by, in the southeast pavilion, is the Hall of Insect Life. The biology of these small but powerful creatures, and their benefit and danger to man, are presented by live specimens in habitat groups and in detailed charts and diagrams. A live beehive, made of glass, enables the spectator to observe the activities of domestic honeybees.

Problems relating to insects are further treated in the Hall of Biological Principles and Applied Biology, first floor, west central wing. Exhibits in this hall deal with general questions of food and water supply, sewage disposal, and the relation of insects, rats, and parasites to public health. Models of disease carriers, showing the characteristic conditions for the spread of epidemics, with methods of cure and prevention, form part of this educational display.

On the first floor, southeast wing, is the Hall of the Woods and Forests of North America, containing an almost complete collection of native trees presented by Morris K. Jesup. The numerous members of great tree families such as beech, oak, pine, and palm, are represented by cross sections of the trunk. The accompanying reproductions of the leaf and flower or fruit of each tree were prepared in the museum laboratories.

In the center of the hall is a forty-five-foot remainder of a fossil tree trunk, several million years old. Another exhibit is a cross section of one of the California Big Trees, sixteen feet in diameter, whose seed was planted in 597 A.D.

The Morgan Memorial Hall of Minerals and Gems, fourth floor, southwest wing, contains collections rivaling those of the British Museum and the Jardin des Plantes. The minerals are arranged according to species, and their qualities and use to man are described. The subject of crystallization is introduced by series of structural models. Notable gems are included here, such as the "Star of India," the largest cut sapphire in the world, the De Long star ruby, the Morgenthau blue topaz, and the Vatican cameo, a carved garnet.

In the southwest tower is the Drummond collection of carved Chinese jade and amber, and Japanese ivory, and sword guards.

Anthropological Exhibits

The museum is also noted for the quantity and quality of its ethnological material, particularly that pertaining to the North American Indians. The Indian exhibits are in the south central wing, the north corridor, and in the southwest and western pavilions and wings on the first floor. The nine great Indian culture areas are represented, each with extensive displays of craft work, charts of cultural and tribal distribution and social and political organization, as well as models showing home life in tents, houses, and villages, physical environment, labor, and ceremonies. Exhibits pertaining to the Central and South American Indians are on the second floor, west wing.

From the North Pacific Coast came the many wonderfully carved totem poles, house posts, grave monuments, and masks, works of the highest aesthetic quality, which excite the admiration of modern artists. A great war canoe occupies the center of the hall.

Eskimo life is represented by implements, clothing, decorative carved objects, and a model of a characteristic ice fishing scene.

The Hall of the Indians of the Woodlands is filled with examples of the dome-shaped huts of Long Island, long rectangular Iroquois bark houses, and the conical wigwams of the Ojibways, together with beautiful bead, quill, and textile work.

The Plains Indians, most of whom depended upon hunting for their existence, had implements and decorative motifs closely related to this pursuit. Interesting examples of their picture writing on skins are to be seen.

CATHEDRAL OF ST. JOHN THE DIVINE

MANHATTANVILLE COLLEGE OF THE SACRED HEART

GORILLA GROUP, AMERICAN MUSEUM OF NATURAL HISTORY

ROOSEVELT MEMORIAL, AMERICAN MUSEUM OF NATURAL HISTORY

FORT TRYON PARK

RIVERSIDE DRIVE NORTH OF GEORGE WASHINGTON BRIDGE

THE CLOISTERS, FORT TRYON PARK

SUGAR HILL, HARLEM

HARLEM SLUM

LENOX AVENUE, HARLEM

JUMEL MANSION, WASHINGTON HEIGHTS

The organization of the religious Dance Societies, the famous Sun Dance and other activities and rituals of the plains are dealt with in detail.

The Southwest Indians are represented by collections of the craft work of their three main divisions, the village inhabitants of the Pueblos and the nomad Apache and Navajo. Silver and turquoise work, pottery, woven blankets and baskets, ceremonial costumes, masks, and images are the chief exhibits. Recesses have been built into the walls for group exhibits showing the daily life of the natives. A special exhibit with models of caves and objects fashioned by the Basket Makers is devoted to the prehistoric culture of the Southwest.

The ancient cultures of Mexico and Central America are depicted in the southwest wing, second floor. Examples are displayed of superb sculpture, jewelry, pottery, ideographic writing, and scientific achievements, notably in astronomy.

In the west wing, South American Indian culture is summarized mainly by exhibits from the culture center, Peru, although craft work from Ecuador, Colombia, Venezuela, and Brazil is also displayed. The Peruvians excelled in pottery, metal work, and textiles. Their belief in immortality is manifested in the "mummy bundles," or fabric wrappings around the dead, and in hundreds of beautiful and useful objects placed in graves for the use of the deceased.

Similar anthropological collections in the western sections of the third and fourth floors are devoted to an exposition, with characteristic objects and models of common and ceremonial life, of the cultures of Africa, Asia, the Pacific Islands, New Guinea, the Philippines, and Malaysia. Ivory, bronze, and ironwork of Africa, costumes and implements of the Siberian tribes, Chinese and Japanese handicraft, a cast of one of the huge monolithic images of Easter Island, and masks and weapons of the Malay Peninsula are only a few of the displays which reveal the high development of these peoples.

In the southwest pavilion on the second floor are exhibits of prehistoric arts and industries as developed by European cave and lake dwellers and North American shellmound dwellers and mound builders. Models of caves, reproductions of cave drawings, and objects illustrating the evolution of domestic and hunting implements predominate.

The Hall of the Natural History of Man in the southwest wing, third floor, deals with human anatomy, showing the physical characteristics, development and growth of the races of mankind. The mechanics, anatomical history, genealogy, embryology, and evolution of the skeletal structure, muscular system, nervous system, and brain of man are the subjects of this exhibit. Another section of this hall, not yet completed (1939), will contain material on individual growth and development, racial classification, human genetics, population problems, and the techniques of physical anthropology.

Fossils

Most prized, perhaps, of all the museum's exhibits are the collections of fossil vertebrates in the eastern and southern sections of the fourth floor. Here, taken out of bogs, swamps, long-closed caves, and ancient geologic strata, or released from thousands of years' imprisonment in frozen ground or stone, are the skeletons of animals that lived from 30,000 to 200,000,000 years ago. Their petrified remains help scientists to reconstruct their lives and times.

First come the great Jurassic and Cretaceous reptiles, the dinosaurs, or "terrible lizards," some vegetarian, but the greatest of them, *Tyrannosaurus,* a beast of prey, swift and fierce. The *Brontosaurus* weighed between twenty-five and thirty tons, while *Ankylosaurus* is called "the most ponderous animated citadel the world has ever seen," its head and body being protected by thick plates of bone.

The Hall of Mongolian Vertebrates exhibits fossils obtained by the Central Asiatic expeditions of the museum, among them the dinosaur eggs that created an international sensation when they were found, and a low relief model of the largest of the baluchitheres, ancient cousins of the rhinoceros—this one, seventeen feet nine inches high at the shoulder.

A chart in the Bashford Dean Memorial Exhibit of Fossil Fishes illustrates the development of 500,000,000 years of ocean life. Sharks used to be much larger than they are now, as the nine-foot model of the jaw of the modern man-eater's ancestor demonstrates.

The evolution of the horse is featured in the Osborn Hall of the Age of Mammals. Among other animals of the Tertiary Period are, surprisingly enough, the camels and rhinoceroses of Nebraska. There are also remains of the first mammals as they began to emerge in the preceding period, the Age of Reptiles.

Early man and his contemporaries, mammoths from France and Siberia, mastodons, one from Newburgh, N. Y., and giant South American sloths, are in the Osborn Hall of the Age of Man. Here, too, is a group of skeletons dramatically posed about a model of the renowned *Rancho La Brea,* a California asphalt pit where so many animals of antiquity met their death. Among them an entrapped saber-toothed tiger is shown about to be attacked by a wolf, who thus involuntarily contributed his share to a knowledge of the principles of evolution.

A hall devoted to geology and invertebrate paleontology contains models of caves and mines and of the structural and historical geology of fifteen selected areas within the United States.

Finally, a corridor is devoted to the modern domesticated horse. Skeletons of Shetland ponies and race and draft horses are compared for structural modifications through breeding.

Hayden Planetarium

The Hayden Planetarium, whose equipment was a gift of the philanthropist, Charles Hayden, has an entrance on Eighty-first Street, and forms a separate architectural unit in the group of museum buildings.

In this fine domed building, science and art are brought together. In the Hall of the Sun on the first floor, an overhead Copernican Planetarium, more than forty feet in diameter, shows the relative sizes and speeds of the planets and their satellites by means of globes revolving around a central sun.

The second floor holds the Theater of the Sky where stars of all seasons and of past, present, and future time appear projected on a great hemispherical screen overhead. The performance is preceded by music, and a lecturer operates a control board for the Zeiss projector, a complex instrument for reproducing the light images of all visible stars. During 1935, the first year of the planetarium's existence, more than 700,000 persons came to see their favorite constellations, the heavens as they appeared over Bethlehem at the birth of Christ, or as they will look to future citizens of the world. Monthly programs treat different aspects of astronomy.

In the corridors throughout the building are photographic transparencies showing heavenly phenomena, a number of famous meteors—among them the 36½-ton mass brought by Robert E. Peary from Cape York, Greenland —a reproduction of the Aztec calendar stone, and the chronometers used by renowned aviators.

A course in celestial navigation is given at the planetarium to aviators and navigators in co-operation with New York University and the Weems System of Navigation in Annapolis.

Museum Activities

As someone has observed, a museum is like an iceberg: only one-eighth of it is visible on the surface. This museum is no exception. Neither the vast amount of research and educational work performed by its explorers, technicians, artists, and teachers, nor its influence throughout the world can be estimated by a casual observer. Behind its exhibition halls are hundreds of classrooms, laboratories, editorial offices, libraries, lecture halls, studios, study collections, and files of vital data. And from the museum go explorers educators, astronomers, and geologists to increase man's knowledge of the external world and to help him win victories over his environment.

The fifth floor of the museum is given over to the administrative offices, the scientific departments, and the library. The workrooms are used for the preparation of fossils, models, and other exhibits. The main library contains more than 117,000 volumes. A second library, founded by Henry Fairfield Osborn, is devoted to vertebrate paleontology.

The museum issues technical publications on its researches and expeditions, and on timely discoveries and theoretical questions. Its popular publications include the general guide, school service series, the journals *Natural History* and *Junior Natural History,* guide leaflets on the collections, and a number of handbooks which may be used as textbooks on subjects illustrated by collections in the museum.

Enormous study collections of hundreds of thousands of specimens in all branches of the natural sciences are available to students and research workers. An idea of their extent may be had from the fact that the insect collection alone consists of more than one million specimens; that of fishes, 10,000; of birds, 750,000, the largest in the world; of fossil mammals, 30,000 catalogued, and of fossil invertebrates, 700,000 specimens catalogued. A fully equipped printing plant is constantly employed.

Lastly, and of tremendous importance, are the educational services of the museum in the form of lectures to children in the public and high schools and to students in colleges and universities, classes and guide services, sponsorship of scientific societies, motion-picture and lantern slide services, circulating collections, radio broadcasts, and nature hikes. The number of people affected by these activities reaches in one year the almost incredible number of 43,000,000.

METROPOLITAN MUSEUM OF ART

5th Ave. and 82d St. IRT Lexington Ave. subway to 86th St.; or 5th or Madison Ave. bus to 82d St. Hours: weekdays 10 A.M. to 5 P.M., Sunday 1 to 6 P.M., legal holidays 10 A.M. to 5 P.M., except Christmas (1 to 5 P.M.). Admission: 25¢ Monday and Friday (free if these days are legal holidays); other days free.

The Metropolitan Museum of Art, one of the great museums of the world, contains the most comprehensive collection of art in America. With

the introduction of a policy of active popular education, which has super-
seded the old lifeless method of exhibiting art objects without plan or explanation, its cultural influence has been strengthened in recent years. It
aims to relate its art collections, from pre-history to the present time, to the
civilization of the peoples who produced them. Exhibits and lectures are
arranged so as to show art as a familiar activity of men, arising from their
daily life, and reflecting their ways of eating, drinking, money-making,
fighting, and praying.

The museum was incorporated April 15, 1870, as the result of a movement among leading New York citizens for the foundation of a "national
gallery and museum . . . for the benefit of the people at large." A modest
purchase of 174 Dutch and Flemish paintings, and of the Cesnola group
of Cypriote antiquities, started the collection, which grew rapidly by bequest, gift, and purchase. A permanent building to house the exhibits was
erected by the city of New York in Central Park and opened to the public
on March 30, 1880. Though far from distinguished for architectural unity,
it has come to constitute an interesting record of American adaptation of
classical and contemporary styles. The first architects were Calvert Vaux
and J. Wrey Mould; the only visible remainder of their work is the arcaded
center of the west façade. In 1888, Theodore Weston added the southwest
wing, designed in the neo-Greek manner.

The central Fifth Avenue section was opened in 1902; it was designed
by Richard Morris Hunt and his son, Richard Howland Hunt, in the "Roman" style made popular by the Chicago Fair of 1893. There is a certain
robust quality in this earlier work that is lacking in subsequent additions
by McKim, Mead, and White.

Incorporated in the buildings are remnants of two old New York landmarks. A part of the old Assay Office (built in 1823) is used as a façade
of the American wing, and the delicate terra-cotta pediment of the old
Madison Square Presbyterian Church, by McKim, Mead, and White
(1906), is incorporated in a façade of the museum library.

The city leases the building to the museum, provides equipment and
makes contributions to its maintenance. Enlargement of the collections,
however, is dependent mainly upon individual bequests and gifts from
philanthropic citizens.

Restrictions of space have prevented a more logical arrangement of the
museum's possessions. The objects in the spacious entrance hall symbolize
the varied character of the collections. At the foot of the central staircase
leading to the galleries of paintings, George Gray Barnard's massive white
marble *Struggle of the Two Natures of Man* represents the heroic-romantic

tradition in American sculpture. At either end of the hall, in strong contrast to this figure, are highly formalized classical sculptures from Egypt and Mesopotamia. The walls are hung with seventeenth-century tapestries, which tell the Biblical story of Judith and Holofernes.

The Egyptian Collection

The fifteen rooms housing the Egyptian collection, on the first floor of the north wing, contain a documentary as well as an artistic record of the ancient culture of the Nile valley from prehistoric times to the introduction of Christianity. Tombs of nobles and the figures of gods, in which the religion and metaphysics of Egypt find expression, are surrounded by painted bas-reliefs, wooden funerary models, household and farm implements, and murals illustrating the life of the common people, their tasks, trades, hardships, and pleasures. Outstanding among these is the Mastaba Tomb, erected about 2460 B.C. for Per-nēb, an Egyptian dignitary; the funerary models of Meket-Rē, part of a most important discovery of the museum's excavations in Egypt; and the Carnarvon Collection of gold, alabaster, glass, and faïence objects. The art of Egypt, from its hieratical statuary, whose symbolism is permeated with death-ritual, to the delicate jewelry of its princesses, is shown in its dual character—as the closed domain of a priestly ruling class, and as endowed with intimate human knowledge and love of natural things.

At the south end of the main entrance hall, a *Winged Bull* and *Winged Lion* from the gateways of the palace of the King Ashur-nasir-apal II introduce the Mesopotamian collection. These, as well as the bas-reliefs of mythological figures, warriors—*Cavalrymen Leading Their Horses Through the Mountains*—and of the martial king himself, the famous *Ashur-nasir-apal and His Cupbearer,* characterize the culture of the Assyrians, dominated by tyrannical government and continual warfare. Two *Lions* are in glazed brick, a medium developed to offset the lack of stone on the plains surrounding Babylon. Early Sumerian art is represented by jewelry from the royal tombs at Ur.

In a room in the north wing on the first floor will eventually be shown early Christian, Byzantine, and early Iranian art.

Greek and Roman Art

The Greek and Roman collection, in a series of rooms and a court on the first floor of the south wing, is arranged chronologically, beginning with the culture of Crete (about 3500 B.C.). Besides the sculpture to be found in the long sculpture hall, including an archaic *Apollo* statue, an

Amazon, probably a Roman copy of a work by the renowned Polykleitos, and a figure of Peace, there are painted ceremonial and household cups and vases, bronze and terra-cotta statuettes, bas-reliefs and wall paintings, showing scenes from the mythology and daily life of the ancients. The personal art of the Tanagra terra-cotta figurines and the Greco-Roman frescoes is also unequaled for grace and the acute perception of details of everyday life.

In the same collection are interesting examples of the art and craft of the Etruscans, a hill people of central Italy, who added their own rugged decorative style to the Greek tradition. Among the exhibits are a colossal terra-cotta *Warrior,* a bronze chariot of the sixth century B.C., remarkably preserved, and a huge terra-cotta *Helmeted Head.* A court in the south wing is built in the manner of a Roman peristyle, with a shallow fish pond in the center, surrounded by green lawns and decorated with Roman and late Greek sculptures.

The Cesnola Collection

In the adjoining room, the Cesnola Collection of Cypriote Antiquities, largest in the world, comprises stone sculpture, bronzes, pottery, and miscellaneous objects unearthed in Cyprus during 1865–1871 by the American consul, General Louis P. di Cesnola. It presents with unusual continuity historic phases of this important center of the ancient world during its long development from 3000 B.C. to Roman times. In the course of time, this island off the coast of Asia Minor was visited, settled, or invaded by Egyptians, Assyrians, Persians, Phoenicians, Greeks, and Romans, and its indigenous culture gave way to that of its conquerors. Particularly remarkable are the carved *Sarcophagus,* the *Male Statue,* and *Head of a Woman.* The Roman glassware, whose iridescent coloring, the result of exposure to damp and oxidation in graves, is so fascinating to connoisseurs, is exhibited in an adjoining room. In a gallery devoted to gold objects are a collection of jewelry, including a tomb group with earrings in the form of Ganymede, a plate from a Scythian sword sheath, and a series of Imperial Roman coins.

China, Japan, India, and the Near East

An impression of the inexhaustible variety of Far Eastern art is conveyed by exhibits of Chinese and Japanese painting, sculpture, and pottery, in a series of rooms in the north wing of the second floor and in the balcony above the entrance hall. The examples of Chinese art range from the great bronzes of the Chou dynasty (1122–256 B.C.) through the T'ang period

(618–906 A.D.), renowned for sculpture, the Sung (960–1279), for painting, and the Ming (1368–1644), for pottery. Chinese art results from the representation not so much of nature itself as of a philosophical or religious idea of nature. This is translated with infinite technical patience into the forms of great ceremonial vessels, contemplative stone Buddhas, unsurpassed porcelain ware—in which the Altman Collection, in the south wing, is also extremely rich—and those paintings in which the artist strives to capture the essence even more than the external appearance of mountains, skies, rivers, and animals. The more intimate aspects of Chinese and Japanese art are also shown, from snuff bottles and carved jades, including the Heber R. Bishop Collection, to rugs, textiles, and costumes, as well as the more recent Japanese color prints, whose charm has won for them almost as much popularity in the western world as at home. A small but varied Indian collection in this section includes early Buddhistic stone sculpture and figures showing the influence of Greece.

In the same wing with the Japanese, Chinese, and Indian collections, the decorative genius of the Mohammedan countries is represented by masterpieces from Egypt, Syria, Mesopotamia, Persia, Turkey, Moorish Africa, and Spain, from the seventh century to the nineteenth century. Superb rugs and textiles from Persia, including the gift of James F. Ballard, Turkish ceramics, Syrian lamps and cups, metalwork and woodwork reveal Islam's preoccupation with design above all other elements. In the Cochran Collection there are excellent examples of Persian miniature painting, which, by its drawings, calligraphy, and novel perspective, has been a source of inspiration to many modern painters, chiefly Henri Matisse.

Included with the Near Eastern collections are the domed room from a Jain temple, and jewelry, jade, and textiles from India and Tibet. The Moore Collection of Near and Far Eastern pottery, metalwork, and glass is of special note.

A large collection of casts of outstanding Greek and Roman sculptures is arranged chronologically for the benefit of students. Also included in galleries at the west end of the first floor is a collection of casts of Renaissance sculpture.

European Arms and Armor

The collection of European arms and armor, in the central hall at the west on the first floor and the large hall in the north wing, traces the development of the armorer's craft from the fourteenth century to its decline in the middle of the seventeenth century. The manner in which the complicated engineering problems of weight, balance, flexibility, and tension of materials were met by master craftsmen is an absorbing study. Horse armor is also shown, as well as axes, maces, swords, and, finally, pistols and small cannon, whose offensive strength, exceeding the resistance of the heaviest body armor, brought to a close the armorer's craft. The William H. Riggs and Bashford Dean Collections rank with the great European groups, and together with the Dino and Morosini Collections, present an impressive source of study in this field. Near Eastern items include helmets, chain mail and plate armor, jeweled swords, and firearms. A corresponding Japanese collection, an outstanding feature of which is its decorative quality, covers the feudal era from the twelfth to the nineteenth century.

In the northwest section of the west wing, first floor, the Crosby Brown Collection of Musical Instruments, consisting of more than 3,600 primitive and modern specimens—among them a piano by Bartolomeo di Francesco Cristofori, inventor of the pianoforte—presents the technical evolution and construction of many of our familiar string, reed, brass, and percussion instruments, and provides an introduction to the musical culture of civilized and primitive peoples throughout the world.

The Morgan Collection

The Pierpont Morgan Collection in a two-story extension, north of the west wing, is a priceless accumulation of European decorative arts from the Gallo-Roman and Merovingian periods to the early nineteenth century. Byzantine and medieval goldsmiths, enamelers, and ivory carvers contribute the most precious section of the collection. The work brought together by Georges Hoentschel of Paris is the most comprehensive group, and consists of sculpture, furniture, textiles, woodwork, ivories, and architectural fragments of the Gothic period, and of French decorative arts of the seventeenth and eighteenth centuries—furniture, decorative paintings, and ormolu fittings. Five Gothic tapestries representing the Sacraments, an Entombment, and a Pietà, the woodwork of a Louis XV room, and a shop front from the Quai Bourbon in Paris, snuff boxes, watches, vanities, scent bottles, and dance programs are also in the Morgan Collection.

Outstanding examples of medieval art in rooms near the Morgan Collection include a tapestry representing King Arthur, and three others of ladies and courtiers in a rose garden, holy figures in stone, stained-glass windows, and an embroidered chasuble of fourteenth-century England.

Modern European and American Sculpture

Rodin's assault on the academic tradition of his time is recorded in the section devoted to modern European sculpture, fronting the south entrance. More than twenty of his pieces are shown, including portrait heads and bronze and marble figures, as well as some of Rodin's original models in terra cotta. His return to Grecian and Renaissance models is carried further by Bourdelle and Maillol, whose exhibited work shows great vigor and plastic solidity. There is an interesting ballet figure by the painter Degas.

The modern American sculpture group, in the corridors flanking the main staircase on the first and second floors, is somewhat small. It expresses mainly the two trends of academic sculpture, the neoclassical (symbolic) and the romantic. Contrasting with the work of such sculptors as Manship, MacMonnies, and French are those of William Zorach and of the expatriate, Jacob Epstein, whose heroic figures exercised a powerful influence in making the British public aware of the modern movement in art.

Painting

The collection of European and American painting, on the second floor, embraces more than 2,300 oils, tempera panels, pastels, and water colors. It includes important private collections bequeathed to the museum as well as contemporary American works bought with income from funds given by George A. Hearn.

The Marquand Gallery, at the head of the main staircase, serves as an entrance hall to the painting exhibits. It contains selected masterpieces by Florentine, Venetian, Dutch, and Flemish masters, among them Raphael, Veronese, Titian, Hals, Van Dyck, and Metsu.

The paintings in other rooms on the second floor are grouped more or less chronologically beginning with Italian, French, and North European primitives. There are examples, including two Giottesque panels, of the early Florentine school which broke with the rigid Byzantine tradition and developed the bases of the later traditions of European and American painting: perspective, spatial composition, atmospheric sense, and freedom of color. There are also works by the softer, lyrical Sienese painters, including Segna di Bonaventura and Pietro Lorenzetti. Among the most interesting Flemish painters are Bosch and Peter Brueghel, the Elder, whose fantasy, masterly drawing, and use of rhythmic patterns influence many artists today in the representation of mass scenes and social symbols. *Crucifixion* and *Last Judgment,* attributed to Hubert van Eyck, show the application of the new oil technique said to have been developed by this artist and his brother to supersede tempera painting. Other important painters in this group are Roger van der Weyden, Hugo van der Goes, Gerard David, and the German, Lucas Cranach. In Botticelli, Mantegna, and Pol-

Iaiuolo, the influence of antique sculpture and painting emphasizes line as the chief element in composition. Venetian painting is introduced by Giovanni Bellini and Carpaccio, whose structural and atmospheric use of color was the starting point of truly modern painting. Works of Titian, Tintoretto, and Veronese show different developments of this original use of color in producing richer and more dramatic effects. A change in Venetian tradition is indicated in Tiepolo's eighteenth-century rococo ceiling painting, which may be compared with Pinturicchio's decoration for the ceiling of the reception hall of a Sienese palace. One of the small adjoining rooms contains drawings by Michelangelo, Rembrandt, Blake, Daumier, and others, and a collection of miniatures featuring the younger Holbein's portrait of Thomas Wriothesley.

Two painters are outstanding in the Spanish collection: El Greco, painter of the famous *View of Toledo* and other renowned masterpieces, who, as a pupil of Tintoretto, developed his teacher's use of strong color and swirling line to produce the structural distortions so forceful in design and emotional intensity, and anticipating the planned distortions of modern art; and Goya, whose portraits and landscapes evidence his genius for psychological characterization as well as for fantasy and allegory with profound social meaning.

Among seventeenth-century Dutch and Flemish painters, Rubens combines the realism of northern art with his robust personal interpretation of Venetian color tradition. Dutch genre, or intimate scene-painting, is represented by Peter de Hooch and Vermeer, the latter renowned for his skillful application of light to textures. Hals' amazing skill in the rendering of textures and his flair for character study are seen in such portraits as that of *Malle Babbe,* a fishwife. There are numerous Rembrandts, in which may be studied the master's method of composing by means of light and shadow in order to express the interior animation of his figures. Other paintings by Rembrandt and Hals are in the Altman Collection in a separate wing, which contains also several Italian and North European primitives, including works by Hans Memling, a Fra Angelico *Crucifixion,* two Holbein portraits, Dutch landscapes, and the Velasquez, *Philip IV.*

The next group comprises French painting of the seventeenth and eighteenth centuries. The structural Renaissance painting of Poussin and of the father of landscape painting, Claude Lorraine, is succeeded by the skillful rococo art of Boucher and by David's "classical" imitations of Republican Rome, spiritual model of the intellectuals of the French Revolution.

English paintings of the eighteenth and nineteenth centuries include those by the conventional portraitists descended from Van Dyck, Reynolds, and Gainsborough; and by Turner, once exaggeratedly hailed by Ruskin as one of the greatest artists of all time.

Beginning with Ingres, Delacroix, Courbet, Corot, and Daumier, the collection of modern French art, enriched by the Havemeyer bequest, includes most of the great masters of Impressionism and those who adopted its use of pure color and diffused light. There are fine examples of Manet, inspirer of the movement; Monet, its purest exponent; Degas, painter of occupations and casual day-to-day existence; and finally Renoir and Cézanne, who, for their color and monumental form, rank with the world's foremost painters. Recent painting is represented by the work of such diverse artists as Picasso, Matisse, Van Gogh, Rousseau, Pascin, and Derain—placed face to face with Rosa Bonheur's *Horse Fair,* perhaps to contrast their paramount interest in design with the earlier romantic devotion to dramatic subjects. A group of miscellaneous small oils runs the gamut from Constable, one of the few important English painters and an ancestor of Impressionism, to the pointillist Seurat, renowned for his spatial compositions.

The water color collection includes mainly the work of American and French artists.

The large collection of early American painting is historically interesting for the subjects of its portraits and its historical tableaux. These are followed by the landscapes of the Hudson River school and by works of George Inness, Winslow Homer, the mystic-ascetic Ryder, the realist Eakins, Whistler, and the flashy Sargent. Contemporary American painting, as seen in the Hearn Fund room, indicates the influence of modern European traditions, either academized or modified creatively in relation with the life and environment of the artists.

The American Wing

The American Wing, a gift of Mr. and Mrs. Robert W. de Forest, is devoted to the decorative arts of the Colonial, Revolutionary, and early Republican periods. On the three floors of the wing, rooms have been reconstructed to convey an accurate sense of the use of the various articles of furniture, metalwork, glass- and silverware, and of their place in the decorative scheme of parlors, dining-rooms, bedrooms, and tavern rooms. Interesting and historically significant are the great hall of the eighteenth-century Van Rensselaer manor house, presented by Mrs. William Bayard Van Rensselaer, and the assembly room from Gadsby's Tavern, Alexandria, Virginia, where Washington attended his last birthday ball. Most striking is the functional character of early American craftsmanship, its careful adherence to the nature of the materials used and the simple severity of its design. American Colonial art is one of the most original of all decorative styles based on classical motifs.

Other galleries throughout the museum contain large exhibits of European decorative arts from the sixteenth to the twentieth century, and of glassware, sundials, clocks, and watches, as well as costumes, textiles, and laces.

Prints

The works of great printmakers are arranged in temporary exhibits on the second floor of the north wing. The museum's large collection of prints is in the Print Study Room, where it may be examined by visitors. Most of the famous graphic artists are represented, including exceptional groups of Rembrandt etchings, Dürer engravings and woodcuts, and examples of Holbein, Goya, Daumier, Blake, Meryon, and Whistler. Historic and technical material on etching, wood block and lithographic processes is in the Print Study Room. The recent revival of interest in the graphic arts makes these collections especially valuable to both artists and students.

To enhance the active use of its treasures, the museum offers lectures, gallery talks, appointments with its instructors, and other educational services. Copying and photographing of exhibits are permitted. Members of the museum may attend special courses; courses for teachers and talks for pupils in public schools, and story hours for children are also given. An auditorium seating 450 persons and five classrooms are in use. An extensive library contains books for reference and photographs, and lantern slides and other material may be obtained for study at a nominal rental through the Extension Division of the museum.

Eight Saturday evening concerts are usually given each year during January and March by a symphony orchestra under the direction of David Mannes, although in 1939 only the four January concerts were given.

MUSEUM OF THE CITY OF NEW YORK

5th Ave., 103d to 104th St. IRT Lexington Ave. subway (local) to 103d St.; or 5th, Madison or Lexington Ave. bus to 104th St. Hours: weekdays 10 A.M. to 5 P.M. (closed Tuesday), Sunday 1 to 5 P.M. Admission: 25¢ Monday, other days free. Sunday lectures, November to March at 4 P.M.

This is New York's Family Album. With painstaking candor, it reveals the city's past—in both its raw and decorous aspects. New Yorkers are fond of this place; they come in large numbers and pass through it slowly, impressed and often amused, as if they were thumbing the pages of their own plush-covered book.

The museum opened in 1923 in the old Gracie Mansion overlooking the East River at East Eighty-eighth Street. Its present home, built in 1931–2 on land provided by the city, faces Central Park at Fifth Avenue between 103d and 104th Streets. Funds for construction were raised by private subscription. Income for maintenance is derived from four sources: city appropriations, endowments, admission fees, and contributions.

The five-story building, designed by Joseph H. Friedlander, the prize-winning architect, is a good example of the modern adaptation of Georgian Colonial architecture. The central section, set back from the building line and flanked by two wings, is executed in red brick, trimmed with white marble. An approach of veined white marble leads to the marble-faced main entrance, above which are four Ionic columns supporting a pediment. To the right and left of the entrance walk are small gardens backed by loggias along the projecting wings. The building's chaste interior, with its exquisitely designed rooms, in cream or light gray tones, and floors for the most part of marble, inset with medallion shapes and borders of contrasting black stone, is characteristic of a mansion of the Federal period. The semicircular entrance hall has a handsome marble floor, a brilliant chandelier, and a curved flying staircase of unusual grace, with marble steps and wrought-iron railings.

The first floor is mainly devoted to historical galleries. The J. Clarence Davies Gallery in the north wing traces the growth of the city from an Indian village to a fair-sized town at the close of the Revolutionary War; while the Altman Foundation Gallery in the south wing continues the account of the city's development from the Federal period to the present. Miniature groups picture events and scenes of the past, including the purchase of Manhattan Island, 1626; Stone Street, 1659; the surrender of New Amsterdam, 1664; the inauguration of Washington, 1789; Bowling Green, 1831—reaching, dramatically, to the construction of the Empire State Building in 1930. Both galleries have many rare and interesting prints and documents of bygone New York; and objects reminiscent of its history, such as a Dutch sleigh, a horse-drawn streetcar, and the tallyho coach.

Dutch furniture and portraits and miniatures of early New Yorkers are displayed in the corridor of the first floor. Here is also a collection illustrating the history of fires and fire fighting; it includes a mid-nineteenth-century fire engine and hose carriage, and a series of models displaying the evolution of the fire engine. On a rear terrace of the south wing, under a loggia overlooking the pleasant garden court, is a copy of the bronze *Romulus and Remus* (at the Capitoline Museum), which was presented in 1928 by the governor of Rome.

On the second floor a room is devoted to memorabilia of George Washington and Alexander Hamilton. In the north wing are costumes that represent the changing fashions from the Dutch period to the end of the nineteenth century. In the south wing is a comprehensive collection of sailboat and steamboat models, engravings of packets and merchantmen, figureheads from old clipper ships—the figurehead of the U.S.S. *Constitution* dominates the east end—and a number of ships' fixtures and nautical instruments; through this collection may be traced the history of the port of New York. Display cases in the platform room at the head of the stairs show a collection of silver by New York craftsmen. Here, and throughout the corridors and smaller rooms, the domestic and commercial details of early American life are abundantly illustrated by furniture, lace, personal ornament, and deeds of sale. Adjoining the silver collection is a small gallery devoted to the history of the New York Stock Exchange. Photomurals, documents, and models show the development of the exchange from 1792 to the present.

A series of models in the Communication Gallery—third floor, north wing—illustrates the rise of communication, from the inauguration of the New York-Boston Post route in 1672, through the mast-and-yard method of barrel signals, to the development of an intricate radio system. One exhibit depicts the great blizzard of 1888, showing the wreckage sustained by sleet-burdened telegraph and telephone lines. Another series of models traces the growth of retail merchandising from the Weigh House Pier of 1660 to early and modern examples of five-and-ten-cent stores. In the south wing on the same floor is recorded the architectural development of the city. Another room is devoted to theatrical and musical history.

On the fourth floor are administration offices and study rooms that contain departments of costume, furniture, and silver; prints, theater, and music. The material in these departments is kept in the custody of curators and may be examined only by appointment. The reference library has a number of rare manuscripts.

On the fifth floor are a bedroom and a dressing room, typical of the 1880's, from the New York residence of the late John D. Rockefeller.

Galleries in the museum, including an auditorium on the ground floor, are used for special exhibitions, held monthly from October to June, and devoted to different phases of the city's past. An important service of the museum is offered through the facilities of its educational department, which supplies guides to public and private school children as well as to adult groups. This department also presents a semiweekly series of motion pictures of New York; midweek illustrated lectures primarily designed for schoolteachers; Saturday afternoon gallery tours for adults and story hours for children; and Sunday afternoon lectures by guest speakers. Membership in the junior museum club is open to any child in New York. A course is offered in museum educational methods in co-operation with the Board of Higher Education, and lecturers are supplied to schools, women's clubs, and other organizations. Schools may avail themselves of series of portable history sets, comprised of cardboard models illustrating various phases in New York history.

CATHEDRAL OF ST. JOHN THE DIVINE

Cathedral Parkway (110th St.) to 113th St., Amsterdam Ave. to Morningside Drive; main entrance on Amsterdam Ave. and 112th St. IRT Broadway-7th Ave. subway to Cathedral Parkway (110th St.); or 8th Ave. (Independent) Washington Heights or Grand Concourse subway (local) to Cathedral Parkway (110th St.); or 9th Ave. el to 110th St.; or 5th Ave. bus No. 4 to Amsterdam Ave. and 110th St. Guide service: Sunday after 11 A.M. and 4 P.M. services.

St. John's has been rising, stone on stone, for almost half a century— a pure masonry structure. Dominating Morningside Heights plateau the cathedral appears to grow out of the masses of jagged gneiss of which Manhattan Island is made. Cut from the cliff emerge the seven clustered apsidal chapels, crowned with peaked verdigris roofs, that emphasize the vertical motif of the whole cathedral. From the apex of the roof a figure of Gabriel with his trumpet salutes the East. Eventually when the cathedral assumes its final form, the crossing tower will dominate the whole mass.

The church grounds comprise eleven and a half acres. South of the cathedral are the synod house, St. Faith's House, the bishop's house, the deanery and the choir school, and the old synod house. These French and English Gothic buildings and the cathedral form a harmonious group.

The ambitious plans proposed by the Right Reverend Horatio Potter in 1872 to erect the largest church in America, began to be realized in 1892 when his nephew and successor, Bishop Henry Codman Potter, purchased the present site—part of the battlefield of Harlem Heights. The cornerstone was laid on St. John's Day, December 27, 1892.

More than twenty million dollars has been expended in the construction (1939). Two-thirds of this was raised in a nation-wide campaign for funds in 1924, when contributions were solicited from all races and religious creeds for a "place of worship for all people." John D. Rockefeller, Jr., a Baptist, gave five hundred thousand dollars.

Construction has advanced in a manner comparable to that of the medieval churches of northern France, with some changes in design and style, occasional years of idleness, and a lack of adequate funds. The first service, in the crypt (beneath the choir), was held in 1899. Twelve years later, in 1911, the choir and the crossing were opened. The foundation stone of the great nave was laid in 1925, the west front was commenced in 1925, and the north transept in 1927.

When completed this cathedral will be the largest church building in America and the largest Gothic cathedral in the world, 601 feet long and 146 feet wide at the nave and 320 feet wide at the transept. It was begun after plans by Heins and La Farge who envisioned a beautiful and harmonious combination of elements inspired by Byzantine and early French and English Gothic architecture. Theirs was the general conception of the church: a great cruciform, with a crossing (surmounted by a lofty tower) broad enough to seat the entire congregation.

In 1911, both the original architects having died, the trustees decided to abandon the "Romanesque" design in favor of "pure Gothic," and the architectural firm of Cram and Ferguson was engaged. An obvious contrast in styles was the result. Eventually, it is planned to alter the earlier parts of the cathedral so that they will conform with the later ones; and the finished edifice, save for certain parts of the apse and the seven apsidal chapels, thus will be essentially the design of one architect, Ralph Adams Cram. The edifice is no mere copy of any existing structure; the architects sought rather to create a cathedral such as might have been fashioned in France in the thirteenth century.

The west front, seen from Amsterdam Avenue at 112th Street, has two towers: St. Peter's (left) and St. Paul's (right); these will be 266.5 feet high when completed. Its five recessed portals are adorned with figures of saints and prophets, martyrs and preachers that were modeled by Lee Lawrie and John Angel. The elaborate carving on the gold-plated bronze doors of the central portal, modeled by John Angel, depicts events from the Old and New Testaments. The doors of the other four portals are of teakwood from Burma.

In the nave the alternation of great lofty clustered piers with lesser ones produces a singular effect of verticality and openness. These piers divide the nave from the spacious side aisles. The vault of the nave, 124 feet high, is in six parts—the first of its kind in America. At the time the cathedral was planned, steel had not yet been proved a lasting construction material; the architects, therefore, chose to build in stone. In the finished church only the framework of the roof above the stone vaulting will be of steel. The use of flying buttresses was also avoided because the architects believed that such exposed masonry would crack in the rigorous climate of New York. Instead, high side aisles that reached to the full height of the nave were employed, thus supplying the necessary buttressing for the nave vaulting and adding greatly to the general impression of spaciousness.

The seven aisle bays for chapels on each side of the nave are dedicated to diverse subjects such as Sports, the Arts, the Labors of Man, the Medical Profession, and the Legal Profession. Above them, where their roofs abut the aisle walls, runs the delicate tracery of the triforium gallery surmounted by stained-glass clerestory windows. A temporary wall now blocks the nave from the crossing, the choir, and high altar.

The north and south transepts, when completed, will each be as wide as the nave itself. The north one, begun in 1927, will be dedicated to the Blessed Virgin Mary, and the other to John the Evangelist.

The choir, enclosed by semicircular arches, may best be seen from the east side of the crossing. The finials of the oak choir stalls are carved in the form of figures of musicians and composers of church music; these were modeled by Otto Jahnsen. In the presbytery is the bishop's throne, a lofty seat of carved oak. The pulpit, of Tennessee marble, has five principal niches, containing scenes, in relief, from the life of Christ. Behind the high altar of Vermont marble is the richly carved reredos. Its central figure is a seven-foot representation of Christ, its size indicative of the scale of the cathedral. Four characters from the Old Testament are on the left, and four from the New Testament are on the right.

Supporting the apse vaulting and roof, eight powerful columns of light-gray granite, fifty-five feet high, form a semicircle behind the sanctuary; each is a memorial. Eventually, the half-dome of the apse, which lacks the mosaics planned for it, will be replaced by Gothic vaulting, and a row of clerestory windows will extend around the upper chancel wall.

The ambulatory separates the choir and sanctuary from the seven apsidal chapels, the baptistery, and the vestry room. In order, from the south side of the choir, the chapels are: St. James, English Gothic, by Henry Vaughn; St. Ambrose, modified Renaissance, by Carrère and Hastings; St. Martin of Tours, early thirteenth-century Gothic, by Cram and Ferguson; St. Saviour, English decorated Gothic, by Heins and La Farge; St. Columba,

Norman, by Heins and La Farge; St. Boniface, English Gothic, by Henry Vaughn; and St. Ansgarius, fourteenth-century Gothic, by Henry Vaughn.

St. Ambrose's is particularly light and graceful—the one Renaissance feature of the cathedral. In St. Boniface's the glass is very fine, as is the vaulting of St. Martin's, where stands a marble figure of Joan of Arc, by Anna Hyatt Huntington.

The baptistery, designed by Cram and Ferguson, is octagonal in plan, and is a masterly accomplishment in workmanship, detail, and symbolism. The font itself, fifteen feet high is of Champville marble, and its panels commemorate the life of John the Baptist.

Among the many gifts to the cathedral are the twelve-foot Menorah lights in the sanctuary on either side of the high altar. They follow the design of those that stood in Solomon's Temple and are the first of their kind used in a Christian cathedral. A pair of teak and gold chests, in the Chapel of St. Saviour, were presented by the King of Siam.

The cathedral serves the Protestant Episcopal diocese of New York which has in its territory 280 parishes and missions, and whose bishop is the Right Reverend William T. Manning.

COLUMBIA UNIVERSITY

116th St. and Broadway. IRT Broadway-7th Ave. subway to 116th St.

Sixty-nine buildings grouped on Morningside Heights constitute the main body of Columbia University, one of the oldest, largest, and best-known educational institutions in the country. Established "for the instruction and education of youth in the learned languages, and in the liberal arts and sciences," Columbia has stretched the word "youth" to include persons of all ages, and its curriculum to embrace almost every field of learning. Each year some thirty thousand students come here to study under a faculty of about three thousand; twelve thousand students attend the summer session.

Columbia College, original nucleus of the university, is still a liberal arts college, but around it have grown schools devoted to the study of medicine, law, dentistry, optometry, engineering, business, architecture, library service, journalism, political science, and philosophy. Teachers College, Barnard College, the College of Pharmacy, 115 West Sixty-eighth Street, the College of Physicians and Surgeons in Columbia-Presbyterian Medical Center (see page 298), the New York Post-Graduate Medical

School, 303 East Twentieth Street, and Bard College at Annandale-on-Hudson are independent corporations within the university. Close association with Union Theological Seminary *(see page 290)* provides Columbia with what is virtually a theological department.

The university is widely known for the range of its scholarship and scientific research, and for its liberal policy in education. The Law School and the Faculty of Political Science, for example, have contributed several professors to the "Brain Trust" of the New Deal—Rexford G. Tugwell, Raymond Moley, A. A. Berle, Jr., and Roswell Magill—as well as Joseph McGoldrick to the comptrollership of New York. The brown Victorian structures of Teachers College are in the "valley," on the block between Broadway and Amsterdam Avenue and 120th and 121st Streets. Since its founding in 1886 as the College for the Training of Teachers, Teachers College has profoundly affected the development of educational technique, and its faculty has acquired unrivaled prestige among educators. It was "T.C.'s" John Dewey whose instrumentalist philosophy led to the abandonment of authoritarian educational methods in favor of learning through experiment and practice. William H. Kilpatrick, a leading interpreter of Dewey's philosophy and a major influence in the progressive-education movement, has taught thousands of teachers from every part of the world. George S. Counts has stressed the relation between economics and education. Edward L. Thorndike, America's leading researcher in aptitudes and intelligence, stimulated the adult-education movement with his discovery that learning capacity does not greatly diminish with age. Many other leaders, such as Rugg, Strayer, Mort, Engelhardt, Patty Hill, and Goodwin Watson, have contributed to T.C.'s pre-eminence. Many younger institutions are staffed with T.C. graduates.

As laboratories for experimental high school and elementary work, Teachers College operates Lincoln School, 425 West 123d Street; Horace Mann School, Broadway at 120th Street; and Horace Mann School for Boys, Riverdale Avenue and 252d Street, the Bronx.

Many great minds have served the Columbia Faculties of Science and Philosophy. Famous in recent generations is the historical school of James Harvey Robinson, Charles A. Beard, James T. Shotwell, Carlton Hayes, Lynn Thorndike, and David S. Muzzey. Robinson and Beard resigned during the war and established the New School for Social Research *(see page 139)* downtown. Beard's resignation was in protest against the expulsion of a colleague for his pacifism. Columbia faculty members have made numerous contributions in chemistry and physics, among them Professor Harold C. Urey's discovery of "heavy water" (the heavy atom or hydrogen isotope in water), which was awarded the Nobel Prize in 1934. Michael Pupin, one of America's outstanding inventors in the field of electricity, was at the university for many years. Franz Boas founded a school of anthropology at Columbia and is a leading authority on the sub ject. Edward MacDowell, widely known for his songs and symphonic tone poems, taught at Columbia at the turn of the century. Criticism of Ameri can drama has been considerably enriched by the work of Professor Brander Matthews, long a faculty member. Many of Matthews' students became playrights, critics, and novelists. The sprightly John Erskine, nov elist and one of the directors of the Metropolitan Opera, was for many years a member of the English Department.

Of significance are the Columbia School of Journalism, the only grad uate school of its kind in the world, the School of Library Service, oldest and largest in the country, and the Department of Extension. The last named offers an amazing variety of afternoon, evening, and Saturday morn ing courses. At the Law School have been educated such men as President Theodore Roosevelt, President Franklin D. Roosevelt, Chief Justice Charles Evans Hughes, and Justices Harlan Fiske Stone and Benjamin N. Cardozo of the Supreme Court of the United States.

Columbia's library, housed largely in new South Hall, is the third larg est university library in the United States. It contains 1,615,000 volumes. Some 40,000 volumes in Avery Hall make up the largest single collection of books on architecture in America, and the fourth largest law library in the world, 200,000 volumes, is in the Law Building.

Barnard College, named for one of the outstanding presidents of Co lumbia University, Frederick A. P. Barnard, was established in 1889. At that time higher education for women was still considered generally to be unnecessary and inappropriate. Despite opposition on the part of trustees, faculty, and students, in 1883 Barnard succeeded in establishing at Co lumbia a course for women equivalent to that offered male students, al though graduates received only a specially invented degree, Bachelor of Humane Letters. It was not until 1889, when a separate college was estab lished for them, that women were granted academic equality with men.

Columbia was chartered as King's College October 31, 1754, although instruction had begun July 17, with a faculty of one preceptor, the Rev erand Samuel Johnson, and a student body of eight. It was the sixth col lege established in the Colonies. Classes were first held in the schoolhouse of Trinity Church, and Trinity provided the first campus, between Church, Barclay, and Murray Streets to the Hudson River (Greenwich Street), from the church farm. A public lottery supplied funds. From the beginning, the college was notable for its charter which established religious freedom for both faculty and students. Among early graduates were Alexander Hamilton (1778), Gouverneur Morris (1768), John Jay (1764), Robert R. Livingston (1765), and De Witt Clinton (1786).

After the Revolutionary War, King's College was rechristened Columbia. Its progress was slow. Although the city was passing through a prosperous phase, it was more fashionable to endow out-of-town colleges than an obscure and struggling local institution. Its position improved, however, in 1814 when the Legislature, in response to an appeal by the trustees, granted to the college the Elgin Botanical Gardens, a tract of land between Forty-seventh and Fifty-first Streets, extending from Fifth Avenue to within a hundred feet of Sixth Avenue. The grant was made because Columbia had not shared in the proceeds of a lottery the State had conducted for the benefit of educational institutions. The college never moved there as planned, but retained ownership of the property, which includes most of the site of Rockefeller Center *(see page 340)*.

So gradual was the growth of Columbia that ninety years after its founding it had but 107 students. In 1857 the college moved uptown to the renovated buildings of a home for the deaf and dumb on Madison Avenue between Forty-ninth and Fiftieth Streets. There, by 1890, it began to assume some of the characteristics of a university. A steady increase in donations accelerated expansion to such an extent that by 1892 the institution had 1,600 students and eighty instructors. The Morningside campus was occupied in 1897, and the title of the college, officially changed in 1896 to Columbia University in the City of New York, was so approved by the State Legislature in 1912.

When the present campus plan was adopted in the 1890's, the architects, McKim, Mead, and White, envisioned a series of small closed courts, formally related to one another and dominated by a great domed central building, Low Memorial Library. Because not all the contemplated units have been built, a certain diffuseness characterizes many of the present views. The one completed quadrangle, between Avery, Schermerhorn, and Fayerweather Halls and St. Paul's Chapel, does achieve the intimate, cloistered effect the architects intended. Little St. Paul's Chapel, built in 1903 by Howells and Stokes, derives an altogether pleasing dignity from beautiful proportions and charming details.

The Low Memorial Library, facing 116th Street, combines some of the grandeur of Roman structure with Greek refinement in a classic building that has been widely praised, although it long ago failed as a usable library. Especial emphasis is given to the stone library by the fact that the surrounding academic buildings are of red brick. In the older structures, limestone trim was wisely limited, but unrestrained use of trim in the more recent work detracts from the serenity of the general effect.

The most recent buildings were not happily designed. Sixteen-story John Jay Hall, at the south end of the college quadrangle, is so disturbingly high that it destroys the harmony of the whole lower end of the campus. South Hall, the new library, fits badly into the group, largely because it clashes in scale with the near-by buildings.

Columbia has not escaped the accusation of applying mass production methods to higher education, and has been called "a factory of education." Certainly a corporation that has six thousand employees, thirty thousand customers, an annual budget of more than ten million dollars, and is one of the largest landowners in the city, cannot avoid the appearance of an industry. The likeness is enhanced by the fact that a large part of the university's capital resources of more than $150,000,000 is invested in real estate and securities of railroads and large industrial corporations, and is supervised by directors and trustees whose names are associated with big business. Harvard is the only wealthier university in the country.

It was during the presidency of Nicholas Murray Butler, who took office in 1902, that the university achieved its present physical and cultural dimensions. Under Dr. Butler's guidance, the growth of Columbia was remarkable even in a period of nation-wide educational expansion. Many institutions, both foreign and domestic, have called him a "great liberal" in granting him academic honors. Some detractors have charged him with being a "devout servant of vested wealth." There is general agreement, however, that he was largely responsible for broadening the appeal of higher education. One of the innovations credited to him is the use of modern publicity methods in the field of learning. For every student enrolled in Columbia when Dr. Butler became president, today there are seven.

THE RIVERSIDE CHURCH

Riverside Drive and 122d St. IRT Broadway-7th Ave. subway to 125th St.; or 5th Ave. bus No. 4 to 122d St.; or Broadway surface car to 122d St. Hours: daily, church 9 A.M. to 5 P.M.; observation tower 10 A.M. to 5 P.M., admission 25¢.

The Riverside Church, set on a commanding eminence overlooking the Hudson, is associated with the names of Dr. Harry Emerson Fosdick, pastor since its beginning, and a member, John D. Rockefeller, Jr., whose financial assistance was largely responsible for the building's construction. Its site is the crest of a hill with a sharp drop to the east, a steep slope to the river on the west, and a descent into the valley crossed by West 125th Street on the north.

Nominally a Baptist organization, the church is characterized by a liberal denominational appeal—indicated, for example, in the fact that the Society of Friends holds services in one of its tower rooms. The Gothic-clothed structure houses the service and recreational units of a complex social enterprise, with clubrooms, classrooms, nurseries, bowling alleys, a library, a theater and gymnasium. In less than a decade since its construction (1929–30) it has become a community center, with some ten thousand people involved in its activities weekly. A full-time staff of 70, along with 143 part-time workers, is required to assist the pastor.

The church, designed by the firm of Allen, Pelton, and Collens, clearly reflects in its details the famous thirteenth-century Cathedral of Chartres, in northwestern France. Its completion in 1929, after a delay caused by a spectacular fire in the tower, was followed by violent critical debate: to some the architecture of the cathedral seemed "a late example of bewildered eclecticism, of cultural servitude to Europe, a travesty on thirteenth-century Gothic," while to others the Gothic style used was considered the one most appropriate for a place of worship.

A basic criticism is that, in using modern steel construction, Gothic architecture is reduced to a mere shell covering the structural members. Thus the exterior buttresses of this church are functionally unnecessary and would be hopelessly inadequate if they alone supported a solid masonry vault. Their smallness has the effect of making the building itself seem smaller than it is, so that its scale is scarcely impressive, even when seen at close range.

No pains were spared in the workmanship of the carving, the stained glass, the metalwork, and the miscellaneous details. In themselves, the decorations constitute a pictorial textbook of Biblical history.

The building appears to be composed of two units; the northern section, which houses the nave, although more than ten stories in height, is like an appendage attached to the tower. The latter rises from a base 100 feet square to a height of 392 feet, and with the belfry is approximately thirty stories high. The nave exterior, boldly designed with pointed buttresses and deeply recessed Gothic-arched rose windows, is faced with Indiana limestone.

The design of the main entrance, or west portal, in the base of the tower, is based upon that of the Porte Royale at Chartres. A seated figure of Christ, surrounded by the four symbols of the Evangelists, is carved in relief in the tympanum. In the concentric arches of the recessed opening are statues of forty-two leading personalities of science, philosophy, and religion. South of the west portal is the chapel doorway, which, like all of the exterior iconography, embodies in carved stone the symbolism of the Nativity and the eternity of life. To the north, Angels of the Apocalypse are ensconced in niches in the upper part of the apse, while the Resurrection Angel with a trumpet is stationed on the ridge, to mark the position of the cross in the chancel below. At the "cloister" entrance on Claremont Avenue three figures above the door represent Faith, Hope, and Charity.

The well-proportioned limestone nave is 215 feet in length, 89 feet in width, and 100 feet in height. The omission of many features of the usual Gothic plan, which ordinarily tend to make the choir appear distant, permits a large number of people to feel that they are close to the chancel. Suppression of a transept, and small chapels, narrow side aisles, and exceptional nave width all contribute to the effect. In addition to the dark oak pews in the nave proper, seating is provided in the triforium gallery and in two galleries at the south end, accommodating 2,500 persons in all.

The bays of the nave are designed with great simplicity, subordinating stonework to the sparkle of stained glass. The apse also is restrained in character. It consists of a decorative background of seven radiating bays with an ascending carved screenwork of white Caen stone. The windows, mosaics of colored light, grow richer toward the apse; here delicate tracery enhances their graceful jambs.

The stained-glass windows, with the possible exception of recent ones installed in the Cathedral of St. John the Divine *(see page 380),* are among the finest in the city. In all there are fifty-one including the two great rose windows above the second gallery which recount the story of the Ten Commandments and the Parables.

The tower's twenty-two stories contain church offices, ministerial studies, Sunday School and club rooms and a late French Romanesque chapel, with a simple vault in eleventh-century style. The Laura Spelman Rockefeller Memorial carillon, the largest in the world, is composed of seventy-two bells. Above the bells is the observation gallery, surmounted by a red beacon that shines at night for the guidance of airmen.

Riverside's history dates back to the small congregation of the Stanton Street Church. In 1841 several hundred of its members acquired a large building not far from its original home and there organized a new body called the Norfolk Street Baptist Church. During the following seventy years the church moved successively to Fifth Avenue, Park Avenue, and, in 1930, to its present site on Riverside Drive.

Triborough Bridge

Entrances: 125th St. and 2d Ave., 122d St. and East River Drive, Manhattan; Southern Blvd. and Cypress Ave., Bronx; 29th St. and 25th Ave., Astoria, Queens. IRT Lexington Ave. subway to 125th St. (bridge bus at Lexington Ave. and 126th St.); or IRT Pelham subway to Cypress Ave., Bronx; or IRT or BMT Astoria subway to 25th Ave. Toll: passenger automobiles 25¢.

With Randall's and Ward's islands as stepping-stones, the Triborough Bridge strides into three boroughs—Manhattan, Queens, and the Bronx. The bridge proper, near the confluence of the Harlem and East Rivers, is a Y-shaped structure comprising four overwater bridges and twelve grade separations (or bridges over land). Its over-all elevated length of 17,710 feet is exceeded only by that of the San Francisco-Oakland Bridge.

Linked with fourteen miles of highway connections, it speeds traffic by shunting through-vehicles away from congested areas and carrying them swiftly across the boroughs.

From Pelham Bay Park in the Bronx, where it taps the Westchester County parkway system, the northern connecting route follows Eastern Boulevard and Whitlock Avenue for six and a quarter miles to a reinforced concrete viaduct between East 132d and East 134th Streets. At that point an overland and overwater bridge, seven truss spans with a total length of 1,600 feet, crosses the Bronx Kills to Randall's Island. The center span, which carries two four-lane roadways and sidewalks, may be converted into a vertical-lift bridge if the Kills should be made navigable.

On Randall's Island this Bronx arm of the bridge meets, at a right angle, the Manhattan arm in the circular swirl of under- and overpasses of what is probably the most ingenious traffic-sorter ever constructed. From there the bridge marches in a single long reach of stilted viaduct and trestle across Little Hell Gate and Ward's Island to turn eastward on suspension cables over Hell Gate (East River) to Astoria, Queens.

No sooner does the roadway come back to earth in Astoria than it drops into an eight-lane depressed thoroughfare to avoid Queens cross traffic. Then, rising again, it follows Astoria Boulevard and Grand Central Parkway, skirting Flushing Bay and the World's Fair site, and more than six miles out in Queens, it leads into the network of Long Island State parkways.

The Manhattan connecting thoroughfare starts at the foot of East Ninety-second Street, runs a mile and a half up the East River shore, and crosses the Harlem River at 125th Street to Randall's Island. This crossing consists of three truss spans, with a total length of 772 feet, and a 310-foot vertical-lift bridge, the largest in the country. Electric motors in two 210-foot steel towers raise the lift span, with its two triple-lane roadways and its sidewalks, eighty feet in the air to permit the passage of large vessels. When it is locked, the span is fifty-five feet above the water.

The East River suspension bridge is the largest overwater unit of the Triborough system. A pair of twenty-and-three-quarter-inch cables passing over two 315-foot steel towers carry eight traffic lanes to a height of 135 feet above the river. The main span is 1,380 feet long, while the two land spans are each 705 feet long. Although it lacks the startling beauty of George Washington Bridge *(see page 399),* this structure has considerable grace. Its twin steel towers are lighter and simpler than those of the George Washington (which were intended to be covered by stonework) ; and its mighty concrete abutments that anchor the cables clearly indicate their function. A striking contrast is furnished by the neighboring Hell Gate span of the New York Connecting Railroad Bridge; its bold arc expresses a triumph over gravity perhaps even more forcefully than the dipping, passive catenaries of the suspension bridge.

Triborough Bridge was begun by the Department of Plant and Structures October 25, 1929, but work was discontinued for lack of funds in the spring of 1932. The Triborough Bridge Authority, which resumed construction in November, 1933, would have preferred to place the Manhattan end at about 100th Street, with the junction on Ward's Island, but it was then too late to shift. The Authority, however, did build part of the East River Drive as an approach, and so reclaimed a mile and a half of blighted water-front area.

To prevent the customary degeneration of underbridge land into unsightly catchalls, these parts of the Triborough right of way were landscaped as parks and playgrounds. At the Astoria end a large riverside park includes a mammoth outdoor swimming pool as well as shady walks and play spaces. On Randall's Island two old institutions, the Children's Hospital and the House of Refuge, were razed and the whole island was transformed into a recreation park around a great municipal stadium. These were made accessible from the bridge. Under the Manhattan ramps at 124th Street another large recreation field was built. When the Manhattan State Hospital is removed, Ward's Island will also become park area.

The bridge was opened for traffic July 11, 1936. Of the total cost of

$60,300,000, New York City appropriated $16,100,000, while the Federal Public Works Administration made a grant of $9,200,000 and bought $35,000,000 of bonds. In 1937 these bonds were bought back from the Government and were refinanced by direct sale to the public.

To the motorist, the Triborough Bridge brings an exhilarating freedom from congestion and stop lights that is worth much more than the toll charge. He must pass but one toll point, and he never crosses the path of another vehicle at grade.

To the pedestrian, the bridge offers one of the most spectacular high-level walks in the country. In recommending that walkers start from the Astoria end, Lewis Mumford wrote: "Here is one of the few places . . . where one can see New York across a foreground of verdure and water and it must be counted one of the most dazzling urban views in the world."

HARLEM RIVER HOUSES

151st to 153d St., Macomb's Place to Harlem River. IRT Lenox Ave. subway to 145th St.; or 8th Ave. (Independent) Grand Concourse subway (local) to 155th St.-8th Ave.; or 9th Ave. el to 151st St.; or 5th Ave. bus No. 2 to 152d St.

In New York City's most overcrowded community, Harlem—where Negroes pay as much as 50 per cent of their incomes for rent, where the rent party is an institution, and where the "hot bed" serves three shifts of sleepers a day—are the Harlem River Houses, a group of apartment buildings that provide more sunlight, fresh air, and certain other advantages of good housing than the residences of fashionable Park Avenue.

Built in 1937 by the Federal Administration of Public Works, Housing Division, the project is a recognition in brick and mortar of the special and urgent needs of Harlem, and the first large-scale modern housing community made available for low-income Manhattan residents at rents they can afford. The houses, a $4,500,000 development, are occupied by 574 Negro families paying rents ranging from $19.28 to $31.42 a month. This development of nine acres (.014 square mile) indicates what may be the solution for 4.4 square miles of Manhattan housing condemned as unfit for human habitation. As a first effort of the present national housing program it has exerted a great influence on the future of that program; and it is significant not only as a step toward solving the problem of the "ill-housed one-third," but also toward raising the housing standards of high-income groups. Indicative of the wide influence of the Federal Government's housing program is the Metropolitan Life Insurance Company's proposed large-scale apartment house development in the Bronx.

The layout of the Harlem River Houses is a testimonial to the designers' ingenuity in mastering a difficult site. With 151st Street as the base, the plot is the shape of a trapezoid split a little to the east of center by Seventh Avenue. One Hundred and Fifty-second Street, closed to traffic, divides the western portion. The architects—Archibald Manning Brown in association with Charles F. Fuller, Horace Ginsbern, Frank J. Forster, Will Rice Amon, Richard W. Buckley, and John Louis Wilson—contrived a pleasing, harmonious arrangement that retains a maximum of useful open area. There are three separate groups of buildings—each group composed of Z-, T-, and L-shaped sections—two west of Seventh Avenue and one east. The east group, designed in relation to the Harlem River, has a more rambling plan than the other two, which are separated by the 152d Street axis and fall into a graciously formal pattern. The western buildings are arranged in a quiet manner around a large rectangular plaza that forms a center for the development and makes it seem more spacious.

The details of the general plan are equally fortunate. A wide playground and park border the Harlem River; while for the use of the younger children there is an ingenious sunken playground in each half of the plaza. The landscaping, supervised by Michael Rapuano, and the sculptures, by Heinz Warnecke, with the assistance of T. Barbarossa, R. Barthé, and F. Steinberger, are excellent. Minor courts are liberally planted, but the well-trodden areas, save for the through paved paths, are laid with cobblestones. The landscaped sloping eastern court, leading first to an amphitheater, and then to the playgrounds, presents an especially pleasing aspect. The Seventh Avenue court of this eastern group has a statue of two playful bear cubs, carved of black basalt. A sunken fountain area in the center of the large plaza has a group of four black basalt penguins, each digging under a wing with its nib. At the southern end of the plaza is a statue of a Negro laborer, while at the opposite end is a group depicting domesticity: mother and child with a dog. These pieces of statuary, ideally suited for their setting, are carved of pink and black marble.

The site of the Harlem River Houses was purchased from the Rockefeller estate for one million dollars. Made of a pleasant red brick, most of the buildings have four stories and basement. All are equal in height, for those on lower levels of the terrain have an additional story. The glass enclosed stairshafts rising above the entrance doors accent the simple pattern formed by wide and ample room windows. There is very little trim and the impression of the whole is one of charming simplicity. A certain carelessness, however, is evident in the material and design of the surface detail. In the words of T. F. Hamlin's enthusiastic article in *Pencil Points,* "The whole, in detailing, looks tired—as if the creative drive and the creator's pleasure, which had sailed so triumphantly through the period of general planning and design, had suddenly failed when it came to the last, completing touches. Harlem River Homes is so generally beautiful that one longs for it to be perfect. What might have been great architecture is merely—very good."

Sixty of the 574 apartments have two rooms with kitchenette; 259 have three rooms, 232 have four rooms, and 23 have five rooms. Each apartment has electric refrigeration and lighting, steam heat, ample closet space, steel casement windows, and a tiled bath; each has cross ventilation. The structural division of the buildings, with no more than four apartments opening on any hallway, insures privacy and quiet. Lewis Mumford has declared that "in essentials of plan and arrangement, these quarters are superior to any comparable area of residential apartments in the city."

A share in a community life is made possible for each tenant by such facilities as four social halls for adult use, a nursery school for children of working mothers, a health clinic operated by the New York City Department of Health, community laundries, and rooms for indoor play. A residents' association promotes group social and cultural activities.

Only Negroes from substandard dwellings are accepted as tenants, and no family is admitted that has an income amounting to more than five times the rent. Another rule requires reasonable proof of an applicant's continuing ability to pay his rent. Thus relatively few Harlem families are eligible. The average income per family—derived from the work of more than one wage earner—in Harlem River Houses is about $1,350. Sixty per cent of the working tenants are unskilled, while 11.6 per cent are semi-skilled.

Forty-five per cent of the development's cost was granted outright by the Federal Government; 55 per cent is to be repaid over a period of sixty years. The houses are operated by the New York City Housing Authority which leases the project from the United States Housing Authority.

Transcending the physical aspects of the development are the social, and one item in the first year's record spoke eloquently: not a single case of delinquency or crime or social disorder was reported for Harlem River Houses. Apartments and courts were maintained with scrupulous care by young and old. A compact, progressive community had emerged, and its very success made the plight of the less fortunate residents of Harlem seem by contrast more bitter than ever.

WASHINGTON HEIGHTS MUSEUM GROUP: MUSEUM OF THE AMERICAN INDIAN—AMERICAN GEOGRAPHICAL SOCIETY—HISPANIC SOCIETY OF AMERICA—AMERICAN NUMISMATIC SOCIETY—AMERICAN ACADEMY OF ARTS AND LETTERS

Broadway, 155th to 156th St. IRT Broadway-7th Ave. subway to 157th St.; or 8th Ave. (Independent) Washington Heights subway to 155th St.
Museum of the American Indian. Hours: weekdays 2 to 5 P.M., closed Sunday and holidays; also closed during July and August. Admission free.
American Geographical Society. Reference library only. Hours: weekdays 9 A. M. to 4:45 P.M., closed Sunday, holidays, and Saturday from June to August. Admission free.
Hispanic Society of America. Hours: weekdays 10 A.M. to 4:30 P.M., Sunday and holidays 1 to 5 P.M., closed Thanksgiving and Christmas. Admission free.
American Numismatic Society. Hours: daily 2 to 5 P.M., closed holidays. Admission free.
American Academy of Arts and Letters. Hours (November to May): weekdays 10 A.M. to 5 P.M., Sunday and holidays 2 to 5 P.M. Admission free.

Occupying land that in the nineteenth century was part of John James Audubon's estate are buildings housing five of the nation's most distinguished museums and learned societies. This cultural center on Washington Heights came into being through the liberality of Archer M. Huntington, who inherited the fortune amassed by his father, Collis P. Huntington, railroad magnate and developer of the Newport News Shipbuilding Company. The son, a poet and scholar, founded thirteen museums. The first of the Washington Heights group, the Hispanic Society of America, was founded in 1904. The building program extended over the next two decades.

The buildings face a court opening on Broadway. The entrance is flanked by twin buildings—the Museum of the American Indian to the south, and the home of the American Geographical Society to the north. Adjacent to the latter is the north building of the Hispanic Society of America, while directly opposite, adjoining the former, is the south building of the Hispanic Society; and farther to the west is the headquarters of the American Numismatic Society. The architect was Charles Pratt Huntington, a nephew of Archer M. Huntington. He died in 1919, having completed all the buildings except the two housing the American Academy of Arts and Letters at the western end of the court. These were designed by Cass Gilbert (north building) and McKim, Mead, and White (south). Huntington evidently planned a monumental composition symmetrically balanced on the axis of the Hispanic Society buildings, and while the court and central plaza are good, the buildings are so poorly related to each other that the effect is sadly weakened. Particularly awkward is the intrusion of the Church of Our Lady of Esperanza, also designed by Huntington. The original conception was further disrupted by the addition of the American Academy buildings, which tend to lengthen the already narrow court and which do not appropriately close the court. The main façades of the buildings face the court, and their rear elevations seen from the side streets are unimpressive and dull.

On the other hand, several of the individual buildings are quite fine, notably the south building of the Hispanic Society, whose well accented doorway and lovely interior arcade are free adaptations from Spanish Renaissance architecture. All the buildings are of Indiana limestone with the exception of the one housing the Numismatic Society. It was made entirely of concrete—embodying a design for which the architect was knighted by King Alfonso XIII.

The Museum of the American Indian—Heye Foundation

The Foundation is the only organization in the world devoted solely to the collection and preservation of cultural material relating to the aborigines of the Western Hemisphere. The museum's nucleus was a collection from New Mexico brought to New York in 1903 and installed in the home of George C. Heye, the institution's founder.

Although the museum attracts a great number of nonprofessional visitors, its exhibits are arranged chiefly for students of anthropology, archaeology and ethnology. Displays on the first floor are devoted to North American Indians and Eskimo tribes. Material relating to the former is also found on the second floor which features the culture of the Northwest Coast, California, and the Southwest desert. The third floor is occupied by exhibits from Mexico, the West Indies, and Central and South America.

The collections present evidence of the close relation between material and spiritual culture in primitive life. Practical implements for achieving certain ends are placed beside magical and symbolic devices presumed to assist or to be equally effective in bringing them about. Ingenious hunting and fishing weapons, decoys, and traps are shown next to the bead, stone, and feather charms, and talismans whose power is not questioned so long as the fish bite and the deer fall.

Outstanding events in the life of nature and mankind—the change of seasons, sowing and harvest, birth, marriage, and death—are emphasized in the hundreds of religious objects and symbols employed in celebration or memorial rites. These include costumes for corn and antelope dances,

GEORGE WASHINGTON, UNION SQUARE

COLUMBUS CIRCLE

METROPOLIS (*Union Square*)

CHELSEA SHAPE-UP

NINTH AVENUE EL

FEEDING THE DUCKS (*Central Park*)

CENTRAL PARK AT NIGHT

CLUBHOUSE, COLONIAL DAMES OF AMERICA (*Smith's Folly*)

GAS PLANT (*Fourteenth Street near East River*)

HARLEM RIVER

HELL GATE BRIDGE

THE SOCIAL GRACES

MUSEUM GUARD

WARMING UP

ABSTRACT THINKING

FASHIONABLE AUCTION

SARDI'S

BURLYCUE

JUNE BUGS

OUTDOOR LIBRARY (*Bryant Park*)

STAMPEDE

A NICKEL A SHINE

thunderbird jewelry, holiday and funeral masks, Kachina dolls, and images of the dead with feathers on their shoulders to insure their flight to heaven.

Particularly interesting are evidences of the great cultures of Mexico, Guatemala, and Peru, which, in some respects, paralleled the early city-states of the Near East and the Mediterranean. Examples of sculpture, mosaic, and metal work, including gold and silver, are especially fine. The preoccupation of the Aztecs with death ritual is evident in sacrificial altars and figures of gods whom human blood might appease. Other interesting and beautiful objects are: a mammoth canoe of the Northwest Coast used for whale hunting; totem and house posts from Alaska; buffalo-hide shields of the Plains Indians; woven costumes from Central America, and native water colors of the hunt and ceremonials. Among the models of typical Indian villages and settlements is one of the Manhattan Indians.

A curious feature is a collection of human heads that have been shrunk to the size of oranges by the Jivaro Indians of Ecuador. This treatment is reserved for enemies. According to M. W. Stirling, Bureau of American Ethnology, "the reduced heads, when skillfully made, are exact miniatures of their former selves."

The museum's display collection is supplemented by material at its study and storage annex, Eastern Boulevard and Middletown Road *(see page 547)*, the Bronx, where all the specimens are available for closer study to properly accredited students. Its extensive library is maintained on deposit at Huntington Free Library and Reading Room, 9 Westchester Square, the Bronx.

The American Geographical Society

This society, founded in 1852 and the oldest geographical society in the United States, is devoted to research in geography and the maintenance of a library and map collection open to public use. Its library of more than one hundred thousand volumes and its collection of nearly an equal number of maps and atlases are the largest of their kind in the Western Hemisphere.

The society publishes books, maps, and a quarterly periodical, the *Geographical Review*. Included in its program of research in the geography of Hispanic America is the production of a great map (to be completed in 107 sheets) on which a large staff has been working for the past eighteen years. The department of mathematical geography is engaged in research into methods of geographical survey, particularly in mapping by aerial photography. The society has also engaged in studies of problems of pioneer settlement throughout the world, and of the geography of the polar regions. It has sponsored a number of recent arctic and antarctic expeditions, and has aided them in planning their work, and through the loan of instruments. The society is interested in the geographical aspects of international relations, and has contributed notably to negotiations leading to the settlement of a number of boundary controversies in Hispanic America, including the Guatemala-Honduras, Bolivia-Paraguay, and Chile-Peru disputes.

The Hispanic Society

This society, an educational institution devoted to advancement of the study of Spanish and Portuguese culture, has, in addition to its large library, containing many original manuscripts and first editions, an extensive collection of documentary and artistic material of the highest quality.

The influence of the various conquerors on the culture of the Iberian Peninsula is clearly indicated in the exhibits: that of the Romans, in sculpture and pottery; of the Moors, in textiles and metal work; and of the Christians, in Gothic and Renaissance art. Conversely, the story of Spain as conqueror is told in numerous documents, maps, charts, and globes relating to the voyages and triumphs of its explorers.

The main collection of paintings is chiefly housed in a gallery encircling the principal hall. Velásquez, whose realism lifted him far above contemporary court painters of the seventeenth century, is well represented. Masterpieces by El Greco, together with the work of members of his school, are exhibited. Among other Renaissance painters shown are Moro, Morales, and Ribera. Intimate and official portraits by Goya illustrate his capacity for profound observation and biting description. A prized possession is an excellent study in oil, made for his great painting, *Third of May,* which depicts the massacre of Madrileños by Napoleon's troops under Murat. In one of the smaller rooms on the second floor, along with numerous modern water colors, are examples of his *Caprices,* graphic works in which Goya makes use of allegory and fantasy to satirize the society of his time.

A separate gallery on the ground floor is devoted to large, mural-size canvases by Joaquín Sorolla y Bastida, depicting life in the various provinces of Spain. A collection of modern Spanish painting is on the second floor in the north building. The equestrian statue of the Spanish hero, *El Cid,* in the court, is the work of Anna Hyatt Huntington, wife of Archer M. Huntington.

The American Numismatic Society

This society, a membership and museum organization, was founded in

1858, for those interested in the art and history of coins, medals, and decorations. Its library and exhibits are, however, open to the public.

Among the objects on display, many were executed by the most skilled metal craftsmen and artists of their time and their beauty is impressive. The coinage of the United States is emphasized. Historical exhibits include pieces struck in the eastern provinces of Rome to finance the war of Brutus against Anthony, emergency currency employed during the siege of Netherlands cities, and coins of large denomination issued in California during the great gold rush. In the large hall are military and civil medals and decorations of all nations, and memorial plaques issued by the society itself.

The American Academy of Arts and Letters

The nation's closest approximation of *l'Académie française* is the American Academy of Arts and Letters, founded in 1904 by the National Institute of Arts and Letters. The institute, which also has its headquarters in the same buildings, was organized in 1898 by the American Social Science Association to further art, music, and literature in America.

The academy's members, limited to fifty, are elected for notable achievement in the arts. William Dean Howells, Augustus Saint-Gaudens, Edmund Clarence Stedman, John La Farge, Samuel L. Clemens, John Hay and Edward MacDowell were the first chosen. The museum contains a permanent display of sculpture, paintings, manuscripts, and other memorabilia of members of both the academy and the institute.

The academy possesses one of the finest small auditoriums in the city, entered from 156th Street. Designed by Cass Gilbert, it excels in general arrangement and in the treatment of its detail.

GEORGE WASHINGTON BRIDGE

Fort Washington Ave. and 179th St., Manhattan, across Hudson River to Fort Lee, N. J. IRT Broadway-7th Ave. subway to 181st St.; or 8th Ave. (Independent) Washington Heights subway to 181st St.; or 5th Ave. bus No. 4 to 178th St. Toll: passenger automobiles 50¢, pedestrians 5¢.

From a distance, George Washington Bridge, most splendid of all Manhattan bridges, is a silver arc above the broad steely plane of the Hudson. Up close the mighty span, linking upper Manhattan and Fort Lee, N. J., dominates the whole setting: the Palisades, the new brick and stone walls of the Riverside cliff dwellers, the wide flood of the river.

Its two great towers, cables, and roadway combine in a form that is graceful, simple, and extraordinarily effective. The design, a superb engineering concept, is based upon function in all its parts, with the exception of the steel arches of the towers—arched openings are expressions of masonry rather than of steel construction. As a matter of fact, the towers were originally intended to be encased in stone, but it is more than probable that this will never be done. Until completion of the San Francisco-Oakland Bay and Golden Gate bridges the George Washington was the longest suspension structure in the world, with a channel span length of 3,500 feet and a total over-all length of 4,760 feet between anchorages. The deck of the bridge, about 115 feet in width and about 250 feet above mean high water, is suspended from four cables. It has two separate roadways (each with three lanes) for east- and westbound traffic, and space in the center for three additional lanes to meet future traffic demands. Provision has been made for a deck twenty-nine feet below the present one either for additional motor traffic, especially busses, or for interstate railway rapid transit service.

The four steel cables, each composed of 26,474 parallel wires, are three feet in diameter and are arranged in pairs on each side of the roadway. Cable sag at the center of the channel span with the present single deck is 316 feet.

The cables are carried by saddles on top of two steel towers, some 600 feet above the river (about twice the height of the Palisades at the Fort Lee end). Each saddle rests on a bed of forty-one eight-inch diameter steel rollers, bolted to the flanges of steel grillage girders that keep the cables clear of the tops of the towers and help to distribute the load to the tower columns.

The New York anchorage is a U-shaped concrete block. The maximum pull of each cable is 62,000,000 pounds. The anchorage is to have a granite facing, similar to that used in the Henry Hudson Parkway structures.

Built, owned, and operated by the Port of New York Authority, the bridge is a part of the complex system of transport routes by which the nation's busiest island seeks to solve its traffic problems. Completed in 1931, it is linked with Manhattan's marginal highway by a series of extensive approaches which also provide a passage to Long Island by way of the Triborough Bridge. It also connects with US 1, 46, and 9W at the Jersey end and with US 1 and 9 at the Manhattan end. During 1937 approximately 8,000,000 vehicles paid toll to cross the bridge, and for the same period the gross income amounted to about $4,700,000. The total cost of the bridge, including rights-of-way, was about $60,000,000. O. H. Ammann of the Authority was the chief engineer and designer; Cass Gilbert, the architect, served in an advisory capacity.

On clear days the view eastward from the bridge includes a good part of Manhattan. Riverside Drive and the Henry Hudson Parkway, with their constant stream of cars, are directly below; Fort Washington and Fort Tryon parks skirt the drives. To the south the ribbons of Manhattan's highways are lost in the thickening cluster of roofs. The funnels of great ocean-going liners in the Hudson River docks, the smoking chimneys of New Jersey industrial towns, the play of the sun about the Himalayan towers of Manhattan are easily discernible.

At night the clear outline of the bridge fades into a fantasy of moving and twinkling lights above the Hudson, while atop the eastern tower the million-candlepower Rogers-Post Memorial Beacon sweeps its reassuring light across fifty miles of darkened sky.

SUBWAYS AND ELS

Until 1939, New York's subway and elevated lines carried about two billion passengers a year over a 281-mile network of main and branch lines in Manhattan, Brooklyn, Queens, and the Bronx (*see subway and el map in pocket*). The gaunt trestle-work of the els brought twilight to miles of streets, the tunnels of the subways honeycomb rocks and rivers and sky-scrapers. Their trains are the first things a good many New Yorkers observe in the morning and the last things a good many more remember at night.

Subways

About 5,500,000 passengers are carried daily by the three subway systems. Tens of thousands more ride the Hudson Tubes (Hudson and Manhattan Railroad) connecting New Jersey and Manhattan. The bulk of this traffic is borne between eight and nine in the morning and five and six in the evening when the crowd of workers moves to and from the business centers of Manhattan.

Typical of mid-town and lower Manhattan's rush-hour is the morning crush at IRT's station at Grand Central. While a crowd of commuters just arrived from the suburbs over New York Central and New Haven trains is storming the turnstiles on its way to downtown offices, a greater crowd from the city is pushing the stiles in the other direction, bound for work in the Grand Central district. These intent and humorless hordes cover uptown and downtown platforms, choke narrow stairways, swamp change-booths, wrestle with closing train doors. Crowds well up from the Queens trains on the lower subway level by way of elevators, escalators, stairways, and graded corridors. Nickels jingle, signal bells clang, turnstiles bang until the faint thunder of footsteps on the wooden passageway connecting the Lexington Avenue lines with the Times Square-Grand Central shuttle sounds human and restful. And through it all trains arrive and depart, delivering and removing crowds, lifting gum-papers and clouds of dust, and jarring the sidewalks, buildings, and windows of the city above.

Beneath the sidewalks of New York the subways have created a second city. Some of the thoroughfares between the turnstiles and the streets have lunch counters, barbershops, shoeshine stands, florist shops, phone booths. Through the use of these facilities the New Yorker could live a rather rounded life without once venturing into the street. He could, for example, stay at the Commodore Hotel, transact business in the Chrysler Building, dine at the Café Savarin, shop at Bloomingdale's, swim in the indoor pool at the Hotel St. George in Brooklyn, see a movie at the Rialto Theatre and, if romance came his way, marry at the Municipal Building. A few of the homeless use the subway as a flophouse and during the worst winters of the 1930's large numbers of unemployed lived here for days.

The three subway systems represent a total investment of $1,650,-000,000, and are owned and operated by the City of New York. These systems are the Interborough Rapid Transit (IRT), Brooklyn-Manhattan Transit (BMT), and Eighth Avenue (Independent). The IRT (station entrances marked by blue lamps) has two major trunk lines: Broadway-Seventh Avenue line, which runs under Manhattan's West Side; Lexington Avenue line, which runs under the East Side. These lines are connected in the mid-town area by a shuttle service under Forty-second Street between Times Square and Grand Central Terminal. Another main trunk line known as the Queens line originates at Times Square and runs east under Forty-second Street and the East River to Long Island City where it forks—one branch extending north through Astoria and another northeast to Flushing. Branches of the two major trunks also serve Brooklyn and the Bronx. The BMT (green and white lamps) was originally built to connect distant parts of Brooklyn with lower Manhattan, but now runs as far north as Sixtieth Street and the East River in Manhattan, and also extends into Queens. The Eighth Avenue (Independent) subway system (green lamps), the most modern of the subways, serves the West

Side and Lower East Side of Manhattan and runs into Brooklyn, Queens, and the West Bronx. Owned and operated by the city of New York, and one of the largest ventures in public ownership and control in the world, the Independent cost more than seven hundred million dollars.

London witnessed the operation of an underground railway in 1853. Seventeen years later, in New York, a pneumatic-driven railroad car made a trial run in a one-block tunnel extending under Broadway from Warren to Murray Street. With this demonstration as proof of the practicability of subways, E. A. Beach, the promoter, sought permission from the city to construct a line from lower Broadway to the Bronx. While the citizens were solidly behind the plan, petitioning public officials and even marching in a torchlight parade to emphasize their support, Beach had to contend with the skepticism of Broadway property owners, and the venture failed. When plans for the first IRT line (from City Hall to West 145th Street) were announced in 1900, Russell Sage remarked: "New York people will never go into a hole in the ground to ride . . . Preposterous!"

In 1904 the first line was opened running from Brooklyn Bridge north to Grand Central Station, then west under Forty-second Street to Times Square by what is now the Times Square-Grand Central shuttle and from that point north under Broadway to 145th Street. Extensions into the Bronx and Brooklyn by way of tunnels under the Harlem and East rivers were made in the following four years. Construction then lapsed until 1913, but between that year and 1931 the BMT and the present additional lines of the IRT were built and opened. In 1932, after seven years of digging, the Eighth Avenue (Independent) trunk line began operation, and extensions were completed in 1933, 1936, and 1937. At present (1939) additional extensions are being made in Brooklyn and the city is building the Sixth Avenue (Independent) subway line in Manhattan at a cost of $57,000,000. To drive a tunnel through the earth below the intersection of Sixth Avenue and Thirty-fourth Street, engineers constructing the Sixth Avenue Line had to solve the complex problem of how to avoid disturbing the already existing tunnels of the BMT, the Hudson Tubes, and the Pennsylvania Railroad—and the underpinning of the Sixth Avenue elevated structure.

With the exception of a few attractive stations, the subways are drab and noisy. Proposals that WPA artists and sculptors decorate the walls of the city-owned stations have been considered. Meanwhile, the romance of the subways of New York may be found in their trajectories, and in the intricacy of their construction and operation.

Elevated Railways

In 1868 when Charles T. Harvey demonstrated a cable-operated elevated train, New Yorkers were confident that the train would plunge into the street below. The trial was a success and subsequent additions to the original half-mile of elevated track from the Battery to Dey Street on Greenwich Street extended the line to West Thirtieth Street.

The trains were undependable: they frequently jammed between stations, compelling nervous passengers to descend to the street by way of hastily erected ladders. Steam locomotives were installed, but their advantages of speed and efficiency were offset by the tons of soot and cinders they poured into streets below, ruining derbies and Prince Alberts, and spoiling the wet wash of housewives, who hurled invective and bricks at the luckless engineers. In 1871, the original company was liquidated.

New companies were formed, and in 1875 the city authorized the construction of the Second, Third, Sixth, and Ninth Avenue elevated lines in Manhattan. Subsequently, el lines were built in Brooklyn and Queens, and electrification, introduced in 1902, aided the practicability of elevated travel.

The antiquated wooden coaches of the els daily carried approximately nine hundred thousand passengers. Owned and operated by IRT and BMT, the els reach into Manhattan, Brooklyn, Queens, and the Bronx. The IRT arteries begin at South Ferry, proceeding northward in parallel routes in Manhattan, then branching into Queens and the Bronx. The BMT lines sprawl across the length and breadth of Brooklyn, and also extend into Queens.

Despite the prevalent idea that "the subway yawns the quickest promise home," the speed of the el is substantially the same as that of the subway. But the el's advantage lies in its rambling trajectory, replete with images of New York which the subway journey (except in brief aerial excursions) lacks. From the vantage point of a window seat, one surveys the slums of Harlem and the East Side; middle-class Tudor City, Chinatown, and the Bowery; the German and Bohemian quarters of Yorkville; the Wall Street district; the flat suburban reaches of Brooklyn; the hilly jumble of the Bronx; and the quiet tree-shaded streets of Queens. Dingy sweatshops, flophouses, dramatic family groups pass in succession. So, too, do scenes of great beauty: skyscrapers at dusk, glittering rivers, dwindling streets.

Because of the unsightliness of the el structures and the lowered real-estate values of streets through which the els run, proposals have been made to abandon the el systems. A major step toward this end was taken in 1938–9 when the city purchased the Sixth Avenue el and razed the el structure. Among the sentimental memories associated with this means of travel will be the station houses, frame structures peaked and gabled in the architectural mode of the Victorian era, heated in winter by big pot-bellied coal stoves. Meanwhile, the el trains continue to rumble up and down New York.

Transit Safety

The maintenance of this vast transportation network requires an organization of unprecedented scope and perfection. Engineers, trackmen, motormen, conductors, dispatchers, mechanics, porters, change-makers, and platform guards—more than 27,000 employees—are all part of the unified scheme. Behind the scenes work those responsible for fundamental transit operations. And still more anonymous, and more numerous, are the inanimate servants: signal and safety devices, checks, trippers, and switches.

The New York subway lines are said to be the safest railroads in the world; the els have an almost equally good record. The IRT, for example, has made this security possible by the operation of fifty-six types of safety devices, as well as by regular inspection of track and equipment, and physical examination of motormen. Should a motorman fail to observe the red stop signal, an automatic tripper would instantly halt the train; should he become ill or die, the second his hand falls from the controller the "dead man's button" stops the train.

Accidents, however, have occurred in the rapid transit systems. In 1929, two Ninth Avenue el trains collided at 110th Street and Eighth Avenue—about fifty-five feet above street level—killing one passenger. Seventeen persons were fatally injured in 1928 when a crowded subway train smashed into a retaining wall just south of Times Square station. But most accidents are of trifling extent, and involve nothing more than the loss of time. Suicides, too, may upset the routine of subway and elevated commerce, but their number is small.

Minor adventures are not infrequent. Strangers get lost in the maze of stations and transit lines, although maps are conspicuously posted in cars and on platforms, and New Yorkers vouchsafe information (at times somewhat incomprehensibly). A small boy, avid for adventure, may set out on a journey to the Bad Lands, and arrive at New Lots Avenue, Brooklyn (which is not bad at all). Or a honeymooning couple, visiting the big town, may be swept apart by the rush of crowds and, as once reported, spend several hours of horrible anxiety before being reunited by the police.

Greater drama resides in the endless flow of activity that crowds the cars and platforms. Beggars, singers, banjo-players, and candy-butchers vie for a few pennies, howl bargains, or stumble silently past the apathetic passengers. Occasionally, a particularly bright singing troupe or an unusually pathetic cripple will meet with warm response. At large stations, pitchmen attract crowds with infinite ease, and disappear before the greenhorn realizes he has been duped.

The five-cent fare—a recurring issue in municipal politics—is not likely to be increased in the immediate or distant future. The New Yorker is extremely sensitive on this point.

The Harbor, The Rivers, and Their Islands

D. Spiegel

The Harbor and Its Islands

STATEN ISLAND FERRY TRIP—STATUE OF
LIBERTY AND BEDLOE ISLAND—GOVERNORS
ISLAND—ELLIS ISLAND

Map on pages 6-7.
To ferries: IRT Broadway-7th Ave. subway (local) to South Ferry; or IRT Lexington Ave. subway (local) to Bowling Green; or 2d, 3d, or 9th Ave. el to South Ferry.

NEW YORK'S harbor is one of the finest in the world; a magnificent water gate that is well protected, open the year round, deep enough for the largest vessels, and spacious enough to hold the entire United States Navy without obstructing normal traffic. Such harbors are few and their importance to a national economy is incalculable. Without this natural advantage, New York could never have advanced to its present position, for water-borne commerce has contributed much to the growth of the city.

The port of New York, in its totality, includes all the navigable waterways within a radius of twenty-five miles from the Statue of Liberty: seven bays (Upper, Lower, Gravesend, Jamaica, Raritan, Newark, and Flushing), four rivers (Raritan, Passaic, Hackensack, Hudson), four estuaries (Arthur Kill, Kill van Kull, East River, Harlem River), several creeks,

and some 771 miles of direct shore line, of which more than 578 miles are
in the five boroughs of New York City. By every significant statistical
measure, this is the busiest seaport in the world. The harbor proper, however, is generally considered to be made up of the Lower Bay, the Upper
Bay, and the Narrows—the three units that form a direct seventeen-mile
route from the open sea to the Battery.

The Lower Bay lies under the western end of Long Island, sheltered by
the curling arm of Sandy Hook, by Rockaway Point, and by the sand shoals
between them. Of the several channels through the shoals and up the bay,
Ambrose Channel, followed by all deep-draft ships, is the most important.
It is dredged 40 feet deep and 2,000 feet wide, and runs 38,000 feet to
the Narrows, where from either side Staten Island and Brooklyn pinch the
harbor into a wasp waist. The Narrows is a mile-wide tidal strait connecting Lower Bay with Upper Bay.

To many landsmen the Upper Bay is the whole harbor, and it is indeed
the center of the port. Five miles long, from the Battery to Staten Island,
four miles wide, from Brooklyn to the Jersey shore, this is at once the
front door of a nation and the service entrance. Long piers reach out from
every shore. Chuffing tugs wrestle determinedly with car floats and clumsy
barges, single-minded ferries cut one another's wakes, tankers with their
snake-nests of deck hose veer westward to the Bayonne refineries, and
occasionally a deep-chested liner rears through the thin haze, easing her
way to a Hudson River berth.

STATEN ISLAND FERRY TRIP

The quickest and best way of seeing the Upper Bay is also the cheapest
—a ferry trip from South Ferry, Manhattan, to St. George, Staten Island,
and return, over the route that Commodore Vanderbilt's *Nautilus* began
traveling in 1817. The Staten Island ferries, operated by the Department
of Docks on a five-cent fare, are a New York institution. The old boats
are double-ended, rather drab old craft with barn-red superstructures, yet
surprisingly swift—they make the five-mile run in twenty minutes. These
are being gradually replaced with sleek, new, partially streamlined boats,
painted a silvery gray.

Even Staten Islanders, many of whom make this trip twice a day, find it
hard to keep their attention on their newspapers as the ferry moves away
from the backdrop of lower Manhattan's fabulous towers. In good weather
they crowd like tourists on the outside decks, while the inside benches are
nearly empty.

On the right of the boat as it pulls away, is the 3,600-foot mouth of the Hudson with the horizontal New Jersey towns along its west bank; obliquely to the left and rear, the tremendous stone piers and airy web of Brooklyn Bridge merge momentarily with Manhattan Bridge high above the East River. Brooklyn, broad and amorphous, stretches away to the east and south, coarse-fringed with ship's funnels and factory smokestacks. In the mouth of the East River is the low-lying strip of Governors Island, dominated by ancient, massive Castle Williams. Once past Governors, the ferry is in the midst of scurrying traffic whose strident voice mingles whistle blasts with the hollow clang of bell buoys and the screams of softly wheeling gulls. Distance subdues the clamor; the bay is unexpectedly quiet.

To the west, the dull brick buildings of Ellis Island are banked low against the Jersey shore. A little farther along, also well over on the New Jersey side, the Statue of Liberty salutes Brooklyn from Bedloe Island. At night the verdigris-coated statue is floodlighted from pedestal to torch.

For most of its route the ferry follows the Upper Bay's principal channel, Anchorage Channel, which runs from the Narrows to a point west of Governors Island. At no place is this course less than forty feet deep and at one point it is about one hundred feet deep. On either side, freighters anchor to wait for dock space or for cargoes. Bay Ridge, Red Hook, and Buttermilk channels follow the Brooklyn shore line into the East River.

Near little Robbins Reef Lighthouse, at the right, outbound ships swing left through the Narrows and make for the ocean, but the ferry continues to St. George, the community that clambers up Fort Hill. To the right the Bayonne Bridge connects Staten Island and New Jersey, arching high across Kill van Kull.

The return trip to the Battery is even more impressive. Manhattan's slender shafts, poised on that narrow bit of land, seem to rise out of the water in one solid pyramiding mass. As the ferry draws closer they resolve themselves into huge cubic blocks, glistening with windows. When night conceals the shore line, the illuminated towers seem suspended in the dark.

STATUE OF LIBERTY AND BEDLOE ISLAND

Boat leaves Battery every hour (every half hour on Saturday and Sunday during the summer); round trip fare 35¢ for adults, 20¢ for children. Statue open daily 9 A.M. to 5 P.M. (to 6 P.M. in September and to 7 P.M. in June, July, and August); admission 10¢.

Perhaps the best-known piece of sculpture in America, Bartholdi's huge female figure of *Liberty Enlightening the World,* commands the Upper Bay from the east end of twelve-acre egg-shaped Bedloe Island.

The 151-foot figure, atop a 142-foot granite and concrete pedestal, portrays Liberty as a woman stepping from broken shackles. The uplifted right hand holds a burning torch, while the left hand grasps a tablet representing the Declaration of Independence, inscribed "July 4, 1776." The statue, of hand-hammered copper plates supported by an inner iron framework, weighs 225 tons. The upheld arm, three hundred feet above sea level, is forty-two feet long and twelve feet in diameter at its thickest; the width of the head is ten feet, of the eyes, two and a half feet. Weathering of the copper has covered the statue with a soft verdigris. A circular stairway of 168 steps leads from the top of the pedestal to the spiked crown. From sunset to sunrise, ninety-two 1,000-watt bulbs floodlight the structure and fifteen more illuminate the torch.

The statue is a gift of the French people to commemorate "the alliance of the two nations in achieving the independence of the United States of America, and attests their abiding friendship." Although the French historian, Edouard Laboulaye, first proposed the gift and helped to form the Franco-American Union for this purpose in 1875, credit for originating the idea of a monument to Franco-American friendship must go largely to Frederic Auguste Bartholdi, who chose the site and modeled the statue. The project became the controlling passion of his life, and he worked indefatigably to raise funds on both sides of the Atlantic to bring the plan to completion. Alexandre Gustave Eiffel, the French engineer, built the supporting framework.

By 1879 one million francs had been raised by popular subscription. The statue was formally presented to the United States in Paris, July 4, 1884; but the American share of the plan, the building of a suitable pedestal, was slow in realization. In 1884, when fifteen feet of masonry had been raised, work ceased for lack of funds, and it was not until a year later, after Joseph Pulitzer of the New York *World* took to writing daily editorials on this state of affairs, that a sum sufficient to complete the pedestal (designed by Richard M. Hunt) was subscribed. The statue was shipped in 214 cases aboard the French ship *Isère* in May, 1885. President Cleveland dedicated the monument on October 28, 1886.

Bedloe Island was called Minissais (lesser island) by the Indians, and Great Oyster Island by the colonists. Isaac Bedloe (or Bedlow), who received it from Governor Nicolls, was the first white owner. His widow is said to have sold it in 1676 to "James Carteret of New Jersey for 81 pounds of Boston money." The Corporation of the city of New York bought it for one thousand pounds in 1758; ownership was transferred to the state of New York for fortification purposes in 1796 with the proviso that the city be allowed to use it as a quarantine station whenever necessary. Between 1793 and 1796 the French fleet had used it as a hospital base. The star-shaped rampart (now the base for the pedestal of the statue) was built in 1811 and later named Fort Wood, for one of the heroes of the Battle of Fort Erie. During more than two centuries of varying ownership, Bedloe Island held a farm, a pesthouse, a gallows, a military prison, and a dump.

The Lighthouse Board had jurisdiction over the statue until 1901, when the War Department assumed control. It was declared a national monument in 1924. In September, 1937, jurisdiction of the island in its entirety passed to the National Park Service of the Department of the Interior. The National Park Service, with WPA help, renovated the statue in 1938, as part of extensive improvements which include landscaping the whole island and providing a more attractive approach to the statue. The new boat landing will face the New Jersey instead of the Manhattan side. The date set for completion of this program is 1942. Annually about three hundred thousand visitors come to the island.

GOVERNORS ISLAND

Ferry (free) leaves South Ferry Barge Office. No pass required; for guide service telephone WHitehall 4-8010 in advance.

Five hundred yards off the tip of Manhattan, Governors Island faces the tall towers of the metropolis; but its neatly squared shores, its trim redbrick barracks, its well-kept buildings, shaded walks, and historic forts surrounded by green lawns suggest a Dutch village.

This is the headquarters for the Second Corps Area, second in importance only to Washington in administrative affairs of the United States Army.

The Government ferryboat, *Gen. Charles F. Humphrey*, lands at the foot of Soissons Place, named for a successful World War engagement of the Sixteenth Infantry Regiment. From here, two roads branch out, one leading to Castle Williams on the right, and the other to Fort Jay on the left.

The star-shaped FORT JAY dominates the island from a knoll. Originally built in 1794, it was reconstructed and renamed Fort Columbus in 1806. Its four bastions of masonry held one hundred guns and a drawbridge approach over a dry moat to a sally port. In 1904 its old name was re-stored. Within the fort is a quadrangle of officers' dwellings; surrounding the bastion works and the patched redbrick walls are the greens of a nine-hole golf course.

The administrative offices, post office, tool shops, and WPA offices and shops are housed in buildings near Fort Jay. The WPA has constructed and repaired officers' dwellings, and beautified the grounds; a mural in the Administration Building, depicting scenes from six American wars, was painted by artists of the Federal Art Project.

CASTLE WILLIAMS, popularly known as "the cheese box" because of its circular shape, was begun in 1807 and completed in 1811 after the de-signs of Lieutenant-Colonel Jonathan Williams. Two hundred feet in di-ameter, with ivied red sandstone walls, forty feet high and eight feet thick, it is casemated with arches for three tiers of guns. Today Castle William is the disciplinary barracks of the U.S. Army.

Near by are the structures built on filled land in the 1930's by the War Department to house the Sixteenth Infantry—complete with barracks, mess- and class-rooms. On the flat expanses of filled land to the south are the polo grounds, small-arms target ranges, and stables. The Sunday afternoon polo matches *(May through October, admission fees 50¢ and 75¢)* draw large numbers of civilian spectators.

BRICK ROW, landscaped in keeping with the military environment, con-sists of eight red-brick two-story houses bordering the parade ground. The frame houses of GENERALS ROW and COLONELS ROW enclose a park. There are also a library, workshops, and a store. At Brick Row, situated in what is now the center of the island, the elevation is about forty feet above the high-water mark. In the chapel are flags of engagements ranging from the Revolutionary to the World War.

At the south end of the island, the triangular SOUTH BATTERY, built in 1812, looks out over Buttermilk Channel to Brooklyn. Once a forbid-ding fortress bristling with guns, it is now the site of the Officers Club.

A few paces from South Battery the square stone tower of the CHAPEL OF SAINT CORNELIUS THE CENTURION, of Trinity Parish, rises above the trees. Within this granite-block building, designed by Charles C. Haight and built in 1906, are preserved a number of military curios, including brass cannon and the oldest army flag of the first United States Infantry.

Governors Island, originally called Nutten Island, was ignored by the Dutch until Wouter van Twiller, second governor of New Netherland, purchased it in 1637 from two Indians for one or two axheads, a few nails, and other trifles. In 1698 the New York Assembly set the land aside "for

the benefit and accommodation of His Majesty's governors." This gave
rise to its present name. At various times the island served as sheep farm,
a quarantine station, a race track, and a game preserve, in addition to
harboring the governor's "pleasure house."

Although the Assembly in 1703 authorized the raising of funds to build
fortifications on the island, none was erected until the urgencies of the
Revolution compelled General Israel Putnam, with a thousand men, to
build them as defense against the British. By the time of the War of 1812
the fortifications were considered to be of such military strength that observers believed they forestalled the threatened British naval attack on
New York City.

During the Civil War, 1,500 Rebel prisoners were held in Castle Williams, and a great number of troops were stationed on the island—the
records mentioning seven regiments as being on duty at one time. In
1863 draft-rioters unsuccessfully tried to storm the island while the troops
were guarding the Subtreasury in Wall Street.

By 1900 the area of Governors Island had dwindled from about 170
acres (its size during the Dutch occupation) to 70 because of wave ero-
sion. The land was replaced with earth dug from subway excavations and
dredged channels, so that today, with 173 acres, Governors Island has
more than regained its former size. On the recovered land more than
seventy buildings were constructed during the World War, and even a
temporary railroad was built.

Today such excitement as the peaceful island knows is created by dress
reviews and competitive sports, to which the public is invited. Most popular are boxing, basketball, football, and polo.

ELLIS ISLAND

Ferry leaves South Ferry Barge Office daily at 9:45 A.M. and 1:45 P.M. Visiting
daily, except Saturday and holidays, 10-11 A.M., 2-3 P.M. Pass from U. S. Department of Labor, Immigration and Naturalization Service, required; telephone WHitehall 4-8860 in advance.

Ellis Island is the headquarters of District No. 3 (southern New York
and northern New Jersey) of the twenty-two Immigration and Naturalization Districts into which the United States is divided. It lies about one mile
southwest of the Battery in Upper Bay. Its shape is that of two parallel
rectangles joined by filled land at their western ends, but separated for the
most part by a narrow rectangular basin which contains a ferry slip.

The bulbous towers of some of the island's buildings give it a faintly Byzantine appearance. The buildings on the east side house administrative offices, a dormitory with space for one thousand beds, a dining hall that can seat a thousand people, rooms for hearings, a recreation room, a room for social welfare workers, a library, and a kindergarten. On the north wall of the dining hall, a mural done by the Federal Art Project depicts the contributions of immigrants to the building of America. Other important units are the general hospital, used now, because of the great decline in immigration, for treatment of American sailors and marines; the contagious-disease hospital; and guarded rooms for dangerous and violent deportees. The most modern building is a ferry house, near the center of the island, built with PWA funds in 1935.

A staff of more than five hundred, under a District Commissioner and a District Director of the Immigration and Naturalization Service of the U.S. Department of Labor, attends to the administration of inspection, boarding, records, registry, bonding, passports, and naturalization matters.

When the Dutch colonists used this island as a picnic ground and called it Oyster Island, it had only about three acres of land. It was known also as Bucking Island, and after the pirate Anderson was hanged there in 1765, as Gibbet Island. In the eighteenth century Samuel Ellis, a Manhattan dealer in general merchandise and owner of a New Jersey farm, bought it. After he died, it passed from his heirs to John A. Berry and, in 1808, to New York State. New York immediately sold the island for ten thousand dollars to the Federal Government. For a time it was used as a government arsenal, to the alarm of near-by Jersey residents who feared an explosion. In 1814 it became the site of Fort Gibson.

By 1890 Castle Garden at the Battery *(see page 308)* could no longer cope with the successive tidal waves of immigrants, and construction of another station on the island was authorized. The name Ellis Island was restored in 1891, and in January, 1892, the station went into operation. Fire destroyed the buildings in 1897, but twenty-eight new ones were constructed.

Two more islands were created by the dumping of earth and rock in 1898 and 1905. Today, although causeways and filled land make one 27½-acre island of the three, employees still designate certain sections as Island No. 1, Island No. 2, and Island No. 3.

Long the wide-open door to the New World, Ellis Island is now barely ajar. In 1907, the station's peak year, 1,285,349 immigrants were admitted. As many as five thousand bewildered aliens passed through some days, so greatly overcrowding the island that living conditions there became notorious. The total fell sharply to 326,700 in 1915 and to 23,068 in 1933. Strict adherence to quota limits checked the influx. Most present-day immigrants do not go to Ellis Island; only those whose eligibility for admission is questioned are examined there. Early in 1939 the quotas of only the Central European countries were filled.

The Rivers and The River Islands

Map on pages 6-7.
Boat trips around Manhattan: Yacht *Tourist* leaves Battery Landing 10:30 A.M. and
2:30 P.M. daily, May to October; round trip $1.50. Yachts *Marilda, Marilda II,* and
Manhattan leave foot of W. 42d St. 10 A.M., 2 P.M., and 7:30 P.M. daily, April 6
to November 1; round trip $2.00.

OF THE three waterways surrounding Manhattan, only the Hudson River
is a true river. It drains water from the Adirondack Mountains, 300 miles
to the north, and the fertile Mohawk Valley; and it drains wheat, automobiles, flour, and many other hinterland products from the Great Lakes
ports by way of the New York State Barge Canal. It was this inland trade
route that gave New York an early advantage over such ports as Boston
and Philadelphia.

The wooded hills through which the Hudson flows make it one of the
most beautiful rivers in America, and the sheer Palisades, forming a
twenty-one mile western wall near its mouth, make it one of the most
spectacular. Where it comes abreast of the northern tip of Manhattan
Island, the Hudson is 4,400 feet wide. The Manhattan shore is lined with
ribbon parks from Inwood Hill to Seventy-second Street; and from Fifty-
ninth Street to the Battery the water front is edged with steamship piers
and ferry slips. On the New Jersey side, the narrow shore front at the base
of the Palisades is taken up, for the most part, by industrial plants, many
of which have their own docking facilities. Fleets of ferries ply between
Manhattan and the railroad terminals in Weehawken (opposite Forty-
second Street), Hoboken (opposite Twenty-third Street), and Jersey City
(opposite the lower end of Manhattan). The river narrows to 2,770 feet
at Fourteenth Street, but this width increases to 3,670 feet at the Battery.
Almost all the larger transatlantic liners that enter the harbor and many

vessels in the coastwise trade berth in the Hudson. From a point near Ellis Island in the Upper Bay, they follow a channel 40 feet deep and from 2,400 to 2,800 feet wide that has been dredged to Fifty-ninth Street. Another channel thirty feet deep serves the New Jersey piers.

The George Washington Bridge (179th Street) and five tunnels connect Manhattan with New Jersey: the Lincoln Tunnel (Thirty-eighth Street), the Pennsylvania Railroad Tunnel (Thirty-second Street), the Holland Tunnel (Canal Street), and two Hudson and Manhattan Railroad crossings (Morton Street and Fulton-Cortlandt Streets). Each of the tunnels has two tubes; the Lincoln and Holland tunnels are for motor vehicles only.

As far as is known, Giovanni da Verrazano was the first European to visit New York Harbor, and he undoubtedly saw the mouth of the Hudson in 1524. Estavan Gomez, a Portuguese Negro, saw it the next year. It was not until September, 1609, that the river was explored by the man for whom it is named, Henry Hudson, who was searching for a new route to the Indies. In 1610 a ship sent out by Amsterdam merchants sailed as far north as Albany. Early Dutch settlers named the Hudson the North River to distinguish it from the Delaware, or South River, and that section of the Hudson which borders Manhattan is still called the North River.

The East River is not strictly speaking a river; it is a salt water estuary, or tidal strait, connecting the Upper Bay with Long Island Sound, and is subject to tidal fluctuations which its varying depth and narrowness accentuate. It separates the western end of Long Island (Brooklyn and Queens) from Manhattan Island and the only mainland borough, the Bronx. From the Upper Bay, between the Battery and Governors Island, to Long Island Sound at Throg's Neck, the river is about sixteen miles long. About eight and one-half miles north of the Battery, where it is joined by another estuary, the Harlem River, the East River turns east toward the Sound.

Near the confluence of the Harlem and the East rivers, and wedged between the Bronx, Manhattan, and Long Island, are Randall's Island and Ward's Island. A little to the south, slender Welfare Island splits the East River up the middle, while in the wider eastern arm of the river, between the Bronx and the northern shore of Queens, Riker's Island and its twin satellites, North Brother and South Brother Islands, lie near the entrance of Bowery Bay.

A forty-foot channel, one thousand feet wide, leads from the Battery to the Brooklyn Navy Yard Basin. Above that point the channel is at least thirty-five feet deep all the way along the west side of Welfare Island, through Hell Gate and east to Throg's Neck; just north of the New York Connecting Railroad Bridge across Hell Gate the river is 168 feet deep at mean low water.

Hell Gate, the narrow channel between Astoria (Queens) and Ward's Island, has borne an ugly reputation among navigators ever since Adrian Block took his *Tyger* through it in 1612; its tortuous course, dangerous rocks, and powerful tidal currents have been the death of thousands of vessels. Washington Irving wrote that at half tide the current roared "like a bull bellowing for more drink," and at full tide slept "as soundly as an alderman after dinner," and compared it to "a quarrelsome toper, who is a peaceable fellow enough when he has no liquor at all, or when he has a skinful, but who, when half-seas-over, plays the very devil." In 1876 a great rocky outcropping of Hallett's Point was blasted out, and later improvements have made the channel much safer, but large vessels from foreign ports still require the help of members of the Hell Gate Pilots Association in making the passage between the Sound and the harbor. The name Hell Gate probably derived from the Dutch *Hellegat* (beautiful pass) which originally was applied to the whole East River.

Ward's and Randall's Islands are separated by Little Hell Gate, which is navigable only by very small boats and is seldom used. Bronx Kill, between Randall's Island and the Bronx, is not navigable.

The deep East River, giving access to long stretches of shore line through the center of the city, has, of course, influenced the nature and direction of the city's development. South Street and the lower Manhattan river front early became the center of maritime affairs, and shipping interests monopolized the shore areas. The increase in the size of ships eventually necessitated moving the docks of the larger liners from the narrow East River to the roomier Hudson; the Brooklyn and South Street piers, however, still accommodate many good-sized vessels.

Although the river has been invaluable to the city's commerce, it has created a serious problem in interborough transportation. Eleven costly tunnels and seven great bridges have been required to connect Manhattan with Brooklyn and Queens. Four of the bridges are suspension spans (Brooklyn, Manhattan, Williamsburg, and the Hell Gate unit of the Triborough); Queensboro is a cantilever; Triborough's 125th Street unit is a vertical lift structure; and the New York Connecting Railroad's Hell Gate Bridge is a steel arched-truss span. All are high enough to permit tall-masted ships to pass under them. To these may be added the Triborough truss span over Bronx Kill and the low bridge between Ward's and Randall's Islands.

The Harlem River, slanting about eight miles around the northern end of Manhattan, is not entirely a natural waterway. The old unnavigable Spuyten Duyvil Creek, which almost encircled Marble Hill, connected the Harlem and Hudson rivers until 1895 when a canal was cut through the flatlands separating Marble Hill from its southern neighbor, Inwood. By obviating the trip around the Battery, the improved Harlem channel, 350 to 400 feet wide and 15 feet deep, shortens the water route between the Hudson River and Long Island Sound by about fourteen miles.

Nine swing bridges, almost identical in appearance, and five fixed bridges cross the Harlem between Manhattan and the Bronx; three subway tunnels burrow under it. Coal hoists, small docks, garbage scows, junk yards, and grimy bridge approaches line both sides of the southern half of the Harlem's length. North of the Yankee Stadium and the Polo Grounds high wooded shores are of some scenic interest. The section that leads past steep Inwood Hill Park and under Henry Hudson Bridge into the Hudson River is strikingly beautiful.

The East River islands, owned by the city for many years, until recently have been jumbles of institutional masonry, ill-assorted piles of prison, hospital, and asylum architecture. Removal of many of the most unsightly buildings and intelligent landscaping by the Department of Parks have given a new beauty to the islands.

Politically, Welfare, Ward's, and Randall's Islands belong to Manhattan; Riker's and North Brother Islands are parts of the Bronx; and South Brother Island is in Queens.

WELFARE ISLAND

Queensboro Bridge from East 59th St. to elevators on island, or ferry (pedestrians only) from foot of East 78th St. to Metropolitan Hospital. Pass from Department of Hospitals required.

Welfare Island, shaped very much like a cigar, is a mile and three-quarters long and at its broadest point 750 feet wide. From one end, off Manhattan's Fifty-first Street, to the other, opposite Eighty-sixth Street, it holds municipal welfare institutions—hospitals and old people's homes—grouped in little landscaped villages with paved streets.

The Queensboro Bridge, crossing high over the island about one-quarter of the way north of the lower tip, gives access to Welfare through a most unusual building, the ELEVATOR STOREHOUSE. The entrance to this ten-story structure, the only vehicular entrance to the island, is on its top floor, flush with the roadway of the bridge, where trucks, ambulances, and other vehicles weighing up to $17\frac{1}{2}$ tons enter large elevators to be lowered to ground level. The building, which was completed in 1916, houses RECEPTION HOSPITAL (a tiny emergency ward and ambulance dispatching office), besides serving as distribution center for supplies used by several municipal departments.

The eighteen light-gray buildings of NEW YORK CITY HOSPITAL occupy the southern end of the island. This is a hospital of a thousand beds with a resident staff of 53 doctors and a visiting staff of 203. It was founded as Penitentiary Hospital in 1832. Despite an early history of scandal and mismanagement, it has come to be recognized, after more than a hundred years of existence, as one of America's fine hospitals, and its staff includes many eminent physicians. Outpatients are treated at a branch at 220 East Fifty-ninth Street.

WELFARE HOSPITAL FOR CHRONIC DISEASES, immediately north of City Hospital, represents one of the most advanced hospital designs in the world. Four four-story pavilions, arranged in chevron-shaped pairs on either side of a more conventional administration building, can accommodate 1,600 patients. The unusual shape of the buildings permits a maximum of sunlight to reach every ward and gives every patient a river view. The peculiar importance of this institution, aside from its design, lies in the fact that it makes research possible in the neglected field of chronic disease. The hospital will be opened in 1939. The architects were Isadore Rosenfield, senior architect of the Department of Hospitals; Butler and Kohn; York and Sawyer.

North of the bridge and the General Storehouse, the spacious new CENTRAL NURSES RESIDENCE, opened in 1938, houses 675 nurses who work in the island's hospitals.

The NEW YORK CITY HOME FOR DEPENDENTS, beyond the Nurses Residence, is a community in itself, with churches, stores, long dormitories, and smaller houses arranged about a central square. There are fifty-six buildings covering almost twenty acres. The home is equipped to furnish food, shelter, recreation, and care for 1,747 indigents, including aged blind people. More than half of the patients are past sixty-five years, and a few are more than ninety.

To the north, the 470-bed CENTRAL NEUROLOGICAL HOSPITAL is devoted to the treatment of organic nervous diseases. Six resident physicians and an attending and consulting staff of thirty-six are aided by the most modern equipment for neurological physiotherapeutics. The hospital was opened in 1909.

The near-by CANCER INSTITUTE, founded in 1923, was one of the first municipal institutions in America given over to diagnosis, care, and treatment of patients suffering from cancer and allied diseases. Two two-story buildings accommodate 200 patients under the care of eight resident doctors and thirty attending physicians and surgeons. The Cancer Institute's clinic, located for convenience at 124 East Fifty-ninth Street, Manhattan, performs diagnoses, treats convalescents, and has accommodations for sixteen patients in a small hospital unit.

METROPOLITAN HOSPITAL occupies the northern end of the island. This century-old institution is one of the largest hospitals in the city (1,385 beds). With some 1,250 employees, it is equipped to give free service of many kinds: general medical, surgical, obstetrical, etc. The main buildings were erected in 1839.

Governor Van Twiller was the first white man to own Welfare Island. In 1637 he obtained it from the Indians as he had Ward's, Randall's, and Governors Islands. Because it was used as pasture for swine, the island (called Minnahanonck by the Indians) became known as Varcken (Hog) Island. The English later corrupted that title to Perkins Island. After Van Twiller lost it in 1652, it passed into the ownership of a man named Flyn.

In 1668 Captain John Manning, a British officer, bought it. He retired to the island after his sword was broken over his head at City Hall for his surrender of New York to the Dutch in 1673.

Robert Blackwell, who had married Manning's stepdaughter Mary, eventually took title to the property and held it until his death in 1717; the island bore his name until April 12, 1921. The old BLACKWELL HOUSE still survives, directly south of the Queensboro Bridge, and is used as a clubhouse for internes.

The city of New York acquired the island July 19, 1828, and constructed charitable and corrective institutions. The original price of the land was $32,500, but fifteen years later the widow of a man named Bell, whose mortgage had been illegally foreclosed, was awarded $20,000 from the city by the courts.

By 1921 the reputation of the workhouse and penitentiary on the island had attained such notoriety that the Board of Aldermen, with Coué-like faith, changed the name from Blackwell's to Welfare Island. Critics called the obsolete buildings "a sin-steeped pile." Reports of serious overcrowding, favoritism, degeneracy, and intramural violence brought frequent scandals. Cliques of favored prisoners virtually ruled the institutions and controlled a heavy traffic in narcotics.

Then, in January, 1934, Austin H. MacCormick took office as Commissioner of Correction. Almost immediately he led a spectacular raid on the island that shattered the ugly system "whereby 200 men lived like kings and 1,200 almost starved." It was recognized, however, that the ancient structures were ill suited to modern penal methods, and the quarters that had housed such notorious convicts as the Tammany leaders, "Boss" Tweed, Billy McGlory, and "Little Abe" Hummel were razed. The prisoners were moved to the new Riker's Island penitentiary. After more than a century's use as a place of punishment, Welfare Island was entirely given over to care of the aged and the ill.

RANDALL'S ISLAND

IRT Lexington Ave. subway, 2d Ave. el, 3d Ave. el, 3d Ave. surface car, 2d Ave. bus, Lexington Ave. bus, or Madison Ave. bus to 125th St.; then by Triborough Bridge bus to Randall's Island.

The program for the transformation of the East River islands has been completed only on Randall's Island, the triangular meeting place for the three arms of the Triborough Bridge. Except for the land required by the Triborough and New York Connecting Railroad Bridge structures, the whole of the island, 194 acres, has been laid out in parks and playgrounds.

Besides the bridges and a few administration buildings, the only important structure is the municipal TRIBOROUGH STADIUM, placed near the southern point of the island. This provides 21,441 permanent seats and space for an additional 8,000. It is used for athletic contests, open-air opera and other musical spectacles, and public meetings. It is equipped with probably the largest movable outdoor stage in the world.

In 1668 the British Governor Nicolls granted the island to customs collector Thomas Delavall. Captain James Montresor bought it for a place of residence in 1772. Of its several early names, Montresor's Island was most commonly used. In 1784 Jonathan Randel (Randal) acquired it. When the city of New York bought the island for sixty thousand dollars in 1835, the misspelled title deed added an extra "l" to Randell that still survives in the island's name.

The Common Council decided in 1843 to move the potter's field from Fiftieth Street and Fourth Avenue to the southern part of the island; in 1845 an almshouse was added. In 1851 part of Randall's was appropriated for the use of the "Society for the Reformation of Juvenile Delinquents," who built there a house of refuge. From that time until it was cleared for the construction of the Triborough Bridge, the island was used by hospitals and corrective institutions for children.

WARD'S ISLAND

Same transit directions as for Randall's Island; then by Little Hell Gate Bridge from Randall's Island.

Ward's Island, approximately square-shaped, is one of the stepping stones used by the Triborough Bridge and the New York Connecting Railroad (Hell Gate) Bridge in crossing the East River. Approaching from the north along nearly parallel lines, both structures swing east from Ward's into Queens.

Slowly, as the MANHATTAN STATE HOSPITAL FOR THE INSANE, which has occupied Ward's for more than forty years, is finally evacuated, the Department of Parks is retrieving the island's 254½ acres for recreational use. By 1943 the eighty buildings that form this institutional community will have been entirely emptied.

A MUNICIPAL SEWAGE DISPOSAL PLANT, one of the three largest in the world, occupies 77½ acres on the northeast corner of the island; it was put into operation by the Department of Sanitation October, 1937. Thirty-seven acres in the southeast corner between the bridges have been cleared by razing ten two-story buildings, erected in 1917 as a military base hospital. This portion will be opened as a park in 1939.

Construction of a new vertical-lift footbridge, 790 feet long, from the foot of 103d Street (Manhattan), has been proposed by the Department of Parks to make the island more readily accessible, and new pedestrian ramps from Triborough Bridge are planned. Meanwhile, all traffic uses the low bridge from Randall's Island across Little Hell Gate.

The British used Ward's Island as a military post during the Revolution. Its early names were Tenkenas, Buchanan's Island, and Great Barn Island, a corruption of Great Barent; but when the Ward brothers, Jasper and Bartholomew, bought it after the Revolution and divided it into farms, the present name came into occasional use. A cotton mill that operated there during the War of 1812 was connected to the foot of East 114th Street (Manhattan) by a bridge, the first over the East River. When the mill closed after the war, the island was deserted.

In 1840 one hundred thousand bodies were moved from the site of Bryant Park to a new potter's field on Ward's. In 1847 a State Emigration

Refuge for "the sick and destitute aliens from the Old World" was established there, and after 1860 the island was used as a secondary immigration station until the Ellis Island station was opened in 1892. The abandoned immigration buildings were then taken over by the New York City Asylum for the Insane, which had been in operation since 1863. The New York State Department of Mental Hygiene assumed control of the asylum in 1896, changed its name to Manhattan State Hospital, and added many buildings.

RIKER'S ISLAND, NORTH BROTHER ISLAND, AND SOUTH BROTHER ISLAND

IRT Pelham subway to Cypress Ave.; then by ferry from E. 134th St., the Bronx. Pass from Department of Correction required.

When Abraham Rycken (later spelled Riker) obtained a patent for Riker's Island in 1664, and through the long years of Riker family ownership, it amounted to only eighty-seven acres of land. Since New York City annexed it from Newtown, Queens, in 1884, the size of the island has increased to four hundred acres, and it is still growing through the dumping of old metal, refuse, cinders, and dirt from subway excavations. For thirty years subterranean fires smoldered in the rubbish, and hordes of rats foraged there.

The island is now entirely given over to the city's MODEL PENITENTIARY, which replaced the obsolete Welfare Island prison in 1935. The twenty-six fireproof brick buildings, costing $9,106,000, constitute one of the most modern and efficient penal institutions in the country. The new prison, with a total capacity of 2,550, houses annually more than 25,000 offenders whose sentences run for not more than three years. The rapid turnover creates many special problems of management.

Much of the made land has been landscaped. A sixty-acre farm cultivated by prisoners is being steadily enlarged; the renowned prison piggery produces more than fifty thousand pounds of pork every year. The modern plant includes a fully equipped hospital with the largest venereal disease clinic in the city, and a large laundry which serves the prison, the Department of Sanitation, and other institutions. The management uses a scientific classification system for determining the needs and attributes of each prisoner in preparation for the prison's unusual educational, vocational, and recreational program.

The Riker's Island ferry passes North Brother Island, the thirteen-acre site of the city's RIVERSIDE HOSPITAL (332 beds) for communicable diseases. "Typhoid Mary" Mallon, a typhoid carrier who unwittingly had started epidemics while employed as a cook, was probably the best-known resident of Riverside; she died in 1938. The burning excursion steamer, *General Slocum,* was beached on North Brother in 1904.

Near-by South Brother Island, owned by the estate of Colonel Jacob Ruppert, is seven acres of unimproved brush.

Brooklyn

Brooklyn

W<small>HEN</small> in 1833 it was proposed that the village of Brooklyn become incorporated into the city of New York, community spirit was already strong enough to resist the overtures from across the river. "Between New-York and Brooklyn," General Jeremiah Johnson, of Wallabout, declared, speaking for the Brooklyn villagers, "there is nothing in common, either in object, interest, or feeling—nothing that even apparently tends to their connexion, unless it be the waters that flow between them. And even those waters, instead of, in fact, uniting them, form a barrier between them which, however frequently passed, still form and must forever continue to form an unsurmountable obstacle to their union."

The general's defiance was fateful. Geographically and hence commercially, Brooklyn was bound to the island of Manhattan; yet it became a city and remained one for sixty-four years. When incorporation finally took place, in 1898, the "insurmountable obstacle" to the union had already been spanned by the mighty Brooklyn Bridge. The Williamsburg and the Manhattan bridges followed and the high-sounding words of General Johnson have long since been lost in the roar of three subways under the river.

So integrated is the borough with the metropolis that it is startling to realize that it is comparable to Chicago in size. Its population of about 2,800,000, like that of the midwestern city, occupies a vast area, some eighty square miles. Brooklyn is one of the greatest maritime and industrial centers of the world. About forty per cent of the foreign commerce moving out of the port of New York clears through Brooklyn's thirty-three miles of developed water front. Seventy steamship freight lines, fourteen trunk railways, and a series of huge shipping terminals, of which Erie Basin and Bush Terminal are the most notable, serve this traffic. Most startling of all, to people who have been led to think of New York City as relatively unproductive, Brooklyn as a manufacturing center ranks fifth in the country.

Brooklyn is best known, however, as a residential quarter; "home borough" is an accepted New York appellation. Industry is largely concentrated within a few blocks of the water front, the business districts concentrated in the downtown section. The remainer of Brooklyn is a vast residential area, the growth of which was determined to some extent by the direction taken by rapid transit lines.

The borough occupies the southwestern extremity of Long Island, and lies southeast of Manhattan, across the East River. Its eastern boundary is coterminous with that of the borough of Queens. To the west are the Narrows and Upper New York Bay and to the south, the Atlantic Ocean. It is like a plain, tilted from a bluff along the East River, opposite the tip of Manhattan, with ridges in the western and central portions that are characteristic of the terminal moraine of all Long Island. It attains a rise of 216.5 feet in Greenwood Cemetery and somewhat less in the northern end of Prospect Park. The 478-acre cemetery and the 526-acre centrally located park are the only permanent open areas of any size in the crosshatch pattern of Brooklyn's streets. These streets are lined, mile after mile, with places to live, a few mansions, large apartment houses, small homes with lawns and gardens, and tens of thousands of two- or three-story flats and one- or two-family houses that run together in rows. The only guiding lines in this maze are the streets leading from the bridges and Prospect Park, radiating fanlike to the borough's limits. Except for Manhattan, Brooklyn has the smallest percentage (about 9 per cent) of undeveloped land of all the boroughs.

In its expansion Brooklyn absorbed twenty-five villages. Many of these communities survive as districts, retaining their names and something of their original characters. Brooklyn Heights, above the wharves and warehouses of the East River and on the site of Fort Stirling, a strong defense work used in the Battle of Long Island (August 27, 1776), still shows Colonial doorways among its more modern apartment buildings. Flatbush, Flatlands, New Utrecht, and Gravesend were all founded in the seventeenth century. Generally speaking, the northern localities—Greenpoint,

INTRODUCTION 433

Williamsburg, Stuyvesant Heights, Navy Yard District, Red Hook—are the poorer ones; the more exclusive sectors are in the Prospect Park neighborhood. The southern half contains many of the newer dwellings, mostly two- and four-family brick or stucco houses built mainly during the post-World War period. Borough Park and Bensonhurst are such new developments.

Ocean Parkway extends through Flatbush which, like Shore Road and Bay Ridge, has a suburban character. The streets are lined with trees, houses are set back in lawns bordered by privet hedges. The average standard of living represented by such communities has been lowered in the last two decades as Manhattan pushed more and more of its people across the river. They migrated by communities and settled as such, imposing a polyglot pattern over the staid lines of suburban Brooklyn.

One-third of the borough's residents are foreign born. It is estimated that the borough has more than twenty separate and distinct Jewish communities, of which Brownsville is the leading one. The 1930 census listed nearly two hundred thousand Italian-born. Ridgewood rivals Manhattan's Yorkville as a German center. In smaller numbers are groups of Scandinavians, Poles, and other nationalities; in the Red Hook vicinity there are many Arabs and Syrians. It is anomalous that Brooklyn, the borough of homes and churches, should have some of the worst slums (Williamsburg, Brownsville, Red Hook) of the nation, yet such is the case.

Village Years

The first purchase of land in Brooklyn (at about what is now Gowanus Bay) was made in 1636, and between 1637 and 1654 Walloons built their houses on Waal-boght (Wallabout Bay). By 1642 a ferry to Long Island had been established by Cornelis Dircksen, operating from Peck Slip, Manhattan, to what is now Fulton Street, and near by, at the intersection of Fulton and Smith Streets, the settlement of Breuckelen (Broken Land) was made. It was named for a village in Holland of similar topography. Lady Deborah Moody, excommunicated from the Puritan Church in Massachusetts because of disbelief in infant baptism, settled in 1643 at Gravesend with her English followers. By 1660 New Utrecht, Midwout, and Bushwick had been established.

The Dutch settlers brought to the New World a community pattern of which the Reformed Church was the center. Even after the Revolution that pattern was strong enough to impress itself upon the village and later upon the city. It was one of order, sobriety, piety.

The villagers were not much concerned with their rights to the water

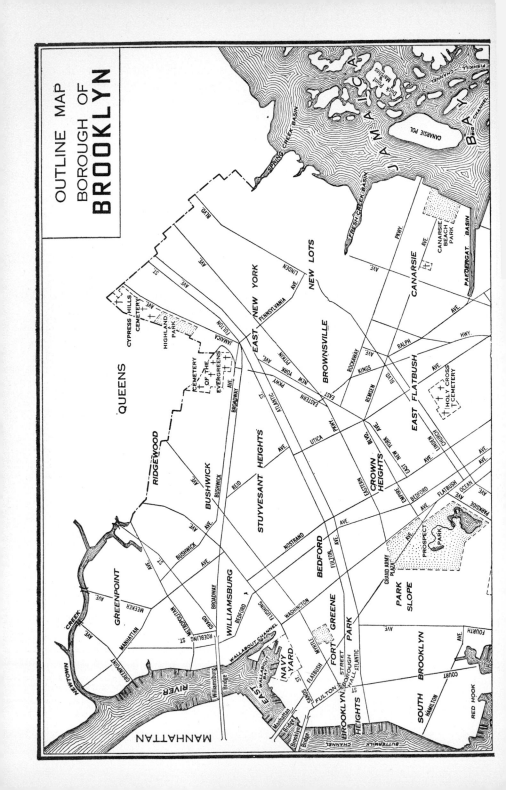

OUTLINE MAP
BOROUGH OF
BROOKLYN

QUEENS

MANHATTAN

EAST RIVER

NEWTOWN CREEK

GREENPOINT

RIDGEWOOD

BUSHWICK

WILLIAMSBURG

STUYVESANT HEIGHTS

CYPRESS HILLS CEMETERY

HIGHLAND PARK

CEMETERY OF THE EVERGREENS

NEW LOTS

EAST NEW YORK

BROWNSVILLE

CROWN HEIGHTS

EAST FLATBUSH

HOLY CROSS CEMETERY

CANARSIE

CANARSIE BEACH PARK

CANARSIE POL.

JAMAICA BAY

Duck Point Marshes

FRESH CREEK BASIN

SPRING CREEK BASIN

PAERDEGAT BASIN

PAERDEGAT BASIN

MILL BASIN

BEDFORD

FORT GREENE PARK

NAVY YARD

WALLABOUT CHANNEL

WALLABOUT BAY

BROOKLYN HEIGHTS

SOUTH BROOKLYN

RED HOOK

PARK SLOPE

PROSPECT PARK

GRAND ARMY PLAZA

BUTTERMILK CHANNEL

Williamsburg Bridge

Manhattan Bridge

Brooklyn Bridge

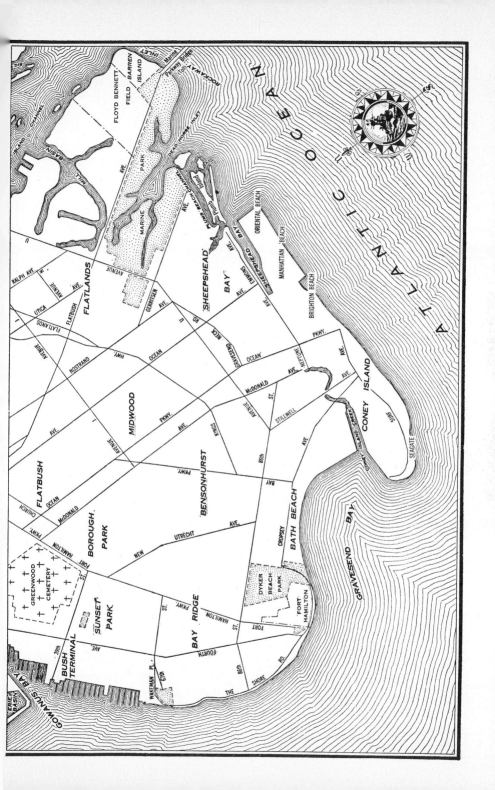

front in those early days. They farmed the hinterland, while enterprising New Yorkers built up the water front, establishing slaughterhouses and tanneries to which Long Islanders brought their cattle.

As time went on, numbers of prosperous Yankees became leading citizens of the island communities, along with the Dutch burghers. They were communicants of St. Ann's Episcopal Church, which, when established in 1784, was invested with all the prestige that belonged to a parish of Trinity Church in Manhattan.

A third religious group, the Methodists, added strength to the mold from which the city was to be formed. The effective missionary zeal of Bishop Asbury's young men, sent into Long Island early, resulted in the founding of the Sands Street Methodist Episcopal Church, which by 1816 was as firmly established as St. Ann's.

In that year Brooklyn, with a population of four thousand, was incorporated as a village. It was about a mile square. The main thoroughfare, Old Ferry Road (now Fulton Street), was lined with houses, taverns, and shops as far as the present Borough Hall.

The possibilities of Brooklyn's growth were manifest. Many small industries were already located there; the Navy Yard was under construction at Wallabout Bay; and most important, the first steam ferry, the *Nassau*, designed by Robert Fulton, was plying the East River. While some saw the future of the village in commercial terms—the Erie Canal was then under construction—most envisioned it as a residential suburb of New York City; now that the ferry was operating, men might work in Manhattan and live on Clover Hill (Brooklyn Heights), advertised as the nearest sylvan retreat to the island.

Many New Yorkers had lots to sell north of Fourteenth Street and were therefore little interested in the future of Brooklyn. Only a minority of those who lived in Brooklyn saw the advantages that might accrue to the village if it were to become part of a wealthy, flourishing city. The majority followed General Jeremiah Johnson to battle and in 1834 the village was given a city charter by the State Legislature.

Brooklyn, the City

By 1840 the city of Brooklyn covered twelve square miles and was inhabited by thirty thousand people. In 1854 it absorbed the townships of Williamsburg and Bushwick. By 1896 its boundaries were made coterminous with those of King's County, and it included the former towns of New Lots, Flatbush, New Utrecht, Gravesend, and Flatlands. In 1898,

INTRODUCTION   437

when it became a borough of Greater New York, Brooklyn had close to a million citizens.

In retrospect Brooklyn, during its period of independence, seems to have been removed from the metropolis, yet stimulated by it. Proximity to the greater city limited its cultural development—Brooklyn was never able to have a rialto of its own—yet it shared a great deal with Manhattan. The great artists of the theater and concert hall appeared in Brooklyn, as well as the foremost lecturers of the day.

During the nineteenth century the Jewish synagogue and the Catholic parish flourished but the Protestant meeting-house dominated the religious life of the community. A succession of religious leaders brought Brooklyn into the national limelight. The first of these was Henry Ward Beecher whose presence at Plymouth Church made Brooklyn a center of the antislavery movement. The Reverend DeWitt Talmage, known for his liberal religious views, preached at the Brooklyn Tabernacle (Presbyterian) from 1869 to 1897. In the present century Brooklyn has had several religious leaders with national following, among them Dr. Samuel Parkes Cadman, one of the founders of the Federal Council of Churches of Christ in America, and Dr. Newell Dwight Hillis.

The churches of Brooklyn were the first to concern themselves with education of the poor. Long before the establishment of public schools, instruction was given in Sunday Schools. The first of these, an interdenominational enterprise, was founded by the humanitarian, Robert Snow, in 1816. Brooklyn's first libraries must also be credited to the churches. Robert Snow's Sunday School, the Apprentices' Library and the Brooklyn Lyceum, stimulated the cultural growth that gave Brooklyn its Institute of Arts and Sciences. The institute directs the Brooklyn Museum, the Brooklyn Botanic Garden, and the Brooklyn Children's Museum, and in addition presents, at the Brooklyn Academy of Music, an annual program of concerts, lectures, and adult education courses.

A free public school was opened in Brooklyn in 1661, the beginning of a public school system that today comprises 224 elementary and 24 high schools, more than one-third of all the public schools in Greater New York. In addition there are more than 40 parochial elementary and more than 200 parochial secondary schools, as well as a large number of Hebrew schools. The numerous institutions of higher learning include Brooklyn College (municipal), Pratt Institute, Long Island University, Brooklyn Polytechnic Institute, St. John's University, Brooklyn Law School, and Packer Collegiate Institute.

At the time of Brooklyn's incorporation as a city in 1834 it already showed signs of its industrial future. Along the East River were numerous docks, warehouses, manufactories. After the consolidation with Williamsburg and Bushwick it ranked third in industry among the cities of New York State. The large Atlantic and Erie basins were built, Newtown Creek became a busy waterway, and to the Williamsburg and Greenpoint river fronts came shipyards, lumberyards, warehouses, distilleries, sugar and oil refineries. Brooklyn's importance in servicing transportation of goods—a major activity today—became evident as early as the 1830's, after the opening of the Erie Canal, and reached its fullest development around the turn of the century, following the construction of connecting railways.

A survival of the city period is the Brooklyn *Eagle,* founded in 1841 and an important paper nationally throughout the nineteenth century. Like its predecessor, Alden Spooner's *Star,* it fostered the literary tradition locally. The name of Walt Whitman is associated with both papers. He was compositor on the *Star* and became editor of the *Eagle* in 1846. He held the latter position for only two years, the publishers being unsympathetic to (among other things) his Free Soil ideas. A point of pride in Brooklyn is the fact that Whitman's *Leaves of Grass* was published there for the first time in 1855.

In the Civil War years the city began to acquire many of its permanent features: Prospect Park was laid out, the County Court House and the City Hall were built, and new streets were constructed. Tracks were laid for the horse railroad, tracks that in subsequent years became so numerous and intricate as to give citizens their sobriquet, the Trolley Dodgers. Downtown Brooklyn as it exists today was shaping up on Fulton Street around the City Hall.

With the completion of the Brooklyn Bridge in 1883 most Brooklynites shared the views of James S. T. Stranahan, founder of Brooklyn's park and boulevard system, who advocated the consolidation of both cities, pointing out that the new bridge would "so affiliate the two in heart and sympathy" that both would seek "a municipal marriage." He likened the situation to that in London and Paris, where the same city lay on both sides of an intervening river. There was little opposition when the merger was voted on in 1895. In 1903 the Williamsburg Bridge was completed and in 1909 the Manhattan was opened. In 1905 the IRT subway was extended to Brooklyn, and in 1913 the BMT crossed to Manhattan. The Eighth Avenue (Independent) subway, opened in 1933, rounded out the borough's system of rapid transit that at present carries half a million Brooklynites to Manhattan offices and shops each morning.

The opening of the subways completed Brooklyn's transition from city to borough and "our village and the city of New York were indeed one people in all the relations of business and social intercourse." Time had underscored the quiet words of Alden Spooner, lost in the rantings of General Johnson.

At present Brooklyn is undergoing many alterations at the hands of city planners, housing experts, Federal Government agencies, and educators. The first noticeable result is that traffic is no longer the unrelieved horror it used to be for the transient motorist. Cross-town streets are being widened, and in the outlying districts wide thoroughfares connect with the Long Island highway system. A circumferential highway is being constructed to run from the foot of Hamilton Avenue in the western part of the borough to Southern State Parkway in Queens.

The shopping and theater district will be allowed to show its face, for the old Fulton Street el structure is to be torn down. A central library building at Grand Army Plaza is being completed (1939). Federal and municipal housing groups are co-operating to eradicate slums. Williamsburg Houses, largest of the nation's slum-clearance, low-rent housing projects, was opened in 1937 and a similar development is under way in Red Hook.

D. Spiegel

Downtown Brooklyn

FULTON FERRY—BROOKLYN HEIGHTS—
FULTON STREET AND VICINITY—NAVY
YARD DISTRICT—FORT GREENE PARK DIS-
TRICT

Area: East River on west and north to Clinton Ave. on east; Atlantic Ave. on
south.
Principal highways: Flatbush Ave. and Fulton St.
Transportation: IRT Broadway-7th Ave. subway, Clark St. to Atlantic Ave. sta-
tions; IRT Lexington Ave. subway, Borough Hall to Atlantic Ave. stations; 8th
Ave. (Independent) Queens-Church Ave. subway, York St. to Jay St. stations;
BMT 4th Ave. subway, Court St. to Pacific St. stations.

DOWNTOWN Brooklyn, the borough's center of business, education,
government, and recreation, and the focal point of its civic life, is on the
site of the old Dutch town of Breuckelen from which the borough derives its name. In addition to the busy Borough Hall and Fulton Street
district at its core, it comprises the historic Fulton Ferry sector at the
Brooklyn Bridge, the quiet and pleasant Brooklyn Heights and Fort
Greene Park residential sections, and the Brooklyn Navy Yard with its
adjacent slums and sprawling factories.

FULTON FERRY, a water-front hamlet in Brooklyn's earliest days, is now a small isolated sector of musty, dilapidated buildings nestling in the shadows of the Brooklyn Bridge *(see page 313)*. The settlement was formed around the ferry landing: beginning with Cornelis Dircksen's regular rowboat crossings in 1642, a number of boat lines operated from both sides of the river, until finally all were merged under the ownership of the New York and Brooklyn Ferry Company in 1839. Before Robert Fulton introduced his steam ferry *Nassau* in 1814, crossings were made in row boats, flat scows with sprit sails, piraguas, and boats propelled by horses walking on treadmills. The last ferry stopped running in 1924.

In the early part of the nineteenth century there was a cluster of houses, taverns, stables, shanties, and stores at Fulton Ferry. The region, originally called "the Ferry," later "Old Ferry" (when a new ferry was established at the foot of Main Street in 1796), blossomed into a pleasant residential neighborhood. The construction of the Brooklyn Bridge destroyed its beauty and the neighborhood became a slum. Fulton Street, in this section, is now a sort of Brooklyn Bowery, with flophouses, small shops, rancid restaurants, haunted by vagabonds and derelicts. Talleyrand once lived in a Fulton Street farmhouse opposite Hicks Street, and Tom Paine in a house at the corner of Sands and Fulton Streets.

1. 170 FULTON STREET, southwest corner of Cranberry Street, is the site of the print shop in which Walt Whitman in 1855 set up type for his *Leaves of Grass,* a fact commemorated by a bronze tablet on the west wall (facing Cranberry Street) of the present building. In view of the poet's close association with this section during the early part of his life, the name "Walt Whitman Plaza" has been urged by civic bodies for the new plaza that extends to the Brooklyn Bridge.

BROOKLYN HEIGHTS, bounded by the East River, Fulton Street, Atlantic Avenue, and Court Street, is an old, distinctive residential quarter, famous in Victorian days for its churches and its clergymen. The Heights section occupies a bluff that rises sharply from the river's edge and gradually recedes on the landward side. Before the Dutch settled on Long Island in the middle of the seventeenth century, this promontory was called Ihpetonga ("the high sandy bank") by the Canarsie Indians. The natives lived there in community houses, some of which were a quarter of a mile long. Apartment dwellings were not brought back to the Heights until the twentieth century, and today there are but few.

The view from the apartments, hotels, and rooming houses along Columbia Heights, the street that edges the bluff, is one of the most exciting in the world; it includes Lower Manhattan, Brooklyn Bridge, Governors Island, the Statue of Liberty and the shipping factories and wharves along the East River. A popular vantage point is the plaza at the foot of Montague Street. The distinguished artist Joseph Pennell found the vistas from his studio atop the Margaret Hotel on the Heights more exciting than those from the London Embankment, and he made many etchings of the harbor. The locale was also made famous by Ernest Poole in his novel, *The Harbor.*

Late in the nineteenth century Brooklyn Heights was an aristocratic neighborhood whose residents set the tone in manners and customs for the elite of the entire city. Many of the brownstone mansions belonged to the merchants whose trading ships docked near by. The piers ran back to warehouses whose roofs were planted with real lawns and trees, forming backyard gardens for the houses above them.

The seclusion of the Heights was destroyed in 1908 when the IRT subway opened the neighborhood to commuters. Many of the patrician inhabitants fled; the old Victorian mansions were partitioned into studios and apartments; and writers and artists were attracted to the region. Many hotels, the Touraine, the Towers, the Bossert, and the huge St. George were erected.

An amusing story is associated with the naming of Cranberry, Pineapple, Orange, Poplar, and Willow Streets, directly west of the Brooklyn Bridge. In the decade before the Civil War these streets bore the names of prominent local families. This fact aroused the ire of a Miss Middagh, a determined member of the Brooklyn aristocracy, who vented her dislike of some of her neighbors by tearing down the street signs bearing their names and substituting placards with botanical titles. When the original

---

KEY TO DOWNTOWN BROOKLYN MAP

1. Site of Printshop *(Leaves of Grass)*
2. Plymouth Church of the Pilgrims
3. Long Island Historical Society
4. Brooklyn Public Library, Central Branch
5. Church of the Holy Trinity
6. Church of the Pilgrims
7. Grace Church, Brooklyn Heights
8. St. Ann's Church
9. Borough Hall
   a. Statue of Henry Ward Beecher
10. Brooklyn Eagle Building
11. St. James Pro-Cathedral
12. U.S. Navy Yard
13. Prison Ship Martyrs' Monument
14. City Prison (Raymond Street Jail)
15. Brooklyn Academy of Music
16. Brooklyn Institute of Arts and Sciences
17. Williamsburgh Savings Bank Building
18. Long Island Railroad Station

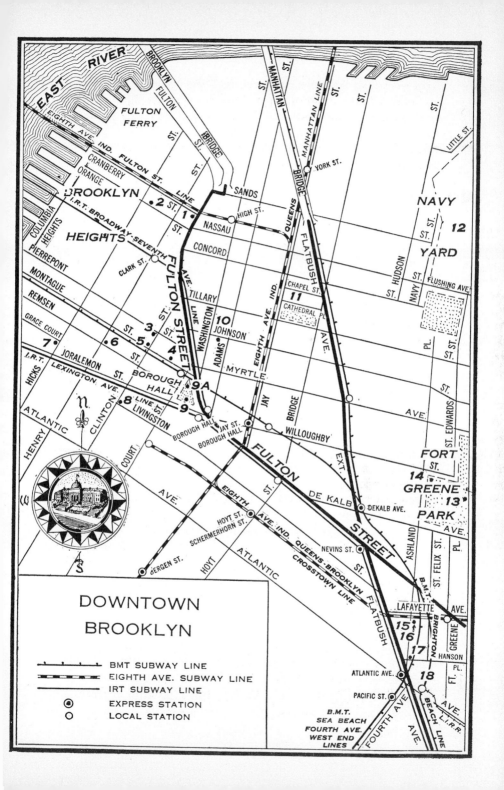

DOWNTOWN
BROOKLYN

BMT SUBWAY LINE
EIGHTH AVE. SUBWAY LINE
IRT SUBWAY LINE
EXPRESS STATION
LOCAL STATION

signs were replaced by the city authorities, she again changed them. This continued until an aldermanic resolution accepted her signs as official. A Heights street retains, however, Miss Middagh's own family name.

After disastrous defeat in the Battle of Long Island, General Israel Putnam and his troops retreated to the Heights. Washington was able to save the remnants of the army by transferring them, under the protection of a dense fog, to lower Manhattan.

2. The PLYMOUTH CHURCH OF THE PILGRIMS, Orange Street between Henry and Hicks Streets, was one of the most influential churches in America during the period (1847–87) when its minister was the eloquent Henry Ward Beecher (1813–87). *(Visitors admitted weekdays 9 a.m. to 5 p.m., Saturday 9 a.m. to 12 m., Sunday 9 a.m. to 1 p.m.)* As a center of Abolitionist sentiment, its pulpit was occupied by such anti-slavery agitators as Wendell Phillips, William Lloyd Garrison, John Greenleaf Whittier, and Charles Sumner. Charles Dickens spoke here on the occasion of his second visit to America in 1867.

Plymouth Church was established in 1846 by a group from the mother Church of the Pilgrims *(see page 446)*, Remsen and Henry Streets, headed by Henry C. Bowen, founder of the *Independent.* In 1934 Plymouth merged with the parent congregation, and both now constitute the Plymouth Church of the Pilgrims.

Henry Ward Beecher rose to a position of undisputed leadership among the clergymen of his time by virtue of his passionate oratory, his uncompromising vigor, and a striking flair for the dramatic. On assuming his pastoral duties at Plymouth Church he at once stated his intention of dealing with the living issues of the day—slavery, war, temperance, and general reform.

One Sunday Beecher astounded his congregation by putting up for sale a mulatto slave girl called "Pinkie." Mimicking a slave auctioneer, he roused his listeners to a fury of compassionate indignation, obtained the money to purchase the girl's freedom, and caught the attention of the entire nation. The girl, Mrs. James Hunt, returned in 1927 to speak from the same platform on which she had been sold.

During the Civil War entire Union regiments on their way to the battlefront paused for services in Plymouth Church. In 1863 Beecher visited England on a speaking tour, and was successful in helping to stem the rising tide of English sympathy for the Confederacy. At the close of the war he was chosen by President Lincoln to deliver the oration at the raising of the flag at Fort Sumter, April 14, 1865.

Beecher was also active in the woman's suffrage movement and was the founder and editor of several periodicals. From 1861 to 1863 he edited the *Independent;* in 1870 he started the *Christian Union* and later the *Outlook.*

The church structure, erected 1849, was designed by J. C. Wells, an English architect. It is in the New England meetinghouse style, a large, severely plain building of dark red brick, without tower, steeple, or other external ornament. The interior consists of a simple rectangular auditorium, with plain white walls and woodwork. The balcony is carried on slender cast-iron columns, and the clear eighty-foot span of the ceiling gives an impression of spaciousness. Nineteen memorial windows, designed by Frederick S. Lamb to represent the *History of Puritanism and Its Influence Upon the Institutions and People of the Republic,* modify somewhat the severity of the interior.

A gallery or arcade at the rear joins the church proper with the Plymouth Institute, built in 1913 by John Arbuckle, Brooklyn coffee merchant. The institute contains a gymnasium and recreational facilities, and serves the church as a parish house. In Memorial Park, the area between the church and the institute, is a bronze statue of Beecher by Gutzon Borglum, erected in 1914.

3. The LONG ISLAND HISTORICAL SOCIETY, Pierrepont and Clinton Streets, owns a collection of historical material so valuable that the building has been nicknamed "Long Island's strongbox." *(Open daily, except Sunday and holidays, 9 a.m. to 6 p.m.; July and August, 9 a.m. to 6 p.m. Monday to Thursday; admission free.)* Since its organization in 1863, the society has assembled one of the finest special libraries in the country. The history of Long Island from earliest Colonial days to the present is told in hundreds of books, pamphlets, and manuscripts; in genealogies and family records; and in portraits, photographs, and sketches of prominent families, places, and institutions.

The society's interests are not limited, however, to local history. It has published American historical works as well as a *Catalogue of American Genealogies,* and its collection of 102,000 books, documents, and pamphlets deal with American and world history. In the field of genealogy the library has but two rivals in the entire country, the New York Historical Society and the New England Historical Genealogical Society. It owns 8,200 volumes dealing with American families.

Among the rarities in its possession are the Samuel Bowne Duryea collection of illuminated manuscripts, a holograph manuscript by Voltaire on the life of Molière, several *Books of Hours,* a set of Audubon's

Birds of America. Among the paintings are portraits of Egbert Benson by Gilbert Stuart and of Chief Justice Marshall by Rembrandt Peale; *The Old Roadway* by George Inness hangs in the foyer. Many fine·antiquities, statues, and paintings are exhibited in the spacious reference room on the second floor. Until a few years ago the society maintained a natural history museum on the fourth floor, but lack of space and funds forced an indefinite loan of much of the collection to other museums in Brooklyn and Manhattan.

The society was originally organized in 1863 by leading citizens of Kings, Queens, and Suffolk counties. Funds for maintenance come from an endowment and membership dues. The four-story red-brick and terra-cotta building, designed by George B. Post, was completed in 1880.

4. The CENTRAL BRANCH OF THE BROOKLYN PUBLIC LIBRARY, 197 Montague Street, between Fulton and Clinton Streets, is an aged brownstone structure opened in 1869. The Brooklyn Public Library began to function under that name in 1897; its progenitor was the Brooklyn Athenaeum Reading Room, founded in 1853. A new central building is now (1939) in process of construction at Flatbush Avenue and Eastern Parkway *(see page 485).*

The Brooklyn Public Library, which contains about 1,153,000 volumes, consists of 35 branch libraries and 546 other agencies of distribution. It serves more than 600,000 borrowers, and approximately 6,700,000 books circulate annually. The library is maintained by the city of New York, with additional income from endowments, fees, and state grants.

5. The CHURCH OF THE HOLY TRINITY (Protestant Episcopal), northwest corner of Clinton and Montague Streets, a handsome dark-red structure built in 1847, is considered one of the most felicitous Gothic designs of Minard Lefever, famous architect of Brooklyn churches. The square east end, the arrangement of the window divisions, and the rich tracery of the ceiling ribs are typically English Gothic. The edifice has a remarkable set of stained-glass windows, designed by William J. Bolton. The congregation was organized in 1846. Its pastor from 1870 to 1895 was Dr. Charles Henry Hall, a leading figure in the councils of the Episcopal Church.

6. The CHURCH OF THE PILGRIMS, northeast corner of Remsen and Henry Streets, part of the Plymouth Church of the Pilgrims *(see page 444),* was located originally at Pineapple and Fulton Streets. The cornerstone of the present building was laid in 1844. Architecturally it belongs to neither the Gothic nor the Classic revivals current when it was built; yet the bold and simple exterior, of good fieldstone masonry, marks the

original work of a master, Richard Upjohn, whose reputation rests on more elaborate and conventional churches in traditional Gothic, like Trinity Church in Manhattan *(see page 310)*. The interior has an unexpected delicacy. Widely spaced slender oak columns and semicircular oak arches support the ceiling; the buff-colored plaster walls and blue ceiling are painted with small repeat patterns. Near the tower corner, under the announcement board, there is a slightly projecting stone, a fragment of Plymouth Rock.

Dr. Richard S. Storrs, who assumed the ministry of the church in 1846 and held it uninterruptedly for almost fifty-four years, rivaled Henry Ward Beecher in popularity.

7. The GRACE CHURCH, BROOKLYN HEIGHTS, Grace Court and Hicks Street, is set amidst large trees, giving the impression of an English parish church. It was designed by Richard Upjohn in 1847, soon after he built the Church of the Pilgrims. In the more conservative design of Grace Church he reverted to the Gothic Revival style.

The simple bays of the exterior are pierced by well-proportioned openings. The pattern of varied tool grooves gives the wall surface a distinctive texture, which accentuates the bold relief of carved moldings, brackets, and capitals. The light interior is roofed with delicate open wood vaulting-trusses. The original wood piers were replaced by stone in 1909 when Herbert Wheaton Congdon repaired the interior. At that time the Pierrepont Memorial Doorway was added. The handsome alabaster altar and reredos and stained glass above the altar were contributed in 1891 as a memorial to certain members of the Bill family. Three of the stained-glass windows in the nave and aisles are by Louis Tiffany.

8. ST. ANN'S CHURCH (Protestant Episcopal), 131 Clinton Street, at Livingston Street, is known as the Mother of Brooklyn Churches. Its parishioners have helped to organize St. Mary's, St. Luke's, two St. Paul's, St. John's, and Christ Church. St. Ann's dates from 1784, when its founding members held services at 40 Fulton Street, then the home of Garret Rappelje. Its first building was erected in 1805 at Washington and Sands Streets. In 1825 it moved into a brick edifice, and in 1869 into its present quarters, a Gothic structure with traceried gables and heavy buttresses, completed in 1869 from plans by Renwick and Sands. In its record books the baptisms of Negroes are noted as "black" and "free black."

FULTON STREET AND VICINITY, between Johnson Street and Rockwell Place, includes the Borough Hall district, the seat of the county and borough governments and the center of business; and Brooklyn's most important shopping and theatrical zones. Fulton Street, the borough's oldest thoroughfare and earliest road of importance on Long Island, was first known as the Old Ferry Road; in the Colonial and Revolutionary periods as King's Highway, and after 1814 as Fulton Street in honor of Robert Fulton. As the city developed into a great metropolis, downtown Fulton Street became the concentration point of subways, street cars, and elevated lines, attracted important public buildings and leading commercial and recreational establishments, and assumed a bustling Main Street air, not unlike State Street, Chicago, or Euclid Avenue, Cleveland. Today the neon signs blink all day long in the false twilight of an overhead el structure, surface cars bang and clatter incessantly, the subway entrances expel and admit passengers, while the streets are clogged with pedestrian and automobile traffic.

In the plaza at the convergence of Court, Fulton, and Joralemon Streets is stately Borough Hall; across Joralemon Street are the fourteen-story Municipal Building, the Kings County Supreme Court, and Kings County Hall of Records. Two blocks north of Borough Hall are the Federal Building and the Brooklyn Eagle Building, the home of the borough's leading newspaper; and two blocks south of the Hall, on Schermerhorn Street, congregate many charitable institutions and juvenile societies, with the Children's Court, the Domestic Relations Court, and the Central Courts Building in their midst. On the Court Street side of Borough Hall Park are the offices of banks and real-estate firms, with many of the real-estate brokers conducting their business on the street in an informal curbstone exchange; while on the periphery of the Borough Hall locality are many of Brooklyn's leading institutions of higher learning, Long Island University, Brooklyn Law School, St. John's University, Brooklyn Polytechnic Institute, and Packer Collegiate Institute.

From Smith Street to Flatbush Avenue, Fulton Street hums by day with an endless procession of shoppers; the department stores, Abraham and Straus, Namm's, and Frederick Loeser and Company, offer as magnificent an array of merchandise as those in Manhattan; and such is the attraction of the Brooklyn market, which is heavily patronized by Long Islanders, that many large Manhattan shops have found it expedient to open branches on Fulton Street.

The amusement center Brooklynites have in mind when they "go downtown to see a movie" is near an open square formed by the intersection of Flatbush Avenue, Nevins and Fulton Streets. Within a small area are the Brooklyn Strand, the Brooklyn Paramount, the Loew's Metropolitan, the Fox, the Orpheum, and the Albee as well as several burlesque and legitimate houses.

Beyond Flatbush Avenue, Fulton Street trails off among rickety dwellings and featureless neighborhoods, with the elevated above and the new Eighth Avenue (Independent) subway below. Early in 1939 plans were announced for razing the el.

9. BOROUGH HALL, in a triangular block formed by Fulton, Court, and Joralemon Streets, is a dignified four-story marble building in post-Colonial style. The front facing the park has a classic portico and a broad flight of marble steps. The building houses the borough president's office. Most of the borough administrative offices are in the Brooklyn Municipal Building on the opposite side of Joralemon Street.

Prior to the consolidation of 1898, the present Borough Hall was the City Hall of Brooklyn. Its cornerstone was laid in 1836, but due to financial difficulties the structure was not completed until 1849. It was originally designed to occupy the entire park, but as completed it fills only the southern end of this space. The building was remodeled in 1895 after a fire, and the overelaborate cupola dates from that period.

STATUE OF HENRY WARD BEECHER (9A), in Borough Hall Park, by J. Q. A. Ward, is a bronze figure about ten feet high standing on a granite pedestal on which are depicted the figures of three children—one a Negro—with wreaths in their hands held up toward the preacher.

10. The BROOKLYN EAGLE BUILDING, Johnson and Adams Streets, houses the borough's major newspaper. The old Eagle Building, at Washington and Johnson Streets, a landmark since 1893, is used as an office building. The Brooklyn *Eagle* was founded in 1841 by a group of Democrats, with Henry C. Murphy, later mayor of Brooklyn, as editor. Walt Whitman edited it from 1846 to 1848, and so vigorously did he oppose the extension of slave states that he was forced out of the editorship; shortly afterward Whitman joined the staff of the radical Brooklyn *Freeman*. In recent years the *Eagle* acquired the Brooklyn *Times-Union,* which had been the Brooklyn *Daily Times* until its acquisition of the Brooklyn *Standard Union.*

11. ST. JAMES PRO-CATHEDRAL, at Jay Street and Cathedral Place, the first Roman Catholic church built on Long Island (1822), serves as a parish church and has been used on special occasions since 1853 by the bishop of the Diocese of Brooklyn, which lacks a cathedral of its own. The building is a simple red-brick structure in High Renaissance style, with a green copper spire over the entrance on Jay Street. It is flanked

on three sides by an old cemetery—said to be the oldest Catholic burial ground on Long Island. The parish was organized in 1822 by a group of seventy Catholics under the leadership of Peter Turner (1797–1863), a bust of whom stands in the churchyard near Jay and Chapel Streets.

The NAVY YARD DISTRICT, spreading south and west of the yard from the East River, is a shapeless grotesque neighborhood, its grimy cobblestone thoroughfares filled with flophouses, crumbling tenements, and greasy restaurants. It is bounded on the west by the Manhattan Bridge; while beyond the dull waters of the East River looms the New York sky line, like the backdrop of a stage set. In the nineteenth century the region was a residential district known as Irish Town, because of the predominantly Irish population. After the turn of the century, business and industry took over parts of the neighborhood and the pleasant homes fell into neglect. The population now is largely composed of laborers from local factories and the Navy Yard.

Sands Street is the principal thoroughfare, extending westward from the Navy Yard to the head of Brooklyn Bridge. Once this street, with its saloons and gambling dens, came close to establishing itself as New York's "Barbary Coast," and during the Prohibition era parts of it were patrolled to keep Navy men away. Today Sands Street still caters to sailors and Navy Yard workers. Shop windows display outfits for sailors; bars and lunchrooms, quiet during the day, become alive at night as their customers arrive. The area north of Sands Street toward the river is crowded with industrial plants, warehouses, and factories which charge the air with their mixed aroma of chocolate, spices, and roasting coffee. Scattered among them are ramshackle frame houses—notorious firetraps of squalid appearance. South of the Navy Yard is a residential district of only slightly better character. Around Sands and Washington Streets is a colony of Filipinos; native food, extremely rare in the eastern part of the United States, is served in a Filipino restaurant at 47 Sands Street. Among the favorite dishes are *adabong gaboy* (pork fried in soy sauce and garlic); *sinigang isda* and *sinigang visaya* (fish soups); *mixta* (beans and rice), and such tropical fruits as mangoes and pomelos, the latter a kind of orange as large as a grapefruit.

12. The UNITED STATES NAVY YARD, Navy Street, Flushing and Clinton Avenues, better known as the Brooklyn Navy Yard, skirts Wallabout Bay, a semicircular elbow of the East River opposite Corlear's Hook, Manhattan. *(Open weekdays 9 a.m. to 5 p.m.; Saturday, Sunday, and holidays*

1 to 4 p.m.; for admission apply at Flushing Avenue and Cumberland Street entrance.) This busy naval city covers a total of 197 acres, 118 on land, 79 on water, and is surrounded by forbidding brick walls with massive iron gateways.

The yard is traversed by more than five miles of paved streets, and contains four drydocks ranging in length from 326 to 700 feet, two huge steel shipways, and six big pontoons and cylindrical floats for salvage work. In addition to the numerous foundries, machine shops, and warehouses, it has barracks for marines, a power plant, a large radio station, and a railroad spur. The activities of the yard in 1938 required the services of about ten thousand men, of whom one-third were WPA workers.

At the south end, facing Flushing Avenue are the officers' quarters, two-story buildings of painted brick, scrupulously neat despite their age (some were built before the Civil War), and bordered by gardens, tennis courts, and carefully kept walks. The commandant's house, oldest structure in the yard, built in 1807, is near the foot of Navy Street at the river. This three-story clapboard building, with peaked roof and encircling porches, is said to have been designed by Charles Bulfinch, the architect who completed the Capitol at Washington.

The site of the Navy Yard originally formed a segment of the Remsen estate, which after the Revolution came into the hands of John Jackson. Here he constructed a dock, and subsequently built a merchant ship, the *Canton,* and a frigate, the *John Adams.* Federal authorities purchased the property for forty thousand dollars in 1801. ╸

Brooklyn Navy Yard is also associated with the early days of the steamboat: the *Fulton* was constructed here in 1814–15 from the inventor's plans. In 1890, the Yard's ways delivered to the sea the ill-fated *Maine.* The Yard Pontoon Service was instrumental in raising the submarines S 51 and S 4.

The most curious item in the Navy Yard is an iron cigar-shaped vessel, near the Sands Street entrance, one of the first submarines ever built. It was constructed in 1864 at a cost of sixty thousand dollars and originally called *Halstead's Folly,* after one of the builders. Subsequently it was given a more flattering title, *The Intelligent Whale.* The craft proved impracticable and was condemned in 1872.

Near the garden of the commandant's house, and at several other points, are guns and trophies captured in the Spanish-American War. At the Sands Street entrance, in the triangular plot known as Trophy Park, a simple marble shaft commemorates twelve American seamen who were killed in 1856 in a battle at Canton, China. At the base of the monument are guns seized with the British frigate *Macedonian* during the War of 1812, and also the iron prow of a Confederate ship captured during the Civil War.

The FORT GREENE PARK DISTRICT, the area around Myrtle Avenue and Cumberland Street, was a silk stocking district in the 1890's. Clinton Avenue was then a fashionable address. Most of the old residences are still standing, but have been converted in recent years into rooming houses and furnished apartments. At the southern end of the neighborhood are several apartment hotels, the Brooklyn Academy of Music, and the Long Island Railroad station. Close at hand along Atlantic Avenue are several central freight depots and large reshipping warehouses.

13. The PRISON SHIP MARTYRS' MONUMENT in Fort Greene Park, Myrtle Avenue and Cumberland Street, designed by Stanford White and dedicated in 1908, rises high above the surrounding plateau and is reached from the street level by a 100-foot-wide stone stairway broken into three flights. The 145-foot fluted granite shaft, supporting a large bronze urn, commemorates the 11,000 patriots who died aboard British prison ships in Wallabout Bay on the site of the Navy Yard during the Revolutionary War. The maltreatment of these prisoners on such infamous hulks as the *Jersey* and the *Whitby,* commanded by the notorious Provost Marshal Cunningham, is recognized as a black mark in British colonial history. Prisoners died from starvation and disease, flogging and other forms of violence, and were buried, usually by their fellow prisoners, in the sands of the bay. Remains of these bodies, found from time to time, were placed in the monument's crypt.

During the Revolution the park site was occupied by Fort Putnam, one of the chain of forts used by Washington in the Battle of Long Island. A garrison was stationed there from 1812 to 1815, and the fort renamed for General Greene. The name was changed to Washington Park in 1847 and some time later to Fort Greene Park.

14. The CITY PRISON (Raymond Street Jail), Ashland Place and Willoughby Street, on the edge of Fort Greene Park, is Brooklyn's "Tombs." (Raymond Street was the former name of Ashland Place.) The dark-gray building, medieval in design, with castellated turrets, comprises a four-story central wing and a six-story annex. Obsolete, inadequate, and unsanitary, it has been repeatedly condemned by investigating Grand Juries. Prisoners are held here pending trial.

The original jail on this site, built in 1839, was replaced by the present building in 1880; the addition was made in 1914. When the main building was completed it was discovered that it had no front entrance; this singular defect was attributed both to the architect, William A. Mundell, and to the Board of Supervisors.

15. The BROOKLYN ACADEMY OF MUSIC, Lafayette Avenue and Ashland Place, is the borough's equivalent of Carnegie Hall. Concerts, recitals, operas, and other musical programs are presented here by the most eminent artists; and lectures are given by noted authors and other personages.

The building was completed in 1908 from plans by Herts and Tallant. Facilities include an opera house seating 2,200, a music hall seating 1,400, a lecture hall with a capacity of 500, and a ballroom accommodating 1,000. Large arched windows in the main façade admirably illuminate the great lounge on the second story.

16. The BROOKLYN INSTITUTE OF ARTS AND SCIENCES, in the Brooklyn Academy of Music building, Lafayette Avenue and Ashland Place, has been the leading cultural organization in Brooklyn for generations. It founded and maintains the Brooklyn Museum *(see page 488)*, the Brooklyn Children's Museum *(see page 496)*, and the Brooklyn Botanic Garden *(see page 485)*. In the Academy building, the institute presents daily from October to May more than two hundred lectures, concerts, recitals, debates, discussions, dramatic performances, travelogues, and forums. It also provides motion-picture programs, field trips, and children's plays. Another department, the Extension School, offers sixty-two courses, in the manner of a university extension school. These services are available to the public at varying fees.

The institute, founded in 1823 as the Apprentices' Library, started with 724 volumes and 150 pamphlets, contributed by citizens who carted them in wheelbarrows to the reading room at 143 Fulton Street. Soon a site was obtained for a new building at Cranberry and Henry Streets, and on July 4, 1825, the cornerstone was laid by General Lafayette, on his last visit to America. In 1843, the library, then in a building on Washington Street, was reorganized as the Brooklyn Institute for the purpose of "enlarging the knowledge in literature, science, and art." It received a large endowment from Augustus Graham, wealthy Brooklyn distiller who had broached the idea for the original library.

After it was reorganized by its director, Franklin W. Hooper, and merged with other societies, the institute was incorporated in 1890 under its present name. In 1895 construction was begun on the Brooklyn

Museum. Support of the institute is derived chiefly from private gifts and endowment, although the city contributes to the maintenance of the museums.

17. The WILLIAMSBURGH SAVINGS BANK BUILDING, 1 Hanson Place, opposite the Long Island Railroad station, is the tallest structure in Brooklyn, 512 feet in height, surmounted by a slim gold-domed tower which is illuminated at night. The tower clock with its four faces, each twenty-seven feet in diameter, is a familiar skymark. The building was completed in 1929 from plans by Halsey, McCormick, and Helmer. The banking room is about sixty-three feet high.

18. The LONG ISLAND RAILROAD STATION, Atlantic and Flatbush Avenues, is used by more than twenty million passengers annually. An average of 133 trains daily enter the station, a low red-brick building which also provides commuters with direct access to the Atlantic Avenue stations of the BMT and IRT subways. The Long Island Railroad, begun in 1834 when it took over the Brooklyn and Jamaica Railroad (1832), is a subsidiary of the Pennsylvania Railroad.

North Brooklyn

Area: East River and Clinton Ave. on the west to Evergreen Cemetery and the borough line on the east; Fulton St. north to Newtown Creek.
Principal highways: Broadway, Bushwick Ave., and Fulton St.
Transportation: BMT Jamaica subway, Marcy Ave. to Eastern Parkway stations; 8th Ave. (Independent) Queens-Brooklyn crosstown subway, Fulton St. to Greenpoint Ave. stations; Fulton St. el, Nostrand to Ralph Ave. stations.

NORTH BROOKLYN is an old, neglected, working-class residential area, built largely around the industrial centers along the East River and Newtown Creek—where Havemeyer, Bliss, Pratt, Arbuckle, Bossert, and Cooper made fortunes in sugar, coffee, lumber, ships, oil, and glue. Williamsburg and Greenpoint are virtually unrelieved slums; Bushwick, Ridgewood, and parts of Stuyvesant Heights achieve a slightly genteel air, a reminder of their more prosperous days in the late nineteenth century.

WILLIAMSBURG, the area extending fanwise from the Williamsburg Bridge to Flushing and Bushwick Avenues, has a large polyglot population. The neighborhood, formerly the most congested residential area in Brooklyn, has lost some sixty thousand inhabitants since the 1920's. Here, with the erection in 1936-7 of Williamsburg Houses, a PWA construction project, began Brooklyn's first experiment in large-scale low-rent housing.
   Originally part of the town of Bushwick, Williamsburg was founded about 1810 and named for a Colonel Williams, the engineer who surveyed it. About 1819 Noah Waterbury established a distillery at the foot of South Second Street, the first industrial plant in the locality. Williamsburg in the middle-nineteenth century was a popular resort; its hotels near the Brooklyn Ferry attracted a wealthy, cosmopolitan crowd, including such gourmets and sportsmen as Commodore Vanderbilt, Jim Fisk, and William C. Whitney. With the opening of the Williamsburg Bridge in 1903 and the resultant influx of immigrant families from overcrowded Manhattan, the district's affluence vanished.

455

1. STATUE OF GEORGE WASHINGTON, west side of Washington Plaza, Broadway and Havemeyer Street, is a bronze equestrian figure mounted on a high granite pedestal. The work of Henry M. Shrady, it was presented to the city in 1901 by James R. Howe, a member of Congress. An enormous volume of traffic—el trains, surface cars, automobiles, wagons, and pedestrians—streams by the statue, for the plaza is the formal Brooklyn terminus of the Williamsburg Bridge *(see page 117)*.

2. WALLABOUT MARKET, Flushing and Clinton Avenues, Brooklyn's only public wholesale market, is a vast clearinghouse for produce from New York and New Jersey farms. The quaintness of buildings inspired by old Dutch prototypes lends an old-world atmosphere to the terminal. The market is housed in blocks of two-story brick structures, each surmounted by a watchtower and a weathercock. The blocks are grouped around a wide plaza called Farmers' Square. A relatively deserted region by day, from midnight to dawn the market bustles with noisy activity: Farmers' Square is a solid mass of vehicles, crates, and barrels, and truck drivers, jobbers, and farmers.

The site of the market, once part of the large tract acquired by the United States for a navy yard, was sold to Brooklyn by Congress in July, 1890.

3. NAVAL HOSPITAL, Flushing Avenue and Ryerson Street, is separated from the Navy Yard *(see page 450)* by Wallabout Market. Its neatly landscaped grounds are enclosed by a high brick wall. Founded in 1834, the hospital has 508 beds, four emergency ambulances and a staff of more than two hundred. The patients—Navy men, war veterans, ECC and, lately, members of the CCC and WPA—have the use of a six-thousand-volume library and may attend nightly movie shows.

4. WILLIAMSBURG HOUSES, Scholes Street to Maujer Street, Leonard Street to Bushwick Avenue, is the largest slum-clearance and low-rent

---

KEY TO NORTH BROOKLYN MAP

1. Statue of George Washington
2. Wallabout Market
3. Naval Hospital
4. Williamsburg Houses
5. Russian Greek Orthodox Church of the Transfiguration of Our Lord
6. Brooklyn Pratt Works (Socony-Vacuum Oil Company)
7. Site of Launching of the Monitor

8. Monitor Memorial
9. South Bushwick Reformed Church ("White Church")
10. St. John's University
11. Geographical Center of New York City
12. 245th Coast Artillery Armory
13. Tompkins Avenue Congregational Church
14. Statue of Robert Fulton

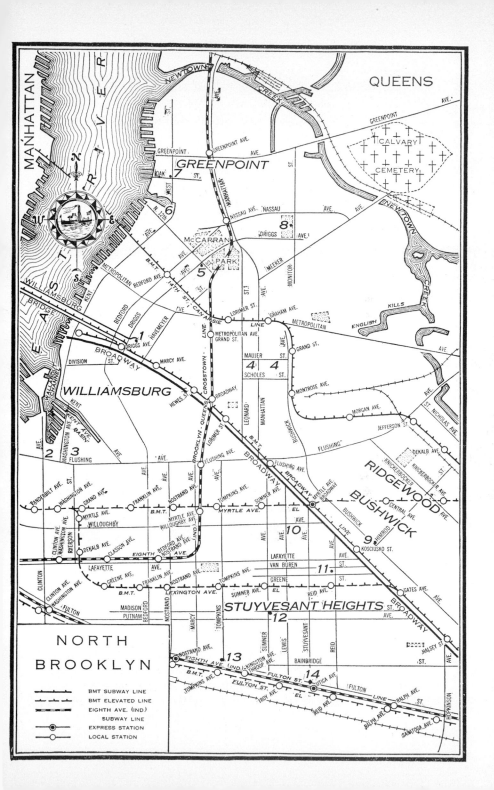

housing project completed under the Federal Housing program (1939). Built at a cost of about $12,800,000, the development includes twenty apartment houses, four stories high, accommodating 1,622 low-income families (about six thousand persons).

Together with a landscaped park and numerous playgrounds, the project covers twenty-five gross acres, formerly twelve slum blocks. The buildings, occupying only about 30 per cent of the gross area, are grouped into four super-blocks, formed by closing two through streets to traffic. Three blocks have six apartment houses each, the other has two houses, the new William J. Gaynor Junior High School, a park, and a playground. Unfortunately, the school is in a rather dull neoclassic style which adds little to the architectural interest of the group.

The houses are placed at a fifteen-degree angle to the streets to orient the buildings toward the sun. The buildings, individually pleasing in design, are of fireproof construction with reinforced concrete floors. Color provides much of their charm—yellow ochre brick, gray cement, blue-gray terra cotta between windows, bright blue doors, and dark blue store front parapets. The floor lines are marked by horizontal bands of concrete, which create an unusual striped effect. Most of the details— entrances, store fronts, etc.—are imaginative and highly successful. The entire group was planned by a committee of architects selected by the New York City Housing Authority, with R. H. Shreve as chairman.

All apartments—two to five rooms—are equipped with electric stoves, refrigerators, and modern plumbing, and supplied with steam heat, hot and cold water. The living room of a typical apartment has a floor area of 150 square feet; the kitchen, 75; and the bedroom, 120.

Williamsburg Houses are under the management of the New York City Housing Authority. Tenants are selected on the basis of income and the need for better housing. No family is eligible whose total income is more than five times the amount of rent plus the cost of utility service. Preference was given to families that had lived on the site of the development, provided they were otherwise eligible as required by law. The first tenants, chosen from a list of more than nineteen thousand applicants, moved into the project in September, 1937, and since then only a few have moved.

Rents, paid weekly in advance, range from $4.45 a week for a two-room apartment to $7.20 for five rooms; electricity for an apartment costs 90 cents to $1.20 a week. Three hundred and ninety-eight residents are employed as clerical workers, 49 as professionals, managers, and officials, 353 as skilled workers, 468 as semiskilled, and 283 as unskilled.

The cultural activities are held in the social and craft rooms of the project and in the community center of the high school. The Authority provides space for classes for mothers in child care and psychology, men's and women's clubs, a glee club, a tenants' council, and youth groups, but these activities are initiated and conducted by the tenants themselves. The tenants also publish a semimonthly paper, the *Projector.*

T. F. Hamlin, in an article in *Pencil Points,* declared that the Williamsburg development offers more of the amenities of good housing than many expensive Park Avenue apartment houses. "In every really important general matter of land usage—in air, in light, in a sense of green and growing things as a concomitant of living; in the creation of an atmosphere of humanity and decency, a place where children would be glad to grow up; in the development of a community that brings with it a new vision of democracy and of progress," he said, "[this development has] qualities that no money can buy."

GREENPOINT, Williamsburg's neighbor to the north, was so named after it was purchased (as a part of Bushwick) from the Indians in 1638, but the grime and smut of industry have long since obliterated the original verdancy. Factories, warehouses, lumberyards, coalyards, and gas storage tanks line the Greenpoint shores of the East River and Newtown Creek, and occupy large parts of the neighborhood. Many of the workers in the plants live near by. The unemployed living here constitute one of the largest relief groups in the city.

Greenpoint is the birthplace of Mae West, the actress. The district's residents are credited with originating the widely publicized "Brooklynese" diction, wherein "erl" stands for oil and "poil" for pearl. "Greenpernt" ranks with Canarsie and the Bronx as a butt for New Yorkers' jokes.

Kent Avenue, now lined with dilapidated piers and abandoned buildings, was a center of shipbuilding after the Civil War. Street names such as Java and India recall the once flourishing trade in coffee and spices with remote lands. The largest contemporary factories are those of the American Manufacturing Company (rope), and the Eberhard-Faber Company (pencils).

5. RUSSIAN GREEK ORTHODOX CHURCH OF THE TRANSFIGURATION OF OUR LORD, North Twelfth Street and Driggs Avenue, is a light-brick structure in Byzantine style whose onion-shaped towers loom out incongruously over the drab Greenpoint sky line. Russians living in Greenpoint and Williamsburg make up its congregation.

6. The BROOKLYN PRATT WORKS OF THE SOCONY-VACUUM OIL COMPANY, Kent and North Twelfth Streets, was the refinery of Charles Pratt and Company before it was absorbed by the gigantic Rockefeller mergers of the 1880's. The original building, a large brick structure erected in 1867, is still in use. The Pratt company was famous for its "Astral Oil," a high-grade kerosene so widely used that it provoked the remark that "the holy lamps of Tibet are primed with 'Astral Oil.'"

7. The ABANDONED IRONWORKS, West Street between Oak and Calyer Streets, was the site of the building and launching of the historic ironclad *Monitor*. Still standing is a long, low brick building in which much of the work was done. Designed by John Ericsson, the "Yankee cheese box on a raft" slid off the ways on January 30, 1862, for its famed encounter with the Confederate armored ram *Merrimac* on March 9 of the same year, a victory that ushered in the era of the iron ship.

8. MONITOR MEMORIAL, in Winthrop Park, Monitor Street between Nassau and Driggs Avenues, depicts an heroic-size bronze figure tugging at a hawser. Designed by Antonio de Filippo, it was erected in 1938.

BUSHWICK and RIDGEWOOD, old-fashioned and respectable, are German-American communities spreading northeast of Broadway. Comfortable brownstones with neat stoops and polished brass give the district an •atmosphere of calm quite unlike that of the usual strident Brooklyn neighborhood.

In 1661 Governor Peter Stuyvesant mapped out the area in the vicinity of what is now Conselyea Street and Bushwick Avenue and named it "Boswijck" (Town of the Woods). The name was later corrupted to Bushwick. After the Battle of Long Island Hessian mercenaries were billeted here; although friction developed between the townsfolk and the troops, some of the soldiers returned at the end of the war and established homes. In 1854 Bushwick became part of the city of Brooklyn. Ridgewood, the region near the Brooklyn-Queens borough line, was settled in the early eighteenth century by the English, who first called it the "Ridge" for its most salient topographical feature.

9. SOUTH BUSHWICK REFORMED CHURCH, Bushwick Avenue and Himrod Street, better known as the "White Church," was organized in 1851 by members of the old Bushwick Reformed Church which dates back to 1654. The white frame building in the Dutch Colonial style, with its solid but graceful spire and green shutters, was completed in 1853 and is a reminder of the older community.

STUYVESANT HEIGHTS, a flat region of brownstone fronts and two-story homes lying east of Nostrand Avenue between Fulton Street and Broadway, contains the city's second largest Negro population. A few imposing church structures, the homes of some old families, and St. John's University are all that remain of a once prosperous middle-class neighborhood. The poorer Negroes, many of them on relief, are largely concentrated in such business and shopping centers as Gates and Sumner Avenues, Fulton and Jefferson Streets, Flushing, Lexington, and Myrtle Avenues—districts which for poverty and squalor are as bad as the worst areas of Harlem.

10. St. John's University, Willoughby and Lewis Avenues, was founded in 1870 as St. John's College. The main building, completed in 1870, houses the original College of Arts and Sciences, the Teachers' College, and the Graduate School. A fourteen-story structure, erected in 1929 at 96 Schermerhorn Street, provides quarters for the Schools of Law, Accounting, Commerce and Finance, and Pharmacy, and a division of the College of Arts and Sciences. The curriculum of the College of Arts and Sciences is based on the traditional Catholic system of education with its emphasis on the humanities. More than nine thousand students annually matriculate at the university.

A new college center is being developed (1939) on the former site of the Hillcrest Golf Club, 176-30 Union Turnpike, Jamaica, where the College of Arts and Sciences and the administrative offices will be moved.

11. The Geographical Center of New York City lies two hundred feet west of Reid Avenue, between Van Buren Street and Greene Avenue.

12. 245th Coast Artillery Armory, 357 Sumner Avenue, second largest armory in the country, was erected in 1894, and occupies about a square block. Its circular towers with narrow slit windows and castellated parapets on the top give it the appearance of a medieval fortress. The architect was R. L. Daus. The 245th was known during the war as the 59th Heavy Field Artillery and fought at St. Mihiel and Meuse-Argonne.

13. Tompkins Avenue Congregational Church, 480 Tompkins Avenue, boasts the largest church structure as well as the second largest church membership of its denomination in the country. The church was organized in 1875, and the present building, a plain brick structure with a belfry at the corner, was dedicated in 1889. It occupies a ground plot of 135 feet by 205 feet, and rises more than 75 feet in height. The congregation numbers 2,440 members.

14. STATUE OF ROBERT FULTON, in Fulton Park, at Fulton Street and Stuyvesant Avenue, is a 10½-foot zinc-and-copper figure showing the inventor of the steamboat resting one hand on a small boat model. Caspar Buberl was the sculptor. The statue was first placed in 1872 in the Brooklyn Ferry House at the foot of Fulton Street. Years later it was found by the Society of Old Brooklynites in a junk pile. In 1930 the statue was rededicated on its present site.

West Brooklyn

SOUTH BROOKLYN—BUSH TERMINAL DIS-
TRICT—SUNSET PARK NEIGHBORHOOD—
BAY RIDGE—BOROUGH PARK, BENSON-
HURST, AND BATH BEACH—CONEY ISLAND

Area: Atlantic Ave. on north to Atlantic Ocean on south; from Ocean Parkway
and Sixth Ave. (Flatbush Ave. to 24th St.) west to Upper Bay, the Narrows, and
Gravesend Bay.
Principal highways: 4th Ave., Shore Road, Bay Parkway, Fort Hamilton Parkway,
Ocean Parkway, and 86th St.
Transportation: BMT West End and Sea Beach subways, Pacific St. to Stillwell
Ave. (Coney Island) stations; BMT 4th Ave. (local) subway, Pacific St. to 95th
St. stations; 8th Ave. (Independent) Queens-Church Ave. subway, Bergen St. to
Church Ave. stations.

THE Brooklyn shore line from the East River to the Narrows carries the
bulk of the borough's shipping industry. The oldest and some of the most
congested residential areas in Brooklyn here adjoin the modern facilities
of a world port. On the sites of the towns of New Utrecht and Gravesend, founded in the seventeenth century, residential districts have been
developed extending from Bay Ridge to Ocean Parkway.

SOUTH BROOKLYN, the headland between Buttermilk Channel and
Gowanus Canal, so called because it was the southern portion of the
original city, is one of the most intensively developed sections of the
harbor water front. Here are the Erie and Atlantic basins, the Todd and
United Shipyards, the busy State Barge Canal Terminal, and miles of
freight railway tracks. Sailors from a hundred foreign ports fill the bars
and rooming houses, and the prevailing atmosphere of a great international seaport is increased by the Syrian shops and coffee houses with
their Arabic signs, on Atlantic Avenue.

The residential blocks are squalid and overcrowded. Red Hook nursed
Al Capone until he was prepared to establish himself in Chicago, and the
district rivaled Manhattan's Hell's Kitchen for years. At present a huge

government housing project is doing much to rehabilitate the neighbor-hood. The name Red Hook, despite its sinister associations, comes from the Dutch *Roode Hoek* (Red Point) which described the color of the soil. The sachem Gouwane sold William Adriaense Bennet and Jacques Bentyn 930 acres here in 1636.

1. The LONG ISLAND COLLEGE HOSPITAL, Henry and Pacific Streets, affiliated with the Long Island College of Medicine, was founded in 1857. Its original staff included a cupper and a leecher. The buildings, designed by D. Everett Waid and William Higginson, were completed in the period from 1897 to 1916, and contain 467 beds. The country's first private bacteriological laboratory, the gift of Cornelius N. Hoagland, M.D., a regent of the hospital, was erected in 1888 at 335 Henry Street, opposite the hospital.

2. ST. THOMAS CHAPEL, Fourth Avenue and Pacific Street, twelve feet high and six feet square, is often called "the smallest chapel in the world." The building, open to the public twenty-four hours of every day in the year, was erected at the end of the war as a peace memorial; one wall contains stones from the Canterbury Cathedral. The chapel belongs to the adjoining Church of the Redeemer (Protestant Episcopal).

3. ATLANTIC BASIN, extending from the foot of Pioneer Street to Hamilton Avenue, rivals the water-front activity of near-by Erie Basin, although it is only half its size and lacks both dry dock and barge ter-minal. Its facilities are part of the two and one-half miles of Brooklyn water front owned by the New York Dock Company whose railroad sheds, warehouses, and massive gray loft buildings extend between the water front and the marginal streets from Brooklyn Bridge to Red Hook. The small lines that use the basin stack the bulkheads with cargoes from

---

KEY TO WEST BROOKLYN MAP

1. Long Island College Hospital
2. St. Thomas Chapel
3. Atlantic Basin
4. Red Hook Houses
5. Erie Basin
6. State Barge Canal Terminal
7. Site of Vechte-Cortelyou House
8. Greenwood Cemetery
9. Bush Terminal
10. New York Port of Embarkation

and Army Supply Base
11. Owl's Head Park
12. Dover Patrol Monument
13. St. John's Church
14. Fort Hamilton
15. Fort Lafayette
16. Dyker Beach Park
17. Israel Zion Hospital
18. Van Pelt Manor House
19. New Utrecht Reformed Church

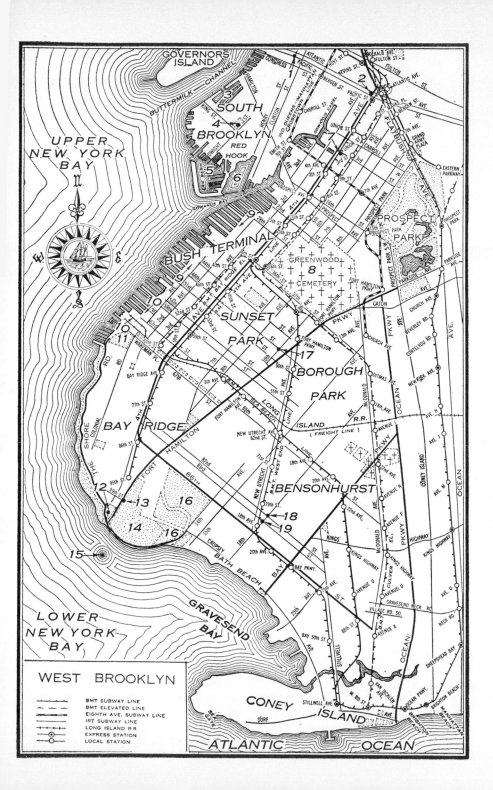

GOVERNORS
ISLAND

BUTTERMILK CHANNEL

UPPER
NEW YORK
BAY

SOUTH
BROOKLYN
RED
HOOK

1

2

3

4

5   6

GOWANUS BAY

BUSH TERMINAL

9

10

10

11

12

13

14

16

16

15

GREENWOOD
CEMETERY
8

PROSPECT
PARK

EASTERN
PARKWAY

PROSPECT PARK

SUNSET
PARK

17

BOROUGH
PARK

BENSONHURST

18

19

LONG   ISLAND   R.R.
(FREIGHT LINE)

BAY RIDGE

SHORE RD.

FORT HAMILTON

NEW UTRECHT AVE.
62nd ST.

CONEY ISLAND

GRAVESEND
BAY

LOWER
NEW YORK
BAY

BATH BEACH

CONEY   ISLAND

ATLANTIC   OCEAN

SURF

WEST   BROOKLYN

BMT SUBWAY LINE
BMT ELEVATED LINE
EIGHTH AVE. SUBWAY LINE
IRT SUBWAY LINE
LONG ISLAND R R
EXPRESS STATION
LOCAL STATION

every port in the world. Lascar, Chinese, and African seamen from the American-South African Line are familiar figures in the neighborhood.

4. RED HOOK HOUSES, King and Dwight Streets, New York's fourth housing project, was under construction in 1939. The project, sponsored by the New York City Housing Authority, was designed by Alfred Easton Poor. It consists of twenty-five buildings, each composed of a number of "cross" units joined together in various ways. The development will offer 2,562 apartments in all at a monthly rate of less than six dollars a room.

The architectural unity of the Queensbridge housing development *(see page 577)* was secured by placing community buildings at the center of the composition. In Red Hook, however, the community buildings are in a corner of the project and the designer has employed a half-mile plaza to unify the entire group. On the side away from the plaza the buildings face large, loosely defined courts.

5. ERIE BASIN, foot of Columbia Street to foot of Van Brunt Street, busiest shipping center in the country, handles the largest part of the Far Eastern and South American shipping in New York harbor. An estimated ten million dollars of merchandise—lumber, scrap iron, automobile parts, raw sugar, coffee beans, rubber—annually clears through the project's five covered piers and twenty-seven warehouses, which cover 135 acres.

Along the 2,500-foot breakwater, an artificial peninsula that shelters the basin from the waters of Upper New York Bay, space is leased for the repair of ships and lighterage activities. The Robins Dry Dock and Repair Company, a subsidiary of the Todd Shipyards Corporation, here operates one of the largest plants of its kind on the eastern seaboard. The breakwater was built largely of ballast dumped from the holds of European vessels.

The development was opened in 1864 and served the Union during the Civil War. After the war its activities were expanded steadily, until today it includes some thirty operations and employs more than seven thousand regular workers.

6. The STATE BARGE CANAL TERMINAL, Henry Street basin adjacent to the Erie docks, is one of the main terminals of the State Barge Canal system. Nearly three hundred barge families, travelers on the Erie and Champlain canals for dozens of years, winter annually at the terminal. Many remember the boisterous, individualistic days when bidding for cargoes was simplified by a hard right to the jaw.

7. The SITE OF THE VECHTE-CORTELYOU HOUSE, in the James J. Byrne Memorial Playground, Fifth Avenue and Third Street, is marked

by a tablet on the wall of the playhouse. The Vechte-Cortelyou House, erected in 1699 and standing till 1897, served as the headquarters of Lord Stirling, the American general. During the Battle of Long Island the general set his small force against the superior numbers of Lord Cornwallis. Stirling's troops were virtually wiped out, but he delayed the British advance long enough to cover the retreat of the main body of the American army.

8. GREENWOOD CEMETERY, Fifth Avenue and Twenty-fifth Street, dates from 1840 and contains almost 450,000 interments. Twenty miles of path wind through its 478 acres on the highest elevation (216.5 feet) in Brooklyn. Near the main entrance is a spacious receiving vault and a columbarium, containing glass-doored marble compartments for the ashes of cremated bodies. Many famous New Yorkers have been buried in Greenwood, among them De Witt Clinton, Mayor William J. Gaynor, Horace Greeley, the Reverend Henry Ward Beecher, Samuel F. B. Morse, and Lola Montez.

The BUSH TERMINAL DISTRICT, west of Fifth Avenue between Twenty-eighth and Sixty-fifth Streets, is the site of the largest freight depot, loft building, and warehouse aggregate in the city. To the east sprawls a poor residential area. A colony of some thirty thousand Norwegians, on Fourth and Fifth Avenues between Fortieth and Sixtieth Streets, retains many of its native customs and tastes. The food stores display Scandinavian delicacies, and the newspaper *Nordisk Tidende* is published weekly.

9. BUSH TERMINAL, from the foot of Twenty-eighth Street to Fiftieth Street, a huge agglomeration of piers, warehouses, manufacturing establishments, and railroad sidings covering two hundred acres of water front, is owned and operated by two independent companies, the Bush Terminal Company and the Bush Terminal Buildings Company. *(Visitors may obtain permission to tour the plant from the office of the Bush Terminal Company at the foot of Forty-third Street, and from the office of the Bush Terminal Buildings Company at Thirty-fifth Street and Third Avenue.)* It was founded in the 1890's by Irving T. Bush on the site of his father's former oil business. The development began with one pier, a warehouse, an old railroad engine, and a towboat, and to publicize the ·enterprise Bush contracted for shipments of hay from Michigan and bananas from Jamaica, stipulating that the merchandise be delivered to the terminal. The project grew steadily until today it comprises 150 building units,

including nineteen loft buildings, each from six to twelve stories, built of steel, concrete, and glass. Thirty-five steamships can be berthed at the eight large piers. All day, amid the clatter of trucks and freight cars, enormous cranes hoist and lower goods amounting to almost one-fifth of all the imports and exports of the port of New York. Some thirty thousand workers are employed by the various companies here.

10. The NEW YORK PORT OF EMBARKATION AND ARMY SUPPLY BASE, from the foot of Fifty-eighth to Sixty-fifth Street, is used for commercial shipments as well as for forwarding supplies to both local and foreign units of the Army. The base, with a storage capacity of half a million tons, contains two eight-story warehouses of reinforced concrete and three two-story piers. The buildings, designed by Cass Gilbert and completed in 1918 at a cost of forty million dollars, are early examples of a nonstylistic, industrial type of architecture. Here the architect refrained from adding extraneous ornament, and the striking effect comes from a skillful arrangement of such vital elements as concrete piers, spandrels, scuppers, windows, and doorways. Two hundred officers and enlisted men and more than a thousand civil employees, under the command of a brigadier general, man the base.

The SUNSET PARK NEIGHBORHOOD, south of Fifth Avenue and Thirty-sixth Street, is inhabited by a large number of Scandinavians and Finns. Local enterprises including small businesses of every type are bound together in the nationally known Finnish Co-operative Association. The apartment house at 816 Forty-third Street, opened in 1916, is supposedly the first co-operative dwelling established in New York City. Within the locality are several Finnish steam baths; the restaurants feature Finnish dishes: *keittokirja* (cabbage soup), *liha pullia* (meat balls), *silli perunat* (herring and potatoes); the homeland's culture is kept alive by Finnish societies; and folk dances are held occasionally at which the women wear the gay peasant costumes of their native land. The bluff of Sunset Park, Fifth Avenue and Forty-second Street, affords a thrilling view of the harbor.

BAY RIDGE, extending from Sixty-seventh Street and Fort Hamilton Parkway to the Narrows, is a spacious and uncrowded residential district. Many Scandinavians including about ten thousand Danes make their homes here. In the late nineteenth century, Bay Ridge was one of Brooklyn's most exclusive suburbs and the Shore Road section still contains many homes of the wealthy. Shore Road, beginning at Owl's Head

Park and skirting the westernmost point of Brooklyn, commands a magnificent view of the Narrows and the Upper New York Bay.

11. OWL'S HEAD PARK, Colonial Road and Wakeman Place, one hundred feet above Shore Road, was formerly part of the estate occupied by Henry C. Murphy, Democratic leader of Brooklyn and first editor of the Brooklyn *Eagle*. Here, in 1866, as State senator, he drafted the bill authorizing the building of Brooklyn Bridge.

12. The DOVER PATROL MONUMENT, at the west end of Fort Hamilton Park, is a granite obelisk designed by Sir Aston Webb and erected in 1931 to commemorate the participation of the U.S. Navy in the World War. Similar monuments have been erected at Cap Blanc Nez, France, and Dover, England. In front of the monument are several piles of Civil War cannon balls and to the west is a large muzzle-loading gun, marked "Fort Pitt, Pa., 1864."

13. ST. JOHN'S CHURCH (Episcopal), Ninety-ninth Street and Fort Hamilton Parkway, founded in 1834, is known as the "Church of the Generals" because it was attended by various military leaders from Fort Hamilton. Here General "Stonewall" Jackson was baptized at the age of thirty, and General Robert E. Lee, then a captain, was a vestryman. The stone and wood building dates from 1834.

14. FORT HAMILTON, foot of Fort Hamilton Parkway, commands the Narrows, entrance to Upper New York Bay, together with Fort Wadsworth, Staten Island. *(Visitors admitted.)* Completed in 1831, it was known originally as the Narrows, but was later renamed in honor of Alexander Hamilton. The fort is the headquarters of the First Division, First Quartermaster Regiment, Band and First Battalion of the Eighteenth Infantry, and the Fifth Coast Artillery; also stationed here are detachments of the Medical Corps, Quartermaster Corps, Signal Corps, and other military units. About one thousand officers and men lead a typical army-post life here; the hundred dull stone, brick, and wooden buildings, standing on 155 acres of enclosed grounds, include barracks and a hospital. Besides the usual parade ground, the post has a fine polo field where games, open to the public, are played.

15. FORT LAFAYETTE, the U.S. Naval Magazine, stands on a one-acre reef offshore opposite Fort Hamilton. The circular brick structure is used to store munitions manufactured in Baldwin, Long Island. It was erected in 1822 and originally named Fort Diamond. During the Civil War the fort was used as a prison.

16. DYKER BEACH PARK, bounded by Seventh Avenue, Eighty-sixth

Street, Fourteenth Avenue, and Gravesend Bay, attracts many golfers to its excellent course. Playgrounds, ball fields, and lawns make up the rest of the 242-acre park.

BOROUGH PARK, BENSONHURST, and BATH BEACH form one undistinguished neighborhood stretching from the southern tip of Greenwood Cemetery down to Gravesend Bay. The western part, along the shore from Bay Ridge to Gravesend, was until the 1890's the town of New Utrecht, first settled in 1652. In that year Cornelis van Werckhoven, a citizen of Utrecht, Holland, and a member of the Dutch West India Company, hearing that the English were making claims on the Dutch possessions on Long Island, came to the New World to found several colonies. He bought land from the Indians, paying a quantity of shirts, shoes, stockings, knives, scissors, and combs, erected a house and mill, and returned to Holland to recruit settlers for his new colony. In 1657 the settlement became a town and was named for Werckhoven's native city.

Gravesend was founded in 1643 on a site marked by the square bounded on three sides by the Old Village Road at McDonald Avenue and Gravesend Neck Road. Lady Deborah Moody, a cultured, strong-willed Englishwoman, led a small flock of colonists to New Amsterdam in search of the religious freedom denied them in England and New England. Receiving a patent from Director-General Kieft and the City Council, and augmented by a group of other Englishmen, the colony settled at Gravesend on lands whose original boundaries included Coney Island. Until her death in 1659, Lady Deborah was a leader in the settlement, and even the testy Peter Stuyvesant sought her opinion from time to time. The exact location of the Moody farm is not known, but it is said that the old Hicks-Platt home, a Dutch stone house reputedly built in 1643, stood on her property (at McDonald Avenue and Gravesend Neck Road). Lady Deborah is buried in the little cemetery opposite the house in the southwest corner of the square.

Bensonhurst today is inhabited mainly by Jewish and Italian families; a few of the latter cultivate small truck farms. Bath Beach, just south of Fort Hamilton, a fashionable resort during the nineteenth century, is a cluster of small houses and ramshackle or abandoned mansions and hotels leading down to a deserted beach. Borough Park, newest of the three communities, is largely a product of the real-estate boom of the 1920's.

17. The ISRAEL ZION HOSPITAL, Tenth Avenue and Forty-eighth

Street, a modern structure of brown brick and limestone trim designed by Mortimer Freehof, contains 450 beds. Among its innovations are a swimming pool for post-paralytic cases, a special department for refugee internes, and the installation of television apparatus in the operating room.

18. The VAN PELT MANOR HOUSE, Eighty-second Street and Eighteenth Avenue, was erected in 1686, though the stone part of the house may be part of an earlier structure built by Jan van Cleef in 1664 or 1672. The beautiful Dutch tiles of the fireplace in the southwest room are said to have been brought from Holland in 1663. Lord Howe and George Washington both used the house during the Revolution and a tablet commemorates the "material aid" given by the Van Pelt family to the American cause. The house is now used by the park department.

19. The NEW UTRECHT REFORMED CHURCH, Eighteenth Avenue and Eighty-third Street, dates back to 1677. The present building, in meeting-house style, was erected in 1828, with stone from the older church, built about 1700. The Liberty Pole in front of the building is the last remaining on Long Island, and the fourth (1910) on this spot since 1783. Among the relics of the church is an hourglass once used to limit the duration of the sermons.

CONEY ISLAND, the sand bar that became the "world's largest playground," fronts a six-mile-long beach on the Atlantic Ocean. *(Season open May 30, ends at close of Mardi Gras, second week after Labor Day; fireworks every Tuesday at 8:30 p.m.; transportation by BMT Coney Island subway, or bus from Times Square, or boat from the Battery, Manhattan; numerous automobile parking lots.)* It is an island in name only, for most of the old tidal Coney Island creek that separated it from the rest of Brooklyn has long been filled in. Though geographically Coney Island includes the whole peninsular strip of land, the name is now applied only to that portion between Ocean Parkway and West Thirty-seventh Street— the Coney of crowds, amusements, noise, and hot dogs. This section is terminated on the west by the high wire fence of Sea Gate, a restricted residential community; guards at the gate do not permit visitors to enter unless so instructed by a resident. On the east is Brighton Beach (named for the famous resort in England), a densely populated year-round residential area, with closely packed apartment houses. Beyond Brighton are Manhattan and Oriental beaches, where the building of apartment houses is prohibited. Brighton and Manhattan have large bathing pavilions, and their surroundings and accommodations are superior to those of Coney Island and more expensive.

Into Coney proper are crammed rows of flimsy shacks, modern apartment houses, two-story residences, an occasional cottage surrounded by lawns, and a wild array of bathhouses, dance halls, freak shows, fun houses, carrousels, roller coasters, penny arcades, assorted game booths, waxworks, ferris wheels, shooting galleries, souvenir shops, restaurants, tearooms, chop suey parlors, hot dog stands, and custard counters to feed and divert the millions. Two miles of excellent boardwalk, a steamboat pier, two large amusement parks, and a number of famous restaurants maintain the popularity of the resort. Surf Avenue, the main thoroughfare, separates the bazaar from the drab community to the north where some one hundred thousand persons live the entire year.

The true origin of Coney's name has never been definitely established, though the most convincing theory holds that Dutch settlers named it *Konijn Eiland* (Rabbit Island) because of its rabbits. In 1829 the first hotel, the Coney Island House, was built at Norton's Point in Sea Gate, and other hotels soon sprang up. In 1844, Eddy and Hart erected the pavilion and bathhouse which began the spectacular career of the place as a summer resort. White paddle boats made regular trips from Manhattan—the water route is still very popular—with cargoes of picknickers. Elegant hotels and restaurants were built along the water front and patronized by New York's wealthy families.

A less genteel, but even more prosperous, period of expansion came during the 1870's under the rule of John Y. McKane, political boss of the township of Gravesend. Large land grants were made by McKane at ridiculously low prices. Several railroads and two boulevards to the island were built. Race tracks opened in Brighton Beach and in near-by Sheepshead Bay, and gambling flourished openly. Championship prize fights starring Jim Jeffries, Tom Sharkey, and Bob Fitzsimmons attracted the sporting set. "Diamond Jim" Brady and Lillian Russell were familiar figures in the dining rooms at Feltman's, Stauch's, Henderson's. In the wake of this gaiety came the three-card monte man, the prostitutes, and the peep shows of the alley called the Bowery. A reform movement in 1910 brought this lush period to a close.

With the introduction of "rides" the island began to take on the aspects of a true amusement park. The Ferris Wheel, a device introduced at Chicago's Columbian Exposition in 1893, carried passengers to great heights; the first scenic railroad, built by LaMarcus Thompson, was one of the wonders of the time; and the roller coaster, designed by Stephen E. Jackman, hurtled crowds over its "gravity road." Steeplechase Park opened in 1897, Luna Park soon followed, and in 1905 Dreamland

Park, later destroyed by fire, opened its exhibits of the "Creation," the "End of the World," and the "Fall of Pompeii."

Coney entered its present phase when the extension of the subway in 1920 made the beach available to millions of lower-income New Yorkers. The beach was widened, and breakwaters and jetties were constructed for its preservation; in 1921 the boardwalk was opened. A plague of hot-dog stands and cheap amusements followed. Coney Island was now a playground of the people, the "empire of the nickel."

Summer crowds are the essence of Coney Island. From early morning, when the first throngs pour from the Stillwell Avenue subway terminal, humanity flows over Coney seeking relief from the heat of the city. Italians, Jews, Greeks, Poles, Germans, Negroes, Irish, people of every nationality; boys and girls, feeble ancients, mothers with squirming children, fathers with bundles, push and collide as they rush, laughing, scolding, sweating, for a spot on the sand.

The mass spreads southward in the direction of the beach and boardwalk and the numerous bathhouses. The bathhouses range from large establishments with sports facilities, swimming pools, and restaurants to minute back-yard dressing rooms. One of the largest is the Municipal Baths, Surf Avenue and West Fifth Street, where lockers rent for ten and twenty-five cents each. From the boardwalk the whole beach may be viewed: bathers splash and shout in the turgid waters close to the shore; on the sand, children dig, young men engage in gymnastics and roughhouse each other, or toss balls over the backs of couples lying amorously intertwined. Luncheon combines the difficulties of a picnic with those of a subway rush hour; families sit in wriggling circles consuming food and drinking from thermos bottles brought in suitcases together with bathing suits, spare clothing, and water wings.

A moving throng covers the boardwalk from the outer rail to the food and amusement booths. The air is heavy with mixed odors of frying frankfurters, popcorn, ice cream, cotton candy, corn-on-the-cob, and *knishes* (Jewish potato cakes). Skee ball, ping pong, beano and other amusements and games of chance are played and watched by hundreds.

After sunset the Island becomes the playground of a mixed crowd of sightseers and strollers. On the Bowery, wedged between Surf Avenue and the boardwalk from Feltman's to Steeplechase, the shouts of competing barkers become more strident, the crowds more compact. Enormous paintings in primitive colors advertise the freak shows, shooting galleries, and waxworks "Chamber of Horrors." Riders are whirled, jolted, battered, tossed upside down by the Cyclone, the Thunderbolt, the Mile

Sky Chaser, the Loop-o-Plane, the Whip, the Flying Turns, the Dodgem Speedway, the Chute-the-Chutes, and the Comet. Above the cacophony of spielers, cries, and the shrieks and laughter, carrousel organs pound out last year's tunes, and roller coasters slam down their terrific inclines. In dance halls and honky-tonks, dancers romp and shuffle to the endless blare of jazz bands.

About midnight, the weary crowds begin to depart, leaving a litter of cigarette butts, torn newspapers, orange and banana peel, old shoes and hats, pop bottles and soiled cardboard boxes, and an occasional corset. A few couples remain behind, with here and there a solitary drunk, or a sleepless old man pacing the boardwalk. The last concessionaire counts his receipts and puts up his shutters, and only the amiable roar of the forgotten sea is heard.

Feltman's, at Surf Avenue and West Tenth Street, is Coney's largest and oldest restaurant. It was founded in 1871 by Charles Feltman, a German baker, who is said to have introduced the frankfurter to this country. The bill of fare always includes clam chowder, oysters, lobsters, and soft-shell crabs. Merriment is provided by Bavarians in costume, who sing folk songs and dance the *Schuplatt'l*. For many years Feltman's has been one of the most popular of all Coney's eating establishments.

On the boardwalk at Twenty-ninth Street is the Half Moon, opened in 1927, Coney's principal hotel and most prominent building. It is fourteen stories high, in modified Spanish style, and was designed by William S. Post. It is a year-round resort that draws a varied patronage: besides its regular quota of vacationing New Yorkers and honeymooners, it attracts sportsmen, concessionaires, and politicians in impressive number, and for the benefits of sun and sea-air, many invalids. Its cuisine is noted. Other well-patronized eating spots are the Assembly and Sea Food, corner of Surf Avenue and Jones Walk; the Clam Bar, on Surf Avenue near West Sixteenth Street; Garguilo's, on West Fifteenth Street between Surf and Mermaid Avenues, and, of course, Childs.

The entrances to the two big amusement parks, Luna and Steeplechase, are on Surf Avenue, the former at West Tenth Street, the latter at West Sixteenth Street. Both include huge salt-water swimming pools. Steeplechase—"The Funny Place"—is a fifteen-acre park, with pavilion, ball-room, and thirty-one rides. It was founded in 1897 by George Tilyou, and his family still operates it.

Luna Park, largest of Coney's fun spots, covers fifty acres glittering with more than a million electric bulbs. Dozens of rides, including the ancient favorite, the "Dragon's Gorge," with its blazing towers, the broad lagoon, and the spacious ballroom make Luna Coney Island's most popular spot. It was built by Frederick Thompson and Elmer S. Dundy in 1903 following the phenomenal success of Thompson's spectacle, "A Trip to the Moon," at the Buffalo exposition in 1901.

An annual event in Coney is Mardi Gras, the week of high jinks ending the season in mid-September, a tradition since 1903. It is a spectacular occasion with carnivals, baby and beauty contests, parades of floats, brass bands, merrymakers in bizarre costumes, and showers of confetti and streamers.

A Coney Island of the future has been projected by Park Commissioner Robert Moses. Less room for the midway and more for bathers is planned: the beach will be widened and the boardwalk lengthened. Landscaped play areas and ten acres of parking space will be provided and a cleaner and more orderly recreation center is foreseen.

Middle Brooklyn

Area: Myrtle Ave. on north to Neptune Ave. and Emmons Ave. (Sheepshead Bay) on south; from 5th Ave., Greenwood Cemetery, and McDonald Ave. east to Nostrand Ave. and Gerritsen Ave.
Principal highways: Flatbush Ave., Bedford Ave., Ocean Ave., and Ocean Parkway.
Transportation: IRT Flatbush Ave. subway, Bergen St. to Flatbush Ave. stations; BMT Brighton Beach subway, 7th Ave. to Sheepshead Bay stations; 8th Ave. (Independent) Fulton St. subway, Clinton Ave. to Nostrand Ave. stations.

THIS section, a long rectangular area extending through the middle of the borough, embraces several of Brooklyn's oldest and choicest residential sectors, virtually untouched by commerce or industry. The borough's domestic character is exemplified here by the Victorian mansions in Bedford, modern apartment dwellings ringing Prospect Park, old houses in Flatbush, newer homes in Midwood, and the cottages and bungalows of Sheepshead Bay.

BEDFORD, in the mauve decade, was one of Brooklyn's most fashionable neighborhoods. Except for one or two quiet, less crowded streets on "The Hill" around Washington Avenue and Ryerson Street, and the newer section around Eastern Parkway, few traces of its past elegance survive. The brownstones of its heyday, faded and neglected for the most part, are now crowded by frame houses, small industrial establishments, and warehouses. The hamlet of Bedford was settled by the Dutch in 1662.

1. PRATT INSTITUTE, Ryerson Street near DeKalb Avenue, a scientific and technical school, was founded in 1887 by Charles Pratt, a Rockefeller associate. The six-story main building, erected in 1887 from plans by William Wingren, is in the Romanesque Revival style; Memorial Hall, designed by John Mead Howells, follows a simplified Byzantine style. Across the street from the main group in a small park is the Pratt In-

stitute Free Library, designed by William Tubby with later additions by
J. Mead Howells. Though the details of the building are Romanesque, the
main outline is Renaissance in character. Its entrance porch, characterized
by diminishing arches, is reminiscent of one designed by Stanford White
for Trinity Church in Boston. The first general public library in Brooklyn,
it serves also as a training school for Pratt Institute library students. Pratt
offers courses leading to certificates and degrees in fine and applied arts,
household science and arts, engineering, science and technology, and
library service.

2. UNDERWOOD MANSION, 336 Washington Avenue, near DeKalb
Avenue, an old-fashioned red-brick and brownstone structure with a glass-
enclosed greenhouse, is the family home of the late John T. Underwood,
typewriter king. Across the lawn, to the right, is the red-brick building
of the Graham Old Ladies' Home, on land donated by Underwood.

3. The HOUSE AT 160 GATES AVENUE was the home of Mollie
Fancher, famous psychic of the late nineteenth century. At the age of
seventeen, after an accident had seriously deranged her nervous system,
Mollie was discovered to possess certain "miraculous" powers enabling
her, among other things, to read letters in sealed envelopes, distinguish
colors in pitch darkness, and tell time by the ticking of a clock. Thousands made annual pilgrimages to her door.

4. The CENTRAL CONGREGATIONAL CHURCH, 15 Hancock Street, was
from 1900 to 1936 the pastorate of the Reverend Dr. Samuel Parkes Cadman, famed for his oratory, and president of the Federal Council of
Churches of Christ in America from 1924 to 1928. Dr. Cadman was especially known in the East for his Sunday radio sermons. The church was
founded in 1854 and moved to its present quarters in 1872. The building,
meant to serve until a permanent structure was erected, presents an unusual appearance. It is entirely covered with light-gray corrugated sheet
iron and topped by clusters of small towers.

5. The MEDICAL SOCIETY OF KINGS COUNTY AND BROOKLYN ACAD-
EMY OF MEDICINE, 1313 Bedford Avenue, founded in 1822, has the
fourth largest medical library in the country—146,000 volumes. The library was established in 1844. In 1938, the society had a membership of
2,743.

6. The STATUE OF GENERAL GRANT, in Grant Square, Bedford Avenue and Bergen Street, a bronze equestrian figure by William Ordway
Partridge, was presented to Brooklyn in 1896 by the Union League Club
of Brooklyn.

7. The CHURCH OF ST. TERESA, Classon Avenue and Sterling Place,

one of the largest parishes in the Brooklyn Diocese, has over fifteen thousand members; more than two thousand children attend the parochial
school. The church structure, built in 1875 in the Romanesque style, has
a richly ornamented interior. It contains a series of paintings depicting
the sufferings of Christ—*The Way of The Cross*—by Francesco Galliardi,
whose works are exhibited in the Vatican. This series is said to be the
only example of the artist's work in the United States.

8. EBBETS FIELD, Bedford Avenue and Sullivan Place, home of the
Brooklyn Dodgers (National League), has a seating capacity of 35,000,
the smallest of the city's three major league baseball parks. It was built in
1912 by Charles Ebbets and the McKeever brothers, former presidents of
the club. The uninhibited Dodgers are known as baseball's eccentrics and
of late have not been among fortune's favorites; altogether they have won
four National League pennants, the first in 1890, the year they entered
the league, the last in 1920. Numbered among Dodger "greats" are Bur-
leigh Grimes, Babe Herman, Dazzy Vance, Nap Rucker, Casey Stengel,
Zach Wheat, and Van Mungo; even Babe Ruth was their coach at one
time. In spite of such an array of talent, scoffers insist that true Dodgers'
strategy has always required outfielders to field balls with their heads and
base runners to run the bases backwards. Dodgers' fans, impervious to
ridicule, have remained loyal to their team throughout the lean years.

The PARK SLOPE DISTRICT, centering about the Grand Army Plaza entrance to Prospect Park at the intersection of Flatbush Avenue and Eastern
Parkway, has been since the mid-nineteenth century Brooklyn's "Gold
Coast." In the quiet streets off the plaza are rows of residences that rival
the mansions on Manhattan's Fifth Avenue. Around the plaza itself, and
towering above the huge Soldiers' and Sailors' Memorial Arch, are tall
apartment buildings, a solid bank of which extends down Eastern Parkway
opposite the new Central Building of the Brooklyn Public Library and
the Brooklyn Museum. Behind the latter are the grounds of the Botanic
Garden, separated from Prospect Park by Flatbush Avenue. The broad,
tree-lined parkway, leading straight to the arch, recalls the Champs
Elysées.

Prospect Park West is an equally fine neighborhood, which west of
Sixth Avenue changes into an area of seedy houses, industrial plants, and
warehouses. In the latter section dwells a small colony of Newfound-
landers, known to the neighborhood as "blue noses" or "fish," who gain
a livelihood on the fishing smacks that go down to the sea from Sheepshead Bay.

MIDDLE BROOKLYN

KEY

1. Pratt Institute
2. Underwood Mansion
3. Home of Molly Fancher
4. Central Congregational Church
5. Medical Society of Kings County
   Brooklyn Academy of Medicine
6. Statue of General Ulysses Simpson Grant
7. Church of St. Teresa
8. Ebbets Field
9. Old First Reformed Church
10. Soldiers' and Sailors' Memorial Arch
11. Prospect Park
    a. Litchfield Mansion
    b. Quaker Cemetery
    c. Battle Pass
    d. Lefferts Homestead
    e. Flatbush Toll House
    f. Monument to the Maryland Regiment
12. Brooklyn Public Library, Central Building
13. Brooklyn Botanic Garden
14. Brooklyn Museum
15. Flatbush Reformed Protestant Church
16. Erasmus Hall High School
17. Brooklyn College
18. Ditmas Homestead
19. Coe House
20. Bennett Homestead

9. The OLD FIRST REFORMED CHURCH, Seventh Avenue and Carroll Street, was formally established in 1660, although services had been held four years earlier. The first church structure was built in 1666 on what is now Fulton Street, between Lawrence and Bridge Streets, and by a genial Dutch custom stood in the middle of the road. In 1792, English was substituted for Dutch in the church service. The present building, fourth on this site, was erected in 1889. It contains Vergilio Tojetti's mural, *The Empty Tomb*.

10. The SOLDIERS' AND SAILORS' MEMORIAL ARCH, in the center of Grand Army Plaza, Eastern Parkway and Flatbush Avenue, a monumental granite arch modeled by John H. Duncan, faces the entrance to Prospect Park. The cornerstone was laid by General W. T. Sherman in 1889, and the arch completed in 1892. It is 80 feet high and 80 feet wide; the aperture is 50 feet high, and has a span of 35 feet. The arch is surmounted by a bronze quadriga by Frederick MacMonnies, the central female figure carrying a banner and sword, and accompanied by two winged figures of Victory. The inner faces of the pier are decorated with equestrian figures of Lincoln and Grant in high relief by W. R. O'Donovan and Thomas Eakins.

In a terraced oval fronting the arch is Bailey Fountain, the $125,000 gift of Frank Bailey. A sculptured group of male and female figures representing Wisdom and Felicity stands on the prow of a ship surrounded by Neptune and his attendant Tritons and a boy grasping a cornucopia. Eugene Savage created the fountain; Edgerton Swarthout designed the base.

11. PROSPECT PARK, bounded by Prospect Park West, Prospect Park Southwest, Parkside, Ocean, and Flatbush Avenues, consists of 526 acres of rolling meadows, picturesque bluffs, and luxuriant verdure. The park is the chief playground of Brooklyn, with picnic grounds, tennis courts, baseball diamonds, ponds, a zoo, a lagoon, parade grounds, bandstand, gravel walks, and broad driveways. The city of Brooklyn purchased most of the area in 1859 at a cost of nearly four million dollars from the Litchfield estate, whose mansion serves as borough headquarters of the Park Department. Delayed by the Civil War, development was begun in 1866 under a commission headed by James S. T. Stranahan, the "Baron Haussmann" of Brooklyn, creator of its park and boulevard system.

One of the main entrances is at Grand Army Plaza, where, to the left of the drive, stands the portrait statue of Stranahan by Frederick MacMonnies. Beyond the plaza, gravel walks flank the Long Meadow, a rolling grassy hollow, affording an unimpaired view for nearly a mile. Folk festivals and native dances are frequently held on the meadow; and May Day is celebrated here by school children. Picnic grounds, and locker and refreshment houses are on the west; to the east is Swan Lake, a circular pond whose swan boat provides amusement for children in summer.

Walks wind across the meadow to Prospect Park West, the first terminating at the Third Street entrance, which is flanked by bronze panthers of heroic size, the work of A. P. Proctor. Near the Fifth Street entrance is the impressive LITCHFIELD MANSION (11A), a Tuscan villa in white stone built in 1855 from designs by Alexander J. Davis. Long a center of Brooklyn social life, the house was acquired by the city in 1892.

At the Ninth Street entrance is the Memorial by Daniel Chester French depicting Lafayette as a general in the Continental Army. Along the walk that leads into the park from this entrance are the greenhouses *(open daily 8 a.m. to 5 p.m.)* where flower shows are held annually; to the north and east are the tennis courts, the carrousel, and the picnic grounds shelter. At the southern extremity of Long Meadow is the fenced-in bluff of the QUAKER CEMETERY (11B), a private graveyard of fifteen acres, established in 1846 and still in use. Simple stones, in the Quaker tradition, mark the graves.

The walk encircling Swan Lake reveals the rough boulders and wooded heights of the moraine ridge which bisects the park in a northeast-southwest direction. At its northern end Swan Lake flows into a brook which trickles eastward through a deep fissure in the ridge, creating a scene of charming wildness—banks strewn with boulders, rising tier by tier, and bridges arching over brook and adjacent bridle path.

The brook ends near the Music Grove, whose bandstand is fronted by tall trees, beneath which are rows of benches. In summer the wide-spreading branches form a leafy ceiling for the audience of Edwin Franko Goldman's Band, the Federal Music Project orchestras, or the occasional vaudeville and drama performances of the Federal Theatre Project.

From the east bank of the brook, walks branch down and cross East Drive. One of these paths leads south to a boathouse where rowboats are rented. Another path leads to BATTLE PASS (11C) (a little north of the zoo), an unusually narrow defile marked by a granite block supporting a bronze eagle. Here the Valley Grove Road, known as the "Porte" or gateway to the hills on the south, crossed the old Kings Highway or Flatbush Turnpike going north, and offered General Sullivan and his men a chance to make a stand in the Battle of Long Island. Through the tragic failure to

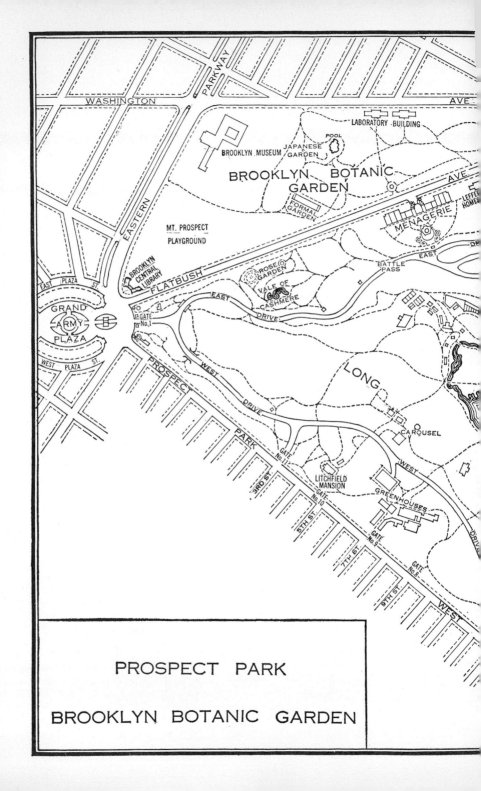

PROSPECT PARK

BROOKLYN BOTANIC GARDEN

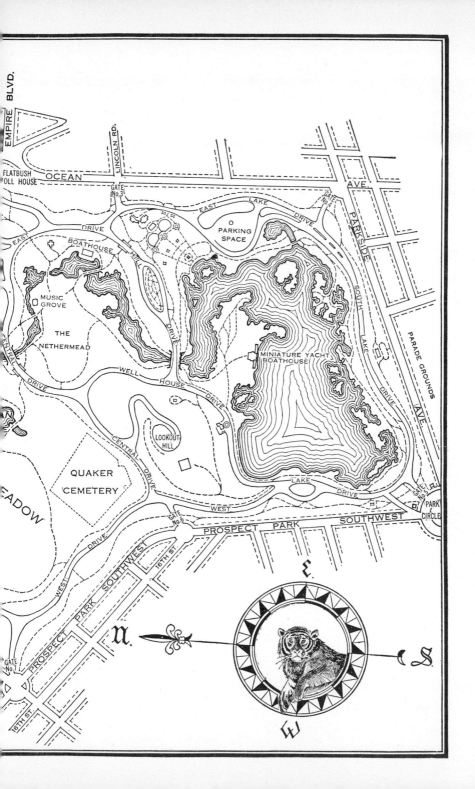

guard the Jamaica Pass in East New York, however, the British were enabled to attack from the rear, capturing Sullivan and forcing the Continentals to retreat.

Farther north along East Drive is the Vale of Cashmere, a natural amphitheater filled with azalea, summersweet, and rhododendron in tropical profusion. A place of retreat, as its poetic name implies, there is a lagoon in the center, with ledges of rhododendron. On the north side, steps lead up to the rose garden, laid out in formal beds around three circular pools.

To the south is the menagerie (rebuilt in 1935), where thousands of visitors daily wind in and out of a neat semicircle of red-brick buildings facing Flatbush Avenue near the Empire Boulevard entrance. *(Open weekdays 11 a.m. to 6 p.m., Saturday, Sunday and holidays 10 a.m. to 6 p.m.; closes one hour earlier in winter; admission free.)* The sunken-barrier moats make it possible to view the animals without the obstruction of bars. Designed by Aymar Embury II, the menagerie is notable for its architecture. The plan centers on the elephant rotunda, to form a group far better integrated than the earlier Central Park Zoo by the same architect. The buildings are decorated with bas-reliefs and murals—the work of WPA artists—depicting scenes from the life of Mowgli, hero of Kipling's *Jungle Books.*

South along the East Drive is the LEFFERTS HOMESTEAD (11D). *(Open Monday, Wednesday, and Friday 1 to 5 p.m.; admission free.)* It was built by Lieutenant Peter Lefferts in 1777 to replace the house burned by the British, and was presented by his descendants to the city in 1918, when it was moved from its original location at 563 Flatbush Avenue. A notable example of the late Dutch Colonial style, it has a low gambrel roof which curves out to form a wide overhang supported by slender columns. The front entrance has a richly paneled door, paned-glass side lights and top light, and an entablature of carved sunburst designs supported by paired shafts. The interior is under the care of the D.A.R. The living and dining rooms, separated by an arch, are on the north side of the main hall; the parlor and real bedrooms are on the south. Above are a children's room with four-poster and trundle beds, a maple room and workroom. The attic, of roughhewn beams, contains a smoke room. The lower two-story wing is used by the caretaker's family.

At the Empire Boulevard entrance is the old FLATBUSH TOLL HOUSE (11E), an octagonal cabin with disclike roof, which marked the division between Flatbush and the town of Brooklyn in Turnpike days. Near the Ocean Avenue-Lincoln Road entrance the walk crosses the drive to the old-fashioned garden on the east. Here are the restaurant and refreshment stands, with statues of Beethoven, Mozart, Von Weber, Grieg, Thomas Moore near by, and, across the drive, Washington Irving. At the head of the terrace, below a flight of stairs, stands a statue, by Henry Kirke Brown, of Lincoln reading his Proclamation.

The view of the lake here is perhaps the best, exuberant foliage shrouding the shores of peninsulas and islets. The lake curves around the southern edge of the park; boating in summer, ice skating in winter, attract many of the park's 75,000 weekly visitors. On the north side of the lake is the miniature yacht boathouse, housing the sloops which dot the wide water front in mild weather.

North of this boathouse is Prospect or Lookout Hill, the central pinnacle of the ridge for which the park is named. About halfway up is the chaste MONUMENT (11F) to the Maryland Regiment that held the Hessians at bay to permit the Continentals to retreat during the Battle of Long Island. The polished granite column with bronze Corinthian capital and white marble globe was designed by Stanford White and erected in 1895 by the Maryland Society of the Sons of the American Revolution. Near by, tiers of stairs lead to the summit of the hill, which affords on clear days a panorama of the densely settled environs of Brooklyn, with the ocean and harbor beyond.

Drive and walk follow the lake shore to the Park Circle entrance at the southwestern tip, notable for the statue, *The Horse Tamers,* by Frederick MacMonnies.

Across Parkside Avenue to the south is the Parade Grounds, frequented by National Guard and American Legion units, a rectangular plain of forty acres, once used by the military and now divided into forty-five baseball diamonds, converted in season into football fields.

12. The CENTRAL BUILDING OF THE BROOKLYN PUBLIC LIBRARY, Flatbush Avenue and Eastern Parkway, finally approaches completion in 1939. The site of the projected building, which was intended to replace the small outmoded structure on Montague Street *(see page 446),* was chosen in 1905, but the foundations were not laid until 1914. From that date until 1937, when the present administration took action, little progress was made. The total cost of the neoclassic building will be five million dollars. Githens and Keally are the architects.

13. BROOKLYN BOTANIC GARDEN, Eastern Parkway, Washington and Flatbush Avenues, is known for its floral displays, and pioneer research and educational work. *(Open daily from 8 a.m. to dusk, except Sunday and holidays, when the gates open at 10 a.m.; admission free.)* Founded in

1910 as a department of the Brooklyn Institute of Arts and Sciences *(see page 453)*, it now occupies a fifty-acre plot, opposite the eastern edge of Prospect Park. The plot is enclosed by tall poplars and shrubs. The Horticultural Garden on the Eastern Parkway side leads to the Overlook, from which the rest of the grounds may be viewed. There are two entrances on Washington Avenue (south of Eastern Parkway), one at the conjunction of Flatbush and Washington Avenues, and one at Eastern Parkway, near the Brooklyn Museum.

The outdoor plantations include a general Systematic Section showing botanical relationships; special gardens including the Japanese, Rose, Rock, Ecological, Native Wild Flower, Water, Wall, Iris, Children's, Shakespeare, and Herb Gardens; horticulture collections and plantings. The Laboratory Building contains the herbarium with some two hundred thousand specimens, an excellent reference library on plant life, and (in the conservatories) a display of economic or tropical plants and other groups, such as those tracing the evolution of plant life.

Probably the most celebrated feature is the Japanese *Niwa,* or landscape garden. Designed and cared for largely by Japanese gardeners, it covers about an acre in the northeast corner just above the Laboratory Building. A typical example of the Japanese talent for condensation, the *Niwa* embodies aspects of four kinds of gardens steeped in religious or social tradition—palace, tea cult, Shinto, and Buddhist temple. It is built around a lake shaped like the Chinese letter meaning "heart" (the center of meditative calm) and is bordered by Japanese iris. The East Indian lotus in the lake is the Buddhist symbol of immortality; its root, flower, and seed pod —which symbolize the past, present, and future—appear at one time. This concept is the basis for the chief Buddhist doctrine, "The Covenant of the Eight Years." The *torii,* or bird-perching gate, in the lake, marks the approach to a Shinto shrine on the rise beyond, where three distinct levels, representing the trinity of Heaven, Man, and Earth, are divided by a gorge and waterfalls. On the path to the shrine is a Kasuga stone lantern with elaborate ornaments and carvings of the zodiac animals, modeled after one in Kasuga Temple Yard in Nara, the ancient capital of Japan.

The Tea House, which has a circular latticework opening on one side, affords a dramatic panorama of the garden. From the north wing a path runs beyond a rustic *torii* to the Moon View House or Waiting Pavilion across the lake. Here, in Japan, guests would await the melodious gong calling them to tea. Just beyond the pavilion is a drum bridge leading to an island with stepping stones, beach, and cave for aquatic birds.

The garden is planted for the most part with hardy specimens such as mountain laurel, azalea, wistaria, and mulberry trees, to insure the proper year-around display. Except for the open lakeside, the whole is enclosed by a bamboo fence.

North of the Japanese Garden is the Herb Garden with varieties of medicinal and culinary herbs. To the west, under the Overlook, are Cherry Walk, popular in May; the esplanade with Norway maples on either side; the lilac collection, of some two hundred varieties, and the Rose Garden, in full flower in June.

Near the Eastern Parkway entrance rests a huge boulder with a bronze tablet memorializing André Parmentier, who in 1825, at Atlantic and Carleton Avenues, established the first botanic garden in Brooklyn. This and twenty-eight other boulders scattered throughout the grounds were unearthed in the excavation of the ridge, the second highest ground in Brooklyn, and part of the terminal glacial moraine deposited during the Ice Age and extending from the Narrows to Montauk Point. Other glacial rocks are utilized in the Wall Garden, running 385 feet along the Mt. Prospect Park embankment, near Eastern Parkway, and in the Rock Garden lying to the south near Flatbush Avenue.

The Rock Garden, built in 1916, contains eight hundred species of Alpine and rock-loving plants from all parts of the world. In the Native Wild Flower Garden, between the Lilac Triangle and Wall Garden, a large number of species found wild within one hundred miles of New York City grow in profusion.

Most of the remaining outdoor area is devoted to the Systematic Section, which winds north to south along the banks of a brook coursing through the grounds. The algae, mosses, and ferns on the south shore of the lake, are succeeded by various classes of gymnosperms (plants with naked seeds) including the conifers. Last come the vast array of angiosperms, or flowering plants, with seeds enclosed in an ovary. In this section the exhibits are arranged in a sequence of plant families from the simpler to the more complex forms.

West of the Laboratory Building and conservatories is the Laboratory Plaza, a formal garden of magnolias and stone vases, and in Conservatory Plaza are two water-lily pools, one containing tropical varieties and the other, hardy specimens. The white stone and stucco Laboratory Building, completed in 1918, was designed by McKim, Mead, and White. Its central and wing sections, two stories high, each surmounted by an octagonal cupola, contain research, lecture, and assembly rooms, and administrative offices, as well as the herbarium and library. In the rotunda of the central section are bronze busts of Linnaeus, Darwin, Mendel, Asa Gray, Robert

Brown, and John Torrey—the work of WPA sculptors—and two symbolic figures by Isabel M. Kimball. Southwest of the conservatories are the Children's House and Garden, pioneer project of its kind, where each year hundreds of boys and girls study nature and practical gardening under supervision. Near by, a Shakespeare Garden exhibits many of the plants mentioned in the poet's plays.

The Botanic Garden is a semi-public institution. The city, which furnished the land and most of the buildings, provides maintenance; the Brooklyn Institute of Arts and Sciences supplies the administrative personnel and scientific material. Garden members are entitled to previews, free docent and technical service, reduced tuition rates and free copies of publications.

14. The BROOKLYN MUSEUM (CENTRAL MUSEUM OF THE BROOKLYN INSTITUTE OF ARTS AND SCIENCES), Eastern Parkway and Washington Avenue, is outstanding not only for its collection of the arts and crafts of primitive Oriental, Egyptian, and American peoples, but for an extensive and progressive educational program that has made it one of the leading educational forces in New York. *(Open weekdays 10 a.m. to 5 p.m., Sunday 2 to 6 p.m.; admission Monday and Friday, adults 25¢, children 10¢, other days free.)* The activities of the Brooklyn Museum include many courses and lectures for children and adults; concerts, folk festivals, demonstrations of art techniques, motion pictures, and touring exhibitions. The museum is used by more than a million people annually.

The building was erected by the city and leased for a nominal fee to the Brooklyn Institute of Arts and Sciences *(see page 453).* Funds for the maintenance of the building and grounds, which are under the jurisdiction of the Department of Parks, are provided by the city. The income from a private endowment is used to pay curators' salaries, to purchase works of art, and for incidental expenses.

The building, constructed in four sections between 1897 and 1925 at a cost of $3,300,000, was designed by McKim, Mead, and White. Of a huge projected plan, only the central portion and one wing have been completed. Like other works by the same architects, it is an impressive monument, but in terms of contemporary museum requirements it is quite outmoded. During the past few years a WPA project has been making the museum one of the most modern and pleasantly arranged in the country. The most striking change has been the removal of a monumental stairway which originally gave access to the third story, and the building of a new entrance hall at the ground level.

In the recent alterations the galleries were completely modernized with respect to color, lighting, and dramatic presentation of material. Architecturally treated walls have given way to plain surfaces, pleasantly colored and ideal as backgrounds for the display of works of art. Maps and educational labels designed for easy reading accompany the exhibits. A progressive directorship has widened the cultural ties between the museum and the community; in the words of the director, "the whole museum is conceived as a place for enjoyment, recreation and education, not as an exclusive palace where art is remote from the common touch."

The entrance hall gives the first hint of the recent transformation. With its interesting forms, levels, contrast of materials, lighting—a maximum of effect with a minimum of expense—it is an example of the best in modern architecture. Devoid of the elaborate decorations which so often clutter up the entrances of public buildings, it contains only a few works of art changed from time to time, and cases for feature exhibits. Among the sculpture now shown there is a bronze cast of Bourdelle's war memorial, *France Saluting America,* which stands in Bordeaux. Adjoining the hall are several galleries for special temporary exhibits. Usually four such exhibitions are on view.

The permanent exhibitions on the first floor embrace the Indian cultures of North and South America, and the primitive cultures of Malaysia, Polynesia, Melanesia, Northern Japan, and Negro Africa. The American Indian collections, including rich specimens of pre-Columbian gold ornaments, are among the finest and most extensive exhibitions of the native arts of the Western Hemisphere to be seen in any museum. The collections of primitive material, though less extensive, reveal the specific qualities of each culture, the materials and techniques used by each race, and the direct relation of the arts and crafts to the daily life of these primitive people. Whether it is an Ecuadorian jaguar in clay, exquisitely woven shrouds from Peru, totemic carvings from the northwest American coast, a stylized frigate bird as a Melanesian fisherman's god, or the sturdy fetish figures from the Congo, each local culture is seen to produce objects which are at once useful and beautiful. In the cases are also musical instruments, bows and arrows, shields, dolls, rugs, shawls, pots, delicate pieces of jewelry, and models of Maya temples.

The offices and classrooms of the educational division, as well as the museum restaurant, are also on the first floor.

A long gallery on the second floor, near the main stairway, serves as an approach to the permanent collection of the art of Persia, India, Japan, and China, which, emerging from a more complicated social organization than that of the primitive peoples, has a wider range and subtlety of form and subject. The great technical advances made by the Oriental craftsmen in metal and pottery are demonstrated in this collection.

The Persian collection includes exhibits of art objects from Persia as well as those lands which were influenced culturally by Persia, such as Turkestan, Mesopotamia, and Turkey. It features paintings of incidents in the lives of heroes, princes, and poets; thirteenth- and fourteenth-century pottery; examples of Persian calligraphy; and rugs, which are still popular in western parlors.

Among the East Indian collections are paintings dating from the sixteenth to the eighteenth centuries that bear witness to the interesting struggle between the Rajput of India and the Moghul invaders: the Rajput paintings are expressive of folk art, with its simple designs and flat color, and contrast with the courtly style sponsored by the invaders, with its European atmospheric effects, subtle tones, and complicated court subjects. Other East Indian exhibits are statues and paintings of Buddhist and Jain religious figures, a chess set, early pottery figurines, heavy gold and silver jewelry, and jade objects of the Moghul aristocracy.

In the Japanese collection, a few workingmen's coats of simple but beautiful design are shown with a large display of lacquer and pottery, costumes, war masks, and arms and armor. A treasure of the Japanese exhibit is a group of Hokusai sketches.

Religious paintings, sculpture, masks, and ceremonial costumes are the main objects in the exhibits from Siam, Tibet, and Korea.

The Chinese collection represents many centuries of civilization during numerous dynasties and religious transitions, in bronze figures, delicate paintings of animals and birds, grave figurines, jades, porcelains, and cloisonné.

The well-equipped library and Department of Prints and Drawings are also on the second floor. A print study room is available to students, while a small gallery near the Print Department is devoted to temporary exhibits of the graphic arts. Among notable items in the print collection are the Goya *Capricios,* Whistler lithographs, Picasso's *Metamorphoses,* Segonzac's *Treilles Muscate,* a first edition of Piranesi's *Carceri,* Maillol's *Art d'Aimer,* Pennell lithographs, and selected prints by Millet, Degas, Manet, Dufy, Bonnard, and Toulouse-Lautrec.

The Greek and Roman collections on the third floor summarize the art of the ancient world from pre-Hellenic times to the decline of the Roman Empire. While the number of exhibits is somewhat limited, essential objects have been chosen which characterize the daily lives of the people of the Aegean and Mediterranean worlds. Large illuminated photomurals of architectural remains, such as a Mycenaean grave circle, the temple of Zeus at Athens, the Colosseum, and the aqueduct at Segovia, supplement Cretan and Greek sculpture, household articles and coins, and Roman glass and frescoes.

Other galleries on the same floor house the Egyptological collections. They consist principally of two collections, one formed by Charles Edwin Wilbour about 1880, the other a loan of the New York Historical Society. The Wilbour collection is especially rich in items of the Amarna period. New objects are acquired through a fund donated by the Wilbour family, by purchase, and through joint expeditions, such as that with the Egypt Exploration Society. A small tomb, royal and private sculpture, jewelry both gold and enamel, textiles, utensils, scarabs, and the mummies of three bullocks are among the displays. Adjoining the Wilbour Gallery is the Wilbour Memorial Library of Egyptology.

In a small room adjacent to one of the Egyptian galleries are twelve Assyrian ceremonial bas-reliefs from the palace of Ashur-nasir-pal, also lent by the New York Historical Society. They are from the same excavations as those at the Metropolitan Museum *(see page 368)*.

The large sculpture court on this floor plays an important role in the museum's life. For want of an auditorium, concerts, lectures, folk festivals, and other cultural activities are held here. Scattered around the sides are representative works of contemporary sculptors, among them Barye, Rodin, Maillol, Meunier, Milles, Epstein, and Ahron Ben-Schmuel.

The gallery of medieval art on the fourth floor provides examples of painting, sculpture, and craftwork from the late Roman Empire to the Renaissance. The Byzantine, or Eastern Empire, and the Western Empire are both represented. Here are textiles of the Copts (Christianized Egyptians of the third to sixth centuries); fifteenth-century carved polychrome figures of Christ; statues from France, Germany, and Spain; tempera altarpieces of the Italian and South German schools; English stained glass; and chasubles of Roman bishops. A small group of icons, mostly from the seventeenth and eighteenth centuries, testify to the persistence in the Greek Catholic Church of the stylized rendering of religious figures and scenes characteristic of near eastern iconography.

An adjoining gallery contains a large collection of peasant costumes and fashionable women's dresses chiefly of the nineteenth century. Different techniques of weaving, embroidery, and other processes of ornamentation are comprehensively illustrated. Extensive study collections of textiles are available to students.

A notable group of Colonial American and Early Republican interiors is also on this floor. Rooms of farmhouses, plantation manors, and merchant homes have been reconstructed with zealous attention to decorative and architectural detail. The rooms range in provenance from New England to South Carolina, in date from 1665 to 1820.

A series of galleries is devoted to the painting, sculpture, ceramics, tapestry, glass ware, furniture, and plastic art of the Renaissance, including the Frank Lusk Babbott and Michael Friedsam collections. While there are no outstanding works of great masters, Italian paintings typical of the chief schools convey the lively charm of Florentine and Venetian artists. A few French, Dutch, and Spanish masters are represented, among them Clouet, Hals, Ter Borch, and Goya.

A comprehensive collection traces the diversity of schools in American painting from the eighteenth century to the present day. The portraits of Copley, Sully, Stuart, and Peale contrast with the work of naïve and refreshing early American painters of lesser renown. Next come the Hudson River painters with their preoccupation with landscape; and these are followed by Impressionists, Realists, and Romanticists. Good examples are to be seen of the work of Albert Ryder, George Inness, John Singer Sargent, Winslow Homer, Thomas Eakins, Childe Hassam, Mary Cassatt, Arthur B. Davies, John Sloan, Alexander Brook, Walt Kuhn, Thomas Benton, and others. Among the water-colorists are Charles Demuth, John Marin, and George Burchfield. Homer and Sargent are each represented by a number of water colors.

Across the rotunda from the Renaissance galleries is a long gallery containing nineteenth-century European painting. Here are represented Delacroix, the great romantic; Corot and other members of the Barbizon school; the Impressionists, Degas, Sisley, Monet and Pissarro; the Realist Courbet; and the father of so many moderns, Cézanne.

FLATBUSH is one of Brooklyn's most desirable residential neighborhoods. It extends south of Prospect Park to Kings Highway, between Nostrand and McDonald Avenues. A few Colonial homes still remain there, and most of the tree-bowered streets, some named for Dutch settlers, have a tranquil, late nineteenth-century air. Roomy homes, with spacious front porches, are separated by lawns and privet hedges. Among them rise numerous modern apartment houses. In World War days, Flatbush's domestic reputation was honored in a popular song called *Nesting Time in Flatbush*.

For more than 250 years after its founding by the Dutch in 1634, Flatbush maintained some degree of isolation from the main stream of metro-

SOLDIERS' AND SAILORS' MEMORIAL ARCH, GRAND ARMY PLAZA, BROOKLYN

BROOKLYN BOTANIC GARDEN

BROOKLYN COLLEGE

LEFFERTS HOMESTEAD, PROSPECT PARK, BROOKLYN

PLYMOUTH CHURCH, BROOKLYN

FLATBUSH REFORMED PROTESTANT CHURCH, BROOKLYN

WALLABOUT MARKET, BROOKLYN

BOROUGH HALL, BROOKLYN

BROOKLYN NAVY YARD

ERIE BASIN, BROOKLYN

CONEY ISLAND, BROOKLYN

politan life. But a succession of real-estate booms, and the advent of the subway in the early 1920's have succeeded finally in drawing it into the orbit of the city.

From the beginning, the community was aided in its aloofness by its situation in the Midwout (Middle Woods). Midwout, in fact, became the name of the community itself, which, by 1652, had expanded sufficiently to receive a patent of township from Peter Stuyvesant. (The southern part is still called Midwood.) The name "Flatbush" was the anglicization of the Dutch 't Vlacke Bos (Wooded Plain), an alternative name for Midwout. Even after the Revolution, Flatbush continued to go its own way, and for fifty years the King's Arms were allowed to hang in the town inn. As late as 1886, a contemporary genially termed the town a "Colonial museum." In 1894 Flatbush was absorbed into the city of Brooklyn.

15. The FLATBUSH REFORMED PROTESTANT CHURCH, Flatbush and Church Avenues, a noted landmark, is one of the oldest existing churches on Long Island. Much of its importance derives from the fact that around it rose the small wooden huts of the early Dutch settlement. The original church was erected in 1654 (under the direction of Peter Stuyvesant), with a stockade for protection against marauding Indian bands. A second church building replaced it in 1698. The present structure, with its slender spire, white-painted belfry, and ivy-covered, buff-colored stucco walls, was built in 1796. An old Dutch bell dating from 1796, still in use, has tolled for the funeral of every President and Vice-President of the United States. The interior, with its stained-glass windows, white walls, ceiling and woodwork, and mahogany rails, radiates a charm that recalls the old Dutch past. In the churchyard are gravestones of an early period, and under the church itself are buried American soldiers killed in the Battle of Long Island.

16. ERASMUS HALL HIGH SCHOOL, Flatbush and Church Avenues, often called the "mother of high schools," began as a small private academy in 1787 with an enrollment of twenty-six boys. It was the first secondary school to be chartered by the Regents of the University of the State of New York and hence is the nucleus out of which grew the vast system of secondary school education in New York. The original academy building, a fine example of Colonial architecture with its hand-carved beams and clapboards, stands in the center of an ivy-towered quadrangle. It was built in 1787 with funds contributed by Alexander Hamilton, Aaron Burr, John Jay, and others. Around it are three-story stone and brick buildings, Collegiate Gothic in design, completed in 1905–1925. In

front of the old academy is a large bronze statue of Desiderius Erasmus, copied from an original (1622) in Rotterdam by Hendrick de Keiser.

The entrance fee to the old Erasmus Hall Academy was one guinea; and tuition was six pounds sterling, a sizable sum in those days. Students came not only from the surrounding countryside, but also from such far-off places as France, Portugal, the West Indies, Brazil, Spain, and Sweden. Discipline was severe and refractory students were punished by solitary confinement in the "brig," an attic above the classrooms, and sometimes even whipped. If the quaint wording of Rule 9 is to be taken literally, however, students who stood in the good graces of teachers were allowed a license undreamed of in modern private schools. This rule states: "No student shall be permitted to practise any species of gaming nor to drink any spirituous liquors nor to go into any tavern in Flat Bush without obtaining the consent of a teacher."

Erasmus became a part of the public-school system in 1896, and today has an enrollment exceeding seven thousand. Its alumni include many stage and screen celebrities and athletes: among them are Barbara Stanwyck, Constance and Norma Talmadge, Jane Cowl, Aline McMahon, Eleanor Holm, Sidney Luckman, and Waite Hoyt. Other graduates are Elmer Sperry, inventor of the Sperry gyroscope; Tessa Kelly, "good angel" of the London slums; and William Duer, an early president of Columbia University.

17. BROOKLYN COLLEGE, Bedford Avenue and Avenue H, one of New York's four municipal colleges, was founded in 1930 as the outcome of a civic campaign for better educational facilities within the borough. It comprises five Georgian Colonial buildings—academic, science, library, gymnasium, and heating plant—formally opened in 1937.

A coeducational college of liberal arts and sciences, it had in 1939 a staff of eight hundred and an enrollment of about twelve thousand, equally divided between day and evening sessions. An additional four thousand are enrolled in the summer school and in the graduate and extension divisions.

The present campus was acquired by the city in 1935, at a cost of $1,600,000, with the aid of a Federal loan and grant. President Franklin D. Roosevelt laid the cornerstone of the gymnasium.

18. The DITMAS HOMESTEAD, 150 Amersfort Place, a late Dutch Colonial farmhouse which houses the Faculty Club of Brooklyn College, was built in 1827 by a branch of the Ditmas family, one of the oldest in Brooklyn. In both front and rear, an exceptionally wide roof eave is used to form a porch. Like much of the Dutch work there is no formal sym-

metry in the façades of this charming house. In pre-Revolutionary days, the site of the Ditmas farm was a flourishing race track, named after the famous Ascot Heath in England.

19. The COE HOUSE, 1128 East Thirty-fourth Street, built in 1793 and moved from its original site at Avenue J and Flatbush Avenue in 1925, is a Dutch Colonial home, with white shingles and blue shutters. The fireplace, a modern addition, is extraordinarily deep and patterned after old stone fireplaces in Holland. The cupboards on the side of the chimney breast as well as the beams of the low ceiling are original.

20. The BENNETT HOMESTEAD, southeast corner of Kings Highway and East Twenty-second Street, a spacious Dutch farmhouse, is said to have been built around 1766 by Hendrick and Andrew Wyckoff. The stay of Hessians during the Revolution is recalled by a name scratched on one of the window panes: Georg Ernst Toepfer, Capt. Reg. de Dittfourth. Noteworthy is the room to the right of the entrance hall, where the panels and cupboards of the mantel wall form a unified design. The Bennett family has owned the house since 1836.

The SHEEPSHEAD BAY NEIGHBORHOOD, whose low wooden houses spread north of Emmons Avenue from the basin, has drawn metropolitan anglers and epicures since its founding in the early 1800's. Fronting the bay are many restaurants noted for their shore dinners. Best known are Lundy's, Villepigue's, Seidel's, the Beau Rivage, and Tappen's.

The Sheephead Bay fishing "fleet," consisting of about fifty boats, is moored to the nine concrete piers along Emmons Avenue built by the city in 1936 at a cost of $180,000. Some of these boats take as many as two hundred passengers on fishing cruises that sometimes extend as far as Atlantic City. The charge per passenger ranges from two and a half to five dollars. Boats leave at six, seven, and eight in the morning, and at midnight.

In the 1870's Sheepshead Bay was also a noted sporting center. At Ocean Avenue, near Jerome, was the track operated by the Coney Island Jockey Club. Near by, in the Holwell mansion, still standing, flourished one of the earliest racing tipster rackets. From the top rooms of the house, "timers" would watch the early morning trials and note the fastest horses. This information would be sold to bookmakers. In 1915, horses gave way to motor cars when the late Harry Harkness, millionaire sportsman, and a group of associates built the $3,500,000 Sheepshead Speedway on this site. It was considered the fastest automobile track in the world. In 1919 the track was replaced by a commercial housing development.

East Brooklyn

CROWN HEIGHTS — EAST FLATBUSH —
BROWNSVILLE—EAST NEW YORK AND NEW
LOTS — CANARSIE — FLATLANDS—BARREN
ISLAND

Area: Fulton St. (Nostrand to Jamaica Ave.) and Jamaica Ave. (to borough
line) on the north to Rockaway Inlet and Jamaica Bay on the south; from Gerrit-
sen and Nostrand Aves. east to the borough line.
Principal highways: Eastern Parkway, Pitkin Ave., Utica Ave., Flatbush Ave., and
Kings Highway.
Transportation: IRT New Lots subway, Nostrand Ave. to New Lots Ave. stations;
IRT Flatbush Ave. subway, President St. to Flatbush Ave. stations; BMT 14th St.-
Canarsie subway, Atlantic Ave. to Rockaway Parkway (Canarsie) stations.

EAST BROOKLYN, the site of some of the earliest settlements on Long
Island, now consists of modern residential communities, a few slum areas,
and bleak, sparsely settled stretches along Jamaica Bay.

CROWN HEIGHTS, for the most part a lower middle-class residential
area, lies on both sides of the ridge of Eastern Parkway. The section was
known as Crow Hill until 1916, when Crown Street was cut through.

1. BROOKLYN CHILDREN'S MUSEUM, Brooklyn Avenue and Park
Place, was the first of its kind in the world. *(Open daily 10 a.m. to 5
p.m., Sunday 2 to 5 p.m.; admission free.)* Founded in 1899 by the
Brooklyn Institute of Arts and Sciences, it is housed in two rambling old
dwellings in Brower Park. An average of five hundred thousand children
come here each year to study the collections, contributed by the institute,
and to take part in actual geological, botanical, or ethnological research
under the guidance of trained staff members. Lectures and educational
movies are scheduled throughout the year. Almost all the exhibits may be
handled by children.

The exhibits include stuffed birds and animals, collections of insects
and minerals, examples of handicraft and costume design, and models

496

depicting such scenes as the primitive hunter with his spear, Galileo at his telescope, Bach at the clavichord, and important incidents in American history.

EAST FLATBUSH, formerly known as Rugby, is a suburban residential district lying south of East New York Avenue between Kings Highway and Nostrand Avenue. It contains chiefly one- and two-family houses. Along the southern fringe are open lots and occasional truck gardens. East Flatbush was developed in the 1920's, and its growth continued through the depression of the 1930's. It was populated largely by the overflow from neighboring localities.

The corner of Rutland Road and East Ninety-fifth Street, in the eastern part, is locally known as the "slave market," because Negro domestic workers gather here daily on the sidewalk and offer their services at hourly rates.

2. KINGS COUNTY HOSPITAL, Clarkson Avenue from New York to Albany Avenues, a municipal institution, established in 1831, is the third largest medical center in the United States. Its bed capacity—2,825—is the largest in the city. In 1938, 61,039 patients were cared for in the hospital, and an additional 401,821 received treatment in the clinics. The resident staff comprises 192 physicians and internes and more than 1,000 nurses. The visiting staff consists of more than 500 leading Brooklyn and Manhattan medical men, who serve without compensation.

Kings County Hospital is really a collection of buildings rather than a group, for there is little sense of a unified whole. The architecture of the buildings is marked by a mélange of influences and a clash of styles: Colonial, Spanish, Georgian, Gothic, and Romanesque—none very definite —are all represented. The main building at East Thirty-eighth Street houses the Acute Hospital. This imposing thirteen-story brick structure, completed in 1931 and officially known as the A B C Unit, was built from plans by Leroy P. Ward and Associates at the cost of about six million dollars. Carved in the stone plaques at each side of the entrance are names of notable sicentists.

Demands for accommodations at Kings County Hospital have increased so rapidly that plans for additional buildings were projected in 1939. These include a chronic hospital, a pathological building, a mortuary, a psychiatric hospital, and a building for the out-patient department.

3. BROOKLYN STATE HOSPITAL, Clarkson Avenue between Albany and Utica Avenues, is under the jurisdiction of the State Department of

Mental Hygiene. It takes nervous and mental cases from Kings County. The institution has 2,725 beds with complete facilities for observation, care, and treatment. The Brooklyn State Hospital was opened in 1895, taking over some of the functions handled by the Kings County Hospital. During the past twenty years all the old buildings have been replaced by fireproof modern structures. The hospital grounds cover twenty-eight acres, and around the nineteen-story central building, opened in 1935, are grouped a number of ward and service buildings. Additions now being constructed will increase the bed capacity to 3,250.

BROWNSVILLE extends from Ralph Avenue to Junius Street, between Liberty and Hegeman Avenues. With more than two hundred thousand people dwelling in its 2.19 square miles, it is the most densely populated district in Brooklyn. The population is predominantly Jewish. A large group of Negroes lives on Rockaway Avenue, Thatford Avenue, and Osborn Street between Livonia and Sutter Avenues. The only Moorish colony in New York is on Livonia Avenue between Rockaway and Stone Avenues. Italians live in the northern section of Brownsville; and on Thatford Avenue near Belmont is a small Arabian and Syrian quarter.

The main thoroughfare, Pitkin Avenue, named for John R. Pitkin, founder of the village of East New York, has large shops, a movie palace, and restaurants; great crowds of shoppers and strollers, day and evening, offer a colorful contrast to the numerous side streets with their dismal houses. The open-air pushcart market on Belmont Avenue, from Christopher Street to Rockaway Avenue, is the cynosure for local housewives, who come to make thrifty purchases. Here Yiddish is the shopkeepers' tongue, and all the varieties of kosher foods, as well as delicacies particularly favored by Jews, are the leading articles of sale. In winter the hucksters bundle up in sweaters and stand around wood fires.

The area now called Brownsville, lying between the villages of East New York and Bushwick, was subdivided by Charles S. Brown in 1865. In 1883 there were 250 frame houses in the village. A group of East Side realtors in 1887 purchased land and erected many dwellings. They encouraged immigrants, chiefly Jews of East European origin, to move here from Manhattan's congested East Side. The extension of the Fulton Street el in 1889 and the IRT subway in 1920–22 made the district completely accessible from Manhattan, where many of the inhabitants work.

Old World customs dominate Brownsville life. There are more than seventy orthodox synagogues; the first, Beth Hamidrash Hagodal, at 337 Sackman Street, was organized in 1889. Numerous *cheders*, where young

EAST BROOKLYN

BMT SUBWAY LINE
BMT ELEVATED LINE
EIGHTH AVE. SUBWAY LINE
IRT SUBWAY LINE
LONG ISLAND R.R.
EXPRESS STATION
LOCAL STATION

KEY

1. Brooklyn Children's Museum

2. Kings Co. Hospital

3. B'klyn State Hospital

4. Site of Howard's Half Way House

5. Highland Park Ridgewood Reservoir

6. Schenck House

7. New Lots Reformed Church

8. Wyckoff Homestead

9. Flatlands Dutch Reformed Church

10. Schenck-Crooke House

11. Lott House

12. Marine Park

13. Floyd Bennett Field

14. Marine Parkway Bridge

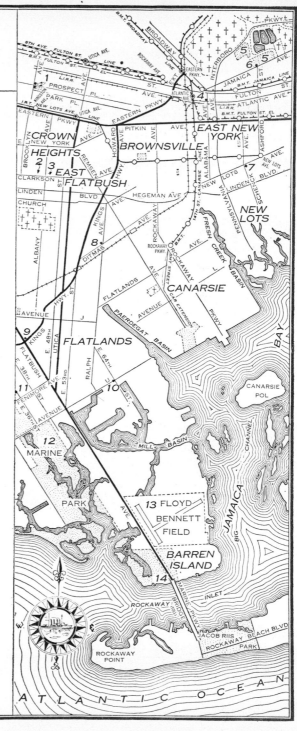

Jews receive instruction in orthodox traditions and customs, dot the neighborhood. On Friday •night and on Jewish holidays the streets of Brownsville are hushed. In all orthodox homes, after nightfall on the Sabbath eve, candles gleam, offering the only light in the room.

Numerous *landsmanschaften,* societies organized by immigrants from the same town or village in the Old World, supply most of the social life for the inhabitants. The *landsmanschaften* are also mutual benefit societies in which regular payments guarantee a doctor's service in case of illness, and a burial plot in case of death.

The building trades claim many Brownsville residents, and on Sunday morning, on the corner of Stone and Pitkin Avenues, carpenters, painters, electricians, and masons assemble to talk shop and find employment. Boss painters and contractors walk from group to group, picking their men. Behind the assembly rises a forlorn building, once a branch of the Bank of the United States, whose sensational bankruptcy in 1930 brought enormous losses to Brownsville residents.

Brownsville has always been hospitable to new social movements. From 1915 to 1921 this district elected Socialists to the New York State Assembly. In 1936 an American Labor Party candidate was elected to the Assembly, only to lose his seat in 1938. In 1916 Margaret Sanger established on Amboy Street the first birth control clinic in America.

EAST NEW YORK and NEW LOTS, lying between Jamaica Avenue and Jamaica Bay, west of Junius Street, are less congested than neighboring Brownsville, but otherwise indistinguishable from it in appearance and social composition. New Lots, then known as Ostwout (East Woods), was settled in 1670 by a group of Dutch farmers who came from the Old Lots section of what is now Flatbush. When incorporated as a town in 1852, it embraced the villages of East New York and Cypress Hills (in the vicinity of Jamaica Avenue) and the area that later became Brownsville. It was annexed to Brooklyn in 1886.

The development of East New York began in 1835 through the enterprise of John R. Pitkin, a wealthy Connecticut merchant who visualized it as a great city rivaling New York. The panic of 1837 smashed his hopes. After 1853 a modest development began. Today the residents of this section are chiefly Italians, Jews, Germans, and Russians who moved in from Brownsville, Bushwick, and other near-by crowded localities. Many of the Slavic families continue to burn candles before icons, and observe religious fetes according to the old calendar. They maintain a small school at 189 Pennsylvania Avenue for instruction in the Russian language and a community house at 120 Glenmore Avenue.

4. The SITE OF HOWARD'S HALF WAY HOUSE, northwest corner of Atlantic and Alabama Avenues, recalls a famous incident of the Revolutionary War in which the proprietor of the inn, an American sympathizer, was coerced by General Howe's forces to guide them to the hill overlooking the unguarded Jamaica Pass just west of what is now the intersection of Fulton Street and Broadway. The occupation of the hill made possible the flanking maneuver that decided the Battle of Long Island in favor of the British. The Half Way House was torn down by the Long Island Railroad in 1902 to make way for its elevated tracks.

5. HIGHLAND PARK, Jamaica Avenue from Warwick Street to Force Tube Avenue, commands a remarkable view of East New York, Jamaica Bay and mid-town Manhattan. On lower ground, facing Jamaica Avenue, are tennis courts, baseball fields, and other playgrounds. Part of this 141-acre park, including Ridgewood Reservoir at its crest, is in Queens County.

6. SCHENCK HOUSE, Jamaica Avenue and Ashford Street (in Highland Park), a stone, Dutch dwelling, was built in 1705 by Johannes Schenck, whose descendants occupied it until 1906. It was then acquired by the city for the use of the park department.

7. The NEW LOTS REFORMED CHURCH, New Lots and Schenck Avenues, erected in 1823, represents the handiwork of the Dutch farmers of New Lots, who decided to build their own church because the trip to the Flatbush Reformed Church (see page 493) was too long and difficult. They hewed, hauled, cut, and planed the lumber, and erected the framework. The structure is the meeting house type with a pitch roof, steeple, and tall, pointed stained-glass windows. In the graveyard are buried members of the old families.

CANARSIE, from Foster Avenue to Jamaica Bay between Paedergat and Fresh Creek basins, is a sparsely settled community laid out on dispiriting flatlands, smoked over by the perpetual reek of fires in the vast refuse dump at its' western end. Its residential section of one- and two-family houses and shacks (most of which resemble those in Charles Burchfield's paintings) is broken by weedy lots and small truck farms cultivated by Italians. Along the uninviting waters of the bay is a forlorn beach resort —an amusement park called Golden City, a fishing boat center, a beach backed by a dump, and beery dance halls—with an outlandish quality that made Canarsie the butt of many vaudeville jokes.

A trolley car extension of the BMT subway runs through a littered lane between the back yards and unkempt gardens of run-down houses. Here and there passengers catch a glimpse of Canarsie's better dwellings, of its village-like business section on Flatlands Avenue, of great stretches of dump and marsh, and of unpaved streets. In the near future Canarsie will undergo changes as the new Circumferential Highway around Jamaica Bay is completed and the shore improved.

Early in the seventeenth century the Dutch farmers from Amersfoort bought this land from Wametappack, sachem of the Canarsie Indians.

8. The WYCKOFF HOMESTEAD, southwest corner of Ralph Avenue and Canarsie Lane, north of Ditmas Avenue, was built between 1639 and 1641. Pieter Clasessen Wijkhof, who came to this country in 1637, occupied the house for forty-four years. Wijkhof was superintendent of Peter Stuyvesant's estate and himself a rich land owner.

The one-story dwelling, a simple Dutch house, has a sweeping, projecting roof. The rounded shingles of white oak on the exterior walls, as well as the handhewn oak rafters in the attic, were fastened with wooden pegs brought over from Holland. The original dwelling was about three-fifths the depth of the present structure.

FLATLANDS, in the southeastern corner of Brooklyn, is a low-lying terrain jutting into Rockaway Inlet and Jamaica Bay, and indented by creeks and small bays. Much of the southern section is unreclaimed marshland. In the residential section in the north are block after block of neat frame or stucco houses. From Marine Park north to Bergen Beach are pathetic communities of squatters, who live in makeshift houses, and eke out a living by fishing and scouring the near-by city dumps for odd necessities. At Bergen Beach, the brooding silence of the dour marshland hangs over old houses and shanties, over small patches of vegetable gardens and decrepit boatyards along the miserable beach front.

Flatlands or New Amersfoort was the name applied by the Dutch to the flat country lying east of Prospect Park Ridge from the Narrows to Hempstead. There was probably a rude settlement in the region now called Flatlands as early as 1624, but the town did not receive its charter till 1667.

9. FLATLANDS DUTCH REFORMED CHURCH, Kings Highway north of Flatbush Avenue, erected in 1848, occupies the site of the original church which was built in 1663 and rebuilt in 1794. A white wooden structure with a well-proportioned steeple, it has a striking simplicity and charm.

In the graveyard are buried members of many noted Dutch families, including the Wyckoffs, Kouwenhovens, Lotts, Stoothoffs, Voorhees, Sprongs, and Suydams.

A plaque on the church lawn identifies Kings Highway at this point as the road along which Lord Cornwallis marched his troops on the night of August 26, 1776, to outflank the Americans at the Battle of Long Island.

10. SCHENCK-CROOKE HOUSE, Avenue U between East Sixty-third and Sixty-fourth Streets, is considered one of the oldest houses in New York City, the original section having been built in 1656. A white house with green shutters and red brick chimneys, it stands in a little hollow back of Public School 236, surrounded by old pine trees. Its Dutch origins are evident in the small twelve-paned windows and early round-end shingles. The slender-pillared front porch formed by an overhanging roof is an eighteenth-century addition.

11. LOTT HOUSE, 1940 East Thirty-sixth Street, exemplifies two stages in the evolution of New York architecture. The north wing, which constituted the original farmhouse, was built by Coert Voorhees in 1676 and acquired by Johannes Lott in 1719; its age is apparent in the small windows, a precaution against Indian raids. The main part of the house was built in 1800 by Hendrick Lott; the high Ionic pillars in front and square pillar in the rear illustrate the change from the earlier period.

12. MARINE PARK, Fillmore Avenue between Gerritsen Avenue and East Thirty-eighth Street, is a two-thousand-acre tract of marshland, cut by sluggish creeks lined with houseboats on stilts and boat landings connected with Flatbush Avenue by long wooden catwalks. Most of this land was donated to the city in 1920 by the Whitney family with the proviso that it be converted into a public park. As yet (1939) little improvement has been made. Plans include a model yacht basin, lagoon, stadium, outdoor theater, riding ring, six recreation areas, baseball fields, and a canal.

13. FLOYD BENNETT FIELD, Flatbush Avenue and Jamaica Bay, one of New York's two municipal airports, covers a rectangular expanse of 387 acres surrounded by fens bordering Jamaica Bay. It was dedicated by Mayor James J. Walker in 1931 and named for Floyd Bennett, the aviator who piloted Admiral Byrd across the North Pole in 1926.

Carefully planned to handle a large volume of traffic and built on reclaimed marshland by hydraulic fill sixteen feet above sea level, Floyd Bennett Field has not been a commercial success because of its distance from the heart of the city. The only commercial planes using it are those of the American Airlines, flying between Boston and New York.

The airport's attractive Administration Building is flanked by eight fireproof hangars, each measuring 120 by 140 feet. Four concrete runways, from 3,200 to 4,200 feet long and from 100 to 150 feet wide, crisscross the field. The two towers at the landing zone are equipped with 5,000,000-candle-power floodlights, which supplement the regular beacon, boundary, and obstruction lights. Blind landings at the field are facilitated by directional radio beam and a special runway bordered by contact lights.

Its site on Jamaica Bay makes Floyd Bennett Field particularly suitable for seaplanes, an advantage impressively demonstrated in 1933 by the visit of twenty-four giant Italian seaplanes under General Italo Balbo on their way home after a transatlantic trip to the Century of Progress Exposition in Chicago. A ramp for seaplanes, 50 by 220 feet, at the eastern end of the field, gives access to ample water space.

Most of the airplanes housed at the field are owned by individuals, flying clubs, and a few flying schools. Many belong to the U.S. Naval and Marine Aviation Base, the Coast Guard, and the New York City Police Department. Courses in aviation are available to civilians. Some private planes specialize in sightseeing trips; more than 85,000 passengers made flights from 1931 to 1938.

The field's strategic location, its long runways and clear approaches have made it a frequent base for long distance flights. The first was the nonstop transatlantic trip of 5,014 miles to Istanbul, Turkey, made in 1931 by Russell Boardman and John Polando. In 1933 Wiley Post began and ended here his sensational solo flight around the world in 7 days, 18 hours, and 49½ minutes. In 1938 Howard Hughes and four companions, embarking from Floyd Bennett Field, circled the globe and reduced Post's record to 3 days, 19 hours, and 8 minutes. Others who have taken off from the airport on noted flights include Clyde Pangborn and Hugh Herndon, Jr., James Mattern and Bennett Griffin, Roscoe Turner, the flying Hutchinson family, and Frank Hawks. The field is the official eastern terminal for all coast-to-coast record flights made under the supervision of the National Aviation Association Contest Committee. The register of the airport, signed by all flyers as they arrive and leave, is a signal collection of names famous in aviation history.

BARREN ISLAND, a small community immediately south of Floyd Bennett Field, and an island in name only, resembles an isolated village in some remote countryside. A cluster of patchwork houses, whose occupants earn their livelihood as housewreckers, huddle around a dirt path leading from Flatbush Avenue. To the south, on Dead Horse Inlet, are the ruins of a fertilizer factory where the families of Barren Island once found employment.

The notorious pirate Gibbs, who met death on the gallows in the early nineteenth century, was said to have buried a portion of his booty on Barren Island, and legend has it that the treasure is still hidden there.

14. MARINE PARKWAY BRIDGE, a toll bridge spanning Rockaway Inlet, links Brooklyn at Flatbush Avenue with Jacob Riis Park on the Rockaway peninsula. *(Passenger automobile toll 15¢.)* It also connects with Rockaway Beach Boulevard and Beach Channel Drive, which run through the seashore resorts.

A bridge of three spans, each providing a channel 500 feet wide, the structure has an overall length of 4,022 feet. At the center is a 540-foot lift span, with a clearance of 55 feet when lowered and 150 feet when raised. The two flanking spans provide a clearance of 50 feet above mean high water. The bridge was built by the Marine Parkway Authority in 1936–7 at a cost of six million dollars (including the parkway). Consulting engineers were Madigan-Hyland, Wadell and Hardesty, and Robinson and Steinman. The consulting architect was Aymar Embury II.

The Bronx

D. Spiegel

The Bronx

THE Bronx, geographically an unbroken extension of Westchester County (of which it was once a political division), is the only New York borough on the mainland. It occupies an area of 42 square miles (with 80 miles of water front), and lies at the northern extremity of the city—in the upper portion of a "Y" formed by the East and Harlem rivers. The Hudson flows past the upper western flank of the borough, and Long Island Sound ends among the islands off the eastern shore. Across the narrow, high-banked Harlem is Manhattan, its long northern extremity snuggling against the Bronx and joined to it by fourteen bridges and three subway tunnels; beyond the flat, irregular shores of the East River is Long Island, linked to the Bronx by the Triborough, New York Connecting Railroad, and Bronx-Whitestone bridges.

Hunt's Point, Clason's Point, Screvin's Neck, and Throg's Neck are large peninsulas of low, salt meadowland jutting into the East River and separated by small bays and streams like Pugsley's Creek, Westchester Creek, and the shallow Bronx River. The last-named descends from the Westchester hills through the middle of the Bronx, while in the northeast the even smaller Hutchinson River empties into Eastchester Bay, which splits Pelham Bay Park. From the northern section of the park extends the Rodman's Neck-Orchard Beach-Hunter's Island peninsula; near by, in the waters of the Sound, are City Island, Hart's Island (site of Potter's Field), and several rocky islets.

The chief topographical features of the borough are three ridges, the worn foothills of the Berkshires and Green Mountains, which give the Bronx its characteristic hilliness. One ridge.extends through Riverdale, between the Hudson and Broadway, its highest point, 284.5 feet, being near Iselin Avenue and 250th Street. A second runs from Van Cortlandt Park to Macombs Dam Bridge, roughly paralleling the Harlem, with the Grand Concourse on its crest. The third, east of the Bronx River, has a noticeable rise in the north, around Edenwald, but falls away into the flats of the East River shore.

Although to the outsider, the Bronx signifies little more than a cocktail, a jeer, or a zoo, the New Yorker knows it as a community of apartment houses peopled by families of average means. About 70 per cent of the Bronx residences are of the multi-family type, a proportion more than twice that for the city as a whole. These dwellings are found chiefly in the West and Middle Bronx, which house three-quarters of the borough's 1,500,000 population. Despite the congestion in several sections, the Bronx has much permanent open space: its parks, among the largest in the city, and cemeteries account for a higher percentage (17 per cent) of the total land area than those in any other borough. A small portion, located almost entirely along the southernmost water front, from Macombs Dam Bridge to Hunt's Point, is devoted to industry. The value of products manufactured in the Bronx in 1935 was $103,177,991, next to the smallest total among the boroughs.

The eastern part of the borough consists of scattered, residential neighborhoods, partly developed: in the north, Edenwald, Eastchester, and Baychester; in the south, Hunt's Point, Clason's Point, Throg's Neck. The oldest neighborhoods, crowded slums (Mott Haven, St. Mary's Park, Morrisania), are in the south, abutting for the most part on the industrial area. Between the Harlem River and Webster Avenue, and centered about the impressive Grand Concourse, are University Heights and Fordham Heights, localities where modern apartment dwellings are massed on hilly streets. In the northwest corner, on a high ridge above the Hudson River, is Riverdale, whose splendid homes and estates, set among quiet lanes, resemble those of fashionable Westchester County. At the opposite side of the borough, a causeway from Pelham Bay Park leads to isolated City Island, where the building of pleasure boats is a leading industry.

The area that is now the Bronx, called Keskeskeck by the Indians, was purchased from them in 1639 by the Dutch West India Company. Two years later, Jonas Bronk, a Scandinavian, became the first white settler of the region when he bought 500 acres between the Harlem River and the

Aquahung. The latter stream soon lost its Indian designation and became known as Bronk's River.

Arriving shortly after Bronk were religious dissenters and other colonists from New England. In 1643 John Throgmorton settled what later became Throg's Neck; the next year, Anne Hutchinson, exiled from Massachusetts for her opposition to theocratic stewardship, came to the banks of the present Hutchinson River; in 1654 Thomas Pell bought a large tract, part of which is now Pelham Bay Park. Their settlements, however, were for the most part unsuccessful, for those that were not wiped out by the Indians were in constant trouble with the Dutch until the British occupation in 1664. More fortunate were the Morris brothers, merchants from Barbadoes, who in 1670 purchased the Bronk estate, giving their name to the present Morrisania. Their descendants included Lewis Morris, a signer of the Declaration of Independence, and Gouverneur Morris, a member of the Constitutional Convention of 1787.

Westchester County (which then included the Bronx) was given over largely to farming during the English Colonial period. Although early visitors found no great wealth among the general population, it would seem that even in large villages every family possessed several acres of farm land. A caste system, perhaps more sharply defined than in other northern colonies, existed here; and as generations passed, life, with the gentleman-farmer, tended toward the comfort and culture of his equals in England and the South, while the mass of people remained always in homespun. The well-to-do sent their sons to Yale, Princeton, and abroad; free schools were not established until late in the seventeenth century and were not separated from the church until the year before the Revolution.

It was during this period that a struggle involving American liberty was precipitated in the Bronx. In 1733 Judge Lewis Morris was summarily dismissed from office after a controversy with Governor Cosby, and in a hotly contested election for the State Assembly, Morris defeated a candidate supported by the Governor. A too-candid newspaper account of the election brought a libel suit by the Governor against the New York editor, John Peter Zenger, which resulted in the vindication of a free press.

The Bronx played no outstanding role in the Revolution. The great families were divided in their allegiance, and the Anglican clergy was, of course, Tory; the small farmers to a large degree held themselves aloof from the Revolution. A number of forts were built or occupied by the British, and though no large-scale battles took place in the Bronx, there were constant encounters and pillagings. Early in the war, according to Rupert Hughes' *Washington*, the British War Office, uninformed as to

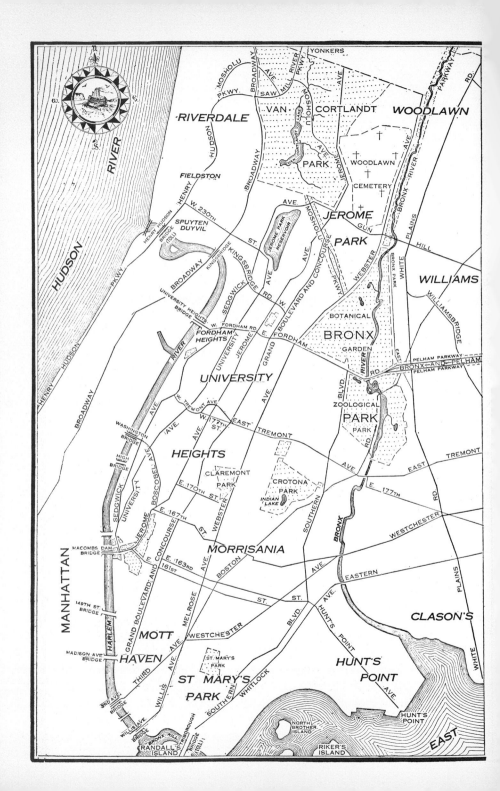

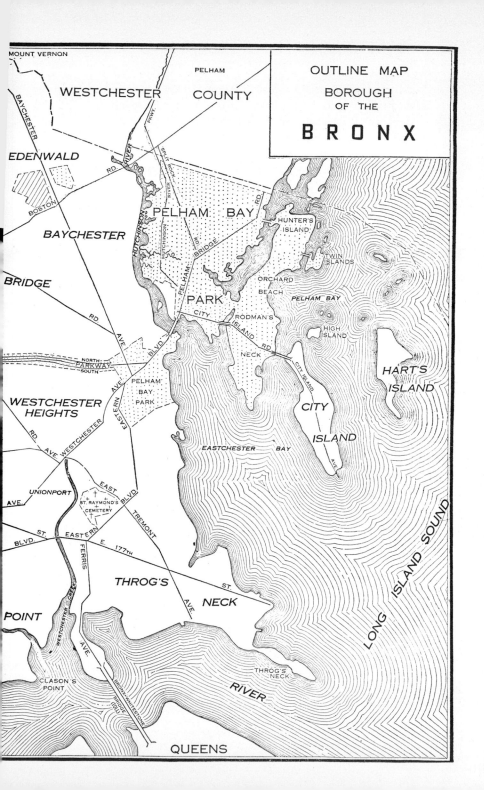

OUTLINE MAP
BOROUGH OF THE
BRONX

MOUNT VERNON

WESTCHESTER COUNTY

PELHAM

EDENWALD

BAYCHESTER

BOSTON RD.

BAYCHESTER

BRIDGE

RD. AVE.

PELHAM BAY

HUTCHINSON RIVER PKWY.

SPLIT ROCK RD.

HUTCHINSON RIVER

HUTCHINSON RD.

PELHAM BRIDGE

HUNTER'S ISLAND

TWIN ISLANDS

ORCHARD BEACH

PELHAM BAY

PARK

CITY ISLAND

RODMAN'S NECK

HIGH ISLAND

NORTH PARKWAY SOUTH

BLVD.

RD.

CITY ISLAND RD.

HART'S ISLAND

WESTCHESTER HEIGHTS

PELHAM BAY PARK

EASTERN AVE.

RD. AVE. WESTCHESTER AVE.

CITY ISLAND

CITY ISLAND AVE.

EASTCHESTER BAY

UNIONPORT

EAST BLVD.

ST. RAYMOND'S CEMETERY

TREMONT

AVE.

ST. BLVD. EASTERN

E. 177TH ST.

FERRIS AVE.

THROG'S NECK

AVE.

LONG ISLAND SOUND

POINT

WESTCHESTER CREEK

AVE.

BRONX-WHITESTONE BRIDGE (TOLL)

CLASON'S POINT

THROG'S NECK

RIVER

QUEENS

Bronx topography, issued orders to Admiral Howe to sail his fleet up the Bronx River and attack "whatever American ships he found there."

There was little change in the Bronx from the close of the Revolution until the middle of the nineteenth century. Despite the exodus of many Tory farmers upon the evacuation of New York, the borough remained a farmers' country, with occasional estates built by wealthy New Yorkers seeking purer air and pleasant wooded hills and streams. The population, 1,761 in 1790, had reached only 8,032 by 1850. The poet Joseph Rodman Drake wrote of it early in the nineteenth century:

> "Yet I will look upon thy face again,
> My own romantic Bronx, and it will be
> A face more pleasant than the face of men."

In 1846, twenty-six years after Drake's death, Edgar Allan Poe brought his wife to Fordham, so that she might benefit by the air, and here *Ulalume* and *Annabel Lee* were written.

Irish immigrants moved in after 1840, many finding employment in building the Harlem Railroad, the Hudson River Railroad, and the Croton Aqueduct; and following the German Revolution of 1848, came an influx of German farmers. From 1850 to 1860 the population was nearly tripled.

Urbanization continued rapidly. Industries were started on the Harlem and East River water fronts and new railroads came through. In 1874 the western townships, Kingsbridge, West Farms, and Morrisania, became wards of New York City; and these were followed in 1895 by the eastern township of Westchester and part of Pelham and Eastchester. Under the Greater New York charter in 1898 these two annexations constituted the borough of the Bronx. (The Bronx became a separate county in 1914.) The population was then about two hundred thousand. A plan to open and grade 420 miles of streets east of the Bronx River was approved by the Board of Estimate in 1903 (although many streets in this section are still only lines on maps). In 1904 the IRT subway was opened to West Farms and the next year to East 180th Street (Bronx Park), supplementing the older elevated road. A real estate boom ensued, and by 1910 the population had reached 430,000. By 1939, with the greater part of the borough available by subway and el, the population had more than tripled. Except for the old neighborhoods along the route of the first subway, the buildings of the Bronx are mostly recent: 92 per cent of the houses were built after 1900. Only Queens has shown more rapid growth in the same period.

To the earlier Irish and Germans, now almost completely assimilated, have been added, since the turn of the century, large numbers of Italians and Russian and Polish Jews, moving up from crowded lower Manhattan. Jews now constitute about half the total population. Negroes, too, in the 1930's, have crossed the Harlem River, settling mostly in Morrisania, while later generations of Irish and other racial groups have come in lesser numbers.

Self-styled the "Borough of Universities," the Bronx has a number of large and outstanding schools: the Bronx Center of New York University, with its Hall of Fame; Fordham University; Manhattan College; a branch of the municipal Hunter College for women; Webb Institute of Naval Architecture; the College of Mount St. Vincent; and several well-known private preparatory schools in Riverdale. Bronx Park, with its great zoological and botanical gardens, is another leading cultural enterprise. The borough has its own newspaper, the Bronx *Home News,* which has a wide circulation.

The Bronx of pleasant woods and streams still lives in its parks. Their large stretches of woodland, bridle paths, golf courses, picnic grounds, lakes, and hiking trails draw many thousands of apartment dwellers the year round. Bronx Park, traversed by the Bronx River, covers more than 700 acres. Pelham Bay Park, with some 2,000 acres and seven miles of water front, is the largest in the city; here the mile-long Orchard Beach was recently developed. Van Cortlandt Park contains nearly 1,200 acres. The three parks are connected by the Mosholu and Pelham Parkways, broad, landscaped boulevards which, together with the Grand Concourse, are notable among the city's fine avenues.

As the city's mainland link with New England, the Bronx is traversed by several important highways. Boston Road (US 1) crosses the borough diagonally to become, across the city line, the old Boston Post Road. Westchester's famous Saw Mill River Parkway connects in Van Cortlandt Park with the new Henry Hudson Parkway. The Bronx River Parkway, among the first model highways, begins in the northern tip of Bronx Park.

Comparatively low-priced land and pleasant surroundings have brought to the Bronx, more than to any other borough with the possible exception of Queens, many large housing projects, private, co-operative, or government aided. In 1939, plans were announced for a huge $35,000,000 development sponsored by the Metropolitan Life Insurance Company. Slum clearance, a relatively small problem in the Bronx, was given impetus when blocks of decrepit dwellings were razed to make way for the approaches to the Triborough Bridge.

Further development of the Bronx, according to the Mayor's Committee on City Planning, will include extensive building of apartment houses and garden apartments, for which large areas are available. By 1939, funds had been appropriated for health centers in three districts, new hospitals, including one for tuberculosis and contagious diseases, and for further improvements of Orchard Beach. Transportation improvements in addition to the Eighth Avenue (Independent) subway (opened in the Bronx in 1933), the Triborough Bridge (1936), and the Bronx-Whitestone Bridge (1939), a direct vehicular link between most of Long Island and New England, will include the projected Burke Avenue vehicular viaduct between Webster Avenue and Bronx Park East, and an airport.

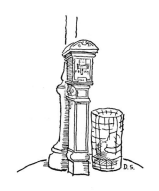

D. Spiegel

West Bronx

Area: Bronx Kills on south to city line on north; from Harlem and Hudson rivers east to Willis Ave., Melrose Ave., Webster Ave. (to E. 211th St.), and Wood-lawn Cemetery.
Principal highways: Grand Concourse, University Ave., and Broadway.
Transportation: IRT Jerome Ave. subway, 149th St. to Woodlawn stations; IRT Broadway-7th Ave. subway, W. 225th St. to 242d St. (Van Cortlandt Park) stations; 9th Ave. el, Sedgwick Ave. to Woodlawn stations; Eighth Ave. (Independent) Grand Concourse subway, 161st St.-River Ave. to 205th St. stations.

THIS section, more densely populated than the eastern part of the borough, is characterized mostly by tall, new apartment houses tenanted on the whole by the families of salaried workers and moderately well-to-do people. The Riverdale section in the north has the smart suburban air of adjoining Westchester County.

The Grand Boulevard and Concourse (commonly called the Grand Concourse) runs about four and a half miles through the center of the West Bronx from Mott Avenue and 138th Street north to Mosholu Parkway near Van Cortlandt Park. The Grand Concourse is the Park Avenue of middle-class Bronx residents, and a lease to an apartment in one of its many large buildings is considered evidence of at least moderate business success. The thoroughfare, 180 feet wide, is the principal parade street of the borough, as well as a through motor route. Along the center the American Legion has planted maple trees in memory of Bronx men who died in the World War.

MOTT HAVEN, bordering the Harlem River and Bronx Kill, at the southwest tip of the Bronx, serves as an industrial overflow for Manhattan. The river front is a jumble of factories, coal- and lumberyards, and railroad yards which make an ugly setting for the Harlem River. Though still dense, Mott Haven's population has been thinning out as the industrial area expands. Within this district are several important government buildings: the two-million-dollar Bronx Central Postoffice Annex (completed in 1937), Grand Concourse and 149th Street; Bronx County Jail (1937), River Avenue and 151st Street, and the Bronx County Building (1934), Grand Concourse and 161st Street.

The section is named for Jordan L. Mott, inventor of the coal-burning stove, who established the Mott Iron Works, at 134th Street and the Harlem River, in 1828; the works remained there until 1906. When Mott bought the land from Gouverneur Morris II, the latter was asked if he objected to the section (then part of Morrisania) being called Mott Haven. "I don't care what he [Mott] calls it," Morris replied; "while he is about it, he might as well change the name of the Harlem and call it the Jordan."

1. BRONX TERMINAL MARKET, Exterior Street between 149th Street and Macomb's Dam Bridge, comprising ten modern brick buildings erected at a cost of $17,000,000 (including the thirty-eight-acre site) during the administration of Mayor .Hylan (1918–25), is a receiving point for the city's fruits and vegetables. The buildings are grouped around a central warehouse and refrigerating plant, and are linked by three miles of yard trackage. Wholesalers rent seventy-four stores. For many years the market, like the municipal piers in Stapleton *(see page 607)*, was known as "Hylan's Folly": the annual cost of maintenance was in excess of $160,000, the annual income from rental $26,000. Improved in 1935 under the LaGuardia administration, it attracted many tenants and became a financial success. The new facilities cost $1,500,000.

2. MACOMB'S DAM BRIDGE, which spans the Harlem River at 161st Street and River Avenue, is on the site of the dam erected in 1813 by Robert Macomb. The waters of the artificial pond operated his mill. Indignant citizens who wanted the river kept open for navigation destroyed part of the dam in 1838. The present span, the third on the site, is a

WEST BRONX

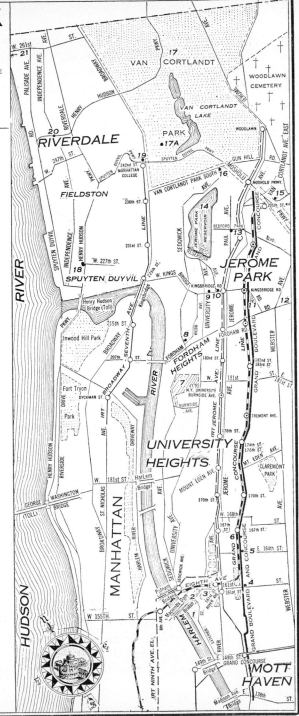

IT SUBWAY LINE
EIGHTH AVE. SUBWAY LINE
IRT ELEVATED LINE
EXPRESS STATION
LOCAL STATION

KEY

1. Bronx Terminal Market
2. Macomb's Dam Bridge
3. Yankee Stadium
4. Bronx County Building
5. Lorelei Fountain
6. Andrew Freedman Home
7. University Heights Center of New York University Hall of Fame
8. Webb Institute of Naval Architecture
9. Fordham Manor Reformed Church
10. 258th Field Artillery (Washington Grays) Armory
11. Poe Cottage
12. Fordham University
13. Bronx Center of Hunter College
14. Jerome Park Reservoir
15. Isaac Varian Homestead
16. Amalgamated Apartments
17. Van Cortlandt Park
    a. Van Cortlandt House
18. Henry Hudson Memorial
19. Manhattan College
20. Campagna Estate
21. College of Mount St. Vincent

swing drawbridge completed in 1896 at a cost of $1,360,000. At its foot is the three-acre Macomb's Dam Park.

3. YANKEE STADIUM, River Avenue and East 161st Street, home of the New York Yankees, is the largest baseball park in the United States. Baseball and football games, boxing matches, and other outdoor events are staged here. Built in 1922 at a cost of three million dollars, the stadium has a normal seating capacity of 75,000, but in September, 1928, at the end of a close and exciting pennant race, it held 83,353 fans, a world's record for attendance at a big league baseball game.

4. BRONX COUNTY BUILDING, 161st Street and Grand Concourse, facing the open space of Franz Sigel Park, is the borough's chief civic center. Ten stories high, and surrounded by a terrace of 125,000 square feet, it dominates the entire scene for miles around. With its fine materials and great simplicity, this neoclassic structure achieves a monumental quality. The building, designed by Joseph H. Freedlander and Max Hausle, was completed in 1934, and cost eight million dollars. It contains the headquarters of the borough president and the Bronx Bar Association as well as the chief courts and offices of Bronx County.

5. LORELEI FOUNTAIN, Grand Concourse and 164th Street, stands in Joyce Kilmer Park, which is dedicated to the author of *Trees*. The sculpture celebrates the legendary siren of Heinrich Heine's lyric, *Die Lorelei,* who lured mariners to their death with her singing and her beauty. A relief portrait of Heine decorates the south side. The fountain, completed about 1893 by the German sculptor Ernst Herter, was intended for Düsseldorf, Heine's birthplace. When the memorial was rejected by the citizens of that town, it was purchased by a group of New York German citizens and presented to the city.

UNIVERSITY HEIGHTS, between about 165th Street and Fordham Road, extends along two ridges, continuations of Westchester County hills. Along the crests of the ridges run the traffic arteries of University Avenue and the Grand Concourse. Tall apartment buildings perch on the top of rocky cliffs or protrude from hillsides, their foundations of rough-hewn masonry exposed. New York University gives the area its name, and near its campus live many well-to-do business and professional people. Even the poorer section to the east near Webster Avenue, inhabited mostly by needle trades workers, is fairly presentable.

University Heights is on the site of the old manor of Fordham, which Governor Lovelace granted in 1671 to Jan Arcer, a Dutchman so skilled in acquiring land from the Indians that he was nicknamed *Koopall* (Buy-all) by his neighbors. The near-by ford of Spuyten Duyvil Creek gave the manor its name. Featherbed Lane, a street in the locality, is said to have been named for a Revolutionary incident in which the local housewives spread their feather beds on the stony road to deaden the hoofbeats of the retreating Colonials, who were thus enabled to avoid the British, join Washington on Harlem Heights and later drive the enemy out of the lane itself. Another explanation of the street's name is that the dirt road was so soft it yielded to the foot like a feather bed.

6. ANDREW FREEDMAN HOME, 1125 Grand Concourse, an attractive building with a French Renaissance flavor, is probably one of the world's most unusual homes for the aged. It was founded in 1916 with a large endowment by Andrew Freedman, a wealthy contractor, once owner of the New York Giants baseball team, who stipulated in his will that admission was to be restricted to "aged and indigent gentlefolk . . . of culture and refinement." The 130 guests, including a czarist general and several retired opera singers, live in private, attractively furnished rooms and are attended by a staff of servants.

7. UNIVERSITY HEIGHTS CENTER OF NEW YORK UNIVERSITY, 181st Street and University Avenue, overlooking the gorge of the Harlem River, has some of the charm of a small-town college campus.

The Heights Center of New York University (see page 133) consists of the undergraduate College of Arts and Pure Science and the graduate divisions of the College of Engineering, enrolling altogether about two thousand men. Its eighteen buildings include several old mansions and stables acquired from previous estates and altered to fit educational purposes. All the modern structures except the gymnasium were designed by Stanford White; they are alike in material and treatment—light yellow brick with gray stone trim. The otherwise plain buildings are enriched by a simple use of classic forms that brings the architecture close in spirit to the Federal period. The group has been justly criticized because the interior of the campus, like that of Columbia University, lacks a view of the river.

The university's Hall of Fame, topping a high cliff at the western edge of the campus, makes a striking landmark that is best viewed from the other side of the river. A 520-foot, semicircular colonnade of granite, the hall has become a national memorial of which the university considers itself the trustee. Along its walls are 150 panels, all destined to be filled with inscriptions celebrating the achievements of outstanding Americans. Candidates for this honor are nominated by the public and chosen by a college of electors consisting of well-known people, and are approved by the Senate of New York University. Above the panels stand bronze busts of the elected persons, the work of eminent artists. Celebrations are sometimes held before the memorials of the individuals on their anniversary days. Among New Yorkers already included in the Hall of Fame are the authors, Walt Whitman, Washington Irving, William Cullen Bryant; the inventors, Samuel F. B. Morse, Robert Fulton, W. T. G. Morton; the philanthropist, Peter Cooper, and the Abolitionist minister, Henry Ward Beecher. The hall itself was the gift of Mrs. Finley J. Shepard (Helen Gould), who also donated the library and Gould Hall to the university. It was dedicated in 1901, when the first twenty-nine figures were unveiled. Seventy-two of the niches are now filled.

The University Heights campus has expanded to an area of about fifty acres since the first eighteen acres were acquired in 1891. Here, during the Revolution, stood British Fort Number 8 which defied assault until the end of the war. Between Butler and South Halls a boulder, a number of guns, and the white mast of the America's Cup challenger, *Shamrock IV,* presented by Sir Thomas Lipton, mark the spot from which the English on November 16, 1776, launched their successful attack on Fort Washington across the river, and forced evacuation of Laurel Hill.

8. WEBB INSTITUTE OF NAVAL ARCHITECTURE, Sedgwick and Webb Avenues, a large red-brick building, is the only school of its kind in the country. *(Visitors admitted weekdays 9 a.m. to 5 p.m., Saturday 9 a.m. to 12 m.)* It was incorporated in 1889 and endowed by William Henry Webb, prominent New York boatbuilder, for the care of aged shipbuilders and for the training of young men as naval architects and marine engineers. Its twofold purpose remains in full effect. Tuition is free, including board and room. Although the student body averages only sixty, the school has considerably influenced the character of American shipbuilding, and graduates of Webb Institute hold positions in most shipbuilding yards. The structure, completed in 1894, was designed by A. B. Jennings. The picturesque massing of its rectangular and curved forms belongs to the period of the Romanesque revival.

Since 1897 Webb Institute has housed the famous Mechanics' Bell, which shipwrights hung a hundred years ago at Goerck and Stanton Streets near the East River. The tolling of the bell marked the end of a ten-hour day, an act of protest against the employers' practice of compelling artisans to work from "dark to dark."

9. FORDHAM MANOR REFORMED CHURCH, 71 Kingsbridge Road, near Jerome Avenue, a trim, red-brick Colonial-style building erected in 1849, served the earliest Dutch congregation in the Bronx, organized in 1696

with a charter granted by William II. The simple interior has box pews enclosed by mahogany rails.

10. 258TH FIELD ARTILLERY (WASHINGTON GRAYS) ARMORY, Jerome Avenue and Kingsbridge Road, is reputed to be the largest and best-equipped armory in the United States. The building, designed by Pilcher and Tachau and completed in 1917, covers an entire block; it is 106 feet high and has a drill floor 300 by 600 feet. The Washington Grays were so named because the original company formed part of the guard of honor at President Washington's first inauguration.

11. POE COTTAGE, in Poe Park, Grand Concourse and Kingsbridge Road, a tiny white-shingled structure dwarfed by the tall apartment buildings of Grand Concourse, was the poet's dwelling place from 1846 to 1849. *(Open daily, except Monday, 10 a.m. to 1 p.m. and 2 to 5 p.m.; Sunday, 1 to 5 p.m.; admission free.)* Here, Poe wrote his child-wife's haunting requiem, *Annabel Lee,* and his *Ulalume.*

The Poes came to Fordham in the spring of 1846, hoping that the country air would prove beneficial to Mrs. Poe who was dying of tuberculosis. He was already famous—*The Raven* had been published the previous year—but honor brought no relief from poverty, and ostracism added to his troubles. The situation was desperate. His mother-in-law, Mrs. Maria Clemm, peddled his unwanted manuscripts and at times scoured the fields for edible herbs to feed the three. Help came through a friend; it was supplemented by funds raised through the pride-racking route of public subscription. But nothing could be done for Virginia: on January 30, 1847, at the age of twenty-six, she died.

Poe hardly survived the winter and his nervous system was shattered. He managed, however, to complete *Eureka* and such final descriptive pieces as *The Domain of Arnheim* and *Landor's Cottage.* His last poems, *To M.L.S., To My Mother,* and *For Annie,* were written here. He left late in June, 1849, for Richmond, leaving Mrs. Clemm at Fordham. In October word was finally brought to her of the death of a "stranger" in a Baltimore hospital who used "the cognomen Edgar A. Poe." As Hervey Allen wrote in the biography, *Israfel,* ". . . the mission which fate had conferred upon Maria Clemm was over. Her reward was a pair of painfully rheumatic, and absolutely empty hands."

The city of New York acquired the house in 1913 and moved it from the original location on the east side of Kingsbridge Road near Fordham Road. Its upkeep was entrusted to the Bronx Society of Arts and Sciences, which restored the exterior and interior, and added a basement. The only actual Poe mementos in the cottage are the bed in which Virginia Poe died, a rocker, a wall mirror, a Bible and a spoon. The square structure with porch and lean-to kitchen and storeroom was built some time before 1816 as a laborer's dwelling. Modest adornments include a paneled door, small-paned windows, and mantels.

12. FORDHAM UNIVERSITY, Fordham Road and Third Avenue, one of the largest Catholic institutions in the country, has an enrollment of 7,500. The university was founded as St. John's College in 1841 by the Right Reverend John Hughes, who later became New York's first Catholic archbishop. In 1846 the Jesuits assumed control, and in 1905 the college was renamed Fordham University, for Fordham Heights, the section in which it is located.

Spread over the large campus is a loosely related group of stone buildings, Collegiate Gothic for the most part, whose harmony of scale and materials makes up for a slight diversity of styles. Most of the seventeen vine-covered structures are comparatively new. The central part of the Administration Building, once the main college building, was erected in 1838 (then Rose Hill Manor House, the spacious home of a gentleman farmer). The latest addition to the campus, Keating Hall, dedicated in 1936 by Patrick Cardinal Hayes, is a three-story edifice used by the Graduate School. The Seismograph Building, erected in 1924 by Mr. and Mrs. William J. Spain in memory of their son, William Lavelle Spain, who died while a freshman at the university, contains six modern quake-recording instruments. It is operated in connection with the Jesuit Seismological Association and the U.S. Coast and Geodetic Survey.

Five of the nine departments of the university have quarters in the Woolworth Building, downtown Manhattan. Women are admitted only to the School of Law, the School of Education, the School of Social Service, the College of Pharmacy, and the Graduate School.

Fordham, in the last decade, has been renowned for strong football teams under the coaching of Major F. W. Cavanaugh (1927–32) and his successor, Jim Crowley. The annual game with New York University, Fordham's traditional rival, is an outstanding sports event in New York.

The JEROME PARK NEIGHBORHOOD, surrounding Jerome Park Reservoir, is a district of comfortable, closely packed, apartment houses, terminating abruptly at the open stretches of Van Cortlandt Park. It is also the site of the Montefiore Hospital, Bainbridge Avenue and Gun Hill Road, a large nonsectarian hospital for chronic diseases. This region was once part of the manor of Colonel Frederick Philipse, a Tory whose lands were confiscated by the Continental Congress.

13. HUNTER COLLEGE, BRONX CENTER, Bedford Park Boulevard and Paul Avenue, is a division of the municipal college for women *(see page 240)*. Only freshman and sophomore classes are held here. The four buildings, designed by Thompson, Holmes, and Converse in a modified Gothic style and completed in 1932, form a quadrangle; they are connected by subterranean passageways. A fifth building is under construction (1939). On the pleasantly landscaped campus are sixteen tennis courts, a hockey field, and a rock garden (built by the Geology Department and modeled after a map of the United States). The buildings, unfortunately, have been placed too far apart and therefore do not appear as a unified group.

14. JEROME PARK RESERVOIR, Reservoir Avenue between Sedgwick and Goulden Avenues, was built in 1906 as part of the Croton system supplying the city with mountain water. Covering ninety-four acres, with a capacity of 773,000,000 gallons, it occupies the site of the Jerome Park race track (1876–90), named for one of its founders, Leonard W. Jerome.

15. ISAAC VARIAN HOMESTEAD, 277 Van Cortlandt Avenue East, corner Bainbridge Avenue, is a simple but well-proportioned Colonial stone house of two stories, said to have been built about 1775. In its vicinity a skirmish occurred between the British and American troops in 1777.

16. AMALGAMATED APARTMENTS, 80 Van Cortlandt Park South near Gouverneur Avenue, is a co-operative building venture initiated by members of the Amalgamated Clothing Workers Union. These were the first apartments to be built and operated under the State Housing Law. The buildings, designed by Springsteen and Goldhammer and erected in 1927–32, are picturesquely grouped around garden courts. The fifth floor section of the façade is decorated with incongruous details derived from English Cottage designs. There are 635 apartments, chiefly with three to five rooms each. The development's many community activities include co-operative services for the supply of groceries, milk, laundry, electricity, and bus transportation.

17. VAN CORTLANDT PARK, Broadway and 242d Street, is a 1,132-acre tract at the northern extremity of the metropolis. Mosholu Parkway, which takes its Indian name from a near-by stream, connects Van Cortlandt Park with other parts of the Bronx, while the Henry Hudson Parkway links it with Manhattan and with Westchester County.

The facilities of the park include two eighteen-hole golf courses and a clubhouse, roller-skating rinks, tennis courts, baseball diamonds, horseshoe pitching courts, bridle paths, archery, hurling, cricket, and hockey fields, skiing hills, hiking trails, and a 36½-acre lake for boating and ice skating. Footpaths meander through dales and gullies and across auto roads and rustic bridges. Sanctuaries are provided in the northern and central parts of the park, where herons, redwings and other marsh birds nest in spring and summer, and game birds stop in season.

The park is the scene of annual intercollegiate cross-country races, and of Rugby games between leading universities. In the warm months hundreds of city children come to play in the day camps conducted by WPA teachers.

The land comprising Van Cortlandt Park, originally a popular hunting ground of the Mohican Indians, became in 1646 part of the patroonship of Adriaen van der Donck, the first lawyer in the province of New Netherland. After his death in 1655, his widow parceled and sold the estate. A portion of it came into the hands of Frederick Philipse, who gave it to his adopted daughter, Eva, wife of Jacobus Van Cortlandt, mayor of New York from 1710 to 1719. Their descendants held the property until 1899, when it was sold to the city.

The VAN CORTLANDT HOUSE (17A) (now a museum), a gray stone structure which stands on a bluff overlooking the lake, near the entrance at Broadway and 242d Street, was built by Frederick Van Cortlandt, son of Jacobus, in 1748. *(Open Tuesday, Wednesday, Friday, and Saturday 10 a.m. to 5 p.m.; Thursday and Sunday 12 to 5 p.m.; admission 25¢ on Thursday, other days free.)* It contains a collection of Dutch and Colonial furniture and an exhibit of ancient arms and documents. A high four-poster bed with steps attached is said to have been used by General Washington when he briefly occupied the home after the Revolution. The L-shaped building is a fine example of New York Georgian architecture. Its hipped roof, pierced by regularly spaced dormers, terminates in a platform or belvedere. Small wooden porches which shelter the south and east entrance doorways are late additions. Carved masks emphasize keystones over the windows. The interior is notable for its hand-carved woodwork. In front of the house a red-brick stairway leads to the old formal Dutch garden, which is surrounded by canals and contains in its center a white marble fountain bearing the seals of the thirteen states. Annually about one hundred thousand visitors come to the Van Cortlandt House.

North of the mansion is VAULT HILL, site of the Van Cortlandt burial ground. Here, in 1781, General Washington ordered campfires burned to deceive the redcoats while he withdrew his army for the decisive Yorktown thrust. The vault itself is said to contain the bones of Augustus Van Cortlandt, Tory clerk of the Common Council of New York.

RIVERDALE, lying west of Van Cortlandt Park along the Hudson, is a quasi-suburban residential community of fine estates, smaller one-family dwellings and some apartment houses. The homes are set along rambling lanes; on the crests of hills overlooking the Hudson; atop ravines that lead to the river; amid flower gardens and picturesque rock formations. Riverdale is the seat of several educational institutions, including Manhattan College, the College of Mount St. Vincent, Riverdale Country School, Horace Mann School for Boys, Fieldston School of the Ethical Culture Society, and Barnard School for Boys. Strict application of zoning regulations permits Riverdale to retain some of the rural character and charm which distinguished the region when it was the property of the Delafield family. (The Delafields founded the community of Fieldston in 1824). The completion of the Henry Hudson Parkway *(see page 284)*, which enters Riverdale by way of Henry Hudson Bridge *(see page 305)*, has resulted in a real-estate boom.

18. HENRY HUDSON MEMORIAL, in Henry Hudson Memorial Park, West 227th Street and Independence Avenue, consists of a hundred-foot column surmounted by a sixteen-foot bronze statue of the navigator, executed by Karl H. Gruppé after a plaster cast by Karl Bitter. Henry Hudson is represented as gazing out over the broad river he explored. Funds for the memorial were raised by popular subscription in connection with the tercentenary of Hudson's discovery in 1909. The Doric column on which the statute stands was erected a few years afterward; the statue itself was not put into position until 1938.

19. MANHATTAN COLLEGE, Spuyten Duyvil Parkway and 242d Street, conducted by the Catholic order of the Brothers of the Christian Schools, was founded as an academy in 1849 and attained collegiate rank in 1863. The present buildings, construction of which was begun in 1921 from plans by James W. O'Connor, are an adaptation based on the Georgian Colonial style. The curriculum of Manhattan College, which emphasizes traditional Catholic training, includes schools of science, engineering, and business. About 1,250 students are enrolled annually.

20. The CAMPAGNA ESTATE, West 249th Street and Independence Avenue, includes what is considered one of the finest villas in the East. The house was designed by Dwight James Baum in Northern Italian Renaissance style, with stucco trim and a hand-made Italian tile roof. The owner, Count Anthony Campagna, won the Architectural League's gold medal in 1923 for the finest Italian gardens in America.

21. COLLEGE OF MOUNT ST. VINCENT, foot of West 261st Street overlooking the Hudson, is a Catholic institution for women, conducted by the Sisters of Charity, whose mother house is on the ninety-six-acre campus. The Sisters purchased the property in 1856 from Edwin Forrest, the famous actor; it included the residence he built in the style of a medieval castle, now used as a museum. The art gallery is noted for its Farnan Collection, which contains paintings attributed to Rembrandt, Lorrain, and Stuart. The gallery is not open to the public.

Middle Bronx

MORRISANIA—WESTCHESTER HEIGHTS—
WILLIAMSBRIDGE — WOODLAWN — EDEN-
WALD—BAYCHESTER

Area: Webster Ave. on the west to Westchester Ave. and Hutchinson River on the
east; from Harlem River and Bronx Kill north to the city line.
Principal highways: Boston Rd., Southern Blvd., and White Plains Rd.
Transportation: IRT White Plains Rd. subway, E. 149th to E. 241st St. stations;
IRT 180th St.-Bronx Park subway, E. 149th to E. 180th St. stations; Third Ave.
el, E. 143d to E. 241st St. stations; Second Ave. el, E. 143d to E. 180th St.
stations.

THE patchwork of the Middle Bronx comprises neighborhoods disparate
in historical development and in contemporary character. The southern
part is a blighted industrial and tenement area; the central, Bronx Park
vicinity, an apartment house district of predominantly Jewish workers and
small businessmen; and the northern section, a composite of middle-class
suburban communities and desolate marshland.

MORRISANIA, an old and neglected section of the Bronx, is part of the
former township of the same name. Seen in the evening from Teller Avenue, it presents some of the contours that must have recommended it to
the Morris family as a site for their manors. Street lamps and lighted
windows distinguish the hills and valleys that are obscured in the day by
tenements and apartment houses.

The name Morrisania is now generally given to the region centering
around Third Avenue and 161st Street. The population is predominantly
Jewish, mixed with Irish, Italian, and German.

Lewis Morris, first owner of the property, died in 1691. In his will he
attempted to cut off the inheritance of his nephew, Lewis Morris II, giving the younger man's "adhering and advizeing with those of bad life
and conversation," as his reasons. The attempt failed and the nephew
became first lord of the manor. His grandson, the fourth Lewis Morris,
was a signer of the Declaration of Independence.

In 1788 Morrisania, then a sparsely settled area, was made a township largely, it was said, through the political influence of Lewis Morris who was trying to sell his estate as a site for a national capital. His description of the region's "healthfulness and salubrity" failed to convince the government. In 1791 Morrisania ceased to be a separate township.

1. CROTONA PARK, Prospect and Crotona Avenues, was named at the whim of an engineer who quarreled with the Park Commission and substituted "Crotona" for the commission's "Bathgate Park." The appearance of the park has very little that is reminiscent of its past as either the estate of the second Gouverneur Morris or the Bathgate family farm. The park contains a large swimming pool, built by the WPA in 1937, and Indian Lake, three and a quarter acres in area. The lake, an artificial one fed by springs and city water, is used for boating and ice skating. The very young, ignoring regulations, fish here with improvised hooks and lines, occasionally surprising spectators by pulling out a catch.

2. NEW YORK COLISEUM, 1104 East 177th Street, a low massive structure, the steel ribs of which were used originally in buildings of the Philadelphia Sesquicentennial in 1927, is the scene of events ranging from bicycle racing to political rallies. It seats fifteen thousand.

3. BECK MEMORIAL PRESBYTERIAN CHURCH, 980 East 180th Street, was organized in 1814 as the West Farms Presbyterian Church. The original building, a frame structure in New England meeting house style, now rarely used, stands on a neglected lot across the street. Adjoining it is an old burial ground. The present church was erected in 1903 with funds left by Charles Bathgate Beck, and renamed in honor of his mother.

4. BRONX PARK, lying in the center of the Bronx, rivals Central Park in the affections of New Yorkers and perhaps surpasses it as a tourist attraction. Within its seven hundred acres of heavy forest and rugged greensward are located the famous botanical garden and the New York Zoological Park, largest in America. The tract averages three-fifths of mile in width and narrows to a giraffe neck towards the north.

A half-hour's ride from Times Square ends in a rural stillness foreign to the crowded city. The quiet is heightened by the splash of waterfalls and the call of birds, while the slanting sunshine is broken into mazy patterns by hemlock, oak, and sassafras. Running from north to south are granite ridges whose crests have been divided by glacial action. In the valleys the soil is generally sandy, but where bogs have been converted into ponds, rich muck is apparent. Bedrock is mostly granite, with layers of gneiss and quartz. Thousands of glacial boulders have been carted

MIDDLE BRONX

——— IRT SUBWAY LINE
– – – IRT ELEVATED LINE
—◎— EXPRESS STATION
—○— LOCAL STATION

KEY

1. Crotona Park

2. New York Coliseum

3. Beck Memorial Presbyterian Church

4. Bronx Park
   New York Zoological Park
   New York Botanical Garden

5. New York Institute for the Education of the Blind

6. Workers Co-operative Colony

7. Hillside Homes

8. Woodlawn Cemetery

9. Edenwald Schools for Boys and Girls (Hebrew Orphan Asylum)

10. Vincent-Halsey House

11. St. Paul's Church

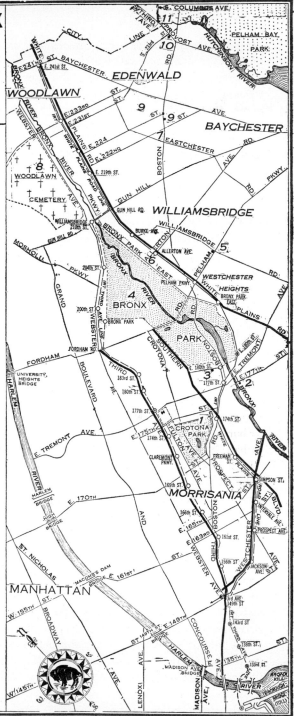

away, but many remain, giving the land a touch of the primeval. The Bronx River, draining a valley fifteen miles long, feeds two lakes—Agassiz and Bronx. At times meandering and almost disappearing, the river is in other places a swift-flowing stream, coursing down waterfalls, rapids, and a steep gorge on its way to join the East River.

The site of the park was acquired by the state in 1884 and four years later title was vested in the city. Two great estates were absorbed by the purchase: the Lorillard homestead, now part of the botanical garden, and the Lydig property, now part of the zoo.

New York Zoological Park

The zoo, founded in 1895, is controlled by the New York Zoological Society, but is maintained by the city. *(Open daily 9 a.m. to a half-hour before sunset April 15 to October 15, 10 a.m. to 6:30 p.m. October 16 to April 14; admission, adults 25¢, children under 12, 15¢, Monday and Thursday, free other days and holidays.)* Although the southern half of Bronx Park was allotted to the society for buildings and enclosures, the zoo, housing about 2,600 specimens (representing almost a thousand species), at present occupies an area about a mile long and three-fifths of a mile wide in the southwestern section; the southeastern part is devoted chiefly to Bronx Lake and woodland walks.

Most visitors arrive by subway (IRT Bronx Park-180th Street line) and use the Boston Road entrance at 182d Street. A short flight of steps from the small plaza near the gate leads to the hoofed-animal ranges. Along the path to the right is the Yak House; American bison, or buffaloes, roam on a twenty-acre range banked by shade trees; wild sheep and goats wander over a ridge of pink granite in which are caves for shelter from both heat and cold.

To the east, on another hill, is the Rocking Stone, a thirty-ton boulder deposited in the glacial period. Pressure applied to its northernmost edge will cause it to teeter back and forth.

The Bear Dens, north of Rocking Stone hill, house members of American, European, and Asiatic species in snug and dry sleeping quarters and large open yards for play and exercise. To the southwest, an enclosed cedar tree shelters a number of racoons, while to the north, in a near-by valley shaded by splendid trees, shy beavers live in their marine retreat.

At the edge of a cluster of oaks, west of the bear dens, is the Reptile House containing, among its amphibians and reptiles, regal pythons, enormous crocodiles and giant tortoises, as well as uncommon bats, including the grisly bloodsucking varieties. In summer many of the non-poisonous

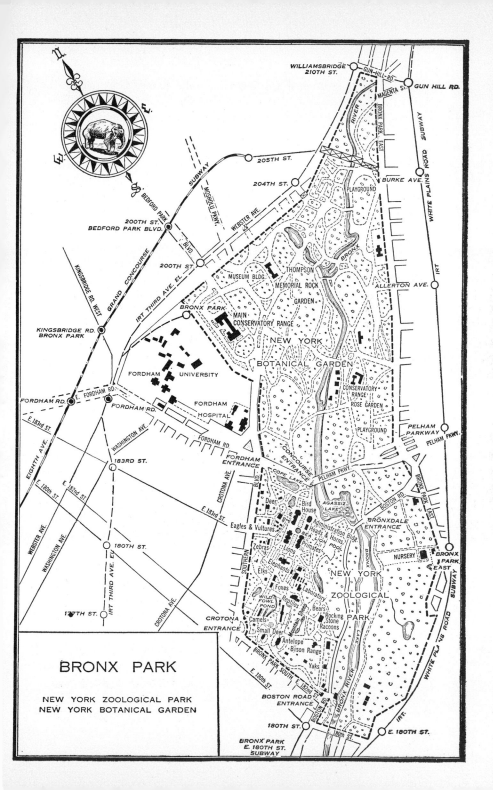

BRONX PARK

NEW YORK ZOOLOGICAL PARK
NEW YORK BOTANICAL GARDEN

snakes inhabit a moat-encircled lawn near the house. Occasionally the giant Komodo lizards, sole survivors of the Dinosaur age, are exhibited. To the northwest stands a huge structure which houses elephants, hippopotamuses, and rhinoceroses in large compartments. Directly north lies the quadrangle of Baird Court around which are grouped a number of exhibition buildings. The sea lions, the vaudevillians of the animal world, honk and cavort in the pool at the center of the court, while the monkeys, apes, baboons, and lemurs in the Primate House near by maintain an incessant racket.

Near the Primate House is the Heads and Horns Museum where exhibits are grouped according to species and geographic distribution. The eleven-foot five-and-a-half-inch tusk of a Sudanese elephant indicates the tremendous size of many of the specimens. Of notable interest is the Combat Collection, containing the heads of animals who died during the mating season, when their antlers interlocked and they were unable to separate and search for food, or defend themselves against enemies.

In the northeastern corner of the court is the Administration Building. Opposite is the rambling Lion House, 244 feet long and 115 feet wide, including the outdoor cages, which hold a splendid collection of beasts of prey—tigers, lions, leopards, pumas, jaguars, and cheetahs. The chief attraction is a recent acquisition, a rare giant panda, captured in Tibet.

The large Bird House, an L-shaped building, occupies the northwestern corner of the court. In 152 indoor and outdoor cages is a colorful, noisy galaxy of more than two thousand native and foreign birds captured in virtually every region of the globe, many with names as strange as their appearance and their cries. In the foot of the L is Parrots' Hall, whose inhabitants are provided with flying cages, pools of running water, umbrageous trees, and rocky ledges. Outside, along the western wall, fourteen large cages shelter members of the crow and blackbird families, natives of American woods and fields.

The great Flying Cage, near the lower end of a section called Bird Valley, a tall arched enclosure of steel pipe and chain net, containing trees, shrubbery, and a hundred-foot pool, is the summer habitat of a mixed flock of large water birds. In winter these birds dwell in the Aquatic Bird House not far to the west; here, too, large migratory water birds find shelter from the winter climate of New York, and eagles and owls roost in large cages outside. In an open glade toward the south stands the Eagle and Vulture Aviary, an enclosed wire structure which exhibits scavengers and birds of prey.

Adjacent to the Flying Cage are Cranes' Park, whose inmates fill the vicinity with their trumpet-like calls, and Goose Aviary, which is also the sanctuary of such rare specimens as the frigate bird, gannet, and saddle-billed stork. Cope Lake to the north is used by Canada geese during the mating season. Just north of Baird Court is the Concourse entrance to the zoo dominated by the Rainey Memorial Gate, a massive structure decorated with animal figures by Paul Manship. A driveway beneath elms, flanked by rhododendron and conifers, leads south from the Memorial Gate to the Italian Gardens and the William Rockefeller Fountain.

Near the Fordham entrance at the corner of Pelham Parkway and Southern Boulevard are several deer ranges, spread over a broad knoll with fine old trees. Farther south is the cheerful Zebra House; wild horses and zebras cavort on a hillock south of the red deer pen. At the south door of the Zebra House is the little Heart-Shaped Pond, the trumpeter swan's retreat.

From the pond to the Crotona Parkway entrance are the corrals of the deer family, the wolf and fox dens, and the elk range with its natural lake. The elk may be viewed at their best in October, when the groves which shelter them acquire brown and russet tints. Ducks and geese ripple the waters of Wild Fowl Pond to the east; near by are the Seal Pools, the Alaskan house, a wild turkey enclosure, the Puma and Lynx House, the Pheasant and Pigeon Aviary, and Prairie Dog Village. The ungainly camel and the long-haired llama (often called the cameloid) greet visitors as they come through the Crotona entrance, while to the southeast the giraffes, kudus, gnus, and other members of the antelope family look down from the commanding heights of Antelope House. Westward are the thirty compartments of the Kangaroo and Wild Swine House, and southward roam a fine herd of fallow deer.

The aim of the founders of the New York Zoological Park was to establish a vivarium which would make "captive animals not only comfortable, but really happy." The longevity of many of the zoo's inmates—some have been in the park for more than thirty years—attests to the excellent treatment they receive. Ailing animals are cared for by an expert veterinarian in a special hospital equipped with the most modern therapeutic and surgical devices. Treatments range from the extraction of hippopotamus molars to the cure of bronchitis in monkeys.

The New York Zoological Society maintains a research laboratory in the park, and publishes excellent popular and technical bulletins, pamphlets, and periodicals.

New York Botanical Garden

The botanical garden, incorporated by the State Legislature in 1891, after a two-year campaign for funds, is maintained by city appropriations, membership fees, and funds from the sale of publications. *(Open daily; admission free.)* In recent years considerable improvements have been effected by PWA and WPA grants.

The garden is separated from the zoological park by Pelham Parkway. From the Bronx Park station of the Third Avenue el, a short walk between clumps of varied pine leads to the Main Conservatory Range, a huge glass building consisting of fifteen subdivisions or "houses." Palms fill the domed house (ninety feet high) that serves as the main entrance. The three houses at the southwest end are devoted to succulent plants of which the garden has more than two thousand species and varieties. One house contains cacti—natives of the New World; another, century plants of the southwestern desert of the United States; a third, the succulent plants of the Old World, notably those that grow in the deserts of South Africa.

Other houses in the main conservatory are devoted to flowering plants of the tropics; economic plants of the tropics, such as bananas and spices, and of the temperate zone, such as coffee and camphor; trees, vines, and epiphytic plants; aroids, such as jack-in-the-pulpit, the brilliant red tail flowers, and gigantic Amorphophallus; and tropical aquatic plants. Two houses have been converted into indoor flower gardens with varying displays; in another a tropical forest has been reproduced, even to the overhead growth that characterizes plant life at the equator.

In the immediate neighborhood of the conservatory are numerous pools and beds where flowers bloom in season. In pools to the southwest are varieties of water lilies, including the sacred "Egyptian," actually Indian, lotus. Crocuses bloom in late March or early April on lawns east of the conservatory; the tall bearded iris comes in May, followed by peonies; day lilies appear about the first of June; cannas, cultivated to enormous sizes, flower in August. Many beds are opposite Fordham Hospital at the southwest corner of the garden; here hardy chrysanthemums survive even the first snows.

The perennial borders facing the southeastern and southwestern sections of the conservatory blossom luxuriantly throughout June, and the colors of delphinium, Canterbury bells, lupine, sweet william, and clematis resemble the colors of an old palette. Near the southeastern bed are dark cedars and flowering shrubs; next to the borders are model gardens.

North of the main conservatory is the museum building, a four-story structure in Italian Renaissance style, which contains the administrative offices of the botanical garden and a herbarium that is one of the finest in America.

In the basement are fossil exhibits, a special laboratory for the study of vitamins and their effect on plant growth, and a lecture hall seating seven hundred. On the first floor are exhibits of preserved economic plants, about seven thousand specimens of drugs, oils, resins, beverages, dyes, foods, spices, and starches, and a herbarium of flora found within a hundred miles of New York.

The second floor contains a museum of systematic botany, with the exhibits arranged in the order of probable evolution from fungi and algae to the angiosperms.

On the top floor are the library (open to students) with 47,000 volumes, the herbarium with 1,900,000 dried specimens from all parts of the world, and laboratories where important research in plant genetics and pathology is conducted. Among recent achievements have been the production of new varieties of seedless grapes and fast-growing poplars to aid reforestation.

In the Thompson Memorial Rock Garden, east of the museum, exotics as well as favorite plants from native meadows, woods, and hills grow in appropriate surroundings.

To the southeast, across the Bronx River, are the nurseries and the great rose garden, which, by masterly cultivation, is made to bloom twice—in June and in October. Also east of the river, near Allerton Avenue, is a second conservatory, temporarily closed to visitors.

Many native wild flowers bloom in the hemlock and deciduous forests that border the Bronx River. (The hemlocks lie between the rock garden and the west bank of the river, and the deciduous trees to the south.) Paths twist through the woodlands, and here, in spring, the maple bears its crimson flowers, and bloodroot and hepatica cover the loam; in summer, the trees provide a sanctuary for native birds; in autumn, the gum trees, the oaks and maples, sassafras and tulip color the banks of the river.

The botanical garden, in addition to its exhibits and research activities, conducts a training school for professional gardeners and extension courses in practical gardening, sponsors radio talks by staff members, publishes scientific and popular periodicals and articles, and co-operates with New York public schools in the teaching of natural science.

WESTCHESTER HEIGHTS lies south of Pelham Parkway between the embankments of the New York, New Haven and Hartford and the New York, Westchester and Boston railroads. Italians of Lombard stock, who for the most part supplanted the original Irish and German settlers, work and reside here. Their homes are two-story frame houses with cupolas or balconies, the walls darkened by soot from the near-by industrial plants and railroad repair shops and yards.

From 1890 to 1904 the fashionable Morris Park race track occupied a site west of the Morris Park station of the New York, New Haven and Hartford Railroad. The pretentious decorations of the grandstand and other structures were designed in Pompeian villa style. Gay life returned to the neighborhood in the Prohibition era when the Woodmansten Inn, a popular night club featuring Texas Guinan and Vincent Lopez, stood near Williamsbridge Road and Morris Park Avenue.

WILLIAMSBRIDGE, east of the Bronx Park Botanical Gardens, has been settled for more than 250 years. As early as 1673, a bridge was built across the Bronx River to carry the traffic of the old Boston Road. Near the eastern end of the bridge a hamlet grew up around the farm of John Williams, whose house stood (until 1903) a little north of the present intersection of Gun Hill Road and White Plains Road. Both the bridge and the hamlet were given Williams' name.

During the Revolution British couriers, carrying dispatches between New York and the New England colonies, almost invariably paused at a small inn near the bridge. While they rested, Peter Bechdolt, the inn's scrawny little hunchback hostler, loosened the shoes of their horses, so that important messages were often delayed because of a mysteriously lamed mount or a cast shoe. For this sabotage of the enemy's communications, Peter was personally thanked by General Washington after the war.

When Williamsbridge was incorporated as a village in 1888, it included the villages of Olinville Number One, Olinville Number Two, Wakefield, and Jerome. The same year, the large oval Gun Hill Reservoir (no longer used) was put into service.

About 1890, a factory that had been established for the manufacture of imitation Gobelin tapestries attracted a number of French tapestry weavers who settled along the Bronx River. Several French restaurants were opened in the colony, and these became popular resorts.

5. The NEW YORK INSTITUTE FOR THE EDUCATION OF THE BLIND, 999 Pelham Parkway, at Williamsbridge Road, is a school for blind and

partially sighted children from five to twenty-one years of age. Here pupils receive free instruction in speech reading, manual communication, Braille, and in vocational and recreational subjects. One of the institute's thirteen buildings is the first ever to be used exclusively for the deaf-blind. Founded in 1831 by Samuel Wood and Dr. Samuel Akerly, the institute has a total enrollment of 223 students. It is supported by private contributions, bequests, and funds from the State government.

6. The WORKERS CO-OPERATIVE COLONY, from Bronx Park East to Barker Avenue between Allerton and Arnow Avenues, organized in 1927, was originally planned to enable trade unionists to purchase their own apartments, but during the early 1930's the ownership of the project passed to a private corporation. The tenants now pay rent, but they elect the board of directors which administers the enterprise. Colony members, both Negro and white, hold spirited discussions on political and economic subjects in the auditorium. The development, occupying two city blocks, comprises four red-brick and stone apartment buildings which fail to make a strong architectural impression because of an ill-advised attempt to put "cute cottage" feeling into so large a housing group. It has a library, kindergarten, clubrooms, and other recreational facilities.

7. HILLSIDE HOMES development, Boston Road at Eastchester Road, is one of the first New York landmarks for southbound motorists on the Boston Road. The 118 red-brick units of this medium-rental housing venture accommodate five thousand people. Nearly two-thirds of the 14½-acre area is in gardens and playgrounds, and generous provision for space and sunlight is a conspicuous feature of the apartments. The project was conceived, not as a mere aggregation of homes, but as a unified community.

On the recommendation of the New York State Housing Board, the Public Works Administration made available $5,060,000, or 88.5 per cent of the estimated cost of the project, at 4 per cent interest. Nathan Straus, who later became administrator of the U.S. Housing Authority, sold the site for the price of seventy cents a square foot, while Starrett Brothers and Eken, the builders, invested the sum of $250,000. The Hillside Housing Corporation is a limited dividend enterprise.

WOODLAWN, a middle-class community east of Woodlawn Cemetery, lies on the far northern marches where New York City cedes to Yonkers and Mount Vernon. In the Revolutionary War Washington stored munitions in the Hyatt homestead that stood on the west bank of the Bronx River near McLean Avenue. To commemorate this incident the settlers called this section Washingtonville. The name was changed in the 1900's to Wakefield and in recent years the community has become known as Woodlawn. From spring through fall groups of hikers mill about the East 241st Street terminal of the IRT White Plains subway, for here begins a two and a half mile trail to sylvan Tibbet's Brook Park in Yonkers.

8. WOODLAWN CEMETERY, East 233d Street and Webster Avenue, occupying four hundred acres of the Fordham ridge, contains the mausoleums of many American tycoons—O. H. P. Belmont, F. W. Woolworth, Collis P. Huntington, Jay Gould, William H. Leeds, and William C. Whitney. Other distinguished men interred here include Admiral David G. Farragut; Charles Scribner, the publisher; Joseph Pulitzer, the newspaper editor; and Herman Melville, author of *Moby Dick*. The cemetery was organized in 1863.

The burial ground is on the site of a Revolutionary engagement. Here in 1778 Colonel Simcoe's British rangers and "Bloody" Tarleton's dragoons ambushed Colonel Gist's troops and his Indian allies.

EDENWALD, the region around East 233d Street and Baychester Avenue, a real-estate subdivision, contains traces of native woodland. Hundreds of frame houses line Kingsbridge Road (here Bussing Avenue), Paulding Avenue, and the Boston Road, while in the central portion of Edenwald are great tracts of untenanted land, clumps of white oak and tulip trees, and an occasional truck garden fenced with bedsprings.

Most of Edenwald was once the estate (called Cragdon) of the Seton family, for whom Seton Park, 233d Street and Seton Avenue, is named. The American Setons were descended from the Scottish family of that name. Among their ancestors was Mary Seton, one of the "Four Marys" who were the "waiting ladies" of Mary, Queen of Scots; another was George, fifth Lord of Seton, who was a Catholic and a stanch supporter of Queen Mary. Ever since William Seton, founder of the American branch of the family, arrived in this country in 1763 his descendants have been distinguished in Catholic affairs. Mother Seton (Elizabeth Ann Bayley Seton) founded the Sisters of Charity (1812); Robert Seton, who died in 1927, was the first Roman Catholic priest in the United States to be elevated to the rank of monsignor.

The Seton Manor once surmounted the hill near the falls of Rattlesnake Creek. In 1903, the city acquired part of the domain as the site for a hospital for contagious diseases; but protests from the residents forestalled the project and the land was unused until the establishment of the park in 1930.

BELOW COLUMBIA HEIGHTS, BROOKLYN

CONEY ISLAND

SNOW ON EASTERN PARKWAY (*Brooklyn*)

CONEY ISLAND

CLAM SHACKS (*Sheepshead Bay, Brooklyn*)

AT THE BRONX ZOO

HOUSES ON STILTS (*Westchester Creek, the Bronx*)

ASTORIA (*Queens*)

JAMAICA BAY

STATEN ISLAND SHORE

SURVIVOR (*Staten Island*)

TOY SHOP, STATEN ISLAND

9. EDENWALD SCHOOLS FOR BOYS AND GIRLS, Boston Road at East 224th Street, units of the Hebrew Orphan Asylum of the City of New York, give instruction, chiefly in the manual crafts, to some 1,500 mentally retarded children. The buildings stand on a pleasantly wooded tract of 123 acres.

BAYCHESTER, the district centering around Baychester Road, east of Boston Road, contains much swampy land, many unpaved streets, a few cultivated patches, and houses spaced as irregularly as pins on a map. It is still untouched by a subway line, though plans call for the extension of the Independent subway to the district. Ten Connecticut families, who purchased land from Thomas Pell and the Indians in 1664, were the first settlers here.

10. VINCENT-HALSEY HOUSE, 3701 Provost Avenue, near East 233d Street, served for two months as the nation's executive mansion when President John Adams moved here in 1797 to escape the yellow fever epidemic raging in Philadelphia, then the Capital. The house was occupied at the time by Colonel William Smith, son-in-law of the President. During the Revolutionary War, the owner of the house, Gilbert Vincent, a blacksmith, was killed by a French officer with the American troops because he refused to shoe the soldier's horse on the Sabbath. In vengeance, Gilbert's brother, Elijah, obtained a commission in the British army. The building has been altered and with its shabby stucco coat is no longer impressive.

11. ST. PAUL'S CHURCH, South Third and South Columbus Avenues, just across the Westchester border, was erected in 1765 to replace an older church built in 1695. This charming old church is of field stone cemented by a mortar of sand and pulverized oyster and clam shells. Among the two hundred parishioners, who contributed oxen, nails, labor, and funds to its construction were members of such New York families as the Roosevelts, Pells, and Van Cortlandts. St. Paul's is a Protestant Episcopal church.

East Bronx

St. Mary's Park—Hunt's Point—Clason's Point—Throg's Neck—City Island
—Hart's Island

Area: Willis Ave., Westchester Ave., and Hutchinson River east to the East River
and Long Island Sound.
Principal highways: Whitlock Ave. and Eastern Blvd.
Transportation: IRT Pelham subway, 3d Ave. to Pelham Bay Park stations.

THE influence of Manhattan on the eastern portion of the Bronx that
borders Long Island Sound and the East River has been negligible. The
settlements along the irregular coast penetrated by Eastchester Bay, Baxter Creek Inlet, Westchester and Pugsley's creeks, and the Bronx River
bear some resemblance to the coastal towns of New England. The only
populous parts of this section lie in the south around St. Mary's Park
and in the north near Pelham Bay Park. The other areas are sparsely developed residential sections, once the site of the manors of early Manhattan millionaires. City Island, the largest of the islands that lie off the
coast, is a picturesque boat-building center.

ST. MARY'S PARK, the nondescript neighborhood surrounding a municipal park of the same name, was part of the land purchased by Jonas
Bronk in 1641 from two Indian sachems, Ranaque and Tackamuck.
Bronksland, his estate, extended along the eastern shore from the Mus-
coota (Harlem) to the Aquahung (Bronx) rivers. His mansion was called
Emmans and stood south of the present junction of Willis Avenue and
132d Street. One historian noted that Bronk "used silver on his table and
had tablecloths . . . and possessed as many as six linen shirts." In the
eighteenth and the first half of the nineteenth century members of the
famous Morris family made their home in this district. The Gouverneur
Morris mansion stood near what is now Cypress Avenue and 132d Street,
and close by was the house of Lewis Morris IV.

1. TRIBOROUGH BRIDGE *(see page 390)*, entrance at Southern Boulevard and Cypress Avenue, connecting the Bronx, Manhattan, and Queens, is linked by Bronx highways with US 1 and the Westchester County parkways.

2. The HELL GATE PLANT OF THE CONSOLIDATED EDISON COMPANY, East 132d Street and the East River, is probably the most valuable piece of property in New York City. The seven-story red-brick building and the water-front site have a combined assessed valuation of $66,734,700. The plant, opened in 1921, has a rated capacity of 605,000 kilowatts, making it the world's second largest electric generating station. The river tunnel that connects the building and the company's Astoria gas plant (Queens) is the longest privately owned one of its kind. About a mile long, 18 feet high and 16¾ feet wide, it carries two huge gas mains (each weighing a ton a foot) and a handcar railway system used for inspection.

3. ST. ANN'S CHURCH, 295 St. Ann's Avenue, is an ivy-covered building in the style of a New England meeting house, modified by doors and windows pointed in the Gothic manner. The church was built in 1841. In its crypt are the bodies of Lewis Morris, signer of the Declaration of Independence; Judge Lewis Morris, first governor of the state of New Jersey (1672); Judge Robert Hunter Morris, mayor of the city of New York (1855); and Ann Carey Randolph, wife of Gouverneur Morris and a descendant of Pocahontas. At the entrance of the church, in a private vault, lie the remains of Gouverneur Morris, a member of the committee chosen to draft the Constitution of the United States in its final form and author of the clause in the New York State constitution providing religious freedom. The building, with its graveyard on a grassy hillock, is a charming spot in an otherwise blighted tenement district.

HUNT'S POINT, now an area of bleak residences, industrial plants, and tidal flats, was a fashionable country section until the Civil War. One of the earliest of the large estates was the Grange, owned by Thomas Hunt. Here in 1688 Hunt built a fine stone mansion which more than a century later became the home of Joseph Rodman Drake, the poet. The site is now part of the Hunt's Point Park, at Hunt's Point Avenue and the East River; the shore here affords an excellent view of Riker's Island. The Indians called the peninsula Quinnahung (a long high place).

4. The AMERICAN BANK NOTE COMPANY, Lafayette and Garrison Avenues, housed in a block-square, five-story brick building, prints paper

money, stamps, bonds, and securities for many foreign governments, as well as a substantial volume of the securities of corporate and financial institutions listed on the New York Stock Exchange. The plates and printing machinery are made on the premises. One of the company's earliest orders was given by Paul Revere, who had been commissioned to have printed a quantity of paper money for the Continental Congress.

5. DRAKE PARK, Hunt's Point and Longfellow Avenues, contains a tiny graveyard in which are buried Joseph Rodman Drake (1795–1820), and members of the Hunt, Leggett, and Willett families. On Drake's monument are inscribed two verses of a poem written upon his death by his most intimate friend, Fitz-Greene Halleck:

"None knew him but to love him,
Nor named him but to praise."

The tombstone of Elizabeth Hunt, wife of Captain Hunt, bears the earliest legible date—1729. The streets near the park are named for poets: Halleck, Drake, Whittier, Longfellow, and Bryant. Another near-by thoroughfare is called Lafayette Avenue, in honor of General Lafayette's visit to Drake's grave in 1824.

6. TEMPLE BETH ELOHIM, 812 Faile Street, is housed in the magnificent country home that was built in 1860 by Colonel Richard M. Hoe, the inventor of the rotary printing press. It is an impressive three-story gray stone structure in the Gothic Revival manner; its interior has been remodeled. Hoe Street, a block west of Faile Street, was named for the inventor.

CLASON'S POINT, an undeveloped residential district, was once the site of a Siwanoy Indian village. Excavations at Sound View and Lacombe Avenues in 1926 yielded a number of Indian relics, now in the Museum of the American Indian *(see page 396)*. In 1643 Thomas Cornell bought the neck of land from the Indians. The land subsequently passed into the hands of the Willett family who held it until 1793, and then sold the eastern part to Isaac Clason and the western to Dominick Lynch. From about 1910 to 1935 the point was a popular shore amusement resort.

7. CLASON POINT INN, south of Sound View Avenue between Newman and Stephens Avenues, contains the stone kitchen wing of the original Thomas Cornell house and parts of the Willett and Clason mansion. The inn, a squat, rambling structure built of rock and wood, was the center of the old Clason Point Amusement Park.

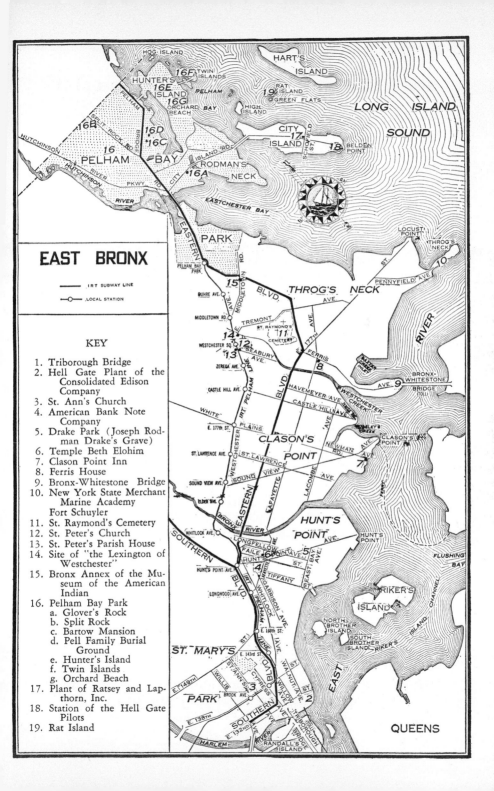

EAST BRONX

— IRT SUBWAY LINE

—O— LOCAL STATION

KEY

1. Triborough Bridge
2. Hell Gate Plant of the Consolidated Edison Company
3. St. Ann's Church
4. American Bank Note Company
5. Drake Park (Joseph Rodman Drake's Grave)
6. Temple Beth Elohim
7. Clason Point Inn
8. Ferris House
9. Bronx-Whitestone Bridge
10. New York State Merchant Marine Academy Fort Schuyler
11. St. Raymond's Cemetery
12. St. Peter's Church
13. St. Peter's Parish House
14. Site of "the Lexington of Westchester"
15. Bronx Annex of the Museum of the American Indian
16. Pelham Bay Park
    a. Glover's Rock
    b. Split Rock
    c. Bartow Mansion
    d. Pell Family Burial Ground
    e. Hunter's Island
    f. Twin Islands
    g. Orchard Beach
17. Plant of Ratsey and Lapthorn, Inc.
18. Station of the Hell Gate Pilots
19. Rat Island

THROG'S NECK, named for John Throgmorton who in 1643 became the proprietor of this long strip of land jutting into the Sound, has numerous small bathing places. After the Civil War the Neck became an exclusive boating and fishing colony of New York millionaires, including Fréderick C. Havemeyer, the sugar magnate, and Collis P. Huntington, the railroad builder. At the turn of the century, large German beer gardens, patronized by Yorkville residents, were established here. Some of the old taverns are still standing.

8. The FERRIS HOUSE, near the southwest corner of Ferris and Lafayette Avenues, erected in 1687, is said to be the oldest house in the Bronx. During the Revolution it was occupied by the Ferris family for whom it was named. The building, which has been considerably remodeled, is now used by an Italian truck farmer.

9. BRONX-WHITESTONE BRIDGE, foot of Ferris Avenue, spans the East River between the Old Ferry Point, the Bronx, and Whitestone, Queens. *(Passenger automobile toll 25¢.)* It provides the most direct vehicular link between Upper New York State (and New England) and eastern Long Island. The crossing, a suspension structure with an over-all length of 3,770 feet, has the fourth longest over-water span in the world (2,300 feet). This span rises 135 feet above water. To reduce maintenance expenses, the towers are surfaced with steel plates, which contrast strikingly with the slender tension members. The crossing was built in 1938-9 at the cost of $18,000,000 and is owned and operated by the Triborough Bridge Authority.

10. The NEW YORK STATE MERCHANT MARINE ACADEMY, Pennyfield Avenue at the East River, the Annapolis of the American Merchant Marine, occupies Fort Schuyler. *(Guide service Saturday, Sunday, and holidays 1 to 5:30 p.m.)* The school, established in 1874 for training youths between seventeen and twenty-one as deck and engineering officers, is under the jurisdiction of the New York State Department of Education. The fifty-acre promontory on which the fort was built was acquired by the Federal Government in 1833 and during the Civil War was used as a prison camp. The garrison was removed in 1911 when new fortifications were built on Fisher's Island at the eastern entrance of Long Island Sound. In 1937 the old fort was leased for fifty years to the state of New York for use by the academy. The S.S. *Empire State,* one-time base force flagship and now the academy's training ship, is docked here. The fort is named for Philip J. Schuyler, the Revolutionary War general.

11. ST. RAYMOND'S CEMETERY, East Tremont Avenue and Eastern

Boulevard, founded in 1856, contains the graves of well-known members of the Bronx political hierarchy—the Bradys, O'Tooles, and Sullivans. There are two units. Old St. Raymond's, with an area of two city blocks, contains St. Raymond's Church, which serves as a chapel for burials in the newer section. New St. Raymond's, consecrated in 1877, covers fifty acres of filled-in swamp land. It was in this cemetery, near the Whittemore Street entrance, that John F. ("Jafsie") Condon one night in April, 1932, paid Bruno Richard Hauptmann a ransom of fifty thousand dollars for the promised return of Charles A. Lindbergh's kidnapped child.

12. St. Peter's Church (Episcopal), Westchester and Seabury Avenues, an ivy-covered stone edifice in Gothic style, is the third built (about 1885) by its congregation; the first was erected on this site in 1702. Many tombstones in the churchyard date from the eighteenth century.

13. St. Peter's Parish House, 2511 Westchester Avenue, opposite St. Peter's Church, served as the state capitol for a few days in the late eighteenth century when a fever plague in lower Manhattan forced the officials to seek safety in near-by towns. The Westchester Boarding School occupied the building in the early nineteenth century, offering in addition to its educational facilities "a daily mail to and from the city and communication, by stage, with the Haerlem Railroad twice a day." The structure is believed to be more than two hundred years old.

14. The Bridge over Westchester Creek, East Tremont Avenue near Westchester Avenue, which in the Revolutionary War connected Throg's Neck, then virtually an island, with the mainland, has been called "the Lexington of Westchester." General Howe made an unsuccessful attempt here to cut off Washington's troops on October 12, 1776, by landing troops at Throg's Neck. When the British marched toward the bridge, however, the Americans ripped up the old plank crossing and opened a heavy fire. Howe was forced to change his plans, and six days later made a successful landing at Rodman's Neck. The present bridge is a small span of steel and concrete.

15. The Bronx Annex of the Museum of the American Indian, Heye Foundation, Eastern Boulevard and Middletown Road, houses the study collections of archaeological and ethnological material relating to the aborigines of the Western Hemisphere. (*Admission by appointment only.*) Typical native houses, reproduced in concrete, and two totem poles, thirty-five and forty-four feet high respectively, are set up on the grounds. Flanking the main entrance are two carved wooden house posts. The main building of the museum is in Manhattan (see page 396).

16. PELHAM BAY PARK, entrance at Eastern Boulevard and Westchester Avenue, largest in the city (1,997 acres), includes Orchard Beach, Hunter's Island, Twin Islands, and Rodman's Neck. Occupying the northeastern corner of the Bronx, it is divided into two main sections, north and south of the Hutchinson River, joined by the Eastern Boulevard causeway. The park provides facilities for picnicking in restful woodlands, golfing on two eighteen-hole courses, and bathing in the quiet waters of Long Island Sound. The city purchased most of the land in 1888.

The park was named for Thomas Pell, an Englishman, who bought 9,166 acres of land here in 1654. The Dutch rulers of New Amsterdam had purchased the same territory in 1640, and Pell was constrained to swear allegiance to them in order to retain his property, and then wait submissively until the English captured the Dutch possessions.

Near the entrance to Pelham Bay Park is a municipal stadium, seating five thousand, used for student contests. An heroic statue, the *American Boy,* by Louis St. Lannes, stands at the top of the concrete bowl. The Mother House, with its collections of birds, fish, and plants is a center for children's nature study. During the summer, a replica of an Indian village is constructed in front of the house to exemplify the mode of life of the Siwanoy Indians, the region's former inhabitants. The near-by Eastchester Bay was once famous for its angling facilities, but pollution spoiled the fishing, and the old pier is little more than a landmark for great flocks of gulls.

About a half mile east of Pelham Bridge Road near City Island Road, GLOVER'S ROCK (16A), as large as a three-story house, commemorates the Revolutionary engagement in which Colonel John Glover and his 550 Marblehead fishermen held General Howe's redcoats at bay, enabling Washington's forces to beat a successful retreat to White Plains on October 18, 1776. This engagement cost the British nearly as many casualties as they suffered at Bunker Hill, and because it saved the Americans from being trapped, was one of the most important early battles of the Revolution.

Another large boulder, SPLIT ROCK (16B), Split Rock Road near the city line, is believed to mark the site of Mrs. Anne Hutchinson's early settlement. This courageous woman, after whom the Hutchinson River is named, had found Puritan New England hostile to her liberal religious views. She arrived in the Bronx region with her fatherless children and a small band of followers in 1643, building a cabin near the present intersection of Split Rock Road and Prospect Avenue. Shortly afterward, all the inhabitants of the settlement, with the exception of Mrs. Hutchinson's young granddaughter, were murdered in an Indian attack. The child was rescued from the Indians two years later.

Mrs. Hutchinson's land came into Pell's possession when he signed a treaty with the Indians in 1654. The spot where this pact was concluded is marked by two fenced-in trees on the lawn of the BARTOW MANSION (16C), an early nineteenth-century country house, Pelham Bridge Road north of Split Rock Road. The interior of the two-story gray stone residence has some excellent Greek Revival details, and includes an elliptical staircase. The International Garden Club, a women's organization, has headquarters here. A garden walk bordered by tall rhododendron bushes leads from the mansion to the PELL FAMILY BURIAL GROUND (16D), in which there have been seven interments, the first in 1748.

HUNTER'S ISLAND (16E), formerly the northernmost island in Greater New York, has been joined to Rodman's Neck on the mainland through the filling in of Orchard Beach. The island, popular with picnickers, was once the property of Thomas Pell, and in the latter part of the eighteenth century it came into the hands of one John Hunter, for whom it was named. A causeway connects its eastern shore with TWIN ISLANDS (16F): here on the southeast side is the Mishow, a great rock near which the Indians conducted religious ceremonies, and on the northeast, a rock called the Gray Mare. Around both Hunter's and Twin islands are treacherous rocks and reefs, and it is said that when a naval engagement took place there during the War of 1812, the Americans were saved by their skill in navigating through these hazards.

ORCHARD BEACH (16G), reached by a four-lane highway from Eastern Boulevard, or by bus from the IRT Pelham subway, attracts many Bronx and Manhattan residents. Its features include a mile-long scarf of white sand imported from the Rockaways and the north Long Island shore, a handsome red-brick bathing pavilion with facilities for six thousand persons *(open daily 9 a.m. to 8 p.m. from May 30 through the week-end after Labor Day; children's lockers 15¢, adults' 25¢)*, parking space for seven thousand automobiles *(fee 25¢)*, and extensive landscaped playgrounds and athletic fields. The Orchard Beach development, a Department of Parks project on which the WPA collaborated, was opened in 1936.

CITY ISLAND, connected to Rodman's Neck by the City Island Avenue causeway, is an important boatyard. The dull rubbed brass of sextants gleams in the shop windows, and white sloops stand like herons in the cradles of the boatbuilders. Clam chowder and popcorn are sold. In the waters that surround the island lie a number of isles and reefs—the Chimney Sweeps, High Island, Rat Island, Middle Reef, Big Tom East and South Nonations, the Blauzes, Hog Island, the Green Flats—named by mariners passing through the Sound.

City Island owes its ambitious name to a scheme devised by its inhabitants in 1761 to erect a municipality complete in itself with a port rivaling New York. The project collapsed, and the 230-acre island became a small town with some of the traits of coastal New England. It severed connections with Westchester to become part of New York City in 1895.

A number of boating clubs have headquarters on the island, and in the summer the surrounding waters are crosshatched with the wakes of every sort of small craft. City Islanders themselves are concerned with the building of boats. Hundreds of skilled workers are employed at this occupation, the island's major industry. George Vanderbilt's *Crusader* and Vincent Astor's *Nourmahal* were built in the yards here. One prominent builder has turned out some five hundred craft during the last thirty years at prices ranging from $300 to $250,000.

A few of the City Islanders still call themselves "clam-diggers," and the island's numerous sea-food restaurants on its main thoroughfare, City Island Avenue, are almost as varied as the pocketbooks they are meant to accommodate. The inhabitants, boasting of the healthful climate, like to repeat the traditional apothegm of New England: " 'Round here we don't die. We just dry up and blow away."

17. PLANT OF RATSEY AND LAPTHORN, INC., on Schofield Street near City Island Avenue, is the American unit of Ratsey and Lapthorn, Ltd. (1796), world-famous sailmakers. *(Visitors admitted.)* Established in this country since 1902, the business is still conducted by members of the Ratsey family. Most of the work in the great sail lofts, where street shoes may not be worn lest the fabrics be damaged, is still done by hand, workers passing through a four-year apprenticeship. Besides patterning suits of sails for nearly all the notable racing yachts, including the America's Cup Defenders, this firm has been chiefly responsible for two of the most striking recent innovations in the industry: the parachute spinnaker and the frostbite dinghy.

18. STATION OF THE HELL GATE PILOTS, on Belden Point (southern tip of City Island), serves as the lookout. When the pilots sight a ship of foreign registry coming down Long Island Sound, one of them goes aboard and guides her through the dangerous whirligig currents of Hell Gate, the twist in the East River near Ninety-fifth Street. Once this was a

thriving business for which scores of pilots fought bitterly; today five pilots suffice for the occasional traffic.

19. RAT ISLAND, about a half mile east of City Island, two acres of bare rock, served as a resting place for escaping convicts from near-by Hart's Island and was the site of the Pelham pesthouse during the yellow fever scares. The island is divided at one end by a natural declivity known as "Devil's Path." For a time Rat Island was the home of a group of writers and artists. One of these was Chester Beecroft, film producer and war correspondent. In 1931 the Mount Vernon Club leased the island and now rents it to vacationists.

HART'S ISLAND, northeast of City Island, contains the REFORMATORY PRISON and the CITY CEMETERY (Potter's Field). *(Ferry at northern end of Fordham Street, City Island; pass must be obtained from Registrar, Department of Correction.)*

The Reformatory Prison, operated by the municipal Department of Correction, cares for approximately 1,200 prisoners transferred from the New York City Penitentiary on Riker's Island in accordance with the department's classification policy. The prisoners here include partially cured drug addicts, aged vagrants, crippled and infirm men, and others who may benefit by the opportunity for exercise and light employment in the open air. Indoor employment includes printing for the Department of Correction, the manufacture of prison clothing, and the repair of furniture for various city departments. Prisoners also do the manual labor in connection with Potter's Field and operate a farm. From 1869, when the body of Louisa Van Slyke, an orphan who died at the old Charity Hospital, was buried in Potter's Field, until 1938, approximately 425,000 interments have been made. The Mortuary Division of the Department of Hospitals at Bellevue Hospital ships weekly to the island an average of about 170 corpses, as well as arms and legs amputated in the city hospitals. The plain pine coffins are laid three deep. A granite cross, erected in 1902, bears the inscription: "He calleth His children by name." Approximately fifty bodies are disinterred annually and removed to other cemeteries, after being identified from photographic records at the mortuary headquarters, or claimed by relatives or friends previously unable to pay for private burial.

In 1774, when the island was acquired by Oliver DeLancey of West Farms, it was known as "Spectacle Island" or "Little Minnefords." It subsequently was owned by the Haight and Rodman families and John Hunter. The city bought the island in 1869.

Queens

D. Spiegel

Queens

QUEENS, by far the largest of the boroughs, covers 121 square miles of the westernmost end of Long Island, about 37 per cent of the city's total area. The East River separates the borough on the west from the Middle and Upper East Side of Manhattan and on the north from the East Bronx. The North Shore is deeply indented by Flushing and Little Neck bays. Newtown Creek, a four-mile tidal arm of the East River, forms part of the western boundary line (between Queens and Brooklyn), which extends irregularly across Long Island to isle-studded Jamaica Bay, semi-circular in shape and about the size of Upper New York Bay. On the south the narrow ten-mile Rockaway peninsula shields Jamaica Bay from the Atlantic Ocean, and on the east Queens merges with Nassau County.

Since the creation of Greater New York in 1898, Queens has grown faster, relatively, than any other borough, yet with the exception of Staten Island it is still the least developed. The "borough of homes" is an amalgam of several score of towns and villages, some three centuries old, others no older than yesterday's real-estate boom. Several of these communities still have independent post-office designations. The neighborhoods of the borough range from intensively industrialized Long Island City and such large-scale residential developments as Forest Hills and Kew Gardens, to the numerous beach colonies and isolated islets of the Rockaways. Long Island City lies opposite mid-town Manhattan; near the Brooklyn-Queens borough line are Maspeth, Ridgewood, Glendale, Woodhaven, Ozone

Park; east of Long Island City and in the central part of the borough, Woodside, Winfield, Elmhurst, Forest Hills, Kew Gardens, Jamaica, Hollis, St. Albans, Queens Village; along the North Shore, Astoria, Jackson Heights, Corona, Flushing, College Point, Whitestone, Bayside, Douglaston, and Little Neck.

The most important business centers are in Long Island City and Jamaica. Queens Plaza, in the former, is the hub of rapid transit to and from Manhattan and Brooklyn, while the Long Island Railroad station in Jamaica is the transfer point to all parts of the island. Jamaica, the first county seat, today shares with Long Island City the borough and county administrative offices. Although an official map of Queens shows a complete street layout, large sections have an almost rural character, and there are still numerous farms. (One truck farm on the North Shore, worked by Chinese, cultivates vegetables native to China for the restaurants of New York.)

In 1938 Queens had 1,700 industrial establishments, 5 per cent of the city's total. More than 1,400 are crowded into the 2.8-square-mile area of Long Island City. It is said that drab and oily Newtown Creek carries more freight annually than the Mississippi River. North of Skillman Avenue is the huge Sunnyside yard of the Pennsylvania Railroad. Queens' chief industry is food processing, especially baking, with metal work, textiles, paints, woodwork, and marble and stone cutting ranking high.

Most of the residences in Queens are of the one- and two-family type; the estimated population (1939) is 1,340,476—17 per cent of the city's total. According to the 1930 census the percentage of foreign-born white stock in Queens was 24 per cent, compared to 33 per cent for the city as a whole. Germans are first in numbers, Italians second; and sizable Negro settlements may be found in Flushing, Jamaica, and Corona.

Topographically, the borough is similar to the rest of Long Island; a northerly chain of hills created by glacial deposits divides it into a North Shore plateau and a South Shore alluvial plain. Little Neck Hill, near the Nassau County line, rises 266 feet above sea level, the highest natural altitude in the borough, and many parts of the irregular terrain in western Queens, where about twenty large cemeteries are located, afford views of the surrounding boroughs.

Many species of plants have proved adaptable to the fertile soil. The northern sections particularly have long been noted for their horticulture. Flushing was the site of what was perhaps the country's first large-scale nursery—established by William Prince in 1737. The southern sections were known for their rich farms. Despite its low altitude, the plain is almost always dry, rain being quickly absorbed in the gravel underbed. Horse racing has been popular in Queens since the British introduced the sport in 1665. Today there are two well-known race tracks, Aqueduct and Jamaica. (Another, Belmont Park, in Nassau County, has an entrance just within the Queens County line.)

Until the pollution of its waters in the 1900's Little Neck Bay was famous for saddle rock oysters and Little Neck clams. Sylvan Alley Park near the Queens-Nassau County line contains a large bird sanctuary for quail, pheasants, geese, pelicans, and heron. In Maspeth, the breeding of homing pigeons is a small industry.

Before Henry Hudson sailed through the Narrows in 1609 searching for the Northwest Passage, he had nosed the *Half Moon* into Rockaway Inlet. The Queens area was then dominated by the Rockaway Indians. The first white settlements were made by the Dutch about 1635. Title to the lands was purchased from the Indians by Governor Kieft in 1639, and Mespat (Maspeth) was founded in 1642, Vlissingen (Flushing) in 1643. Between these two towns, another, Middleburg (becoming Newtown in 1665), was founded in 1652 by Dutch, French, and English. Jamaica dates from 1650, and it, too, was settled largely by the English. Numerous other settlements sprang up, the Dutch tending to settle in the west, the English in the east.

The dispute between England and Holland concerning territorial jurisdiction led to friction between the settlers, though their community of interests worked to unite them. Queens County was organized in 1683— one of the twelve counties constituting the British province of New York —and was named in honor of Catherine of Braganza, Queen of Charles II. In the same year Flushing, Newtown, and Jamaica were incorporated, these townships dominating the county until 1870.

Numerous seventeenth- and eighteenth-century houses survive. Among them are the Bowne House (1661) and the Quaker Meeting House (1696) in Flushing, the Onderdonk Farmhouse (1731) in Maspeth, and the King Mansion (about 1750) in Jamaica.

At the outbreak of the Revolution the majority of people in Queens County were British sympathizers, and the force that the Continental Congress sent against them merely stiffened their resistance to the Revolution. After the Battle of Long Island (Brooklyn, 1776) the county was occupied for the duration of the war by British troops. In 1783 a group of Tories from Queens emigrated to Newfoundland.

The century following the Revolution was for Queens an age of agricultural expansion. In 1790 its population (exclusive of the towns that

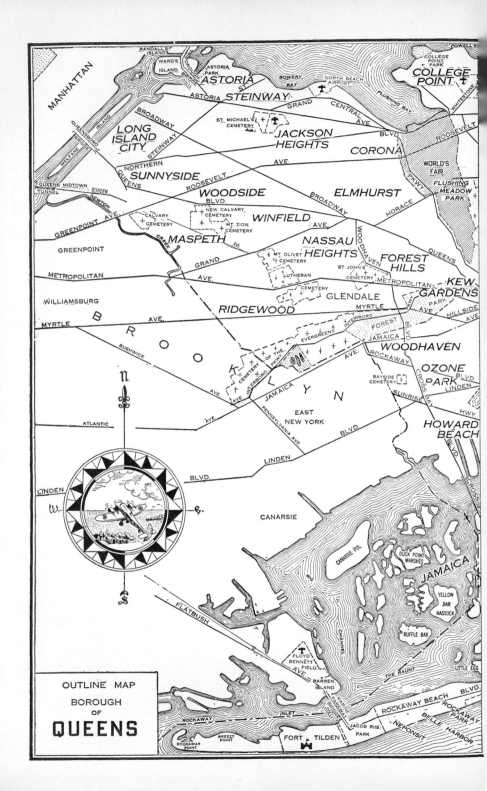

OUTLINE MAP
BOROUGH
OF
QUEENS

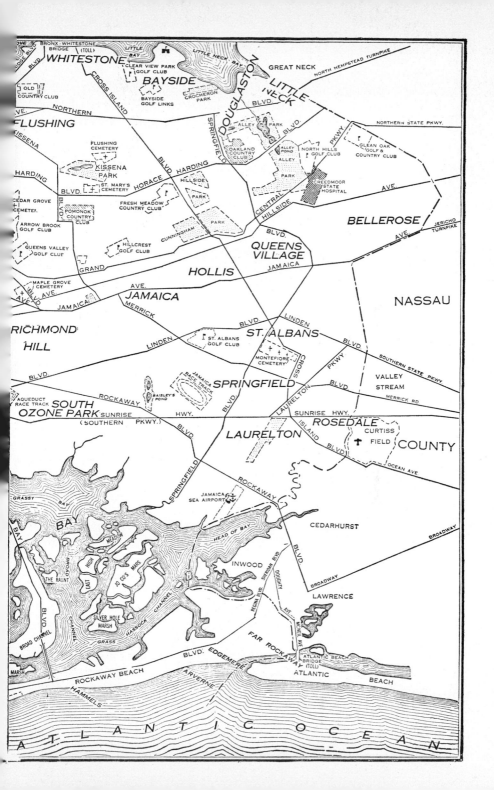

were later to form Nassau County) was 6,159; in 1850, 18,593; and in 1890, 87,050. Toward the end of the nineteenth century the industrialization along the East River and Newtown Creek began, though a few factories had been established there much earlier. Edward Smith and Company opened a paint factory in Long Island City in 1827; William Steinway built his piano factory in Astoria in the early 1870's and laid out a company town for his workers. The growth of industry in Long Island City in the 1890's was accompanied by a growth of graft, and "Paddy" Gleason, mayor of Long Island City, performed the role of Manhattan's "Boss Tweed."

The North and South Shores began attracting large numbers of summer visitors and well-to-do residents in the 1880's. North Beach, the site of the present North Beach Airport, became a popular recreational spot, while the distant Rockaways, reached by the Long Island Railroad, developed into a fashionable resort with large hotels and mansions.

Queens was consolidated with New York City in 1898 and Long Island City, Newtown, Flushing, Jamaica, and the Rockaways became the five wards of the borough. The towns voting against absorption—Hempstead, North Hempstead, and Oyster Bay—were organized into a new county, Nassau. A period of enormous growth began in Queens with the opening of the Queensboro Bridge between Long Island City and Fifty-ninth Street, Manhattan, in 1909, and of the Pennsylvania Railroad Long Island Tunnel under the East River in 1910. At that time the population of the borough was 284,041 and the assessed valuation of real estate, three hundred million dollars. Two decades later the population had almost quadrupled; the assessed valuation multiplied sixfold.

The height of the boom came in the 1920's, following the construction of the Queens branches of the IRT and BMT subways. For five years the average annual cost of new buildings was $165,000,000. This unnatural development had its drawbacks. Huge graft in the construction of sewers was revealed. Large areas of flimsy houses built for speculation soon became potential slums. The 1929 depression was severely felt, and many families, unable to meet the payments on their homes, were evicted.

In 1938, however, about 70 per cent of new building in the city was done in Queens; and for several years previously immense sums had been spent in the borough to construct bridges, tunnels, parks, schools, highways, streets, sewers, and disposal plants. This expansion has been partly due to the 1939 World's Fair, but natural growth made necessary such public improvements as the Triborough Bridge, connecting the Bronx, Manhattan, and Queens (1936); the municipal Eighth Avenue (or Independent) subway extension to Jamaica (completed in 1937); the Bronx-

Whitestone Bridge (1939); and the Queens Midtown (vehicular) Tunnel under the East River between Long Island City and Thirty-eighth Street, Manhattan (to be opened in 1939).

A good portion of the inhabitants of Queens now dwells within a half-mile of a subway or elevated station, with five-cent fare transit from Astoria, Flushing, Kew Gardens, Jamaica, Ozone Park, and Ridgewood to Manhattan and Brooklyn. In addition there are 71 route miles of electric railroad, and bus routes and trolley lines touch every community. Queens has three airports, including the $15,000,000 municipal North Beach Airport. The borough's 300 schools, including the municipal Queens College, have an attendance of about 225,000. The public library system, centered at Jamaica, circulates through 29 branches and various extension services more than 3,600,000 volumes annually. There are 425 churches, and more than 100 parks and playgrounds. Nine hospitals include the new $6,000,000 Queens General Hospital in Jamaica. Local news is carried by a dozen weekly and three daily periodicals.

The Mayor's Committee on City Planning estimated in 1936 that the ultimate population of Queens will probably be 1,900,000. The borough is being rapidly integrated with the city as a whole, its community lines becoming less distinguishable. As the built-up areas increase, Queens neighborhoods tend to lose their half-rural air and come to resemble the highly developed localities of the other boroughs. Queens Plaza, for example, may follow to some extent the pattern of the Grand Central district of Manhattan.

A $12,000,000 civic center to unite the scattered government offices will be erected on a site adjoining Queens College, if Federal approval and co-operation are obtained. The Queensbridge housing project, bordering the East River in Long Island City, was under construction in 1939. The picturesque North Shore, with its excellent boating facilities, may regain its popularity as a bathing region following the completion of the sewage disposal program. Further improvements are scheduled for Rockaway Beach, whose splendid Jacob Riis Park was opened in 1937, and the Eighth Avenue (Independent) subway may soon be extended to that peninsula. When the World's Fair is over, its site will become one of the city's finest parks. Jamaica Bay and its islands may be converted into a municipal recreational center, which will be linked to the new Circumferential (Belt) Highway along the Brooklyn and Queens shore line. Queens, favored by its position between Manhattan and rural Long Island, will, it seems, remain primarily a residential borough less congested than the Bronx, Manhattan, or Brooklyn.

D. Spiegel

North Queens

ASTORIA—STEINWAY—JACKSON HEIGHTS—
CORONA—FLUSHING—COLLEGE POINT—
WHITESTONE — BAYSIDE — DOUGLASTON
AND LITTLE NECK

Area: East River on west and north to city line on east; south to Broadway (East River to 73d St.), Roosevelt Ave. (73d St. to National Ave.), Corona Ave., and Horace Harding Blvd.
Principal highways: Astoria Ave., Grand Central Parkway, and Northern Blvd.
Transportation: IRT and BMT Astoria subways, 30th Ave. to Ditmars Blvd. stations; IRT and BMT Flushing subways, 104th St. to Main St. stations; bus from Flushing to College Point, Whitestone, Bayside, Douglaston, and Little Neck; Long Island R.R. to Corona, Flushing, Bayside, Douglaston, and Little Neck.

THE North Shore of Queens is a series of peninsulas separated by bays of the East River: Bowery Bay, Flushing Bay, Powell's Cove, Little Bay, and Little Neck Bay. The western half, from Astoria to Flushing, is a well-developed residential area with a few industries, and is served by the three subway systems. East of Flushing are spacious, more fashionable suburbs similar to the wealthy communities in adjoining Nassau County. New highways and bridges and major improvements created for the 1939 World's Fair, in Flushing, are transforming the North Shore, most of which has remained unchanged for years.

ASTORIA, the community in the northwest corner of Queens, was originally called Hallett's Cove. It was incorporated as the village of Astoria in 1839 after a bitter factional fight in which friends of John Jacob Astor were charged with having engaged in skulduggery to accomplish the acceptance of the name.

Stephen A. Halsey worked untiringly to develop the village. He built factories, stores, shops, and dwellings, and induced tradesmen to settle here. These activities led many local historians to refer to him as the "father of Astoria."

Late in the nineteenth century schooners brought mahogany and other costly woods from foreign countries to the lumber yards along the Astoria shores of the East River. Many of the local residents who officered these ships had homes with towers and widow's walks of the Nantucket type.

In 1654 Governor Stuyvesant granted William Hallett, the first settler here, a patent of 1,500 acres. The property remained in the possession of the Hallett family for about 150 years.

1. The PETER RAPALYE HOUSE, 9-07 Main Avenue between Welling Court and Vernon Boulevard, built in the late eighteenth century, is one of the many reminders of the prominent Rapalye family *(see page 565)*. This red-shingled, green-trimmed building with its beamed ceilings and big open fireplaces, was a tavern in the mid-nineteenth century. Here farmers bound for Manhattan markets amused themselves while their boats lay in the near-by cove awaiting a change of tide. It is said that the original Manhattan cocktail was mixed at the bar in the basement, an

---

KEY TO NORTH QUEENS MAP

1. Peter Rapalye House
2. Triborough Bridge
3. Astoria Park
4. New York Connecting Railroad Bridge
5. Jacob Rapalye House
6. Astoria Plant of the Consolidated Edison Company
7. Steinway Mansion
8. Lent Homestead (Isaac Rapalye House)
9. Holmes Airport
10. North Beach Airport
11. Flushing Meadow Park New York World's Fair 1939
12. St. George's Episcopal Church
13. Old Quaker Meeting House
14. John Aspinwall House
15. Bowne House
16. Flushing Airport
17. William K. Murray House
18. Kissena Park
19. Lawrence House
20. Queens College
21. Poppenhusen Institute
22. Chisholm Mansion
23. Bronx-Whitestone Bridge
24. Fort Totten
25. Graveyard of the Zion P. E. Church
26. Alley Park

honor also claimed for the old Manhattan Club, Madison Avenue and Twenty-sixth Street, Manhattan.

2. TRIBOROUGH BRIDGE *(see page 390)*, Astoria Boulevard and Stein-way Street, connects Grand Central Parkway and New York State 25 on Long Island with the East River Drive in Manhattan and US 1 in the Bronx.

3. ASTORIA PARK, Twenty-fifth Avenue and Nineteenth Street, a neatly

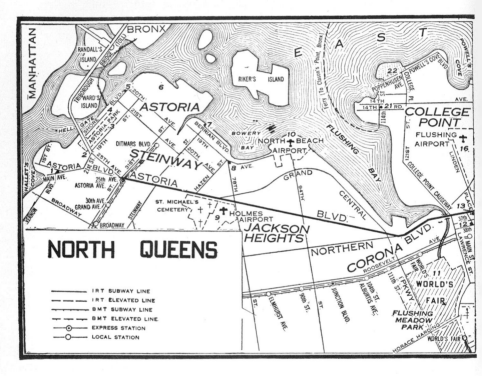

landscaped area of fifty-six acres, provides an excellent view of Hell Gate Bridge, Randall's Island, Ward's Island, Hell Gate Channel, and the skyscrapers of mid-town Manhattan. In the southern part where the Tri-borough Bridge curves smoothly down to earth, the WPA has built a series of playfields and a pink-tiled swimming pool, 330 feet in length and 165 feet in width. Here the 1936 Olympic swimming trials were held.

4. The NEW YORK CONNECTING RAILROAD BRIDGE, Shore Boulevard and Twenty-second Road, paralleling the Bronx-Queens section of the Triborough Bridge, is nationally known for its magnificent bow-shaped span of steel across Hell Gate Channel (between Astoria and Ward's

Island). Far more significant, though less publicized, is the fact that the bridge is a vital part of the railroad connecting the Pennsylvania and the New York, New Haven and Hartford systems, making possible direct rail travel between New England and the South and West. The crossing, completed in 1917, comprises in addition to the arch span of 1,087 feet, a 350-foot bascule bridge over the Bronx Kills, a 1,200-foot bridge of the bow string type over Little Hell Gate, and three miles of concrete viaduct

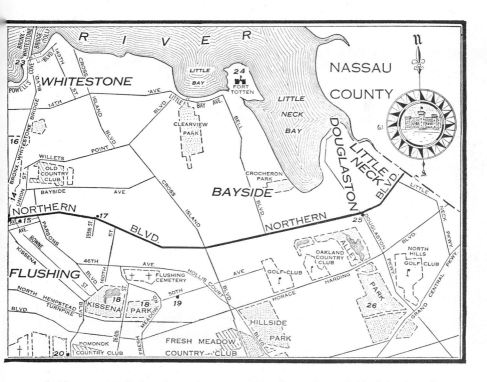

(bridge approaches and trestles across Ward's and Randall's islands). It was designed by Gustav Lindenthal and cost about $15,000,000.

5. The JACOB RAPALYE HOUSE, Shore Boulevard between Twentieth and Twenty-first Avenues, ancestral home of several branches of the Rapalye family, was built in 1749 by the only one of six brothers who sympathized with the colonists in the Revolution. It is now owned and occupied by the Consolidated Edison Company. The white clapboard building with its white stone base and low pitched roof is in an excellent state of preservation. It stands on a wide lawn overlooking Hell Gate Channel.

The family cemetery, in a private playground a short distance east of the house, has been reserved "forever for the descendants of Jacob Rapalye." Two crumbling headstones, the inscriptions of which are almost obliterated, stand sentinel over the old graves.

6. The ASTORIA PLANT OF THE CONSOLIDATED EDISON COMPANY, Twentieth Avenue and Twenty-first Street, the largest gas manufacturing plant in the world, occupies 383 acres of land, including what was once Berrien's Island. The works can manufacture daily 71,500,000 cubic feet of gas, and has two water-sealed holders with a capacity of 15,000,000 cubic feet apiece.

STEINWAY, the vicinity of Steinway Street, was named for William Steinway, Manhattan piano manufacturer who in the early 1870's established a branch factory here on a four-hundred-acre site along the Bowery Bay. He was motivated by the desire to remove large numbers of his employees from the influence of labor organizers and to provide additional production facilities. Around his plant he laid out a company town with a kindergarten, a free library, a bathhouse, a park, and athletic fields. The firm of Steinway and Sons still operates a factory in the neighborhood.

7. STEINWAY MANSION, near the foot of Steinway Street and the East River, built in the 1870's by William Steinway, was a show place of its day, and around the circular brick driveway leading to the porte-cochere came the carriages of society. The house, an ivy-covered dark-gray granite structure with a square tower and cast-iron pillars, surmounts a knoll overlooking the East River.

8. The LENT HOMESTEAD, Nineteenth Road near Seventy-eighth Street, was built by Abraham Lent about 1729. His father, who had assumed the name Lent, was the oldest son of Abraham Riker (Rycken), early Queens landowner and progenitor of the well-known Riker family. Isaac Rapalye married into the family, and bought the homestead in 1797. In the rear of the house is a graveyard where lie buried not only the Rikers and Lents but also the exiled Irish revolutionaries, Dr. William J. Macneven and Catherine Ann Tone, to whom the Riker family had extended hospitality. When additions were made to the original stone house, the entire structure was shingled. The building is also known as the Isaac Rapalye House.

JACKSON HEIGHTS, north of Roosevelt Avenue and centering around Eighty-second Street, was called "the cornfields of Queens" by Mayor Gaynor as recently as 1914. Integrated development of what was then

farm land has resulted in a middle-class community of "garden" apartment houses and single homes, with tennis courts, playgrounds, community gardens, and a golf course. Jackson Heights has the modest distinction of being the only community outside Manhattan served by the
Fifth Avenue bus line.

9. HOLMES AIRPORT (also known as the Grand Central Air Terminal),
Astoria Avenue and Grand Central Parkway, one of the best developed
private fields in the East, comprises 190 acres of land, a dirigible hangar
and four oiled runways ranging from 2,800 to 3,300 feet in length. It is
patronized by operators of small and medium sized craft.

10. NORTH BEACH AIRPORT, Grand Central Parkway and Ninety-
fourth Street, scheduled for opening in the summer of 1939, is New York's
second municipal airport—Floyd Bennett Field in Brooklyn is first—and
the most important land- and seaplane terminal in the East. Situated on a
432-acre tract projecting into the East River between Bowery and Flushing bays, the field is only twenty minutes ride, by way of Grand Central
Parkway and Triborough Bridge, from mid-town Manhattan.

The seaplane division is designed to accommodate regular transatlantic
airplane travel and will be used by Pan American Airways, Air France
Transatlantique, Imperial Airways, Royal Dutch, and Deutsche Lufthansa.
Its facilities will eventually include two hangars holding twelve to fourteen planes; a marine traffic terminal connecting with the hangars by
tunnel; an administration building containing waiting and baggage rooms,
and offices for navigation, flight control, health, customs, and immigration; and a platform ramp on Flushing Bay for landing passengers.

The landplane field will be used as the eastern terminus for the planes
of the Transcontinental and Western, the American, the United, and the
Eastern air lines, replacing Newark Airport in this respect. Its facilities
will comprise four concrete runways measuring 4,688, 4,168, 3,900, and
3,532 feet, unobstructed runway approaches of several hundred feet, and
an administration building flanked by six hangars.

The cost of the airport is estimated at $22,000,000, of which 70 per
cent will be borne by the WPA. Work was begun early in 1938.

CORONA, on both sides of Roosevelt Avenue west of the World's Fair
site, was called West Flushing in 1856 when the Fashion Race Track was
opened there. The track, named for a race horse, operated until 1866.
When the land was first subdivided, in 1870, the name was changed to
Corona to express the hope of making this the "crowning community" of

Long Island. Today Corona is a drab section of closely packed two-story houses, largely populated by people of Italian descent.

FLUSHING, east of the Flushing River, was one of Manhattan's leading summer colonies during the middle of the nineteenth century. Its later development as a residential community was rapid. More than two hundred apartment houses have been constructed since 1910 and the highways being built to the World's Fair of 1939 on the Flushing meadows promise a further growth.

When George Washington wrote of visiting "Mr. Prince's fruit gardens and shrubberies," he was describing a horticultural establishment that has had a lasting influence on Flushing's appearance. The Linnaean Gardens, established in Flushing by William Prince in 1737, was the first large nursery in the country. Today, as a result of the commercial cultivation of trees and shrubberies, Flushing contains 140 genera including 2,000 species of trees, among them the row of Chinese taxodium on Parsons Boulevard, just south of Northern Boulevard; the white dwarf horse chestnut, Japanese maple, and arborvitae at the old Bowne House; and the ginkgo, ilex, and other exotic varieties in various localities.

Flushing (Vlissingen), first settled in 1643 by the Bowne family *(see page 569)*, was the scene of a long and successful struggle for religious toleration against the Dutch authorities of New Amsterdam by a small band of English Quaker refugees from Vlissingen, Holland.

11. FLUSHING MEADOW PARK, Northern Boulevard and Grand Central Parkway, contains the site of the New York World's Fair 1939 *(see page 627)*; the land includes the old "Corona Dump," which was graded and landscaped for the fair. After the fair, the 1,216½-acre site will be made into one of the largest municipal parks in New York. All of the investment of $27,648,721 made by the city went into permanent improvements in or near the park, including a $4,000,000 sewage treatment plant, street grading, and a subway branch. A $1,100,000 "glass house," the city's exhibition hall for the fair, will be used for indoor recreation in the new park.

12. ST. GEORGE'S EPISCOPAL CHURCH, Main Street and Thirty-eighth Avenue, a Gothic-style, gray stone edifice with a tower surmounted by a shingled spire, dates from 1853, and is the third erected on the site since the congregation's founding in 1702. The architect was Richard Upjohn. Its interior has walls of a soft terra-cotta color and decorative open wood arches and trusses. Among its relics are a wooden model of the first church, a weathervane used in 1760, and an old foot stove. Francis Lewis,

a signer of the Declaration of Independence, was a vestryman here from 1765 to 1790.

13. The OLD QUAKER MEETING HOUSE (Society of Friends), Northern Boulevard opposite Linden Place, opened in 1696, is an austere, vine covered, gray-shingled building with a hipped roof. Men and women were originally required to use separate entrances—the two doors under a porch facing the graveyard on the south. The interior has a beamed ceiling and handmade, unpainted benches. Except from 1776 to 1783 when the British used it as a prison, hospital, and stable, the structure has served continuously as a meeting house. In the burial ground is an elm tree planted to commemorate George Washington's stay in Flushing in 1789 and 1790.

14. The JOHN ASPINWALL HOUSE, 138-28 Northern Boulevard, a long yellow-shingled building erected by a New York merchant in 1760, served as a headquarters for British officers. Somewhat remodeled, it is still a fine residence, notable for its wide arched and paneled hallway and luxuriously appointed rooms.

15. BOWNE HOUSE, Bowne Street near Thirty-seventh Avenue, was built in 1661 by John Bowne on land purchased from the Indians for eight strings of white wampum. The proscribed Society of Friends, which at first met secretly in the woods of Flushing, later assembled in this house. The unsymmetrical roof of the main portion of the house has small shed dormers; two stories above ground on the north, the roof slopes down to the first story on the south. The rooms, each on a different level, contain old furniture and heirlooms, including the mahogany four-poster used by William Penn on his visit here to Samuel Bowne in 1700, the walking stick with which John Bowne killed a bear on a near-by road, and the couch used by George Fox, founder of the Society of Friends. Above the dining room hearth are mahogany drawers for the Quakers' long pipes, and in the eight-foot kitchen fireplace hang old pots and kettles.

Across the street, in front of 36-40 Bowne Street, a tablet on a granite boulder marks the spot where, under two giant oaks, George Fox preached to the Friends in 1672.

16. FLUSHING AIRPORT, Thirty-second Avenue and Linden Place, occupying an area of three hundred acres, is a privately owned field used chiefly by amateur pilots. It has three hangars, two flying schools, a repair shop, and an overhauling station.

17. WILLIAM K. MURRAY HOUSE, 40-25 155th Street, a well-preserved Dutch Colonial house built in 1775, was once the home of the family for which Murray Hill in Manhattan is named. It is a white-shingled house of three stories with a gambrel roof. The kitchen wing is of recent date.

18. KISSENA PARK, North Hempstead Turnpike and Kissena Boulevard, is a 219-acre park, equipped with a golf course, tennis courts, ball fields, picnic grounds, and boating facilities on Kissena Lake. Fresh water springs feed the lake, which is joined to Flushing Creek. The park was the site of the Parsons Nurseries (founded in 1838), one of those for which Flushing was famous, and contains varieties of oak, larch, dogwood, and maple trees.

19. LAWRENCE HOUSE, Fiftieth Avenue, between Hollis Court Boulevard and Fresh Meadow Road, was built shortly after 1743 by Samuel Lawrence. A descendant of Lawrence occupies the dwelling.

20. QUEENS COLLEGE, 65-30 Kissena Boulevard, one of the four municipal colleges, occupies nine red-tile-roofed buildings of Spanish Mission design, which are well grouped on a commanding site. It was opened in October, 1937, and under the direction of Dr. Paul Klapper, president, is developing a progressive program of undergraduate education. About eight hundred students matriculate at the school.

COLLEGE POINT, now a quiet residential area, was a lusty industrial community in the second half of the nineteenth century. Around its rubber works, ribbon mills, toilet goods plants, and brewery lived large numbers of Swiss and German immigrants who, one historian observed, demanded a "lax interpretation of the excise laws." On Sundays the beer gardens and picnic groves attracted German-born Manhattanites.

In the seventeenth century this district was the northwestern section of William Lawrence's estate. His descendants sold part of the land here in 1790 to Eliphalet Stratton, and the village that subsequently grew up was known as Strattonsport. In 1836 the Reverend William A. Muhlenberg, educator and philanthropist, began building St. Paul's College, an Episcopal divinity school. Although the project was never completed, the idea caught the fancy of the inhabitants, and when the village was incorporated, the name was changed to College Point. In the post-bellum period the Poppenhusen family controlled large tracts of real estate and many industrial enterprises here. Adolph Poppenhusen for a time was the majority stockholder of the Long Island Railroad.

College Point fronts Flushing Bay, East River, and Powell's Cove; its shore line forms the outline of a dog's head. In early Colonial days it was part of Tew's Neck (later called Lawrence's Neck).

21. The POPPENHUSEN INSTITUTE, 114-04 Fourteenth Road, one of the first free evening schools for adults in the country, was established and

endowed in 1868 by Conrad Poppenhusen, industrialist. Although its original purpose was to train young men in the manufacturing trades, it now also gives evening courses in arts, trades, languages, and commercial subjects. A bust of Poppenhusen stands a few blocks away in a little park at College Place and Eleventh Avenue.

22. CHISHOLM MANSION, College Point Park, College Place and Poppenhusen Avenue, a local landmark, was erected in 1848 by Mrs. John Rogers, a sister of the Reverend William A. Muhlenberg. She presented it as a wedding gift to her daughter, Mrs. William Edings Chisholm, and the house remained in possession of the Chisholm family until 1930, when it was acquired by the city of New York. In 1937 the building, a three-story structure with a two-story ell in the rear, was used as the summer City Hall.

WHITESTONE proper, off the chief North Shore traffic route, remains a venerable Long Island community. Its half-dozen blocks radiating from Fourteenth Avenue at 150th Street contain old frame houses, a library, and the offices of the Whitestone *Herald.* Surrounding this center are the modern houses of the Beechhurst development, strung along the Sound from Whitestone Landing to Little Bay, and the Malba community to the west, bordering Powell's Cove on the East River. The whole Whitestone district has about 15,000 inhabitants.

Settled about 1645 by Dutch farmers who paid the Matinecock Indians one ax for every fifty acres of land, it took its name from a large white rock at the landing. Whitestone Landing is a jumble of little fishing piers and houses on stilts where tackle and bait are sold and skiffs rent for a dollar a day. Whitestone was called Clintonville when DeWitt Clinton was governor of New York State, but took back its original name in 1854. Part of the village was once known as Cookie Hill in honor of a cake-and-candy woman who was put off the Sound steamer, *Lynneus,* at the landing. An imperturbable Manhattanite, she sold out her stock of sweets and crullers to a crowd of Whitestone men and boys.

23. BRONX-WHITESTONE BRIDGE *(see page 546),* foot of Parsons Boulevard, crosses the East River to Eastern Boulevard, the Bronx, which connects with US 1. A new two-mile approach to Flushing leads to Grand Central Parkway and New York State 25, for points on Long Island.

BAYSIDE, a wedge-shaped district whose base abuts the western shore of Little Neck Bay, is a middle- and high-income residential community.

Large areas are still undeveloped. William Lawrence, who came here in 1664 to establish his home, was the first settler. A majority of Baysiders were Tories during the Revolution, and as such were twice attacked by whaleboat parties of raiders from New Rochelle.

24. FORT TOTTEN, the northeastern tip of Bayside, with a garrison of nine hundred enlisted men and officers, is headquarters of the Sixty-second Coast Artillery and of New York's harbor eastern defense system. *(Visitors admitted 9 a.m. to 9 p.m.)* Its mobile antiaircraft batteries are among the most modern of their kind. Built in 1862 as a military post known as Willett's Point, it was converted into a coast artillery fort in 1901 and given its present name.

The fort is situated at the confluence of the East River, Long Island Sound, and Little Neck Bay, and commands an excellent view of the Bronx and the site of old Fort Schuyler at Throg's Neck. In seasonable weather the troops parade on Friday afternoons.

DOUGLASTON and LITTLE NECK occupy the northeasternmost part of Queens. More than three-quarters of the families own their homes, which range in scale from thirty-room mansions to undistinguished five-room frame houses.

Douglaston, west of Little Neck and situated on a promontory jutting into Little Neck Bay, has a fine view of Long Island Sound. The houses are rambling and spacious, and many are surrounded by rock gardens and trees of great beauty. Numerous varieties of evergreen, poplar, elm, and yew flourish. In spring the Kentucky coffee tree scatters its blossoms among blooming magnolias. Weeping willows stand along the bay shore, and oaks grow side by side with sycamore, horse chestnut, and tulip trees. Peculiar to Douglaston is the cherry ginkgo, or Chinese maidenhair tree, and the Chinese weeping cypress. The yards of even the smallest homes are graced by trim Swiss stone pines.

The bay, a yachting center, contains the shellfish beds that yielded the famous Little Neck clams. The city condemned the beds in 1909 when the bay water was found to be impure.

What is now Douglaston was first settled in the late seventeenth century by Thomas Hicks—ancestor of Elias Hicks, founder of the Hicksite Branch of the Society of Friends—and a party of sympathizers, who forcibly evicted the Indians from the land. The entire section was known as Little Neck until 1876, when William B. Douglas donated the station for the Long Island Railroad in the western part. His father, George Douglas, in 1835 had purchased the manor now used as the Douglaston Club House from Wynant Van Zandt, a prosperous New York merchant and alderman. The development of Marathon Village in 1872 was the first of a series of realty promotions which culminated in the early 1920's when several old farms were broken up into building lots. A combined population of two thousand in Douglaston and Little Neck in 1920 had risen in 1930 to more than eight thousand, its present approximate level.

25. The GRAVEYARD OF THE ZION P.E. CHURCH, Northern Boulevard and Douglaston Parkway, contains the burial place of Bloodgood H. Cutter, the Long Island farmer-poet, who is celebrated as the "poet lariat" of Mark Twain's *Innocents Abroad*. Here are also interred the remains of the Matinecock Indians, removed from what was formerly a tribal cemetery on Northern Boulevard near Little Neck Parkway. The church is popularly called by the local inhabitants the "White Church on the Hill"; its white spire and gold cross are visible for miles.

26. ALLEY PARK, at 223d Street, Grand Central Parkway to Northern Boulevard, has five hundred acres, most of which is woodland. Within the area are a twenty-three-acre bird sanctuary, a nature trail, extensive bridle paths, athletic fields, tennis courts, picnic areas, outdoor fireplaces, and automobile parking fields. Alley Pond and Oakland Lake provide fishing and skating in season. A plaque on a boulder across the road from the pond commemorates George Washington's passage through this region, April 24, 1790, on his tour of Long Island. The park was named for the "Alley," a commercial and manufacturing center occupying part of the area in the eighteenth century. In the section of the park called Devil's Hollow have been found arrowheads, tomahawks, and the remains of what was probably a dumping ground for a wampum "factory."

Middle Queens

Area: East River and Newtown Creek on west to the city line on east; from Broad-
way (East River to 73d St.), Roosevelt Ave. (73d St. to National Ave.), Corona
Ave., and Horace Harding Blvd. south to Liberty Ave. and Linden Blvd. (Sutphin
Blvd. to city line).
Principal highways: Queens Blvd. and Jamaica Ave.
Transportation: 8th Ave. (Independent) Queens subway, Queens Plaza to 169th
St. stations; BMT Jamaica subway, Eastern Parkway to Sutphin Blvd. stations;
Long Island R.R. and bus from Jamaica to Hollis, St. Albans, and Queens Village.

MIDDLE QUEENS contains most of the borough's distinctive features: the
great industrial plants of Long Island City, the chain of cemeteries in
Maspeth and Ridgewood, the "garden homes" belt from Jackson Heights
to Kew Gardens, the subway suburbs in and around Jamaica (the gateway
to Long Island); and the peripheral communities adjoining the city line.
Site of the first settlements in Queens and now the borough's most developed area, Middle Queens took on its modern aspects in the 1910's
with the opening of new or improved transit facilities.

LONG ISLAND CITY, fronting the East River and Newtown Creek
around the approach to the Queensboro Bridge, is a labyrinth of industrial plants whose harsh and grimy outlines rise against the soot-laden sky.
Within an area of a few square miles, gridironed by elevated lines, railroad yards, and bridge approaches, are gathered about 1,400 factories,
producing chiefly spaghetti, candy, sugar, bread, machinery, paint, shoes,
cut stone, and furniture. Its bakeries alone turn out about five million
loaves weekly; its paint and varnish factories, about ten million gallons
a year; its stoneyards handle about 90 per cent of the cut stone and marble

imported into the United States. On the oily waters of Newtown Creek, which separates Queens from Brooklyn, tugboats and barges plow busily all day long, entering with coal and raw materials and leaving with manufactured products.

Hunter's Point, near the mouth of the creek, was settled by Burger Jorissen shortly after the founding of New Amsterdam. Attractive farms dotted the region until the nineteenth century, when its location near the tidal East River and its proximity to Manhattan attracted industries. Consolidation of the river-front towns of Hunter's Point, Blissville, Dutch Kills, and Middletown into Long Island City occurred in 1870. Here was the center of county activities, as Court House Square, dominated by the stately red-brick County Court House (also called the Supreme Court House), still testifies.

Queensboro Bridge Plaza, the terminus of the Queensboro Bridge *(see page 211)*, is a great bottleneck of traffic, as well as an important business center. Outstanding among surrounding structures is the classic white limestone building of the Long Island City Savings Bank, established in 1876. The old Brewster Building, on the north side of the plaza, distinguished by its tall red clock tower, housed until 1938 the Brewster Company, which originally produced fine carriages and later became the American assembly plant of Rolls-Royce automobiles.

Ravenswood, the section of Long Island City flanking the East River, north of the Queensboro Bridge, is one of those blighted neighborhoods for which New York is noted. There is hardly a sprout of vegetation, and the drab cobblestone streets stretch sordidly to the river front. The only escape from the general ugliness is the neatly landscaped Rainey Park, facing the

---

KEY TO MIDDLE QUEENS MAP

1. Queens Midtown Tunnel
2. Sunnyside Yard of the Pennsylvania and Long Island Railroads
3. Bodine Castle
4. Queensbridge Houses
5. Eastern Service Studios
6. Church of the Most Precious Blood
7. Madison Square Garden Bowl
8. Sunnyside Gardens
9. Boulevard Gardens Apartments
10. Onderdonk Farmhouse
11. Site of the Moore Homestead
12. St. James Episcopal Church
13. Renne House
14. West Side Tennis Club Stadium
15. Forest Hill Gardens
16. Forest Park
17. King Mansion
18. Prospect Cemetery (Old Jamaica Burial Ground)
19. First Presbyterian Church
20. Queens General Hospital
21. Site of Increase Carpenter's Inn
22. Creedmoor State Hospital

river on Thirty-third Street, where, on hot summer evenings, hundreds of strollers come for a scent of flowers and a breath of cool air. The section is inhabited chiefly by Italians.

1. QUEENS MIDTOWN TUNNEL, entrance at Borden Avenue and Eleventh Street—under construction (1939)—will connect Queens with Forty-second Street, Manhattan *(see page 209)*.

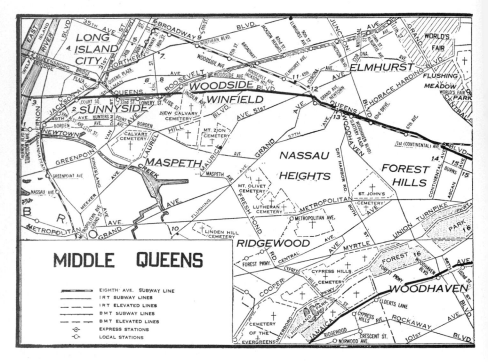

MIDDLE QUEENS

EIGHTH AVE. SUBWAY LINE
IRT SUBWAY LINES
IRT ELEVATED LINES
BMT SUBWAY LINES
BMT ELEVATED LINES
EXPRESS STATIONS
LOCAL STATIONS

2. The SUNNYSIDE YARD OF THE PENNSYLVANIA AND LONG ISLAND RAILROADS (also used by the Lehigh Valley and the New York, New Haven and Hartford roads) is wedged in between Skillman and Jackson Avenues for more than a mile. Its seventy-nine tracks have a total length of approximately forty miles. The yard was opened in 1910, simultaneously with Pennsylvania Station in Manhattan and the railroad tunnel under the East River.

3. BODINE CASTLE, 43-16 Vernon Boulevard, half-hidden behind the fence of a lumberyard, which it serves as an office, was once a show place of Queens County. It is said to have been built in the eighteenth century

by a French nobleman, who, forced to flee his native land, desired to recreate a bit of old-world atmosphere, a castle replete with tower, keep, secret passageways, dungeons, and landscaped gardens reaching to the water's edge. Later the nobleman, discovering a love affair between his daughter and a young workman, confined them both in dungeons. When the village authorities interfered, he gave up the castle in disgust and returned to France. About 1850 it received its name, Bodine Castle, from

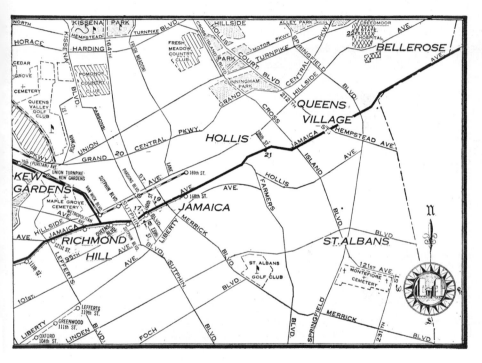

a subsequent owner. At one time it was a rendezvous of New York aristocracy, its guests including James Fenimore Cooper.

4. QUEENSBRIDGE HOUSES, north of Queensboro Bridge Plaza, between Vernon Boulevard and Twenty-first Street, is the fifth low-rent, government-financed housing project in the city since 1936. Twenty-six brick dwelling structures, six stories high with elevators, a community building, and a children's center, all arranged around open polygonal courts, will cover less than one quarter of the project's 62.5 acres; the remaining land will be landscaped park and recreation space. When completed late in 1939, the 3,161 apartments will house approximately

11,400 people. Ninety per cent of the estimated cost of $15,000,000 was supplied by a Federal loan, and 10 per cent by a municipal loan. The development was planned by the Queensbridge Project Associated Architects (William F. Ballard, chief architect), and will be operated by the New York City Housing Authority.

5. EASTERN SERVICE STUDIOS, Thirty-fifth Avenue between Thirty-fourth and Thirty-sixth Streets, was completed in 1919 by Famous-Players Lasky Corporation (later known as Paramount Pictures), and at present is used for the making of comedy and educational shorts, including the *March of Time,* and occasional feature films. Such pictures as Ernst Lubitsch's *Smiling Lieutenant* and Ben Hecht and Charles MacArthur's *The Scoundrel* and *Crime Without Passion* were produced here.

6. The CHURCH OF THE MOST PRECIOUS BLOOD (Roman Catholic), Thirty-seventh Street near Broadway, is a highly original adaptation of the "modernistic" style of architecture developed in such skyscrapers as the Chrysler Building and exemplified by the use of a multiplicity of overlapping forms, wide variety of decorative materials, and angular ornament. It was designed by Henry J. McGill and erected in 1931.

7. MADISON SQUARE GARDEN BOWL, Forty-fifth Street and Northern Boulevard, is an outdoor arena with a seating capacity of eighty thousand. The Madison Square Garden Corporation erected it in 1932 for summer sports events, chiefly boxing. Here, on June 29, 1933, Primo Carnera won the world's heavyweight championship by knocking out Jack Sharkey, and two years later, on June 14, 1935, James Braddock captured the same title from Max Baer by a decision.

SUNNYSIDE, at the junction of Queens Boulevard and Roosevelt Avenue, and WOODSIDE and WINFIELD, just east of it, occupy a plateau which until two decades ago was largely a barren, mosquito-infested tract. Rural touches still remain: the sound of locusts and croaking frogs in vacant lots overgrown with wild shrubs; and stretches of dirt road. The extension of the subway in 1918 invited a boom—it took only a few minutes to reach Manhattan—and enterprising builders erected semi-detached houses in the English manner, with tiny shrubbery plots in front and communal yards and gardens in the rear, as well as huge apartment houses set in spacious grounds.

8. SUNNYSIDE GARDENS, covering an area of approximately seventy acres between Forty-third and Fifty-first Streets, from Thirty-ninth Avenue to Queens Boulevard, is a community of one-, two-, and three-family

homes and apartment houses built during the prosperous years after 1924 by the City Housing Corporation, a limited-dividend enterprise. It was an early demonstration of satisfactory housing within the limitations of the average city block and has had a great influence on subsequent developments. The Gardens is notable for its skillful site planning, its large park areas, and its recreational facilities. Henry Wright, Clarence S. Stein, and Frederick L. Ackerman were the architects.

During the depression of the 1930's, many home owners in Sunnyside found themselves unable to meet the mortgage payments; eviction notices were bitterly fought by collective action. Doors were barricaded with sandbags and barbed wire, and sheriffs were showered with flour and pepper. But it was a losing battle, and more than 60 per cent of the original buyers lost their homes through foreclosure.

9. BOULEVARD GARDENS APARTMENTS, Fifty-fourth Street and Thirty-first Avenue, a successful limited-dividend housing development, consists of ten six-story buildings occupying 24 per cent of an 11.64-acre plot. The site plan differs from that of the usual housing project: the buildings are set in a park instead of being grouped around grass courts. This arrangement creates a feeling of openness and provides abundant light and air. The development, financed with the help of PWA, cost about $3,700,000 and was built in 1935 after plans by T. H. Engelhardt.

MASPETH, at the head of Newtown Creek, surrounded on three sides by cemeteries, is a dreary residential and industrial neighborhood with an enthralling view of the smoke-plumed skyscrapers of downtown Manhattan and downtown Brooklyn. The name Maspeth derives from an Indian tribe, the Mespat. The first white settlement near Maspeth Creek (as the branch of Newtown Creek is called) took place in 1642. The village was of importance in the Revolutionary War; from the porch of the Old Queen's Head Tavern, which stood near the corner of Fifty-eighth Street and Maspeth Avenue, General Howe watched his troops embark triumphantly, after the Battle of Long Island, down Maspeth Creek for Manhattan.

10. The ONDERDONK FARMHOUSE, 1820 Flushing Avenue, is the best preserved of a group of Colonial homes, with their white picket fences, barns, and cobblestone walks, surviving amidst the factories near Newtown Creek. The Onderdonk house, a two-story stone dwelling built in 1731, has a charm lent by such features as a gambrel roof, beaded floor beams, basement cattle stalls, and small-paned window sashes. The main

wing is now used as a business office, while the kitchen wing houses the caretaker's family.

RIDGEWOOD, between Metropolitan Avenue and Evergreen Cemetery, a preponderantly German-American neighborhood, is the Queens extension of the Brooklyn community of the same name *(see page 460).*

ELMHURST, around Queens Boulevard and Grand Avenue, represents the metamorphosis of part of the important old town of Newtown into modernity. It is dotted with nineteenth-century estates and dwellings, rapidly giving way, as a result of the extension of the Eighth Avenue (Independent) subway, to apartment houses and small homes. In the vicinity of Broadway, Queens Boulevard, and Grand Avenue are a few historic buildings, streets, and graveyards, vestiges of old Newtown. The nucleus of the settlement in this area was Middleburg, founded by English Puritans under Dutch auspices in 1652. Out of the vicissitudes of English-Dutch rivalry emerged "New Towne" (1665), embracing the southwestern half of what is now Queens County. Its identity was almost entirely lost by the time of consolidation with the greater city in 1898. In the apple orchards of Newtown were raised the famous "Newtown Pippins," which were extensively exported to England, where they fetched as much as twenty dollars a barrel. About 1840 Samuel Lord opened a drygoods store in Newtown, which ultimately became the Lord and Taylor department store in Manhattan.

11. The SITE OF THE MOORE HOMESTEAD, Broadway, between Forty-fifth Avenue and Eighty-second Street, still holds the barn, carriage shed, and coal shed. The main house (constructed in 1661) was demolished during the building of the Eighth Avenue (Independent) subway in 1937. It was the home of Samuel Moore, son of the Reverend John Moore, first minister of Newtown. A famous member of the Moore family was Benjamin Moore, Protestant Episcopal bishop of New York (1801) and rector of Trinity Church (1809).

12. ST. JAMES EPISCOPAL CHURCH, northeast corner of Broadway and Corona Avenue, belongs to a parish that was established in 1704 by the Reverend William Urquhart, a missionary from England. The present edifice dates from 1848. A churchyard in the rear contains tombstones two centuries old. A block away, at Broadway and Fifty-first Avenue, is the original church, erected in 1735 and subsequently modernized; it is still used as a parish hall. This gray wooden structure, which lacks its steeple,

is the only public building of Colonial times still standing in the community.

13. RENNE HOUSE, southwest corner of Queens Boulevard and Fifty-seventh Avenue, served for a time as General Howe's headquarters during the Revolution; and here, it is said, he wrote a report of the Battle of Long Island. The three-story frame dwelling, with a high basement, porch and three sharp dormers, was built by Samuel Renne.

NASSAU HEIGHTS, adjoining Elmhurst on the southwest, is a real-estate development of comfortable little houses on a rise of land amid large tracts of sandy soil, brush, and unkempt grass. At night the great plains of Queens below twinkle with electric lights, with the details of the landscape dissolved in shadows. After the German Revolution of 1848, a large number of political refugees bought land here, which their descendants held until 1938. Earlier names given the elevation were Bishoff's Hill and Poverty Hill. For many years an observatory, where maps of the surrounding country were made, stood on the summit.

FOREST HILLS, on the wooded heights around the northeast end of Forest Park, is a fashionable middle-class garden community. The many English Tudor and Colonial homes and apartments, with their neatly landscaped grounds, set off this patrician spot from prosaic surrounding localities. The region, known as Whitepot from a legend that the land was purchased from the Indians for three white pots, was settled probably about the time of the founding of Middleburg, 1652. The name clung to the neighborhood until a real-estate company in the first decade of the present century began to subdivide the land. It dubbed the development "Forest Hills" as a matter of course, and under that name has grown a community nationally known for its tennis club and celebrated residents, among them Helen Keller; Dale Carnegie; Burns Mantle, the drama critic; and Hal Kemp, the orchestra leader.

14. The WEST SIDE TENNIS CLUB, Tennis Place and Burns Street, is the tennis capital of the country, scene of the National Singles Championships and the International Davis and Wightman Cup matches. Its twenty-three grass, twenty-three clay, and twelve special courts, completed in 1923, are as renowned as those of Wimbledon and Auteuil. The stadium seats 13,500. Many of the visiting stars stay at the towered Forest Hills Inn in the square near by. The club was founded in 1892.

15. FOREST HILL GARDENS, Burns and Ingram Streets, Puritan and

Herrick Avenues and Union Turnpike, a housing development, has the appearance of an old English village. The uniform red roofs, houses joined together along curving streets, and the verdant terraces and gardens achieve an extraordinary harmony. Deep within the gardens is the village green with its tall flagstaff and memorial to local youths who fought in the World War. The project, inspired by the English "Garden Cities," was initiated in 1906 by the philanthropic Mrs. Russell Sage as a low-cost housing community. It was designed by Grosvenor Atterbury. In 1923, when about half completed, management was taken over by an organization of residents, the Forest Hill Gardens Corporation, which set up restrictive standards. What was planned as a poor man's community thus became a rich man's haven, and now to own a home in Forest Hill Gardens is a mark of social distinction.

16. FOREST PARK, whose eastern section separates Forest Hills from Kew Gardens and Richmond Hill, is the largest recreational park in Queens. Its 538 acres, lying on the crest of a terminal moraine which forms the "backbone" of Long Island, contain dense woods, numerous hillocks, and kettle holes, and provide excellent sites for bridle trails, a golf course, and other recreational facilities. Interborough Parkway, with its fine intermittent views of Manhattan peaks and Jamaica Bay, cuts through the park.

KEW GARDENS, east of Forest Park, resembles Forest Hills, and has the quiet atmosphere of a secluded village. Its expensive houses range from ornate Spanish to rugged Tudor and dignified Colonial styles; the streets are shaded by gnarled locusts, tremendous spreading maples and elms, and formal poplars. The profusion of trees and shrubbery, as well as the numerous rock gardens, attract many varieties of birds. The shopping center on Lefferts Avenue consists of a row of Tudor shop fronts, sometimes flanked by tubs of dwarf blue spruce.

Sixty years ago the region was farm land owned by the Lefferts family, and where now elegantly bedizened ladies drink tea at formal garden parties, lazy milch cows used to switch at flies in the pasture. Kew Gardens was so named becaue of the fancied resemblance of its setting to the Royal Botanical Gardens at Kew in England. For a considerable period it was part of Richmond Hill.

RICHMOND HILL and WOODHAVEN, south of Forest Park are stodgy suburbs whose rows of frame dwellings contrast sharply with the opulent mansions of adjoining Kew Gardens and Forest Hills. The real-estate history of Richmond Hill (which strangely enough has no promontory) goes back to 1868, when Albon P. Man, a banker, bought the large Lefferts farm and began the development of one of the earliest residential communities on Long Island. Woodhaven's career began about twenty years earlier, when John R. Pitkin (whose name clings to the leading thoroughfare in Brownsville and East New York) subdivided the territory and called it Woodville. It was not till the 1860's, however, when Lalance and Grosjean, manufacturers of light metal ware, established their factory on Atlantic Avenue and Ninety-first Street, that the village (now called Woodhaven) experienced a boom.

JAMAICA, the community around Jamaica Avenue and Parsons Boulevard, is the geographical center of Queens. Most of the important Brooklyn and Queens highways that lead to Nassau County and eastern Long Island pass through Jamaica. It is a terminus of the BMT and Independent subways and the principal transfer station of the Long Island Railroad. Along the main thoroughfare, Jamaica Avenue, there has evolved a comprehensive suburban shopping center.

The original settlement, called Rustdorp, was made by the English in 1650. In the same year a charter was obtained from Governor Stuyvesant and the name was soon changed to Jamaica, from the Jameco Indians, the aboriginal settlers. Because of its proximity to Brooklyn and Manhattan, Jamaica early in the eighteenth century became a trading center for the farmers of Long Island; here was brought the produce of the truck farms for which the island was famous. The real growth of Jamaica stems from the electrification of the Long Island Railroad in 1910 and extension of the subways in the 1920's.

In the main, Jamaica is, like other parts of Queens, a rectangular pattern of streets, cheap modern homes and patches of greensward, among which one comes occasionally upon a house, public building, or graveyard that recalls the rural Long Island civilization of the eighteenth or nineteenth century. Near the railroad tracks are industrial plants. In the old town south of the railroad embankment about 15,000 Negroes dwell in miserable shacks, lacking sanitary and recreational facilities. At the opposite pole, around Edgerton Road to the north, are splendid new houses and broad lawns, with the Grand Central Parkway cutting through under raised streets.

17. KING MANSION, in King Park, Jamaica Avenue and 153d Street, is a stately eighteenth-century shingled dwelling that was once the home

of the Federalist Rufus King, one of the framers of the Constitution, one of the first two senators from New York, and first minister to England. *(Open Monday, Wednesday, and Saturday 1:00 to 4:30 p.m.; admission free.)*

The mansion was built for the most part before 1750. It was purchased by King in 1806, and remained in the possession of the family until 1896, when the village of Jamaica acquired the house and surrounding park of eleven and a half acres. King Mansion has a harmonious combination of Dutch and Georgian Colonial motifs. The main wing of three stories and an attic, covered by a gambrel roof, has an entrance portico supported by fluted Doric columns. The two-story kitchen and servants' wing, originally a short distance from the house, has a gabled roof and covered porch. The only rooms open to the public are those off the main hall on the first and second floors of the main wing, containing furniture and relics presented by Colonial societies.

18. PROSPECT CEMETERY, 159th Street near Jamaica Avenue, which dates from 1662, was Jamaica's first public burial ground. In the early days of Jamaica persons of wealth were often buried in church—laymen under their pews, and clergymen in the chapel or beneath the pulpit. Less distinguished folk were buried in the churchyard. Interred in Prospect Cemetery are the remains of James H. Hackett, the actor, and Egbert Benson, Thomas Wicks, and Henry Benson, Revolutionary statesmen.

19. The FIRST PRESBYTERIAN CHURCH, 164th Street near Jamaica Avenue, organized in 1662, is probably the oldest Presbyterian congregation on the continent. It became the center of a bitter controversy, precipitated by Lord Cornbury, first British governor of the colony, when he attempted to abrogate the freedom of worship enjoyed by the Presbyterians under Dutch rule and to enforce the English statutes of conformity with Anglican worship. The congregation balked at these measures, and Lord Cornbury's agents seized (1704) the church property and tithes. The courts finally returned the property in 1728. During the Revolution the church was used as a military prison by the British. The present edifice, New England Colonial in style, was erected in 1813.

20. The QUEENS GENERAL HOSPITAL, 161st Street and Eighty-second Drive, built in 1931–5, is the main unit of a group of municipal hospitals here. It has 642 beds in the central section and eventually will have 141 in the pavilion for contagious diseases. Underground tunnels lead to nine accessory buildings. The two long, low-roofed bungalows of gray stucco constitute the Queensboro Hospital for Communicable Diseases, the original nucleus of the medical center. The three-million-dollar Tri-

borough Hospital for Tuberculosis, being built (1939) near by, will accommodate 530 patients, and emphasize modern therapeutic methods by utilizing open balconies and roofs, solaria and upper-floor walls of clear glass.

HOLLIS, centered about Jamaica Avenue and Farmers Boulevard, is the first of the open verdant suburbs beyond the subway's reach, which string out like wayside stations along main traveled roads. In the nineteenth century, families from near-by farms used to gather at the East Jamaica tollgate, in the vicinity of Jamaica Avenue and 186th Street, for country dances and shooting matches. Frederick W. Dunton's purchase of a tract of land here in 1884 signaled the end of the agricultural age. Dunton, a railroad magnate, named the district Hollis for his birthplace in New Hampshire; a believer in astrology, he laid out streets (north of what is now Hillside Avenue) in circles, like the orbits of planets, preserving the Indian trail which ran through the village. The greater part of Hollis, however, developed later, follows the gridiron block plan. Most of the homes are set back from the street, have flagstone walks, and are surrounded by dogwood trees which bloom in profusion.

21. The MARKER at St. Gabriel's Episcopal Church, Woodhull and Jamaica Avenues, calls attention to the historic site of Increase Carpenter's tavern, where General Nathaniel Woodhull, president of the Provincial Congress of New York, was captured and mortally wounded while driving livestock out of the enemy's reach shortly after the Battle of Long Island in 1776.

QUEENS VILLAGE, intersected by Springfield Boulevard, is linked with Hollis by the principal shopping street, Jamaica Avenue, which in earlier days was the main artery for travelers and produce wagons bound for Brooklyn and New York. The site was first subdivided in 1871 by Alfred M. Wood, onetime mayor of Brooklyn, when it received the name of Queens, later changed to Queens Village to avoid confusion with the name of the borough. Some of the dwellings erected in the following decade are still standing in the vicinity of Springfield Boulevard and 100th Avenue, their carriage houses converted into garages.

The smooth terrain of this part of Long Island, first known as the "Plains," has attracted race courses ever since horse racing was introduced into the colonies in 1665. The Belmont Park track, whose western gates are just within the Queens boundary, serves to keep alive this tradition in the neighborhood, and devotees congregate at the Track Tavern at Springfield Boulevard and Hempstead Avenue. In 1927 the village achieved nation-wide notoriety as the scene of the murder in the Ruth Snyder-Judd Gray case.

22. CREEDMOOR STATE HOSPITAL, northeast corner of Winchester Boulevard and Hillside Avenue, under the jurisdiction of the State Department of Mental Hygiene, was a part of Brooklyn State Hospital, but since 1935 has been an independent unit, caring for more than four thousand patients. Of the forty-nine buildings within the 312-acre enclosure, the most important are buff brick structures, erected since 1926 at a cost of about ten million dollars. Within the grounds is a large truck farm which furnishes much of the vegetables used in the institution.

ST. ALBANS, south of Hollis, forty years ago consisted of about three hundred residents and a general store, and the Long Island Railroad trains stopped only when signaled. Ambitious citizens, anticipating its development, dignified it by borrowing the name of a London suburb. Today, St. Albans has approximately thirty thousand inhabitants, about seventy trains stop daily, and within its narrow limits is the elegant St. Albans Golf Club, with a course winding over land said to be worth five hundred thousand dollars.

South Queens

Area: Liberty Ave. and Linden Blvd. (Sutphin Blvd. to city line) on north to Atlantic Ocean on south; from the Brooklyn borough line east to the city line.
Principal highways: Rockaway Blvd., Southern Parkway (Sunrise Highway), Cross Bay Blvd., and Rockaway Beach Blvd.
Transportation: Long Island R.R. (from Atlantic Ave. and Pennsylvania Stations) to all points in South Queens; IRT New Lots subway to New Lots Ave. station, then by bus to the Rockaways; IRT Flatbush Ave. subway to Flatbush Ave. station, then by bus to the Rockaways.

SOUTH QUEENS is cut into two sections by Jamaica Bay. North of the bay are modest, commuter neighborhoods untapped by subway lines and containing two race tracks, Aqueduct and Jamaica. Across the bay's islands one highway and the Long Island Railroad trestle run to the long thin arm of the Rockaway peninsula, which shelters the bay from the Atlantic Ocean. The beaches and seaside communities strung along this sand bar comprise the most frequented ocean resort in the metropolitan area, with the exception of Coney Island.

OZONE PARK, SOUTH OZONE PARK, and HOWARD BEACH, thriving communities developed after 1900, were once part of a farming region, dotted by a meager string of fishermen's huts along the northern shore of Jamaica Bay. As in much of Brooklyn and Queens, the architectural monotony of block upon block of boxlike frame and brick houses, some fronted by a patch of lawn, lends to these communities a prosaic suburban air. Howard Beach is no longer a popular summer colony, since swimming is prohibited in the polluted waters. Boating and fishing, however, continue to be popular sports. The narrow lanes of Shellbank and Hawtree basins, extending inland for half a mile, accommodate small craft, with anchorages at their owners' back yards.

587

1. The AQUEDUCT RACE TRACK (Queens County Jockey Club), between Rockaway Boulevard and Southern Parkway, 107th to 113th Street, was opened in 1894. *(General admission $2.50, women $1.75; clubhouse $5.00, women $3.50.)* Its course, 1¼ miles long and 80 feet wide (90 feet in the backstretch), contains the longest homestretch of any track in the country—770 yards. The stands seat 12,000, but when top-flight horses race attendance is twice that figure. In the past, record crowds have been attracted by Man o' War, Osmand, Roseben, Silver Fox, Naturalist, Irish Lad, King James, Fitzherbert, Seabiscuit, and War Admiral. It was here that Man o' War won his famous victory over John P. Grier in 1920.

Numerous handicaps, such as the Dwyer, Queens County, Carter, and Gazelle races, draw crowds to the June and September meetings. The Brooklyn Handicap, the largest stake race, pays more than nine thousand dollars to the winner.

The track is named for an aqueduct that runs past the southern end of the field carrying water from Long Island reservoirs to parts of Queens and Brooklyn.

SPRINGFIELD, LAURELTON, and ROSEDALE, at the southeastern extremity of the borough, are undistinguished products of the Queens building boom of the 1920's. Springfield, a placid community during most of the year, takes on a festive air during the spring and autumn meetings of near-by Jamaica Race Track. The village was settled in the seventeenth century, and its cemetery, first used in 1760, contains the remains of many early settlers. Laurelton and Rosedale are traversed by the arterial Sunrise Highway and Rockaway Boulevard that link Brooklyn with South Shore villages.

South of Laurelton are the meadows of Jamaica Bay, lush with salt hay and tall swamp tassel, and indented by small tiderace creeks and drainage ditches. Groups of houses built on pilings cling to the slightly elevated northern and western fringes of the swampland and sprawl along the highways which cross the marshes. The improvement of Conduit Boulevard (now known as Sunrise Highway) in 1926–9 induced a small building boom in the more habitable section of the district.

The pollution of the waters has driven bathers away from Idlewild Point, once a popular beach resort. South of Cornell Basin is a dismal area of swamp and dunes, penetrated by Long Pond, Thurston and Salt creeks, and facing the marshy islands and hassocks of Jamaica Bay.

2. The JAMAICA RACE TRACK (Metropolitan Jockey Club), Baisley

HIGH BRIDGE OVER THE HARLEM AND BRONX APARTMENT HOUSES

BRONX COUNTY COURT BUILDING, GRAND CONCOURSE

FORDHAM UNIVERSITY, THE BRONX

MUSEUM BUILDING, NEW YORK BOTANICAL GARDEN, THE BRONX

HALL OF FAME, NEW YORK UNIVERSITY, THE BRONX

BRONX PARK

HILLSIDE HOMES, THE BRONX

CITY ISLAND BOATYARD, THE BRONX

KING MANSION, JAMAICA, QUEENS

BOWNE HOUSE, FLUSHING, QUEENS

HOMES IN QUEENS

BOULEVARD GARDENS APARTMENTS, WOODSIDE, QUEENS

FOREST HILLS, QUEENS

CEMETERY, QUEENS

BROAD CHANNEL, JAMAICA BAY, QUEENS

ROCKAWAY BEACH, QUEENS

NEWTOWN CREEK, QUEENS-BROOKLYN

OLD DUTCH REFORMED CHURCH, PORT RICHMOND, STATEN ISLAND

STILLWELL-PERINE HOUSE, DONGAN HILLS, STATEN ISLAND

BRITTON COTTAGE, NEW DORP, STATEN ISLAND

CHURCH OF ST. ANDREW, RICHMOND, STATEN ISLAND

CONFERENCE (BILLOPP) HOUSE, TOTTENVILLE, STATEN ISLAND

BAYONNE BRIDGE, PORT RICHMOND, STATEN ISLAND

GARIBALDI MEMORIAL, STAPLETON, STATEN ISLAND

VANDERBILT MAUSOLEUM, DONGAN HILLS, STATEN ISLAND

STATEN ISLAND ZOO, WEST NEW BRIGHTON

CLOVE LAKES PARK, WEST NEW BRIGHTON

Boulevard between 165th and 169th Streets, is favored by sprinters because of its wide turns and short homestretch, 385 yards. *(General admission $2.50, women $1.75; clubhouse $5.00, women $3.50.)* It is used exclusively for flat racing and unlike other New York tracks has no steeplechase course on the infield. It was opened in 1903.

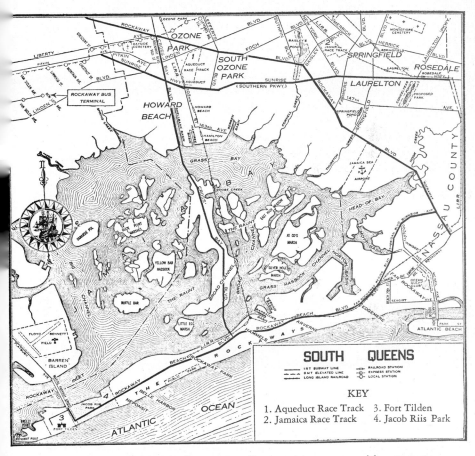

SOUTH QUEENS

KEY

1. Aqueduct Race Track   3. Fort Tilden
2. Jamaica Race Track   4. Jacob Riis Park

Jamaica usually begins the metropolitan racing season with a twenty-one-day meeting in April. The Wood Memorial, its most famous race, is regarded as a dress rehearsal for the Kentucky Derby. Another meet is held in October. The track's wooden grandstand seats 15,000 and its brick clubhouse 1,500, although 25,000 people on April 30, 1937, saw Melodist, a 15-to-1 shot, win the Wood Memorial. Other annual races are the Paumonok, Stuyvesant, Jamaica, and Excelsior Handicaps; the

Rosedale Stakes and the Youthful Stakes. Jamaica has resounded to the hoofs of such thoroughbreds as Man o' War, Gallant Fox, Twenty Grand, Zev, King Saxon, Equipoise, War Admiral, and Pompoon.

The JAMAICA BAY ISLANDS, sprawled among the twenty square miles of shallow Jamaica Bay, are marshy flats on which about four thousand people dwell in comparative isolation within the corporate limits of New York City. All but two per cent live on Broad Channel island; the remainder are scattered over the Raunt and other tiny islands. Cross Bay Boulevard and the Long Island Railroad connect the region with the mainland and the Rockaways. Most of the children travel by bus, provided by the Board of Education, to school in the Rockaways.

The few islands that are above high tide were not permanently settled until about 1880, when a fishing village was established on Big Egg Marsh (now known as Broad Channel). Here, before the city's open sewers contaminated Jamaica Bay, fluke, flounder, weakfish, oysters, and clams were abundant.

Modernization of Broad Channel began in 1915, when a drive was started to make Jamaica Bay a great port, and a Mr. Henry A. Meyer and fellow enthusiasts chartered a ship and toured Europe, advertising Jamaica Harbor. Nothing came of this venture and in the meantime Pierre Noel, a realtor, organized the Broad Channel Corporation which leased land from the city for thirty years. Lots were sublet, streets laid out, and electric and water plants built. When Prohibition came, the island was nicknamed "Little Cuba." Yacht clubs and night clubs opened, and rum running was widespread. A relic of that gay period is the abandoned Enterprise Hotel, a house on stilts, reached with difficulty by climbing a fence and treading a catwalk.

In 1925 Cross Bay Boulevard was built, beaches were developed, and a business district sprang up. At present a great many people stop at Broad Channel in the summer, and fish, mostly with improvised lines, from the two bridges at either end of the island. On the eastern side the shore dips and curves; here the cottages are whitewashed and trim. In other sections long rows of ramshackle buildings lean over the water on their uncertain stilts. Poverty and decay marks the dirt streets and battered houses whose gardens are decorated with mounds of bleached shells. Men in sailor caps and dungarees tinker with boats, and housewives may be seen working over kerosene stoves. The sea has played many pranks with Broad Channel. Hard northeasters have bashed in fishermen's huts and sent roofs spinning into the bay.

The Raunt, in the middle of the bay, contains only a few dozen jerry-built shacks, and the driver of the bus that crosses the bay will stop at this desolate island only upon request. A new wooden footbridge spans the channel between the boulevard and the Raunt. The houses with their crazy catwalks stand above the mud. There is no gas or fresh water. Large tanks used to catch rain water are to be seen everywhere. When the supply runs low, the inhabitants row over to Broad Channel and borrow some.

Feeble attempts at gardening are evident in many places where platforms are raised on stilts and filled with pale gray soil. To be assured of absolute privacy, the colonists only need to pull in the gangplanks which rest like drawbridges on the common duckboard walk.

Beyond the Raunt are many lonely and forbidding islands, some spotted with frail shacks inhabited by such characters as Old Doc. This veteran of the Boer War is sovereign of his island; he stomps about on his peg leg like a character out of *Treasure Island*. Visitors are barred by a pack of wolfish dogs. Occasionally, Old Doc rows into Broad Channel for victuals or a chat with cronies.

The ROCKAWAYS, a narrow windswept peninsula, jutting from the southern mainland of Queens like a sharp splinter, takes its name from the tribe of Indians who inhabited this region. In the pre-railroad era, Far Rockaway was reached by stagecoach over a turnpike from the Brooklyn ferry landing, and its relative inaccessibility made it a fashionable resort second only to Saratoga Springs. With the construction of railroads in 1868, 1872, and 1878, extensive building activity took place in the section. By 1900 society leaders had retreated eastward to the exclusive folds of the Hampton dunes, and the area became a resort for lower middle-class families. Neponsit, Belle Harbor, and Far Rockaway retain traces of the Rockaways' former splendor. In 1925 Rockaway was the scene of a disastrous real-estate boom, following the Florida example, in which millions of dollars were made and lost by frenzied speculators.

There are no industries on the peninsula save those which cater to the needs of the summer visitors and the 45,000 permanent residents. The principal business and shopping street is Rockaway Beach Boulevard, which runs almost the entire length of the peninsula and connects with Cross Bay Boulevard, the main highway to central Queens and Brooklyn. In summer the Rockaways acquire the color, congestion, and gaiety of Coney Island. On weekends as many as a million people throng the five-mile long boardwalk, lie on the white beaches, and swim in the surf.

More than a hundred hotels, most of them in Arverne, Edgemere, and Far Rockaway, cater to vacationists.

Flounders, weakfish, sea bass, kingfish, fluke, porgies, and bluefish abound, and the permits obtained from the borough president's office allow fishing between 8:30 P.M. and 8:00 A.M. from March to late September. In 1935 Francis Low caught a tuna off the Rockaways weighing 735 pounds, establishing a national record.

In winter the ocean-bound strip is a quiet suburb. The beach is deserted, save for flocks of gulls that wheel in the air, and nearly all the bungalows, shops, hotels, and bathhouses along the boardwalk are closed, like theaters out of season.

At the western end of Rockaway are Fort Tilden and Jacob Riis Park. Adjoining the latter is Neponsit, a tiny town about twelve by four blocks in area, composed of substantial homes. Its business district is limited to one block, and zoning restrictions prevent building of houses costing less than three thousand dollars. Concrete walks leading up from the dirt road —there are many unpaved streets in Neponsit—cut white lines in the green lawns surrounding the residences; gaily striped awnings shade the spacious porches, and wicker chairs and tables are set upon the terraces.

Neponsit merges into Belle Harbor, with its fine summer homes where dwell many New York officials. The absence of apartment houses and bungalows gives this section an exclusive air.

Near the terminus of Cross Bay Boulevard is Rockaway Park, containing an amusement park, a bungalow colony, and a public beach.

Hammels, east of Rockaway Park, with a winter population of about 7,500, is a permanent settlement as well as a summer resort. Many of the shops are open the year round, and a few imposing private dwellings are set in the midst of cheaply constructed frame houses, inhabited by Jews, Italians, Irish, and Negroes who constitute a majority of the residents. At the foot of Beach Eightieth Street is a narrow inlet bearing the romantic name of Barbadoes Channel. Here is a small shipyard devoted to the repair of motor launches.

East of Hammels is a superior seaside community, Arverne. About the time of the Civil War the Vanderbilts were said to have been impressed by the beauty of the beach and decided to make it their summer home. In the last quarter of the nineteenth century many families prominent in business and manufacturing had their summer residences here. Among them were the Sterns and Strauses of department store wealth and the Scheers of diamond fame. Today the permanent residents are chiefly small businessmen. Edgemere, the locality adjacent to Arverne, is largely a bungalow resort.

Far Rockaway, which extends from Edgemere to the Queens-Nassau County line, is the widest part of the peninsula and the highest above sea level. Since 1925, the town has become the commercial hub of the Rockaways, with fewer summer citizens in proportion to the total population than neighboring communities. Here are located the main post office, a railroad station, a branch of the public library, most of the chain stores, theaters, banks, and apartment houses.

3. FORT TILDEN, occupying about three hundred acres at the western end of Rockaway peninsula was established February 19, 1917, on land purchased by the Federal Government from the State of New York. The fort was named for Samuel J. Tilden, the Presidential candidate defeated by Rutherford B. Hayes in 1876. Together with Fort Hancock, located at Sandy Hook, Fort Tilden constitutes the outer coast defense of New York harbor.

The guns of the post are of 16-inch and 6-inch caliber. The 16-inch battery, the largest in service, has a range of 50,000 yards and fires 2,100-pound projectiles. In addition to the seacoast defenses, Fort Tilden has three 3-inch antiaircraft guns on fixed mounts.

The fort is a match for any potential invader, although the casual visitor may not be aware of it. Guns appear from the sand dunes, then disappear as if by magic. Smaller cannon mounted on rubber-tired wheels can be dragged to strategic spots by tractors and trucks to augment the fixed defenses. Many a harmless looking dune is a potential dump for powerful munitions.

The fort often bustles with the excitement of sham battles and extensive drills. Every summer the Sixty-second Antiaircraft Regiment executes new maneuvers, a battalion of coast defense artillerymen experiments with the big guns, and swooping airplanes simulate war conditions in mock attacks on New York.

4. JACOB RIIS PARK, flanked by Fort Tilden on the west and the Neponsit Children's Hospital on the east, is named for the journalist who crusaded for recreational facilities for the city's poor. The park contains no commercial amusements, but provides 9,600 lockers *(open daily 10 a.m. to 8 p.m. from Decoration Day to Labor Day; children's lockers 15¢, adults' 25¢, dressing room 50¢)*, parking space for 13,000 cars *(fee 25¢)*, a cafeteria with a capacity of 1,500, handball courts, paddle tennis, and

shuffleboard games, and an eighteen-hole pitch-and-putt golf course. The recreational facilities are strung over a mile of water front, accommodating 100,000 persons.

The area was a wasteland known as the Hatch Tract when it was obtained by the city through condemnation proceedings in 1912. Before it was named Riis Park the section was called Telawana Park. In January, 1936, the New York Park Commission, employing WPA funds and labor, began the last phase of construction. The park was opened in June, 1937. A month later the Marine Parkway Bridge *(see page 505)* spanning Rockaway Inlet to the beach was opened.

The view from the park is extremely attractive. On the southwest, far across the ocean, is the high jut of the Jersey shore. To the north, the serrated sky line of lower Brooklyn and downtown Manhattan, about fifteen miles away, is silhouetted behind Jamaica Bay. Planes cut patterns in the sky over near-by Floyd Bennett Airport. At night, the lightships *Ambrose* and *Scotland,* moored off the Atlantic Highlands, flash their warning gleams, while distant Coney Island shows its filigree of electric lights.

Richmond

D. Spiegel

Richmond

STATEN ISLAND—officially known as Richmond—is separated from Manhattan by the five-mile corridor of Upper New York Bay, a half-hour ride by ferry. A pear-shaped island 13.9 miles long and 7.3 miles broad at its widest point, it follows closely the contours of the New Jersey coast, to which it is connected by three immense bridges spanning Arthur Kill and Kill van Kull. Owing perhaps to its isolation from Manhattan—the ferry providing the only public transportation—the community has maintained an air of rural self-sufficiency, in spite of the fact that many of its inhabitants work in Manhattan and New Jersey. It is the borough least known to New Yorkers, who vaguely think of it as the terminus of an inexpensive and popular ferry ride.

Extending like an arched spine down the six miles from St. George to La Tourette Park is a range of hills—Todt Hill (409.239 feet) is the highest—of greater elevation than found elsewhere on the Atlantic coast between Maine and Florida. East of the central ridge lies a long coastal plain. A less distinct range begins at the Narrows and extends westerly, with some southerly divergences, to the shore of Arthur Kill. The rest of the borough's 36,600 acres is flat country, and in the northwest, near Port Ivory, stretch lonely lowlands and fetid salt marshes.

Factories topped by high smoking chimneys are grouped along the north and the northeast shores. Farther inland modest middle-class communities, many of them independent towns and villages at the time of the consolidation of Greater New York in 1898, cluster about the few main roads: on Hylan Boulevard are Rosebank, New Dorp, Richmond, and Tottenville; on Bay Street, St. George, Tompkinsville, and Stapleton; on Richmond Terrace, New Brighton, Port Richmond, and Mariners Harbor. Large estates and pretentious mansions extend along the central ridge. The localities are linked by bus lines and the Staten Island Rapid Transit, whose main depot is near the ferry shed at St. George.

Staten Island, with a population of 175,000, is a borough of small, single-family homes. It has the highest percentage (74 per cent) of native-born residents in the city; many of the inhabitants of the older communities (Tottenville, Port Richmond, New Brighton) are descendants of early settlers. The foreign population, chiefly Italian, Scandinavian, and Polish, is concentrated in the industrial localities (Stapleton, Port Richmond, Mariners Harbor, West New Brighton).

Giovanni da Verrazano, Italian-born explorer sailing under the French flag, discovered the island in 1524. Eighty-five years later Henry Hudson rediscovered it and, according to legend, named it Staaten Eylandt, in honor of the States-General of the Netherlands, sponsor of the expedition. The Dutch colonists who subsequently attempted settlement here found as their neighbors the Unami Indians, a branch of the Delaware tribe, who called the land Eghquaons (later anglicized to Aquehonga), meaning "high, sandy banks." The Indians on the east end of the island were known locally as the Raritans, and on the west end, as the Hackensacks.

At least three organized attempts, beginning in 1630, were made to colonize the island, but in each case the settlements were wiped out by the Indians. It is likely that isolated *bouweries*—small stock farms characteristic of Dutch settlements—were common throughout this period. The Peach War (1655) was precipitated when Van Dyck, attorney general of New Netherland, shot and killed an Indian woman who was picking peaches in his orchard. The Whisky War (1643) had been provoked by similar incidents. Each time peace was concluded, negotiations for a formal sale of the land to the whites took place. The Dutch bought the island five times; in 1649 Cornelis Melyn, a colonist, had complained of intimations that it was time to buy it again: "They supposed that ye Island by reason of ye war, by killing, burning & driving us off, was become theirs again." In the Federal period, when New Jersey made unsuccessful claims to Staten Island, one of the strong arguments of New York State was that Governor Lovelace of New York Province had last bought it from the Indians in 1670.

OUTLINE MAP
BOROUGH
OF
RICHMOND
[STATEN ISLAND]

In 1661, nineteen Dutch and French settlers established Oude Dorp (Old Town), believed to be the first permanent settlement on the island, near the present site of Fort Wadsworth. Other settlements followed soon after.

When the English captured New Amsterdam in 1664, Staten Island became part of the province of New York and was named Richmond County, in honor of the Duke of Richmond, son of King Charles II. There is a tradition that the Duke of York, to decide the dispute between New Jersey and New York ducal proprietors over Staten Island, said that the island would be awarded to citizens who could circumnavigate it in twenty-four hours. Captain Christopher Billopp sailed around Staten Island, and as a reward in 1687 Governor Andros granted him 1,600 acres at the southernmost tip, where he established the manor of Bentley on the site of what is now the village of Tottenville.

The British discouraged any kind of manufacturing in their colonies, and stock raising became one of the leading occupations here. The thirty-five miles of water front also influenced the development of the island. The natural oyster beds had been well known to the Indians, and were so prolific that it was not until the 1830's that artificial culture was begun. In addition, the rise and fall of the tide operated numerous saw and grist mills. Shipbuilding took its place early as an important industry.

The British captured Staten Island at the opening of the Revolutionary War and held it until Evacuation Day. The Conference or Billopp House as it is sometimes known, in Tottenville, was the scene of a meeting in September, 1776, between Lord Howe and three delegates of the Continental Congress—Benjamin Franklin, John Adams, and Edward Rutledge—to try to settle differences without further bloodshed. The conference came to no decision and the war went on. On an eminence (known as the "Watering Place") in St. George, commanding the harbor, stood Fort Hill, occupied by British troops for the duration of the conflict. Lord Stirling, an American commander, made an unsuccessful attempt to capture the fort in January, 1780.

In the postwar period ferry service by sailboat between the island and New York was irregular and hazardous. Among the early operators was Cornelius ("Commodore") Vanderbilt, who was born near Stapleton in 1794, and who established the first regular ferry service across the bay. The municipal ferry system was not inaugurated until 1890.

Until the 1830's Staten Island remained chiefly a farming and fishing community. The development of fashionable bathing resorts in the northern part of the island, about 1830, rapidly transformed this sparsely settled farm region into an urban community. The descendants of the first landowners were crowded out by socially prominent families from New York and the South. Coincidentally, a literary colony sprang up in West New Brighton. James Russell Lowell and Francis Parkman, the historian, came here for rest and treatment by the famous oculist, Dr. McKenzie Elliot. Edgar Wilson Nye, better known as Bill Nye, the humorist, lived here for a time. Charles Mackay, a correspondent for the London *Times,* in 1865 eulogized the island in his poem, *A Home in Staten Island.* Judge William Emerson moved from Massachusetts in 1837 and established a home, "The Snuggery," near Clifton. Among his guests were his famous brother, Ralph Waldo, and the naturalist philosopher, Henry David Thoreau.

Other visitors and residents were the prima donnas, Jenny Lind and Adelina Patti; Giuseppe Garibaldi, Italian patriot, who lived here in the 1850's, during his exile from Italy; and George William Curtis, essayist and editor of *Harper's Weekly* (1863–92), who made his home here for more than twenty-five years. The island is the birthplace of the labor leader, Ella Reeve ("Mother") Bloor, and of Alan Seeger, killed in France in 1916 soon after he wrote the prophetic *I Have a Rendezvous with Death.* Edwin Markham, author of *The Man with the Hoe,* has lived here for many years.

During the Civil War many southern planters sent their women to Staten Island for safety. The Draft Riots were particularly severe on the island and a number of Abolitionists had to fortify their homes, maintaining a day and night watch against the mobs.

After the Civil War the rapid industrialization of New Jersey towns along the Arthur Kill and Kill van Kull spread across the rivers to the north and northeast shores of the island, particularly around the ferry landings. In 1860 the first railroad on the island had been built; it operated between Clifton and Tottenville. Sewage from oil refineries and other industrial plants polluted the waters, and by 1916 the fishing and oyster dredging, which had been the main source of income for a large part of the population, was brought to an end. Shipbuilding, always important, became the leading industry. The borough also contains many building materials' manufactories and yards, lumber mills, and printing and publishing establishments. Despite the fact that Staten Island has the only free port area in the country, it carries on little maritime commerce.

A number of fashionable finishing schools here attract students from all over the East. The Staten Island Institute of Arts and Sciences, a local cultural center, maintains a public museum, while the Staten Island Historical Society preserves a number of historic homesteads. The borough has its own zoo, at Barrett Park, with a reptile department that is especially well known. An independent community spirit is evident in the wide circulation of the Staten Island *Advance,* a daily newspaper. The bathing beaches on the south shore, particularly South and Midland, are popular summer retreats of New Jersey families. Several parks, notably La Tourette near Egbertville, furnish playground and recreational facilities.

When the city carries out its long-standing plan for a vehicular tunnel connecting Staten Island with Brooklyn across the Narrows, this borough will become a thoroughfare for traffic between Long Island and New Jersey and its present rural-residential character may change.

East and South Richmond

St. George—Tompkinsville and Stapleton—Dongan Hills and Richmond—
Pleasant Plains and Tottenville

Area: St. George on the north to Tottenville on the south; from New York Bay
west to Victory Blvd. (Bay St. to Manor Rd.), Manor Rd. (Victory Blvd. to
Rockland Ave.), La Tourette Park, Richmond Creek, Fresh Kills, and Arthur Kill.
Principal highways: Bay St., Hylan Blvd., Richmond Rd., and Amboy Rd.
Transportation: Bus or Staten Island Rapid Transit from St. George.

ALONG the east and south shores of Staten Island, a long coastal plain
backed by a hilly inland region, are some of the island's oldest communities, and many interesting old homes, including the historic Conference
or Billopp House. The main roads pass through pleasant rural areas and
frequently afford arresting views of Lower New York Bay and Atlantic
Ocean.

ST. GEORGE, clambering up Fort Hill, is metropolitan in its aspect and
movement, and serves as the civic, business, cultural, and transit center of
Staten Island. The nucleus of the town is the municipal ferry shed;
through it passes most of the island's working population, going to and
from Manhattan, and clustered around it are the terminals of the Staten
Island Rapid Transit and bus lines, and the seats of the borough and
county governments.

603

Although modern apartment and two-story houses predominate, the town, which rises abruptly toward the southwest, still contains some old gabled mansions typical of nineteenth-century Staten Island, erected in an era when wood and labor were cheap and space was not at a premium.

1. The STATEN ISLAND INSTITUTE OF ARTS AND SCIENCES, Wall Street and Stuyvesant Place, is the co-ordinating body for most of the cultural and scientific activities on the island. *(Open weekdays 10 a.m. to 5 p.m., Sunday 2 to 5 p.m.; admission free.)* Chief among its affiliates are the Staten Island Bird Club, Microscopical Society, Nature Club, Art Association, and Belles Lettres Society. The institute was founded as the Natural Science Association of Staten Island on November 12, 1881, with the aim of forming a collection principally of Staten Island objects. The association opened a public museum in Borough Hall in 1907, after adopting its present name. The various collections grew rapidly. Ten years later the museum acquired its own home, a two-story building, to which two floors were added in 1928.

The institute's museum, occupying the first floor and part of the second, includes exhibits of Staten Island marine life, fauna, and natural history,

KEY TO EAST AND SOUTH RICHMOND MAP

1. Staten Island Institute of Arts and Sciences
2. Borough Hall
3. County Court House
4. Foreign Trade Zone No. 1 (Free Port)
5. U.S. Marine Hospital
6. Mariners Family Asylum of the Port of New York
7. Garibaldi Memorial
8. Austen House
9. U.S. Quarantine Station
10. Hoffman and Swinburne Islands
11. Fort Wadsworth
12. Clove Meeting House Cemetery
13. Stillwell-Perine House
14. Todt Hill
15. Moravian Cemetery
    Moravian Church
    Vanderbilt Mausoleum
16. Rose and Crown Monument
17. Miller Field
18. Britton Cottage
19. Lake-Tysen House
20. Old Richmond County Courthouse
21. Burial Ground of the Rezeau-Van Pelts
22. Staten Island Historical Society Museum
23. Church of St. Andrew
24. La Tourette Park
    La Tourette Mansion
25. Vorleezers House
26. Staten Island Marine Park
27. Cropsey Homestead
28. Church of the Huguenots
29. Purdy's Hotel
30. Mount Loretto
31. Outerbridge Crossing
32. Howat Ceramic Works
33. Conference or Billopp House

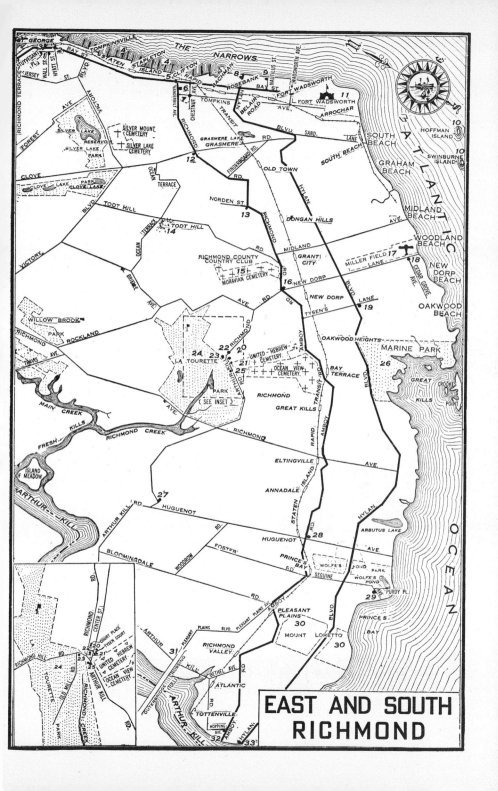

EAST AND SOUTH
RICHMOND

as well as a small collection of live snakes, fish, and invertebrates. The collection of cicadas assembled by William T. Davis is the largest privately owned collection in the United States. In the southwest wing three models, built by Ned J. Burns, sculptor, reproduce in miniature the interior of the Billopp House, a wigwam and its occupants, and an Indian attack on Dutch settlers. Several collections of relics, including the possessions of both settlers and Indians, depict Colonial life on the island. The historical section of the museum library has, in addition to standard histories, an assortment of old maps, original documents, copies of early newspapers, and other periodicals. Exhibits in an art gallery on the second floor are changed monthly.

The institute co-operates with the public school system by providing illustrated lectures for school children in natural history, woodlore, and other subjects. In addition, it shows educational motion pictures at regular intervals in its auditorium, and sponsors classes in drawing and sculpture. The building also serves as the headquarters for amateur nature study and camera clubs.

2. BOROUGH HALL, Richmond Terrace and Hyatt Street, dominates the group of public buildings that make up the civic center near the summit of Fort Hill. Four stories high, of red brick and stone, with a clock tower rising forty feet above the slate roof, it resembles a French town hall. It was completed in 1906 after plans by Carrère and Hastings. In the main vestibule, twelve brilliantly colored murals, painted by F. C. Stahr, depict episodes in the early history of Staten Island.

3. COUNTY COURT HOUSE, adjoining Borough Hall on Richmond Terrace, is the seat of government of Richmond County. The main wing contains the offices of the county clerk and other officials, while the rear wing houses the county court. The building was designed in Italian Renaissance style and the portico in Greek Revival. The whole, completed in 1919, clashes with the Borough Hall in style, scale, and spirit, although designed by the same firm of architects.

TOMPKINSVILLE and STAPLETON are contiguous localities, virtually indistinguishable from each other, on the east shore of Staten Island, between St. George and Fort Wadsworth. Numerous plants, large and small, give the neighborhood a "factory town" aspect. Near the water front squat the shabby houses of laborers, while on fashionable Grymes Hill, slightly west of Stapleton, rise many fine residences. In the vicinity of Canal Street is the largest Italian colony on the island. On the Stapleton shore is the free port, the first of its kind in the country.

4. The FOREIGN TRADE ZONE NO. 1, comprising Piers 12, 13, 15, 16, off Bay Street and eighteen adjoining acres of land and warehouse space, is used for the transshipment and the re-export, duty free, of foreign goods. Neither manufacturing nor the permanent exhibition of commodities, however, is permitted within the port—its main deviation from European prototypes. The port is under the jurisdiction of the Commissioner of Docks and subject to the regulations of the Free Trade Zones Board. It was established in 1936 chiefly to utilize a portion of the twelve costly municipal wharves along the Stapleton water front, built by Mayor John F. Hylan's administration to meet an anticipated increase in New York maritime traffic; the piers fell into desuetude and were dubbed "Hylan's Folly."

5. UNITED STATES MARINE HOSPITAL, Bay Street and Vanderbilt Avenue, a Federal hospital operated by the United States Public Health Service, is open to personnel of the Merchant Marine and Coast Guard, and to certain classes of Government employees. Constructed in 1933–6 by the PWA at a cost of two million dollars, the tawny-colored brick buildings with a silver tower cover an area of eighteen acres. Louis A. Simon was the supervising architect. This hospital was originally on Bedloe Island but was removed in 1883 to make room for the Statue of Liberty.

6. MARINERS FAMILY ASYLUM OF THE PORT OF NEW YORK, 119 Tompkins Avenue, adjoining the U.S. Marine Hospital, was founded in 1843 by the Female Bethel Society of New York to provide quarters "for aged widows, wives, sisters, and daughters of seamen of the port of New York." Twenty-two women form the present family in the tall square edifice which was erected in 1843. This refuge, the only institution of its kind in the country, is supported by voluntary contributions. The present building was dedicated in 1855.

7. The GARIBALDI MEMORIAL, Chestnut and Tompkins Avenues, in the heart of Stapleton's Little Italy, commemorates the Italian liberator's brief American residence. From 1851 to 1853 Garibaldi resided at the home of Antonio Meucci, where he supported himself as a candlemaker. Meucci's house, a small frame cottage which was moved from its location across the street, is sheltered under a monumental concrete structure whose classic columns contrast with the cottage's simplicity. A bust marks the grave of Meucci on the weedy lawn fronting the house.

8. The AUSTEN HOUSE, 2 Hylan Boulevard, one of the best-preserved early Staten Island homes, stands on a knoll overlooking the Narrows. Its main wing is believed to have been built prior to 1669. The vine-covered frame cottage demonstrates the charm that Colonial builders were able to

achieve with simple architectural lines. The long horizontals are punctuated by three unevenly spaced, sharp-peaked dormers added in the nineteenth century; a wide overhang protects the wall below. The rooms are appropriately filled with period furniture and historic relics. The present owner, a descendant of the John Austen who bought the cottage in 1835, has converted the house into a tearoom.

9. The UNITED STATES QUARANTINE STATION, Nautilus and Bay Streets, examines persons on vessels from foreign ports for typhus, leprosy, cholera, plague, yellow fever, anthrax, and psitticosis (parrot fever). No quarantinable case has gained admission to the port of New York since 1921 when the Federal Government took over the station from New York State. The eight-acre site, prior to 1872, was part of the estate of the O'Learys, a prominent New York family.

10. HOFFMAN and SWINBURNE ISLANDS, in Lower New York Bay, about a quarter of a mile east of the Quarantine Station, are artificial islands constructed in 1872 to serve as quarantine stations. They were abandoned following the curb on immigration in the 1920's. During 1938 Hoffman Island was reconditioned for use by the Training School of the U.S. Maritime Service, which prepares trained seamen under the supervision of the U.S. Coast Guard.

11. FORT WADSWORTH, Bay Street and Wadsworth Avenue, guards the Narrows, the water gate to Upper New York Bay. *(Visitors must obtain permission from the post adjutant.)* On the opposite side of the strait is Fort Hamilton *(see page 469).* Fort Wadsworth is garrisoned by the Second and Third Battalions of the Eighteenth Infantry, a detachment of the Fifth Coast Artillery, units of the Quartermaster Corps and the Medical Department, and the Headquarters Company of the First Infantry Brigade. Its main fortification is called Fort Tompkins.

A fortification occupied the site as early as 1663. The British were in possession during the Revolution. On Evacuation Day, 1783, the commander of a British warship, goaded by the jeers of the onlooking victorious rebels, fired at the fort a shot that may be considered the last one of the Revolution. A fort, built here by New York State in the War of 1812, was replaced in 1847 by the present defenses. In 1865 it was renamed in honor of Brigadier General James S. Wadsworth, who was killed in the Battle of the Wilderness.

DONGAN HILLS and RICHMOND, the vicinity near the junction of Amboy and Richmond Roads, embrace a number of once independent villages, some dating from Colonial times. Dongan Hills, rich in hematite deposits, was founded in the seventeenth century as a mining town, and named for Thomas Dongan, governor of the province of New York (1683–8). It contains Todt Hill, the highest point on the seaboard between Maine and Florida. In the first known description of Richmond (1700), it is called "Coccles Town," probably in reference to the oyster or clam shells (cockle or "coccle" shells) taken out of the neighboring Fresh Kills. Corrupted to the libelous "Cuckoldstown," the name—no doubt by common consent—became "Richmond Town" at about the time of the Revolution. In the nineteenth century the town was the seat of the county government. It occupies the geographical center of the island.

The strand east of Dongan Hills, between Fort Wadsworth and Staten Island Marine Park, was once known as South Beach, a fashionable summer resort in the 1890's. It has never regained its former status, although in recent years the beach has become a favorite of residents of near-by New Jersey industrial towns. The attraction of a two-million-dollar boardwalk, constructed by the WPA in 1938, and easy accessibility by way of the projected Brooklyn-Staten Island vehicular tunnel (if and when built), may again make it a popular retreat for New Yorkers. The beach now comprises six units—South, Graham, Midland, Woodland, New Dorp, and Oakwood—of which Midland Beach, with its amusement facilities, is most frequented.

12. CLOVE MEETING HOUSE CEMETERY, southwest corner of Richmond and Clove Roads, is a small unfenced burial ground, marked by crumbling and broken tombstones, half-hidden by bushes and weeds. One stone dates from 1811. Near by, more than a century ago, stood the Clove Meeting House, belonging to a Baptist congregation.

13. STILLWELL-PERINE HOUSE, 1476 Richmond Road, near Norden Street, is a public museum owned by the Staten Island Historical Society. (Open weekdays 9 a.m. to 5 p.m.; admission free.) The original part of this stone cottage, a one-story white structure with sloping shingled roof, was built in 1680. The additions—some with English peaked dormers, others with Dutch shed dormers—achieve a general harmony of appearance although their motifs and styles differ. Acquired by the Perine family in 1764, the house remained in its possession until 1913. The rustic air which clings to the cottage and its modest grounds is enhanced by a brook which runs beside the house, flowing under Richmond Road. The dwelling contains a secret chamber opening into the "Beam Room," so called because of its heavily beamed ceiling.

14. TODT HILL, Todt Hill Road and Ocean Terrace, rises 409.2 feet

above sea level at Dongan Knoll. Landscaped estates and imposing mansions, commanding a fine view of the island and Lower New York Bay, cover the hillside.

The hill was called Yserberg, or Iron Hill, by the Dutch who worked it as an iron ore (hematite) depository as early as 1664. The mines were abandoned when imported Cuban hematite made them unprofitable. The open green hill, still patched with woodlands, was a favorite retreat in the last part of the nineteenth century, and Jenny Lind, the Swedish soprano, often rode horseback on these slopes.

The Dutch word "todt" means "death," but its application to the hill has never been satisfactorily explained. The hollow fronting Todt Hill is known as the valley of the Iron Hill, or Mersereau's Valley, the latter name deriving from the legend of a native youth who rescued his sweetheart from a British officer during the occupation in 1777.

15. MORAVIAN CEMETERY, Todt Hill Road and Richmond Road, which contains the Vanderbilt Mausoleum, belongs to the New Dorp Moravian Church (United Brethren). Rising two hundred feet above Richmond Road and covering eighty neatly terraced acres on the southerly slope of Todt Hill, the site was used as a cemetery long before it was taken over by the United Brethren Church, more than a hundred years ago. One of the earliest gravestones bears the epitaph of Colonel Nicholas Britten, dated 1740. In the section set aside for the exclusive use of Moravians, the dead were segregated according to sex, but this practice has since been discontinued. The remainder of the graveyard is nonsectarian.

The Greek Revival church, whose square pillars are a common variation of the columnar Greek portico, is at the entrance of the cemetery; it replaced one that was built in 1762. The present building was erected in 1845 and later improved with funds donated chiefly by Cornelius and William H. Vanderbilt, whose ancestor, Jacob Van Der Bilt, was converted to the Moravian faith in the eighteenth century. The original church and parish house is now used as the cemetery office.

The Vanderbilt Mausoleum, a massive granite building in Romanesque style, with bronze doors, set in the side of a hill, cost about a million dollars. Here are the remains of most of the Vanderbilt family, including Commodore Cornelius Vanderbilt and his son William. The first Jacob Van Der Bilt, his wife and their son Jacob, are buried in an adjoining plot.

16. The ROSE AND CROWN MONUMENT, at the triangle formed by Richmond Road, New Dorp Lane, and First Street, is a large roughhewn piece of granite, near the site of the Rose and Crown House, a Colonial tavern which became General William Howe's headquarters during the

British occupation of Staten Island. Behind the monument is a tablet erected in honor of the men of New Dorp killed in the World War.

17. MILLER FIELD, extending from Hylan Boulevard to the ocean along New Dorp Lane, is a Federal aviation field, named in honor of James Ely Miller, first A.E.F. aviator to be killed in combat in France. It contains the headquarters of the Twenty-Seventh Division Aviation Corps of the New York National Guard, and the barracks of the Headquarters Company First Brigade and the First Division Tank Company of the U.S. Army. At the foot of the field is the Elm Tree Beacon, which together with a beacon in the Moravian Cemetery, is used as a landmark by navigators in Lower New York Bay. The beacon derives its name from an elm tree which once stood here.

18. The BRITTON COTTAGE, New Dorp Lane, east of Cedar Grove Avenue, in the heart of the New Dorp beach colony, is a shingled, ivy-covered Colonial structure, now owned by the Staten Island Institute of Arts and Sciences, which acquired it from the Britton family. *(Open weekdays 9 a.m. to 5 p.m.; admission free.)* Although the exact date of construction is unknown, it is believed that part of the main house was built by Nathaniel Britton before 1699. The interior has a musty smell of old wood, seasoned by the sea wind for many decades. The house, appointed with Colonial furnishings, has low, heavily beamed ceilings, and large windows. The kitchen fireplace, of unusual size, can hold an eight-foot log.

19. The LAKE-TYSEN HOUSE, on the grounds of the Tysen Manor Golf Club, 630 Tysen's Lane, east of Hylan Boulevard, is an excellent example of an early Dutch farmhouse. It is reported to have been built by Daniel Lake prior to 1740; a number of additions were made at a later date. Its low-pitched gambrel roof swings out over the porch.

20. The OLD RICHMOND COUNTY COURTHOUSE, Center Street and Court Place, built in 1837, is now used as a community center. This building, designed in Greek Revival style, is notable for the excellent proportions of its main elements, which achieve interest and beauty without the use of extensive ornament. Large modern window panes somewhat disrupt the uniformity of the scale. The court was transferred in 1920 to a new building in St. George. In the rear is the county jail (enclosed by a high iron railing) constructed in 1860 and rebuilt in 1896.

21. The BURIAL PLOT OF THE REZEAU-VAN PELTS, adjoining the courthouse on the west, is a private cemetery, about two hundred years old. The largest tombstone marks the grave of Susannah Van Pelt, who died in 1802 at the age of ninety-nine. Fragments of the original iron

fence which once surrounded the plot are considered fine examples of ironwork.

22. The STATEN ISLAND HISTORICAL SOCIETY MUSEUM, opposite the old county courthouse at Court Place and Center Street, is housed in the old county clerk's and surrogate's office, a two-story brick structure of Colonial design, built in 1848 and restored in 1933-5 by the WPA. *(Open weekdays 10 a.m. to 5 p.m., Sunday and holidays 2 to 5 p.m.; admission free.)* Its collections emphasize the agricultural history of Staten Island and trace various phases of local arts and crafts. Reproductions of small shops—wheelwright, cooper, carpenter, and cobbler—complete with their rude tools, dramatize the early industries of the island. The museum also contains exhibits of Colonial furniture and household effects, and an extensive library of photographs, manuscripts, and printed material relating to Staten Island.

23. CHURCH OF ST. ANDREW (Episcopal), near the junction of Richmond, Richmond Hill, and Old Mill Roads, was founded in 1708 and granted a charter by Queen Anne in 1713. The first church, a simple Colonial edifice, was built that same year, and although damaged during the Revolution, and twice razed by fire, the original walls remain. The church was served by a number of distinguished clergymen including the Right Reverend Samuel Seabury, first American bishop, who was consecrated at Aberdeen in 1784. The present ivy-covered structure built in 1872 in Victorian Gothic style, has the air of a quiet English rural church. It is surrounded by an old cemetery in which some of the first Staten Island families are buried. A number of gifts presented by Queen Anne to the church, including a chalice and paten, are now in the Metropolitan Museum of Art. The church bell, also donated by the Queen, is still·in use.

24. LA TOURETTE PARK, north and west of the junction of Richmond and Richmond Hill Roads, comprises 580 acres of tufted groves, hillocks, twisting brooks, and landscaped playfields. The clubhouse for the golf course, formerly the home of the La Tourette family, dates from 1830. The spacious mansion is surrounded by wide verandas. Old Staten Islanders believe that the troubled ghost of David La Tourette, vexed at the profanation of his home, occasionally roams through the building.

25. VORLEEZERS HOUSE, 63 Arthur Kill Road, south of Center Street, is reputed to be one of the oldest Dutch frame buildings in New York. The name, in Dutch, means "the house of a person who reads scriptures." The two-story frame house, now without its shutters and roof overhang, is believed to have been erected before 1696 and is the oldest known elementary school building in the country and the first church on Staten

Island. From 1705 to 1872 it was occupied by the Rezeau and Van Pelt families. The structure was about to be razed in 1936, but the Staten Island Historical Society arranged to have the municipality purchase and convert the building into a museum. (In 1939 it was being restored.)

26. STATEN ISLAND MARINE PARK, between Hylan Boulevard and Lower New York Bay, from Emmet Avenue to Great Kills, a 1,256-acre municipal playland under construction (1939), will include landscaped athletic fields, a boardwalk promenade, beach, bathhouses, dining hall, yacht basin, boathouse, and parking space for 9,800 automobiles.

27. CROPSEY HOMESTEAD, 1922 Arthur Kill Road, between Arden and Huguenot Avenues, a shingled one-story frame house said to have been built in 1767, has two rooms, with a narrow stairway leading to the attic. Its two-part Dutch door is less than six feet high. Jasper Francis Cropsey, a landscape painter who died in 1900, was the last of the family to occupy the dwelling.

28. The MEMORIAL CHURCH OF THE HUGUENOTS, Amboy Road and Huguenot Avenue, is built of stone quarried on the Long Island estate of Ernest Flagg, the architect of the church. The squat, rambling structure was dedicated in 1924 as the national monument of the Huguenot-Walloon Tercentenary, which commemorated the coming of the first group of settlers, thirty-four families of French Huguenots and Walloons. It contains a number of memorials donated by Huguenot societies and descendants of early Huguenot colonists. One inscription is dedicated to "Abraham de Veaux, 1674, Huguenot settler near the Raritan"; others are dedicated to Admiral Coligny; Angelique Guion; and William, Prince of Orange. The exterior is overcomplicated for so small a church, but the interior arrangement is original and impressive.

29. PURDY'S HOTEL, Seguine Avenue and Purdy Place, a two-hundred-year-old homestead, was used as headquarters by General Vaughan when the British forces occupied the island in 1776. It is a one-story house with a two-story addition at a lower level. The walls are of stone, covered with shingle and clapboard. The exterior is in the usual Dutch farmhouse style, but enclosed porches have been added and other minor changes made. The house is named for a former owner who operated it as a hotel in the days when Seguine Avenue was a busy fishing and boating center.

PLEASANT PLAINS and TOTTENVILLE, at the southern tip of the island, are former fishing villages, the streets of which at one time were surfaced with oyster shells. A few small fishing and pleasure craft crisscross the waters which once held numerous oyster boats and fashionable yachts. Tottenville is a compact, quiet residential community. Old families of English descent have lived here for generations, often in the same home.

Tottenville is the latest name of the village and was adopted after protracted and acrimonious disputes. The place had intermittently been called Totten's Landing, Bentley Dock, Unionville, Mount Hermon, Arensville, and the Neck. It is named for the Totten family, once numerous on the island.

30. MOUNT LORETTO, fronting Raritan Bay (west of Sharrot Avenue and south of Amboy Road), is a 650-acre estate conducted by the Mission of the Immaculate Virgin for the Protection of Homeless and Destitute Children, Inc., a Catholic institution. Founded in 1870 by the Reverend John C. Drumgoole as a home for newsboys, at 54 Warren Street, Manhattan, the mission was established here ten years later. It comprises the St. Joseph's Home for Boys, St. Elizabeth's Home for Girls, the Duval Cottage for orphaned baby girls, and St. Joseph's Asylum for Blind Girls. The personnel of nearly two hundred includes seventy-six Sisters of St. Francis. In 1937 it cared for 1,057 children.

31. OUTERBRIDGE CROSSING, Pleasant Plains Boulevard and Page Avenue, is the southernmost of the three Staten Island-New Jersey bridges built and maintained by the Port of New York Authority. (Passenger automobile toll 50¢.) It connects Tottenville with Perth Amboy, New Jersey, across Arthur Kill, and leads to roads that link with US 1 and 9. The cantilever structure is the longest of the island bridges, the total length of its truss spans being 2,100 feet. The main span, 750 feet long, clears 135 feet above the water. The bridge was opened June 29, 1928, and named for Eugenius H. Outerbridge, the Authority's first chairman. It cost about ten million dollars. O. H. Ammann was the designer, assisted by Allston Dana; Waddell and Hardesty were the consulting engineers.

32. HOWAT CERAMIC WORKS, 85 Hopping Avenue, established in 1934, is one of the few plants in the United States that have perfected the technique of casting statues, busts, and smaller statuary in porcelain. (Visitors admitted weekdays 4 to 5 p.m.) The firm uses an oil-burning kiln of its own design.

33. The CONFERENCE OR BILLOPP HOUSE, at the foot of Hylan Boulevard, was the scene of important but futile peace negotiations after the Battle of Long Island. (Open daily, except Monday, 10 a.m. to 6 p.m. May to October; 10 a.m. to 5 p.m. November to April; admission free.) At the request of Lord Howe, the British admiral, the Continental Congress

appointed a delegation of three—Benjamin Franklin (a friend of Lord Howe), John Adams, and Edward Rutledge—to meet with him on September 11, 1776. The discussion proved fruitless, for the Americans refused to barter for peace unless the British granted independence to the colonies.

The delegation returned to Perth Amboy aboard Howe's barge. As the boat entered the wharf Franklin offered some gold and silver coins to the sailors but the commanding officer intervened. "As these people are under the impression that we have not a farthing of hard money in the country," Franklin later explained to his companions, "I thought I would convince them of their mistake. I knew at the same time that I risked nothing by an offer, which their regulation and discipline would not permit them to accept." The group then traveled to Philadelphia, where its report was submitted to Congress.

The land on which the house stands was included in a patent of 932 acres granted in 1676 to Christopher Billopp, a British Navy captain who two years earlier had come to America with Governor Andros. In 1687 Thomas Dongan, Andros' successor, granted the patent and an additional 668 acres to Captain Billopp as the manor of Bentley.

The house, built by Billopp prior to 1688, was for many years the island's most imposing mansion. The property was inherited by Thomas Farmar, Jr., third son of the captain's daughter, Anne. Under the terms of the will the heir assumed the name of Thomas Billopp. Christopher, Thomas' eldest son, became the next proprietor of the estate. A Tory colonel, he frequently entertained British officers, including Lord Howe, and his house was kept under constant surveillance by the Americans entrenched on the New Jersey shores of the near-by Arthur Kill. At the time of the historic meeting redcoats were quartered in the mansion. Colonel Billopp died in 1827.

The house, subsequently used as a factory, fell into neglect. Many efforts were made to restore it, but none was successful until 1925, when the Conference House Association was organized. The real-estate company that had acquired the property deeded the house and an acre of land to the city in 1926; three years later the Municipal Assembly made the association custodian of the building.

With the exception of a pillared two-story porch which was not replaced, the structure has been restored to its original condition. Two stories and an attic in height, it has exterior walls of local stone. The basement kitchen has been repaired with glazed brick (made in Holland) to simulate the original flooring; at one end of the room is a massive

fireplace; at the opposite, an arched brick vault that was used as a wine cellar. The beams in the Conference Room (left of the entrance), like those in
the kitchen, attic, and other parts of the house, are the handhewn orig-
inals. The laths, split by hand, are fastened to the beams by hand-made
wrought-iron nails.

The interior has been appointed with pieces associated with the Colonial
period. The D.A.R. and Philemon rooms on the first floor are noteworthy,
as well as the Colonial chamber and the room set aside for a Benjamin
Franklin National Museum on the second floor. The restoration was under
the immediate supervision of Chester A. Cole.

North and West Richmond

Area: Kill van Kull on the north to Fresh Kills and Richmond Creek on the south; from Arthur Kill east to La Tourette Park, Manor Rd. (Rockland Ave. to Victory Blvd.), and Victory Blvd. (Manor Rd. to Bay St.)
Principal highways: Richmond Terrace, Forest Ave., and Victory Blvd.
Transportation: Bus and Staten Island Rapid Transit from St. George.

THE north shore of Staten Island is a heavily populated residential area extending inland from the industrial establishments that fringe the narrow Kill van Kull. The western section, save for the neighborhoods of Mariners Harbor and Travis, is largely a stretch of meadowland, dotted with a few truck farms.

NEW BRIGHTON, west of St. George between Westervelt and Davis Avenues, formerly one of the most fashionable summer resorts in the East, is now a quiet residential community. A few stately mansions, some of them abandoned, provide a link with the years of the nineteenth century when southern planters and wealthy New Yorkers patronized the elegant hotels and villas of the neighborhood. Richmond Terrace, a fashionable drive in the 1890's, is now lined with a disheartening row of small stores, beer gardens, factories and shipyards facing the Kill van Kull and the equally desolate shore of near-by New Jersey.

1. The NEVILLE HOUSE, 806 Richmond Terrace, between Clinton and Tysen Streets, said to have been built in 1770, is one of the best-preserved of Staten Island houses. The two-story stone building was formerly the home of Captain John Neville, whose activities, after his retirement from the U.S. Navy, caused the place to be known as "The Stone Jug." In the early 1900's it was used as a tavern and hotel. The bar became too great an attraction to the inmates of Sailors' Snug Harbor, so the Harbor purchased and closed the place.

2. SAILORS' SNUG HARBOR, Richmond Terrace between Tysen Street and Kissell Avenue, a home for retired seamen, occupies an estate of one hundred acres overlooking the Kill van Kull. *(Visitors admitted weekdays 9 a.m. to 4 p.m.)* Here the mariners spend their declining days provided with everything from food and shelter to tobacco and movies. To be admitted a mariner must be sixty-five, an American citizen, and prove that he has been at sea at least five years. The institution has a capacity of one thousand, but the number is usually a hundred or so below the mark. To the amusement and disdain of some of the inmates a ferryboat captain and several towboat men have been admitted. The old tars wear blue uniforms.

The Harbor was founded in 1801 by the will of Captain Robert Richard Randall, son of a privateer, who bequeathed the bulk of his fortune for the establishment and support of a "home for aged, decrepit, and worn-out sailors." Randall's property consisted principally of a Manhattan farm of twenty-one acres, covering a large portion of what is now the Washington Square district. The income of the estate is used for the maintenance of the Harbor.

The Staten Island site was purchased in 1831 and the asylum was opened August 1, 1833, when twenty sailors were admitted. The Harbor contains more than fifty buildings, some connected by passageways; eight are used for dormitories and mess halls. The most prominent structure is a chapel in the style of the late Italian Renaissance; its dome can be seen from any vantage point on the North Shore. Other buildings house the hospital, the electric plant, a lecture hall, and a morgue. The Harbor maintains its own cemetery. The grave of Captain Randall is near the entrance to the executive building, and a statue of the philanthropist executed by Augustus Saint-Gaudens and unveiled May 30, 1884, stands near by.

3. SILVER LAKE PARK, Forest Avenue and Victory Boulevard, embraces 207 beautifully landscaped acres surrounding Silver Lake Reservoir, which draws its water from the Catskills, 119 miles away. The reservoir was built in 1917 and has a capacity of 435,000,000 gallons.

WEST NEW BRIGHTON, between Davis Avenue and Bodine Creek, has the tempo and appearance of an average American suburb. Francis Parkman, the historian, took a house in the neighborhood in 1848. Here, despite "an extreme weakness of sight . . . a condition of brain prohibiting fixed attention . . . and an exhaustion and total derangement of the nervous system," he wrote six lines a day for his *History of the Conspiracy of Pontiac.*

During the Civil War Abolitionists operated a station of the underground railroad in this neighborhood, and on one occasion they kidnapped a Negro maid from a Southern woman visiting the town. During the Draft Riots a mob invaded the community, trampling and stoning to death several Negroes and putting to flight many others.

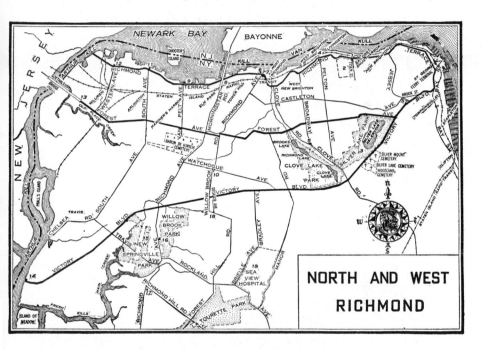

NORTH AND WEST RICHMOND

KEY TO NORTH AND WEST RICHMOND MAP

1. Neville House
2. Sailors' Snug Harbor
3. Silver Lake Park
4. Kreuzer-Pelton House
5. Staten Island Zoo
6. Port Richmond Hotel
7. Old Dutch Reformed Church
8. Bayonne Bridge
9. Captains' Row
10. Cruser Pero House
11. Bethlehem Steel Company Shipyard

Brewer Shipyard and Dry Dock
12. Port Ivory
13. Goethals Bridge
14. Slip of the Carteret Ferry
15. New Springville Park
16. Public School 27
17. Barne Tysen House
18. Christopher House
19. Sea View Hospital
Richmond Borough Hospital
New York City Farm Colony

Until 1932 a settlement centering around Broadway was known as Factoryville for the number of its industrial establishments, or as Corktown, the latter a more or less oblique reference to a favorite pastime of the inhabitants.

4. The KREUZER-PELTON HOUSE, 1268 Richmond Terrace, foot of Pelton Avenue, is an attractive stone house built about 1730. It bears the names of two of its many owners. In front of the house is a terrace, high above the street and shored by a stone wall. During the British occupation the building was used as headquarters by Cortlandt Skinner, a Tory militia commander. Among the guests in the house were Prince William Henry, later William IV of England, and Major André.

5. STATEN ISLAND ZOO, Broadway and Clove Road, is nationally known for its reptile collection. *(Open daily 10 a.m. to 5 p.m., Sunday and holidays 10 a.m. to 6 p.m.; closes one hour earlier in winter; admission free.)* Boas, pythons, cobras, and viperines, including the bushmaster and the fer-de-lance, are among the occupants of a modern, glass-enclosed reptile house. The excellence of this collection prompted the Staten Island Zoological Society to sponsor the first International Snake Exhibit, held in 1936 in Grand Central Palace. Small mammals, birds, and tropical fish and amphibia complete the zoo's exhibits. Features of the zoo's modern equipment are glass shingles admitting the maximum of sunlight, outdoor cages, and surroundings simulating the native habitat of the exhibits. An animal hospital, laboratory, library, administration offices, lecture rooms, and a large auditorium are on the second floor where studies of the zoo's collection are made by biology classes, adult groups, and visiting scientists and curators.

The $300,000 building, a T-shaped brick structure of Georgian design, was opened in 1936. The site was bequeathed to the municipality by Mrs. Julia O. Hardin and called at her request the Clarence T. Barrett Park in honor of her brother-in-law. The zoo is administered by the Staten Island Zoological Society.

PORT RICHMOND, the shopping and entertainment district for the surrounding communities, centers on Richmond Avenue. The two-story buildings, neon signs, garish façades, and Saturday night shopping crowds make the avenue the Main Street of the North Shore.

6. PORT RICHMOND HOTEL, 2040 Richmond Terrace, a barracks-like building facing the Bayonne ferry terminal, was once the elegant St. James Hotel. It was erected about 1787. A plaque on the building identifies it

as the last home of Aaron Burr, host here at many banquets. Burr died here on September 14, 1836.

7. OLD DUTCH REFORMED CHURCH, Richmond Avenue south of Richmond Terrace, Greek Revival in style, dates from 1844. The congregation was organized in 1663 (or 1665). The original building, a log structure around which the community now known as Port Richmond grew, was erected on land donated in 1714 by Governor Hunter. The deed is among the church relics. A tablet on the building commemorates Staten Islanders who fought in the Revolution, including the five Mersereau brothers. On the headstone of Cornelius Mersereau in the church burial ground is the verse:

> My flesh shall slumber in the ground
> Till the last trumpets joyfull sound,
> Then burst the chains in sweet surprise
> And in my Savior's Image rise.

8. BAYONNE BRIDGE, Morningstar Road and Hooker Place, the silvery outlines of which can be clearly seen from the Staten Island ferry, connects the industrial north shore of the island with Bayonne, New Jersey, and leads to the Holland Tunnel. (Passenger automobile toll for bridge 50¢.) It was completed in 1931 at a cost of thirteen million dollars. The 1,675-foot main span, a great steel arch spanning Kill van Kull without intermediate piers, is the longest of its kind in the world. The crossing was designed and built under the direction of O. H. Ammann, chief engineer of the Port of New York Authority. Cass Gilbert was the consulting architect for the approaches. The total length of the bridge, including approaches, is 8,100 feet and the clearance above water at mid-span is 150 feet.

9. CAPTAINS' ROW, Richmond Terrace between Van Name and Van Pelt Avenues, still contains a number of the dignified and spacious mansions with two-story porticos that belonged to the masters of the lucrative oyster and clipper ships of the 1850's and 1860's. Perhaps the most colorful of these captains was John J. Housman, a blustery, outspoken man, savage in his attacks on the proslavery element. When the Union Army embarked for Richmond, Virginia, by way of the James River, it was he who selected pilots from Mariners Harbor for the trip.

Subsequently, factories polluted the waters of the Kill van Kull where the rich oyster beds were planted; and by 1880 the steamboat had replaced the clipper ship: the prosperity of Captains' Row was at an end.

10. CRUSER PERO HOUSE, northwest corner of Watchogue Avenue and Willowbrook Road, a one-story structure built about 1739, is a good example of an early Staten Island farmhouse. The heavy stone walls have few windows. The triangular end gables are framed in wood and faced with siding. The high pitch roof is original, but the dormer window is a modern addition. A landscaping firm now occupies the premises.

MARINERS HARBOR, the northwestern shoulder of Staten Island, is now a busy industrial area of soap works, oil refineries, and shipyards. There are very few reminders of the oyster fishing industry that prospered here in the middle-nineteenth century.

11. PLANT OF BETHLEHEM STEEL COMPANY, 3075 Richmond Terrace, and the BREWER SHIPYARD AND DRY DOCKS, 2945 Richmond Terrace, are two of the leading shipbuilding and repair companies on the island. The former grew out of the Staten Island Shipbuilding Company, established during the war; it has built nearly nine hundred hulls since 1929, including many ferryboats and numerous vessels for the U.S. Navy. Its yards contain four shipways, each four hundred feet long, and five dry docks. The Brewer Shipyard constructs barges and makes ship repairs. Near by on Kill van Kull is Shooters Island, once the site of the Townsend Downey yards. Former Kaiser Wilhelm's yacht, the *Meteor,* was built here.

12. PORT IVORY, along Richmond Terrace west of Catherine Street, named after a nationally advertised soap, comprises the 121 acres of ground and the thirty-six buildings of Procter and Gamble, manufacturers of soaps and edible oils. The company employs about 1,300 persons.

13. GOETHALS BRIDGE, Forest Avenue and McKinley Street, rises high above the marshlands of northwestern Staten Island. *(Passenger automobile toll 50¢.)* The cantilever structure, constructed under the direction of O. H. Ammann and named in honor of General George W. Goethals, chief engineer of the Panama Canal, crosses Arthur Kill to Elizabeth, New Jersey. It has a main span of 672 feet, a total length of 8,600 feet, and a clearance over the water of 135 feet. The Goethals, a sister span of the Outerbridge Crossing *(see page 614),* was opened in 1928 and cost about seven million dollars.

TRAVIS, the village in the vicinity of Travis Avenue and Victory Boulevard, took the name of Linoleumville in 1873 when the American Linoleum Company established a plant here. The company was one of the depression casualties and the plant closed in 1931. A few years later the disillusioned village resumed its original name of Travis.

The region, settled by English and Dutch farmers, is inhabited chiefly by families of Polish and German descent.

14. The SLIP OF THE CARTERET FERRY, at the foot of Victory Boulevard and the Arthur Kill, is on the site of New Blazing Star Inn, an important stagecoach stop between Philadelphia and New York in the early nineteenth century. The ferry was discontinued in 1929. A granite marker with a bronze tablet, about one hundred feet from the shore, indicates the site of an engagement between American and British troops on August 22, 1777.

15. NEW SPRINGVILLE PARK, bisected by Travis Avenue between Victory Boulevard and Richmond Avenue, contains 182 acres of salt-water marsh preserved as a bird sanctuary. In the fall, ringneck pheasants, blue jays, cardinals, and crows are fed at a station maintained by the Staten Island Bird Club. When the creeks and streams are frozen, black ducks are given food along the banks. Meadow larks winter in near-by salt marshes, and in summer nesting cover is provided for redtails, sparrow hawks, and owls.

16. PUBLIC SCHOOL 27, on the east side of Richmond Avenue, north of Rockland Avenue, is one of the few remaining one-room, one-teacher schoolhouses in the city limits. It serves children from farms in the vicinity.

17. BARNE TYSEN HOUSE, Richmond Avenue south of Richmond Hill Road, one hundred feet off the road, is set on a large and uncultivated plain. A stone structure with a single pitch roof, it is believed to have been built in the early eighteenth century. Governor Andros granted the site to the Tysen family in 1677. The structure has been abandoned.

18. CHRISTOPHER HOUSE, near 805 Willowbrook Road, behind Willowbrook Public Tennis Courts (see marker on Willowbrook Road), was used for secret meetings of the Committee of Safety during the American Revolution. The "Great Swamp," near which it stood has since been partially filled in and converted into Willowbrook Park. The original one-room stone house was built about 1756, and later enlarged by Joseph Christopher. The present building has low ceilings, small windows, and an open porch with wooden pillars.

19. SEA VIEW HOSPITAL, RICHMOND BOROUGH HOSPITAL (FOR COMMUNICABLE DISEASES), and the NEW YORK CITY FARM COLONY, are three units of an institutional group that occupies 379 acres bounded by Manor Road, Brielle Avenue, Steers Street, and Rockland Avenue. Sea

View Hospital is one of the largest (1,446 beds) tuberculosis hospitals in the world. A separate building houses the occupational therapy division with its workshops where patients are vocationally rehabilitated. The farm colony is used as an asylum for the aged.

Books About New York

Books About New York

DESCRIPTIVE

Asbury, Herbert. *The Gangs of New York.* New York, Alfred A. Knopf, 1928. 373p. illus.

Browne, Junius Henri. *The Great Metropolis.* Hartford, American Pub. Co., 1869. 700p. illus.

Crockett, Albert Stevens. *Peacocks on Parade.* Life in New York 1890–1914. New York, Sears Pub. Co., 1931. 314p. illus.

Dreiser, Theodore. *The Color of A Great City.* New York, Boni and Liveright, 1923. 287p. illus.

Federal Writers' Project, New York City. *New York Panorama.* New York, Random House, 1938. 526p. illus.

Footner, Hulbert. *New York, City of Cities.* Philadelphia, J. B. Lippincott Co., 1937. 338p. illus.

Irving, Washington. *Knickerbocker's History of New York.* (Numerous reprints.) New York, Doubleday, Doran and Co., 1928. 427p. illus.

Irwin, Will. *Highlights of Manhattan.* New York, D. Appleton-Century Co., 1937. rev. ed. 432p. illus.

Johnson, James Weldon. *Black Manhattan.* New York, Alfred A. Knopf, 1930. 248p. illus.

Markey, Morris. *Manhattan Reporter.* New York, Dodge Pub. Co., 1935. 320p.

Morand, Paul. *New York.* Translated from the French by Hamish Miles. New York, Henry Holt and Co., 1930. 322p. illus.

Parry, Albert. *Garrets and Pretenders.* A book on Bohemianism with particular reference to Greenwich Village. New York, Covici, Friede, 1933. 383p. illus.

FICTION

Dos Passos, John. *Manhattan Transfer.* New York, Harper and Bros., 1925. 404p.

Gold, Michael. *Jews Without Money.* New York, H. Liveright, 1930. 309p. illus.

Halper, Albert. *Union Square.* New York, Viking Press, 1934. 257p.

Howells, William Dean. *The Coast of Bohemia.* New York, Harper and Bros., 1899. 340p.

James, Henry. *Washington Square.* (Various editions.) New York, Harper and Bros., 1889. 266p. illus.

Ornitz, Samuel. *Haunch, Paunch and Jowl.* New York, Boni and Liveright, 1924. 300p.

Poole, Ernest. *The Harbor.* New York, Macmillan Co., 1925. 387p. illus.

Porter, William Sydney (O. Henry, pseud.). *The Four Million.* New York, Doubleday, Page and Co., 1909. 261p.

Van Vechten, Carl. *Nigger Heaven.* New York, Alfred A. Knopf, 1926. 286p.

Wharton, Edith. *Age of Innocence.* New York, D. Appleton and Co., 1920 (reprint). 364p.

BIOGRAPHIES OF FAMOUS NEW YORKERS

Barrett, Walter. *The Old Merchants of New York City.* New York, Carelton, 1863–6. 4v.

Carter, John Franklin (Jay Franklin, pseud.). *LaGuardia.* New York, Modern Age Books, 1937. 176p.

Duffus, Robert L. *Lillian Wald, Neighbor and Crusader.* New York, Macmillan Co., 1938. 371p. illus.

Hamm, Margherita Arlina. *Famous Families of New York.* New York, G. P. Putnam's Sons, 1902. 2v. illus.

Hapgood, Norman, and Moskowitz, H. *Up from the City Streets: Alfred E. Smith.* A biographical study in contemporary politics. New York, Harcourt, Brace and Co., 1927. 349p. illus., plates, portraits.

Josephson, Matthew. *Robber Barons.* New York, Harcourt, Brace and Co., 1934. 474p.

Lynch, Dennis Tilden. *"Boss" Tweed.* New York, Boni and Liveright, 1927. 433p. illus.

Patterson, Samuel W. *Famous Men and Places in the History of New York City.* New York, Noble and Noble, 1923, 245p. illus.

Smith, Arthur D. Howden. *Commodore Vanderbilt.* New York, McBride and Co., 1929. 339p. illus.

Ulmann, Albert. *New Yorkers. From Stuyvesant to Roosevelt.* New York, Chaucer Head Book Shop, 1928. 267p. illus.

Van Loon, Hendrik W. *Life and Times of Peter Stuyvesant.* New York, Henry Holt and Co., 1928. 336p.

Winkler, John K. *Morgan the Magnificent.* New York, Vanguard Press, 1930. 313p.

NATURAL SETTING

Gratacap, L. P. *Geology of the City of New York.* New York, Henry Holt and Co., 1909. 232p. illus., maps.

HISTORY

Bolton, Reginald Pelham. *Indian Life of Long Ago in New York City.* New York, Joseph Graham (Bolton Books Schoen Press), 1934. 162p. illus.

Brown, Henry Collins. *Fifth Avenue, Old and New.* New York, Fifth Avenue Association, 1924. 126p. illus., maps.

Collins, F. A. *The Romance of Park Avenue.* New York, Auspices Park Avenue Association, 1930. 107p. illus.

Fitzpatrick, Benedict. *The Bronx and Its People.* New York, Lewis Historical Pub. Co., 1927. 4v. illus., maps.
Flick, Alexander C., editor. *History of the State of New York.* New York, Columbia University Press, 1936. 10v. illus.
Gilder, Rodman. *The Battery.* Four centuries on Manhattan Island's tip. Boston, Houghton Mifflin Co., 1936. 304p. illus., maps.
Harlow, Alvin F. *Old Bowery Days.* New York, D. Appleton and Co., 1931. 564p. illus.
Hazelton, Henry Isham. *The Boroughs of Brooklyn and Queens, Counties of Nassau and Suffolk, Long Island, New York, 1609–1924.* New York, Lewis Historical Pub. Co., 1925. 7v. plates, portraits, maps.
Hill, Frederick Trevor. *The Story of a Street.* (Wall Street.) New York, Harper and Bros., 1908. 170p. illus.
Jenkins, Stephen. *The Greatest Street in the World.* Broadway from Bowling Green to Albany. New York, G. P. Putnam's Sons, 1911. 509p. illus., maps.
Lamb, Martha J. *History of the City of New York.* New York, A. S. Barnes and Co., 1877. 768p. illus., maps.
Leng, Charles W., and Davis, William T. *Staten Island and Its People.* New York, Lewis Historical Pub. Co., 1930. 4v. illus.
McKay, Richard C. *South Street.* New York, G. P. Putnam's Sons, 1934. 460p. illus.
Mott, Hopper S. *New York of Yesterday.* (Old Bloomingdale.) New York, G. P. Putnam's Sons, 1908. 597p. illus., diagrs., maps.
Perine, E. T. B. *Here's to Broadway.* New York, G. P. Putnam's Sons, 1930. 321p. illus.
Stiles, Henry R., editor-in-chief. *History of Kings County, 1683–1884.* New York, W. W. Munsell and Co. 2v. illus.
Stokes, Isaac Newton Phelps. *The Iconography of Manhattan Island, 1498–1909.* New York, R. H. Dodd, 1915–28. 6v. illus., diagrs., charts.
Wilson, James Grant, editor. *The Memorial History of the City of New York From Its First Settlement to 1892.* New York, New York History Co., 1892-3. 4v. illus., maps.
Wilson, Rufus Rockwell. *New York, Old and New.* Its story, streets and landmarks. Philadelphia, J. B. Lippincott Co., 1909. 2v. illus.

GOVERNMENT

Crump, Irving, and Newton, John W. *Our Police.* New York, Dodd. Mead and Co., 1935. 263p. illus.
LaGuardia, Fiorello. *New York Advancing.* New York, Municipal Reference Library, 1939. World's Fair edition. 272p. illus., charts.
Northrop, William B. *The Insolence of Office.* The story of the Seabury investigation. New York, G. P. Putnam's Sons, 1932. 306p.
O'Connor, Richard. *Police Promoter.* An abstract of ordinances, sanitary and legal codes, and the old charter. New York, Delehanty Institute, 1930, 687p.
Rankin, Rebecca. *Guide to the Municipal Government of the City of New York.* New York, The Eagle Library, Inc., 1939–40. 115p.

COMMERCE, INDUSTRY, AND FINANCE

Bishop, Joseph Bucklin. *A Chronicle of 150 Years.* The Chamber of Commerce of the State of New York, 1768–1918. New York, Charles Scribners Sons, 1918. 311p. illus.

Bonner, William T. *New York, the World Metropolis, 1623–1924.* (Including facsimile of first New York City directory.) New York, R. L. Polk and Co., 1924. 958p. illus.

Edwards, Richard, editor. *New York's Great Industries.* New York, New York Historical Pub. Co., 1884. 304p.

Harrington, Virginia D. *The New York Merchant on the Eve of the Revolution.* New York, Columbia University Press, 1935. 389p.

Lanier, Henry Wysham. *A Century of Banking in New York, 1822–1922.* The Farmers' Loan and Trust Co. edition. New York, Gillis Press, 1922. 335p. illus.

Myers, Gustavus. *History of Great American Fortunes.* Chicago, C. H. Kerr and Co., 1911. 3v. plates, portraits.

Rochester, Anna. *Rulers of America.* A study of finance capital. New York, International Pubs., 1936. 368p. charts.

HOUSING, REAL ESTATE, AND CITY PLANNING

Arent, Arthur. "One-Third of A Nation," included in *Federal Theatre Plays.* New York, Random House, 1938. 121p.

Bauer, Catherine. *Modern Housing.* Boston, Houghton Mifflin Co., 1934. 330p. illus., diagrs.

Committee on Regional Plan of New York and Its Environs. *Regional Plan of New York and Its Environs.* New York, Regional Plan of New York and Its Environs, 1929–31. 2v. illus., diagrs., maps. v. I. The Graphic Regional Plan. v. II. The Building of the City.

Committee on Regional Plan of New York and Its Environs. *Regional Survey of New York and Its Environs.* New York, Regional Plan of New York and Its Environs, 1927–9. 8v. illus., diagrs., maps, charts. v. I. Major Economic Factors in Metropolitan Growth and Arrangement. v. II. Population, Land Values and Government. v. III. Highway Traffic. v. IV. Transit and Transportation. v. V. Public Recreation. v. VI. Buildings: Their Uses and the Spaces About Them. v. VII. Neighborhood and Community Planning. v. VIII. Physical Conditions and Public Services.

Duffus, Robert L. *Mastering a Metropolis.* An authorized account of the most important findings of the Committee on the Regional Plan of New York and Its Environs. New York, Harper and Bros., 1930. 302p. illus.

Ford, James. *Slums and Housing.* (Special reference to New York City.) Published under the auspices of the Phelps-Stokes Fund. Cambridge, Harvard University Press, 1936. 2v. illus., diagrs., maps.

Laidlow, Walter. *Statistical Sources for Demographic Studies of Greater New York.* New York, Columbia University Press, 1920. 819p. illus.

Mayor's Committee on City Planning. *Progress Report of the Mayor's Committee on City Planning.* New York, Mayor's Committee on City Planning, 1936. 122p. tables, diagrs., charts.

Mumford, Lewis. *Culture of Cities.* New York, Harcourt, Brace and Co., 1938. 586p. illus.

Post, Langdon. *The Challenge of Housing.* New York, Farrar and Rinehart, 1938. 309p. plates, maps.

Pound, Arthur. *The Golden Earth.* The story of Manhattan's landed wealth. New York, Macmillan Co., 1935. 303p. illus.

Real Estate Record and Building Guide. *A History of Real Estate and Building in New York.* New York, Real Estate Record and Building Guide, 1914. 143p. illus., tables, maps.

Riis, Jacob August. *How the Other Half Lives.* New York, Scribners, 1890. 304p. illus.

EDUCATION

Board of Education, New York. *The Elementary Schools of the City of New York.* Their problems and the efforts that are being made to solve these problems. (The annual reports of the district superintendents in the field, 1933–4.) New York, Board of Education, 1934. 241p.

Bureau of Child Guidance, Board of Education. *Five-Year Report of the Bureau of Child Guidance of the Board of Education (1932–37).* New York, Board of Education, 1937. 159p.

Campbell, Harold G. *All the Children.* Annual report of the superintendent of schools, City of New York. New York, Board of Education, 1937. 145p. illus.

Chase, Josephine. *New York at School.* New York, Public Education Association of the City of New York, 1927. 268p.

Graves, Frank Pierrepont. *Report of a Study of New York City Schools.* Albany, University of the State of New York Press, 1933–4. 2v. diagrs., charts.

Mosenthal, Philip James, and Horne, Charles F., editors. *The City College.* Memories of sixty years. New York, G. P. Putnam's Sons, 1907. 565p. illus.

Robson, John William, editor. *A Guide to Columbia University.* Includes some account of its history and traditions. New York, Columbia University Press, 1938. 213p. illus.

SOCIAL WELFARE

Betts, Lillian Williams. *The Leaven in a Great City.* New York, Dodd, Mead and Co., 1902. 315p. illus.

Brace, Charles Loring. *The Dangerous Classes of New York and Twenty Years Work Among Them.* New York, Wynkoop and Hallenbeck, 1872. 448p. illus.

Brandt, Lillian. *An Impressionistic View of the Winter of 1930–31 in New York City.* New York, Welfare Council of New York City, 1932. 91p.

Greene, Elizabeth. *Report of A Survey of Mental Hygiene Facilities and Resources in New York City.* New York, State Charities Aid Association, 1929. 206p.

Huntley, Kate Eleanor. *Financial Trends in Organized Social Work in New York City.* New York, Columbia University Press, 1935. 330p. illus.

Kennedy, Albert Joseph. *Social Settlements in New York City.* New York, Columbia University Press, 1935. 599p. illus.

Klein, Philip, in collaboration with Ruth Voris. *Some Basic Statistics in Social Work.* New York, Columbia University Press, 1933. 218p. maps.

Pipkin, C. W. *Social Politics and Modern Democracies.* New York, Macmillan Co., 1931. 2v.

Shulman, H. M. *Slums of New York.* A study of four slum areas in 1926 and in 1931-2. New York, A. and C. Boni, 1938. 394p.

Simkhovitch, Mary Kingsbury. *Neighborhood—My Story of Greenwich House.* New York, W. W. Norton, 1938. 411p.

Wald, Lillian D. *The House on Henry Street.* New York, Henry Holt and Co., 1915. 317p. illus.

Ware, Caroline F. *Greenwich Village, 1920-1930.* Boston, Houghton Mifflin Co., 1935. 496p.

RELIGION AND CHURCHES

Berrian, William. *An Historical Sketch of Trinity Church, New York.* New York, Stanford and Swards, 1847. 386p. illus.

Billington, Ray Allen. *The Protestant Crusade, 1800-1860.* New York, Macmillan Co., 1938. 514p. illus.

Disoway, A. M., and Poillon, Gabriel. *The Earliest Churches of New York.* New York, James G. Gregory, 1865. 416p. illus.

Goldstein, Israel. *A Century of Judaism in New York.* New York, Congregation B'nai Yeshurun, 1930. 460p. illus.

Greater New York Federation of Churches. *The Negro Churches of Manhattan (New York City).* New York, Greater New York Federation of Churches, 1930. 36p.

Greenleaf, J. *A History of the Churches, of All Denominations, in the City of New York, From the First Settlement to the Year 1846.* New York, E. French, 1846. 379p.

Hall, Edward Hogawan. *A Guide to the Cathedral Church of St. John the Divine.* New York, Layman's Club of the Cathedral, 1928. 132p. illus.

MacAdam, George. *The Little Church Around the Corner.* New York, G. P. Putnam's Sons, 1925. 347p. illus.

McNally, Augustin Francis. *Guide to St. Patrick's.* New York, Brown McNally Associates, 1932. 112p. illus.

Ryan, Leo Raymond. *Old St. Peter's, the Mother Church of Catholic New York, 1785-1935.* New York, U. S. Catholic Historical Society, 1935. 282p. illus.

St. Mark's Church in the Bowery. Published by the Vestry. New York, T. Whittaker, 1899. 194p. illus.

Shea, John Dawson Gilmary, editor. *The Catholic Churches of New York City.* New York, L. G. Goulding and Co., 1878. 748p. illus.

The Riverside Church. A Handbook of the Institution and Its Building. New York, The Riverside Church, 1931. 127p. illus.

Wenner, George. *The Lutherans of New York.* New York, Petersfield Press, 1918. 160p. illus.

BOOKS ABOUT NEW YORK 633

LABOR

Commons, John R. *History of Labor in the United States.* New York, Macmillan Co., 1918–35. 4v.

Hardy, Jack. *The Clothing Workers.* A study of the conditions and struggles in the needle trades. New York, International Pubs., 1935. 256p.

Hillquit, Morris. *Loose Leaves from a Busy Life.* New York, Macmillan Co., 1934. 339p.

Ireland, Tom. *Child Labor as a Relic of the Dark Ages.* New York, G. P. Putnam's Sons, 1937. 336p.

Lorwin, Lewis (Louis Levine, pseud.). *The Women Garment Workers.* A history of the International Ladies' Garment Workers' Union. New York, B. W. Huebsch, 1924. 608p.

McKee, Samuel. *Labor in Colonial New York, 1664–1776.* New York, Columbia University Press, 1935. 193p.

Richardson, Dorothy. *The Long Day.* The story of a New York working girl, as told by herself. New York, Century Co., 1905. 309p.

Walsh, Raymond. *C.I.O., Industrial Unionism in Action.* New York, W. W. Norton, 1937. 293p.

NEWSPAPERS

Baehr, H. W., Jr. *Since the Civil War.* New York Tribune. New York, 1936. Dodge Co. 420p.

Bessie, Simon Michael. *Jazz Journalism.* The story of the tabloid newspapers. New York, E. P. Dutton and Co., 1938. 247p. illus.

Davis, Elmer. *History of the New York Times.* New York, the New York Times, 1921. 434p. illus.

Nevins, Allan. *The Evening Post.* A century of journalism. New York, Boni and Liveright, 1922. 590p. illus.

O'Brien, Frank M. *Story of the Sun.* New York, George H. Doran Co., 1918. 445p. illus.

Seitz, Don Carlos. *James Gordon Bennett.* Indianapolis, Bobbs-Merrill Co., 1928. 405p. illus.

Seitz, Don Carlos. *Joseph Pulitzer, His Life and Letters.* New York, Garden City Publishing Co., 1927. 478p. illus.

Villard, Oswald Garrison. *Some Newspapers and Newspapermen.* New York, Alfred A. Knopf, 1933. 335p.

Walker, Stanley. *City Editor.* New York, Frederick A. Stokes Co., 1934. 336p. illus.

STAGE, SCREEN, AND RADIO

Avidson, Linda (Mrs. D. W. Griffith). *When the Movies Were Young.* New York, E. P. Dutton and Co., 1925. 256p. illus.

Brown, John Mason. *Two on the Aisle.* Ten years of the American theatre in performance. New York, W. W. Norton, 1938. 321p.

Frohman, Daniel. *Daniel Frohman Presents.* Fifty years of the New York stage. New York, C. Kendall and W. Sharp, 1935. 397p. illus.

Hornblow, Arthur. *A History of the Theater in America from Its Beginnings to the Present Time.* Philadelphia, J. B. Lippincott Co., 1919. 2v. illus.

Ireland, Joseph N. *Records of the New York Stage from 1750–1860.* New York, T. H. Morrell, 1866–7. 2v.

Isman, Felix. *Weber and Fields, Their Tribulations, Triumphs and Associates.* New York, Boni and Liveright, 1924. 345p. illus.

Mantle, Burns Robert. *A Treasury of the Theatre.* New York, Simon and Schuster, 1935. 1,643p.

Martin, John. *American Dancing.* New York, Dodge Pub. Co., 1936. 320p. illus.

Moses, Montrose J., and Brown, John Mason. *The American Theater as Seen by Its Critics (1752–1934).* New York, W. W. Norton, 1934. 391p.

Nathan, George Jean. *The Theatre of the Moment.* A journalistic commentary. New York, Alfred A. Knopf, 1936. 310p.

Odell, George C. D. *Annals of the New York Stage.* New York, Columbia University Press, 1927–31. 7v. illus.

Ramsaye, Terry. *A Million and One Nights.* The history of the motion picture. New York, Simon and Schuster, 1926. 2v. illus.

Variety. *Radio Directory.* Personalities, laws, sponsors. New York, Variety, 1937–8.

Woollcott, Alexander. *Going to Pieces.* New York, G. P. Putnam's Sons, 1928. 256p.

MUSIC

Goldberg, Isaac. *Tin Pan Alley.* New York, John Day Co., 1930. 341p. illus.

Huneker, James Gibbons. *Philharmonic Society of New York City.* New York, The Society, 1917. 130p.

Kolodin, Irving. *The Metropolitan Opera (1883–1935).* New York, Oxford University Press, 1936. 589p.

Marks, Edward Bennet. *They All Sang.* From Tony Pastor to Rudy Vallee, as told to Abbott J. Liebling. New York, Viking Press, 1934. 321p. illus., plates.

Odell, George C. D. *Annals of the New York Stage.* (See Stage, Screen, and Radio.)

Peyser, Ethel Rose. *The House That Music Built.* The Story of Carnegie Hall. New York, McBride and Co., 1936. 371p. illus.

ART AND ARCHITECTURE

Art Commission of the City of New York. *Catalog of the Works of Art Belonging to the City of New York.* New York, the Art Commission of the City of New York, 1909 and 1920. 2v. illus.

Bailey, Rosalie Fellows. *Pre-Revolutionary Dutch Houses and Families in Northern New Jersey and Southern New York.* Introduction by Franklin D. Roosevelt. New York, W. Morrow, 1936. 612p. illus.

Carpenter, Frederick V. *A Sketch Book of New York.* New York, Bridgman, 1927. 62p. illus.

Ferriss, Hugh. *Metropolis of Tomorrow.* New York, Washburn, 1929. 140p. illus.

Hamlin, Talbot A. *The American Spirit in Architecture.* New Haven, Yale University Press, 1926. 353p. illus.

Kimball, Sidney Fiske. *American Architecture.* New York, Bobbs-Merrill Co., 1928. 262p. illus.

Levy, Florence N. *Art in New York.* New York, Art Service, 1938. 63p. illus.

Schuyler, Montgomery. *American Architecture.* New York, Harper and Bros., 1892. 211p. illus.

Index

Index

Case, Charlotte Anne, 309
Case, Frank, 177
Cassatt, Mary, paintings by, 492
Castle Clinton, 308
Castle Garden, 308, 416
Castle, Montague, stained glass by, 358
Castle Williams, 414, 415
Catalogue of American Genealogies, 445
Cathedral of St. John the Divine, 380-383
Cather, Willa, 134
Catherine, Queen of Braganza, 557
Catholic Youth Organization, 152
Catlin, George, painting by, 95
Cavanagh's (restaurant), 153
Cavanaugh, Major F. W., 524
Center Theatre, 333, *338*
Central Congregational Church, 477
Central Courts Building (Brooklyn), 448
Central Harlem Health Center, 257, 263
Central High School of Needle Trades, 154
Central Neurological Hospital, 422
Central Park, 246, *350-356*
Central Park South, *229-231*, 232
Central Park West, 275; neighborhood, 275-284
Central Railroad of New Jersey, 70
Century Apartments, 278
Century Theatre, 278
Cesnola (Louis P. Di) Collection of Cypriote Antiquities, 369, *371*
Cézanne, Paul, paintings by, 134, 241, 349, 376, 492
Chaliapin, Feodor, 324
Chambellan, René P., sculpture by, 335, 340
Chambers Street, 101
Chandler, Beatrice, sculpture by, 213
Chanfrau, Frank S., 119
Chanin Building, 225
Chanin, Irwin S., architect, 275, 279
Chanler, Robert, grave of, 297
Chapel of Ease of Trinity Church (St. George's Church), 190
Chapel of the Intercession (Trinity Church), 296, 312
Chapel of St. Cornelius the Centurion (Trinity Church), 414
Chaplin, Charlie, 349
Chapman, Frank M., 363
Charles and Company, 225
Charles II, King, 64, 600
Charlotte Temple (novel), 312
Chase National Bank, 89
Chatham Club, 107
Chatham Square, 120
Chelsea, 151-155
Chelsea Piers, 72
Chemists' Club, 215
Cherry Hill, 114
Cherry Lane Theater, 142
Cherry Street, 114, 115
Children's Aid Society, 100, 157
Children's Court (Brooklyn), 448
Children's Court (Manhattan), 197
Chimney Sweeps (island), 550
Chinatown, 104-108

Chinatown Emporium, 106
Chinese in New York, *104-108*, 556
Chinese Exclusion Act, 104
Chinese Journal, 106
Chinese Republic News, 105
Chinese School, 106
Chisholm family, 571
Chisholm Mansion, 571
Chisholm, Mrs. William Edings, 571
Choate, Joseph H., 248
Cholera epidemics, 115
Christ Church, 447
Christadora House, 110
Christian Union (periodical), 445
Christopher House, 623
Christopher, Joseph, 623
Christus, Petrus, paintings by, 239
Chrysler Building, *224*, 319
Chrysler Company, 224
Chrystie Street House, 153
Church of All Nations, 110
Church of the Annunciation, 292
Church of the Ascension, 135
"Church of the Generals," 469
Church of the Guardian Angel, 152
Church of the Holy Communion, 152
Church of the Holy Cross, 158
Church of the Holy Trinity, 446
Church of the Most Precious Blood, 578
Church of Notre Dame de Lourdes, 290
Church of Our Lady of Guadalupe, 151
Church of Our Lady of the Miraculous Medal, 268
Church of Our Lady of Mount Carmel, 270
Church of the Pilgrims (Plymouth Church of the Pilgrims), 444, *446*
Church of the Redeemer, 464
Church of St. Andrew (Episcopal), 612
Church of St. Andrew (Roman Catholic), 100
Church of St. Benedict the Moor, 159
Church of St. Catherine of Siena, 246
Church of St. Cecilia, 268
Church of St. Francis de Sales, 268
Church of St. John the Evangelist, site of, 346
Church of St. Mary the Virgin, 178
Church of St. Nicholas, 77
Church of St. Paul the Apostle, 281
Church of St. Teresa, 477
Church of St. Vincent Ferrer, 246
Church of St. Vincent de Paul, 154
Church Street, 77
Church of The Transfiguration, 212
Church of The Transfiguration of Our Lord, 459
Churches
    Baptist: Abyssinian Baptist Church, 263; First Baptist Church, 283; First Swedish Church, 243; Judson Memorial Baptist Church, 134; Metropolitan Baptist Church, 261
    Christian Science: First Church of Christ The Scientist, 280
    Congregational: Broadway Tabernacle, 174; Central Congregational Church, 477; Plymouth Church of the Pil-

ABOUT THE AUTHORS

The Federal Writers' Project was established in 1935 as part of Federal #1, a project to provide work relief for artists and professionals under the Works Progress Administration. In the next four years the project produced works on local history, folkways, and culture in addition to the magisterial *American Guide Series.*

William H. Whyte is the author of numerous books, including *The Organization Man* and, most recently, *The Social Life of Small Urban Spaces.* In 1969 he wrote the text of the *Plan for New York City* for the New York City Planning Commission.

OTHER PANTHEON
TITLES OF INTEREST

America's Forgotten Architecture, The National Trust for Historic Preservation

The Architect's Eye: American Architectural Drawings from 1799 to 1978, Deborah Nevins and Robert A.M. Stern

Building the Dream: A Social History of Housing in America, Gwendolyn Wright

Housing by People: Towards Autonomy in Building Environments, John F.C. Turner

Solar Houses: 48 Energy-Saving Designs, Louis Gropp